Legal Research
and Writing
for Paralegals

Legal Research and Writing for Paralegals

Fourth Edition

Deborah E. Bouchoux, 1950 -
Georgetown University
Washington, D.C.

PUBLISHERS

111 Eighth Avenue, New York, NY 10011
www.aspenpublishers.com

Aspen Publishers
Attn: Permissions Department
111 Eighth Avenue, 7th Floor
New York, NY 10011

Printed in the United States of America

ISBN 0-7355-5105-7

2 3 4 5 6 7 8 9 0

Library of Congress Cataloging-in-Publication Data

Bouchoux, Deborah E., 1950–

  Legal research and writing for paralegals/Deborah E. Bouchoux.–4th ed.
    p. cm.
  Includes index
  ISBN 0-7355-5105-7
    1. Legal research–United States. 2. Legal composition. 3. Legal assistants–United States–Handbooks, manuals, etc. I. Title.

KF240.B68 2005
340'.072'073–dc22

                                    2005050027

About Aspen Publishers

Aspen Publishers, headquartered in New York City, is a leading information provider for attorneys, business professionals, and law students. Written by preeminent authorities, our products consist of analytical and practical information in such topical areas as business law, corporate compliance, and legal ethics.

For customer service or to comment on our products, please contact our Customer Care Center at 1-800-901-9075.

For my husband, Don, and my children,
Meaghan, Elizabeth, Patrick, and Robert,
who have provided immeasurable support
and inspiration in helping me achieve my
goal of writing a legal research and writing
textbook for paralegal students

Summary of Contents

Section III Legal Writing 585

Appendices

Contents

Section I
Legal Research:
Primary Authorities   1

Chapter 1   Finding the Law   3

Chapter 2   The Federal and State Court Systems   29

Chapter 3   Statutory Law   61

Chapter 4 Case Law and Judicial Opinions 105

Chapter 5 The Use of Digests, Annotated Law Reports, and *Words and Phrases* 155

Contents

Section II
Legal Research:
Secondary Authorities
and Other Research
Aids   193

Chapter 6   Encyclopedias, Periodicals, Treatises, and Restatements   195

Chapter 7   Miscellaneous Secondary Authorities   243

Chapter 8 Legal Citation Form 283

Chapter 9   Updating and Validating Your Research   361

Chapter 10   Special Research Issues   419

Chapter 11 The Digital Library: LEXIS, Westlaw, and Non-Print Research Sources   481

Chapter 12   E-Research: Legal Research Using the Internet   527

Chapter 13   Overview of the Research Process   557

Section III
Legal Writing 585

Chapter 14 Back to Basics 587

Chapter 15   Strategies for Effective Writing   613

Chapter 16 Legal Correspondence 649

Chapter 17   Legal Memoranda   671

Chapter 18   Legal Briefs   687

Chapter 19 Postwriting Steps 709

Appendices

Preface

You will soon discover that legal research is truly a "hands-on" subject. While there are numerous books to be found that discuss methods and techniques, there is no substitute for actually performing the task of legal research. A simply analogy can be drawn to driving a car: You may find several manuals that discuss driving and provide tips on better driving, but simply reading about operating a car is not a substitute for actually driving a car yourself. Similarly, you will learn the most about legal research, about which shortcuts are invaluable, and which techniques are non-productive, only by doing legal research. To that end, library assignments are placed at the conclusion of each chapter so you can see and use the books discussed in each chapter. You should never have to use a book or set of books that have not been discussed in the chapter you have finished reading or any preceding chapter. Take the time to explore the books by reviewing the foreword, table of contents, and index found in each volume. Familiarize yourself with all of the features of the books or electronic resources you use, and you will simplify your legal research.

Performing legal research can be both frustrating and gratifying. It can be frustrating because there is often no one perfect answer and because there are no established guidelines on how much research to do and when to stop. On the other hand, legal research is gratifying because you will be engaged in a task that requires you to *do* something and one in which you will be rewarded by finding the right case, statute, or other authority.

You should view legal research as an exciting treasure hunt — a search for the best authorities to answer a question or legal issue. In this sense, the task of using and exploring the law library or the Internet for answers to legal issues or questions should be a welcome relief from the assignments of other classes, which may be passive in nature and involve copious amounts of reading.

I would encourage you to research with other students if you are comfortable doing so. Often you will learn a great deal by comparing notes with others who may be able to share successful strategies for effectively using various books or electronic resources or finding the answers to research problems. Naturally, sharing ideas and tips for research techniques should not be viewed as an excuse not to do the work yourself or a license to use answers discussed by others. In other words, you should research with other students (if you find it useful to do so) but you should never write together. Not only is this practice dishonest, but it will prevent you from effectively learning the skill of legal research. Ultimately, an employer is not interested in how many "points" you obtained on a class exercise or what grade you obtained, but in whether you can be depended upon to research an issue competently. As adult learners and professionals, you should concentrate on learning the skill of legal research rather than focusing on the number of right answers you can obtain.

While this text shows case names and book titles in italics, underlining or underscoring is also acceptable according to *The Bluebook: A Uniform System of Citation* (Columbia Law Review Ass'n et al. eds., 18th ed. 2005) and ALWD & Darby Dickerson, *ALWD Citation Manual* (2d ed., Aspen Publishers 2003), which are the standard reference tools for citation form. There is variation among practitioners, so check with your firm or office to determine if there is a preference.

When you begin reading this book, most of you will be unfamiliar with cases, statutes, constitutions, or the numerous other legal authorities. As you progress in class and through the chapters and assignments in this text, you will readily be able to measure your progress. When you complete this text and your legal research class, you will have gained thorough mastery of legal research and writing techniques as well as familiarity with the numerous sets of law books and electronic resources that you will be required to use in your profession.

This fourth edition of the text introduces several new features, including the following:

- A section at the end of each chapter, entitled "State Your Answer," offers additional questions relating to the materials discussed in each chapter. These questions require you to access relevant Internet sites and locate the type of information an employer will require you to retrieve, such as the name of your state's secretary of state, local court rules, and so forth. Where possible, these questions are specific to your state. Learning how to navigate through cyberspace will add to your arsenal of legal research tools.
- A new feature, called "The Final Wrap-Up," provides practical and pragmatic information on citing and using various research resources, such as cases, codes, and periodicals. This feature provides advice on when to use a certain set and whether it may be cited in various legal documents.
- "Practice Tips" are included in each chapter, offering realistic and helpful suggestions for workplace success.
- Chapter 8 on legal citation form has been significantly revised to include information relating to the *ALWD* citation manual. *Bluebook* examples conform to the 18th edition of *The Bluebook*, published in 2005. Moreover, the examples of citation form given at the end of each chapter display citations in both *Bluebook* and *ALWD* form.

Additionally, new charts and diagrams are included, such as a chart showing all state encyclopedias and a list of abbreviations commonly used in legal writing and note taking. Reflecting the continuing and dramatic effect of the Internet on legal research and the ever-increasing accessibility of resources in cyberspace, new material discussing the controversy surrounding the use and citation of unpublished opinions is included in Chapter 4, and links for Web-based tutorials are given when applicable. Moreover, information is included relating to legal listservs, newsgroups, and blawgs. Finally, the chapters relating to legal writing are enhanced through the addition of information relating to using thesis statements and the CRAC method of legal analysis.

The vast number of legal authorities available in both a conventional law library and through digital law libraries means that effective legal researchers are flexible. Sometimes the materials you need are not on the shelves and you will need to switch directions. Sometimes new methods of locating materials emerge. In any event, you will find legal research an interesting hunt for the authorities you need, whether in conventional print sources, on LEXIS or Westlaw (the computer-assisted legal research systems), or on the Internet.

Deborah E. Bouchoux

August 2005

Acknowledgments

I would like to express my deep appreciation to the many individuals who contributed greatly to the development of this text and its fourth edition. First, I would like to express my gratitude to Susan M. Sullivan, the Program Director of the University of San Diego Paralegal Program, who provided me with my first opportunity to teach and who suggested I write a legal research and writing text. She has been a good friend and colleague.

My current Program Director, Gloria Silvers, of the Paralegal Studies Program at Georgetown University in Washington, D.C., has also been a tremendous influence and help to me, and I thank her for her continuing encouragement.

Thank you to Alex Butler for his assistance in obtaining photostats for the text and to Gayle P. Gregg of Kaufman & Canoles for providing numerous sample pages and forms.

Many thanks also to the various reviewers who evaluated the manuscript on behalf of the publisher. Throughout the more than 20 years I have taught I have also received continuing evaluation from my students, who have offered their comments and insight regarding methods of teaching, productive assignments, and effective writing strategies.

Finally, my deepest appreciation to my editor, Troy Froebe, and to the following individuals at Aspen Publishers: Betsy Kenny, Melody Davies, and Kathryn Porzio, all of whom offered encouragement and support throughout the development of this text. Their thoughtful comments and suggestions were welcomed and greatly contributed to this fourth edition.

I would like to acknowledge the following publishers who permitted me to reproduce copyrighted material for this text.

Chapter 2: The Federal and State Court Systems

Figure 2-3: Reprinted with permission from *Federal Reporter Second Series*, copyright © 1998 by Thomson/West.

Most of the statistical information in this chapter was obtained from http://www.uscourts/gov and http://www.supremecourtus.gov.

Chapter 3: Statutory Law

Figures 3-4 and 3-5: Reprinted with permission from Titles 11 and 42 of U.S.C.A., copyright by Thomson/West.

Figure 3-6: 15 U.S.C.S. § 288. Reproduced by permission of LexisNexis. Further reproduction of any kind is strictly prohibited.

Figure 3-7: Cover of Cumulative Supplement, 35 U.S.C.S. §§ 271-end. Reproduced by permission of LexisNexis. Further reproduction of any kind is strictly prohibited.

Figure 3-8: Reprinted with permission of Thomson/West.

Figure 3-10: U.S.C.S. General Index. Reproduced by permission of LexisNexis. Further reproduction of any kind is strictly prohibited.

Figure 3-11: Reprinted with permission from U.S.C.A. Popular Name Table, copyright © 1993 by Thomson/West.

Figure 3-12: Va. Code Ann. § 18.2-53. Reproduced by permission of LexisNexis. Further reproduction of any kind is strictly prohibited.

Chapter 4: Case Law and Judicial Opinions

Figure 4-1: Reprinted with permission from 595 S.E.2d 697, copyright © 2004 by Thomson/West.

Figure 4-2: Reprinted with permission from 108 S. Ct. 2830, copyright © 1992 by Thomson/West.

Figure 4-3: Reprinted with permission from *West's Law Finder*, copyright © 1988 by Thomson/West.

Figure 4-6: Reprinted with permission from 108 S. Ct. 2611, copyright © 1992 by Thomson/West.

Chapter 5: The Use of Digests, Annotated Law Reports, and *Words and Phrases*

Figure 5-2: Reprinted with permission of Thomson/West.

Figure 5-3: Reprinted with permission from *Descriptive Word Index to Ninth Decennial Digest*, Part 2, copyright © 1988 by Thomson/West.

Figure 5-4: Reprinted with permission from 29 *Ninth Decennial Digest*, Part 2, page 783, copyright © 1988 by Thomson/West.

Figure 5-5: Reprinted with permission from 44 *Ninth Decennial Digest*, Part 2, Table of Cases, page 1015, copyright © 1988 by Thomson/West.

Figure 5-6: Reprinted with permission from 29 *Ninth Decennial Digest*, Part 2, page 956, copyright © 1988 by Thomson/West.

Figures 5-7, 5-8, and 5-10: Reprinted with permission from American Law Reports, copyright by Thomson/West.

Figure 5-11: Reprinted with permission from *Words and Phrases*, copyright by Thomson/West.

Chapter 6: Encyclopedias, Periodicals, Treatises, and Restatements

Figure 6-1: Reprinted with permission from 87 C.J.S., copyright by Thomson/West.

Figure 6-2: Reprinted with permission from 25 Am. Jur. 2d, copyright by Thomson/West.

Figure 6-3: Reprinted with permission from *Deeds* § 87:77, *Am. Jur. Legal Forms 2d*, copyright by Thomson/West.

Figure 6-4: Reprinted with permission from General Index Update to Am. Jur. 2d, copyright by Thomson/West.

Figure 6-6: Reprinted with permission of the publisher, California Western Law Review, Vol. 41, Number 1, Fall 2004, copyright © 2004.

Figure 6-7: Reprinted with permission of *California Lawyer*, copyright © 2004.

Figure 6-8: Reprinted from "Subject and Author Index" and "Table of Cases" from *Index to Legal Periodicals & Books*, reprinted with permission of the H.W. Wilson Company.

Figure 6-9: Reprinted from *O'Neal's Close Corporations* (3d ed. 2003) copyright © 2003 by Thomson/West.

Figure 6-11: Copyright © 1965 by the American Law Institute. Reprinted with permission. All rights reserved.

Chapter 7: Miscellaneous Secondary Authorities

Figure 7-1: Reprinted with permission from *Black's Law Dictionary* 1002 (6th ed. 1990) copyright © 1990 by Thomson/West.

Figure 7-2: Reprinted with permission from *Martindale-Hubbell Law Directory* 1389B. Copyright © Martindale-Hubbell.

Figure 7-3: Reprinted with permission from *Martindale-Hubbell Law Directory*, Wisconsin Law Digest, copyright © 1990 and 1991 by Martindale-Hubbell.

Figure 7-4: Reprinted with permission from *Martindale-Hubbell Law Directory*, Mexico Law Digest, copyright © 1992 and 1993 by Martindale-Hubbell.

Figure 7-5A: Reprinted with permission from *Virginia Forms* Form 9-1002, by Frank J. Gallo, reproduced by permission of LexisNexis. Further reproduction of any kind is strictly prohibited.

Figure 7-6: Reprinted with permission Unif. Prob. Code § 2-102, from *Uniform Laws Annotated, Master Edition*, copyright © 1983 by National Conference of Commissioners on Uniform State Laws.

Figure 7-7: Reprinted with permission from *Directory of Uniform Acts and Codes*, copyright © 1983 by Thomson/West.

Figure 7-8: California Civil Jury Instructions. No copyright is claimed to the text of the jury instructions, directions for use, sources and authorities. Material located at http://www.courtinfo.ca.gov/reference/4_34juryinst.htm.

Chapter 9: Updating and Validating Your Research

Figure 9-1: Reprinted with permission from *Shepard's Virginia Citations*, August 2004, © 2004. Reproduced by permission of LexisNexis. Further reproduction of any kind is strictly prohibited.

Figure 9-4: Reprinted with permission from *Shepard's Michigan Citations*, copyright © 1990. Reproduced by permission of LexisNexis. Further reproduction of any kind is strictly prohibited. The material in this publication is not current and does not reflect the new format and information published by LexisNexis.

Figure 9-5: Reprinted with permission from *Shepard's Northwestern Citations*, copyright © 1993. Reproduced by permission of LexisNexis. Further reproduction of any kind is strictly prohibited. The material in this publication is not current and does not reflect the new format and information published by LexisNexis.

Figure 9-6: Reprinted with permission from *Shepard's United States Citations*, Eighth Edition, 2004, Bound Vol. 1–7, page 703, copyright © 2004. Reproduced by permission of LexisNexis. Further reproduction of any kind is strictly prohibited.

Figure 9-7: Reprinted with permission from *Shepard's Federal Citations,* Vol. 5, 1990, page 141, copyright © 1990. Reproduced by permission of LexisNexis. Further reproduction of any kind is strictly prohibited. The material in this publication is not current and does not reflect the new format and information published by LexisNexis.

Figure 9-10: Reprinted with permission from *Shepard's Virginia Citations*, Bound Vol. 2, 1995, page 621, copyright © 1995. Reproduced by permission of LexisNexis. Further reproduction of any kind is strictly prohibited.

Figure 9-11: Reprinted with permission from *Shepard's Federal Statutes Citations*, Bound Supplement, 2003-2005, Vol. 2, page 37, copyright © 2003-2005. Reproduced by permission of LexisNexis. Further reproduction of any kind is strictly prohibited.

Figures 9-13 and 9-14: Reprinted with permission from *Shepard's Federal Statutes Citations*, Bound Supplement, 2003-2005, Vol. 1, pages 3 and 43, copyright © 2003-2005. Reproduced by permission of LexisNexis. Further reproduction of any kind is strictly prohibited.

Figure 9-15: Reprinted with permission from *Shepard's Federal Circuit Case Name Citator*, copyright © 1992. Reproduced by permission of LexisNexis. Further reproduction of any kind is strictly prohibited. The material in this publication is not current and does not reflect the new format and information published by LexisNexis.

Figures 9-16 and 9-17: Reprinted with permission from *How to Shepardize*, pages 9 and 10. Reproduced by permission of LexisNexis. Further reproduction of any kind is strictly prohibited.

Figure 9-18: KeyCite Screen. *Research Guide for Paralegals*, page 57. Reprinted with permission from Thomson/West.

Figure 9-19: KeyCite Screen. Westlaw *Quick Research Guide* page 21. Reprinted with permission from Thomson/West.

Chapter 10: Special Research Issues

Figure 10-9: Reprinted with permission from *Shepard's Federal Statute Citations*, Bound 1996, Vol. 6, page 1109, copyright © 1996. Reproduced by permission of LexisNexis. Further reproduction of any kind is strictly prohibited.

Chapter 11: The Digital Library: LEXIS, Westlaw, and Non-Print Research Sources

Figures 11-1, 11-2, 11-3, and 11-4: LEXIS screens. Reproduced by permission of LexisNexis. Further reproduction of any kind is strictly prohibited.

Figures 11-6 and 11-7: Westlaw screens. Reprinted with permission of Thomson/West.

Chapter 12: E-Research: Legal Research Using the Internet

Figure 12-1: FindLaw screen. Reprinted with permission of Thomson/West.

Figure 12-2: Reprinted with permission of Washburn University School of Law.

Public Domain Materials

No copyright is claimed in the material shown in the following figures: 2-1, 3-2, 7-8, 10-1, 10-2, 10-3, 10-4, 10-5, 10-6, 10-7, 15-1, Appendix B, Appendix C, Appendix D.

Legal Research
and Writing
for Paralegals

Legal Research: Primary Authorities

Finding the Law

We are under a Constitution, but the Constitution is what the judges say it is, and the judiciary is the safeguard of our liberty and of our property under the Constitution.

Charles Evans Hughes (1907)

Chapter Overview

In this chapter we will discuss the role of paralegals in legal research and writing, the ethical duty to perform research competently, types of law libraries and their uses, and the sources of law in the United States. We will also examine the classification of law books as either primary or secondary sources. Finally, there is a brief introduction to the major law book publishers, who will be compared in greater detail in later chapters.

A. The Paralegal's Role in Legal Research and Writing

1. Legal Research and Writing as Core Competencies

Paralegals are expected to perform the task of legal research competently and cost effectively. In fact, the American Association for Paralegal

Education (AAfPE), a national organization that serves the needs of paralegal educators and institutions offering paralegal education programs,
identifies legal research as one of the "core competencies" that a successful
paralegal must possess.

Performing legal research today is both easier and more difficult than
it was just a generation ago. It is easier because many sources are available
on the Internet, making it quick and easy to find statutes, cases, and other
legal authorities. It is more difficult because the Internet makes so many
sources accessible that tracking down the right authority can seem like
finding a needle in a haystack.

Today's paralegals are expected to know how to use conventional
print sources, the computer-assisted research services LEXIS and Westlaw, and the Internet to find the best answer to a research problem as
quickly and effectively as possible.

Once you have conducted legal research, you will need to communicate the results of that research. In fact, the cornerstone of the legal profession is communication—communication with a colleague, client,
adverse party, or judge. In most cases the communication will be in written
form. Even in those instances in which you communicate orally, you will
often follow up with a written letter or memo to a file. Effective legal
writing is not only a task expected of paralegals but also one of the core
competencies identified by AAfPE for success in the paralegal profession.

2. *Ethical Duty to Research Accurately*

Perhaps the most fundamental aspect of the attorney-client relationship is
the client's absolute trust and confidence in the competence of the attorney.
This duty of competence is imposed on paralegals as well who are required
to exercise the ordinary skill and knowledge that would be expected of
similar paralegals in similar circumstances. In fact, Guideline 1 of the
American Bar Association's Model Guidelines for the Utilization of
Legal Assistant Services specifically requires that attorneys take reasonable measures to ensure that a paralegal's conduct is consistent with the
attorney's obligations, meaning that obligations imposed on attorneys
are likewise imposed on paralegals. Thus, attorneys are responsible for
ensuring that their paralegals are competent to perform assigned work,
including legal research and writing.

While it is important to "know" the law, particularly in a field in
which you may intend to specialize, it is even more important to be able
to "find" the law. In this sense, proficiency in legal research is the foundation for a successful career as a paralegal. Your employer will not be as
interested in your final grade in any specific class as much as your ability
to find accurate answers to questions relating to topics even though you
may not have been exposed to those topics in school. If you cannot perform
legal research tasks accurately and efficiently, you will not be a successful
paralegal despite excellent grades in your coursework.

In fact, the duty to perform accurate legal research has been
addressed in a number of cases, including *People v. Ledesma*, 729 P.2d

839, 871 (Cal. 1987), in which the court noted that an attorney's first duty is to investigate the facts of a client's case and to research the law applicable to those facts. In sum, the ethical duty to conduct adequate research required of attorneys is shared by paralegals as well.

Moreover, the failure to research adequately may lead to liability for legal malpractice. In one of the earliest cases on this subject matter, *Smith v. Lewis*, 520 P.2d 589 (Cal. 1975), *overruled on other grounds, In re Marriage of Brown*, 544 P.2d 561 (Cal. 1976), the California Supreme Court affirmed a lower court decision awarding $100,000 to be paid to a former client by an attorney who had failed to conduct adequate legal research. The court held that the attorney was obligated to undertake reasonable research and stated, "[e]ven as to doubtful matters, an attorney is expected to perform sufficient research to enable him to make an informed and intelligent judgment on behalf of his client." *Id.* at 596. In sum, you will be expected to perform competent legal research not only because your employer will insist on it but also because ethical standards demand it.

Now that we have established the role of paralegals in legal research and writing and the ethical duty shared by paralegals with attorneys to conduct competent legal research, we can address two critical questions where legal research is performed and what sources are used.

B. Law Libraries

1. Types of Law Libraries

As noted in the introduction to this text, legal research is a "hands-on" skill, requiring you to know how to use a law library. Your first task, therefore, is to locate a law library that you may use. There are approximately 3,600 law libraries in the United States. Following is a list of the most common types of law libraries with a brief description of each:

> *Law School Libraries* All accredited law schools have their own law libraries, most of which will have tens of thousands of volumes in print and nonprint forms such as CD-ROM, microforms, electronic bulletin boards, and the Internet. If you are attending a paralegal program at a four-year university that is affiliated with a law school, you will undoubtedly have access to the law library at the law school. Even if you do not attend a paralegal program affiliated with a law school, you may have access to a law school library if it has been designated as a Federal Depository Library, or a partial or selective depository, meaning that certain publications of the United States government, generally statutes and court decisions, will be sent to the library for review and access by the general public. In many cases, local public libraries or university libraries are designated as federal depositories. You can easily determine whether a library is a Federal Depository Library by

calling the reference librarian at the library and inquiring. Some law libraries, however, while providing access to the general public to review the depository collection, will prohibit access to any other portion of the law library. The location of the approximately 1,350 depository libraries can be retrieved at the following Web site: http://www.gpoaccess.gov/libraries.html.

Paralegal School Libraries Some paralegal programs maintain their own law libraries, although these are typically much smaller and contain far fewer volumes than law school libraries. Generally, only students who attend these programs have access to these law libraries.

Local Law Libraries Often a county or city will maintain a law library, and these are usually open to members of the general public. These law libraries vary in size, with the largest law libraries being found in the largest counties. Often they are located near a courthouse. The American Association of Law Libraries provides a list of state, county, and court law libraries at the following Web site: http://www.aallnet.org/sis/sccll.

Government or Agency Law Libraries Various governmental agencies, such as the Department of Justice, maintain their own law libraries. These law libraries typically serve only agency employees, and members of the general public will have no access. The Library of Congress, located in Washington, D.C., was established by the United States Congress in 1800 primarily to provide reference and research assistance to members of Congress. It has an excellent law library, which is open to any member of the general public.

Courthouse Law Libraries Many courts, both federal and state, maintain their own law libraries. Court law libraries are often found in the courthouse for the county seat. Some law libraries are open to the public while others restrict access to courthouse personnel, attorneys, and their paralegals.

Bar Association and Private Group Law Libraries Often bar associations or private groups, such as insurance companies or real estate boards, will maintain law libraries. These are usually open only to members of the association or group.

Law Firm Libraries Almost every law firm will maintain a law library, some of which are nearly as extensive as a law school or courthouse law library. These law libraries are available for use only by members or employees of the firm.

You should consult a telephone book and call law schools, courthouses, and county offices in your area to determine whether members of the general public have access to those law libraries and to obtain the hours for each. Be particularly careful of law school libraries that tend to schedule their hours of operation around the law school calendar and will often close unannounced after final exams or during semester breaks.

Additionally, many public and college or university libraries are increasing their collections of law books. While these libraries typically offer only the major sets of books, such as the cases of the United States Supreme Court, federal statutes, and statutes from the state in which they are located, these public or college libraries may afford a quick answer to some legal research questions.

Finally, law libraries now exist in cyberspace with vast collections of legal materials available for free "24/7." These virtual law libraries afford quick and easy access to a significant number of legal resources. Conducting legal research in cyberspace through the Internet is discussed in Chapter 12.

2. *Arrangement of Law Libraries*

There is no one standard arrangement for law libraries. Each law library is arranged according to the needs of its patrons or by decision of the law librarian. The best introduction to a law library is a tour given by a staff member and you should inquire whether orientation tours of the law library are given. If you cannot arrange for a tour, obtain a copy of the library handbook or guide that will describe the services offered, set forth the library's rules and regulations, and provide a floorplan of the law library. Spend an hour wandering around the law library and familiarizing yourself with its arrangement, organization, and collections. You will notice that there may be duplicate volumes of some books or even duplicate sets of books. In general, books that are widely used will have duplicates to ensure ease of use and accessibility. In many cases you can judge legal books by their titles, which usually describe their contents.

While some law libraries still use a card catalog (identical in its alphabetical organization and arrangement to the card catalogs you may have used through your schooling) to help you locate the books, treatises, and periodicals in the library, the more modern approach is the online catalog or OPAC (online public access catalog).

Most of the online catalogs are very easy to use, and you should not be intimidated. The law library staff is usually quite willing to provide instruction, and training sessions can be completed in only a few minutes. Typically, you will type in or "enter" the title, author, or subject matter you are interested in and you will then be provided with the "call number." The shelves or "stacks" in the law library are clearly marked, and locating a book is merely a matter of matching up the call number provided by the card catalog or online catalog with the appropriate stack label.

Most law school and large law firm law libraries use the Library of Congress classification system to arrange their books. The Library of Congress classification system is an alphanumeric system that arranges books on the shelves in subject order. Materials are organized according to twenty-one branches of knowledge. Each book is marked with a three-line classification number, consisting of an alphanumeric combination, meaning a combination of letters, a whole number, and a decimal. For example, a book may be classified as "KF503.181." The designation "KF" is the Library of Congress identifier for American legal publications.

An unusual feature of law libraries is that, in general, they are not circulating libraries. That is, unlike other libraries that circulate their volumes by allowing one to check out books, law libraries seldom allow patrons to check out books. You can imagine your frustration if you were unable to read a case because someone had already checked out the volume containing the case. Books that are not widely used, however, may often be checked out by individuals who possess library identification cards.

———————————— Practice Tip ————————

The Law Library

Familiarize yourself with your law library by investing half an hour to wander through the stacks and gain a sense of how the library is arranged. Experiencing the way the stacks are organized will imprint itself on your memory. This initial investment will save time for you later when you need to recall, for example, where the books relating to corporate law or litigation are located.

---

3. Law Library Staff

Most of the larger law libraries are serviced by full-time law librarians who are not only lawyers who have been awarded a Juris Doctor degree but who also possess a Masters Degree in Library Science. Most library staff are extremely helpful and responsive to questions; however, you should diligently try to locate a book or answer before you approach library staff for help. In law school libraries, the individuals who sit at the front desk are often law students who may not be thoroughly knowledgeable about the arrangement of the library or its collections. Therefore, if you have a question, be sure to address it to one of the professional law librarians (in this regard, the reference librarians are particularly helpful) rather than a student who may be more interested in studying at the front desk than helping you locate a book. Many reference librarians are available for research consultations by appointment. While law librarians will provide useful research tips and suggestions, they will not provide legal advice.

4. Law Library Courtesy

You should assume that everyone who uses the law library is as busy as you and therefore you should observe standard library etiquette by reshelving properly every book you use (unless the law library you use prohibits reshelving or has a separate preshelving stack for books that are to be reshelved). Nothing is more frustrating than taking time out of a busy schedule to drive to a law library and search for the appropriate sources only to realize that a needed volume is missing. If you take books to a study carrel to read or to the photocopier to reproduce a page, you must reshelve them when you are finished. This is particularly true in school situations in which your fellow classmates will in all likelihood have the same assignments as you and will thus need to use the same books.

Do not deface the books by turning pages down or marking an answer. Finally, do not resort to unfair conduct by hiding or intentionally misplacing books. There is no excuse for such overzealous tactics that not only impede learning but also reflect poorly on one who is purporting to be a member of a profession devoted to the law.

5. Other Library Services

Most law libraries offer a variety of other services to ensure students can conduct productive research. For example, if you are working on an extensive project, your law library may reserve a carrel for you and allow you to store books and materials there. Similarly, you may be able to reserve a group study room so you can meet with other students to brainstorm a research project. Law librarians can provide you with permits and letters of introduction to other law libraries in the area so you can retrieve materials not available at your law library. If certain materials are not maintained at your law library, the reference librarian may assist you in borrowing materials from other institutions through interlibrary loans. The ease of facsimile and online transmission results in ready access to a wealth of materials from all over the nation and the world.

Practice Tip

Legal Abbreviations

In the beginning of your legal career, you may become confused by the numerous abbreviations used for legal books, case reports, and journals. To determine the meaning of abbreviations such as "Ala." (for *Alabama Reports*) or "C.J.S." (for *Corpus Juris Secundum*), check Appendix A in *Black's Law Dictionary* (8th ed. 2004), which provides an extensive list of abbreviations commonly used in law.

C. Sources of Law in the United States

1. Cases and Our Common Law Tradition

If your task is to be able to find the law, one may well ask, "What is the 'law' we are talking about?" There are numerous definitions of the word "law." On an academic or philosophical level, law is a system of rules that governs society so as to prevent chaos. On a practical level, on the other hand, as indicated by the quotation at the beginning of this chapter, Governor of New York, and later United States Supreme Court Chief Justice Charles Evans Hughes suggested that the law "is what the judges say it is." This second view may give you cause for concern. If the law is what a judge says, what if the judge rules against you because of your race, or sex, or religion? What if the judge is not familiar with an area of the law? The American legal system has certain safeguards built into it to protect litigants from such scenarios.

The American legal system is part of what is referred to as the "common law" tradition. "Common law" is defined in part by *Black's Law Dictionary* 293 (8th ed. 2004) as that body of law that derived from judicial decisions rather than from statutes or constitutions. Common law is often referred to as "judge-made law."

This common law system began in England several hundred years ago. Since at least 1300 A.D., people who may have been training to be lawyers began "taking notes" on what occurred during trials. When judges were called upon to decide cases, they then began referring to these written reports of earlier cases and following the prior cases in similar situations. The English referred to this system as the "common law" because it was applied equally all throughout England and replaced a less uniform system of law. This system of following similar previous cases was considered the most equitable way of resolving disputes: People who are involved in like situations should be treated in the same manner.

This concept of following previous cases, or precedents, is called *stare decisis*, which is a Latin phrase meaning "to stand by things decided." In its broadest sense, the doctrine of stare decisis means that once courts have announced a principle of law, they will follow it in future cases that are substantially similar. It is this doctrine of stare decisis that serves to protect litigants from judges who may not be familiar with an area of the law. If the judge is required to follow precedent, he or she cannot rule against you based on your race, sex, or religion. Similarly, these precedents will guide a judge who is unacquainted with a certain area of the law. In this way, stare decisis advances fairness and consistency in our legal system.

Moreover, stare decisis promotes stability in our judicial system. It would not only be chaotic but manifestly unfair if judges treated each case that came before them as being severed from our great body of legal tradition and then rendered different and inconsistent rulings on a daily basis. You can imagine the frustration of a client who seeks advice of counsel on the division of property in a dissolution of a marriage only to be informed that the division depends on which judge hears the case: that Judge Jones divides property in a marital dissolution on a 50/50 basis; Judge Smith divides the property on a 40/60 basis; and Judge Anderson divides the property differently each day depending upon his mood. The client's rights would be totally dependent upon an arbitrary assignment to a judge. Such a result is not only unjust but unpredictable. Thus, stare decisis not only encourages stability in our legal system but also aids those in the legal profession in advising clients as to the likely disposition of their cases.

Under this system or doctrine of precedent following, "the law" was thus found in the written decisions of the judges, and these decisions served as precedents that were followed in later cases involving substantially similar issues. Thus, the first source of law in the United States is judge-made case law.

2. Constitutions and Statutes

A second source of law in the United States is constitutions and statutes. A constitution sets forth the fundamental law for a nation or a state. It is the document that sets forth the principles relating to organization and regulation of a federal or state government. We have a United States Constitution, our supreme law of the land, and each state has its own constitution. A statute, or law, is defined by *Black's Law Dictionary* 1448 (8th ed. 2004) as "a law passed by a legislative body."

In the United States, legislatures did not become particularly active in enacting statutes until the early to mid-1800s when the United States economy began changing from a very rural base to a more urban base. This major change in American society was coupled with a tremendous population growth, due largely to immigration, and it became clear that rather than deciding disputes on a case-by-case basis, which was slow and cumbersome at best, broader laws needed to be enacted that would set forth rules to govern behavior of the public at large. For example, when people live miles apart from one another and interact on a sporadic basis, few disputes will arise. On the other hand, when people are crowded into apartment buildings and work in densely populated urban areas, the number of problems greatly increases, and there is a concomitant need for general regulation by law or statute.

3. Administrative Regulations

A third source of law in the United States is the vast number of administrative rules and regulations promulgated by federal agencies such as the Federal Communications Commission ("FCC"), the Food and Drug Administration ("FDA"), the Occupational Safety and Health Administration ("OSHA"), and numerous other agencies. Agencies exist in the individual states as well, and these also enact rules and regulations.

The agencies play a unique role in our legal system because they function quasi-legislatively and quasi-judicially. You may recall from basic history and civics classes that our government is divided into three branches: the legislative branch, which makes laws; the judicial branch, which interprets laws; and the executive branch, which enforces laws.

Each division is to exercise its own powers, and, by a system known as "checks and balances," each functions separately from the others.

The agencies, on the other hand, perform two functions: They act as a legislature by promulgating rules and regulations that bind us; and they act as a judiciary by hearing disputes and rendering decisions.

While you may not have given a great deal of thought to the impact of the agencies in your daily life, their influence is significant and far-reaching. For example, the radio you listen to and the television you watch are regulated by the FCC; the cosmetics you use and the food or aspirin you ingest are regulated by the FDA; and the safety of your workplace is regulated by OSHA.

4. The Executive Branch

While the primary function of the federal executive branch is to enforce the law, it does serve as a source of law in three ways. First, treaties are entered into by the executive branch with the advice and consent of the United States Senate. These agreements between two or more nations do affect your daily life and serve as a source of law because they may relate to trade and import matters, economic cooperation, or even international boundaries and fishing rights. Second, the president, our chief executive, can issue executive orders to regulate and direct federal agencies and officials. Third, the executive branch exerts influence on the law through policies on enforcing laws.

For example, if various federal laws relating to possession of small amounts of drugs are rarely enforced, the *effect* is as if the law does not exist despite the fact that a statute clearly prohibits such acts. Nevertheless, while such an approach by the executive branch influences the law as well as societal behavior, such influence on the law is indirect and remote. In the event the government then prosecutes an individual for violation of such a previously unenforced law, the individual usually cannot raise the previous laxity as a defense. In a related example, in 1980, when the Selective Service System was reinstated to require United States males born in 1960 or later to register with the Service, several conscientious objectors refused to register. The federal government immediately prosecuted some of these individuals, who then asserted as a defense that they had been singled out for prosecution because they had been vigorous opponents of this draft registration. This defense, commonly known as "selective enforcement," is rarely successful and was not successful in the draft registration cases. To use a simple analogy, if you are cited for speeding, you cannot successfully assert that either all people who speed should be likewise cited or that none should. You would accept that you had simply been unluckier than other speeders. On the other hand, if only women are cited or only Hispanics are cited, such would appear to be the result of discrimination based on sex or ethnic origin, and a defense of selective enforcement alleging such invidious discrimination might well be successful.

D. Legal Systems of Other Countries

While every country has its own system of law, most systems are classified as either being part of the common law tradition, described above, or part of the civil law tradition. Civil law systems developed from Roman law. The Roman emperor Justinian I commissioned a comprehensive code of laws known as *Corpus Juris Civilis*, meaning "Body of Civil Law," to set forth all of the law of the Roman Empire. As a result, countries whose systems of law follow the Roman scheme of law with thoroughly comprehensive codes are said to be part of the civil law tradition. Even today many countries' codes of civil law are derived from the original Roman codes.

In general, civil law countries place much heavier reliance on their collections of statutes than on their much smaller collections of cases. These statutes are designed to address every conceivable legal issue that might arise, and it is these statutes that provide the ultimate answers to legal questions. Cases considered by judges rarely form the sole basis for any decision in civil law countries. Germany, France, Japan, Mexico, Korea, Spain, Italy, China, Austria, and the countries of Latin America are considered civil law countries.

In general, English-speaking countries or those that are prior British Commonwealth colonies are part of the common law system, which is greatly dependent on cases used as precedents, which in turn are followed in future cases that are substantially similar. Non-English-speaking countries are usually part of the civil law system, which is greatly dependent on codes or statutes intended to apply to every legal question or dispute. Because of the thoroughness of the Roman codes, statutes came to be known as the "written" law while the common law, relying as it does on judge-made case law, is often referred to as the "unwritten" law.

It is interesting to note that every state in the United States, except Louisiana, and every Canadian province, except Quebec, is part of the common law tradition. Because Quebec and Louisiana were settled by the French, their legal systems are largely patterned after the law of France, a civil law country. In fact, the Civil Code of Louisiana is closely based on the Code Napoleon, the French legal code enacted in 1804. In practice, however, even in many countries with systems based on civil law, case law still plays a significant role.

E. Legal System of the United States

The nature of our federalist system of government seeks to apportion power between our central or federal government and the 50 separate states and the District of Columbia. The founders of the Constitution feared that an overly strong federal government with concentrated power would ultimately engulf the separate states. Therefore, the Tenth Amendment to the Constitution was adopted. This amendment reserves to the individual states any powers not expressly granted or delegated to the federal government.

As a result, while the United States adheres to a uniform common law tradition, there is no one single legal system in this country. We have federal laws enacted by the United States Congress and federal cases decided by our federal courts, including the United States Supreme Court. Moreover, unless an area of the law has been preempted by the United States Constitution or the federal government, each state and the District of Columbia is free to enact laws as well as decide cases dealing with state or local concerns. Even within each state are smaller political subdivisions such as cities and counties, which enact local ordinances and regulations.

Thus, there is a tremendous body of legal literature on the shelves of law libraries: federal cases and federal statutes; Connecticut cases and Connecticut statutes; Florida cases and Florida statutes; Utah cases and Utah statutes, and so forth. Additionally, both the federal government and state governments promulgate administrative regulations, attorneys general issue opinions regarding legal problems, and experts publish commentary regarding the law. As early as 1821, Supreme Court Justice Joseph Story complained, "The mass of law is . . . accumulating with an almost incredible rapidity. . . . It is impossible not to look without some discouragement upon the ponderous volumes, which the next half century will add to the groaning shelves of our jurists." This statement was made about the time volume 19 of the *United States Reports* was published. As of 2002, the *United States Reports* covered more than 530 volumes.

All of the great mass of legal authorities can be classified as either primary authority or secondary authority. That is, every book in any law library is a primary authority or a secondary authority. See Figure 1-1.

Primary authorities are official pronouncements of the law by the executive branch (treaties and executive orders), legislative branch (constitutions, statutes, and administrative regulations and decisions), and judicial branch (cases). The key primary authorities are cases, constitutions, statutes, and administrative regulations. Thus, primary sources are those created by a governmental entity.

If a legal authority does not fall within one of the previously mentioned categories, it is a *secondary* authority. Secondary authorities may consist of legal encyclopedias, which provide summaries of many areas of the law; law review articles written about various legal topics; books or other treatises dealing with legal issues; law dictionaries; annotations, or essays about the law; and expert opinions on legal issues. In general, the secondary authorities are not the law but rather provide comment, discussion, and explanation of the primary authorities and, more important, help you locate the primary authorities.

It is critical to understand thoroughly the differences between primary and secondary authorities because only the primary authorities are *binding* upon the court, agency, or tribunal that may be deciding the legal issue you are researching. That is, if your argument relies upon or cites a case, constitution, statute, or administrative regulation that is relevant to a legal issue, it *must* be followed. All other authorities, for example, the secondary authorities, are *persuasive* only. If your argument cites *Black's Law Dictionary* for the definition of *negligence*, a court might be *persuaded* to adopt such a definition, but it is not *bound* to do so. On the other hand, if you cite a relevant case that defines *negligence*, a court must follow that definition.

Even though the secondary authorities are not binding on a court, they are often extremely effective research tools and provide excellent introductions to various legal topics. Nevertheless, you should keep in mind the purpose of the secondary authorities — to explain the primary authorities and locate the primary authorities that, if relevant, must be followed by a court.

In addition to the various authorities previously discussed, there are other books in the law library that are in the nature of practical guides or finding tools. These include books such as digests, which help you locate cases (see Chapter 5), form books, which provide forms for various legal documents such as wills, deeds, and contracts (see Chapter 7), and sets of books called *Shepard's Citations*, which help you update the authorities you rely upon in any legal writing (see Chapter 9). While these books are not true secondary authorities, their principal function is either to assist in locating primary sources or to serve as practical or finding guides for those in the legal profession.

The Final Wrap-Up

Using and Citing Primary and Secondary Authorities

Use: Use primary authorities to support the legal assertions you make. Use secondary authorities to summarize and explain the primary authorities and to help you locate the primary authorities.

Citation: You may cite to any primary authority. If a primary authority is on point, it must be followed in your jurisdiction. You may cite to most secondary authorities. Many are highly authoritative (such as the Restatements and many treatises). Others, however, are elementary and weak (for example, most legal encyclopedias) and should be used to familiarize yourself with an area of law and to direct you to the primary authorities.

F.   Law Book Publishing

As shown in Figure 1-1, the collection and variety of books in a law library are incredibly extensive.

Compared to the litigation explosion of the last 30 years, the early period of American history produced a fairly small number of cases. But just as the change in American society from agrarian and rural to an industrial and urban population resulted in a need for statutes to establish standards for behavior, this change also resulted in increased litigation and attendant case decisions.

For example, in the United States Courts of Appeal alone, the number of cases filed between 1994 and 2003 increased by nearly twenty-two percent. According to the National Center for State Courts, the nation's courts (both state and federal and trial and appellate courts) processed more than 90 million cases each year from 1984 to 1993. The vast majority was handled by state courts, which processed approximately

Figure 1-1
Primary Authorities (binding)

Authorities	Source
Cases (federal and state)	Judiciary
Constitutions (federal and state)	Legislature
Statutes (federal and state)	Legislature
Administrative regulations (federal and state)	Administrative agencies
Executive orders (federal only)	Executive branch
Treaties (federal only)	Executive branch

Secondary Authorities (persuasive)

Authorities
Encyclopedias
Law review articles
Periodical publications
Treatises and texts
Dictionaries
Attorneys general opinions
Restatements
Annotations
Foreign sources
Form books
Practice guides (such as jury instructions or non-judicial opinions on ethics)

88 million of these cases. The National Center concluded that the "trend for most types of state court cases is characterized by rapid growth." Most cases filed in the trial courts, approximately 90 percent, never come to trial. Of those state court cases that go to trial, only slightly more than 10 percent are appealed and result in a published opinion due to the fact that trial court opinions are rarely published. Nevertheless, even that number, added to the cases decided and published by the federal courts, results in approximately 50,000 cases being published each year. Additionally, Congress and the state legislatures publish thousands of pages of statutes, and thousands of pages of administrative rules and regulations are also published annually.

Thus, a tremendous amount of publication of legal authorities, both primary and secondary, occurs each year. You cannot expect to know all of the law contained in these authorities; however, you can be reasonably expected to be able to locate and use these legal authorities. That is the goal of legal research.

The actual publication of these authorities is conducted by only a handful of publishing companies. The giant in the legal publishing industry is West Group, headquartered in Eagan, Minnesota ("West").

In the mid-1990s, West was purchased for $3.4 billion by The Thomson Corporation, a Canadian publishing and information conglomerate. In the United States, the company retained its identification as "West." In 1996, West then merged with a number of other large law book publishers, namely Bancroft-Whitney, Clark Boardman Callaghan, and Lawyers Cooperative Publishing, to form West Group ("West"), which now has more than 8,000 employees, making it the preeminent provider of information to the legal market in the United States. In 2001, West acquired FindLaw (http://www.findlaw.com), which is the leader in free online legal information and services and the highest-trafficked legal Web site. In addition to being the provider of Westlaw, West annually publishes over 66 million books and 500 CD-ROM libraries.

The merger of Lawyers Cooperative Publishing ("Lawyers Co-op") into West has been of particular interest inasmuch as these two companies were for years the major publishers in the law book industry, offering competing products and services. For example, West has published federal statutes in a set known as U.S.C.A. while Lawyers Co-op published the same statutes in its set, U.S.C.S. Similarly, West has published cases from the United States Supreme Court in a set called *Supreme Court Reporter* while Lawyers Co-op published those same cases in a set called *United States Supreme Court Reports, Lawyers' Edition*. Lawyers and other legal professionals would purchase one set rather than the other based on price, convenience, habit, and ease of use, or perceived advantages of one set over the other.

Because the possibility of West acquiring a virtual monopoly on legal publication existed, West was ordered to divest itself of some of the publications it acquired through its merger. Thus, U.S.C.S. is now owned by LexisNexis Group ("LEXIS"), a division of Reed Elsevier PLC, and will continue to compete head-on with West for readers of federal statutes. You will likely notice some differences in the presentation of Lexis's name on its various publications. For example, some of its publications are marked "LexisNexis," others are marked "LEXIS Publishing," and still others are marked "LEXIS Law Publishing." For simplicity, this text will generally use "LEXIS Publishing" to refer to conventional print sources and "LEXIS" or "LexisNexis" to refer to the company's online or computer-assisted legal research system.

The numerous combinations and acquisitions of publishing companies has resulted in changes in some features of some law books. For example, for years a set of books called *American Law Reports* was published by Lawyers Co-op. It therefore referred its users to other Lawyers Co-op books. In 1998, the set was acquired by West and thus it now directs readers to West-owned law books. Moreover, some of the features of the set changed slightly after West acquired it. Thus, as books are described in this text, it is possible that some of their features and layout have changed over the years with recent books in a set appearing slightly different from earlier published books in the set.

Law book publishers also face increasing competition from emerging technologies. As discussed in Chapter 11, many cases now appear in CD-ROM format at a price significantly less than print versions, or on the Internet at no cost. These inroads on print publication have caused decreases in circulation of print materials. For example, subscriptions to West's *South Western Reporter*, publishing decisions from Texas, Missouri, Arkansas, Kentucky, and Tennessee have fallen 21 percent since 1993.

Finally, the acquisition of West by Thomson comes amid increasing competition and consolidation in the legal publishing arena. In 1994, Dutch publisher Wolters Kluwer purchased legal and tax publisher Commerce Clearing House Inc. In 1994, Anglo-Dutch publishing powerhouse Reed Elsevier PLC purchased LexisNexis, the online legal research system, from Mead Corporation for $1.5 billion. In sum, the world of legal publishing, long dominated by the giants West and Lawyers Co-op, is changing, partly due to increased competition and conglomeration and partly due to pressures brought to bear by the Internet, which allows 24-hours-a-day free access to many legal materials.

West publishes primary and secondary sources, for example, cases, statutes, and constitutions, as well as encyclopedias and other nonbinding authorities. Throughout the chapters ahead, there are frequent discussions and comparisons of West and other publishers, including analyses of similarities and distinctions between methods and organization of their publications.

In general, there are three major "families" of legal publishers, each of which incorporates other law book publishers: The Thomson Corporation (including the former West Publishing, now called West Group, Bancroft Whitney, and Clark Boardman Callaghan); Reed Elsevier PLC (including LexisNexis, Matthew Bender, Michie Company, Shepard's, and Martindale-Hubbell); and Wolters Kluwer (including Aspen Publishers, Inc. and Commerce Clearing House). More information on legal publishers can be found at the following Internet site: *A Legal Publishers List: Corporate Affiliations of Legal Publishers* (2004), http://www.aallnet.org/committee/criv/resources/tools/list.

Additionally, some companies such as Commerce Clearing House, Clark Boardman Callaghan, and Bureau of National Affairs specialize in the publication of looseleaf services — that is, sets of books dealing with various legal topics and contained in ringed binders. The hallmark of these looseleaf volumes is that they publish information on legal topics that are subject to frequent change and that if placed in hardback volumes would quickly become out-of-date. Publication of materials in looseleaf binders allows frequent updating by replacement of individual outdated pages with current pages. The looseleaf sets are thus "evergreen."

One of the common features shared by the primary sources (cases, constitutions, statutes, and regulations) as they are initially published is that they are arranged in chronological order. That is, cases are published in the order in which the court issued the decisions. A court will not designate a month as landlord-tenant month and only hear cases dealing with landlord-tenant law before moving on to some other topic, but rather may hear a case involving burglary followed by a contract dispute followed by a probate matter. The cases appear in volumes of books, called "court reports," in chronological order.

Similarly, during any given session, a legislature will enact laws relating to motor vehicles, regulation of utilities, and licensing of real estate salespeople. The initial publication of these statutes is in the order in which they were enacted rather than according to subject matter.

This type of organization makes research difficult. If you were asked to locate cases dealing with landlord-tenant law, you would find that they have not been brought together in one specific location but rather may be scattered over several hundred volumes of cases. It is clear then that a method of obtaining access to these primary authorities is needed and, in general, the secondary authorities and digests will assist you in locating the primary authorities. For example, a secondary source such as a legal encyclopedia will describe and explain landlord-tenant law and will then direct you to cases that are primary or binding authorities relating to this area of the law. These cases, when cited in a legal argument, under the doctrine of stare decisis, must be followed by a court, while the encyclopedia discussion is persuasive only and need not be followed by a court.

G.   Non-Print Research Media

Until fairly recently, almost all legal research was performed using conventional print volumes in law libraries. With the advent of computer-assisted legal research (see Chapter 11) and Internet legal research (see Chapter 12), legal professionals use a variety of media to get the right answers to their research questions and are no longer tied to the law library. Good researchers must be adept at both methods of performing legal research: using conventional print sources and using newer technology sources such as CD-ROM, commercial databases such as LEXIS and Westlaw, and the Internet. Using newer technologies allows legal professionals to perform research at their desks or even on the road.

Some methods are more efficient and cost-effective than others. For example, if you need general background information about an area of law, you should consider browsing an encyclopedia or treatise in print form. If you need information about a new or evolving area of law, computer-assisted legal research will likely provide the most current information. If you need to refresh your memory about a statutory provision, it may be more cost-effective for the client if you quickly review the statute in print form rather than going to the expense of logging on to LEXIS or Westlaw. Moreover, you need to flexible in using all methods of legal research if case materials are unavailable: Books can disappear from library shelves and networks can go down.

Thus, effective legal researchers are creative and adaptable. A recent survey by the American Bar Association reported that the responding attorneys spent 37 percent of their total research time using fee-based Internet or online services such as LEXIS or Westlaw and a nearly equal amount of time, namely, 34 percent, using conventional print resources. Time spent using other media such as CD-ROM made up about 12 percent of their total research time. Legal Technology Resource Center, American Bar Association, *2001 ABA Legal Technology Resource Center Survey Report, Executive Summary* xi (2001).

Successful legal researchers thus combine research media to obtain information for clients. Knowing which media to use requires an analysis of many factors, including the complexity of your task, the costs involved, and time constraints. Many teachers urge students first to become familiar with the conventional print tools before becoming too wedded to computer-assisted or Internet legal research. Strong skills in manual legal research provide a good foundation for using LEXIS, Westlaw, and the Internet more effectively. Thus, this text will fully examine the conventional print research tools before discussing newer technologies such as computer-assisted legal research and Internet legal research.

H. Change in Our Legal System

While stare decisis promotes stability, fairness, and uniformity in our legal system, blind adherence to established precedents in the face of changing societal views and mores may result in injustice. For example, in 1896, the United States Supreme Court held that "separate but equal" public facilities for blacks and whites were lawful. *Plessy v. Ferguson*, 163 U.S. 537 (1896). This precedent served to justify segregation for more than 50 years. In 1954, however, in *Brown v. Board of Education*, 347 U.S. 483 (1954), the Supreme Court overruled its earlier decision and held that segregation solely according to race in public schools violated the United States Constitution. A strict adherence to stare decisis would have precluded a second look at this issue and would have resulted in continued racial segregation.

Similarly, the view of women has changed in our case law. In *Bradwell v. State*, 83 U.S. (16 Wall.) 130, 141 (1872), a concurring justice noted: "The paramount destiny and mission of woman are to fulfil the noble and benign offices of wife and mother. This is the law of the Creator." One hundred years later, Justice Brennan acknowledged, "There can be no doubt that our Nation has had a long and unfortunate history of sex discrimination. Traditionally, such discrimination was rationalized by an attitude of 'romantic paternalism' which, in practical effect, put women, not on a pedestal, but in a cage." *Frontiero v. Richardson*, 411 U.S. 677, 684 (1973).

Thus, it is clear that as society changes, the law must also change. A balance must be struck between society's need for stability in its legal system and the need for flexibility, growth, and change when precedents have outlived their usefulness or result in injustice. In discussing the fact that the United States Supreme Court can overrule its precedents to correct an injustice, Woodrow Wilson remarked that the Court sits as "a kind of constitutional convention in continuous session." It is the function of our courts to achieve both of these seemingly contradictory goals: the need for stability and the need for change.

In recent years the United States Supreme Court has shown an increased willingness to depart from its previous rulings. From 1789 to 1954 the United States Supreme Court overruled only 88 of its precedents. From 1954 to 1990, however, the Court overruled 108 of its precedents.

Nevertheless, you should not view these changes as abrupt and unsettling frequent events. Change often occurs slowly and always occurs in an ordered framework. This order is a result of the structure of our court systems into a hierarchy of lower courts, which conduct trials, and higher courts, which review the conduct of those trials by appeal.

Change in established legal precedent comes about by rulings of higher courts, which then bind lower courts in that judicial system or hierarchy. For example, a small claims court in Portland, Oregon, cannot overrule *Brown v. Board of Education*. Because *Brown v. Board of Education* was decided by the United States Supreme Court, it can only be overruled by the United States Supreme Court. Similarly, a decision by the highest court in Minnesota, binds all of the lower courts in Minnesota and a decision by the Ninth Circuit Court of Appeals is binding on all courts within that circuit, but not in other circuits. Nevertheless, lower courts often attempt to evade precedents by striving to show those precedents are inapplicable to the cases then before them. For example, a lower court might hold that a precedent established by a court above it dealing with the interpretation of a written contract is not binding because the lower court is interpreting an oral contract. Lower courts thus often reject precedent or refuse to follow precedent on the basis that those precedents are inapplicable to their case or can be distinguished from their case. This flexibility in reasoning results in a rich, complex, and often contradictory body of American case law. According to *Hart v. Massanari*, 266 F.3d 1155, 1173 (9th Cir. 2001), "This ability to develop different interpretations of law among the circuits [and courts] is considered a strength of our system. It allows experimentation with different approaches to the same legal problem so that when the Supreme Court eventually reviews the issue it has the benefit of 'percolation' within the lower courts."

Thus, stare decisis means more than simply following settled cases. It means following settled cases that are factually similar and legally relevant to the case or problem you are researching. Such a factually similar and legally relevant case from a court equivalent to or higher than the court that will hear your particular case is said to be "on point" or "on all fours" with your case. The goal of legal research is to be able to locate cases on point with your particular case. Such cases are binding upon and must be followed by the court hearing your case.

In the event you cannot locate cases on point in your judicial hierarchy (possibly because your case presents a novel issue not yet considered in your jurisdiction), you should expand your search for cases on point to other jurisdictions. That is, if your case presents an issue not yet decided by the Minnesota courts, often called a case "of first impression," search for on-point cases in other states. If you locate a Wisconsin case on point, it is *not* binding in Minnesota. It may, however, be *persuasive* to the Minnesota court. If the Minnesota court adopts the view espoused in the Wisconsin case, it is then a precedent in Minnesota and according to the doctrine of stare decisis is binding upon that Minnesota court and all others lower than it in Minnesota.

Among the factors that may be considered by the Minnesota court in adopting the Wisconsin view are whether the Wisconsin case is well reasoned and well written, whether Minnesota and Wisconsin have some tradition in relying upon and respecting each other's cases, whether the Wisconsin case was issued by one of the higher Wisconsin courts, and whether the Wisconsin view is shared by other jurisdictions or approved by legal scholars. See Figure 1-2.

Change in our legal system can occur not only as a result of judges expanding or overruling precedents found in cases but through

Figure 1-2
Stare Decisis and Our Judical Hierarchy

- Primary law comprises cases, constitutions, statutes, treaties, executive orders, and administrative regulation. All other legal authorities are secondary.
- Primary law from your state or jurisdiction is binding within your state or jurisdiction.
- Primary law from another state or jurisdiction is persuasive only in your state or jurisdiction.
- If your state or jurisdiction adopts the law or position of another state or jurisdiction, then that position is now binding within your judiciary hierarchy.
- Secondary law (no matter where it originates) is persuasive only.
- Higher courts in any given judicial hierarchy bind lower courts in that hierarchy.
- Higher courts can depart from a previously announced rule if there are compelling and important reasons for doing so.

repeal or amendment of a statute by a legislature or even through judicial interpretation of a statute. You may notice as you read statutes that many are broadly written, ambiguous, or vague. In such a case, judges may interpret the meaning of the statute, clarify ambiguous terms, explain the language of the statute, or declare the law invalid. For example, a statute may require a landlord to provide three days' notice to a tenant before evicting a tenant for nonpayment of rent. A question may arise as to the meaning of this provision if the third day occurs on a national holiday. If the statute does not address this issue, a court is free to determine that if the third day occurs on a Sunday or holiday, the tenant will be given an extra day's notice. While a court cannot *change* the plain meaning of a statute, it is free to *interpret* the statute. Thus, even when you locate a statute that appears directly to address your research problem, you cannot stop researching. You must read the cases that have interpreted the statute because it is judicial interpretation of a statute rather than the naked language of a statute that is binding under the doctrine of stare decisis. This research requirement brings us full circle to the practical definition of "the law" given before — that the law is what the judges say it is. In statutory construction, the law is not always what the statute says but rather what a judge says it means.

You have seen that a case from a higher court in one state or jurisdiction is binding upon lower courts in that state or jurisdiction and may be persuasive authority in other states. In contrast, a statute has no effect whatsoever anywhere other than in the jurisdiction that enacted it. When the Kansas legislature is enacting statutes relating to the licensing of real estate salespersons, it is unaffected by statutes in Nevada relating to the same topic. Any Nevada statutes on this topic lack even persuasive effect outside Nevada's jurisdictional boundaries.

I. Identifying the Holding in a Case

You can readily see that the foundation of the American legal system lies in its rich and varied body of case law. While analysis of cases will be discussed in great detail in Chapter 4, you should be aware that under the concept of stare decisis, only the actual rule of law announced in a case is binding. That is, only the holding of the case is authoritative. The holding is referred to as the *ratio decidendi* or "reason of the decision." The remainder of the language in the case is referred to as *dictum*, which is usually used as an abbreviated form of *obiter dictum*, meaning a remark "in passing." *Black's Law Dictionary* 485 (8th ed. 2004) provides that dictum is "a statement of opinion or belief considered authoritative because of the dignity of the person making it." Dictum in a case is persuasive only.

On some occasions, a court may speculate that its decision would be different if certain facts in the case were different. This type of discussion is dictum and while it may be persuasive in other cases, it is not binding authority.

In many cases, distinguishing the holding from the dictum is easily done. Often a court will set the stage for announcing its holding by using extremely specific language similar to the following: "We hold that a landlord may not commence an action to evict a tenant for nonpayment of rent without providing the tenant with a written notice to either pay rent or forfeit possession of the leased premises." On other occasions, finding the holding requires a great deal more persistence and probing.

You may notice that some cases are difficult to read and are written using archaic and outmoded language. Do not get discouraged. Reading cases takes a great deal of patience and experience. You will find, however, that the more cases you read, the more skillful you will become at locating the holding, distinguishing dicta from the holding, and understanding the relevance of the case for the future.

J.   Case Citation Form

While case citation will be discussed in much more depth in Chapter 8, the sooner you begin examining the books in which our cases are published or reported and the sooner you begin reading those cases, the more confident you will become about your ability to research effectively.

All cases follow the same basic citation form: You will be given the case name, the volume number of the set in which the case is published, the name of the set in which the case appears, the page on which it begins, and the year it was decided (and the deciding court, if not apparent from the name of the set). For example, in "reading" the citation to the United States Supreme Court case *Brown v. Board of Education*, 347 U.S. 483 (1954), you can readily see the following:

1.   The case name is *Brown v. Board of Education*;
2.   It is located in volume 347;
3.   It is found in a set of books entitled *United States Reports*;
4.   It begins on page 483 of volume 347; and
5.   It was decided in 1954.

State court cases are cited much the same way. The citation *State v. Paul*, 548 N.W.2d 260 (Minn. 1996) informs you that:

1.   The case name is *State v. Paul*;
2.   It is located in volume 548;
3.   It is found in a set of books entitled *North Western Reporter, Second Series*;
4.   It begins on page 260; and
5.   It is a Minnesota case decided in 1996.

While this text shows case names and book titles in italics, underlining or underscoring is also acceptable according to *The Bluebook: A Uniform System of Citation* (Columbia Law Review Ass'n et al. eds., 18th ed. 2005) ("*The Bluebook*") and ALWD & Darby Dickerson, *ALWD Citation Manual* (2d ed., Aspen Publishers 2003) ("*ALWD*"). As discussed in Chapter 8, although *The Bluebook* is the standard reference tool for citation form, *ALWD* is gaining in popularity due to its commonsense rules and user-friendly format. The citation examples given previously comply with both *Bluebook* and *ALWD* rules. There are additional citation systems as well and variation among practitioners, so check with your firm or office to determine if there is a preference.

CyberSites

http://www.westpub.com or http://www.thomson.com	Information about West Group products and services
http://www.lectlaw.com	Inter-Law's 'Lectric Library, a variety of legal information together with links to other law-related sites
http://www.ilrg.com	Internet Legal Resource Guide, a comprehensive guide to legal resources available online
http://www.hg.org/publishers.html	HierosGamos Web site, offering a list of legal publishers together with their addresses and telephone numbers
http://www.lawguru.com/lawlib	Internet Law Library (formerly the U.S. House of Representatives Internet Law Library) with useful links to a large number of legal resources
http://www.loc.gov/law/guide	Guide to Law Online, prepared by the U.S. Law Library of Congress, Public Services Division, providing an annotated guide to sources of information and law available online and links to useful and reliable sites for legal information

Writing Strategies

Always support arguments with cases on point. Precedents that differ significantly from your case will not only *not* be helpful, they may actually hurt your case by causing the reader to believe that there is no authority to support the position you advocate.

Carefully scrutinize the cases you find for their weight (what level is the court that rendered the decision?), their date (when was the case decided?), their issues (are the legal issues involved in the cases you find similar or identical to ones in your case?), and the facts (are the facts involved in the cases you find similar or analogous to the ones in your case?).

Use only the "best" decisions to support your argument. Be merciless. Discard cases that provide the adversary with any ammunition. When you have selected the cases that will best advance your position, use analogy to show the reader how similar they are to your case so the reader can easily see why these cases are controlling.

Use active voice and vivid and forceful language when constructing your argument. Personalize your clients by identifying them by name ("Jean White") and depersonalize adverse parties by referring to them by a "label" (the "defendant," the "company").

Assignment for Chapter 1

1. a. Give the name of the case located at 531 U.S. 70 (2000).
   b. Who argued the case for the Petitioner?
2. a. Give the name of the case located at 447 U.S. 303 (1980).
   b. Who delivered the opinion of the Court?
   c. Who dissented?
3. a. Give the name of the case at 502 U.S. 301 (1992).
   b. Give the date the case was argued.
   c. Give the date the case was decided.
   d. Locate a case in this volume in which the defendant's name is *Bryant* and give the name of the case.
   e. Give the citation for the *Bryant* case.
   f. What part did Justice Thomas take in the *Bryant* case?

State Your Answer

1. Use Table T.1 of *The Bluebook* or access http://www.ncsconline.org (the Web site for the National Center for State Courts) and locate and access your state's judicial Web site. Who is the current chief justice or senior judge of your state's highest court?
2. Access the site for the American Association for Law Libraries and identify the state, court, or county law libraries in your state or nearest locality.
3. Access the site for GPO Access and identify at least one federal depository library for your state or nearest locality.
4. Access Cornell Law School's Legal Information Institute at http://www.cornell.edu. Select "Lexicon" and provide the definition for stare decisis.

The Federal and State Court Systems

The Republic endures and this is the symbol of its faith.

Chief Justice Charles Evans Hughes (on the occasion
of the laying of the cornerstone for the
Supreme Court building in 1932)

A. **Federalism**
B. **Establishment of Federal Court Structure**
C. **Jurisdiction**
D. **Ground Rules for Cases**
E. **The Federal Court Structure**
F. **State Court Organization**
G. **Citation Form**

Chapter Overview

As we discussed in Chapter 1, there is no one legal system in the United States. There are 52 legal systems: one system composed of cases and statutes decided and enacted by federal courts and the federal legislature, namely the United States Congress, and another system composed of cases and statutes decided and enacted by the state courts and state legislatures for each of the 50 states and the District of Columbia.

This chapter will provide an overview of the federal and state court systems. To perform research tasks, you should understand these court structures so when you are confronted with a research assignment or a case citation you will readily understand the hierarchy of cases within a given court structure, giving greater emphasis to cases from higher courts such as the United States Supreme Court and the United States Courts of Appeal than to cases from the federal trial courts, the United States district courts, or the lower state courts.

A. Federalism

As you no doubt remember from basic American history or civics classes, there are three branches in the federal government: the legislative branch, which is charged with making federal law; the executive branch, which is tasked with enforcing the law; and the judicial branch, whose function is interpreting the law. See Figure 2-1 for a chart showing the organization of the government of the United States.

That we have federal courts that exist separate and apart from state courts is a result of a feature of our system of government called federalism. The principle of federalism developed from the time of the drafting of the Constitution.

At the time of the Constitutional Convention in 1787, there were two conflicting ideas held by the framers of the Constitution. On the one hand, the framers recognized the need for a strong central or "federal" government to act in matters of national concern and to reduce George Washington's fear that the fledgling nation had "thirteen heads, or one head without competent powers." On the other hand, the delegates to the Convention were wary of delegating too much power to a centralized government; after all, almost all of the delegates had served as soldiers in the Revolutionary War, which had been fought against a monolithic government insensitive to the rights of the newly emerging colonies. This principle of states' rights was seen as the best protection against an encroaching central government.

The solution was a compromise: For those delegates devoted to a strong national government, the principle developed that the national government could exercise only those powers expressly delegated to it. These powers were specifically enumerated in Article I, Section 8 of the Constitution, which states that, among other things, the federal government has the power to borrow money, collect taxes, coin money, establish post offices, declare war, raise and support armies, and make any other laws "necessary and proper" for carrying out these delegated powers. This "necessary and proper" clause is often called the "elastic" clause as it makes clear that the federal government not only has the powers expressly delegated to it in Article I, Section 8 but can also take action that is not specifically mentioned so long as it is "necessary and proper" to enable it to carry out the delegated powers.

As is readily seen, these specifically enumerated powers are extremely important, and those delegates in favor of states' rights were concerned that, as a result of the compromise, the federal government was too strong and would eventually "swallow up" the states. In fact, Patrick Henry refused to attend the Convention because of his opposition to granting any additional power to the national government and expressly warned that the Constitution "squints toward monarchy. Your President may easily become King." However, the Constitution was immediately modified by the addition of ten amendments collectively known as the Bill of Rights, which were designed to protect individual liberties. The Tenth Amendment, in particular, was enacted to reassure those in favor of states' rights that

Figure 2-1
The Government of the United States

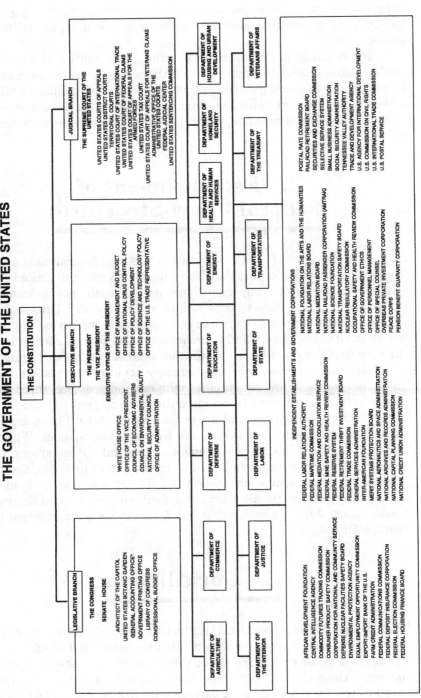

THE GOVERNMENT OF THE UNITED STATES

*Officially renamed Government Accountability Office, effective July 7, 2004.

the federal government would not be able to encroach on the rights of the 13 new states or their citizens. The Tenth Amendment, often referred to as the "reserve" clause, provides that any powers not expressly given to the national government are reserved to, or retained by, the individual states.

The result of the historic Constitutional Convention is our "living law" — a unique federalist system in which the states have formed a union by granting the federal government power over national affairs while the states retain their independent existence and power over local matters. In a system based on federalism, power is shared between the national and state governments.

B. Establishment of Federal Court Structure

Article III, Section 1 of the Constitution created the federal court system. This section provides in part that "the judicial power of the United States shall be vested in one Supreme Court and in such inferior courts as Congress may from time to time ordain and establish." Thus, only the existence of the Supreme Court was ensured. It was left up to Congress to determine its composition and to create any other federal courts. In fact, the very first Congress began to work on establishing a functioning federal court system and enacted the Judiciary Act of 1789. This Act created 13 district courts in prominent cities with one judge apiece, three circuit courts to be presided over by no more than two Supreme Court justices and a district court judge, and above these, the United States Supreme Court consisting of a chief justice and five associate justices. While the Judiciary Act of 1789 has been amended several times (among other reasons, to increase the number of Supreme Court justices), the basic structure of our federal court system remains as it was in 1789: district courts, intermediate circuit courts of appeal, and one United States Supreme Court. Judges appointed to these courts are often referred to as "Article III judges."

C. Jurisdiction

The jurisdiction (or power to act) of the federal courts does not extend to every kind of case or controversy but only to certain types of matters. You will learn a great deal more about this topic in your litigation or civil procedure classes, but a brief explanation is in order here for you to understand fully why some research assignments will be researched through the exclusive use of federal law and others will be researched through the exclusive use of the law of a particular state.

There are two types of cases that are resolved by federal courts: those based on federal question jurisdiction and those based on diversity jurisdiction.

1. *Federal Question Jurisdiction*

The federal courts are empowered to hear cases that involve a federal question, namely, any case arising under the United States Constitution, a United States (or federal) law, or any treaty to which the United States is a party. Additionally, federal courts may decide controversies between states or between the United States and foreign governments and any cases involving the U.S. government. Cases arising under the Constitution include cases alleging racial, sexual, or age discrimination; cases involving freedom of speech, freedom of the press, freedom of religion; cases involving a defendant's right to a fair trial; cases involving federal crimes such as bank robbery or kidnapping; and any other such actions pertaining to a federal law or the Constitution.

It may be easier for you to remember the scope of federal question cases if you keep in mind a simple analogy. If a *7-11* convenience store in your neighborhood were burglarized, you would expect your local law enforcement officials to investigate the crime. On the other hand, if a bank in your area were burglarized, you would expect the investigation to be handled by the FBI, our federal law enforcement officials. Similarly, *federal* questions, namely those arising under federal law or the Constitution, are resolved by *federal* courts while more local matters are typically resolved by state courts.

2. *Diversity Jurisdiction*

The other category of cases that is handled by federal courts is determined not by the issue itself (as are federal question cases) but by the status of the parties to the action.

Imagine you are a New York resident on vacation in Montana where you become involved in an automobile accident with a Montana resident. You may have some concern whether a court in Montana would treat you, an outsider, the same as it would treat its own residents, particularly in a locality in which the residents elect the judge.

To ensure that litigants are treated fairly and to eliminate any bias against an out-of-state litigant, the federal courts may resolve cases based on the diversity of the parties; that is, in general, federal courts may hear cases in civil actions between: (i) citizens of different states; and (ii) citizens of a state and citizens of a foreign nation. Diversity cases accounted for nearly 40 percent of the civil trials in federal courts in 2003.

Note that diversity jurisdiction is conditioned upon satisfying another key element: The amount in controversy must exceed $75,000 exclusive of interest and court costs. For example, if a resident of Oregon sues a resident of Nevada for breach of contract and alleges (in good faith) damages in the amount of $80,000, the matter may be instituted in federal court.

Diversity must be complete; all plaintiffs must be citizens of different states from all defendants. A federal court in a diversity case will apply the state law of the state in which it is located. For example, if an Ohio resident sues a Texas resident for $100,000 for breach of contract in a Texas federal court, the federal court will rely on Texas's law in reaching its decision. In early 2005, Congress passed the Class Action Fairness Act of 2005, which amends the federal diversity statute (28 U.S.C. § 1332) by granting district courts original jurisdiction in civil actions in which the matter in controversy exceeds $5 million. The legislation is intended to send most large multistate class actions to federal court (although the matter will be heard in state court if the primary defendant and more than one-third of the plaintiffs are from the same state).

Over the years, the federal courts have increased the monetary amount in diversity cases in order to prevent the federal courts from becoming inundated with cases. Until 1988, the monetary amount was $10,000. When it became apparent that almost any routine "fender bender" resulted in damages in excess of $10,000, Congress increased the monetary limit to the amount of $50,000. In October 1996, the limit was increased again to its present requirement of $75,000. There is no monetary jurisdictional limit for cases instituted in federal court based on federal questions; that is, if a plaintiff alleges she has been wrongfully discharged from her employment due to sexual discrimination, she need not allege damages in excess of $75,000.

Diversity jurisdiction has its detractors, notably Chief Justice William H. Rehnquist, who since 1987 has urged elimination of diversity jurisdiction as a basis for initiating an action in federal court. Because total elimination of diversity jurisdiction appears unlikely, Chief Justice Rehnquist has alternatively suggested that diversity jurisdiction be curtailed so as to prevent citizens of one state from suing citizens from another state in federal court. It is believed such a modification to diversity jurisdiction would eliminate "forum shopping," that is, the selection of a particular federal court for certain perceived advantages, among them the strategy of making it difficult for individuals to defend themselves in a court not located near their residences.

Another criticism of diversity jurisdiction, especially in cases brought by a citizen of one state against a citizen of another state, is that the federal courts are becoming "clogged up" deciding non-federal questions such as routine automobile accident cases, which are better resolved by the state courts.

If a plaintiff brings a case in state court that could have been brought in federal court (based on either subject matter or diversity jurisdiction), the defendant may remove it to federal court. If removal was improper (because the court lacked jurisdiction), the case must be remanded or returned back to the state court.

See Figure 2-2 for chart of federal jurisdiction.

Figure 2-2
Federal Jurisdiction

Federal jurisdiction may be based upon the following:

- **Federal question:** Any case arising under the U.S. Constitution or any federal law (28 U.S.C. § 1331 (2000)); or
- **Diversity:** Generally, cases in which all plaintiffs are from different states from all defendants and in which the matter in controversy exceeds $75,000. (28 U.S.C. § 1332 (2000)).

Additionally, cases originally filed in state court may be removed to a federal court, as follows:

- **Removal:** If a case is originally filed by a plaintiff in state court and federal jurisdiction exists, the case may be removed to federal district court by the defendant. 28 U.S.C. § 1441 (2000).
- **Remand:** If it is determined that a case was improperly removed because it lacked subject matter jurisdiction, it must be remanded or returned to the state court. 28 U.S.C. § 1447 (2000).

3. *Concurrent Jurisdiction*

Often one hears about cases that are being litigated in a state court when it seems clear the action involves a federal question, for instance, racial discrimination. In such cases, concurrent jurisdiction may exist, meaning the plaintiff alleged a cause of action that violated both state law and federal law. In the example mentioned above, the basis for the action, racial discrimination, violates both California law and federal law. The plaintiff in such a case then has a choice whether to proceed in state court or federal court. The decision in which court to bring an action when concurrent jurisdiction exists is often made on the basis of tactics and strategy. For example, a plaintiff may wish to proceed in a federal court because it is not as crowded with cases as the local state court, thus resulting in a more speedy trial and resolution. Moreover, any diversity jurisdiction case regardless of the amount of money involved may be brought in a state court rather than a federal court.

4. *Exclusive Jurisdiction*

Some matters are handled exclusively by federal courts and are never the subject of concurrent jurisdiction. For example, by federal law all bankruptcy cases are resolved by the United States Bankruptcy Courts (discussed below). Other examples of cases that are handled exclusively by federal courts are maritime, copyright, and patent cases.

Because issues relating to jurisdiction are often complex, always ask your supervising attorney if you have a question relating to the jurisdiction of a case.

D.   Ground Rules for Cases

Even if a federal question is involved or even if the requirements for diversity jurisdiction are satisfied, there still remain some ground rules that must be satisfied before a federal court will hear a case.

   In large part, these ground rules are rooted in Article III of the Constitution, which establishes the jurisdiction of federal courts and restricts federal courts to resolving "cases" and "controversies." This limitation has been construed to mean that federal courts will only resolve an actual controversy. Moreover, the actual controversy must exist througout the matter, and not merely at the date the action is initiated. With very few exceptions, federal courts will not consider issues that are "moot" or already resolved. In fact, it is a fraud on a court to continue with a case that is moot. An exception to this requirement is demonstrated by the well-known case *Roe v. Wade*, 410 U.S. 113 (1973), in which a pregnant plaintiff challenged a Texas law prohibiting abortion. By the time the case reached the United States Supreme Court, the plaintiff had given birth and placed the baby for adoption. The United States Supreme Court could have dismissed the case claiming it was moot — namely, that the issue had already been effectively decided upon the birth of the child and that even if the court awarded the relief the plaintiff had requested, declaring abortion lawful, the plaintiff's situation would not be affected by the ruling. However, in *Roe* the United States Supreme Court, realizing that such a case would inevitably be rendered moot by the time it would reach the Court, made an exception and heard the case.

   A close corollary to this ground rule that federal courts will not consider questions that are moot is that federal courts will not render advisory opinions, even if asked by the president. The federal courts view themselves as constitutionally bound to resolve actual ongoing disputes, not to give advice. For example, President George Washington once sent the Supreme Court 29 questions on treaties and international law, asking for advice. The justices refused on the dual bases that under the Constitution, they could not share powers and duties with the executive branch and that they were forbidden to issue advisory opinions.

   Finally, a plaintiff must have personally suffered some actual or threatened injury; that is, the plaintiff must be adversely affected by some conduct of the defendant and cannot base a claim on the rights or interests of some other persons. No matter how convinced you may be that a law is unconstitutional, you cannot challenge it unless *your* rights are directly affected. This requirement is referred to as "standing." For example, in *Sierra Club v. Morton*, 405 U.S. 727 (1972), the Sierra Club brought an action to prevent development of Mineral King Valley into a commercial resort. The Court concluded that the Sierra Club lacked standing as it had not alleged that it or any of its members would be affected by the defendant's activities in developing Mineral King Valley. The Court noted that standing does not exist merely because one has an interest in a controversy or a matter is personally displeasing; one must have a personal stake in the outcome of the controversy.

In a more colorful example, in late 1999, a judge rejected a suit filed by a political opponent of Minnesota governor and former wrestler Jesse Ventura that sought to stop Governor Ventura from refereeing a wrestling match. Although the plaintiff claimed that the governor's appearance would violate a state law against using public office for personal gain, the judge stated the plaintiff had no standing because he had failed to provide evidence that he would suffer harm as a result of Governor Ventura's involvement in a Worldwide Wrestling Federation match.

E. The Federal Court Structure

1. District Courts

The district courts are the trial courts in our federal system. At present, there are 94 district courts scattered throughout the 50 states, the District of Columbia, and the territories and possessions of the United States. There is at least one district court in each state, and the more populous states, such as California, New York, and Texas, may have as many as four within their territorial borders. Other less populous states, such as Alaska, Idaho, and Utah, each have only one district. There are also district courts located in Puerto Rico, Guam, the Northern Mariana Islands, and the Virgin Islands. While there may not be a federal district court located in your hometown, there is at least one in your state, thus providing you with ready access to the federal courts. See Figure 8-1 in Chapter 8 for a list of all district courts.

These district courts have jurisdiction over a wide variety of cases. One day a district court judge may hear a case involving a bank robbery and the next day may resolve a civil rights question followed by a case involving a crime committed on an Indian reservation. Bankruptcy courts are considered units of our district courts with judges appointed by the courts of appeal for terms of 14 years. Each of our 94 districts includes a United States bankruptcy court.

The more than 600 judges who sit in federal district courts are, as are all of the judges in the federal court system, nominated by the president and confirmed with the advice and consent of the United States Senate. The number of judges assigned to a particular district court will vary depending upon the number of cases the court is called upon to adjudicate. There may be as few as one district court judge assigned to a district court, or there may be nearly 30, as is the case for the increasingly busy Southern District of New York. In the event of a shift in the population that increases the caseload of a district, the United States Congress will add or approve new judgeships to enable the district court to keep pace with its increasing litigation demands. At present, there are 680 judgeships authorized in the district courts.

In early 2000, Representative Robert Andrews (Dem. N.J.) introduced legislation to split New Jersey, a single federal judicial district, into two districts, one for the northern part of the state and one for the southern part. The creation of new districts is quite rare: The last time a new district was created by splitting a district was in 1971 in Louisiana, due to geographical distance that impeded the timely administration of justice. The four criteria necessary to establish a new federal judicial district are geography, caseload, judicial administration, and community convenience. At the time of publication of this text, the proposal to divide the New Jersey district in two had died.

The district court judges, who are paid $158,100 per year, usually sit individually; that is, they hear cases and render decisions by themselves rather than as a panel or group as the judges for our intermediate courts of appeal and our United States Supreme Court justices sit.

The vast majority of all federal cases end at the district court level; only approximately 10 percent of these federal cases are appealed. In contrast to the new filings for the United States Courts of Appeal and the United States Supreme Court, which continue to show a marked increase each year, civil filings in the district courts are relatively stable, with an increase of 10 percent in civil filings between 1994 and 2003. This stability is generally attributed to the 1988 legislation that increased the jurisdictional amount in diversity cases from $10,000 to $50,000 and 1996 legislation that increased the jurisdictional amount from $50,000 to $75,000. Immediately after the legislation became effective, filings for diversity cases dropped sharply. Moreover, the number of trials completed in the district courts has dropped slightly, as litigants have taken advantage of various forms of alternative dispute resolution programs, including mediation and arbitration. Additionally, prisoner petitions declined after the enactment of the Prisoner Litigation Reform Act, aimed at reducing prisoner petitions. Finally, product liability cases such as those involving breast implants and asbestos cause moderate fluctuations from year to year.

2. *United States Courts of Appeal*

The 13 United States Courts of Appeal, sometimes called the circuit courts, are the intermediate courts in our federal system. The theory of our judicial system is that a litigant should have a trial in one court before one judge and a right to an appeal in another court before a different judge. This structure serves to satisfy the cause of justice and to ensure that a litigant who may have been denied any rights at the trial in the district court will have a second opportunity before a different panel of judges in these intermediate courts of appeal. In fact, a statute directs that no judge may hear an appeal of a case originally tried by him or her.

In a civil case, either side may appeal the verdict. In a criminal case, the defendant may appeal a guilty verdict, but the government may not appeal if a defendant is found not guilty. Either side in a criminal case may appeal with respect to the sentence that is imposed after a guilty verdict.

It is critical to distinguish between the district courts, where the trial occurs, evidence is presented, witnesses testify, and a decision is rendered, and the courts of appeal, whose primary function is to review cases from these district courts. The courts of appeal do not retry a case. They do not receive additional evidence or hear witnesses. They merely review the record and the briefs of counsel to determine if a prejudicial error of law was made in the district court below. A second important function of the United States Courts of Appeal is to review and enforce decisions from federal administrative agencies such as the National Labor Relations Board or the Securities and Exchange Commission. Judicial review in cases involving certain federal agencies or programs, for example, disputes over Social Security benefits, may occur first in a federal district court rather than in one of the courts of appeals.

The United States is divided into 12 geographical areas called "circuits," and there is a court of appeal in each of these circuits. Additionally, there is a Court of Appeals for the Federal Circuit, as discussed below. Figure 2-3 shows the grouping of states that comprise each circuit. It is not critical to know which states or district courts fall within the boundaries of which circuits. Maps of the circuit courts are readily available in the front of each volume of West's *Federal Reporter*. You should certainly know which circuit covers the state in which you will be working and that each circuit is assigned a number and will have several states (and their district courts) within it. For example, the Ninth Circuit covers California and most of the western states.

Thus, if a trial occurs in the Northern District of California, the appeal is filed in the Ninth Circuit. Similarly, if a trial occurs in the Southern District of New York, the appeal is filed in the Second Circuit. All lower federal district courts that fall within the jurisdiction of a federal circuit court are bound by its decisions. Each of the intermediate circuit courts of appeal is free to make its own decisions independent of what other circuits have held; however, in practice, the circuit courts are often guided by decisions from other circuits. Decisions by the U.S. Supreme Court often resolve conflicts among the circuits — not only those in the lower circuit courts but in all other courts in the nation.

The Eleventh Circuit was created in 1981 to relieve some of the pressure the Fifth Circuit was facing due to an ever-increasing caseload caused by population growth. The Fifth Circuit, which had covered Texas, Louisiana, Mississippi, Alabama, Georgia, and Florida, was split, and a new Eleventh Circuit was created by the United States Congress to handle cases from Alabama, Georgia, and Florida (leaving only Texas, Louisiana, and Mississippi in the Fifth Circuit).

Since the 1940s, proposals have been made to split the huge Ninth Circuit in two. At the time of writing of this text, legislation is pending in Congress (H.R. 109-211) that would reorganize the Ninth Circuit by leaving California, Guam, Hawaii, and the Northern Mariana Islands in the Ninth Circuit, create a new Twelfth Circuit (to be composed of Arizona, Nevada, Idaho, and Montana), and create a new Thirteenth Circuit (to be composed of Alaska, Oregon, and Washington). The primary reason advanced for dividing the Ninth Circuit is that it is simply too large, making for inconsistent law. Many of the judges in the Ninth Circuit are opposed to the split, including Chief Judge Mary Schroeder, who testified

Figure 2-3

The Thirteen Federal Judicial Circuits (See 28 U.S.C.A § 41)

before Congress that advances in technology, including computer-assisted legal research, e-mail, and an automated docketing system have improved the circuit's efficiency. Many experts believe that because most of the judges in the Ninth Circuit oppose the split, Congress should not effect it. As Chief Judge Schroeder remarked in July 2004, "Divorce is expensive. This family is going to stay together."

In addition to the 11 "numbered" circuits (First Circuit, Second Circuit, and so forth), there is a Circuit Court of Appeals for the District of Columbia and a circuit court created in 1982 that merged the United States Court of Customs and Patent Appeals and the United States Court of Claims into a new court known as the Court of Appeals for the Federal Circuit, located in Washington, D.C. This court has exclusive jurisdiction over patent appeals and many practitioners believe it has strengthened our patent system. Patent cases comprise about 30 percent of its caseload. This court also handles certain specialized appeals such as those from the United States Court of International Trade, the Trademark Trial and Appeal Board, the United States Court of Appeals for Veterans Claims, the United States Court of Federal Claims, and other specialized courts.

There are more than 170 justices who sit for the 13 United States Courts of Appeal, with each court of appeals having from six to 28 justices assigned to it, depending on the caseload for the circuit. The justices usually hear the appeals from the District Courts as a panel of three justices, although they may sit *en banc* with all justices present. These federal justices are also appointed by the president and earn an annual salary of $167,600. The workload of the United States Courts of Appeal has increased substantially, primarily due to a rise in the number of criminal appeals from decisions of the United States District Courts and in appeals of administrative agency decisions. Despite the steady increase in filings, no additional judgeships have been created for the Courts of Appeal since 1990. The United States Courts of Appeal typically issue more than 15,000 opinions each year, although not all opinions are published.

For the vast majority of litigants, these intermediate courts of appeal represent the last opportunity to prevail. As you will see, the popular notion that everyone has access to the United States Supreme Court is unfounded; for most litigants the court of appeals is the last chance to win, as one who wishes to appeal a case to the United States Supreme Court is largely dependent on the Court's discretion in accepting a case for review.

3. *United States Supreme Court*

The United States Supreme Court consists of eight associate justices and one chief justice. While the chief justice is paid more than the associate justices ($203,000 to their annual salaries of $194,300), and while he has prestige and certain authority by virtue of seniority, the chief justice's vote counts equally with that of any associate justice. Nevertheless, as the presiding officer of the Supreme Court, he is responsible for administration of the Court and leadership of the federal judicial system. Upon the death or resignation of a chief justice, the president may either appoint one of the eight existing associate justices to the position of chief justice or may appoint an "outsider" as chief justice. That is, there is no seniority system whereby an associate justice works his or her way up to the chief justice position.

As are all approximately 1,700 judges in the federal system, the Supreme Court justices are appointed by the president and hold office "during good behavior." This means they are not subject to mandatory retirement and may sit as federal judges until they voluntarily resign or die. As an example of the lack of a mandatory retirement, Judge Giles Rich, of the United States Court of Appeals for the Federal Circuit, sat on the bench until his death in 1999 at age 95. While federal judges can be impeached by the Congress, this drastic remedy is seldom used, and only a handful of judges has been removed through impeachment and conviction by Congress of treason, bribery, or other high crimes and misdemeanors. To further ensure the independence of the federal judiciary, the Constitution prohibits any decrease in federal judges' salaries during their term in office. These two protections ensure that an independent judiciary decides cases free from popular passion and political influence.

The individuals who sit on the United States Supreme Court (or state supreme courts) are usually referred to as "justices" while the individuals who sit on lower courts are referred to as "judges." Occasionally, individuals who sit on intermediate appellate courts are also referred to as "justices," although in general the term "justice" is reserved for individuals on the United States Supreme Court or a state supreme court.

The Supreme Court has not always had nine justices. When the Court was established in 1790, there were only six justices. The number of justices has changed several times; at one point there were ten justices. The present composition of nine justices has existed since 1869. The most recent attempt to alter the size of the Supreme Court occurred in 1937 when President Franklin D. Roosevelt presented a plan to the Senate for reorganization of the Court. President Roosevelt's proposal called for adding an additional justice each time any justice reached the age of 70 and did not voluntarily retire, to a maximum of 15 justices. Fierce public outcry immediately met this attempt to "pack" the Supreme Court and there has been no serious discussion of altering the number of justices since that time.

Federal Court Caseloads

- From 1998-2003, the total number of weighted civil and criminal filings per United States District Court judgeship climbed 8 percent, and from 1994-2003, bankruptcy filings per authorized judgeship, soared 88 percent.

- The increase in bankruptcy cases is linked to the filings of personal bankruptcies, which passed the 1.5 million mark in 2003. In fact, nonbusiness bankruptcy cases accounted for 98 percent of all filings. Despite this surge, the last increase in authorized bankruptcy judgeships occurred in 1992.

(continued)

Federal Court Caseloads (Continued)

- While the number of criminal cases filed in the United States district courts climbed 53 percent between 1994-2003, the number of civil cases filed during this same period climbed only 10 percent.
- Most of the work of the United States district courts relates to its civil caseload. In 2003, civil cases constituted approximately 78 percent of total filings, and criminal cases accounted for 22 percent. Of the civil cases, actions brought under statutes (such as civil rights and employment actions) comprise the majority, followed by tort actions and personal injury cases, and then by contract actions. Of the criminal cases, 70 percent involve drugs, firearms, and immigration law violations.
- The Department of Justice (which is responsible for prosecuting federal crimes and representing the government in civil actions) is the most frequent litigator in the federal court system.
- Between 1999 and 2003, the number of appeals to the United States Courts of Appeal climbed nearly 13 percent.
- The increase in appeals filed in the United States Courts of Appeal (22 percent increase from 1994-2003) resulted from a significant surge in appeals of administrative agency decisions, primarily those relating to immigration matters. In fact, appeals of decisions of the Board of Immigration Appeals climbed 379 percent in 2003.

Because there is no mandatory retirement for federal judges, many have served for extremely long periods—notably Chief Justice John Marshall, widely regarded as the finest jurist produced by the United States, who served 34 years, and Associate Justice William O. Douglas, who served for 36 years. On average, Supreme Court justices have served for approximately 15 years.

In addition to their primary activities of hearing Supreme Court cases and writing opinions, each justice is assigned to one of the federal judicial circuits for the purpose of handling special and emergency matters such as stays of execution and injunctions. For example, in mid-2000, Associate Justice Anthony Kennedy, then assigned to the Eleventh Circuit, which includes Florida, rejected an emergency request to allow Elian Gonzales, a Cuban child, to remain in the United States. Similarly, in spring 2005 Justice Kennedy (after his referral to the Court) denied an application by Floridian Terri Schiavo's parents to reinsert her feeding tube. Because there are 13 federal circuits and only 9 Supreme Court justices, some justices are assigned to more than one circuit. Assignment to the circuits is made by the chief justice at the beginning of each term. A listing of the assignments is found in the front of each volume of *United States Reports*.

The United States Supreme Court is currently located in Washington, D.C. Initially, the Court met in New York City, the original capital of the United States. When the national capital was relocated to

Philadelphia, the Court established its offices there. When Washington, D.C., became the permanent national capital in 1800, the Court again moved and was located in the United States Capitol. In 1929, former President William Howard Taft, who had been appointed as chief justice of the Court after his presidential term, persuaded Congress to construct a permanent building for the Court. The Supreme Court building was completed in 1935, almost 150 years after the Court was created.

By federal law the term of the United States Supreme Court commences on the first Monday in October. Typically the term ends at the end of June or early July nine months later. During the summer recess the justices continue working and reviewing the many petitions for relief the Court receives during the year. The last month of the term is often referred to as the "June crunch" as the Court struggles to finalize and release opinions before the summer recess. In the last two months of the Court's 2003-2004 term, it produced decisions in approximately 50 percent of its cases, some of which were the most complex on its docket.

Many interesting traditions endure in the Court. The justices are seated at the bench by seniority: The chief justice occupies the center seat and the most senior associate justice sits to his right; the next most senior associate justice sits to his left and this procedure continues, with the newest member of the Court occupying the chair at the extreme right of the bench. Formal pictures of the justices also reflect this seniority arrangement.

Though seldom used, white quill pens are still placed on the tables in the Court, just as was done 200 years ago. One of the more impressive traditions is the "conference handshake," which was instituted by Chief Justice Melville W. Fuller in the late 1800s. As the justices take their seats on the bench and at the beginning of the case conferences at which they meet to review cases, each justice formally shakes hands with each of the other justices. This handshake serves as a visible reminder that while the justices may offer differing views of the law, they are united in their purpose of interpreting the United States Constitution. Because the Court has retained so many traditions, one legal historian has called it "the first Court still sitting."

Until William H. Rehnquist became chief justice, the caseload of the United States Supreme Court increased dramatically each year. In just the nine-year period between 1994 and 2003, the number of cases appealed in the federal system grew more than 20 percent. According to the Supreme Court Historical Society, over a recent 25-year period the number of appeals filed in the federal courts has grown more than six times as quickly as the country's population. While the Supreme Court justices have recognized they are overburdened and while various suggestions have been made to decrease their staggering caseload, Associate Justice Stevens once remarked that the justices were too busy to resolve the problem of being too busy. In recent years, however, the Court has been reducing its docket and producing far fewer opinions. During the 1980s, the Court routinely decided roughly 150 cases per term. In its 2003-2004 term, the Court issued only 79 written opinions, although the average number of pages and footnotes per opinion has increased steadily over the years.

By the authority of the Constitution, the United States Supreme Court has the jurisdiction to act not only as an appellate or reviewing court but also in very limited instances can act as a court of original jurisdiction or a trial court for cases involving controversies between two states and many cases affecting ambassadors, public ministers, and consuls. While the Supreme Court can conduct a trial in these cases, it prefers that trials be conducted in the district courts below. As might be expected, few litigants elect to have their trial conducted in this highest court as there is no avenue for an appeal if a party loses a trial before the United States Supreme Court. In cases involving controversies between two or more states, the United States Supreme Court has original and exclusive jurisdiction. For example, in 2000, Maryland initiated an action in the Supreme Court against Virginia regarding each state's rights to the Potomac River. In December 2003, the Court ruled in favor of Virginia. The Supreme Court typically hears less than five original jurisdiction cases per term. See Figure 2-4 for an outline of jurisdiction of the United States Supreme Court.

The most important function of the United States Supreme Court is its appellate jurisdiction; that is, its authority to review decisions from lower courts. Cases may come to the Supreme Court from the lower federal courts or from the highest court in any state.

While a few cases, such as some cases under the Interstate Commerce Act, are directly appealable from the district courts to the United States Supreme Court, the vast majority of federal cases that the Supreme Court reviews proceed to the court in the expected "stair-step" fashion: trial in the district court, an intermediate appeal to the appropriate circuit court, and a final appeal to the United States Supreme Court. In the 2003-2004

Figure 2-4
Jurisdiction of United States Supreme Court

I. ORIGINAL JURISDICTION (28 U.S.C. § 1251 (2000))
    A. Controversies between two or more states (exclusive jurisdiction)
    B. Actions in which ambassadors or other public ministers of foreign states are parties (non-exclusive jurisdiction)
    C. Controversies between the United States and a state (non-exclusive jurisdiction)
    D. Actions by a state against the citizens of another state (non-exclusive jurisdiction)
II. APPELLATE JURISDICTION (28 U.S.C. §§ 1253-1259 (2000))
    A. Cases from federal courts
        1. United States District Courts (special statutes allow some direct appeals as well as appeals from three-judge district courts granting or denying injunctive relief to be directly appealed to United States Supreme Court)
        2. United States Courts of Appeal
            (a) Certiorari
            (b) Certification (granted only in exceptional cases)
    B. Cases from highest state courts that present a federal question

term, 68 of the Court's 79 written cases came from the federal appellate courts, 2 from the federal district courts, and the remainder from state appellate courts.

Additionally, special statutes might allow for direct appeal to the Supreme Court. For example, you might recall that in mid-2000, the Department of Justice asked that the United States Supreme Court review the Microsoft antitrust case under a special federal statute that would have resulted in the case moving from the United States District Court directly to the Supreme Court, skipping over the intermediate court of appeals. The Supreme Court declined the case, and it was sent to the Court of Appeals for the District of Columbia. In 26 years, only two such cases have gone directly to the Supreme Court under special legislation that provides that government-initiated antitrust cases of general public importance should receive direct consideration by the Court.

The most widely used means to gain access to the United States Supreme Court from the lower circuit courts of appeal is the writ of *certiorari. Certiorari* is a Latin word meaning "to be more fully informed." *Black's Law Dictionary* 241 (8th ed. 2004). A litigant who has lost an appeal in the intermediate circuit court will file a document or petition with the Supreme Court called a Petition for Writ of Certiorari. The fee for filing the Petition for Writ of Certiorari is $300. This petition will set forth the litigant's (or appellant's) basis for appeal and will enumerate the errors that were allegedly committed by the lower court(s). The Supreme Court will either grant the petition and direct the lower court to send its records and files to the Supreme Court for review (in which instance the case is often referred to as being "cert worthy") or will deny the petition, meaning that the lower court decision will stand. In the vast majority of cases, issuance of the writ, or "granting cert," is discretionary with the Supreme Court, and seldom does a litigant have an absolute right to have the Supreme Court review a case.

Nearly 8,000 petitions for certiorari are filed with the United States Supreme Court each year, and the justices typically grant cert in fewer than 100 of these cases. Full written opinions are issued in about 75 cases, and the remaining cases are disposed of without oral argument or formal written opinions.

Deciding which of the 8,000 petitions for certiorari to grant (which will result in the United States Supreme Court's hearing the appeal) may be as important as the actual decision ultimately reached. While some proposals for court reform have suggested a second-tier court just below the United States Supreme Court to review the petitions for certiorari and decide which of the appeals the justices should hear, the justices have steadfastly resisted such an idea, contending that their screening function in determining which appeals to hear is critical in importance. A Supreme Court historian once stated that deciding which petitions for certiorari should be granted is "arguably the most important stage in the entire Supreme Court process."

Each justice is entitled to four law clerks who are usually top graduates of the nation's best law schools. Many of the justices themselves, including Chief Justice Rehnquist and Associate Justices Stevens and Breyer, have served as law clerks. These law clerks routinely work

70 to 90 hours per week (as do many of the justices) and prepare memoranda for the justices summarizing the petitions for certiorari that have been filed. Eight of the nine present justices make use of a "cert pool," pooling their law clerks who take turns evaluating the cert petitions and writing memos. Justice Stevens prefers to rely on his own clerks. All of the justices review all of the petitions or the clerks' memoranda discussing the petitions, and they meet on Wednesdays and Fridays in "conference" to discuss the petitions for certiorari. Once again, the justices sit in prescribed order by seniority at the conference table with the chief justice sitting at the east end. No notes are taken, and no one other than the nine justices is ever present at these secret case conferences. For certiorari to be granted, only four of the nine justices need vote to accept the case for review. This process is often referred to as "the rule of four."

There are no clearly articulated or published criteria followed by the justices in determining which petitions will be deemed "cert worthy." The guideline most frequently given is that certiorari will be granted when there are "compelling" reasons for doing so. These "compelling" reasons are, of course, determined by the justices. In general, however, a review of the cases accepted by the Supreme Court reveals some common threads: If the lower federal courts of appeal are in conflict on a certain issue and are issuing contradictory opinions, the Supreme Court often grants certiorari so it can resolve such conflicts; if a case is of general importance, the Court will grant certiorari; or if a state court of last resort has decided an important federal question in a way that conflicts with a decision of another court, certiorari is often granted. These three factors considered by the Court are also set forth in Rule 10 of the Rules of the Supreme Court.

Denial of the writ of certiorari is not to be viewed as a message to the petitioner from the Court that it has fully reviewed and researched all aspects of the case and it is satisfied the lower court's ruling is correct but rather that for reasons of judicial economy not every case can be heard. The Supreme Court cannot possibly review every case that litigants desire to appeal, and the appeal process must end somewhere. In most cases originating in the federal court system, the litigant had a trial conducted by a judge who was appointed by the president and confirmed by the Senate; an appeal then followed in one of the circuit courts of appeal before a panel of judges appointed by the president and confirmed by the Senate. This should be sufficient to satisfy the cause of justice. In fact, in 1925, Chief Justice William Howard Taft (formerly President Taft) stated, "[N]o litigant is entitled to more than two chances, namely, to the original trial and to a review." Denial of a writ of certiorari is the chief means the justices have of controlling their caseload and ensuring they continue to issue opinions on a timely basis.

Practice Tip

Denials of Certiorari

Be a savvy reader. Understand that the denial of certiorari is not an endorsement or affirmation of lower court action but merely a determination by a court that it will not take a case.

Once the petition for certiorari has been granted, the attorneys or parties are notified and instructed to submit their written arguments, called briefs, which are then filed with the Court and made available to the public.

Oral arguments are heard two weeks of every month on Mondays, Tuesdays, and Wednesdays through April. Fridays are generally reserved for discussion of cases and voting on petitions for certiorari. A typical day begins with a case at 10:00 A.M., and another at 11:00 A.M. followed by a lunch break from 12:00 noon to 1:00 P.M. The afternoon session will also be devoted to two cases, one at 1:00 P.M. and another at 2:00 P.M. In recent years, however, the Court has not heard cases in the afternoon, probably due to its decreased caseload. At least six justices must be present to hear a case. The two-week sessions when the Court hears arguments and delivers opinions are called "sittings," and the two-week sessions when the justices consider business before the Court and write opinions are called "recesses."

Usually only one-half hour is allotted to each side for oral argument. Timing is regulated by a lighting system. After 25 minutes, a white light is turned on, notifying the speaker that only five minutes remain for oral argument. A red light signals the end of the 30-minute oral argument period. During the oral argument, the justices may ask questions and often interrupt the speaker. It is rare for a case to exceed the one hour allotted for oral argument. Cameras are not authorized in the courtroom, and spectators are not permitted to take notes.

After oral argument, the justices again meet in conference and discuss the case. A preliminary vote is taken to determine the Court's disposition of the case. This is the time when the power and prestige of the chief justice are shown. If the preliminary vote is 5-4 with the majority in favor of affirming and the chief justice is in the majority, he may assign the opinion to be drafted by any of the associate justices in the majority group or may decide to author the opinion himself. When the chief justice is not in the majority, the senior associate justice in the majority group will make the assignment.

While one justice is drafting the majority opinion, others may be writing separate dissents or concurring opinions (see Chapter 4). Drafting the majority opinion may take weeks or months, and the law clerks often write the first drafts. Justice Brennan once disclosed that he circulated ten drafts of an opinion before one was approved. When the opinion is complete, it is circulated to the other justices for comments. Justices who were originally in the majority may, after reviewing the opinion, change their votes, and it is possible that what initially appeared to be a majority may vanish and the original dissenters may become the majority. While the average length of time between oral argument and issuance of the opinion is only a few months, in some instances there may be a period of nearly a year before the final opinion is released. All cases argued during a term are decided before the summer recess begins.

Finally, the last revisions are made to the opinion and it is released to the public and authorized for printing in the *United States Reports*, the official publication of the Court's work. Only the final version of the opinion is printed and only it is the law, serving as a legal precedent under the doctrine of stare decisis.

In its 2003-2004 term, the Court continued its practice of overturning lower court judgments in the vast majority of the cases that it fully reviewed. Specifically, the Court reversed or vacated lower court rulings approximately 75 percent of the time. The U.S. Court of Appeals for the Ninth Circuit is the most frequently reversed court and it continued to face heavy scrutiny by the Supreme Court. Cases from the Ninth Circuit accounted for nearly one-third of the decisions issued by the Supreme Court in its 2003-2004 term.

Although the popular view of the Supreme Court is that the justices are often divided, with one exception, their unanimity rate has remained above 40 percent since the early 1990s. Nearly half of the Court's written decisions were made with every justice agreeing as to the ultimate result (although there was disagreement in the rationale for the result in about 15 percent of these cases). When the Court is evenly divided (as may be the case if a justice has recused himself or herself due to a conflict of interest), the ruling of the lower court stands, and no nationwide precedent is set.

While the vast majority of cases arrive at the United States Supreme Court from the various United States courts of appeal by means of the writ of certiorari, there is one other means by which cases from the United States Courts of Appeal may be reviewed by the United States Supreme Court: certification. Certification is the process by which a court of appeals refers a question to the United States Supreme Court and asks for instructions. Certification is not done for the benefit of the parties to the case. It is done at the desire of the court and typically involves questions of grave doubt. The Court itself refers to its certification jurisdiction as "exceptional."

One example is a case in which conflicting decisions had been rendered by several of the courts of appeal regarding the right of the Secretary of Labor to deport Chinese citizens. Because of these conflicting decisions, one of the courts of appeal "certified" the case to the United States Supreme Court, asking for direction and instruction. Similarly, in mid-2004, after the Supreme Court issued a decision relating to federal criminal sentencing guidelines, the Court of Appeals for the Second Circuit certified a case to the Supreme Court and issued a set of three questions for the Court. The Second Circuit noted the rarity of the certification process by remarking that it had not certified a case for more than twenty years and stating that a prompt answer to the questions was needed to avoid a major disruption in the administration of criminal justice.

The certification procedure does not play a significant role in the Court's caseload. Certification is discretionary with the Court and is granted only for exceptional cases. In addition, a party may appeal directly to the United States Supreme Court from an order granting or denying injunctive relief in any case determined by a three-judge district court.

Cases from state courts may be appealed to the United States Supreme Court from the highest court in a state if and only if a federal question is involved. Even then, the Court may, in its discretion, refuse to grant certiorari, thus rendering the state court decision final. State court cases seeking access to the United States Supreme Court have no absolute right to an appeal and are entirely dependent on the Court granting certiorari, which it does for roughly 1 percent of cases. See Figure 2-5 for a diagram of federal court structure.

4. *Specialized Courts*

In addition to the district courts, the intermediate circuit courts of appeal, and the United States Supreme Court, certain specialized courts exist in the federal judicial system to determine particular issues. These include the following:

- the United States Court of Appeals for the Armed Forces (previously United States Court of Military Appeals), which is the final appellate court to review court-martial determinations of the various branches of the military;
- the United States Tax Court, which issues decisions in tax matters relating to income, gift, and estate taxes;
- the Court of International Trade (previously called the Customs Court), which handles trade and customs disputes;
- the United States Court of Appeals for Veterans Claims, which reviews determinations regarding matters pertaining to veterans of the armed services such as disability determinations; and
- the United States Court of Federal Claims (formerly called the United States Claims Court), which considers and determines certain claims (other than in tort) seeking monetary damages from the United States government, for example, claims by contractors working on federal projects. Approximately one fourth of the court's cases involve tax refund suits. In every case, the defendant is the federal government.

A review of some recent Court of Federal Claims cases reveals a case filed by federal employees for wrongful termination, one brought by landowners who alleged a government reservoir flooded their land, and one seeking damages under the National Vaccine Injury Compensation Program. In fiscal year 2003, the court disposed of 732 complaints and awarded judgments totaling $878 million (on claims made that would have totaled $40 billion if granted). The average claim made against the government is more than $1 million.

As a matter of historical perspective, it is useful to know that the district courts, intermediate courts of appeal, and the United States Supreme Court are referred to as "constitutional courts" as they exist under Article III of the Constitution, and their judges (the "Article III judges") are protected as to tenure and salary reductions. Most of the specialized courts described above are created under Article I of the Constitution and are referred to as "legislative courts" or Article I courts; their judges are appointed for specific terms.

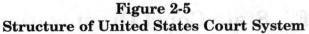

Figure 2-5
Structure of United States Court System

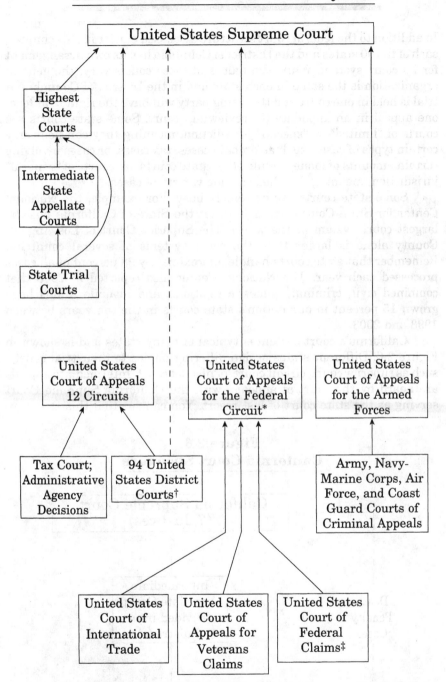

*The Court of Appeals for the Federal Circuit also receives cases from the Patent and Trademark Office, the Board of Contract Appeals, the Merit Systems Protection Board, and the International Trade Commission.

†A few cases are directly appealed from the United States District Courts to the United States Supreme Court.

‡Formerly, the United States Claims Court.

F. State Court Organization

In addition to the federal court structure discussed earlier in this chapter, each of the 50 states and the District of Columbia has its own arrangement for its court system. While the names of these courts vary, the general organization is the same in each state and in the District of Columbia: A trial is held in one court and the losing party will have the right to at least one appeal in an appellate (or reviewing) court. Some state courts are courts of "limited" or "special" jurisdiction, meaning they can hear only certain types of cases, such as probate cases, tax cases, or cases involving certain amounts of money, while other state courts are courts of "general" jurisdiction, meaning they hear a wide variety of cases.

Some state courts are extremely busy. For example, the National Center for State Courts has noted that the State of California has the largest court system in the world. The Superior Court of Los Angeles County alone is larger than the court systems of several countries. Remember that state courts handle approximately 98 percent of all cases processed each year. The National Center also reported in 2003 that combined civil, criminal, domestic relations, and juvenile filings have grown 15 percent in our nation's state courts in the ten years between 1993 and 2003.

California's court system is typical of many states and is shown in Figure 2-6. Different states assign differing names to their trial courts, such as superior court, circuit court, or district court. Intermediate appeals are heard by the court of appeals, with the California Supreme Court serving as the state court of last resort. You can see that this structure

Figure 2-6
California Court Structure

is extremely similar to the federal court structure in which a trial is held in the district court, an intermediate appeal follows in the United States Courts of Appeal, and a final appeal may occur in the United States Supreme Court.

While the majority of courts have a two-tier appellate system, in ten states (Maine, Montana, Nevada, New Hampshire, North Dakota, Rhode Island, South Dakota, Vermont, West Virginia, and Wyoming) and in the District of Columbia there is no intermediate court of appeal, and dissatisfied litigants proceed directly from the state trial court to the court of last resort in the state, usually called the supreme court. For example, in North Dakota a breach of contract case alleging damages of $50,000 would be tried in the North Dakota District Court. The party who loses would appeal directly to the North Dakota Supreme Court. (See Figure 2-7.)

In almost all states, the highest state court is called the supreme court. Maryland, however, calls its highest court the court of appeals. New York also calls its highest court the court of appeals and calls one of the courts below it, which handles felonies and miscellaneous civil actions, the supreme court, which can cause a great deal of confusion. When reading cases from New York, therefore, exercise a great deal of caution and remember that the decisions of its highest court, the court of appeals, bind all other courts in New York, while its supreme court is not New York's highest court despite its name. Similarly, the decisions of Maryland's highest court, the court of appeals, bind all other courts in Maryland. Likewise, the court of last resort in the District of Columbia is called the court of appeals.

Figure 2-7
North Dakota Court Structure

North Dakota
Supreme Court
(5 Justices)

District Court
(All civil actions; felonies
and misdemeanors)

Municipal Court
(City ordinance
violations and
DUI cases)

Decisions by the highest courts in all states are rendered by odd-numbered panels of judges (or justices) who function in a collective manner similar to the justices of the United States Supreme Court. Seventeen of the 50 states are composed of a five-member supreme court; 28 of the states are composed of a seven-member supreme court; and five of the states are composed of a nine-member supreme court.

The average salary for justices on the highest state courts is $125,292. The average salary for judges sitting on the state intermediate appellate courts is $121,697; and the average salary for state trial court judges is $112,724. Note that most of these salaries are lower than the starting salaries paid to new attorneys in the nation's largest law firms, which range from $125,000 to $140,000.

While all judges in the federal system are appointed by the president and are confirmed by the United States Senate, there is great variation among the states with regard to the selection of state court judges. Many states use a merit selection method (somewhat similar to the federal presidential appointment method) in which the governor appoints a judge from a list of nominees provided to him or her by a judicial nominating commission. Other states elect their judges either by vote of the state legislature or the general population for specific terms.

For information about all federal and state courts, see *Want's Federal-State Court Directory* (Robert S. Want ed., 30th ed. 2005), (212) 687-3774. This annual directory provides thorough information about federal and state courts and judges and also provides charts showing the organization of each state court system. Generally, each state's judicial Web site also includes basic information about the judicial system in that state. Table T.1 of *The Bluebook* provides a reference to each state's judicial Web site.

Practice Tip

Reading Citations

Gain as much information from citations as you can. When you see the word "App." in a case citation, immediately think to yourself that the case is likely not from the state's highest court. Similarly, the absence of the word "App." in a citation is probably a signal that the case is a strong one and is from your state's court of last resort.

The state trial courts are often referred to as courts of first resort: Witnesses appear and testify, evidence is introduced, and a decision is rendered by a judge or jury. State appellate courts do not retry a case. Rather, they review the record or transcript from the trial court below, read the written briefs submitted by the attorneys for each party, listen to oral arguments in some cases, and then render a decision. No evidence is presented and no witnesses testify. It is often said that appellate courts cannot make factual determinations and are restricted to deciding issues of law. For example, if a jury convicts Defendant Smith of manslaughter, the appellate court cannot overturn or reverse this judgment on the basis that Smith seems like a fine, upstanding individual and the appellate court cannot believe Smith would have committed such an atrocious act. The trial court has already determined a fact: Smith murdered the victim. With few exceptions, it is not within the province of an appellate court to substitute its judgment for that of the jury. The appellate court may, however, reverse the judgment and order a new trial on the basis that prejudicial hearsay was incorrectly admitted at trial, that the jury instructions were improper, or that evidence used at the trial to convict Smith was obtained without a search warrant. Such issues are ones of law rather than fact. Appellate courts typically review only questions of law, not factual determinations that have already been made by a judge or jury at the trial below. Thus, it is often said that trial courts try cases while appellate courts try trial courts.

G. Citation Form

1. Federal Cases (The Bluebook and ALWD)

    a.   United States Supreme Court cases:
        Vestron, Inc. v. Lowell, 347 U.S. 483 (1965).
    b.   United States Courts of Appeal cases:
        Bailey v. Talbert, 585 F.2d 968 (8th Cir. 1989).
    c.   United States District Court cases:
        Peters v. May, 697 F. Supp. 101 (S.D. Cal. 1988).

2. State Cases (The Bluebook and ALWD)

Cite to the regional reporter for the region in which the court is located, if the opinion appears in that reporter. Otherwise, cite to the state's official report. Do not use parallel citations unless required by local rules:

    Janson v. Keyser, 415 N.E.2d 891 (Mass. 1976).

███ *Supreme Court Dicta*

- In its 2003 term, the Supreme Court reversed 75 percent of the cases it received from the Ninth Circuit, 25 percent of the cases it received from the Fourth Circuit, and 67 percent of the cases it received from the state courts.
- In 2000, when the Supreme Court heard *Bush v. Gore*, 531 U.S. 98 (2000), just four days elapsed between the time the Court agreed to hear the case and when it issued its decision, which represented the quickest turnaround in the Court's history.
- Three of the current justices (Justices Rehnquist, Stevens, and Breyer) served as law clerks to the Court.
- From 1999-2004, the justices recused themselves more than 500 times. Justice Stephen Breyer led the list with 181 recusals (primarily in cases involving rulings by his brother, a federal judge). Chief Justice Rehnquist did not sit out a case during this period.
- The annual salary of the first chief justice was $4,000. The salary of the current chief justice is $203,000.
- By law, the chief justice sits on the boards of three significant Washington cultural institutions, including the Smithsonian Institution.
- William Howard Taft is the only chief justice in history to have previously served as president.
- The United States Supreme Court reverses cases from the Courts of Appeal approximately 75 percent of the time.
- The cost of an appeal to the Court can be as high as $500,000 with printing costs alone topping $7,000.
- After Chief Justice Rehnquist presided over President Clinton's impeachment trial the Supreme Court law clerks gave him a T-shirt with the following slogan: "I presided over a presidential impeachment and all I got was this lousy T-shirt."
- In 1999, Justice Breyer used the pronoun "I" in a Supreme Court opinion violating a 200-year-old tradition, begun by Chief Justice John Marshall, of speaking collectively by using the pronoun "we" in majority opinions.
- Each October before the Court begins its session, several justices attend a "Red Mass" at the Roman Catholic Cathedral of St. Matthew (where President Kennedy's funeral Mass was held), where the church blesses the forthcoming term as well as the work of other civic leaders. In 1999, six justices attended the Mass, named for the red vestments worn by its celebrants.
- Chief Justice Rehnquist, who has been on the Court since 1972, is the only one of the current justices never to have served as a trial judge.
- A 1995 nationwide poll by the *Washington Post* revealed that while 59 percent of those polled could name the Three Stooges, only 17 percent

(continued)

Supreme Court Dicta *(Continued)*

could name three of the nine United States Supreme Court justices. Justice Sandra Day O'Connor was the most frequently named justice identified by 31 percent of those polled, while Justice John Paul Stevens was identified by only 1 percent despite his 20-year tenure on the high Court.

- Although 47 states have allowed television coverage of at least some court proceedings, television coverage of oral arguments has been forbidden by continuous order of the Supreme Court.

- After leaving office, President John Adams stated, "My gift of John Marshall [appointed by Adams as chief justice in 1801] to the people of the United States was the proudest act of my life." One Court observer remarked that to try to describe Marshall's eloquence "would be to attempt to paint the sunbeams."

- According to Justice Joseph Story, on rainy days the early justices would enliven case conferences with wine. On other days, even if the sun was shifting, Chief Justice John Marshall would order wine anyway, saying, "Our jurisdiction is so vast that it must be raining somewhere."

- Until 1969, there was no copying machine at the Supreme Court. Justices often read blurry eight-carbon copies of draft decisions. Justice Bernnan (1956-1990) never used a word processor and handwrote all drafts and opinions. At present, Justice Souter is reportedly the only justice who does not use a word processor for writing his opinions.

- Injuries suffered by Chief Justice Marshall, often referred to as "the man who made the Court Supreme," in a stagecoach crash while riding circuit court were said to have hastened his death.

- Harlan Fiske Stone (appointed chief justice in 1941), a former farm boy, once said, "Had I realized what I'd be doing later in my career I'd have hung on to that pitchfork."

CyberSites

www.supremecourtus.gov	The Web site of the United States Supreme Court provides information about the Court, its docket, a schedule of oral arguments, opinions, Court rules, visitor information, and bar admission forms.
http://www.uscourts.gov	The Federal Judicial home page provides information about the U.S. federal courts and links to the U.S. Supreme Court, the U.S. Courts of Appeal (with a map of the Federal circuits), U.S. District Courts, and U.S. Bankruptcy Courts.
http://www.fjc.gov	The Federal Judicial Center provides educational and research services relating to the federal courts, including online access to numerous publications and statistical reports.
http://www.firstgov.gov	FirstGov is the federal government's official Web portal with links to all units of the federal judicial branch and a vast array of excellent information about the federal government.
www.supremecourtus.gov	The Web site of the Supreme Court provides access to the Court's docket, opinions, and rules. Background information about the Court is provided, together with links to other useful sites.
http://www.supremecourt history.org	The site of the Supreme Court Historical Society offers excellent information about the history and background of the Supreme Court, with several useful guides explaining how the Court works and its traditions.
http://www.loc.gov/law/ guide/us.html	The Library of Congress site provides excellent information about the U.S. judiciary as well as various online guides to law and legal issues.
http://www.ncsconline.org	The National Center for State Courts offers information about state courts, including statistical tables for state court caseloads and an organizational chart for each state's judicial system.
(202) 479-3360	Today's Supreme Court decisions.
http://www.oyez.org	This site allows ordering of "The Supreme Court's Greatest Hits," a multimedia CD-ROM resource providing access to Supreme Court oral arguments, text, and images.
http://www.findlaw.com	FindLaw, a well-known legal site, provides easy access to federal and state cases as well as a wide variety of other law-related information and links.
http://www.law.cornell.edu	This Web site provides decisions of the Supreme Court, cases from other federal courts, and state court cases.

Writing Strategies

When selecting cases to discuss and analyze in your writing, examine citations carefully for the signals they will give you about the level of the court that rendered the decision. When viewing a "U.S." citation, immediately think "highest court in the country"; when viewing an "F.2d" or "F.3d" citation, immediately think "intermediate federal appellate courts"; when viewing an "F. Supp." or "F. Supp. 2d" citation, immediately think "trial court—lowest court in the federal system."

While there is nothing wrong with district court cases, you should prefer cases from higher courts over lower courts, everything else being equal.

Examine opinions for clues regarding the strength and viability of a case. If the precedent you rely on was a 9-0 decision, refer to it as a "unanimous decision" or a decision by an "undivided court." Refer to cases relied upon by an adversary, if applicable, as decisions rendered by a "bare majority" or a "divided court."

If you cannot find cases as recent as you would like, try to enhance the stature of older cases by describing them as "well-established," "well-settled," or "landmark" cases. Select cases from your circuit and remind the reader of this in your writing by stating, "This circuit has held . . . ," or "Since 1967, the law in this circuit has been . . . ."

Discuss *your* argument. Do not shift the focus away from your position to your adversary's by spending all of your time refuting your adversary's contentions.

Assignment for Chapter 2

1. a. Give the name of the case located at 531 U.S. 57 (2000).
   b. Give the holding of the case.
   c. During the period of time covered by the cases in the volume, which United States Supreme Court justice was assigned or allotted to the Tenth Circuit?
   d. Locate a case in this volume in which the plaintiff's name is *Buckman Co.*
      (i) Give the full name and citation of this case.
      (ii) Who was the United States attorney general at the time this case was decided?
2. a. Locate a case in volume 502 of the *U.S. Reports* in which the plaintiff's name is *Byers* and give the name and citation of this case.
   b. Give the result reached in this case.
3. To which circuits are the following states assigned?
   a. Utah
   b. Connecticut
   c. Missouri
4. a. Give the name of the case located at 154 F.3d 161 (4th Cir. 1998).
   b. Which judge issued the opinion of the court?
5. a. Give the name of the case located at 33 F. Supp. 2d 78.
   b. Which of the United States District Courts decided this case?
   c. Who represented the defendant in this case?

State Your Answer

1. Access the site http://www.uscourts.gov and review the map of federal circuits and districts.
   a. In which circuit is your state located?
   b. In which district court would you file a complaint for age discrimination?
2. Access the site for the National Center for State Courts at http://ncsconline.org and locate the "State Court Structure Charts."
   a. How many justices sit on your state's highest court?
   b. What are the names of your state's courts?
3. Within the site for the National Center for State Courts, select "Court Statistics Project" and then locate "State Court Caseload Statistics." Review Table 2. How many total cases (including both mandatory and discretionary petitions) were filed in your state's highest court?

Statutory Law

A plural Legislature is as necessary to good Government as a single Executive. It is not enough that your Legislature should be numerous; it should also be divided.

Benjamin Franklin (1789)

A. **Federal Legislation**
B. **State Legislation**
C. **Statutory Research Overview**
D. **Citation Form**

Chapter Overview

Recall from Chapter 1 that courts are free to interpret statutes. Thus, this chapter focuses on statutory law because the logical progression many researchers follow when given a task is to first determine whether a statute relates to the issue. If so, they begin by reading the statute itself and then reviewing the cases and other sources that interpret it.

In this chapter we will thus discuss the enactment of federal and state legislation and will then focus on the publication and codification of statutes. In order to conduct research efficiently and effectively, you will need a clear understanding of the procedure by which laws are passed and the sets of books in which they are found. Following this, we will focus on research techniques that will enable you to locate statutes.

A.   Federal Legislation

1.   *Enactment of Federal Statutes*

The chief function of the Congress of the United States is its lawmaking task. Congress is a bicameral (two-chamber) legislature. It comprises

100 members of the Senate and 435 members of the House of Representatives ("House").

The framers of the Constitution anticipated that most legislation would originate in the House. This expectation arose from the fact that the House is considered more representative of the country's population and its desires. Every state, without regard to its size, sends two senators to Congress. On the other hand, states that are less populous, such as Montana or Alaska, send far fewer representatives to the House than heavily populated states such as New York or California. While the Senate can introduce most types of legislation, the drafters of the Constitution correctly anticipated that most legislation would commence in the House. For example, during the 108th Congress, from January 1, 2003, until November 1, 2004, 6,842 bills and resolutions were introduced in the House while 3,630 were introduced in the Senate. Nevertheless, the Constitution provides that only the House of Representatives can originate revenue-raising bills. By tradition, the House also initiates appropriation bills. Legislation can be proposed by anyone, including members of Congress, executive departments of the federal government, private individuals, or lobbyists. These individuals or groups transmit their proposals to their representative.

There are several steps in the enactment of legislation (we will assume legislation is originating in the House):

- A bill, which is a proposed law, is introduced by its sponsor in Congress by being handed to the Clerk of the House or by being placed in a wooden box called the "hopper."
- The bill is numbered. If the bill originated in the House, it will be labeled "H.R." Those bills introduced in the Senate are labeled "S."

Examples
(i)   H.R. 412 (from the first session of the 108th Congress): "To enhance the operation of the AMBER Alert communications network in order to facilitate the recovery of abducted children, to provide for enhanced notification on highways of alerts and information on such children, and for other purposes."

(ii) S. 326 (from the first session of the 108th Congress): "To amend the Uniform Code of Military Justice to apply to prosecutions of child abuse cases in courts-martial an extended statute of limitations applicable to prosecutions of child abuse cases in United States District Courts, and for other purposes."

The numbering of the bills is always sequential; that is, "H.R. 41" indicates the forty-first bill introduced in a particular congressional session.

- The bill is now printed in slip form (as an individual pamphlet) by the Government Printing Office and given to each representative and sent to the appropriate committee. For example, if the bill deals with the military, it will be referred to the House (or Senate) Armed Services Committee. If it involves the judiciary, it will be referred to the House (or Senate) Judiciary Committee. The House has 19 permanent committees, and the Senate has 17. Additionally, several select committees exist, such as the Senate Select Committee on Ethics. Much of the work involved in enacting federal legislation is done by these committees or by their subcommittees. Until 1975, the Speaker of the House could refer a bill to only one committee. In modern practice, the Speaker may refer an introduced bill to multiple committees for consideration of those provisions of the bill within the jurisdiction of each committee concerned. Generally, the Speaker must designate a primary committee of jurisdiction on bills referred to multiple committees.

- The committee will now place the bill on its calendar. The committee's initial action is usually to request interested agencies of the government to comment upon the proposed legislation. The committee may hold hearings regarding the proposed legislation and interested parties, lobbyists, experts, and consumer advocates may testify either voluntarily or by subpoena. Cabinet officers and high-ranking civil and military officials of the government may also testify.

- After studying the legislation and holding hearings, the committee will take one of three actions: It will report (recommend) the bill without any revisions; it will report the bill with revisions and modifications; or it may "table" the bill, or fail to take any action on it, which effectively kills the bill. The committee will hold a "mark up" session and then issue a written statement, called a report, which explains the purpose of the bill, the intent of the bill, and why the bill has been approved or modified. Generally, a section-by-section analysis is given. Committee reports are perhaps the most valuable single element of the legislative history of a law. They are used by the courts, executive departments, and the public as a source of information regarding the purpose and meaning of the law.

- After the bill has been returned to the chamber in which it originated, it is placed on the calendar and scheduled for debate on the floor of the House (or Senate, if the bill was introduced in the Senate). While there are certain limits for the duration of debate in the House, debate in the Senate is usually not subject to any limits. The House Rules Committee may call for the bill to be voted on quickly if it is important or urgent.

- Voting occurs after debate, typically by electronic voting device.

- After a bill is passed in the chamber in which it originated, it is sent to the other chamber, which may pass the bill in its then present form. When a final bill is passed by one chamber, it is called an "engrossed" bill. More likely, however, the bill will be sent to the appropriate committee for analysis. This committee may also approve the measure, modify it, or table it. A report will be issued by the committee explaining the action taken by it.

- After the bill is reported out of the committee, it will be scheduled for debate and voting in the second chamber.
- If the bill is passed and the version agreed to by the second chamber is identical to the one passed by the first chamber, it will be sent to the president for signature.
- If the versions passed by the House and Senate differ, the measure is sent to "conference," the function of which is to reconcile these differing versions and produce compromise legislation acceptable to both chambers. The conference is typically comprised of senior members or "conferees" of the House and Senate committees that studied the bill, although in recent years junior members of the committee have been appointed as well as other members interested in the measure who were not on the committees. This has led to increased conference sizes, such as the 1981 conference on a budget reconciliation bill in which 250 members of Congress, divided into 58 subgroups, participated.
- The conference may continue for weeks or months as the conferees struggle to harmonize the conflicting versions of the bill. After agreement is finally reached, the conferees will prepare a report setting forth their conclusions and recommendations. This compromise measure must again be voted on by both the House and Senate.
- When the reconciled bill has been passed by both the House and Senate, it is printed by the Government Printing Office in a process called "enrollment" and is then certified as correct and signed by the Speaker of the House and then the vice president.
- The bill is now sent to the president for signature. If the president approves the bill, he will sign it, date it, and usually write the word "approved" on the bill, which has now been printed on parchment. Once the president has signed the bill, it is referred to as a "law" or a "statute" rather than a "bill." If the president fails to take action within ten days, excluding Sundays, while Congress is in session (January 3 until mid-summer), the bill will become law without his signature. If Congress adjourns before this ten-day period and the president fails to sign the bill, it will die. This is often referred to as the "pocket veto." An "act" is a series of statutes related to the same topic, such as the Lanham Act, which is numerous statutes all dealing with federal trademark law.
- If the president vetoes, or rejects, the bill by refusing to sign it, Congress may override this veto and enact the measure if both the House and Senate vote to approve it by a two-thirds majority. Failure to secure this two-thirds vote will result in the president's veto being upheld.
- When the bill is signed, it is assigned a number in sequential order. For example, Pub. L. 108-120 would indicate the 120th public law enacted during the One Hundred Eighth Congress.
- A bill that is not enacted in a particular Congress does not carry over to the next Congress; it must be re-proposed in a following

Congress if legislation is desired. For example, the Brady Bill, dealing with the sale of firearms, was introduced in several Congresses before finally being enacted into law. Far more bills are introduced in any session than are passed. For example, between January 1, 2003, and November 1, 2004, 10,472 bills were introduced in the House and Senate, but only 414 (about four percent) had become law.

See Figure 3-1 for a diagram showing how a bill becomes a law.

Figure 3-1
How a Bill Becomes Law

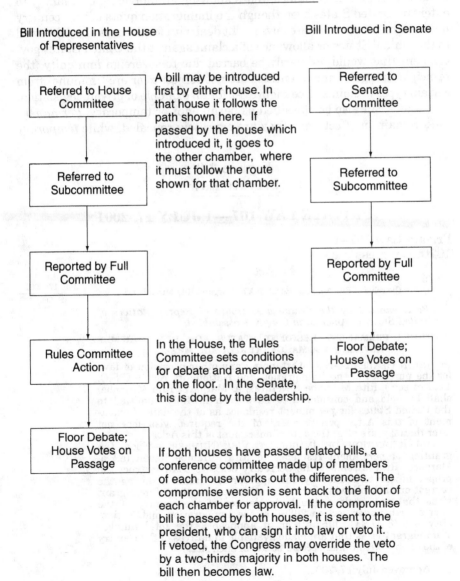

Bill Introduced in the House
of Representatives

Bill Introduced in Senate

Referred to House Committee

A bill may be introduced first by either house. In that house it follows the path shown here. If passed by the house which introduced it, it goes to the other chamber, where it must follow the route shown for that chamber.

Referred to Senate Committee

Referred to Subcommittee

Referred to Subcommittee

Reported by Full Committee

Reported by Full Committee

Rules Committee Action

In the House, the Rules Committee sets conditions for debate and amendments on the floor. In the Senate, this is done by the leadership.

Floor Debate; House Votes on Passage

Floor Debate; House Votes on Passage

If both houses have passed related bills, a conference committee made up of members of each house works out the differences. The compromise version is sent back to the floor of each chamber for approval. If the compromise bill is passed by both houses, it is sent to the president, who can sign it into law or veto it. If vetoed, the Congress may override the veto by a two-thirds majority in both houses. The bill then becomes law.

2. Classification of Federal Statutes

After the bill is enacted into law by the president signing it or by act of the United States Congress in overriding a presidential veto by a two-thirds vote of each chamber of Congress, it is sent to the Archivist of the United States, who will classify each law as public or private and will direct its publication.

Public laws are those that affect the public generally, such as tax laws, laws relating to federal lands, laws relating to bankruptcy, and the like.

Private laws are those that affect only one person or entity or a small group of persons, granting them some special benefit not afforded to the public at large. The most common private laws are those dealing with immigration or naturalization; for instance, those allowing an individual or a family to enter the United States even though the immigration quota of that country has been met. Other private laws might deal with forgiveness of a debt owed to the United States or allowance of a claim against the United States government that would ordinarily be barred due to sovereign immunity (the principle that government entities are not subject to or are "immune" from certain types of claims). See Figure 3-2 for an example of private legislation.

Laws can also be classified as permanent or temporary. *Permanent laws* remain in effect until they are expressly repealed, while *temporary*

Figure 3-2
Private Law

PRIVATE LAW 107—1 JULY 17, 2001

Private Law 107–1
107th Congress

An Act

For the relief of Rita Mirembe Revell (a.k.a. Margaret Rita Mirembe).

July 17, 2001
[S. 560]

Be it enacted by the Senate and House of Representatives of the United States of America in Congress assembled,

SECTION 1. PERMANENT RESIDENT STATUS FOR RITA MIREMBE REVELL (A.K.A. MARGARET RITA MIREMBE).

(a) IN GENERAL.—Notwithstanding any other provision of law, for the purposes of the Immigration and Nationality Act (8 U.S.C. 1101 et seq.), Rita Mirembe Revell (a.k.a. Margaret Rita Mirembe) shall be held and considered to have been lawfully admitted to the United States for permanent residence as of the date of enactment of this Act, upon payment of the required visa fees not later than 2 years after the date of enactment of this Act.

(b) REDUCTION OF IMMIGRANT VISA NUMBERS.—Upon the granting of permanent residence to Rita Mirembe Revell (a.k.a. Margaret Rita Mirembe), the Secretary of State shall instruct the proper officer to reduce by the appropriate number, during the current or next following fiscal year, the total number of immigrant visas that are made available to natives of the country of the alien's birth under section 203(a) of the Immigration and Nationality Act (8 U.S.C. 1153(a)) or, if applicable, the total number of immigrant visas that are made available to natives of the country of the alien's birth under section 202(e) of such Act.

Approved July 17, 2001.

laws have limiting language in the statute itself, such as the following: "This law shall have no force or effect after December 31, 2004."

As you might expect, the vast majority of laws are permanent, as it would be extraordinarily inefficient for lawmakers to pass legislation that continually expires. Nevertheless, there are situations in which temporary legislation is enacted. For example, in the mid-1970s, to address a critical shortage in oil and to conserve gasoline, the United States Congress enacted legislation reducing the speed limit on federal highways from 65 to 55 miles per hour. The original statute provided it would expire in one year. Near the end of that year period, after Congress heard testimony relating to decreased fuel consumption and decreased mortality rates attributed to this reduction in speed, it extended and made permanent the original temporary legislation. Various spending measures, appropriations bills, and tax laws are often temporary.

3. *Publication of Federal Statutes*

a. *United States Statutes at Large*

As each law is passed, it is published by the United States Government Printing Office as a looseleaf unbound pamphlet or sheet of paper (or several sheets, depending upon the length of the law), referred to as a "slip." At the end of each congressional session, these slips are taken together and are placed in chronological order in a hardback set of volumes called *United States Statutes at Large*. Keep in mind that a session is one year and that there are two sessions for each Congress because a new Congress comes into existence every two years upon the election of the members of the House of Representatives. All of our federal laws since 1789 are contained in more than 110 volumes of *United States Statutes at Large*. This set is often referred to as our "session laws," because it includes all the slips from one legislative session in chronological order.

Because it can take as long as a year after the end of a congressional session for the applicable volume of *United States Statutes at Large* to arrive at a law library, you should know there are several alternate sources available that will provide you with the exact wording of a federal statute. In this regard, you should never rely on a summary or synopsis of any legislation. You must obtain and analyze the exact wording of the statute in order to ensure that your research is correct because a mere summary, in a news publication or otherwise, cannot convey the explicit nature of statutory language.

To obtain the exact wording of a federal statute without waiting as long as one year for the hardback bound volumes of *United States Statutes at Large* to become available, consult the following:

(1) *Slip Laws*

The slips themselves are available in certain libraries throughout the United States. Nearly 1,300 libraries scattered throughout the nation (including law libraries) have been designated as United States Government Depository Libraries, which will receive certain selected government materials, notably slip laws. In a large city there may be several depository libraries. For example, there are nine in Los Angeles, California. Often these depositories are large law school libraries or the libraries in courthouses in a county seat. To find out if a library is a depository library, simply call the reference librarian at a few of the libraries in your area (both law school libraries and at the largest courthouse in your region). The reference librarian will inform you if the library has been designated as a government depository. If so, any member of the public will have access to the depository materials, including the slip laws. These slips may be available as early as five to seven days after the law is enacted. Alternatively, to locate federal depository libraries, access http://www.gpoaccess. gov/libraries.html.

(2) United States Code Congressional and Administrative News Service ("USCCAN")

This publication is issued monthly by West, which prints in a softcover or pamphlet form the complete text of all of the public laws passed during the previous month as well as newly enacted federal regulations, executive orders, and presidential proclamations. A law firm or law library subscribes to this publication in much the same way an individual might subscribe to *Time Magazine, Sports Illustrated*, or *Gourmet*, although the cost is substantially higher — for example, approximately $600 per year for 12 issues of USCCAN, as opposed to approximately $20 per year for 12 issues of *Gourmet*. At the end of each congressional session, the pamphlets comprising USCCAN are published in hardback volumes.

(3) United States Law Week

This weekly publication is a product of the Bureau of National Affairs, which prints the complete text of the more significant public laws enacted during the previous week (as well as summaries of recent cases decided). While *United States Law Week* will thus give you more rapid access than USCCAN (because *United States Law Week* is weekly and USCCAN is published only monthly), *United States Law Week* does not provide you with *all* of the public laws passed during the week preceding its publication but only those the publisher deems most important. Similar to USCCAN subscriptions, law firms and law libraries will subscribe to *United States Law Week* much the same way individuals arrange to receive publications they may be interested in (once again, however, the cost may be significantly higher — the current subscription rate for *United States Law Week* is approximately $700 per year).

(4) Government Printing Office

Slip laws can be purchased from the United States Government Printing Office. Call (202) 512-0000 or toll free at (888) 293-6498 for information or (202) 512-1800 to place an order.

(5) U.S.C.S. Advance *Pamphlets*

A monthly pamphlet issued by the publisher of U.S.C.S. and called *U.S.C.S. Advance* publishes the text of newly enacted public laws passed during the previous month. There are no hardbound volumes. Summaries of proposed legislation are also given, together with tables that pinpoint the sections of the United States Code that have been affected by recent legislation or regulatory action.

(6) *Congressional Representatives*

You should also consider contacting the sponsor of the legislation or your congressional representative(s) to ask for the complete text of a recently enacted law. Most representatives have local telephone numbers, which can be found in your telephone book or local newspaper, and most of them have assistants or "staffers" who are very helpful and skillful in locating the information you need and sending it to you at no cost. Alternatively, access the THOMAS site (http://thomas.loc.gov) and select either "House Directory" or "Senate Directory" to locate phone numbers and addresses of all members of Congress. All congressional representatives and their staffers have immediate access to Congressional Research Service, a division of the Library of Congress, the primary function of which is to provide research and reference assistance to the United States Congress. If your first request for information is not successful, call again. Often the information you request will be provided to you within a matter of days.

(7) *The Internet*

Rapid access to federal statutes can also be found on the Internet. One of the best sites for legislative information is "THOMAS—Legislation Information on the Internet," a site provided by the Library of Congress that offers the text of proposed and enacted legislation, committee information, calendars for hearings scheduled, and House and Senate Directories. Access http://thomas.loc.gov. Alternatively, access GPO Access at http://www.gpoaccess.gov/plaws/index.html. A sample page from THOMAS is shown as Figure 10-1 in Chapter 10. Research using the Internet will be fully discussed in Chapter 12.

As discussed above, at the end of each congressional session, the slip laws are compiled chronologically into the bound set of volumes called *United States Statutes at Large*. *United States Statutes at Large* contains both public and private laws, although private laws are typically found in a much smaller section near the end of each volume.

While *United States Statutes at Large* offers a wonderful historical overview of the order in which the United States Congress has enacted laws for the previous 200 years, it suffers from glaring deficiencies from a legal researcher's point of view:

- The arrangement of *United States Statutes at Large* is chronological rather than by subject or topic. Thus, if you were asked to find all of the federal laws relating to trademarks, you might find them scattered over more than 115 volumes rather than being contained in volumes devoted solely to the topic of trademarks.

- Subsequent amendments to or even a repeal of a previously passed law will not appear together with that law but will appear in the volumes relating to the session in which those amendments or repeals were enacted. That is, if a law enacted in 1970 was amended in 1980 and repealed in 1990, you would need to look at three separate volumes of *United States Statutes at Large* — those for 1970, 1980, and 1990 — to obtain the complete history and current status of this legislation.

- There is no one comprehensive index to *United States Statutes at Large*. Even though each volume of *United States Statutes at Large* contains an index and a table of contents, there is no one cumulative index to tell you which specific volumes to examine if you were charged with the responsibility of locating all of the federal laws relating to copyrights, for example. Rather, you would be forced to pick up each volume of the set and examine its index to determine if any laws relating to copyrights were contained in that volume.

(8) LEXIS and Westlaw

You can also gain rapid access to federal statutes (together with their legislative history, including committee reports and debates) through either of the two online legal research services, LEXIS, offered by Lexis-Nexis, and Westlaw, offered by West. These services are fully described in Chapter 11.

b. United States Code

Because the organization of *United States Statutes at Large* makes research using the set so difficult, it became readily apparent that a set of books should be developed to eliminate these barriers to efficient research. The process of developing a set of books that compiles the currently valid laws on the same subject together with any amendments to those laws is referred to as "codification."

The first codification of *United States Statutes at Large* occurred in the mid-1870s. A second codification or edition followed a few years thereafter but the set or "code" in current use originates from 1925, when Congress authorized preparation of the *United States Code* (U.S.C.).

All of the statutes enacted into law and contained in *United States Statutes at Large* were analyzed and categorized by subject matter so that at the completion of this project there were 50 categories or "titles" of federal statutes. For instance, Title 7 contains statutes dealing with agriculture; Title 25 contains statutes dealing with Indians; Title 38 contains statutes dealing with veterans' benefits; and Title 50 contains statutes dealing with war and national defense. The 50 titles are further divided into chapters and sections. A citation to any statute in the *United States*

Code indicates the number of the title, the name of the set, the section number, and the year of the code, as follows:

42	U.S.C.	§	1396	(2000)
Title	*Set*	*Abbr. for section*	*Section no.*	*Year of code*

It is not important to know what subject each of the 50 titles refers to. It is sufficient to understand that there are, in fact, 50 groups of statutes or titles, that they are arranged alphabetically, and that these 50 titles are permanently established, meaning that any federal statute relating to agriculture will always be found in Title 7, that any federal statute dealing with Indians will always be found in Title 25, and so on. See Figure 3-3 for a listing of the 50 titles of the *United States Code.*

The *United States Code* is "official," a term whose sole meaning is that publication of the set is directed by a statute or that the set is designated as "official" by a statute or court order. The actual printing of the set is done either by the United States Government Printing Office or at its express instruction. In fact, West has helped organize and maintain the *United States Code* since 1926. The *United States Code* is revised and a new edition published by the Government Printing Office every six years. During this six-year period, statutes may be amended or even repealed. Changes to federal statutes during the course of the six years are reflected in annual hardbound supplements placed on the shelf after Title 50. However, these annual cumulative supplements often take eight months to two years to be printed. Thus, researchers often rely on one of the annotated versions of the *United States Code* for more rapid updating and other useful research features, as described below.

c. Annotated Versions of the *United States Code*

While the *United States Code* is an efficiently organized set in that all federal statutes relating to bankruptcy have been brought together, all federal statutes relating to crimes have been brought together, and so forth, researchers typically want something more than a mere recitation of a statute. If you will remember the point made in Chapter 1, that under the concept of stare decisis, it is not the naked statutory language that controls but a court's interpretation of that statute (particularly in instances in which the statute is vague or ambiguous), you can readily see why the *United States Code*, while organized in an easy-to-understand scheme, is still unsatisfactory to researchers. That is because researchers prefer to read a statute and immediately be directed to cases that have construed or interpreted that statute.

Because the *United States Code* simply recites the exact text of a federal statute and immediately thereafter recites the exact text of the next federal statute without providing any comment regarding the law or any reference to any cases that may have interpreted that law, two private publishers, West and the former Lawyers Cooperative Publishing (now LEXIS Publishing), separately assumed the task of providing this necessary information to those in the legal profession. Because the publication of these two sets is not directed by statute, these publications are referred to as "unofficial." Both of these sets are referred to as "annotated" codes, meaning they contain "notes" referring readers to cases interpreting statutes.

Note that the classification and organization of all of the federal statutes, both official and unofficial, is identical so that once a statute is assigned to a title and given a section number, it retains those designations for all purposes.

Example: 17 U.S.C. § 105 (2000)
17 U.S.C.A. § 105 (West 1996)
17 U.S.C.S. § 105 (LexisNexis 2001) (*for The Bluebook*)
17 U.S.C.S. § 105 (LEXIS 1994) (*for ALWD*)

Figure 3-3
Titles of *United States Code*

1. General Provisions	29. Labor
2. The Congress	30. Mineral Lands and
3. The President	Mining
4. Flag and Seal, Seat of	31. Money and Finance
Government, and the States	32. National Guard
5. Government Organization	33. Navigation and Navigable
and Employees	Waters
6. Surety Bonds	34. Navy (see Title 10, Armed
7. Agriculture	Forces)
8. Aliens and Nationality	35. Patents
9. Arbitration	36. Patriotic Societies and
10. Armed Forces	Observances
11. Bankruptcy	37. Pay and Allowances of the
12. Banks and Banking	Uniformed Services
13. Census	38. Veterans' Benefits
14. Coast Guard	39. Postal Service
15. Commerce and Trade	40. Public Buildings, Property,
16. Conservation	and Works
17. Copyrights	41. Public Contracts
18. Crimes and Criminal	42. The Public Health and
Procedure	Welfare
19. Customs Duties	43. Public Lands
20. Education	44. Public Printing and
21. Food and Drugs	Documents
22. Foreign Relations and	45. Railroads
Intercourse	46. Shipping
23. Highways	47. Telegraphs, Telephones, and
24. Hospitals and Asylums	Radiotelegraphs
25. Indians	48. Territories and Insular
26. Internal Revenue Code	Possessions
27. Intoxicating Liquors	49. Transportation
28. Judiciary and Judicial	50. War and National
Procedure	Defense

(1) United States Code Annotated

West publishes an annotated version of the *United States Code* titled *United States Code Annotated*, universally referred to as "U.S.C.A." The word "annotated" means "with notes," and one of the most useful features of U.S.C.A. is the notes provided to researchers who use U.S.C.A. These include references to additional primary and secondary materials.

U.S.C.A. is a set of approximately 300 volumes, all of which are relatively small in size for law books (approximately 5½″ × 9½″) and all of which are a deep maroon color. U.S.C.A. is divided into the very same groupings or 50 "titles" as the *United States Code* and contains the exact wording of the federal statutes contained in the *United States Code*. There is a multivolume general index to U.S.C.A.

The front of each volume of U.S.C.A. contains a list of the 50 titles of the *United States Code*. Therefore, you need not memorize which statutes are contained within each title because you can readily determine this information.

You may have observed that there are only 50 titles to the *United States Code* (and U.S.C.A.), and yet U.S.C.A. comprises approximately 300 volumes. This arrangement arises out of the fact that some titles, such as Bankruptcy, contain numerous statutes and "spill over" into more than one volume, while other titles, such as Coast Guard, have far fewer statutes and can be contained in less than one volume. Thus, seven volumes of U.S.C.A. are devoted to bankruptcy statutes while the statutes relating to the Census and the Coast Guard are combined in one volume.

U.S.C.A. is not valuable because it provides the exact text of federal statutes — the *United States Code* provides that as well. U.S.C.A. is valuable because of the "extra" features provided to researchers. Those are displayed in Figure 3-4 and are as follows:

(a) Historical and Statutory Notes

Following the statute you will find an overview of the history of a particular statute, including the Public Law Number, the effective date of the statute, its citation to *United States Statutes at Large*, an indication of the date certain parts or subsections of the statute were added or deleted, and a basic summary of the evolution of this particular federal law.

(b) Cross References

Following the historical notes you will be sent to other federal statutes that may be of assistance in helping you understand this federal statute.

(c) Library References

In its section called "Library References," U.S.C.A. directs you to other sources in the law library, including form books, practice manuals, texts and treatises, jury instructions, encyclopedias, and law review articles that also deal with the topic covered by the statute. Additionally, you will be given West's topic name and key number assigned to the subject covered by the statute so you may access West's digests (discussed in Chapter 5).

(d) Westlaw Electronic Research

U.S.C.A. will provide you with guidance in developing search queries so you can conduct further research relating to the statute on WESTLAW, West's computerized legal research system (see Chapter 11).

(e) *Code of Federal Regulations*

Following the library references you may be directed to sections of the *Code of Federal Regulations* (see Chapter 10) that relate to this statute.

Figure 3-4
Sample Pages from U.S.C.A. (Title 42)

§ 1395.   Prohibition against any Federal interference

Nothing in this subchapter shall be construed to authorize any Federal officer or employee to exercise any supervision or control over the practice of medicine or the manner in which medical services are provided, or over the selection, tenure, or compensation of any officer or employee of any institution, agency, or person providing health services; or to exercise any supervision or control over the administration or operation of any such institution, agency, or person.

(Aug. 14, 1935, c. 531, Title XVIII, § 1801, as added July 30, 1965, Pub.L. 89–97, Title I, § 102(a), 79 Stat. 291.)

Historical Note

Short Title. For Short Title of Pub.L. 89–97, which enacted this subchapter, see Short Title of 1965 Amendment note, set out under section 1305 of this title.

Legislative History. For legislative history and purpose of Pub.L. 89–97, see 1965 U.S. Code Cong. and Adm.News, p. 1943.

West's Federal Practice Manual

Analysis of major federal benefits for disabled persons, see § 6034.
Medicare, see § 5741.

Code of Federal Regulations

Professional Standards Review Organization hospital review, see 42 CFR 466.1 et seq.

Notes of Decisions

Administrative review 8
Construction 1
Control over medical practice 4
Cost limitations 5
Judicial review 9
Purpose 2
Recoupment 6
Rules and regulations 3
Waiver 7

1. Construction

Interpretation of a complex statute such as this subchapter by the administrative officer charged with the responsibility of administering it is entitled to considerable deference and, if reasonable, is not to be rejected by a court merely because another interpretation may also be reasonable. Health Care Service Corp. v. Califano, C.A.Ill.1979, 601 F.2d 934.

Figure 3-4 (continued)

This subchapter is remedial in nature and is to be construed liberally to effectuate the Congressional purpose of insuring that adequate medical care is available to the aged. Whitman v. Weinberger, D.C.Va.1974, 382 F.Supp. 256.

This subchapter is remedial and is to be construed liberally. Reading v. Richardson, D.C.Mo.1972, 339 F.Supp. 295. See, also, Lord v. Richardson, D.C.Ind.1972, 356 F.Supp. 232; Pippin v. Richardson, D.C.Fla. 1972, 349 F.Supp. 1365; Bohlen v. Richardson, D.C.Pa.1972, 345 F.Supp. 124, affirmed 483 F.2d 918; Sowell v. Richardson, D.C. S.C.1970, 319 F.Supp. 689; Carey v. Finch, D.C.La.1970, 316 F.Supp. 1263.

This subchapter is remedial and therefore is to be construed liberally to effectuate the legislative purpose of insuring that adequate medical care is available to the aged throughout the country, and it is necessary to interpret provisions of this subchapter in a sensible, nontechnical manner. In re Schnelle's Estate, 1974, 353 N.Y.S.2d 902, 77 Misc.2d 857.

2. Purpose

This subchapter providing Federal health insurance for aged and disabled was enacted for specific purpose of providing coordinated and comprehensive approach to Federal health insurance and medical care for the aged. Turecamo v. C.I.R., C.A.2, 1977, 554 F.2d 564, 46 A.L.R.Fed. 912.

Purpose of this subchapter is to insure that adequate medical care is available to the aged throughout the country. Hultzman v. Weinberger, C.A.Pa.1974, 495 F.2d 1276.

The purpose of medicare is to provide health services to the elderly at minimal cost to them. Diplomat Lakewood Inc. v. Califano, D.C.D.C.1978, 453 F.Supp. 442, reversed on other grounds 613 F.2d 1009, 198 U.S. App.D.C. 276.

It was Congress' purpose in this chapter and in this subchapter to limit the availability of judicial review in order to prevent courts from being deluged with a multiplicity of complaints. Lodi Memorial Hospital v. Califano, D.C.D.C.1978, 451 F.Supp. 651.

Purpose of this subchapter is not merely to protect its beneficiaries against major health care expenditures, but to make the best in modern medicine more available. Rastetter v. Weinberger, D.C.Ariz.1974, 379 F.Supp. 170, affirmed 95 S.Ct. 767, 419 U.S. 1098, 42 L.Ed.2d 795.

In accomplishing this subchapter's purpose of making the best in modern medicine more available, Congress may legitimately proceed toward that end by one step at a time, addressing itself to the phase of the problem which seems most acute to the legislative mind. Id.

Intent of this subchapter is not only to make benefits available to defray hospital costs but also to alleviate costs of treatment in posthospital extended care facilities. Schoultz v. Weinberger, D.C.Wis.1974, 375 F.Supp. 929.

One purpose of this subchapter is to insure the availability of adequate medical care for the aged. Lord v. Richardson, D.C.Ind.1972, 356 F.Supp. 232.

3. Rules and regulations

Whatever legal rights the patients might have against nursing home for its failure to maintain its status as a qualified facility, the enforcement by the Department of Health, Education and Welfare [now Department of Health and Human Services] and by the Pennsylvania Department of Public Welfare of their valid regulations did not directly affect the patient's legal rights or deprive them of any constitutionally protected interest in life, liberty or property. O'Bannon v. Town Court Nursing Center, Pa.1980, 100 S.Ct. 2467, 447 U.S. 773, 65 L.Ed.2d 506, on remand 626 F.2d 1114.

In judging whether medicare regulations are valid under reasonably related test, interpretation of statutory scheme by Secretary is entitled to considerable deference, and party challenging regulations shoulders difficult burden of proving that regulations conflict with purpose of enabling legislation. River Garden Hebrew Home for the Aged v. Califano, D.C.Fla.1980, 507 F.Supp. 221.

Congress intended judgmental process in health care delivery systems to be influenced and animated by consciousness of costs of medical care, and any effect of maximum allowable cost regulations upon drug prescription habits in medical profession was consistent with Congressional intent; regulations did not constitute Federal supervision or control over practice of medicine within meaning of this section prohibiting such Federal supervision or control. American Medical Ass'n v. Mathews, D.C.Ill.1977, 429 F.Supp. 1179.

Even though medicare provider submitted its request for reimbursement for the years 1966 and 1967 before promulgation of regulation requiring that interest expenses incurred in construction be capitalized rather than expensed, where reimbursement was denied on the basis of that regulation, the provider could complain of impropriety in the manner

75

(f) Notes of Decisions

These notes or "annotations" are the most valuable part of U.S.C.A., for it is these notes that will direct you to cases that have interpreted the statute you have just read.

If a case has discussed, interpreted, or construed the statute you are reviewing, U.S.C.A. will provide you with a citation to that case. Moreover, West has realized that a case citation standing alone might not be particularly helpful to a researcher. Therefore, you will not only be given the case citation but also a brief one-sentence description of the case so you do not waste time pulling endless cases off the library shelves but instead can make an informed decision as to which cases to review based upon the quick summary or "annotation." Although West's goal is to serve as a comprehensive tool for researchers, U.S.C.A. will not send you to every case that may interpret or mention a statute. Nevertheless, you will be sent to a sufficient cross-section of cases so you can embark upon your research tasks.

Because some statutes have been interpreted in hundreds of ways on hundreds of occasions, U.S.C.A. does not merely give you a long list of annotations but organizes or indexes these annotations for you under numbered catchlines. For instance, if you have read a statute and want to read cases that interpret the statute generally, you may be directed to read the annotations listed under the catchline called "Note 1." Note 1 will then give you quick summaries of several cases that discuss this statute in a general fashion. The annotations are arranged alphabetically under numbered notes so you can readily locate court decisions on any section or portion of the statute you are researching. For example, suppose you are researching 42 U.S.C.A. § 1395(y) (West 2000 § Supp. 2004), relating to exclusions from health insurance coverage. The annotations are arranged as follows:

Notes of Decisions

Generally   3
Ability of spouse to care for patient   5
Construction   1
Custodial or supportive care   6
Estoppel   13
Evidence   12
Hearing   10
Jurisdiction   9
Necessity of services   4
Notice and hearing   10
Personal comfort items   7
Pleadings   11
Purpose   2
Reasonableness and necessity of services   4
Remand   15

Thus, if you are interested in the reasonableness and necessity of services, you would review the annotations listed under Note 4. You must then read the cases to which you are directed. While the brief digests or summaries are extremely well done and are written by attorney-editors, they cannot convey the subtle nuances of a case and are never a substitute for full analysis of a case. It is possible there may be no annotations following a statute, which would indicate that the statute has not been the subject of litigation and thus has not been interpreted or construed by any cases. See Figure 3-5 for a sample page of U.S.C.A. annotations.

Figure 3-5
U.S.C.A. Annotations

Library References

Bankruptcy ⊜837.   C.J.S. Bankruptcy § 1051 et seq.

Notes of Decisions

Generally 1
Collective bargaining agreements within section 2
Determination of disputes 3
Instructions to trustees 4
Jurisdiction 5

1. Generally

Under former section 205(n) of this title which provided that no judge or trustee acting under this title could change wages or working conditions of railroad employees except in manner prescribed in Railway Labor Act, section 151 et seq. of Title 45, district court acting as reorganization court erred in ordering suspension of previously negotiated railroad employee protection agreements and impoundment of funds which would otherwise have been paid to employees. Railway Labor Executives' Ass'n, Broth. of Locomotive Engineers and Congress of Ry. Unions v. Patton, C.A.Ohio 1974, 500 F.2d 34, certiorari denied 95 S.Ct. 682, 419 U.S. 1090, 42 L.Ed.2d 682.

2. Collective bargaining agreements within section

Under provision of former section 205(n) of this title that no judge or trustee could change wages or working conditions except in manner prescribed in Railway Labor Act, section 151 et seq., of Title 45, air carrier's collective bargaining agreements with pilots and stewardesses were governed by Railway Labor Act and could be changed only in conformity therewith, and referee could not authorize disaffirmance without compliance with Railway Labor Act. In re Overseas Nat. Airways, Inc., D.C.N.Y. 1965, 238 F.Supp. 359.

3. Determination of disputes

Bankruptcy court had no right to intervene to determine dispute between trustees of debtor railroad and two unions, where it did not clearly appear whether Railway Labor Act, section 151 et seq. of Title 45, had been violated or complied with, or that the threatened action of permitting yard conductors rather than road conductors to operate certain trains would be prejudicial to the public interest, since such matter was for determination of the Railway Adjustment Board. Order of Ry. Conductors of America v. Pitney, N.J.1946, 66 S.Ct. 322, 326 U.S. 561, 90 L.Ed. 318, rehearing denied 66 S.Ct. 525, 327 U.S. 814, 90 L.Ed. 1038.

4. Instructions to trustees

Instructions of the bankruptcy court to railroad trustees with respect to question whether, under contracts with unions, road conductors or yard conductors should operate certain trains, amount to no more than a decision any other carrier would make about the course to be followed and, while binding on the trustees and subject to appellate review, would not finally settle the dispute. Or-

Finally, U.S.C.A. not only contains a multivolume general index at the end of the set, but each title is separately indexed and each volume in the set is kept current by an annual cumulative pocket part or by separate softcover supplements, the importance of which will be discussed below.

(2) United States Code Service

LEXIS Publishing also publishes an annotated version of the *United States Code entitled United States Code Service Lawyers Edition* and referred to as "U.S.C.S." Similar in arrangement to U.S.C.A., U.S.C.S. is a set of approximately 200 volumes, which conform in size to most law books in that they are approximately 7″×10″. The volumes comprising U.S.C.S. are black and have aqua trim that is displayed on the spines of the book. Like U.S.C.A., this set also contains a multivolume general index. U.S.C.S. is divided into the same 50 titles as U.S.C. and U.S.C.A. and contains the identical wording of the federal statutes published in *United States Statutes at Large*.

While U.S.C.A. contains approximately 300 volumes and U.S.C.S. contains approximately 200 volumes, you should not make the assumption that U.S.C.A. is more valuable than U.S.C.S. or that U.S.C.A. gives you far more information than U.S.C.S. provides. Rather, the individual volumes in U.S.C.S. are quite large compared to the smaller size volumes used for U.S.C.A., and therefore, while the number of books in each set differs, the material contained within the books is substantially similar.

Like U.S.C.A., U.S.C.S. is "unofficial," meaning that it is published by a private publishing company without any government direction or mandate. Just as provided by U.S.C.A., U.S.C.S. contains the text of the federal statutes. If you are curious why these various sets (U.S.C., U.S.C.A., and U.S.C.S.) are all available, all of which provide the wording of the federal statutes, you should note a simple analogy to automobiles. All automobiles provide the same service: transportation. Yet consumers develop distinct preferences for Chevrolets, Fords, or Toyotas and may select one make of automobile over another based on habit, perceived differences, or various options available.

Similarly, all of the codifications mentioned herein (U.S.C., U.S.C.A., and U.S.C.S.) provide the same coverage: federal statutes. Yet consumers, namely law firms and law libraries, may choose to purchase one set over another based on various perceived advantages or options available.

Among the features provided by U.S.C.S. are the following:

(a) History; Ancillary Laws and Directives

Immediately following the text of the federal statute you will be provided with information relating to the effective date of the statute and amendments and revisions made to the statute. A citation to *United States Statutes at Large* is provided. This feature of U.S.C.S. is virtually identical to that feature of U.S.C.A. titled "Historical Notes," as both features show the evolution and development of the statute.

(b) *Code of Federal Regulations*

U.S.C.S. may direct you to sections of the *Code of Federal Regulations* that relate to this statute.

(c) Cross References

U.S.C.S. will direct you to other federal statutes that will assist in your interpretation of the statute in question as well as other sources, often other LEXIS Publishing sources.

(d) Research Guide

U.S.C.S. will direct you to other sources in the library (books, forms, encyclopedias, annotations, law review articles, for example) that may be helpful in construing and interpreting this statute. This feature of U.S.C.S. is equivalent to the feature of U.S.C.A. titled "Library References," although it is somewhat broader in scope than the Library References given by U.S.C.A. in that you are directed to numerous other sources, including a wider variety of law review articles.

(e) Interpretive Notes and Decisions

These notes or annotations are the most important of the features offered by U.S.C.S. Functioning identically to the annotations found in U.S.C.A., these notes will direct you to cases that have interpreted or discussed the statute being researched. Just as given by U.S.C.A., U.S.C.S. will provide you not only the citations to cases that have construed this statute but a short digest or summary of the cases to enable you to research more efficiently by selecting only those cases that appear promising. Just as seen in U.S.C.A., U.S.C.S. will organize the annotations for you by numbering them so that all of the cases discussing one part of the statute are brought together, all of the cases discussing another part of the statute are brought together, and so on. See Figure 3-6 for sample pages from U.S.C.S.

As you can see, the unofficial sets, U.S.C.A. and U.S.C.S., are substantially similar: Both provide the exact wording of the public federal statutes; both provide information relating to the history of the statute; both direct you to other sources in the library to enhance your understanding of the statute; and both provide you with citations and summaries or "annotations" of cases interpreting the statute.

Beyond this, both sets share additional features in common:

- The front of each volume of U.S.C.A. and U.S.C.S. contains a listing of the 50 titles of the *United States Code*;
- The citations to U.S.C.A. and U.S.C.S. are nearly identical in form. For instance, if a statute is found at Title 42, Section 1352, it will be cited: 42 U.S.C. § 1352 (2000), 42 U.S.C.A. § 1352 (West 2003), and 42 U.S.C.S. § 1352 (LexisNexis 2000). Thus, once a law is categorized within one of the 50 titles of the United States Code and assigned a section number, it will retain this title and section number for U.S.C.A. and U.S.C.S.;

- Both U.S.C.A. and U.S.C.S. have conversion tables that allow you to locate a federal statute if the only information you have is the public law number or the *U.S. Statutes at Large* citation. You can convert these citations into a citation to U.S.C.A. or U.S.C.S. For example, if you know a statute is 108 Stat. 381, tables in the last volumes of U.S.C.A. and U.S.C.S. located after the volumes for Title 50 will convert this citation to 20 U.S.C. § 1085 so you can readily locate the statute; and

Figure 3-6
Sample Pages from U.S.C.S. (Title 35)

§ 288. Action for infringement of a patent containing an invalid claim

Whenever, without deceptive intention, a claim of a patent is invalid, an action may be maintained for the infringement of a claim of the patent which may be valid. The patentee shall recover no costs unless a disclaimer of the invalid claim has been entered at the Patent and Trademark Office before the commencement of the suit.

(July 19, 1952, ch 950, § 1, 66 Stat. 813; Jan. 2, 1975, P. L. 93-596, § 1, 88 Stat. 1949.)

HISTORY; ANCILLARY LAWS AND DIRECTIVES

Prior law and revision:
This section is based on 35 USC, 1946 ed., § 71 (R. S. § 4922).
The necessity for a disclaimer to recover on valid claims is eliminated.
See 35 USCS § 253.
Language is changed.

Amendments:
1975. Act Jan. 2, 1975 (effective 1/2/75, as provided by § 4 of such Act), substituted "Patent and Trademark Office" for "Patent Office".

CROSS REFERENCES

Court of Appeals jurisdiction of appeals from judgments in civil actions for patent infringement which are final except for accounting, 28 USCS § 1292(a)(4).
Venue of civil action for patent infringement, 28 USCS § 1400(b).
Action by owner against United States in Court of Claims where invention described in and covered by patent is used or manufactured by or for United States without license of owner, 28 USCS § 1498(a).
Disclaimer, 35 USCS § 253.

RESEARCH GUIDE

Am Jur:
1 Am Jur 2d, Abatement, Survival, and Revival § 101.
20 Am Jur 2d, Costs § 63.
60 Am Jur 2d, Patents § 486.

Figure 3-6 *(Continued)*

Forms:

14 Am Jur Legal Forms 2d, Patents §§ 196:264–196:267.

Annotations:

Propriety of reference under Federal Civil Procedure Rule 53(b). 1 L
Ed 2d 1796.

Right to jury trial in patent infringement action in federal court. 18
ALR Fed 690.

Modern status of federal rules of res judicata in patent litigation. 4
ALR Fed 181.

Res judicata effect of federal consent decree in patent cases. 4 ALR
Fed 214.

Texts:

3 Deller, Patent Claims (2d ed) § 561.

4 Deller's Walker on Patents (2d ed) §§ 271, 278, 279, 282, 284, 287,
288.

Law Review Articles:

Zarley, Jury Trials in Patent Litigation. 20 Drake L Rev 243.

Newitt & Nelson, The Patent Lawyer and Trial by Jury. 1 John
Marshall J of Practice & Procedure 59.

INTERPRETIVE NOTES AND DECISIONS

1. Generally
2. Action on valid claims
3. Deceptive intent
4. Disclaimer of invalid claims
5. Costs recovery

1. Generally

These provisions have no application where
entire patent was void. Williams Calk Co. v
Kemmerer (1906, CA3 Pa) 145 F 928.

These provisions apply to reissued patents.
Rawson & Morrison Mfg. Co. v C. W. Hunt Co.
(1906, CA2 NY) 147 F 239.

Notwithstanding fact that some of plaintiff's
claims are valid and others invalid, and that
plaintiff therefore has grounds to sue for damages for patent infringement, plaintiff cannot
prevail where his attorney retired from patent
office immediately after signing notice of allowance of plaintiff's original patent, participated in
patent, acted as paid consultant in obtaining
plaintiff's patent reissues and acted as attorney in
prosecution of plaintiff's patent infringement suit.
Kearney & Trecker Corp. v Giddings & Lewis,
Inc. (1971, CA7 Wis) 452 F2d 579, 1971 CCH
Trade Cases P 73735, 171 USPQ 650, cert den
405 US 1066, 31 L Ed 2d 796, 92 S Ct 1500.

Original patent claims held valid and infringed
are unenforceable because of fraud involved in
using retired patent examiner to prosecute reis-

sue applications. Kearney & Trecker Corp. v
Cincinnati Milacron, Inc. (1977, CA6) 562 F2d
365, 195 USPQ 402.

2. Action on valid claims

Action could have been maintained for infringement of other parts of invention although
no disclaimer was filed, but in such case plaintiff
could not have recovered costs. Hall v Wiles
(CC NY) F Cas No 5954.

If plaintiff omitted to make a disclaimer, but
brought suit for violation of patent and he was
entitled to be protected in a portion of claims set
up in his patent he was still entitled to damages
for the valid portion of his claim, provided he
was not guilty of neglect in filing disclaimer.
McCormick v Seymour, (CC NY) F Cas No
8727, affd 60 US (19 How) 96, 15 L Ed 557.

Where it appeared that plaintiff was original
inventor of the parts of his invention secured by
alleged infringed claims, he was not required in
order to entitle himself to a decree for infringement, to make disclaimer of other claims. American Bell Tel. Co. v Spencer (1881, CC Mass) 8
F 509; Whitney v Boston & A. R. Co. (1892, CC
Mass) 50 F 72.

Plastic garment tag patent containing claim on
prior art concept falling within general concept
of inventor and not asserted against infringer
does not fall within 35 USCS § 288, because

- Both U.S.C.A. and U.S.C.S. are kept current by the most typical method of updating legal research volumes: annual cumulative pocket parts. Statutes are subject to frequent repeal or amendment, and this method allows the codes to be kept current without requiring the entire set of volumes in U.S.C.A. or U.S.C.S. to be replaced. A slit or "pocket" has been created in the back cover of each volume of U.S.C.A. and U.S.C.S. Sometime during the first quarter of each year the publishers of U.S.C.A. and U.S.C.S. mail small, softcover pamphlets called "pocket parts" to law firms, agencies, and law libraries that have subscribed to U.S.C.A. and U.S.C.S. These pocket parts slip into the slits in the back of each volume of U.S.C.A. and U.S.C.S. and provide current information about the statutes in that volume, including changes or amendments to the statute and references or annotations to cases decided since the hardback volume of U.S.C.A. or U.S.C.S. was placed on the library shelf.

  Pocket parts are prepared annually. When the pocket part is received for 2004, for example, the law librarian removes and discards the old 2003 pocket part and replaces it with the new 2004 pamphlet. The pocket parts are *cumulative*, meaning that if a hardback volume was received in 2000, the 2004 pocket part found in the back of that volume will have all of the changes and updates relating to the statutes in that volume from 2001, 2002, and 2003. See Figure 3-7 for sample pages from a pocket part.

On occasion, and over a period of time, the pocket parts may become too thick to fit into the slit cut into the back of each hardbound volume of U.S.C.A. or U.S.C.S. On such occasions, the publishers will issue a softcover supplement that functions in the same way as a pocket part but sits on the library shelf next to the volume it updates.

There are few invariable or inflexible rules in legal research, but one of them is that you must always consult a pocket part (or softcover supplement) if the volume you are using is updated by a pocket part pamphlet. If you wish, you may elect to check the pocket part before reviewing the hardbound volume itself. *When* you review the pocket part is not critical; *that* you review it is critical. Oftentimes, research in a university law library can be frustrating as a volume will contain a slit or opening for a pocket part and yet no pocket part is found. If this is so, you should assume that a pocket part does exist but that it has been misplaced because the publishers of both U.S.C.A. and U.S.C.S., as a courtesy to researchers, will provide either a pocket part for each volume or a notice, which slips into the pocket and will inform you "this volume contains no pocket part." See Figure 3-8.

You can easily see the advantage of the pocket parts and supplements: rapid supplementation of the statutes and annotations at a cost much lower than replacing the nearly 300 volumes of U.S.C.A. or the approximately 200 volumes of U.S.C.S. each year. Nevertheless, the expenses associated in maintaining any law library are substantial.

To enhance the updating of U.S.C.A., West provides an additional pamphlet service. These Statutory Supplements are designed to accelerate

Figure 3-7
Front Page of Pocket Part to U.S.C.S.

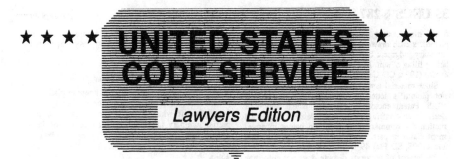

★ ★ ★ ★ UNITED STATES ★ ★ ★
CODE SERVICE

Lawyers Edition

Issued in

April 2000

CUMULATIVE SUPPLEMENT

By The Publisher's Editorial Staff

35 USCS
Patents
§§ 271–End

LEXIS Publishing™

LEXIS®·NEXIS®· MARTINDALE-HUBBELL®
MATTHEW BENDER®· MICHIE™· SHEPARD'S®

IT-132

Figure 3-7 (*Continued*)
Sample Page from Pocket Part to U.S.C.S.

35 USCS § 287, n 9   PATENTS

fringe more recent patent than patents marked on plaintiff's cash drawers results in granting of partial summary judgment barring damages prior to 6 years before filing of suit. M-S Cash Drawer Corp. v Block & Co. (1992, CD Cal) 26 USPQ2d 1472.

Since material issue of fact exists as to whether or not plaintiff's letter to defendant contains words "U.S. Patent enclosed" provided actual notice of design patent infringement, court denies defendant's motion for summary judgement on patent infringement claim in part. Bazz, Inc. v Catalina Lighting, Inc. (1998, SD Fla) 49 USPQ2d 2009.

Settlement of previous dispute does not constitute notice of patent infringement, but later letter indicating patent number does constitute notice, so that summary judgment against collection of damages before date of letter is granted. Konstant Prods., Inc. v Frazier Indus. Co. (1992, ND Ill) 25 USPQ2d 1223, summary judgment den, in part, summary judgment gr, in part (ND Ill) 1993 US Dist LEXIS 7957.

10. Persons notified

Patent making provision of 35 USCS § 287 is not defense available to government under 28 USCS § 1498 for using patent rights. Motorola, Inc. v United States (1984, CA FC) 729 F2d 765, 221 USPQ 297.

11. Actual knowledge of infringer

Indirect evidence that defendant knew of plaintiff's patents falls short of actual notice of infringement from plaintiff who did not mark products, so that partial summary judgment against recovery of damages before notice is granted. Hoover Universal v Graham Packaging Corp. (1996, CD Cal) 44 USPQ2d 1596.

IV. PROCEDURE

13. Generally

Notice provisions are effective to limit damage amounts, but do not operate during liability determination to allow withholding of information in resistance to interrogatories because of failure of patentee to mark with patent notice. Ampex Corp. v United States (1980,US Ct Cl) 207 USPQ 440.

§ 288. Action for infringement of a patent containing an invalid claim

RESEARCH GUIDE

Federal Procedure:

Patents, Fed Proc, L Ed, § 60:1055.

Am Jur:

60 Am Jur 2d, Patents §§ 806, 928, 929, 930, 931, 938-940, 941, 943, 948, 972, 973, 1046, 1094, 1113, 1123, 1233.

Forms:

13A Fed Procedural Forms L Ed Patents §§ 52:1, 381, 461, 481.

Intellectual Property:

4 Chisum on Patents (Matthew Bender), Patent & Trademark Office Procedures § 11.07.

Texts:

Deller, Patent Claims (2d ed).

INTERPRETIVE NOTES AND DECISIONS

2. Action on valid claims

Plaintiff's disclaimer of claims 1, 2, and 11 and simultaneous retention of undistinguishable claims 3 through 6 does not preclude plaintiff's enforcement of. valid and distinguishable claims 7, 8, 10, and 14 by action for infringement. Allen Archery, Inc. v Jennings Compound Bow. Inc. (1981, CD Cal) 211 USPQ 206.

4. Disclaimer of invalid claims

Maytag rule under predecessor statute that patentee who disclaimed invalid claim and failed to disclaim indistinguishable claim invalidated entire patent does not apply under USC § 253 and § 258, so that disclaimer of some claims and failure to disclaim indistinguishable claims do not invalidate entire patent. Allen Archery, Inc. v Jennings Compound Bow, Inc. (1982, CA9 Cal) 686 F2d 780, 216 USPQ 585.

Failure of patentee to disclaim invalid patent claim does not prevent patentee from enforcing any remaining claims that are otherwise valid in same patent. Allen Archery, Inc. v Browning Mfg. Co. (1987, CA FC) 819 F2d 1087, 2 USPQ2d 1490.

Withdrawing patent claims from suit without disclaimer does not invalidate patent without clear and convincing proof of bad faith. National Business Systems, Inc. v AM International, Inc. (1982, ND Ill) 546 F Supp 340, 217 USPQ 235.

Question of delay is irrelevant to filing of terminal disclaimer for claims subject to defense of obviousness-type double patenting. Bayer AG & Miles, Inc. v Barr Laboratories, Inc. (1992, SD NY) 798 F Supp 196, 24 USPQ2d 1864.

5. Costs recovery

Delay by patentee in disclaiming invalid claims affects only recovery of costs and does not invalidate otherwise valid claims. Allen Archery, Inc. v Jennings Compound Bow, Inc. (1982, CA9 Cal) 686 F2d 780, 216 USPQ 585.

Reissue of patent in suit is procedure for amending and correcting patent and accomplishes same result as disclaimer and thus preserves successful plaintiff's right to recover costs. Wycoff v Motorola, Inc. (1981, ND Ill) 217 USPQ 639.

Although patentee fraudulently concealed prior art from PTO, that event took place many years ago, and plaintiff fairly and expeditiously conducted trial so that even though patent is held invalid for fraud on PTO and for several other grounds, case is not exceptional and attorney fees to defendant are denied. Torin Corp. v Philips Industries, Inc. (1985, SD Ohio) 625 F Supp 1077, 228 USPQ 465.

Recent Annotatio in Pocket Part

Figure 3-8
Notice That No Pocket Part Exists

This Volume
Contains
No Pocket Part

Refer to
Separate
Soft Bound Supplement
to this Volume
for
Latest Updating Material

S1291b

the updating of statutes in U.S.C.A. before the publication of next year's pocket part. They include the public laws passed since the publication of the most recent pocket part and that relate to sections of the *United States Code*. Therefore, after you check the pocket part (published yearly) or supplement to determine if a statute has been amended or repealed, check the Statutory Supplements (published bimonthly) to determine if even more recent changes have occurred. Because the Statutory Supplements are not cumulative, you will have to check each one. These Statutory Supplements update all 50 titles of U.S.C.A., and thus are shelved after the end of Title 50. When new pocket parts are published at the beginning of each year, they will include all of the information previously included in the Statutory Supplements, which are then discarded.

Similarly, the publisher of U.S.C.S. publishes pamphlets called *Cumulative Later Case and Statutory Service*, which are designed to update the statutes found in U.S.C.S. Issued three times each year, these supplements contain statutory amendments and annotations to new cases. Each pamphlet is cumulative so that you need only consult the most recent issue. When the yearly pocket part for a volume of U.S.C.S. is published, the previous pamphlet will be discarded.

The publishers of U.S.C.S. also issue a monthly pamphlet to each subscriber of U.S.C.S. This is the *U.S.C.S. Advance*, and it includes materials issued after publication of the *Cumulative Later Case and Statutory Service*, such as newly enacted public laws, presidential proclamations and executive orders, and other presidential documents. Each monthly issue of *Advance* includes a cumulative index. A section titled "Current Awareness Commentary" includes highlights of new legislation, summaries of pending legislation, and "Supreme Court Update" discusses recent United States Supreme Court cases and cases accepted for review by the Court. See Figure 3-9 for a chart showing how to update research of federal statutes.

When a statute is located under a particular title and section, for example, 42 U.S.C.A. § 1223 or 42 U.S.C.S. § 1223, any amendment or further information relating to it in the pocket parts (or supplementary pamphlets) will also be located under the same title and section number. Similarly, the pocket parts use the same annotation titles or catchlines as the hardbound volumes so researchers can readily locate the latest decisions interpreting a statute.

When necessary, the publishers of U.S.C.A. and U.S.C.S. will issue replacement volumes for the hardback volumes in the set by simply mailing the law firm, agency, or law library a new volume together with a bill for the new volume.

Finally, you may be able to do some updating using various online sources. For example, the site for the Office of the Law Revision Counsel at http://uscode.house.gov/uscode.htm lists the sections of the United States Code affected by recently enacted laws. Similarly, the site GPO Access, maintained by the Government Printing Office at http://www.access.gpo.gov/uscode, attempts to ensure that its online references to the U.S. Code are always current.

d. Use of U.S.C., U.S.C.A., and U.S.C.S.

As you now know, there are three sets of codes you may use to locate and interpret federal statutes: U.S.C., U.S.C.A., and U.S.C.S. It is unlikely you will use U.S.C. very often because U.S.C.A. and U.S.C.S. provide you with the exact wording of the federal statutes found in U.S.C. together with extremely useful annotations, which refer you to cases interpreting and construing the statutes. Moreover, the updating of U.S.C. is much slower than that for U.S.C.A. or U.S.C.S. Nevertheless, you may choose to use U.S.C. when you are primarily interested in reviewing only the statutory language itself rather than any judicial decisions interpreting the statutes.

When you are interested in researching the history of a statute, finding other sources in the law library that discuss or refer to that statute, and, most important, reviewing judicial decisions that have interpreted the statute, use U.S.C.A. or U.S.C.S. There are some differences between them. For example, U.S.C.S.'s section titled "Research Guide" refers you to far more sources in the library than does U.S.C.A.'s comparable section titled "Library References." In general, U.S.C.A. will direct you to other West publications, and U.S.C.S. will direct you to other LEXIS Publishing or Reed Elsevier publications. Additionally, the organization of the annotations within each set differs in that U.S.C.A. uses an alphabetical

Figure 3-9
Updating Federal Statutory Research

U.S.C.	*U.S.C.A.*	*U.S.C.S.*
Read statute in main hardbound volume.	Read statute in main hardbound volume.	Read statute in main hardbound volume.
Check annual hardbound supplements.	Check annual pocket part or softcover supplements.	Check annual pocket part or softcover supplements.
Check slip laws, *U.S. Law Week*, or USCCAN.	Check U.S.C.A.'s Statutory Supplements.	Check U.S.C.S.'s *Cumulative Later Case and Statutory Service* and then the *Advance* pamphlets.
	Check slip laws, *U.S. Law Week*, or USCCAN.	Check slip laws, *U.S. Law Week*, or USCCAN.
Check the GPO Web site at http:// www.access.gpo.gov/ uscode or at http:// www.gpoaccess.gov/ legislative.html	Check the GPO Web site at http:// www.access.gpo.gov/ uscode or at http:// www.gpoaccess.gov/ legislative.html	Check the GPO Web site at http:// www.access.gpo.gov/ uscode or at http:// www.gpoaccess.gov/ legislative.html

arrangement while U.S.C.S. uses a topic approach. Finally, U.S.C.A. and U.S.C.S. may each refer you to cases that the other set does not. In general, West's publication, U.S.C.A., attempts to be as comprehensive as possible, sending you to nearly all cases interpreting or discussing a federal statute, while the publisher of U.S.C.S. aims to provide researchers with the most significant cases, eliminating what it believes to be outmoded or repetitive cases, stating that U.S.C.S. contains "no vague or marginal cases to wade through and weigh before getting to the heart of [a] problem."

Another difference is that the language contained in U.S.C.A. is identical to the official text of the *United States Code* while the language in U.S.C.S. is identical to the text of *United States Statutes at Large*. Thus, the language found in U.S.C.S. replicates the language of statutes as enacted by Congress. Only on rare occasions, however, will an error in reprinting a statute occur in the *United States Code*, and this difference may be more imagined than real.

Most experts agree that these differences are not significant for most research projects. Therefore, for the typical research project you will ordinarily use U.S.C.A. *or* U.S.C.S. but not both. Using both sets would be analogous to driving to work in a Ford and then walking home and driving to work again in a Chevrolet. In most respects, U.S.C.A. and U.S.C.S. are *competitive* sets, meaning they are equivalent. The choice of which set you ultimately use may depend on habit or convenience. If your first employer has purchased U.S.C.A. and you become familiar with the organization and arrangement of this set, you may find that you prefer to use U.S.C.A. Many people prefer U.S.C.S. due to the larger size of the books and larger and bolder typeface, which is easy to read. Some researchers prefer an integrated approach to all legal research and will consistently use all West publications when possible, thereby gaining access to all of West's books and its proprietary key number/digest system (see Chapter 5), while others prefer to use books published by LEXIS to obtain access to its other publications.

In summary, if you are engaged in an extremely detailed research project, you should consult both U.S.C.A. and U.S.C.S. Ordinarily, however, one set will be sufficient for most of your research needs and most law firms, corporations, and agencies purchase only one set or the other.

The exercise placed at the end of this chapter will require you to use both U.S.C.A. and U.S.C.S., and you may find you have an immediate preference for one set over the other.

Practice Tip

Annotations

Never fully rely on the one-sentence annotations or descriptions of cases provided by U.S.C.A., U.S.C.S., or any other annotated set. It is not possible to convey complex case analysis in one sentence. Similarly, never quote from an annotation. They are not the law but rather very brief summaries of the law found in the cases.

e. Research Techniques

There are three primary techniques you may use to locate federal statutes: the descriptive word approach, the title/topic approach, and the popular name approach.

(1) Descriptive Word Approach

This method of locating statutes is one that you have undoubtedly used before in other research projects. For example, if you were asked to find out how far Earth is from Mars, you would probably elect to use an encyclopedia; however, you would not simply start reading at page 1 of volume 1, hoping you would eventually stumble upon the information. You would consult the general index at the end of the encyclopedia set and look for various words that describe the problem such as "Earth," "Mars," "planets," or "solar system." The index would then direct you to the appropriate volume and page number. This is the descriptive word approach.

Both U.S.C.A. and U.S.C.S. have a multivolume general index, which is arranged alphabetically and is usually located after Title 50, the last volume in both U.S.C.A. and U.S.C.S. These index volumes are softcover books that are replaced each year. When you have been assigned a legal research problem, you should try to think of key words or phrases that describe this problem. To assist in developing descriptive words or phrases, consider the following questions: *Who* is involved? *What* is the issue under consideration? *Where* did the action take place? *When* did the action occur? *Why* did the issue develop? *How* did the problem arise? You should then insert these words or phrases into the general index of U.S.C.A. or U.S.C.S., which will then direct you to the appropriate title and section of the code. See Figure 3-10.

The indices for U.S.C.A. and U.S.C.S. are both very "forgiving." For example, if you selected "landlord" and the statute is indexed under "tenant," both U.S.C.A. and U.S.C.S. will guide you to the appropriate word, as follows:

Landlord. Tenant, this index.

U.S.C.A. and U.S.C.S. will direct you to the appropriate statute by listing the title first and then identifying the specific statute section, as follows:

Citizenship, 8 § 1409

You are thus directed to Title 8, Section 1409.

If you have difficulty thinking of an appropriate word to insert into the index, you might consider using a thesaurus to provide you with synonyms or antonyms. Generally, however, such a practice will not be necessary as the indices for both U.S.C.A. and U.S.C.S. are excellent finding tools and have indexed statutes under numerous words or topics. Thus, you need not distill your research problem into one perfect word; even phrases such as "sudden infant death syndrome" are found in the general index to U.S.C.A. and U.S.C.S., and there are typically numerous cross-references and entry words in these indices that will lead you to the correct statute.

Figure 3-10
Sample Page from U.S.C.S. General Index

207   **PODIATRISTS**

PLUMAS NATIONAL FOREST
Addition of lands to, 16 § 482i
Bucks Lake Wilderness, designation, 16 § 1132 nt

PLUMS
Agricultural Adjustment Act, orders regulating handling applicability, 7 § 608c(6)
Defined, export standards for grapes and plums, 7 § 599
Export standards. See Interstate and Foreign Commerce, generally, this index
Importation prohibitions during time marketing order in effect, 7 § 608e-1
Marketing promotion including paid advertising, research and development projects, orders regulating handling under Agricultural Adjustment Act, 7 § 608c(6)

PLURAL NUMBER
Singular included in words of statute importing plural number, 1 § 1

PLUTONIUM
Atomic energy, development and control of, 42 § 2011 et seq.
Atomic Energy Commission, distribution to International Atomic Energy Agency, 42 § 2074
Energy Research and Development Administration, shipment by air, prohibition, exceptions, 42 § 5817 nt
EURATOM Cooperation Act,
    Amount and use authorized to be acquired from community, 42 § 2295
    Authorization for sale or lease to community, 42 § 2294
    Restriction on amounts acquired from community, 42 § 2295
International terrorism. Terrorists and Terrorism, generally, this index
Licensing of shipments by air transport, restrictions on NRC, 42 § 5841 nt
Nuclear reactors, production in, guaranteed purchase prices, 42 § 2076
Shipments by foreign nations through United States air space, 42 § 5841 nt
Special nuclear material,
    As meaning, atomic energy, 42 § 2014
    Plutonium produced through use of, guaranteed purchase prices, 42 § 2076
Terrorists and Terrorism, generally, this index

PNEUMOCONIOSIS
See BLACK LUNG DISEASE, generally, this index

PNEUMONIA
Medical and other health services defined to include pneumococcal vaccine and its administration, 42 § 1395x

POCOSIN WILDERNESS
Designation, Croatan National Forest, 16 § 1132 nt

PODIATRIC SERVICE
Veterans Health Administration. Veterans Affairs Department, generally, this index

PODIATRISTS AND PODIATRY
Air Force, retention in active status of certain reserve officers, 10 § 8855
Armed Forces, reserve officers, podiatry as specialty, retention in active status until certain age, 10 § 3855
Child abuse, reporting incident on Federal land or facility, victims' protections and rights, 42 § 13031
Community Mental Health Centers, generally, this index
Consumer-patient radiation health and safety. Radiation, generally, this index
Domestic volunteer services, civil actions for malpractice or negligence of, 42 § 5055
Group Practice Facilities Mortgage Insurance, generally, this index
Health Maintenance Organizations, generally, this index
Health Professionals Educational Assistance Program. Veterans Affairs Department, generally, this index
Indian child protection and family violence prevention. Child Abuse and Neglect, generally, this index
Indian health care and services. Indians, generally, this index
Labor-management relations. Veterans Affairs Department, generally, this index
Laboratories, specimens for examination, etc., acceptance or solicitation, certificate requirements, exemption, 42 § 263a
Malpractice, generally, this index
Military Selective Service Act, exemption from training and service under, etc., 50 Ap § 456
National Health Service Corps Scholarship Program. Public Health Service, generally, this index
Primary health care training, health professions education. Public Health Service, generally, this index
Scholarship Program, Health Professionals Educational Assistance Program. Veterans Affairs Department, generally, this index
School of podiatry,
    Grants,
        Health professions teaching personnel, training, traineeships and fellowships for. Public Health Service, generally, this index
        Scholarships. Public Health Service, generally, this index
    Health professions education. Public Health Service, generally, this index
    Improvement of quality of, grants and contracts. Public Health Service, generally, this index
    Indian health care and services. Indians, generally, this index
    Student loans. Public Health Service, generally, this index
Uniform health professions data reporting system, 42 § 295k
Veterans Health Administration. Veterans Affairs Department, this index

Figure 3-10 *(Continued)*
Sample Page from U.S.C.S. General Index

GENERAL INDEX

CHIRICAHUA NATIONAL MONUMENT

Chiricahua National Monument Wilderness, designation, 16 § 1132 note
Establishment, 16 § 431 note

CHIROPRACTORS

Social security, services included under medical assistance programs, 42 § 1396d

CHISTOCHINA

Public lands, Copper River, native village subject to withdrawal of public lands from appropriation under Alaska Native claims settlement, 43 § 1610

CHITINA

Public lands, Copper River, native village subject to withdrawal of public lands from appropriation under Alaska Native claims settlement, 43 § 1610

CHLORACNE

Veterans' benefits, disability and death compensation, 38 § 1116

CHLORAMPHENICOL

Food, Drug, and Cosmetic Act (this index)

CHLORIDES OF POTASSIUM

Mineral leasing and prospecting permits, 30 § 281

CHLORINE

Water Supply Systems (this index)

CHLOROFLUORCARBONS

Air pollution control, nonessential products containing, 42 § 7671i

CHLORTETRACYCLINE

Food, Drug, and Cosmetic Act (this index)

CHOCTAW-CHICKASAW SUPPLEMENTAL AGREEMENT

Generally, 16 § 151

CHOCTAW TRIBE

Choctaw-Chickasaw Supplemental Agreement, 16 § 151
Disposition of estates, 25 § 375d
Minerals, reservation of, 25 § 414
Per capita payments, 25 § 120

CHOICE

Election or Choice (this index)

CHOLERA

Anti-Hog-Cholera Serum and Hog-Cholera Virus (this index)
Veterans' benefits, cholera included in term chronic disease, 38 § 1101

CHONDROSARCOMA

Veterans' benefits, disability and death compensation, 38 § 1116

CHORAL PERFORMANCES

National Foundation on the Arts and the Humanities Act of 1965, 20 § 952

CHRISTA MCAULIFFE FELLOWSHIP PROGRAM

Generally, 20 § 1113 et seq.
Evaluation of applications, 20 § 1113d
Repayment provisions, 20 § 1113e
Selection of fellowships, 20 § 1113c
Use of funds, 20 § 1113a

CHRISTIAN SCIENCE

Income tax, 26 § 1402
Medicare, post-hospital extended care in Christian Science skilled nursing facilities, defined, 42 § 1395x
Sanatoriums. Social Security (this index)

CHRISTMAS DAY

Patriotic customs, display of flag, 36 § 174

CHRISTMAS ISLAND

Trade Agreement Acts, designation under trade act as beneficiary developing country, 19 § 2462 note

CHROME

Southern Rhodesia, prohibition, importation into U.S., suspension of operation of amendments concerning by President, 22 § 287c note

CHRONIC DISEASES

Disease (this index)

CHRONIC ECONOMIC DEPRESSION

Public works, research into causes, 42 § 3151

CHRONIC HAZARD ADVISORY PANEL

Consumer product safety, 15 § 2077

CHRYSLER CORPORATION LOAN GUARANTEE

Generally, 15 § 1861 et seq.
Aggregate amount of nonfederally guaranteed assistance, computation and components, 15 § 1863
Agreement between board and Chrysler Corporation for employee stock ownership plan, 15 § 1866
Annual comprehensive assessments by Transportation Secretary, 15 § 1871
Appropriations, authorization, 15 § 1874
Assignment or sale of guarantee to foreign entity prohibited, 15 § 1864
Assistance from other than federal government to fund employee stock ownership plan, 15 § 1866
Audits by General Accounting Office, 15 § 1869

CHRYSLER CORPORATION LOAN GUARANTEE—Cont'd

Authority of board
– generally, 15 § 1863
– limitations, 15 § 1867
– protection of government's interest, 15 § 1870
– termination, 15 § 1875
Automobile industry
– federal regulations, assessment of economic impact by Transportation Secretary, 15 § 1873
– long-term study and annual comprehensive assessment by Transportation Secretary, 15 § 1871
Bankruptcy, 15 § 1870
Benefits. Wages and benefits, infra
Board
– generally, 15 § 1862
– agreement with Chrysler Corporation for employee stock ownership plan, 15 § 1866
– authority
– – generally, 15 § 1863
– – limitations, 15 § 1867
– – protection of government's interest, 15 § 1870
– – termination, 15 § 1875
– defined, 15 § 1861
– investigatory powers, 15 § 1869
Capital, defined, 15 § 1863
Cash to be obtained from disposition of corporate assets, defined, 15 § 1863
Chrysler Corporation Loan Guarantee Act of 1979, 15 § 1861 et seq.
Collective bargaining agreements, modification
– generally, 15 § 1865
– maximum reductions in wages and benefits, 15 § 1865
Commitments
– generally, 15 § 1863
– terms, 15 § 1864
Common stock, employee stock ownership plan, 15 § 1866
Compensation. Wages and benefits, infra
Computation of aggregate amount of nonfederally guaranteed assistance, 15 § 1863
Concessions
– defined, 15 § 1863
– employees to make, 15 § 1865
Contracts, 15 § 1864
Contracts entered into by corporation, effect, 15 § 1870
Definitions
– generally, 15 § 1861
– board, 15 § 1861
– borrower, 15 § 1861
– capital, 15 § 1863
– cash to be obtained from disposition of corporate assets, 15 § 1863
– concession, 15 § 1863
– corporation, 15 § 1861
– financial commitment, 15 § 1863
– financing plan, 15 § 1861
– fiscal year, 15 § 1861
– labor organization, 15 § 1861
– operating plan, 15 § 1861
– persons with existing economic stake in health of corporation, 15 § 1861
– wages and benefits, 15 § 1861

After you have been directed to the appropriate title and section, you can readily locate the statute by scanning the library shelves. U.S.C.A. and U.S.C.S. are arranged by titles 1 through 50, and the spine of each volume that faces you is clearly marked to facilitate your research efforts.

This descriptive word approach (sometimes called the "index method" because you use the general index to find statutes) is usually the easiest and most efficient way to locate a statute, particularly for beginning researchers. This is the technique you should use until you are extremely familiar with the organization of U.S.C.A. and U.S.C.S. and feel comfortable using the next method of statutory research: the title/topic approach.

(2)   *Title/Topic Approach*

As you know, all of the statutes in U.S.C.A. and U.S.C.S. are divided or categorized into 50 titles. It is possible that you may be so familiar with the contents and organization of U.S.C.A. and U.S.C.S. that when presented with a legal research problem, you bypass the general index and immediately proceed to remove the appropriate title from the library shelf.

Thus, if you consistently performed research in the area of bankruptcy and were asked a question relating to the filing of a petition under the United States Bankruptcy Act, you may be able to immediately recognize that this subject is covered by Title 11. You would proceed to the appropriate volume(s) relating to Title 11 and begin examining the statutes and annotations therein.

At the very beginning of Title 11 is a table of contents, which gives you an outline of the bankruptcy statutes so you can select the appropriate one. Additionally, after the very last bankruptcy statute you will be given an index to all of the bankruptcy statutes in Title 11 and you may use this to focus in on the specific statute you are seeking.

This title/topic method is best employed by researchers who are sufficiently familiar with U.S.C.A. and U.S.C.S. so they can confidently select the one particular title of the 50 titles available and review the statutes therein. Because it is possible that some statutes may be covered under more than one title and because this title/topic approach presumes a great deal of knowledge about U.S.C.A. and U.S.C.S., you should avoid using this method when you are just beginning to perform legal research.

(3)   *Popular Name Approach*

Many of our federal statutes are known by a popular name — either that of the sponsors of the legislation (Gramm-Rudman-Hollings Act, Taft-Hartley Act, Sarbanes-Oxley Act of 2002) or that given to the legislation by the public or media (National School Lunch Act, Freedom of Information Act, AMBER Alert Act). If you are asked to locate one of these statutes, you can easily do so in either U.S.C.A. or U.S.C.S.

To find such a statute in U.S.C.A., locate the volume entitled *Popular Name Table*, which lists in alphabetical order federal laws known by their popular names. Simply look up the law you are interested in and you will be directed to the appropriate title and section. See Figure 3-11 for a sample page from the *Popular Name Table*.

Figure 3-11
Sample Page from U.S.C.A. *Popular Name Table*

Child Protection and Obscenity Enforcement Act of 1988
Pub.L. 100–690, Title VII, Subtitle N, §§ 7501, 7511 to 7514, 7521 to 7526, Nov. 18, 1988, 102 Stat. 4485 to 4503 (Title 18, §§ 1460, 1465 to 1469, 1961, 2251, 2251 note, 2251A, 2252 to 2254, 2256, 2257, 2257 note, 2516; Title 19, § 1305; Title 47, § 223)

Child Protection and Toy Safety Act of 1969
Pub. L. 91–113, Nov. 6, 1969, 83 Stat. 187 (Title 15, §§ 401 note, 1261, 1262, 1274)

Child Protection Restoration and Penalties Enhancement Act of 1990
Pub.L. 101–647, Title III, Nov. 29, 1990, 104 Stat. 4816 (Title 18, §§ 1460, 2243, 2251 note, 2252, 2257, 2257 note; Title 28, § 994 note)

Child Sexual Abuse and Pornography Act of 1986
Pub.L. 99–628, Nov. 7, 1986, 100 Stat. 3510 (Title 18, §§ 2251, 2255, 2421, 2422, 2423, 2424)

Child Support Enforcement Act
See Federal Child Support Enforcement Act

Child Support Enforcement Amendments of 1984
Pub.L. 98–378, Aug. 16, 1984, 98 Stat. 1305 (Title 26, §§ 6103, 6402, 7213; Title 42, §§ 602, 602 note, 603, 606, 606 note, 651, 652, 652 note, 653, 654, 654 note, 655 to 657, 657 note, 658, 658 note, 664, 666, 667, 667 note, 671, 1305 note, 1315, 1396a)
Pub.L. 100–485, Title III, § 303(e), Oct. 13, 1988, 102 Stat. 2393 (Title 42, § 606 note)
Pub.L. 101–239, Title VIII, § 8003(a), Dec. 19, 1989, 103 Stat. 2453 (Title 42, § 606 note)

Child Support Recovery Act of 1992
Pub.L. 102–521, Oct. 25, 1992, 106 Stat. 3403 (Title 18, §§ 228, 228 note, 3563, Title 42, §§ 3793, 3796cc, 3796cc–1 to 3796cc–6, 3797, 12301 note)

Children With Disabilities Temporary Care Reauthorization Act of 1989
Pub.L. 101–127, Oct. 25, 1989, 103 Stat. 770 (Title 42, §§ 5117 notes, 5117a, 5117a note, 5117c, 5117d)

Children's Bureau Act
Apr. 9, 1912, ch. 73, 37 Stat. 79

Children's Justice Act
Pub.L. 99–401, Title I, Aug. 27, 1986, 100 Stat. 903 (Title 42, §§ 290dd–3, 290ee–3, 5101, 5101 notes, 5103, 5105, 10601, 10603, 10603a)

Children's Justice and Assistance Act of 1986
Pub.L. 99–401, Aug. 27, 1986, 100 Stat. 903 (Title 42, §§ 290dd–3, 290ee–3, 5101, 5101 notes, 5103, 5105, 5117, 5117 notes, 5117a to 5117d, 10601, 10603, 10603a)

Children's Nutrition Assistance Act of 1992
Pub.L. 102–512, Oct. 24, 1992, 106 Stat. 3363 (Title 42, §§ 1771 notes, 1769, 1769 note, 1776, 1786, 1786 notes)

Children's Television Act of 1990
Pub.L. 101–437, Oct. 18, 1990, 104 Stat. 996 (Title 47, §§ 303a, 303a note, 303b, 393a, prec. 394, 394, 394 note, prec. 395, prec. 396, prec. 397, 397, 609 notes)
Pub.L. 102–356, § 15, Aug. 26, 1992, 106 Stat. 954 (Title 47, § 303b)

China Aid Act
Feb. 7, 1942, ch. 47, 56 Stat. 82

China Aid Act of 1948
Apr. 3, 1948, ch. 169, title IV, 62 Stat. 158

China Appropriation Act
Feb. 12, 1942, ch. 71, 56 Stat. 89

China Area Aid Act of 1950
June 5, 1950, ch. 220, title II, 64 Stat. 202

China Trade Act (Corporations Act)
June 6, 1932, ch. 209, §§ 261–264, 47 Stat. 232

China Trade Act, 1922
Sept. 19, 1922, ch. 346, 42 Stat. 849 (Title 15, §§ 141–162)
Feb. 26, 1925, ch. 345, 43 Stat. 995–997 (Title 15, §§ 144, 146, 147, 149, 150, 160, 162)
Oct. 15, 1970, Pub. L. 91–452, title II, § 217, 84 Stat. 929 (Title 15, § 155)

To locate such a statute in U.S.C.S., you should consult the *Popular Name* table found in a separate volume of U.S.C.S., which lists the federal statutes known by a popular name in alphabetical order. Just as with U.S.C.A., you will be directed to the appropriate title and section.

The *United States Code* also includes a table, "Acts Cited by Popular Name," in the volume for Title 50.

Shepard's Acts and Cases by Popular Name: Federal and State organizes federal and state statutes in alphabetical order, providing you with citations to federal as well as state laws and cases known by popular names. For federal laws, this compact set also provides a citation to *United States Statutes at Large* and gives the public law number as well as the year the statute was enacted. *Shepard's Acts and Cases* is kept current by soft-cover supplements.

Finally, if you have only a public law number (such as P. L. 107-114) or a reference to the statute from *Statutes at Large* (such as 86 Stat. 471), both U.S.C.A. and U.S.C.S. have separate volumes marked "Tables" after Title 50 of the respective sets, allowing you to translate and convert a public law number or a *Statutes at Large* citation into a citation to U.S.C.A. or U.S.C.S.

Practice Tip

Infra *and* Supra

When using indexes for almost any set of law books, you may encounter the words *infra* (meaning "below") and *supra* (meaning "above"). These are signal terms that direct you to other pages within the index. For example, if you look up the word "tenant" in an index, you may see the instruction "See landlord, *supra*," meaning that you should look at the entries listed under the word "landlord" given previously in the index.

---

f. Final Research Steps

After you locate the statute you are interested in, read it carefully. Examine the historical notes and review the library references to determine whether other sources in the library provide further information on this statute or the subject matter it discusses. Then read the annotations carefully and decide which cases you will read in full based on your initial reading of the brief descriptions of these cases. Finally, check the pocket part and any of the interim pamphlets or supplements (which are usually arranged exactly like the numbering used in the hardback volumes) to determine if the statute has been amended or repealed and to look for annotations or references to cases that have interpreted the statute subsequent to the publication of the hardbound volume. If you have any difficulty performing statutory research, you may call either LEXIS ((800) 897-7922) or West ((800) 733-2889) to receive personal assistance from reference attorneys.

g. United States Constitution

While the United States Constitution is not one of the 50 titles of the *United States Code*, nevertheless both U.S.C.A. and U.S.C.S. contain volumes for the Constitution. You will be provided with the text of the Constitution and its amendments and then, by the use of annotations, you will be referred to cases that interpret the Constitution. For example, after you read the First Amendment, you will be directed to thousands of cases that have construed the First Amendment. You will also be provided with reference guides and cross-references to other materials to help you better understand the constitutional provision you are researching. Unannotated versions of the United States Constitution can be found in U.S.C. and in the *Am. Jur. 2d Desk Book* (see Chapter 6) and at various Internet sites, such as http://thomas.loc.gov.

Depending upon the arrangement of the law library you use, the volumes for the Constitution may precede Title 1 on your library shelves, may be located as the last volumes after Title 50, or may appear alphabetically within the set between the volumes for Conservation and those for Copyrights.

The three primary research approaches discussed above, namely, the descriptive word approach, the title/topic approach, and the popular name approach, should also be used when you are presented with a constitutional research issue. Be sure to refer to the pocket parts or softcover supplements for the applicable volumes to locate the newest cases interpreting constitutional provisions.

B. State Legislation

1. Enactment of State Statutes

The process of enacting and publishing legislation at the state level is substantially similar to the process described above for the federal level. Most state legislatures closely conform to the United States Congress with regard to their organization and manner of enacting law. Just as the United States Congress is divided into two chambers — the Senate and the House of Representatives — each state except for Nebraska has a legislature divided into two chambers. Such a legislature is referred to as a bicameral legislature. Nebraska has a one-house or unicameral legislature. The names given to the two chambers may vary from state to state. For example, the two houses in California are the Senate and the Assembly; the two houses in Louisiana are the Senate and the House of Representatives; and the two houses in Maryland are the Senate and the House of Delegates. More than four-fifths of the state legislatures meet on a yearly basis, while the remaining legislatures meet every two years.

Similar to the process of enacting federal law, much of the work in enacting state law is done by committees. When a final version of a bill is agreed upon, it will be sent to the governor of the state for signature, at which time it is referred to as a "law" or "statute" rather than a bill.

Additional information regarding the names of the lawmaking bodies for each of the states and the process of enacting legislation can be obtained from almost any general information encyclopedia or at the Web site of the National Conference of State Legislatures at http://www.ncsl.org.

2. Publication and Codification of State Statutes

Many states, particularly the most populous ones, initially publish their laws in slip form, similar in appearance to federal slip laws. At the end of the state's legislative session, these slips are taken together and compiled into books, which are generally referred to as "session laws." While some states may not use the words "session laws" and may name their compiled statutes "acts and resolves," or "statutes," or some other name, the generic title given to volumes that set forth a state's laws in chronological order is "session laws."

These session laws are analogous to *United States Statutes at Large*. That is, the volumes of session laws will contain the laws of a particular state in the order in which they were enacted. Just as researchers required *United States Statutes at Large* to be better arranged, or "codified," in order to bring together all the current laws on the same subject and eliminate laws that had been repealed, codification of the session laws of each state has also taken place. These state codifications may be called "codes," "compilations," "revisions," or "consolidations," depending on the state.

Some states arrange their statutes by titles and chapter, such as Virginia: Va. Code Ann § 8.01-108 (2000). Other states, usually the more populous ones, arrange their statutes in named titles, such as California: Cal. Evid. Code § 312 (West 1995). Thus, numbering and format vary from state to state.

Most states have annotated codes, meaning that after you are provided with the wording of the state statute, you will be directed to cases that interpret the statute. West publishes annotated codes for approximately 20 states and Michie Publishing Company (now part of LEXIS Publishing) publishes for most of the remaining states. A few states use other publishers. An identification of the publisher for each state's statutes can be found in Table T.1 of *The Bluebook* and Appendix 1 of *ALWD*.

While the publication of each state's statutes will vary somewhat and while the publication may be official or unofficial, most state codes share the following features:

(i)   The constitution of the state will be contained in the code;

(ii) The statutes will be organized by subject matter so that all of the corporation statutes are together, all of the penal statutes are together, all of the workers' compensation statutes are together, and so forth;

(iii) There will be a general index to the entire set and often each title will be separately indexed, so that after you read the last evidence statute you are given an index to all of the evidence statutes, and so forth;

(iv) The statutes are kept current by annual cumulative pocket parts, which will be placed in the back of each hardback bound volume or by supplements placed on the shelves next to the volumes being updated;

(v) Annotations will be provided to direct you to cases interpreting the statutes, typically through the use of a one-sentence summary of the case similar to the arrangement and organization of annotations provided by U.S.C.A. and U.S.C.S.;

(vi) Historical notes, which explain the history and amendments to the statute, and library references, which will direct you to other sources in the law library to assist you in interpreting the statute, will typically be provided (see Figure 3-12 for a sample page of a state statute); and

(vii) Conversion tables are provided in each volume so that if a state statute has been repealed or renumbered, you will be informed of the repealing or provided with the new section number of the statute.

Figure 3-12
Sample Page from Code of Virginia

§ 18.2-53. Shooting, etc., in committing or attempting a felony. — If any person, in the commission of, or attempt to commit, felony, unlawfully shoot, stab, cut or wound another person he shall be guilty of a Class 6 felony. (Code 1950, § 18.1-68; 1960, c. 358; 1975, cc. 14, 15.)

The purpose of this section is to deter the use of specific forms of violence and thus lessen the risk of bodily harm to the potential victims of felonious crime. To effectuate this purpose, the General Assembly employed the only appropriate means available, viz., the imposition of punishment for the use of such violence in addition to the penalty prescribed for the primary felony. Blythe v. Commonwealth, 222 Va. 722, 284 S.E.2d 796 (1981).

Legislative intent regarding multiple punishments. — Defendant's punishment for two counts of malicious wounding resulting from the stabbing of two victims and for two counts of stabbing/cutting the same victims during the commission of a felony does not offend the double jeopardy clause because the General Assembly intended to impose multiple punishments when enacting this section. Hall v. Commonwealth, 14 Va. App. 892, 421 S.E.2d 455 (1992).

The legislative intent to authorize cumulative punishment is clear in this section, despite the absence of an express statement to that effect. Blythe v. Commonwealth, 222 Va. 722, 284 S.E.2d 796 (1981).

Section 19.2-294 does not prohibit defendant's prosecution in a single trial for aggravated malicious wounding and use of a firearm in the commission of the aggravated malicious wounding. Powell v. Commonwealth, No. 0554-89-1 (Ct. of Appeals Oct. 6, 1992).

Intent to wound does not preclude intent to steal. — The mere fact that appellant had the intent to commit malicious wounding did not exclude the hypothesis that he also formed the intent to steal victim's property. Saunders v. Commonwealth, 18 Va. App. 825, 447 S.E.2d 526 (1994).

3. *Research Techniques*

The same techniques used to locate federal statutes are used to locate state statutes. They are as follows:

a. Descriptive Word Approach

This method requires you to determine which words or phrases relate to the issue you are researching and then locate those words or phrases in the general index, which will then direct you to the appropriate statute.

b. Title/Topic Approach

This technique may be used when you have become so familiar with your state code that you bypass the general index and immediately locate the particular title or chapter that deals with the research problem.

c. Popular Name Approach

This method of locating statutes is used in those instances in which a state statute is known by a popular name, such as the the "Megan's Law" in your state. You can locate this statute by simply looking up the name of the act or statute in the alphabetically arranged general index.

For example, suppose you wish to determine whether the directors of a corporation may conduct a board meeting by conference call. If you elect to use the descriptive word approach, you should consider inserting some of the following words into the general index in order to be directed to the appropriate statute: "directors," "board of directors," "corporations," "meetings," or "conference calls." Researchers who are familiar with their state's code may use the topic approach and immediately locate the volumes in the state code that contain statutes dealing with corporations and review the separate index at the end of all of the corporations statutes or the table of contents, which appears at the beginning of the statutes dealing with corporations.

After locating the statute, read it carefully, examine the historical notes and library references, if any, analyze the annotations you believe appear promising, and examine the pocket part (or supplements) to ensure the statute is still in force and to locate newer cases, which may have interpreted the statute. You must then read the relevant cases in full.

You may observe that the numbering system for some state codes is unusual, with large gaps between some sections; for example, § 1815 might be followed by § 1832. Such a gap may indicate that sections 1816 through 1831 have been repealed or renumbered. Consult any conversion tables that appear in the volume to determine whether sections 1816 through 1831 have been repealed or whether they have been renumbered and subsumed within some other title or chapter in the code.

On other occasions you may notice that the numbering of state statutes is not by whole numbers but rather by decimals or subsections. For instance, § 410 may not be followed by § 411, but by § 410.10, § 410.20,

§ 410.30, and then by § 411. This numbering scheme typically indicates that after the state legislature enacted statutes that were numbered as § 410 and § 411, other statutes were enacted that dealt with the same general topic or subject matter and thus needed to be inserted between § 410 and § 411.

Finally, there is no one set of books that will provide you with all of the laws for all 50 states. Such a set would be unwieldy, expensive, and generally not very useful, as researchers in one state are usually not interested in the statutes of another state. There is, however, a set of books that will provide you with some of the laws of all of the states. This set is the *Martindale-Hubbell Law Directory*, which is fully discussed in Chapter 7.

The Final Wrap-Up

Use and Citation of Annotated Codes

Use: Use annotated codes to find relevant statutes. Then use the annotations or one-sentence case summaries to locate cases on point. You may also use the various research references to expand and supplement your research efforts because these will direct you to useful forms, helpful law review articles, and so forth.

Citation: You may (and should) cite to and quote from the statutes you find in an annotated code, but you may never cite to or quote from the annotations (case summaries) or any research references. You must retrieve the cases and references cited, read and analyze them, and then you may cite to these sources.

4. Uniform and Model Laws

Uniform or model laws are those drafted for topics of the law in which uniformity is desirable and practical. For example, a set of laws relating to the formation, operation, and dissolution of partnerships, called the Uniform Partnership Act (1997), has been adopted in every state but Louisiana. Once adopted in a state, a Uniform Law is then a state statute like any other and can be located using any of the research techniques discussed above. Many states, however, often make changes and modifications to the Uniform Laws, resulting in laws that are highly similar from state to state but that are not perfectly uniform. Uniform and model acts are discussed in detail in Chapter 7.

C. Statutory Research Overview

When you are undecided whether to begin a project by examining federal or state statutes, keep in mind that some matters are exclusively presumed to be federal in nature. For example, establishing a uniform currency system is the province of the federal government, which eliminates the confusion that would result if each state developed its own types of coins. On the other hand, states have the power to enact laws relating to local concerns, such as establishing the death penalty in the state, residency laws for obtaining a divorce, and statutes of limitation for breach of contract matters. If you are uncertain whether an area is governed by federal or state law, examine the federal statutes first. If the topic is not covered by federal statute, proceed to examine your state statutes.

When you locate a statute, quickly review the entire scope of the statutes governing the topic. Generally, terms used in the act or statutory scheme are first defined. Definitions are usually followed by the rules announced in the statute and then by penalties for violations of the statute. Assume that each word in the statute is there for a purpose and the words are to be given their plain meaning. If the statute is vague or ambiguous, examine the cases that discuss the statute to determine how courts have interpreted the statute. You can also examine the legislative history of the statute by reviewing the documents considered by the legislature when it enacted the law, such as the transcripts of committee hearings and committee reports. Legislative history research is fully discussed in Chapter 10. Remember that it is the court's interpretation of a statute rather than the naked statutory language that is controlling under our system of law. It is the province of our courts to apply and interpret statutes and even strike down statutes as unconstitutional.

D. Citation Form

1. Federal Statutes (*The Bluebook* and *ALWD*)

11 U.S.C. § 1327 (2000).
11 U.S.C.A. § 1327 (West 2004).
The Bluebook: 11 U.S.C. § 1327 (LexisNexis 2001)
ALWD: 11 U.S.C. § 1327 (LEXIS 2000)

2. State Statutes (*The Bluebook* and *ALWD*)

Ind. Code Ann. § 14-201 (West 1998).
Wash. Rev. Code § 8.907 (1997).

CyberSites �

http://www.loc.gov	Library of Congress home page
http://www.senate.gov	United States Senate home page
http://www.house.gov	United States House of Representatives home page (includes access to United States Code)
http://thomas.loc.gov	THOMAS contains full text of pending bills, key legislation, committee and congressional information, references to the Congressional Record, the text of historical documents, and information about the legislative process.
http://www.gpoaccess.gov/ index.html	GPO Access: United States Government Printing Office site offers access to bills, public and private laws, United States Code, United States Constitution, and various congressional documents and reports, and bills.
http://www.findlaw.com	FindLaw, one of the best known legal sites, provides easy access to federal and state statutes as well as a wide variety of other law-related information and links to other sites.
http://uscode.house.gov/ uscode.htm	The site for the Office of the Law Revision Counsel provides information about the United States Code, allows searching of the United States Code, and provides classification tables listing sections of the United States Code affected by new laws.
http://www4.law. Cornell.edu/uscode	The site of Cornell University provides easy access to the United States Constitution and to federal statutes, including a list of titles of the United States Code, a list of federal statutes by popular names, and a form allowing rapid access to specific sections of the Code.
http://www.loc.gov/law/guide	The Guide to Law Online, offered by the Library of Congress, provides an index to federal public laws, links to the United States Code, as well as to state statutes.
http://www.senate.gov/ legislative/common/ generic/Doc_Room.htm; (202) 224-7860	The Senate Document Room provides information on the status and availability of Senate legislative documents. Documents can be ordered by fax or online at orders@sec.senate.gov.
http://clerk.house.gov/clerk/ Offices_Services/lrc.html; (202) 226-5200	The Legislative Resource Center for the House of Representatives provides public access to all published House documents.
www.ncsl.org/public/ leglinks.cfm	The National Conference of State Legislatures offers direct links to all state legislatures, their constitutions, bills, statutes, and other legislative information.

Writing Strategies

Examine statutes as carefully as possible. Every word and phrase is meaningful. If the statute is contrary to the client's position, look to see if your issue fits within any exceptions to the statute. Review the law review articles you are directed to by the cross-references to determine if any guidance is given as to what situations the statute was designed to address or remedy.

Statutes can be long and complex. To avoid having to reproduce all of a lengthy statute in your writings, say "in pertinent part N.Y. Gen. Bus. Law § 26 (McKinney 2004) provides . . . ."

If the statute supports the client's position, say so forcefully: "Cal. Gov't Code § 426 (West 1995) [requires] or [mandates] or [imposes] . . . ."

If the statute contradicts the client's position, try to shift the focus away from the statute and toward the cases interpreting the statute that may provide you with more latitude due to vague or imprecise language: "In the seminal case interpreting Ind. Code Ann. § 14-11-1-6 (West 1998), the court . . . ."

Assignment for Chapter 3

1. What title of the United States Code relates to Shipping?
2. Use U.S.C.A. and cite the title and section that govern the following:
   a. Research relating to lupus.
   b. Definitions of African elephants.
3. Use either U.S.C.A. or U.S.C.S. and cite the title and section that govern the following:
   a. Smallpox vaccines and vaccinations.
   b. Beer as being nonmailable.
4. Use the Popular Name tables as directed and cite the title and section for the following:
   a. Use U.S.C.A. and give the citation for the short title of the Sarbanes-Oxley Act of 2002.
   b. Use U.S.C.A. and give the citation for Jennifer's Law.
   c. Use either U.S.C.A. or U.S.C.S. and give the citation for the Boggs Act.
   d. Use either U.S.C.A. or U.S.C.S. and give the citation for the Muhammad Ali Boxing Reform Act.
5. Use either U.S.C.A. or U.S.C.S. and describe the counseling available for veterans who are victims of sexual trauma.
6. Use the U.S.C.A. volumes for the Constitution. Answer the following questions and cite the best case to support your answer. Give case names only.
   a. Under the First Amendment (Freedom of Religion), does requiring mandatory chapel attendance for cadets and midshipmen at federal military academies violate the Establishment Clause?
   b. Under the Eighth Amendment, is denial of warm food cruel and unusual punishment?
7. Use U.S.C.A. Give an answer to the question and cite the best case to support your answer. Give case name only.
   a. Under 18 U.S.C.A. § 1302, is "keno" a "lottery" within the meaning of internal revenue laws?
   b. What encyclopedia reference are you directed to in order to better understand this statute?
8. Use U.S.C.S. Answer the following questions and cite the best case to support your answer. Give case names only.
   a. Under 29 U.S.C.S. § 152, are interns, residents, and fellows employed by medical centers "employees"?
   b. Under 15 U.S.C.S. § 1052, may a trademark including the letters "U.S." prominently displayed be registered as a trademark?
9. Use *U.S. Statutes at Large.*
   a. What is the short title of Public Law 107-296?
   b. Give the citation for this law in *U.S. Statutes at Large.*
   c. What was its designation in the House of Representatives?
10. Use *U.S. Statutes at Large.*
    a. For whose relief was Private Law 106-14 enacted?
    b. What was the purpose of Private Law 106-5?

State Your Answer

1. Access one of the Internet sites for the United States Senate and identify your state's two senators.
2. Access the National Conference on State Legislatures (www.ncsconline.org) and select the appropriate topics and links.
   a. Identify the two legislative bodies in your state (one in Nebraska).
   b. Determine whether your state imposes term limits on its legislative representatives. If it does, describe those limits.
3. Use FindLaw (http://www.findlaw.com) to link to your state's statutes. Review the business organizations or corporations statutes for your state and give your state's definition of the term "corporation."
4. Use either *The Bluebook* or *ALWD* and determine which publisher (if any) publishes the compiled statutes in your state. Note that some states publish only officially and no publisher will be identified.

Case Law and Judicial Opinions

It is evident that I consider stare decisis essential to the rule of law.

Supreme Court Associate Justice Lewis F. Powell, Jr. (1990)

Chapter Overview

In this chapter we will discuss judicial opinions and provide you with an understanding of the publication of cases, the elements of a typical court case, and the types of opinions written by judges. We will present the elements of analyzing and briefing cases and introduce the *National Reporter System*, a thorough and comprehensive series of case reporters, which publishes decisions from state and federal courts.

A. Selective Publication

1. *Standards for Publishing Cases*

At the conclusion of Chapter 1, you were required to locate certain published cases. This emphasis on locating cases is a cornerstone of the legal profession, primarily because of our common law tradition of reliance on case law as precedent. You will recall from Chapter 1 that the concept of stare decisis requires that a court follow a previous case from that jurisdiction if the case is materially similar to the case then before the court, although higher courts may depart from previously decided cases if a change in the law is deemed important. Due to the litigious nature of our society, each year approximately 60,000 new cases are published, and each one of these adds to the great number of cases or precedents that you may need to locate to persuade a court to rule in a client's favor. While the assignment in Chapter 1 required you to locate cases, it was easy to accomplish because the citations to the cases were given to you.

Seldom, if ever, does such a lucky event occur in the workplace. Generally, you will be provided only with an overview of the legal problem or question involved, and you will then be required to locate cases on point without the aid of a specific citation or often any direction whatsoever. In Chapters 5, 6, and 7 you will read about several publications that will help you locate relevant cases. Before you begin to locate cases, however, you will need a clear understanding of the elements of a typical court case and the process of publication of cases.

You may be surprised to learn that not all cases are published or "reported." In general, and with the exception of some trial cases from our federal courts, trial court decisions are not published. If you consider the overwhelming number of routine assault and battery cases, divorce or dissolution actions, prosecutions for driving while intoxicated, or cases relating to the possession of narcotics, you can readily see why trial court decisions are not usually published. Many of these cases add little to our body of precedents and relate only to the litigants themselves. If we were to publish the more than 88 million cases that are processed annually in our state courts, our bookshelves would soon collapse of their own weight. As a result, usually only decisions of appellate courts are published. Because approximately 10 percent of cases are appealed, even the reporting of appellate court decisions results in a mass of publication. Therefore, in general, only appellate court cases that advance legal theory are published. Nearly 80 percent of cases disposed of by federal courts are unpublished. Generally, only the decisions of the courts of last resort in a jurisdiction are published in full. For example, all of the decisions of the United States Supreme Court and the California Supreme Court are published in full, but the decisions of the lower federal courts and lower California courts are not.

In many instances, the courts themselves decide whether a case merits publication. For example, in California, California Rule of Court 976(b) specifies which appellate court cases shall be officially published:

- those that establish a new rule of law or alter or criticize an existing rule;
- those that resolve an apparent conflict of authority in the law;
- those that involve a legal issue of continuing public interest; or
- those that make a significant contribution to legal literature.

In most jurisdictions, including California, unpublished cases cannot be cited or used as precedents. You should not interpret the fact that many cases are not published as a conspiracy to prevent people from obtaining access to cases. Unless a case is sealed (usually for national security reasons, to maintain trade secrets, or for the protection of a minor), the case file is readily accessible at the courthouse that handled the case. If you know the name of the case, you can determine its docket number in a Plaintiff-Defendant Index at the courthouse. You may then ask a court clerk to allow you to review the file, and you will have access to all of the pleadings filed in the case as well as the judge's decision and the final judgment. If you need a case from another jurisdiction, consult your yellow pages directory and locate an "attorneys service" company. These companies will locate and copy case files and pleadings for you for payment of a fee.

You can see, therefore, that publishing every case decided in the United States this year would not be of any great value to researchers and would simply result in needless publication. Thus, a certain amount of "weeding out" or selectivity occurs in the publication of cases.

2. The Controversy Surrounding Unpublished Opinions

As discussed above, generally a court decides which cases to publish by designating them for publication after determining that the cases meet the court's standards for publication. In recent years, however, the issue of selective publication of cases has sparked a great deal of controversy. In *Anastasoff v. United States*, 223 F.3d 898 (8th Cir. 2000), the court ruled that allowing judges to ignore unpublished cases was unconstitutional and gave them arbitrary power. Although the decision in *Anastasoff* was later vacated as moot on other grounds, *see Anastasoff v. United States*, 235 F.3d 1054 (8th Cir. 2000), the issue regarding the precedential value of published decisions remains an open question that continues to engender heated debate.

As courts have published their opinions on their own Web sites and released them to LEXIS and Westlaw, the online legal research systems, the public has been able to access these otherwise unpublished decisions, and attorneys and litigants have wanted to refer to, cite to, and rely upon these unpublished decisions to support their arguments and their clients' positions. Moreover, in 2001 West created the *Federal Appendix*, a set that prints the unpublished federal courts of appeals decisions, together with headnotes, key numbers, and topic names, making these unpublished cases even more readily available to researchers.

The camps favoring and disfavoring citation to unpublished decisions are firmly divided. Nine of the country's thirteen circuit courts of appeal (the First, Third, Fourth, Fifth, Sixth, Eighth, Tenth, Eleventh, and District of Columbia Circuits) allow lawyers and judges to cite unpublished decisions, although they vary widely on how much weight should be given to these opinions. Most agree that an unpublished opinion of a circuit is not binding although it may be persuasive authority. The Ninth Circuit Court of Appeals, the largest and most prolific circuit, is vehemently opposed to allowing citation to unpublished decisions. *See Hart v. Massanari*, 266 F.3d 1155 (9th Cir. 2001). The Federal Circuit is in accord with the Ninth Circuit.

State courts also differ in their treatment of unpublished decisions, with 22 states allowing citation of unpublished decisions, although most of these concur that these unpublished decisions are not binding precedent under the theory of stare decisis. Others, such as California, strictly prohibit courts and parties from citing or relying upon opinions not certified for publication. Cal. R. Ct. 977(a).

The most recent catalyst for discussion has been proposed Federal Rule of Appellate Procedure 32.1, which would allow the citation of unpublished decisions in all federal courts of appeal. The proposed rule has been the most controversial amendment ever proposed to the federal appellate rules and has caused significant controversy (more than 500 written comments from judges have opposed it). In April 2005 the rule was approved by committee, and as of the writing of this text, it will be sent with a recommendation for consideration by the Judicial Conference.

Some of the arguments advanced by each side can be summarized as follows:

Arguments for Allowing Citation	*Arguments Against Allowing Citation*
— unpublished decisions are already accessible and easy to research	— unpublished decisions are primarily written for the parties to the litigation and often aren't carefully written (in fact, many are written by law clerks); moreover, the reasoning in these cases is untested and left uncritiqued by later commentary and cases
— none of the nine circuits and twenty-two states that allow citation to unpublished opinions have noted any dire consequences	— judges will feel compelled to draft more carefully worded opinions, which will bog down the writing and issuing of opinions and cause them to neglect their other responsibilities

—lawyers routinely cite the words of novelists, cartoonists, and nearly every spoken word in the English language; why shouldn't they be able to cite the court's own words found in its unpublished opinions?

—uniformity is needed within the federal circuits so practitioners practicing in more than one circuit are not at a disadvantage

—issuing unpublished opinions allows judges to spend time on the issues and cases that merit more critical attention and shape the law

—legal researchers would face the nearly impossible task of researching not only the millions of published cases but unpublished ones to determine if they include anything helpful to a client; only the mega firms have the resources to perform this task, thus placing small firms and poor litigants at a disadvantage

—allowing unpublished opinions to be cited would increase the number of citable opinions more than four or fivefold in federal courts (and twelvefold in California alone), increasing the costs research and access to the judicial system for the public

As of late 2004, pursuant to the E-Government Act of 2002, all federal appellate courts must provide access over the Internet to all of their opinions, regardless of whether such opinions are to be published, thus further complicating the issue by making available thousands of additional cases each year. Will it be legal malpractice not to locate the numerous unpublished authorities that might support a client's position? At present, there is no legal obligation to locate authorities that may be persuasive only; thus, failure to cite to such unpublished opinions would probably not constitute malpractice. In fact, a proposed California law (California Senate Bill 1655) that would have allowed California attorneys to cite unpublished opinions for their persuasive value expressly stated that attorneys who did not cite relevant unpublished cases could not be sued for malpractice. The lawmaker who proposed the legislation agreed to drop it after the Chief Justice of the California Supreme Court agreed to study the issue.

Although the trend in various courts appears to favor the abolition of no-citation rules, many expert commentators have commented that it is unlikely that the proposed federal appellate rule would be enacted in the face of the significant opposition it has encountered. Thus, the status of citation to unpublished decisions is still unsettled at the time of the writing of this text. While some individuals fear an avalanche of cases, others look forward to being able to review and cite literally thousands of additional cases.

As a researcher, you will have access to unpublished decisions (from the courts' own Web sites, through LEXIS and Westlaw, and through various Internet sources). You will need to know and comply with your state and applicable federal rules regarding citing to these unpublished cases when you prepare documents for filing with courts.

B.   Elements of a Case

When an appellate court has reviewed the transcript of the trial below, read the written arguments (called "briefs"), which were submitted by the parties, and perhaps heard oral argument, the court will render its decision in a written opinion. It is this opinion that will be published (assuming it advances legal knowledge) and that will now serve as a precedent under the doctrine of stare decisis.

Cases that are published or reported typically contain the following elements. (See Figure 4-1 on pages 111-113):

1.   Case Name

The name or title of a case identifies the parties involved in the action and also provides additional information about the nature of the proceeding. There are several types of case names.

> *Smith v. Jones.*   This case name is the most common and indicates by the use of the signal "v." (for "versus") that the matter is adversarial in nature. The first listed party, Smith, is the plaintiff, who has instituted this action against Jones. Usually the case name will remain the same if the case is appealed, although some courts may reverse the order by placing the name of a defendant who lost the trial below and instituted the appeal first. For example, if Jones lost the trial and appealed the decision, the case might then be identified as *Jones v. Smith*, even though the original plaintiff was Smith. *The Bluebook* and *ALWD* require that only the first listed plaintiff and first listed defendant be identified in a case citation. Nevertheless, a case may involve several plaintiffs and defendants or may be a consolidation of several cases so a court can resolve cases dealing with the same legal issue at one time.
>
> *In re Smith.*   The phrase "in re" means "regarding" or "in the matter of." This case name designates a case that is not adversarial in nature. That is, rather than one party instituting an action against another, this case involves only one matter or party, such as a

Figure 4-1
Sample of a Published Case

Case Name

STATE of North Carolina
v.
John BOYD.

Docket Number — No. COA03–37.

Deciding Court — Court of Appeals of North Carolina.

Date of Decision — Jan. 6, 2004.

Case Summary or Synopsis

Background: Defendant was convicted in the Superior Court, Mecklenburg County, J. Gentry Caudill, J., of conspiracy to sell a controlled substance and was acquitted of sale of a controlled substance, contributing to the delinquency of a minor, and employing and using a minor to commit a controlled substance offense. He appealed conviction and sentence.

Holdings: The Court of Appeals, Wynn, J., held that:

(1) even if issue had been properly preserved for appeal, evidence was sufficient to sustain denial of defendant's motion to dismiss charge of conspiracy to sell a controlled substance, and

(2) defendant's acquittals did not preclude trial court from considering sentencing aggravating factor that defendant involved a person under 16 in commission of conspiracy.

Affirmed.

Headnote

1. Criminal Law ⊂⇒1044.2(2)

Defense counsel, who did not avail himself of his opportunity to move to dismiss conspiracy charge at the close of State's evidence, could not renew nonexistent motion at close of all evidence, as was required to attack on appeal sufficiency of evidence supporting conviction for conspiracy to sell a controlled substance. Rules App.Proc., Rule 10(b)(3).

2. Conspiracy ⊂⇒47(12)

Even if issue had been properly preserved for appeal, evidence was sufficient to sustain denial of defendant's motion to dismiss charge of conspiracy to sell a controlled substance; evidence showed defendant ap-

proached undercover police officers in response to juvenile's call, that officer told defendant he wanted to find some cocaine, that defendant told officer to pull his car over and wait while he went down the street to get "it," that defendant and juvenile crossed street, and that juvenile returned and handed officer clear plastic bag containing a rock of crack cocaine, which officer paid for with a marked twenty dollar bill.

3. Sentencing and Punishment ⊂⇒98

Fact that defendant was acquitted of contributing to the delinquency of a minor and employing and using a minor to commit a controlled substance offense did not preclude trial court from considering the sentencing aggravating factor that defendant involved a person under 16 in the commission of conspiracy to sell a controlled substance. West's N.C.G.S.A. § 15A–1340.16(d)(13); § 15A–1340.4(a) (Repealed).

———

Appeal by Defendant from judgment entered 13 August 2002 by Judge J. Gentry Caudill in Superior Court, Mecklenburg County. Heard in the Court of Appeals 28 October 2003.

Names of Counsel

Assistant Attorney General Martin T. McCracken, for the State.

Robert W. Ewing, Winston-Salem, for the Defendant.

Author of Opinion

WYNN, Judge.

From his conviction for Conspiracy to Sell a Controlled Substance, Defendant, John Boyd, argues on appeal that the trial court erred by failing to grant his motion to dismiss, and considering as an aggravating sentencing factor that he involved a person under 16 years of age in the commission of a crime. We find no error in Defendant's trial.

At trial, the State's evidence tended to show that on 25 October 2001, while conducting undercover drug buys, Charlotte Police Officers Eric Duft and Susan O'Donohue stopped two juveniles in the Colony Acres Drive neighborhood and asked for some "hard" or "rock"—slang terms for the drug crack cocaine. In response, Quintine Hamp-

111

Figure 4-1   (*Continued*)

ton, one of the youths, pointed across the street and yelled for "J.B." to come over to the car. Responding to Hampton, Defendant approached the officers' car. Officer Duft reiterated his desire to find some "hard," but before discussing the drug request, Defendant asked the officers whether they were police. Officer Duft denied being a police officer and assured Defendant he "just wanted to get hooked up." Apparently satisfied, Defendant told Officer Duft to pull his car over and wait while he went down the street to get "it."

The officers then observed Hampton and Defendant cross Colony Acres Drive before losing sight of them. After two or three minutes, Hampton returned alone and handed Officer Duft a clear plastic bag containing a rock of crack cocaine. Officer Duft paid Hampton with a marked twenty dollar bill. Thereafter, Defendant and Hampton were arrested separately.

After estimating that he had conducted approximately 200–300 similar undercover drug buy stings, Officer Duft testified that "it is common for more than one person to be involved in the [drug] transaction" and sometimes, "they will use a younger person to sell them [because] [t]here is less consequences for a juvenile than there is for an adult." The arresting officer testified that, when Defendant was apprehended, "He stated to me; and I, quote, 'I did not sell shit. All I did was get a piece of the rock.'" At the close of the State's evidence, defense counsel did not "care to be heard" on the conspiracy charge, but did move to dismiss all remaining charges; the motions were denied.

In his defense, Defendant denied the statement attributed to him by the arresting officer. Rather, Defendant testified that he was walking towards Hampton to warn him that Officers Duft and O'Donohue were police officers. When Defendant "couldn't catch [Hampton's] bicycle" he turned around to go home. Defendant maintained "I don't have nothing to do with it."

Ultimately, the jury convicted Defendant of Conspiracy to Sell a Controlled Substance but acquitted him of the remaining charges of Sale of a Controlled Substance, Contributing to the Delinquency of a Minor [1], and Employing and Using a Minor to Commit a Controlled Substance Offense.[2] The trial judge found one aggravating factor (that Defendant involved a person under the age of 16 in the commission of the offense) outweighed mitigating factors (that Defendant had a support system in the community and was gainfully employed) and sentenced Defendant in the aggravated range of 18 to 22 months imprisonment. Defendant appealed.

[1] Defendant first argues the trial court erred by denying his motion to dismiss the charge of Conspiracy to Sell a Controlled Substance. For procedural reasons, we disagree.

N.C.R.App. P. 10(b)(3) provides that "a defendant in a criminal case may not assign as error the insufficiency of the evidence to prove the crime charged unless he moves to dismiss the action. . . ." The rules further provide that by presenting evidence after the close of the State's case, a defendant waives any previous motion to dismiss, and in order to preserve an insufficiency of the evidence argument for appeal, defendant must renew his motion to dismiss at the close of all evidence.

[2] At the close of the State's case, the trial judge in the instant case asked defense counsel whether he cared to make "any motions for the defendant?" Defense counsel responded:

> Yes, Your Honor. I think, taking the evidence in the light most favorable to the state, their strongest case seems to be for conspiracy. And so, I don't care to be heard on that . . . I'll ask you to dismiss the sale, at the close of evidence.

---

1. N.C.G.S. § 14.316.1: "to knowingly or willfully cause, encourage or aid any juvenile within the jurisdiction of the court to be in a place or condition, or to commit an act whereby the juvenile could be adjudicated delinquent, undisciplined, abused or neglected."

2. N.C.G.S. § 90–95.4: "to hire or intentionally use a minor to violate G.S. § 90–95(a)(1)."

Figure 4-1 *(Continued)*

STATE v. BOYD   N. C. **699**

Cite as 595 S.E.2d 697 (N.C.App. 2004)

At the close of all evidence, Defense counsel renewed prior motions to dismiss: "We would rest and renew our motions to dismiss; and, re-adopt our arguments, special as they relate to the sale, conspiracy, contributing to the delinquency of a minor; and, the engaging a minor in drug trafficking." By that statement, defense counsel renewed his argument that he "didn't care to be heard" on the conspiracy charge because "their strongest evidence seems to be for conspiracy." Defense counsel did not avail himself of his opportunity to move to dismiss the conspiracy charge at the close of the State's evidence, and thus, he could not renew a nonexistent motion at the close of all evidence. Accordingly, we are precluded from reviewing the merits of Defendant's argument. *See State v. Stocks,* 319 N.C. 437, 439, 355 S.E.2d 492, 492 (1987) (holding that "a defendant who fails to make a motion to dismiss at the close of all the evidence may not attack on appeal the sufficiency of the evidence at trial."). We note, however, that even if this issue had been properly preserved for appeal, the evidence in the record sustains the trial court's denial of Defendant's motion to dismiss this charge.

[3] Defendant next argues that because Hampton's age was an element of the crimes for which he was acquitted, Contributing to the Delinquency of a Minor and Employing and Using a Minor to Commit a Controlled Substance Offense, the trial court erred by considering the sentencing aggravating factor that he "involved a person under 16 in the commission of a crime." We disagree.

In North Carolina, a trial court may consider any aggravating factors it finds proved by the preponderance of the evidence that are reasonably related to the purposes of sentencing. N.C.G.S. § 15A–1340l.4(a). N.C.G.S § 15A–1340.16(d)(13) allows a court to aggravate a defendant's sentence from the presumptive range when "defendant involve[s] a person under the age of 16 in the commission of the crime."

In *State v. Marley,* 321 N.C. 415, 424, 364 S.E.2d 133, 138 (1988), our Supreme Court stated that "once a defendant has been acquitted of a crime he has been set free or judicially discharged from an accusation; re-

leased from ... a charge or suspicion of guilt." Therefore, our Supreme Court held "to allow the trial court to use at sentencing an essential element of a greater offense as an aggravating factor, when the presumption of innocence was not, at trial, overcome as to this element, is fundamentally inconsistent with the presumption of innocence itself." In *Marley,* the defendant had been tried for first degree murder upon the theory of premeditation and deliberation. The jury found the defendant guilty of second degree murder. Thus, one can infer from the jury's verdict in *Marley* that the jury determined there was insufficient evidence of premeditation and deliberation.

In this case, it cannot be inferred from the jury's acquittal of Defendant on the contributing to the delinquency of a juvenile and employing and intentionally using a minor to commit a controlled substance offense charges that it found there was insufficient evidence to conclude beyond a reasonable doubt that Hampton was a minor. Indeed, the parties in this case stipulated Hampton was thirteen years old. Unlike Marley, where the difference between first degree murder and second degree murder was the jury "decided that there [was] not sufficient evidence to conclude beyond a reasonable doubt that defendant premeditated and deliberated the killing," *Marley,* 321 N.C. at 424, 364 S.E.2d at 138, in this case, we are unable to explain rationale behind the jury's verdict. Thus, by convicting Defendant of conspiracy to sell a controlled substance, the jury concluded that Johnny Boyd and Quintinie Hampton were conspirators. Therefore, we uphold the trial court's consideration as an aggravating sentencing factor that Defendant involved a person under the age of 16 in the commission of a crime.

No error.   **Decision**

Judges TIMMONS–GOODSON and ELMORE concur.

bankruptcy proceeding, a conservatorship, disbarment, or a probate matter that relates to the rights of one individual.

State v. Smith (or *United States v. Smith*). This case name generally indicates a criminal proceeding. In our legal system, when a crime is committed, the state will prosecute the action on behalf of its citizens, all of whom have been injured by the crime. Some jurisdictions identify these cases as *People v. Smith*, and four jurisdictions (Kentucky, Massachusetts, Pennsylvania, and Virginia) are known as "Commonwealths" and will identify their criminal cases as *Commonwealth v. Smith*.

In re Johnny S.   Case names that indicate only a party's first name or initials (such as *In re J.B.*) are typically used to designate matters that involve minors. Often these cases relate to delinquency actions involving minors, adoption proceedings, or child custody proceedings. For purposes of privacy, the minor's surname is omitted from the published opinion.

Ex rel. Smith.   The phrase "ex rel." is short for "ex relatione" meaning "upon relation or information." Such a case name indicates a legal proceeding instituted by an attorney general or some other state or governmental official on behalf of a state but at the instigation of a private party who has an interest in the matter. A case involving adjudication of contractor Smith's claims against the United States Postal Service might be titled *United States ex rel. Smith*.

Ex parte Smith.   "Ex parte" means "on one side only" and usually refers to an action by or for one party without notice to or any contest by the other party.

Complaint of M / V Vulcan.   A case with this type of title will involve maritime or admiralty matters or will deal with a ship or sailing vessel. "M/V" means "motor vessel."

United States v. 22,152 Articles of Aircraft Parts.   Such an oddly named case typically involves the forfeiture or seizure of illegal goods or contraband. For example, this case was a forfeiture action brought by the United States government, which sought title to aircraft parts that a purchaser had attempted to illegally export to Libya. *United States v. $200,000 in United States Currency* was an action brought by the government seeking forfeiture to the government of $200,000 seized by the United States Customs Department at Miami International Airport.

Practice Tip

Citations in Cases

The citations that appear in published cases are generally not in correct *Bluebook* or *ALWD* form. For space reasons, these published cases often take shortcuts in citing cases and other authorities. Rely on *The Bluebook* or *ALWD* when citing legal authorities.

2. *Docket Number and Deciding Court*

Immediately beneath the case name you will be provided the docket number of the case. When the first paper or pleading in a case is filed, the clerk of the court will stamp a number on the papers. This number, referred to as a docket number, serves to identify and track this case as it progresses through the court. Courts do not identify cases by name, primarily due to the possibility of duplication and confusion. To request information about a case or obtain copies of the pleadings or motions submitted in a case, you must provide the docket number to the clerk, who will then retrieve the file for you. Often docket numbers provide information about a case. For instance, a docket number of "CV-03-862-CAJ" indicates the case was a civil case filed or instituted in 2003, it was the 862nd case filed that year, and it has been assigned to Judge Carolyn A. Jackson. Following the docket number, the deciding court is often identified.

3. *Date of Decision*

The date the case was decided by the court will be given. If two dates are given, one will be identified as the date the case was argued and the other will be the date the decision was issued by the court. For citation purposes, the critical date is the year of decision.

4. *Case Synopsis or Summary*

Before you are presented with the actual opinion of the court, you will be provided with a paragraph summarizing the nature and background of the case, an identification of the parties, the name of the lower court judge, a description of what occurred at the court(s) below, the name of the judge authoring this opinion, and what this court's decision is. This introductory paragraph, often referred to as a case synopsis (or occasionally as a "syllabus"), provides a quick overview of the general nature of the case and by what procedure it arrived at this court. This summary is typically prepared not by the court that issued the opinion but rather by the editors at West, LEXIS Publishing, or some other publishing company and is intended to serve merely as a convenience to legal professionals. Thus, while it serves as a quick introduction to the case, it may never be quoted from or relied upon as authority. A case synopsis merely helps you weed out irrelevant cases.

5. *Headnotes*

Before the actual opinion of the court, you will be provided with short paragraphs, each of which is assigned a number and a name. These are called headnotes or digest paragraphs. (For the present time, ignore the pictorial design of the "Key" followed by another number. This Key Number System will be thoroughly described in Chapter 5.) For instance, you may be presented with the following headnote:

3. Criminal Law
To convict defendant of aiding and abetting offense against the United States, Government must prove defendant was associated with criminal venture, participated in it as something defendant wished to bring about, and sought by his or her actions to make it succeed.

Each point of law discussed in the case is assigned a headnote. If a case discusses 20 issues of law, there will be 20 headnotes. These headnotes usually are prepared by the editors of the companies that publish the court reports and serve as a table of contents or index to the case. They allow you to determine, usually in less than one minute, whether the case is worthy of additional analysis. For example, someone in your law office may realize you are researching an assault and battery issue and may recommend that you read the case *Gingles v. Edmisten*, 590 F. Supp. 345 (E.D.N.C. 1984). When you retrieve this case, you discover the case is 40 pages long. It is possible that you could spend two hours reading this case only to realize, on the last page, that *Gingles v. Edmisten* is not at all on point and that you were steered in the wrong direction.

Headnotes help reduce the time you might spend reading a case that ultimately proves to be of no value to you and serve to give you a brief glimpse at the legal topics discussed in a case. By examining the headnotes, each of which is usually only a sentence in length, you can make an informed decision whether to read the case in full or whether to put the case aside.

If the issues you are researching are assault and battery, quickly scan the headnotes looking for the words "assault" or "battery." If none of the headnotes deal with these issues but rather deal solely with "licenses," "deeds," and "trusts," you can make a quick determination to set the case aside rather than spend hours reading a case that does not discuss the issues in which you are interested.

If your examination of the headnotes reveals that headnote 6 discusses battery, you should then examine the case and locate a boldface, bracketed "6." This **[6]** corresponds with and directs you to the portion of the case devoted to the discussion of battery. Because the headnote is usually only a single sentence, you should now read this section **[6]** of the case in full. If this reading looks promising, you should return to the beginning of the case and read the entire case.

Because the headnotes are typically prepared by publishers rather than judges, you cannot rely on the headnotes as authoritative, and you should never quote from the headnotes. You should rather use the headnotes to assist you in making an initial determination whether the case will be helpful to you and then to locate the most relevant portion of the case. Like the case synopsis, use the headnotes to help you weed out irrelevant decisions.

6. *Names of Counsel*

You will be provided with the names and locations of the law firms and the individual attorneys in those firms who represented the appellant and the appellee. You may wish to contact the attorneys, especially if the case presents a novel issue or represents a change in the law. While you can readily obtain copies of the briefs and papers filed in a court case from the clerk of the court, discussing the case with the attorney involved may be of particular help to you, and often the attorneys may be flattered that they are being contacted as experts in this field.

7. *Opinion*

The commencement of the opinion of the court is almost always marked by an identification of the judge or justice who authored the opinion. For example, "Petersen, C.J." would indicate Chief Judge or Chief Justice Petersen. Everything that follows the identification of the author is the court's opinion. Most opinions start with a recital of the facts in the case because without factual background, the rest of the opinion exists in a vacuum. The court will then apply the law of the jurisdiction involved to the facts in this particular case. Precedents may be cited and statutes or other authorities may be relied upon.

As you read the opinion in the case, keep in mind the key distinction between the holding in the case and *dicta*, extraneous comments made by the court that cannot serve as authority. You will notice that there are different types of opinions:

Majority opinions are those written by a member of the majority after the court has reached its decision. A majority opinion is one in which more than half of the judges or justices agree. The holding, or ratio decidendi, announced in the majority opinion is the law and serves as binding authority on lower courts in that jurisdiction.

Per curiam *opinions* are opinions issued by the whole court and no specific author will be identified. Per curiam decisions are usually short, often deal with uncontroversial matters, and are often considered weak precedent. Per curiam decisions are not necessarily unanimous. One highly controversial decision, *Bush v. Gore*, 531 U.S. 98 (2000), was a nonunanimous per curiam decision. After the opinion, Chief Justice Rehnquist (with whom Justices Scalia and Thomas joined in a concurring opinion) wrote, "We join the *per curiam* opinion. We write separately because we believe there are additional grounds that require us to reverse the Florida Supreme Court's decision." *Id.* at 111.

Concurring opinions are opinions written by justices who agree with the actual result reached in a case, for example, that the case should be reversed, but would rely on authorities other than those depended upon by the author of the opinion. A concurring opinion often uses language such as the following: "I agree the lower court erred and its decision should be reversed; however, while my learned brethren rely on Civil Code § 52, I would rely on Probate Code § 901." For example, in *Lynch v. Donnelly*, 465 U.S. 668, 687 (1984), Justice O'Connor's concurring opinion began as follows: "I concur in the opinion of the Court. I write separately to suggest a clarification of our Establishment Clause doctrine." A concurring justice is essentially telling others in the majority, "You got the right answer but for the wrong reason." While some concurring justices may set forth an actual opinion giving the reasons they concur, others may simply state, "I concur," and give no opinion.

Plurality opinions are those in which a result is reached but due to the existence of numerous concurring opinions, there is no common legal ground upon which the majority has agreed. If no opinion receives more than half of the justices' votes, the opinion receiving the most number of votes is called a plurality opinion. While a plurality opinion resolves the dispute between the litigating parties, it is a weak opinion because it does not reflect the will of a majority. In fact, the reasoning of the plurality is not binding in future cases although it may be highly persuasive.

Dissenting opinions are those written by members of the minority who disagree with the result reached. Just as is seen with concurring opinions, a dissenting judge may write a full opinion giving the reasons for the dissent or may simply indicate, "I dissent." If a certain case hurts your legal position, read the dissent carefully, as it may suggest arguments against the majority opinion.

Memorandum opinions report routine decisions. They provide a holding or result but little, if any, reasoning therefor. The decisions of the United States Supreme Court that merely reflect that a writ of certiorari has been denied are examples of memorandum opinions. Other memoranda opinions may state only, "For the reasons given by the court below, we also affirm." See Figure 4-2 for examples of memorandum opinions.

Chamber or in-chambers opinions are written by a United States Supreme Court justice in his or her capacity as the justice assigned to a circuit rather than in the capacity of writing for the majority. An in-chambers opinion is usually used to dispose of an application by a party requesting some form of interim relief, such as a temporary injunction or a stay of a judgment or order of a lower court. For example, in a matter arising out of the Kobe Bryant sexual assault case, the trial court issued an order prohibiting the press from publishing certain transcripts that the press received by an inadvertent e-mail transmission. The press requested a stay of the order, and Justice Breyer, writing an in-chambers opinion as circuit justice, denied the application for a stay. *Associated Press v. District Court for the Fifth District of Colorado*, No. 04A73 (U.S. July 26, 2004). For another example, a decision by a Supreme Court justice to stay an execution of a convicted murderer in his or her assigned circuit is a chamber opinion.

Figure 4-2
Sample Page from West's *Supreme Court Reporter* Showing Memorandum Decisions

1

486 U.S. 1058, 100 L.Ed.2d 930

**Hugh J. SHANNON, petitioner,
v. UNITED STATES. No.
87–6952.**

Case below, 836 F.2d 1125.

Petition for writ of certiorari to the United States Court of Appeals for the Eighth Circuit.

June 13, 1988. Denied.

2

486 U.S. 1059, 100 L.Ed.2d 930

**Frans Jacobus Smit THERON,
petitioner, v. UNITED STATES
MARSHAL. No. 87–6954.**

Case below, 832 F.2d 492.

Petition for writ of certiorari to the United States Court of Appeals for the Ninth Circuit.

June 13, 1988. Denied.

3

486 U.S. 1059, 100 L.Ed.2d 930

**ALBERTA GAS CHEMICALS LIMITED,
et al., petitioners, v. E.I. du PONT de
NEMOURS AND COMPANY, et al.
No. 87–652.**

Former decision, 484 U.S. 984, 108 S.Ct. 499.

Case below, 826 F.2d 1235.

June 13, 1988. The motion of petitioners to file reply brief under seal is granted. Petition for writ of certiorari to the United States Court of Appeals for the Third Circuit denied.

Memorandum Opinion

4

486 U.S. 1059, 100 L.Ed.2d 930

**NATIONWIDE CORPORATION and Nationwide Mutual Insurance Company,
petitioners, v. HOWING COMPANY, et
al. No. 87–1047.**

Former decision, 484 U.S. 1056, 108 S.Ct. 1008.

Case below, 625 F.Supp. 146; 826 F.2d 1470.

Petition for writ of certiorari to the United States Court of Appeals for the Sixth Circuit.

June 13, 1988. Denied.

Justice WHITE took no part in the consideration or decision of this petition.

5

486 U.S. 1059, 100 L.Ed.2d 930

**N.W. ENTERPRISES, INC., petitioner,
v. TEXAS. No. 87–1370.**

Petition for writ of certiorari to the Court of Appeals of Texas, Fourteenth District.

June 13, 1988. Denied.

Justice BRENNAN and Justice MARSHALL would grant the petition for a writ of certiorari and reverse the judgment of conviction.

6

486 U.S. 1059, 100 L.Ed.2d 931

SECURITIES INDUSTRY ASSOCIATION, petitioner, v. BOARD OF GOVERNORS OF the FEDERAL RESERVE SYSTEM, et al. No. 87–1513.

Case below, 839 F.2d 47.

119

En banc opinions are those in which all justices in a court of appeals participate. For example, if all of the justices in the Ninth Circuit sit together to decide a case (rather than the case being heard by a panel of three judges, as is the usual procedure), the decision is said to be rendered *en banc*, literally "in the bench."

Some Supreme Court cases, such as *Bush v. Gore*, produce several separate opinions and sorting them out can be difficult. Remember that only the majority opinion is the law that is binding on lower courts. Dissenting opinions and concurring opinions are not the law and while they may be persuasive, they are not mandatory authorities that must be followed.

Practice Tip

Headnotes

Never quote from either the synopses or the headnotes in a published case. While these editorial enhancements are very helpful to researchers, they are not the law but rather the publisher's interpretation and summary of the law. Recognize these features for what they are — tools to help you pick the right cases to read and focus on the most pertinent parts of the case.

---

8. *Decision*

The final element in a case is the actual decision reached by the court. The final decision may be to *affirm* or uphold the determination of the lower court, to *reverse* or overturn the determination reached below, or to *remand* or return the case to the lower court for further action consistent with the court's findings. A court may also *vacate* a case or dismiss it entirely. While, strictly speaking, the word "decision" refers only to the final disposition of a case, in many instances and in common usage, the words "opinion," "judgment," "decision," "case," and "holding" are used interchangeably to refer to an entire case from the name of the case to the final decision.

C. Publication of Cases

1. *Official and Unofficial Publication*

Now that you are familiar with the elements of a case, you should become familiar with the publication of cases and the features provided in the casebooks, which will assist you in your research efforts. The books in which cases are published are referred to as "reporters," and each one has a specific abbreviation. If cases are published pursuant to some statutory directive or court rule, the sets of books in which they are collected are referred to as "official" reports. Cases published without this type of governmental mandate are collected in sets of books referred to as "unofficial" reporters. Although the terms "report" and "reporter" are often used interchangeably, the term "report" usually refers to an official set of cases, such as the *U.S. Reports* or *California Reports*, while the term "reporter" usually refers to an unofficial set, such as the *Supreme Court Reporter* or *Pacific Reporter*.

Keep in mind that the terms "official" and "unofficial" have nothing to do with the quality or accuracy of the cases. Cases found in "official" sets are neither better nor more precise than those found in "unofficial" sets. The terms "official" and "unofficial" relate solely to the method of publication, not to the legal status of the cases. In the rare event of some discrepancy between two versions of a case, however, the official or government-approved version will govern.

When decisions are rendered by a court, they are initially available in slip form; that is, as looseleaf sheets of paper, or in small pamphlets. For example, a decision released by the highest court in Wisconsin, the Wisconsin Supreme Court, will initially be published in slip form. It may also be published on the Court's Web site and on various Internet sites and will be available on LEXIS and Westlaw. At this stage, the opinion will consist solely of the case name, date of decision, names of attorneys, opinion, (and concurring or dissenting opinions, if any) and decision. Many of the extra features discussed above, such as the headnotes and the introductory paragraph or synopsis, will not yet be present. Wisconsin publishes all of its decisions officially and therefore the case will appear next in softcover temporary volumes called *advance sheets* and thereafter in hardbound volumes known as *Wisconsin Reports, Second Series*.

Because the case itself is not copyrighted and is in the public domain, you would be free to take the case, photocopy it, perhaps add a few extra features, such as your own form of headnotes, place it in a set of volumes that you publish, and give the set your name. Such a publication would be "unofficial," as there is no statute that directs you to publish this case. The case in your privately published volume would be word for word the same as that which appeared in the official *Wisconsin Reports* — after all, what the judge has said in issuing the opinion is "etched in stone." What may distinguish your unofficial set of case reporters from the official set would be the "extra" features such as headnotes, the case summary or syllabus, and the like. These extra features are often called "editorial enhancements."

This type of duplication of case publishing by private individuals (or companies) is exactly what has occurred, and there now exist official and unofficial sets, each of which might publish the same case and each of which might add special or extra features to the sets. This is why you cannot quote from or rely exclusively on the headnotes or case synopsis — they are not usually prepared or written by the court but by a publishing company, and therefore are not the law. Similarly, the availability of cases on the Internet (see Chapter 12) arises out of the fact that cases are not copyrightable. Thus, they can be copied, posted on the Internet, and disseminated to others.

2. *Series of Cases*

You may have observed that some of the case reports on the shelves are marked *Atlantic Reporter* or *Federal Reporter*, while others indicate *Atlantic Reporter 2d Series* or *Federal Reporter 3d Series* on the spine. In some states, such as California, where there is an abundance of reported cases, some of the spines indicate *California Reports 3d Series* and even *California Reports 4th Series.*

The switch to a new series does not occur at regularly scheduled intervals, and you cannot predict when the next series will commence. It is believed that the change to a new series is done to prevent the volume numbers from getting too high. For example, volume 300 of the *South Western Reporter* is followed by volume 1 of the *South Western Reporter, Second Series*, and volume 999 of the *Federal Reporter*, Second Series is followed by volume 1 of the *Federal Reporter, Third Series*. If the volume numbers were to reach 1806, for example, the likelihood of transposing the numbers and making an error in citation form are much greater.

You do not need to know which years are covered by which series. It is sufficient that you know, for example, that any case published in *Southern Reporter 2d* is newer than any case published in *Southern Reporter*, and so forth.

3. *Advance Sheets*

After a case is released by a court in slip form, publishers add the editorial enhancements such as the headnotes and then gather and publish the cases in temporary softcover books or pamphlets referred to as "advance sheets." These advance sheets are published to provide rapid access to cases and are often available within a couple of weeks after a decision is issued by a court. West publishes advance sheets for its reporters (usually each week) and sends them to law libraries, agencies, and law firms that subscribe to its services, much the same way you might subscribe to *Time Magazine* or *Sports Illustrated.*

The advance sheets are placed on the shelves next to the hardbound volumes they relate to and are meant to last only until a permanent hardbound volume is published, typically a few months. Upon receipt of the permanent volume, the advance sheets are discarded. The permanent volumes will share the identical volume number and pagination as the earlier advance sheets. Therefore, you may readily rely upon and quote from cases appearing in the advance sheets because the citation to the page a quote appears on in the advance sheet will be identical to the page a quote appears on in the later published hardbound volume. West is so exacting that if a word is hyphenated between pages 242 and 243 of an advance sheet, it will likewise be hyphenated between pages 242 and 243 of the later permanent volume. After a case is printed in a West advance sheet but before publication in hardbound form, West returns the case to the authoring judge for additional comments or corrections, which are then included in the final print version.

D. Publication of State Cases

1. *West's* National Reporter System

In 1879, West Group ("West") created and published the *North Western Reporter*. The *North Western Reporter* is unofficial; it is published by West, a private company, which is acting independently and without any direction or order from any governmental authority. In most instances, the cases "picked up" by West and published in its *North Western Reporter* were already being published officially. West, however, believed that by grouping neighboring states together from the northwest region of the United States and by adding extra features to its sets of books, it could provide better service to those in the legal profession and could create a market for its publications. The set was so successful that West followed it by creating reporters for other geographical regions of the United States. The set of books published by West that collect state and federal cases are collectively referred to as the *National Reporter System*. In these sets of books West publishes all the cases released by courts for publication as well as adding thousands of cases not released for official publication and those that were reported as memorandum decisions.

The states that comprise each unit of the *National Reporter System* can be readily seen in the map shown as Figure 4-3 and are as follows:

North Western Reporter N.W., N.W.2d	Iowa, Michigan, Minnesota, Nebraska, North Dakota, South Dakota, and Wisconsin
Pacific Reporter P., P.2d, P.3d	Alaska, Arizona, California, Colorado, Hawaii, Idaho, Kansas, Montana, Nevada, New Mexico, Oklahoma, Oregon, Utah, Washington, and Wyoming
North Eastern Reporter N.E., N.E.2d	Illinois, Indiana, Massachusetts, New York, and Ohio
Atlantic Reporter A., A.2d	Connecticut, Delaware, Maine, Maryland, New Hampshire, New Jersey, Pennsylvania, Rhode Island, Vermont, and Washington, D.C.
South Western Reporter S.W., S.W..2d, S.W.3d	Arkansas, Kentucky, Missouri, Tennessee, and Texas
Southern Reporter So., So.2d	Alabama, Florida, Louisiana, and Mississippi
South Eastern Reporter S.E., S.E.2d	Georgia, North Carolina, South Carolina, Virginia, and West Virginia

These geographical units were the first units created by West. It is not important to memorize or know which state is published or covered in which unit. It is sufficient if you understand the general structure of West's *National Reporter System*: It is a set of books, published unofficially, which reports many cases already published officially by many states themselves. You should know, however, which unit covers the state in which you will be working. As you can see from the map in Figure 4-3, West's grouping of the states is not a perfect geographical division. Certainly no one would view Kansas or Oklahoma as Pacific states and yet their cases have been placed in the *Pacific Reporter*. Thus, while a knowledge of geography may be helpful in considering which unit publishes decisions from a certain state, you cannot be absolutely certain unless you review the list that is found in the front of each and every volume of the books in the *National Reporter System* units.

No one state has ruled on every issue, and researchers in a state are often required to search for cases outside their home or forum jurisdiction. West's grouping of cases from neighboring states affords legal practitioners the ability to engage in such research. Although a case from one

Figure 4-3
National Reporter System Map Showing the States Included in Each Reporter Group

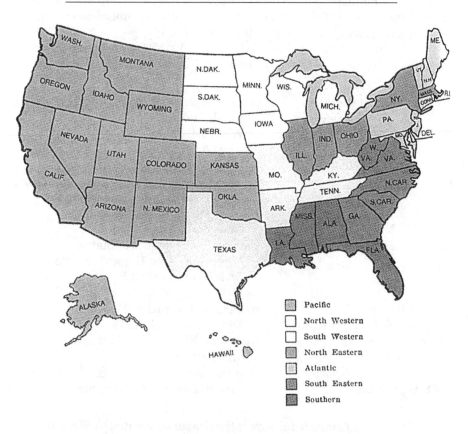

The National Reporter System also includes the Supreme Court Reporter, the Federal Reporter, the Federal Supplement, Federal Rules Decisions, West's Bankruptcy Reporter, the New York Supplement, West's California Reporter, West's Illinois Decisions, West's Military Justice Reporter and the Federal Claims Reporter.

state is not binding outside its jurisdictional borders (see Chapter 1), in the absence of its own binding authority a state might adopt the position announced by another state. If it does, under our concept of stare decisis, the principle then binds the lower courts within that state.

Because West believed that New York, California, and Illinois published so many cases, it created units just for those states: the *California Reporter* (created in 1959 to publish cases from the California Supreme Court, the California Courts of Appeal, and the Appellate Departments of California's Superior Courts); the *New York Supplement* (created in 1956, which publishes decisions of various New York courts); and *Illinois Decisions* (created in 1976 to publish cases from the Illinois Supreme Court and Appellate Court). Thus, a case citation to a California case may appear as follows:

> *Taylor v. Conrad*, 34 Cal. 3d 102, 698 P.2d 109, 206 Cal. Rptr. 911 (1983).

This citation indicates there are three sets of books in which you could locate this California case: the official *California Reports*, the unofficial *Pacific Reporter*, and the unofficial *California Reporter*. These three citations are called "parallel" citations. The publication of cases in more than one location can be a great service to a researcher: If the volume of *California Reports* that you need is missing from the shelf, you can elect to read the case in the *Pacific Reporter* or the *California Reporter*. Remember that the opinion issued by the court in *Taylor v. Conrad* will be the same no matter which of the three sets you select to locate the case. What the judge has stated in the opinion will not be revised by West's books in any manner. What will differ, however, may be the color of the set, the quality of the paper used, the typeface, and the editorial enhancements such as headnotes and the case summary or synopsis.

As is common with well-established and popular sets, all of the regional units have reached the second series (S.E.2d, A.2d, N.E.2d, N.W.2d, and So. 2d), and two reporters have reached their third series (P.3d and S.W.3d).

If you are puzzled why multiple sets of case reporters are needed, you should simply bear in mind that many different types of automobiles are also available in the United States. It is possible to buy a Ford, a Chevrolet, a Nissan, or a Toyota. Each car will provide the same function: transportation. Yet an individual may develop a preference for one manufacturer or may select one model over another based on considerations of price or available options. The same is true for law firms, corporations, and agencies. Some may elect to purchase official reports rather than unofficial reporters based upon price or some other consideration, and some may prefer the many extra and integrated features found in West's *National Reporter System*.

One of the advantages of the *National Reporter System* units lies in its grouping of states. A law firm in South Carolina that purchases the official *South Carolina Reports* will acquire a set of books that contains cases from South Carolina. If that firm purchases the *South Eastern Reporter*, however, it will acquire a set of books that contains decisions not only from

South Carolina but from Georgia, North Carolina, Virginia, and West Virginia. This allows legal professionals in states without a rich or complex body of case law to review decisions from other states, which decisions might be relied upon if a case of first impression arises in South Carolina. West also markets several state-specific versions of its regional reporters. For example, in Massachusetts a law firm can purchase a set called *Massachusetts Decisions* comprising only the Massachusetts cases from the *North Eastern Reporter*. Lists of the sets of books published by West is available on its Web site at http://west.thomson.com.

West's *National Reporter* units often publish cases that would not otherwise be published in the official state reports. This is because West will publish cases that have been designated "not for publication" due to the fact that these cases do not advance legal theory or are duplicative of other already published cases. While West promotes its *National Reporter System* by noting that it publishes thousands of cases that are not published in the official state reports, one of the publishers of the official sets views this as a drawback. Marketing materials for the publisher of the official *California Reports* state, "Up to 25% of the cases in each unofficial reporter volume are depublished or otherwise superseded. Nonadmissible in court . . . the bottom line—are you paying good money for bad law?"

Interestingly enough, and perhaps because of its publishing expertise, West has been recognized as the official or primary source of decisions in a majority of the states. Thus, while *Arizona Reports* and *Ohio State Reports* are the official sets of the respective states, the actual publication of the books is accomplished by West. Similarly, some states have adopted West's regional reporters as their official state reporters.

Additionally, the availability of unpublished opinions on the computerized legal research systems, LEXIS and Westlaw, on the Internet, and in the newly published *Federal Appendix* has contributed to the increasing proliferation of cases. As noted earlier, courts attempt to reduce the mass of legal publication by enacting court rules prohibiting citation of cases in court documents unless those cases have been marked "for publication." Others require authors citing unreported cases to include a copy of the case together with any document citing the case. In any event, at present, an unreported case is not binding precedent under the doctrine of stare decisis but is rather persuasive authority only. As noted, the issue whether researchers should be allowed to cite to unpublished opinions in documents submitted to courts has generated considerable controversy, leaving both federal and state courts highly divided as to whether to allow such citation.

2. Citation Form

While citation form will be covered in depth in Chapter 8, at this point you should know one importance of distinguishing an official citation from an unofficial citation. Many state citation rules require that citations to state court cases include a citation to the official state report followed by a citation to West's regional reporter. Thus, you will need to know the units in West's *National Reporter System* so that when you are confronted with a case citation such as *Neibarger v. Universal Cooperatives*, 439 Mich. 512, 486 N.W.2d 612 (1992), you will know that because the *North Western Reporter* is one of West's *National Reporter System* unofficial regional units, the citation to it should follow the official *Michigan Reports* citation. Under *The Bluebook* and *ALWD* (unless local rules require otherwise), the citation would include only the West regional reporter and not the official citation, as follows: *Neibarger v. Universal Cooperatives*, 486 N.W.2d 612 (Mich. 1992).

3. *Discontinuation of Some Official Reports*

Because of the success and accuracy of West's *National Reporter System*, and because many researchers preferred using and buying the regional reporters with their convenient grouping of cases from neighboring states and user-friendly editorial enhancements, many states have ceased publishing their cases officially. In fact, between 1948 and 1981, 20 states discontinued officially publishing their cases. Another reason for the discontinuation of official reports in many states is the expense of publishing cases that West will also be publishing. In the states shown below there are no longer parallel citations, and the only citation to cases from these states are to the appropriate geographical unit of West's *National Reporter System* (although, as noted above, for many of these states West publishes specialized state-specific reporters, for example, the *Alabama Reporter, Florida Cases*, and the *Maine Reporter*):

State that Never Published Cases Officially	States That Have Discontinued Official Publication and Year of Discontinuance	States that Continue to Publish Officially
Alaska	Alabama (1976)	Arizona
	Colorado (1980)	Arkansas
	Delaware (1966)	California
	District of Columbia (1941)	Connecticut
	Florida (1948)	Georgia
	Indiana (1981)	Hawaii
	Iowa (1968)	Idaho
	Kentucky (1951)	Illinois
	Louisiana (1972)	Kansas
	Maine (1965)	Maryland
	Minnesota (1977)	Massachusetts
	Mississippi (1966)	Michigan
	Missouri (1956)	Montana
	North Dakota (1953)	Nebraska

State that Never Published Cases Officially	States That Have Discontinued Official Publication and Year of Discontinuance	States that Continue to Publish Officially
	Oklahoma (1953)	Nevada
	Rhode Island (1980)	New Hampshire
	South Dakota (1976)	New Jersey
	Tennessee (1971)	New Mexico
	Texas (1962)	New York
	Utah (1974)	North Carolina
	Wyoming (1959)	Ohio
		Oregon
		Pennsylvania
		South Carolina
		Vermont
		Virginia
		Washington
		West Virginia
		Wisconsin

E. Publication of Federal Cases

1. United States Supreme Court Cases

a. Publication

United States Supreme Court cases are published in the following three sets of books. Most law firms or offices will purchase only one set.

(1) United States Reports (U.S.)

The *United States Reports* is official. It is published by private firms under contract with the United States Government Printing Office and comprises more than 530 volumes. Approximately 5,000 pages are published each year. Initially, cases from the United States Supreme Court were published in sets of books named after the individuals responsible for publishing the set. Thus, the initial 90 volumes of this set have names on the spines such as Dallas, Cranch, Wheaton, and Peters. In 1875, it became apparent that it was unsatisfactory to name a set after an individual who would inevitably retire or die. Therefore, in 1875, the set that reported United States Supreme Court cases was named the *United States Reports*. The older volumes were later numbered consecutively. Citations to these older cases appear as follows: *Turner v. Fendall*, 5 U.S. (1 Cranch) 117 (1801). When you observe such a citation, you should simply realize the case is very old. Cases in *United States Reports* appear initially as bench opinions, which are small pamphlets issued to the press and the public on the day opinions are announced by the Court. Several days later the case will be printed in slip form and then in brown softcover advance sheets. Some months later, the hardbound volumes are published and sent to law firms, law libraries, and other subscribers.

(2) Supreme Court Reporter (S. Ct.)

The *Supreme Court Reporter* is published by West and is unofficial. It is another unit of West's *National Reporter System*. This set began its coverage in 1882 and reports in full every decision rendered by the United States Supreme Court since that time. Cases initially appear in advance sheets, which are issued twice a month. The advance sheets are later discarded and replaced by semi-permanent volumes, which remain on the bookshelves for two or three years until the final permanent corrected and hardbound volumes are available.

(3) United States Supreme Court Reports, Lawyers' Edition (L. Ed.)

United States Supreme Court Reports, Lawyers' Edition (and *Lawyers' Edition 2d*), is published by LEXIS Publishing and is unofficial. It was created in response to a need among lawyers for less expensive books reporting Supreme Court cases than the official ones then being published. It contains all decisions issued by the Supreme Court since 1789. This set contains many useful editorial features such as quick summaries of the holdings of the cases, summaries of the briefs of counsel for the parties in the cases (given for older cases), research references, and, for some cases, annotations or essays written by LEXIS's staff attorneys on significant legal issues raised in the case. Be careful when reading older cases reported in *Lawyers' Edition* as it may be easy to confuse the arguments being advanced by counsel with the actual opinion of the Court. Make sure you rely only on information appearing after the authoring justice's name. Any information that precedes the majority opinion has usually been prepared by the publisher, and while it is extremely valuable and useful, it is not the law. Cases initially appear in advance sheets about twice per month, and these advance sheets are discarded when the permanent volumes are received.

There are thus three parallel cites for all United States Supreme Court cases, and you can locate the 1986 case, *Batson v. Kentucky*, in three locations: 476 U.S. 79, 106 S. Ct. 1712, and 90 L. Ed. 2d 69. In the event of any conflict in versions of the cases reported in these volumes, the version of a case found in the official *U.S. Reports* governs.

Both of the unofficial sets reporting cases from the United States Supreme Court (S. Ct. and L. Ed.) include a section called "Syllabus," given before each opinion published in the set. The Syllabus is a comprehensive summary of the case to follow. While it is prepared by the Court's Reporter of Decisions, it is not the opinion of the Court itself. Therefore, it is a useful feature but cannot be quoted from. Be careful to rely only on the case itself, not on any of the editorial enhancements that accompany a case. Locate the name of the author of the opinion. This name signals the start of the opinion. Everything given after it is "fair game."

b. Rapid Access to United States Supreme Court Cases

As described above, all of the sets that publish United States Supreme Court cases issue advance sheets. Nevertheless, even the advance sheets may take four to six weeks to be received. Very rapid access to United States Supreme Court cases can be achieved through the following sources:

(1) Slip Opinions

After the bench opinion is made available to the public, the United States Supreme Court issues its opinion in slip form. These slip opinions are available at the United States Supreme Court the day a decision is announced. The slips are then immediately sent to law libraries, law book publishers, and other subscribers. The slip opinions can typically be located in law libraries within five to ten days after the date of decision. The slips will contain only the decision of the Court; they will not include any editorial features such as headnotes.

(2) Computer-Assisted Research

As we will discuss more fully in Chapter 11, the computer-assisted research services LEXIS and Westlaw usually have the full text of a United States Supreme Court case within one hour after the decision is released. Other computer-assisted legal research services such as Loislaw also offer immediate access to these cases.

(3) United States Law Week

You may recall from Chapter 3 that *United States Law Week*, a weekly publication of The Bureau of National Affairs, Inc. ("BNA"), publishes some of the federal laws passed during the previous week. *United States Law Week* is perhaps better known, however, for publishing in looseleaf form (for example, looseleaf pamphlets, which are then maintained in ringed binders), the full text of United States Supreme Court opinions from the preceding week. Just as you may subscribe to *Architectural Digest* or *Better Homes and Gardens*, law firms and law libraries subscribe to *United States Law Week* to obtain rapid access to recent United States Supreme Court decisions. In addition to publishing the United States Supreme Court cases, *United States Law Week* also indicates which cases have been docketed or scheduled for hearing by the Court, summaries of cases recently filed with the Court, a calendar of hearings scheduled, and summaries of oral arguments made before the Court. *United States Law Week*'s print service is complemented by its e-mail notification service, called *Supreme Court Today, Case Alert and Legal News*, which provides subscribers with e-mail alerts every day the Court decides a case or grants or denies review. Highlights and summaries of arguments are also included.

(4) Newspapers

Many law firms and law libraries subscribe to legal newspapers, which report news of interest to legal professionals. Often these newspapers will print United States Supreme Court cases in full as well as cases from lower federal courts or cases from the courts in the state in which the newspaper is published. These newspapers are generally available within a few days after the decision is rendered.

(5) West Document Retrieval

West provides a variety of services allowing ready access to cases. Specifically, West Document Retrieval provides public records, court documents, and so forth by overnight delivery, e-mail, or fax. Call 1-877-DOC-RETR.

(6) Internet

As discussed in Chapter 12, Supreme Court cases are now available at no cost on the Internet. Cases appear on the Internet within a day of their release. The most authoritative site is that of the Supreme Court itself at http://www.supremecourtus.gov. The text of each opinion is posted to the Court's site within hours after the opinion is announced.

2. United States Courts of Appeal Cases

The set of books that publishes cases from the intermediate courts of appeal (for example, First Circuit, Second Circuit) is the *Federal Reporter* (abbreviated "F.") and the *Federal Reporter, Second Series* and *Third Series* (abbreviated as "F.2d" and "F.3d"). The *Federal Reporter* was created by West in 1880 to publish decisions from the United States Courts of Appeal. While the primary function of the *Federal Reporter* is to publish decisions from these intermediate federal courts, it has published cases from various other courts as well. See Figure 4-4.

This set of reporters is unofficial and is yet another of the units in West's *National Reporter System*. In fact, the *Federal Reporter* is the *only* set that reports decisions from these intermediate courts of appeal. Although only approximately 20 percent of the cases for the Courts of Appeal are published, the *Federal Reporter* grows by about 20 to 25 hardbound volumes each year. There is no official reporter for these cases. Thus, there are no parallel cites for cases from the circuit courts. The only citation that you will encounter is to the *Federal Reporter* or *Federal Reporter, Second Series* or *Third Series*. As is typical of publication of court decisions, the cases are initially published in softcover advance sheets that are later replaced by hardbound permanent volumes.

While the overview of the *Federal Reporter*, as shown in Figure 4-4, is a useful historical guide, it is sufficient to know that the chief role of the *Federal Reporter* is to report decisions from the United States Courts of Appeal.

As discussed earlier, in 2001 West began publishing a new set of books, the *Federal Appendix*, which publishes unpublished courts of appeals cases. The set is part of the *National Reporter System*. Each case includes West's editorial enhancements, such as case synopses, key numbers, headnotes, and so forth. Also discussed earlier, the use and citation of unpublished cases is a controversial matter, with some courts allowing citation of unpublished cases and some courts strictly prohibiting such. As a researcher, you will be able to access unpublished decisions (through LEXIS and Westlaw, the online legal research systems, and now through the *Federal Appendix*), but you must understand and comply with all federal and court rules regarding citation to such opinions when you submit documents to a court.

3. *United States District Court Cases*

You will recall from Chapter 2 that the United States District Courts are the trial courts in our federal system. You may also recall that Section A of this chapter noted that trial court decisions are not usually published. An exception to this general rule lies in the *Federal Supplement* and *Federal Supplement Second Series* (abbreviated as "F. Supp." and "F. Supp. 2d"), created in 1932 by West and which publish decisions from the United States District Courts, our federal trial courts. While the *Federal Supplement* and *Federal Supplement Second Series* publish decisions from other courts as well (see Figure 4-5), their key function is to report decisions from these United States District Courts, although they publish only about 15 percent of the cases heard by our federal district courts. The *Federal Supplement* and *Federal Supplement Second Series* are other unofficial West publications and are a part of West's *National Reporter System*. The *Federal Supplement* and *Federal Supplement Second Series* comprise the sole set of books that publish United States District Court cases. Thus, there are no parallel citations

Figure 4-4
Coverage of the *Federal Reporter*

1880-1912	U.S. Circuit Court Cases
1911-1913	Commerce Court of the United States (Court abolished in 1932)
1880-1932	U.S. District Courts (after 1932, cases reported in *Federal Supplement*)
1929-1932, 1960-1982	U.S. Court of Claims
1891-Date	U.S. Courts of Appeal
1929-1982	U.S. Court of Customs and Patent Appeals (covers years court was in operation)
1943-1961	U.S. Emergency Court of Appeals
1972-1993	Temporary Emergency Court of Appeals

Figure 4-5
Coverage of the *Federal Supplement*

1932-1960	U.S. Court of Claims
1932-Date	U.S. District Courts
1956-Date	U.S. Court of International Trade (formerly the United States Customs Court)
1968-Date	Judicial Panel on Multidistrict Litigation
1973-1996	Special Court, Regional Rail Reorganization Act (abolished in 1996)

for United States District Court cases. Just as with other case reports, cases appear first in advance sheets and later in hardbound volumes.

4. Cases Interpreting Federal Rules

Yet another unit in West's *National Reporter System*, the *Federal Rules Decisions* set, publishes United States District Court cases since 1939 that interpret the Federal Rules of Civil Procedure and, since 1946, cases that interpret Federal Rules of Criminal Procedure, cases interpreting Federal Rules of Evidence, Federal Rules of Appellate Procedure, Federal Sentencing Guidelines, and other rules. *Federal Rules Decisions* (abbreviated as "F.R.D.") publishes these cases in advance sheets and then in replacement hardbound volumes. They do not otherwise appear in the *Federal Supplement*. Thus, the name of this set, *Federal Rules Decisions*, is perfectly descriptive of its function: It publishes cases that construe federal rules, whether those rules relate to rules of procedure for civil cases, rules of procedure for criminal cases, rules of evidence, and so forth.

F. Star Paging

Citation form will be thoroughly discussed in Chapter 8, but for now it is sufficient if you are aware that many state rules require that citation to state cases include all parallel cites. Thus, if you are referring to the case *Guysinger v. K.C. Raceway, Inc.*, in a brief for a court in Ohio, the correct citation form may be as follows: *Guysinger v. K.C. Raceway, Inc.*, 54 Ohio App. 3d 17, 560 N.E.2d 584 (1990).

The *Bluebook* requires that for United States Supreme Court cases, you are to cite only to the official *United States Reports*. That is, for citation form purposes, it is as if the unofficial sets, West's *Supreme Court Reporter* (S. Ct.) and LEXIS Publishing's *Supreme Court Reports, Lawyers' Edition* (L. Ed.), do not exist (unless the citation to the *United States Reports* is unavailable). The *ALWD* rule is substantially similar, although *ALWD* permits parallel citations for United States Supreme Court cases.

Obviously, therefore, the publishers at West and LEXIS were in a dilemma. It would be extremely difficult for these publishers to attempt to market their sets of books because no matter how wonderful and useful the extra features contained in these unofficial sets might be, law firms and other users would be highly unlikely to purchase a set of books that could not be cited or quoted.

The publishers at West and LEXIS Publishing thus developed a technique of continually indicating throughout their sets which volume and page a reader would be on if that reader were using the official *United States Reports*. This technique of indicating page breaks in the official set is called "star paging" because the early method of indicating when a new page commenced was through the use of a star or asterisk (*).

LEXIS Publishing indicates its page breaks with a boldface reference in brackets, as in **[516 US 14]**. West uses an inverted "T." For example, if you are reading a case in West's *Supreme Court Reporter*, each page therein will provide you with the parallel citation to the official *United States Reports*. This citation is usually found in the upper corner of each page. As you are reading through the opinion, you might see language such as the following:

"We therefore hold|that the law of implied indemnity. . . ."
              218

Such an indication informs you that if you were reading this case in the *United States Reports*, after the word "hold" you would have turned the page to page 218. The first word on page 218 in that volume of the *United States Reports* would be "that."

Star paging is entirely self-correcting. If you have any doubt that you are converting the page numbers accurately, you can always retrieve the appropriate volume of the *United States Reports* and verify that the first word on page 218 is "that." As a result, no matter which set of unofficial books you use for United States Supreme Court cases, you can readily tell the page you would be on if you were holding the official *United States Reports*. Figure 4-6 shows a sample page illustrating star paging. Star paging is also found in some other West sets, such as in *California Reporter* and in the *New York Supplement* directing you to pagination for the official California and New York reports.

G.   Specialized *National Reporter System* Sets

There are additional sets of books that are also a part of West's *National Reporter System Series*. These reporters, however, publish very specialized cases and are as follows:

1.   *West's* Military Justice Reporter

This set publishes decisions from the United States Court of Appeals for the Armed Forces and the Military Service Courts of Criminal Appeals.

Figure 4-6
Sample Page from West's *Supreme Court Reporter* Showing "Star Paging"

Reference to volume and page in official *United States Reports*

487 U.S. 677

MORRISON v. OLSON
Cite as 108 S.Ct. 2597 (1988)

2611

ter the addition of "Consuls" to the list, the Committee's proposal was adopted, *id.*, at 539, and was subsequently reported to the Convention by the Committee of Style. See *id.*, at 599. It was at this point, on September 15, that Gouverneur Morris moved to add the Excepting Clause to Art. II, § 2. *Id.*, at 627. The one comment made on this motion was by Madison, who felt that the Clause did not go far enough in that it did not allow Congress to vest appointment powers in "Superior Officers below Heads of Departments." The first vote on Morris' motion ended in a tie. It was then put forward a second time, with the urging that "some such provision [was] too necessary, to be omitted." This time the proposal was adopted. *Id.*, at 627–628. As this discussion shows, there was little or no debate on the question whether the Clause empowers Congress to provide for interbranch appointments, and there is nothing to suggest that the Framers intended to prevent Congress from having that power.

Star Paging (the word "to" appears on page 675 of volume 487 of the *United States Reports*, while the word "impair" appears on page 676 of the volume)

We do not mean to say that Congress' power to provide for interbranch appointments of "inferior officers" is unlimited. In addition to separation-of-powers concerns, which would arise if such provisions for appointment had the potential to [676]impair the constitutional functions assigned to one of the branches, *Siebold* itself suggested that Congress decision to vest the appointment power in the courts would be improper if there was some "incongruity" between the functions normally performed by the courts and the performance of their duty to appoint. 100 U.S. (10 Otto), at 398 ("[T]he duty to appoint inferior officers, when required thereto by law, is a constitutional duty of the courts; and in the

present case there is no such incongruity in the duty required as to excuse the courts from its performance, or to render their acts void"). In this case, however, we do not think it impermissible for Congress to vest the power to appoint independent counsel in a specially created federal court. We thus disagree with the Court of Appeals' conclusion that there is an inherent incongruity about a court having the power to appoint prosecutorial officers.[13] We have recognized that courts may appoint private attorneys to act as prosecutor for judicial contempt judgments. See *Young v. United States ex rel. Vuitton et Fils S.A.*, 481 U.S. 787, 107 S.Ct. 2124, 95 L.Ed.2d 740 (1987). In *Go–Bart Importing Co. v. United States*, 282 U.S. 344, 51 S.Ct. 153, 75 L.Ed. 374 (1931), we approved court appointment of United States commissioners, who exercised certain limited prosecutorial powers. *Id.*, at 353, n. 2, 51 S.Ct., at 156, n. 2. In *Siebold*, as well, we indicated that judicial appointment of federal marshals, who are "executive officer[s]," would not be inappropriate. Lower courts have also upheld interim judicial appointments of United States Attorneys, see *United States v. Solomon*, 216 F.Supp. 835 (SDNY 1963), and Congress itself has vested the power to make these interim appointments in the district courts, see 28 [677]U.S.C. § 546(d) (1982 ed., Supp. V).[14] Congress, of course, was concerned when it created the office of independent counsel with the conflicts of interest that could arise in situations when the Executive Branch is called upon to investigate its own high-ranking officers. If it were to remove the appointing authority from the Executive Branch, the most logical place to put it was in the Judicial Branch. In the light of

---

13. Indeed, in light of judicial experience with prosecutors in criminal cases, it could be said that courts are especially well qualified to appoint prosecutors. This is not a case in which judges are given power to appoint an officer in an area in which they have no special knowledge or expertise, as in, for example, a statute authorizing the courts to appoint officials in the Department of Agriculture or the Federal Energy Regulatory Commission.

14. We note also the longstanding judicial practice of appointing defense attorneys for individuals who are unable to afford representation, see 18 U.S.C. § 3006A(b) (1982 ed., Supp. V), notwithstanding the possibility that the appointed attorney may appear in court before the judge who appointed him.

2. *West's* Veterans Appeals Reporter

This set publishes cases decided by the United States Court of Appeals for Veterans Claims, created in 1988, and previously named the United States Court of Veterans Appeals.

3. *West's* Bankruptcy Reporter

The *Bankruptcy Reporter* publishes selected decisions that are not found in the *Federal Supplement* and that are decided by the United States Bankruptcy Courts, the Bankruptcy Appellate Panels, and the United States District Courts. Additionally, this set reprints bankruptcy appeals handled by the United States Courts of Appeal and the United States Supreme Court.

4. *West's* Federal Claims Reporter

This set (previously called *United States Claims Court Reporter*) publishes decisions from the United States Court of Federal Claims (formerly called the United States Claims Court) from its conception in 1982 as well as Court of Federal Claims appeals handled by the United States Courts of Appeal and the United States Supreme Court.

5. *Federal Cases*

Until 1880, when West began publishing cases from the lower federal courts, there was no one comprehensive set of books that reported decisions from these courts. While several sets existed, none were adequate. Therefore, in 1880, West collected all of these lower federal court cases together and republished them in a set of books titled *Federal Cases*. *Federal Cases* is a very unusual arrangement of cases as it publishes these lower federal court cases that preceded the establishment of the *National Reporter System* in *alphabetical* order rather than *chronological* order, as is the usual format. If you examine *Federal Cases*, you will note that each case is assigned a consecutive number, with the first case referred to as No. 1, *The Aalesund*, and the last case referred to as No. 18,222, *In re Zug*.

Due to the fact it covers much older cases, *Federal Cases* is typically available at only larger law libraries. You should compare the relatively small number of volumes, 30, which cover lower federal court cases from 1789 to 1879 in *Federal Cases* with the current total of approximately 3,000 volumes covering cases from 1880 to the present in the *Federal Reporter* and *Federal Supplement*, thus demonstrating again the dramatic increase in litigation in this country.

H. Features of West's *National Reporter System*

The case reporters in West's *National Reporter System* possess a number of useful editorial features that aid in and simplify legal research. These features are found in both the advance sheets and the permanent hard-bound volumes (except as noted) and are as follows:

1. Tables of Cases Reported

There will be at least one alphabetical table of cases in each volume of West's *National Reporter System* sets. For example, in any volume of the *Supreme Court Reporter*, there will be a complete alphabetical list of all of the cases in that volume. This feature is useful if you know the approximate date of a Supreme Court case and need to examine a few volumes of the set to locate the specific case itself. Additionally, you may have inadvertently transposed the numbers in a citation and be unable to locate the case you need. The table of cases will allow you to look up the case you desire and then locate the specific page on which it appears. Cases can be found by using either the plaintiff's or the defendant's name.

Some sets of books have two tables of cases. For instance, any volume in the *Pacific Reporter* will contain one complete alphabetical list of the cases in that volume as well as an alphabetized list of the cases arranged by state so that the Alaska cases are separately alphabetized, the Arizona cases are separately alphabetized, and so on. Similarly, any volume in the *Federal Reporter* will possess one complete alphabetical list of the cases in that volume and will also separately arrange and alphabetize the First Circuit cases, then the Second Circuit cases, for example.

2. Tables of Statutes and Rules

The Table of Statutes will direct you to cases in a volume that have interpreted or construed any statutes or constitutional provisions. Thus, if you are interested in whether any recent cases have interpreted N.Y. Banking Law § 317 (McKinney 2001), you can consult the table of statutes in any recent volume of the *North Eastern Reporter* and you will be directed to the specific page in the volume that interprets that statute.

Similarly, there are tables listing all federal rules of civil and criminal procedure, federal rules of appellate procedure, and federal rules of evidence that are construed by any cases in a particular volume.

3. Table of Words and Phrases

This table alphabetically lists words or phrases that have been interpreted or defined by any cases in a volume of the *National Reporter System*.

For example, you can consult the Table of Words and Phrases and determine if the words "abandonment," "negligence," or "trustee" have been defined by any cases in a volume, and you will be directed to the specific page in a volume on which such a word is judicially defined.

4. List of Judges

This feature is found only in the hardbound volumes of the *National Reporter System* and lists all of the judges sitting on the courts covered by that particular volume. Thus, any hardbound volume of the *Federal Reporter* will provide a list of First Circuit judges, Second Circuit judges, and so on.

5. Key Number System

While West's Key Number System will be described in full in the next chapter, for the present it is sufficient to know that in the back of each hardbound volume in West's *National Reporter System* (except the *Bankruptcy Reporter* and the *Federal Claims Court Reporter*), West will provide a brief summary of each case in the volume arranged by topic and key number.

I.   Finding Parallel Cites

You have seen that many cases can be found in more than one place. This is because many cases are published officially and unofficially. The different citations to a case are known as *parallel cites*.

On some occasions, you may have one cite and may need the other parallel cite. This could be due to the fact that citation rules require all parallel cites or it could be for the very practical reason that the volume you need is missing from the library bookshelf and you must obtain the parallel cite to locate the case you need. There are several techniques you can use to find a parallel cite.

1. Cross-References

Many cases provide all parallel cites. For example, if you open a volume of *California Reports* to the case you need, at the top of each page you are given all parallel cites for this case. Similarly, West's reporters will provide the official citation(s) for cases they report unofficially.

2. National Reporter Blue Book *and State Blue and White Books*

If you have an official cite for a state court case and you need the unofficial parallel cite, you can use a set published by West and titled the *National Reporter Blue Book*. This set contains complete conversion tables showing parallel cites. For example, if you look up the official cite, 321 N.C. 111, you are immediately provided with the unofficial citation, 361 S.E.2d 562.

Similarly, most states that continue to publish their cases officially have available what are known as "State Blue and White Books," which provide conversion tables with parallel citations. For example, the *Nebraska Blue and White Book* is a single volume with blue pages giving citations from the official reports to the unofficial regional reporter (when you have an official citation) and the white pages giving the parallel citation from the regional reporter back to the official reports. The various Blue and White Books are published by West. Most law libraries include only the Blue and White Book for the state in which they are located.

3. Shepard's Citations *and KeyCite*

As you will learn in Chapter 9, when you Shepardize or KeyCite either an official or an unofficial citation, you are given the parallel cite.

The Final Wrap-Up

Using and Citing Cases

Use: Use cases to support the legal assertions you make. Focus on the relevant facts and the reasoning relied upon by the deciding court. Did the court establish a new rule of law? Is the holding limited to the particular facts of the case or is it broad enough to serve as a precedent in later cases? Also use cases to direct you to other authorities, both primary and secondary. Most court opinions cite numerous other legal authorities, many of which may be helpful to you.

Citation: Because cases are primary authority and because they are binding in your jurisdiction (assuming they are on point), your documents will probably cite cases more than any other authorities. Use proper citation form (according to *The Bluebook, ALWD,* or local rules).

4. *State Digests*

West has published sets of books called "digests" for each state except Delaware, Nevada, and Utah. These digests (discussed in detail in the next chapter) contain tables of cases, which provide parallel citations. Thus, if you look up a case by name in the *Wisconsin Digest*, you will be provided with the citation for the case in the *Wisconsin Reports* as well as in the *North Western Reporter*.

J. Summary of West's *National Reporter System*

West's *National Reporter System* is a series of sets of case reporters that publish cases from state appellate courts and from federal trial and appellate courts. All of the sets of books in the *National Reporter System* are unofficial because the books are published privately by West rather than pursuant to some statutory directive or mandate. Although West's *National Reporter System* is the largest collection of case reporters, West is not the only publisher of cases. For example, LEXIS Publishing publishes United States Supreme Court cases in its set *United States Supreme Court Reports, Lawyers' Edition*.

West publishes state court cases in various regional units, each of which contains cases from a particular geographical area. The state court units are as follows:

> *North Western Reporter*
> *Pacific Reporter*
> *North Eastern Reporter*
> *Atlantic Reporter*
> *South Western Reporter*
> *Southern Reporter*
> *South Eastern Reporter*

Because the states of New York, California, and Illinois decide so many cases, West also created the following separate sets just for these states:

> *New York Supplement*
> *California Reporter*
> *Illinois Decisions*

Federal cases are published in these sets of books:

Supreme Court Reporter	(cases from the United States Supreme Court)
Federal Reporter	(cases from the United States Courts of Appeal)
Federal Supplement	(cases from the United States District Courts)

Federal Rules Decisions	(cases interpreting federal rules of civil and criminal procedure and other rules)

Finally, West publishes four other sets, each of which is descriptively titled: the *Military Justice Reporter*, the *Veterans Appeals Reporter*, the *Bankruptcy Reporter*, and the *Federal Claims Reporter* (formerly the *United States Claims Court Reporter*).

All of the books in West's *National Reporter System* possess a variety of useful features and all are participants in West's *Key Number System*, which is described in full in Chapter 5.

You can readily see that there are numerous sets of reporters, each identified by its own particular abbreviation. There is an excellent reference tool of abbreviations and acronyms used in legal literature, from "Ct. Cl. R." (for Court of Claims Rules) to "S.L.R.B." (for State Labor Relations Board). See Mary Miles Prince, *Bieber's Dictionary of Legal Abbreviations* (5th ed. 2001), published by William S. Hein & Co., Inc., of Buffalo, New York. A copy may be kept in the reference section of your law library. Additionally, the front of each volume of West's general encyclopedia, *Corpus Juris Secundum* (C.J.S.) includes a thorough table of legal abbreviations. Finally, the new *Black's Law Dictionary* (8th ed. 2004) includes an extensive list of legal abbreviations in its Appendix A. See Figure 4-7 for a summary of case law publication.

Figure 4-7
Summary of Case Law Publication

	Highest Court	Intermediate Appellate Courts	Trial Courts
Federal Cases	United States Supreme Court a. *United States Reports** b. *Supreme Courts Reporter* c. *United States Supreme Court Reports, Lawyers' Edition* d. *United States Law Week*	United States Courts of Appeal cases are published in *Federal Reporter* (F., F.2d, and F.3d)	United States District Court cases are published in *Federal Supplement* (F. Supp. and F. Supp. 2d)
State Cases	State Supreme Courts (example of official sets are *California Reports** and *Georgia Reports**)	State Appellate Courts (example of official sets are *California Appellate Reports** and *Georgia Appeals Reports**)	Generally, trial court cases are not published

(*designates official set)

K. Briefing Cases

The importance of cases in our common law system has already been discussed. You will also recall that in our legal system it is not sufficient to merely read a statute assuming that it will provide the answer to a question or problem because it is the task of our courts to interpret and construe statutory language. Thus, reading, interpreting, and analyzing cases are of critical importance to all involved in the legal profession.

Few people find it natural to read cases. The language used by courts is often archaic, and the style of writing can make it difficult to comprehend the court's reasoning. The most common technique used to impose some order or structure on the confusing world of case law is case briefing. Do not confuse the word "brief" in this context, in which it means a summary of the key elements of a case, with the written argument an attorney presents to a court, which is also called a "brief." A case brief is a short, written summary and analysis of a case.

Practice Tip

Finding Authorities

Be a smart researcher. When you read cases, be alert to references to other cases and legal authorities cited in the opinion. These may help you in your research tasks.

It is extremely common for law students to brief cases so in the event they are called upon in class to discuss a case, they will have a convenient summary to use. Moreover, practicing attorneys often desire to have cases briefed so they may save time by reading the briefs first and then, based upon the initial reading, analyze only selected cases in full. In some instances, months can go by between hearings in court, or new attorneys and paralegals may join the legal team. The case briefs for a matter handled by the team should be sufficiently readable and useful that new team members can be immediately brought "up to speed" by reviewing the briefs.

Perhaps the primary reason for briefing cases, however, is to learn how to focus on the important parts of the case in order to obtain a thorough understanding of the case and its reasoning. While you may be tempted to view case briefing as busywork and may believe you can understand a case by simply reading it through, research has shown that people tend to read quickly and see words in groupings. Briefing a case will force you to slow down and concentrate on the critical aspects of the case.

Preparing a case brief requires you to tear the case apart and rebuild it in a structure that helps you and others understand it. Case briefing helps develop your analytical skills and forces you to focus on the critical parts of a court's opinion. In a sense, you are taking notes on the cases you read, and just as explaining a difficult concept to another helps you understand it better, preparing a case brief will help clarify your comprehension of the case. As discussed below, after you have mastered case briefing and thus trained yourself to analyze cases properly, you may be able to dispense with separately prepared written briefs and be able to brief cases by merely underlining or highlighting the key portions of cases.

The first briefs you prepare may be nearly as long as the case itself. This is because it takes practice to learn to recognize the essential elements of a case. Initially, every part of the case will seem critical to you. With time, however, you will develop skill at briefing and will be able to produce a concise summary of cases. Ideally, a case brief should be no more than one typed page, although longer and more complex cases may require a longer brief.

There is no one perfect form for a case brief. Some large law firms provide suggested formats. If no form is given to you, you should use a style that best suits you and helps you understand the case and its significance as a precedent for the research problem on which you are working. Read through a case at least once before you begin to brief it so you will have a general idea as to the nature of the issues involved and how the court resolved these issues. Resist the temptation to read only the headnotes or to skim the case. A close scrutiny of the case may reveal critical analysis likely to be overlooked in a cursory reading. See Figure 4-8 for some reading strategies.

It may take you several readings of a case to understand it thoroughly. You may need to take notes and prepare a diagram or flowchart showing the path the case followed in reaching this court and the relationship of the parties to each other.

Figure 4-8
Case Reading Strategies

Consider the following strategies to help you better understand the cases you read and to help prepare case briefs.

- During your first reading, just skim the headnotes and the case. Focus on who the parties are and what relief they wanted from the court. Ask, "What is the plaintiff's gripe?" and "What is the defendant's defense?"
- Figure out what happened at the court(s) below and then determine what this reviewing court's decision is. Knowing the court's decision in advance will help you make sense of the case when you read it more thoroughly.
- Look for clues. Watch for language in the court's opinion such as "It is critical to note that," "although we have previously held that," and other signals that what follows such expressions is key to the court's decision.
- Look up all Latin words and any words you don't understand.

Good case briefs share the following elements:

- They use complete sentences.
- They do not overquote from the opinion.
- They do not include unnecessary, distracting citations.
- They are brief, ideally one page in length.

The most common elements to be included in a case brief are the following:

1. *Name of case.*
2. *Citations.* All parallel citations should be included as well as the year of decision. These citations will enable you and others to retrieve the case later if you need to relocate it. Use correct citation form.
3. *Procedural history.* This is a brief summary of the holdings of any previous court(s) and usually includes the disposition of the case by this court. A procedural history describes how the case got to this court and how this court resolves the case. It will be significant whether the prior decision is a trial court decision or an appellate court decision. Consider briefly identifying the parties and stating the nature of the action, the relief they were seeking, or the defenses they raised. Then proceed to discuss what the court(s) below held and the final disposition by this reviewing court. In many instances, the procedural history or background can be summed up in one or two brief sentences.

   Example: The case was appealed by the defendant to the Florida Supreme Court after a jury verdict awarding monetary damages to the plaintiff employee for sexual harassment. The Florida Supreme Court affirmed the decision of the Florida District Court of Appeals.

4. *Statement of facts.* A case brief should include a concise summary of the facts of the case. You need not include all facts but rather only the significant facts relied on by the court in reaching its decision. Facts that affect the outcome of a case are called "relevant facts" or "material facts." Identify the parties by name and indicate whether a party is a plaintiff, defendant, and so forth. The facts are more readable if they are presented in a narrative rather than outline or "bullet" format. Discuss facts in the past tense. A chronological presentation of the facts is usually the most helpful to a reader. Thus, tell a story in plain English, giving enough facts that the issue the court is being called upon to decide is apparent from reading these facts. Although a chronological presentation is the most typical way facts are presented, if the facts have no temporal relationship to each other, consider grouping the facts by topic or by the claims or causes of action presented by the plaintiff. If certain facts are disputed, note such.

5. *Issue(s).* You must formulate the question(s) or issue(s) being decided by this court. Focus on what the parties asked the court to determine. In some instances, courts will specifically state the issues being addressed. In other instances, the issues are not expressly provided and you will have to formulate the issue being decided. Phrase the issue so that it has some relevance to the case at hand. Thus, rather than stating the issue in a broad fashion ("What is an assault?" or "Did the lower court err?"), state the issue so it incorporates some of the relevant facts of the case ("Does a conditional threat constitute an assault?"). Keep your issues or questions to one sentence in length.

   If you have trouble determining the issue, locate the rule the court announces and then convert this into question form.

Example of rule:	The goodwill of a celebrity is a marital asset that can be evaluated and distributed in a marriage dissolution.
Example of issue:	Is a celebrity's goodwill acquired during a marriage a property asset that can be evaluated and distributed in a proceeding dissolving the marriage?

   In any event, the issue should be phrased so that it can be answered "yes" or "no." If there are several issues, number each one and place each at the left margin. Do not number a single issue.
   There are three ways issues can be phrased: a direct question, the "whether" format, or the "under" format. A direct question might ask, "Is pointing an unloaded gun at a person an assault?" The "whether" format would phrase the same question as follows: "Whether pointing an unloaded gun at a person is an assault." The "under" format would result in the following phrasing: "Under California law, is pointing an unloaded gun at a person an assault?" Generally, any of these formats is acceptable, although some attorneys dislike the "whether" form of issue because it results in a fragment rather than a complete sentence.

6. *Answer(s)* or *Holding(s).* Provide an answer(s) to the question(s) being resolved by this court. Rather than merely stating "yes" or "no," phrase the answer in a complete sentence and incorporate some of the reasons for the answer. For example, if the issue is "Does a conditional threat constitute an assault?," rather than merely state "no," state, "A conditional threat does not constitute an assault because a condition negates a threat so the hearer is in no danger of present or immediate harm." If you have set forth three issues, you will need three separate answers. Each answer should be no more than two sentences in length. Strive for one-sentence answers. Do not include citations. A brief answer or holding such as "the court below did not err in distributing the value of a celebrity's goodwill" is not helpful to the reader. Each holding should directly respond to the issues you have phrased.

Example: Yes. All assets acquired during a marriage are subject to division. The goodwill earned by a celebrity is no different from any other asset acquired during a marriage.

4. *Reasoning*. The reasoning is the most important part of a brief. This is the section in which you discuss *why* the court reached the conclusions it did. Were prior cases relied upon? Did the court adopt a new rule of law? Is the decision limited to the facts of this particular case or is the decision broad enough to serve as binding precedent in similar but not identical cases? Did the court discuss any social policy that would be served by its decision? Fully discuss the reasons why the court reached its decision and the thought process by which it arrived at this decision. Make sure you apply the court's reasoning to the facts of your case. Re-read your issue(s) and answer(s) and then ensure that the reasoning is directly responsive to these and answers the *why* question. Citations may be included in this section but are often not necessary. Use your own words in summarizing and explaining the court's reasoning rather than overquoting from the case. This will help ensure that you understand the rationale for the court's decision. Many briefs include the authoring justice's name. Don't be concerned that there will be repetition in your case brief. As you have seen, the brief answer or holding nearly parrots the language of the issue. The same or similar language will reappear as part of your reasoning section. A case brief is not meant to be a thrilling work of literature. It is meant to help you develop your analytical skills and provide a convenient summary of a case.

5. *Holding*. Include the actual disposition of this case, such as "affirmed" or "reversed."

Practice Tip

Formulating Issues

To gain experience in formulating issues for case briefs and other court documents, review the briefs filed with the U.S. Supreme Court and examine the "Questions Presented." The Supreme Court requires all petitions for writs of certiorari and all principal briefs to set forth the questions the Court is asked to review. Review these questions to sharpen your skills at writing your own question and issue statements. The briefs may be accessed through the Supreme Court's Web site at http://www.supremecourtus.gov. Select "Docket" and then "Merit Briefs." Alternatively, the briefs may be accessed through FindLaw at http://supreme.lp.findlaw.com/supreme_court/briefs/index.html.

You may include an additional section in your brief summarizing concurring or dissenting opinions.

Following is a suggested format for a typical case brief:

United States v. Wellons
32 F.3d 117 (4th Cir. 1994)

Procedural History

Defendant Wellons was convicted in the U.S. District Court for the Southern District of West Virginia of various offenses related to the possession and intent to distribute heroin and cocaine, and he appealed, arguing that the search that revealed the narcotics violated his Fourth Amendment rights. The Fourth Circuit Court of Appeals affirmed.

Statement of Facts

Wellons and two others left Pennsylvania in a rental car. Wellons was not listed as an authorized driver on the rental agreement. After his companions left him, Wellons drove the car to return it to the rental agency. He was stopped by a state trooper for exceeding the speed limit. When Wellons could not find the rental agreement, the trooper contacted the rental agency, which confirmed that Wellons was not an authorized driver. The trooper also asked that another trooper with a drug-sniffing dog be sent to the scene. The trooper asked for permission to search the vehicle and Wellons declined. The dog then arrived on the scene and indicated the presence of narcotics. A subsequent warrantless search of the automobile and Wellon's luggage revealed cocaine and heroin.

Issue

May a defendant who is an unauthorized driver assert a right of privacy in a rented automobile such that a police search of the automobile violates his search and seizure rights under the Fourth Amendment?

Answer

No. One who is an unauthorized driver of a rental car has no legitimate privacy interest in the car, and thus a police search of the car does not violate the Fourth Amendment.

Reasoning

Only when a police search intrudes upon a space in which an individual has a legitimate expectation of privacy will the search violate that individual's Fourth Amendment rights. In this case, Wellons, as an unauthorized driver of the rented car, had no legitimate privacy interest in the car, and thus a police search did not violate his Constitutional rights. Even though a driver may have the renter's permission to drive the car, a person not listed as a valid driver on the rental agreement has no legitimate expectation of privacy, and thus a search of the vehicle cannot violate his Fourth Amendment rights. Wellons may have had the authorized renter's agreement to drive the car, but he did not have the permission of the rental agency that owned the car. Moreover, Wellons cannot assert an expectation of privacy in the luggage found in the automobile. A person who cannot assert a legitimate claim to a vehicle cannot reasonably expect that the vehicle is a private repository for his personal effects, whether or not they are enclosed in a container such as luggage.

Holding

The Fourth Circuit Court of Appeals affirmed the decision of the court below.

The preceding brief follows a very standard format. A more thorough and comprehensive brief would include the name of the author of the majority opinion, a reference to how many justices were in the majority and how many dissented (for example, 7-2), a summary of any dissenting and concurring opinions, a summary of each party's contentions and legal arguments, a discussion of social policies furthered by the decision, and a final section including your comments and criticism of the case. In most instances, such a thorough brief is not needed, and the format above should suffice for most purposes. See Figure 4-9 for a form for a case brief.

After you have gained experience in case briefing, you may be able to use a technique some experts have referred to as "Technicolor briefing" in which you use colored pens and highlighters to mark sections of cases as you read them. You will photocopy the cases you need to brief and annotate the critical sections in the margins. For example, use "PH" to mark the procedural history section of the case, "I" to designate the issue the court is deciding, and so forth. In law school, this technique is usually called "book briefing" because you brief the cases in your textbooks by these notes rather than preparing a separate brief.

Develop a system of abbreviations to help you mark and annotate the cases you read. See Figure 4-10 for a list of commonly used legal abbreviations.

Case Brief Assignment

Prepare a brief of the case *PepsiCo, Inc. v. Redmond*, 54 F.3d 1262 (7th Cir. 1995).

L. Citation Form

1. *Federal Cases (The Bluebook and ALWD)*

a. Cases from the United States Supreme Court:
    Roe v. Wade, 410 U.S. 113 (1973) (*ALWD* allows parallel citations).

Figure 4-9
Case Brief Form

Case Name: _____

Case Citation: _____

Procedural History: _____

_____

_____

_____

Statement of Facts: _____

_____

_____

_____

_____

Issues:

1. _____

2. _____

3. _____

Answers:

1. _____

2. _____

3. _____

Reasoning: _____

_____

_____

_____

Holding: _____

b. Cases from the United States Courts of Appeal:
    Traylor v. Cohen, 597 F.2d 109 (4th Cir. 1988).
c. Cases from the United States District Courts:
    Allen v. Carr, 686 F. Supp. 207 (W.D. Tex. 1980).

2. *State Cases (The Bluebook and ALWD)*

Local state rules often require citation to the official report followed by a parallel citation to a regional reporter, as follows:
    Baker v. Dolan, 281 S.C. 114, 204 S.E.2d 909 (1995).
    Both *The Bluebook* and *ALWD* require legal professionals to follow all applicable local rules. Unless local rules require parallel citations, under both *The Bluebook* and *ALWD*, the citation would include only West's regional reporter and not all parallel citations, as follows:
    Baker v. Dolan, 204 S.E.2d 909 (S.C. 1995).

Figure 4-10
Common Legal Abbreviations

Π	plaintiff
Δ	defendant
§	section
C	complaint
K	contract
x, x/c	cross, cross-complaint
app	appeal
atty	attorney
c/a	cause of action
cert	certiorari
dep	deposition, deponent
J, J'ment	judgment
JNOV	judgment notwithstanding the verdict
Re:	regarding
SJ	summary judgment
S/F	statute of frauds
S/L	statute of limitations
v., vs.	versus, as opposed to
w/	with
w/o	without

CyberSites

http://www.uscourts.gov	Federal Judiciary home page with links to federal courts and information about the federal court system.
http://www.supremecourtus.gov	The Web site of the United States Supreme Court provides information about the Court, its docket, Court rules, and access to its opinions.
http://www.loc.gov/law/guide	This site, called Guide to Law Online, provides access to cases from the United States Supreme Court, the Courts of Appeal, and the District Courts, as well as links for state cases.
http://www.gpoaccess.gov/index.html	GPO Access provides access to United States Supreme Court cases.
http://www.law.emory.edu/FEDCTS	The Federal Courts Finder provides a map of the United States. Click links to go to specific circuits.
http://www.law.cornell.edu	This site provides United States Supreme Court rulings since 1990 and 600 important Court cases prior to 1990. Cases from lower federal courts are also provided as are links to state court cases.
http://www.vls.law.vill.edu/locator/fedcourt.html	This site provides access to United States Supreme Court, United States Courts of Appeal, and United States District Court cases through the Villanova University School of Law.
http://www.washlaw.edu	Washburn Law School's site offers links to federal and state cases as well as links to numerous excellent law-related sites.
http://www.findlaw.com	FindLaw, one of the best known legal sites, provides easy access to federal and state cases as well as providing a wide variety of other law-related information and links to other sites.
http://www.lawschool.westlaw.com	Westlaw's site for law students offers a guide to briefing cases. Enter "briefing cases" in the search box.

Writing Strategies

In discussing cases, it is not enough to merely summarize or repeat the court's holding. You must *analyze* the case and show the reader why and how it applies to your situation.

By briefing cases, you will force yourself to concentrate on the critical elements of a case: its procedural background, the facts, the issues, the reasoning, and the holding. When you later discuss the case in a memo or court brief, you will be "pre-programmed" to analyze the case properly by virtue of the training you acquired by preparing case briefs.

In written projects, discuss cited cases in the past tense. Any discussion in a project in the present tense ("the Defendant argues," "a duty is owed," "the Plaintiff appeals") will be interpreted as referring to *your* case, not a cited case on which you are relying.

In discussing cases, you need not give all of the facts. Give sufficient facts, however, so a reader can see why the case is controlling. If the facts are strikingly similar to those in your case, recite them in greater detail to allow the reader immediately to grasp why the result reached in the cited case governs your case.

Confront cases that are contrary to your position head-on. Assume the adversary will locate these cases. You will minimize their impact if you discuss them yourself. Emphasize why such cases are not controlling by distinguishing them from your case. Show the reader that the facts and issues in such unfavorable cases are so different from those in your case that they cannot be relied upon.

Use "location" to minimize the impact of unfavorable cases. Discuss them briefly and only after you have set forth your strongest arguments. Discuss them in the middle of a project rather than at the beginning or end, where they will draw more attention.

Assignment for Chapter 4

1. Give the name of the case located at 667 N.W.2d 467 (Minn. Ct. App. 2003) and state what the case involves.
2. Use 39 P.3d. What case in this volume construes the meaning of "dwelling"?
3. Give the author of the opinion for the case located at 540 U.S. 544 (2004).
4. Use 710 N.E.2d. What case in this volume construes Mass. Gen. Laws ch. 272, § 17?
5. Locate the case at 846 A.2d 318 (D.C. 2004).
   a. Give the name of the case.
   b. What does headnote 7 discuss?
6. What is the name of the case located at 163 F.3d 238 (5th Cir. 1998)?
7. What is the name of the case located at 308 F. Supp. 798 (S.D.N.Y. 1970)?
8. What is the name of the case located at 679 F. Supp. 360, and which U.S. district court decided this case?
9. What is the name of the case located at 54 F.R.D. 282 (W.D. Pa. 1971), and briefly state the topic the case discusses.
10. In which National Reporter System series do the decisions of the following states appear?
    a. Kentucky
    b. Ohio
    c. Connecticut
11. Give the name of the case located at:
    a. 622 N.W.2d 1
    b. 272 S.E.2d 706
    c. 195 So. 248
12. Give the parallel citations for the case located at 116 S. Ct. 356.
13. Locate the case at 121 S. Ct. 447. How does page 39 of the parallel *United States Reports* begin?
14. Locate the case at 144 L. Ed. 2d 196. How does page 219 of the parallel *United States Reports* begin?
15. Use the *National Reporter Blue Book* (2005 Cum. Supp.) and give the parallel citations for the following cases.
    a. 252 Ga. Ct. App. 45
    b. 165 N.J. 205
    c. 167 Or. Ct. App. 1

State Your Answer

1. Use either *The Bluebook* or *ALWD* and identify the names of the sets of books that report case decisions from your state's courts.

2. Use either *The Bluebook* or *ALWD* and prepare the following citation (assume it is being cited in an internal office memorandum at your firm): *Anderson v. Diaz*, a case decided by your state's highest court in 2003 and reported in volume 709, at page 404 of the relevant reporter.

3. Access the site for the Center for Individual Freedom (http://www.centerforindividualfreedom.org) and select "Legal" and review the statistics for the 2003 term of the United States Supreme Court. What was the reversal rate (expressed as a percentage) for your circuit during the 2003 term?

4. Access the site MegaLaw at http://www.megalaw.com and select "State Law." Locate the site for your state's courts or judicial system and determine which court rules can be accessed through your state's site.

The Use of Digests, Annotated Law Reports, and *Words and Phrases*

Binding authority ... cannot be considered and cast aside; it is not merely evidence of what the law is. Rather, case law on point is the law.

Hart v. Massanari, 266 F.3d 1155, 1170 (9th Cir. 2001)

A. **Using Digests to Locate Cases**
B. *American Law Reports*
C. *Words and Phrases*
D. **Citation Form**

Chapter Overview

This chapter will complete the discussion of primary authorities (statutes, constitutions, and cases) by explaining the use of digests, which serve as comprehensive casefinders. Additionally, you will be introduced to annotated law reports, which can "speed up" the research process and provide you with an exhaustive overview of an area of the law. These annotated law reports combine elements of both primary and secondary sources and thus form a bridge between the primary sources of statutes, constitutions, and cases, which have been discussed, and the secondary authorities of encyclopedias, law reviews, treatises, and other sources, which follow. Finally, you will be provided with a discussion of *Words and Phrases*, a set of books created by West, which can be used to determine the legal meaning of certain words and phrases, and then direct you to primary authorities supporting those interpretations.

A.   Using Digests to Locate Cases

1.   *Introduction*

It is improbable that an individual with whom you work will simply hand you a list of citations and ask you to retrieve and photocopy the cases cited. It is far more likely that you will be presented with a description of a research problem and be tasked with determining the answer. For example, an attorney might describe a client's current problems with her landlord by posing the following scenario: The firm's client rented a house from her landlord. Two months later the client noticed the roof was leaking and notified the landlord repeatedly of this problem to no avail. A recent storm caused water to leak through the roof, causing $20,000 damage to the client's expensive furniture and rug. You may be asked to research whether the landlord is liable for the damage and whether the tenant may withhold rent from the landlord until the $20,000 damage amount is satisfied.

This common type of research assignment requires you to search for cases that are "on point," which will serve as precedents and provide an answer to the client's questions. Of course, if an area of the law is likely to be dealt with by statutes, you should remember to consult initially your annotated code to review the applicable statutes and then examine the annotations following the statutes, which will direct you to cases that interpret the statute.

You will recall that cases are usually published in chronological order. That is, there is no one set of books called *Landlord and Tenant Law* that will contain all cases dealing with landlords and tenants. Such cases are scattered throughout the numerous sets of books. For instance, each volume in the *Nevada Reports* may contain a few cases covering this particular subject matter. You cannot simply start with Volume 1 of the *Nevada Reports* or some other set of reports hoping to eventually stumble upon the right case. Such a research technique is not only inefficient and time-consuming, it may well be ineffective, as it is possible you could examine the more than 100 volumes of the *Nevada Reports* only to discover that Nevada has not yet considered this particular issue.

Legal research requires a much more systematic approach to locating pertinent cases, and this systematic approach is aided through the use of sets of books called "digests." While there are several varieties of digests, all of them function in a similar fashion: Digests assist you by arranging cases by subject matter so that all of the assault cases are brought together, all of the bribery cases are brought together, all of the contract cases are brought together, and so on. These digests, however, do not reprint in full all of the assault cases, but rather print a brief one-sentence summary or "digest" of each assault case and then provide you with a citation so you can determine which cases you should retrieve and examine in full. In this way, digests serve as guideposts, which help direct you to the specific cases you need so you can research as efficiently and effectively as possible. Because the digests are written by publishers (primarily West) and are mere summaries of cases, the digest entries cannot be quoted from or relied upon. The cases the digests direct you to, however, will serve as binding authority.

2.　*The* American Digest System

While there are different types of digests, the majority are published by West, which realized shortly after it introduced its *National Reporter System* that legal professionals needed a method of finding the cases published therein. The most comprehensive digest set published by West is the *American Digest System*, which will be described here in detail. Once you understand how to use the *American Digest System*, you will also understand how to use the other West digests because all digests are organized in substantially the same manner.

　　The *American Digest System* is an amazingly thorough set of books that aims at citing and digesting every reported case so you can readily locate *all* cases in a given area of law, such as corporations, trusts, negligence, or landlord-tenant law. In the *American Digest System*, West brings together all cases relating to a legal issue from *all* of the units of the *National Reporter System*. Thus, if you were researching the defenses to battery, you would be able to locate cases from the *Supreme Court Reporter, Federal Reporter, Federal Supplement, North Western Reporter, Pacific Reporter*, and others, all of which deal with defenses to battery. The *American Digest System* is therefore most useful when you have an extensive research project and you desire to know how several jurisdictions (both federal and state) have treated a specific legal topic.

　　West describes its combination of headnotes and topics and Key Numbers as part of the "greatest time-saving system ever invented to help [researchers] find cases worthy of further analysis."

3.　*Organization of the* American Digest System

To understand how to locate cases using West's *American Digest System*, it is necessary to understand how the System is organized. You will recall from Chapter 4 that when a decision is issued by a court, it consists of a case name, a docket number, a date of decision, names of counsel, and the opinion itself. West receives a copy of the case, scans or keyboards it on Westlaw, and assigns it to its editors. These editors are attorneys who thoroughly read the case and through a 26-step process, draft the brief synopsis (which appears after the case name and which concisely summarizes the case) and the headnotes for the case. If the case discusses seven areas of law, it will have seven headnotes. If the case discusses 12 areas of the law, it will have 12 headnotes. These headnotes are the brief paragraphs that precede the opinion of the court. Each headnote is given a consecutive number, a topic name (Insurance, Covenants, Deeds, Venue, for example) based on the area of law the headnote deals with, and a "Key Number" (a pictorial design of a key and a number). Thus, a typical headnote in a case published in any West set of court reports looks like the following:

7.   Gifts 🔑= 22
Constructive delivery is sufficient where donor's intention to make the gift plainly appears and the articles intended to be given are not present or, if present, are incapable of manual delivery.

Such a headnote is the seventh one in the case, its topic is "Gifts," and its Key Number is 22.

The case is now complete, consisting of the original elements as provided by the court and the additional features (synopsis and headnotes) provided by West's editors. The case will be printed in an advance sheet, which is mailed to agencies, judges, law firms, law libraries, and other subscribers. The headnotes alone, however, are taken by West and published in a monthly pamphlet called the *General Digest*. Last month's *General Digest*, therefore, contains *all* of the headnotes of *all* cases published by West in its *National Reporter System* (*North Western Reporter, Pacific Reporter, California Reporter, Federal Reporter*, and so on). The headnotes are arranged alphabetically by topic name such as Abandoned and Lost Property, Abatement and Revival, Abortion and Birth Control, and Absentees. Within each topic name, the headnotes are arranged by Key Number, such as Absentees 1, Absentees 2, and Absentees 3.

The monthly softcover issues of the *General Digest* are later brought together ("cumulated") and published in hardcover volumes. West then began bringing together and publishing the hardcover volumes of the *General Digest* in ten-year groups called "Decennials." The word "decennial" is literally defined as a ten-year period. Thus, the *First Decennial* contains all headnotes from all of the units of the *National Reporter System* for the period 1897-1906. The *Second Decennial* contains all headnotes from all of the units of the *National Reporter System* for the ten-year period 1906-1916. For obvious reasons, the *American Digest System* is sometimes called the *Decennial Digest System*.

You should be aware that West has also created a set of books called the *Century Digest* to cover the time period 1658 to 1897 (the date coverage of the *First Decennial* commences). The *Century Digest* uses a classification scheme different from the Key Number System used in the *Decennials*. It is unlikely you will use the *Century Digest* very often, if ever, as it digests cases that are very old. West does, however, provide crossreference tables in the *First* and *Second Decennial Digests* so you can readily locate cases in the *Century Digest* if you have a topic name and a Key Number. Figure 5-1 shows the time period covered by each of the *Decennials*.

As you can see, starting in 1976, West began issuing the *Decennials* in two five-year parts. This change was brought about by the explosion in

Figure 5-1

Century Digest	1658-1897
First Decennial	1897-1906
Second Decennial	1907-1916
Third Decennial	1916-1926
Fourth Decennial	1926-1936
Fifth Decennial	1936-1946
Sixth Decennial	1946-1956
Seventh Decennial	1956-1966
Eighth Decennial	1966-1976
Ninth Decennial, Part 1	1976-1981
Ninth Decennial, Part 2	1981-1986
Tenth Decennial, Part 1	1986-1991
Tenth Decennial, Part 2	1991-1996
Eleventh Decennial, Part 1	1996-2001
General Digest, 10th Series	2001-Date

case law. Thus, the *Tenth Decennial* covers a ten-year period but is issued in two parts — *Part 1*, which covers 1986-1991, and *Part 2*, which covers 1991-1996.

General Digest is the name of the set of books currently in use. As soon as the next five-year time period is completed, the name of the *General Digest, 10th Series*, will change to *Twelfth Decennial, Part 1*, and the current set will then be called the *General Digest, 11th Series*.

It is not necessary to memorize the time periods covered by each *Decennial* unit. It is sufficient to understand the general structure of the *Decennial* units: Each *Decennial* covers a ten-year period and each *Decennial* will contain all of the headnotes from all of the units of the *National Reporter System* for its particular ten-year period.

If you possess the headnote presented earlier relating to constructive delivery of gifts (**Gifts 22**), you can locate all American cases from 1658 until last month that relate to this specific subject matter. You can accomplish this task by taking the following actions:

- Locate the *Decennial* volumes for a recent time period such as the *Eleventh Decennial, Part 1*.
- Find the volume covering the letter "G" (for "Gifts").
- Look up "Gifts."
- Locate Gifts 22.

You will now be presented with all United States Supreme Court cases decided between 1996-2001 relating to constructive delivery of gifts, then all United States Court of Appeals cases relating to this subject, all United States District Court cases, all Alabama cases, all Alaska cases, all Arizona cases, and so on. Each case will be described with a one-sentence summary (the "digest") and you will be provided a case citation, enabling you to locate the case and read it in full if you determine the case may be helpful. The paragraph entries in the digest are basically the headnote paragraphs from the cases in West's reporters, now rearranged by subject matter.

After you have located cases in the *Eleventh Decennial, Part 1,* follow the same strategy for the *Tenth Decennial, Part 2,* the *Tenth Decennial, Part 1,* the *Ninth Decennial,* and so forth. In this way you will be able to find all cases decided in federal and state courts from 1658 (using the *Century Digest*) until last month (using the *General Digest, 10th Series*), which relate to constructive delivery of gifts.

4. *West's Digest Topics*

The fact that you can locate all cases on a similar point of law from 1658 until last month arises from West's remarkable consistency in assigning topic names and Key Numbers to legal issues. In order to efficiently and systematically organize cases under topic names and Key Numbers, West developed its own outline of the law. It should be noted that this outline of the law was developed exclusively by West for its own purposes. You may or may not agree with the organization scheme developed by West. You may believe additional topic names should exist. West's outline is not an official pronouncement of the subjects discussed in cases. It has no judicial or academic authority. It is simply West's organizational blueprint for its Key Number System, representing its decision that there are more than 400 topics of law that a case may discuss.

A complete list of West's digest topics is shown in Figure 5-2. The list is also found at the beginning of any West digest volume.

A case may discuss one of these more than 400 topics in a variety of ways. For example, cases may discuss infants in many different respects. The Key Numbers are assigned as follows: Each Key Number relates to the manner in which a point of law is discussed. This subtopic is represented by a number, the "key number." Thus, if a case relates to the prevention of cruelty to an infant, West will title the pertinent headnote **Infants 15**; if a case relates to the effect of marriage of an infant (in a legal sense, an "infant" is simply someone who has not yet attained the age of majority), West will title the pertinent headnote **Infants 10**; and if a case relates to emancipation of an infant by a parent, West will give the pertinent headnote the topic and Key Number **Infants 9**. Each topic name and Key Number combination thus represents a specific point of law and each provides links to other similar cases.

It is unnecessary to commit to memory the list of topic names; it is sufficient if you have a general understanding of West's System. It may be easiest to understand West's system if you imagine that West possesses an immense chart with all of the topics and Key Numbers listed on it. Every time a portion of *any* case in *any* unit of the *National Reporter System* discusses prevention of cruelty to infants, the headnote will be given the topic name "Infants" and the Key Number 15. The headnote will then be printed initially in the monthly pamphlet *General Digest* and will later be printed in the hardbound copies called *Decennials*. You will be able to locate other cases on this area of the law by taking this topic name

Figure 5-2
West's List of Digest Topics

The West Key Number System

ALPHABETICAL LIST OF DIGEST TOPICS

1	Abandoned and Lost Property	69	Cancellation of Instruments	131	District and Prosecuting Attorneys
2	Abatement and Revival	70	Carriers	132	District of Columbia
4	Abortion and Birth Control	71	Cemeteries	133	Disturbance of Public Assemblage
5	Absentees	72	Census		
6	Abstracts of Title	73	Certiorari	134	Divorce
7	Accession	74	Champerty and Maintenance	135	Domicile
8	Accord and Satisfaction			135h	Double Jeopardy
9	Account	75	Charities	136	Dower and Curtesy
10	Account, Action on	76	Chattel Mortgages	137	Drains
11	Account Stated	76a	Chemical Dependents	138	Drugs and Narcotics
11a	Accountants	76h	Children Out-of-Wedlock	141	Easements
12	Acknowledgment	77	Citizens	142	Ejectment
13	Action	78	Civil Rights	143	Election of Remedies
14	Action on the Case	79	Clerks of Courts	144	Elections
15	Adjoining Landowners	80	Clubs	145	Electricity
15a	Administrative Law and Procedure	81	Colleges and Universities	146	Embezzlement
		82	Collision	148	Eminent Domain
16	Admiralty	83	Commerce	148a	Employers' Liability
17	Adoption	83h	Commodity Futures Trading Regulation	149	Entry, Writ of
18	Adulteration			150	Equity
19	Adultery	84	Common Lands	151	Escape
20	Adverse Possession	85	Common Law	152	Escheat
21	Affidavits	88	Compounding Offenses	154	Estates in Property
23	Agriculture	89	Compromise and Settlement	156	Estoppel
24	Aliens			157	Evidence
25	Alterations of Instruments	89a	Condominium	158	Exceptions, Bill of
26	Ambassadors and Consuls	90	Confusion of Goods	159	Exchange of Property
27	Amicus Curiae	91	Conspiracy	160	Exchanges
28	Animals	92	Constitutional Law	161	Execution
29	Annuities	92b	Consumer Credit	162	Executors and Administrators
30	Appeal and Error	92h	Consumer Protection		
31	Appearance	93	Contempt	163	Exemptions
33	Arbitration	95	Contracts	164	Explosives
34	Armed Services	96	Contribution	165	Extortion and Threats
35	Arrest	97	Conversion	166	Extradition and Detainers
36	Arson	98	Convicts	167	Factors
37	Assault and Battery	99	Copyrights and Intellectual Property	168	False Imprisonment
38	Assignments			169	False Personation
40	Assistance, Writ of	100	Coroners	170	False Pretenses
41	Associations	101	Corporations	170a	Federal Civil Procedure
42	Assumpsit, Action of	102	Costs	170b	Federal Courts
43	Asylums	103	Counterfeiting	171	Fences
44	Attachment	104	Counties	172	Ferries
45	Attorney and Client	105	Court Commissioners	174	Fines
46	Attorney General	106	Courts (see also Topic 170b Federal Courts)	175	Fires
47	Auctions and Auctioneers			176	Fish
48	Audita Querela	107	Covenant, Action of	177	Fixtures
48a	Automobiles	108	Covenants	178	Food
48b	Aviation	108a	Credit Reporting Agencies	179	Forcible Entry and Detainer
49	Bail	110	Criminal Law	180	Forfeitures
50	Bailment	111	Crops	181	Forgery
51	Bankruptcy	113	Customs and Usages	183	Franchises
52	Banks and Banking	114	Customs Duties	184	Fraud
54	Beneficial Associations	115	Damages	185	Frauds, Statute of
55	Bigamy	116	Dead Bodies	186	Fraudulent Conveyances
56	Bills and Notes	117	Death	187	Game
58	Bonds	117g	Debt, Action of	188	Gaming
59	Boundaries	117t	Debtor and Creditor	189	Garnishment
60	Bounties	118a	Declaratory Judgment	190	Gas
61	Breach of Marriage Promise	119	Dedication	191	Gifts
62	Breach of the Peace	120	Deeds	192	Good Will
63	Bribery	122a	Deposits and Escrows	193	Grand Jury
64	Bridges	123	Deposits in Court	195	Guaranty
65	Brokers	124	Descent and Distribution	196	Guardian and Ward
66	Building and Loan Associations	125	Detectives	197	Habeas Corpus
		126	Detinue	198	Hawkers and Peddlers
67	Burglary	129	Disorderly Conduct	199	Health and Environment
68	Canals	130	Disorderly House	200	Highways

161

Figure 5-2 *(Continued)*

201 Holidays	256 Mayhem	313a Products Liability	360 States
202 Homestead	257 Mechanics' Liens	314 Prohibition	361 Statutes
203 Homicide	257a Mental Health	315 Property	362 Steam
204 Hospitals	258a Military Justice	316 Prostitution	363 Stipulations
205 Husband and Wife	259 Militia	316a Public Contracts	365 Submission of Controversy
205h Implied and Constructive Contracts	260 Mines and Minerals	317 Public Lands	366 Subrogation
206 Improvements	265 Monopolies	317a Public Utilities	367 Subscriptions
207 Incest	266 Mortgages	318 Quieting Title	368 Suicide
208 Indemnity	267 Motions	319 Quo Warranto	369 Sunday
209 Indians	268 Municipal Corporations	319h Racketeer Influenced and Corrupt Organizations	370 Supersedeas
210 Indictment and Information	269 Names	320 Railroads	371 Taxation
211 Infants	270 Navigable Waters	321 Rape	372 Telecommunications
212 Injunction	271 Ne Exeat	322 Real Actions	373 Tenancy in Common
213 Innkeepers	272 Negligence	323 Receivers	374 Tender
216 Inspection	273 Neutrality Laws	324 Receiving Stolen Goods	376 Territories
217 Insurance	274 Newspapers	325 Recognizances	376 Theaters and Shows
218 Insurrection and Sedition	275 New Trial	326 Records	378 Time
219 Interest	276 Notaries	327 Reference	380 Towage
220 Internal Revenue	277 Notice	328 Reformation of Instruments	381 Towns
221 International Law	278 Novation	330 Registers of Deeds	382 Trade Regulation
222 Interpleader	279 Nuisance	331 Release	384 Treason
223 Intoxicating Liquors	280 Oath	332 Religious Societies	385 Treaties
224 Joint Adventures	281 Obscenity	333 Remainders	386 Trespass
225 Joint-Stock Companies and Business Trusts	282 Obstructing Justice	334 Removal of Cases	387 Trespass to Try Title
226 Joint Tenancy	283 Officers and Public Employees	335 Replevin	388 Trial
227 Judges	284 Pardon and Parole	336 Reports	389 Trover and Conversion
228 Judgment	285 Parent and Child	337 Rescue	390 Trusts
229 Judicial Sales	286 Parliamentary Law	338 Reversions	391 Turnpikes and Toll Roads
230 Jury	287 Parties	339 Review	392 Undertakings
231 Justices of the Peace	288 Partition	340 Rewards	393 United States
232 Kidnapping	289 Partnership	341 Riot	394 United States Magistrates
232a Labor Relations	290 Party Walls	342 Robbery	395 United States Marshals
233 Landlord and Tenant	291 Patents	343 Sales	396 Unlawful Assembly
234 Larceny	292 Paupers	344 Salvage	396a Urban Railroads
235 Levees and Flood Control	294 Payment	345 Schools	398 Usury
236 Lewdness	295 Penalties	346 Scire Facias	399 Vagrancy
237 Libel and Slander	296 Pensions	347 Seals	400 Vendor and Purchaser
238 Licenses	297 Perjury	348 Seamen	401 Venue
239 Liens	298 Perpetuities	349 Searches and Seizures	402 War and National Emergency
240 Life Estates	299 Physicians and Surgeons	349a Secured Transactions	403 Warehousemen
241 Limitation of Actions	300 Pilots	349b Securities Regulation	404 Waste
242 Lis Pendens	302 Pleading	350 Seduction	405 Waters and Water Courses
245 Logs and Logging	303 Pledges	351 Sequestration	406 Weapons
246 Lost Instruments	304 Poisons	352 Set-Off and Counterclaim	407 Weights and Measures
247 Lotteries	305 Possessory Warrant	353 Sheriffs and Constables	408 Wharves
248 Malicious Mischief	306 Postal Service	354 Shipping	409 Wills
249 Malicious Prosecution	307 Powers	355 Signatures	410 Witnesses
250 Mandamus	307a Pretrial Procedure	356 Slaves	411 Woods and Forests
251 Manufactures	308 Principal and Agent	356a Social Security and Public Welfare	413 Workers' Compensation
252 Maritime Liens	309 Principal and Surety	357 Sodomy	414 Zoning and Planning
253 Marriage	310 Prisons	358 Specific Performance	450 Merit Systems Protection (Merit Systems Protection Board Reporter)
255 Master and Servant	311 Private Roads	359 Spendthrifts	
	313 Process		

and Key Number (**Infants 15**) and inserting it into the various *Decennial* units. You will then be directed to other cases, both federal and state, that discuss this issue and that were decided within the relevant ten-year periods. According to West, "the beauty of the ... System is that the key number assigned to a point of law is uniform throughout all of West's digests."

You may have noticed that some of the Key Numbers have been subdivided, such as **Criminal Law 1169.1(5)**. This occurs as an area of the law expands and novel theories are developed. West will categorize its Key Numbers, such as **Criminal Law 1169**, into subdivisions to reflect the varying and developing ways in which this topic is discussed by courts, as shown by the following list:

Criminal Law 1169	Admission of evidence
Criminal Law 1169.1	Admission of evidence in general
Criminal Law 1169.1(5)	Admission of evidence relating to arrest and identification

Similarly, as new causes of action or new defenses arise, West will add new topics, such as "Racketeer-Influenced and Corrupt Organizations," "Abortion and Birth Control, and "Franchises." In this way, West keeps current with case law as it expands and develops. Finally, some headnotes have more than one key number because they relate to more than one legal topic. At present, there are more than 100,000 individual key numbers.

5. *Locating a Topic and Key Number*

Until now, we have assumed that you knew a topic name and Key Number and inserted it into the various *Decennial* units to locate cases. We will now assume that you are starting your research project from "square one" and that the only information you have is the description of the research problem, for example, the landlord-tenant issue described in the beginning of this chapter. There are three strategies you can use to obtain a topic and Key Number that you can use to locate on-point cases.

a. **Descriptive Word Approach**

Each of the *Decennial* units includes a volume (or volumes) titled "Descriptive Word Index." West has selected certain words and phrases and listed these alphabetically in its Descriptive Word Indexes. You use these indexes exactly as you do the indexes for U.S.C.A. and U.S.C.S. as described in Chapter 3. That is, you simply brainstorm by thinking of words and phrases that describe the problem you are researching, such as landlord, tenant, or lease. Remember to consider the Who, Where, When, Why, and How questions discussed in Chapter 3 to assist you in developing a list of descriptive words or phrases. Look up these words in any Descriptive Word Index and you will be provided with a topic and Key Number just as you were given a title and section when you located statutes in U.S.C.A. or U.S.C.S.

If you have difficulty thinking of words to use, think of synonyms (renter), antonyms (owner), defenses a party might assert (consent, waiver), the type of relief a party might seek (injunctive relief, damages, rescission of the lease), or the cause of action a plaintiff might plead (breach of contract, negligence). These should assist you in thinking of words to look up in the index. Just as you have seen with the indexes for U.S.C.A. and U.S.C.S., the Descriptive Word Indexes in the *American Digest System* are very "forgiving." Many topics are indexed under more than one entry, making it easy for you to locate the all-important topic name and Key Number.

When attempting to locate a topic name and a Key Number by using this Descriptive Word Index method, you should use the Descriptive Word Index to one of the newer *Decennial* units such as the *Eleventh Decennial Digest, Part 1*. If you cannot locate a topic name and a Key Number in the *Eleventh Decennial Digest, Part 1*, try the *Tenth Decennial (Parts 1 and 2)* as it is possible that no cases discussed this particular legal issue during 1996-2001, the time period covered by the *Eleventh Decennial Digest, Part 1*. You could also use one of the Descriptive Word Indexes for the *General Digest*. There is a cumulative Descriptive Word Index in every tenth volume of the *General Digest*.

The Descriptive Word method is the easiest and most reliable way of locating a topic name and a Key Number, and this should be the approach you use until you have become thoroughly familiar with West's *Key Number System*. In fact, West advises that this method of search will generally prove most useful and should always be used first unless the researcher knows the specific topic. See Figure 5-3 for a sample page from the Descriptive Word Index to the *Ninth Decennial Digest, Part 2*, which demonstrates how to locate a topic name and a Key Number through the Descriptive Word approach.

b.   Topic Approach

You may recall that in locating statutes, the topic approach calls for you to bypass the general index at the end of a set of statutes and go directly to the appropriate title and begin examining the statutes. The topic approach to locating a topic name and a Key Number is exactly the same. Thus, if you were using the topic approach for the landlord-tenant problem described herein, you would bypass the Descriptive Word Index and go immediately to the "L" volume of a *Decennial* unit such as the *Eleventh Decennial Digest, Part 1*, and look up the phrase "Landlord and Tenant." Prior to the digest listing of the headnotes (**Landlord and Tenant 1, Landlord and Tenant 2**, and so on) you will be given an overview of the coverage of this topic, Landlord and Tenant, much like a book's table of contents. All of the Key Numbers digested under **Landlord and Tenant** will be described in an index or outline fashion, and you may then scan the entries to determine the appropriate Key Number and proceed to look up and examine the headnotes listed or digested under **Landlord and Tenant**.

Figure 5-3
Sample Page from Descriptive Word Index

LANDLORD = Guide Word

LANDLORD AND TENANT—Cont'd
GUIDE dogs, waiver of pet restriction inapplicable to dog neither trained nor used as guide dog. **Land & Ten 134(1)**
HABITABILITY. **Land & Ten 125**
Implied warranty—
Coextensive with Residential Rental Agreements Act. **Land & Ten 125(1)**
HEALTH regulations, see this index **Health and Environment**
HEAT, see this index **Heat**
HEAT violation, notice as condition precedent to prosecution. **Health & E 39**
HOLDING over—
Damages—
Landlord's proper measure of damages for tenant's willful holdover. **Land & Ten 144**
Estoppel, effect on. **Land & Ten 62(4)**
Extension by. **Land & Ten 90**
Month to month tenancy. **Land & Ten 115(3)**
Renewal by. **Land & Ten 90**
Rent, amount while holding over. **Land & Ten 200.9**
Sufficiency to create new tenancy. **Land & Ten 90(4)**
Tenancy at sufferance, creation by. **Land & Ten 119(2)**
Tenancy at will, creation by. **Land & Ten 118(4)**
Year-to-year tenancy. **Land & Ten 114(3)**
HOMESTEAD, see this index **Homestead**
HOMICIDE conviction arising from death of tenant's guest—
Due process guarantees. **Const Law 258(3)**
HOTELS—
Duties owed to renter's patrons—
Providing guard for coat rack. **Inn 11(3)**
HUNTING rights. **Land & Ten 134(3)**
HUSBAND and wife—
Lease of community property. **Hus & W 267(3)**
Administration of community. **Hus & W 276(6)**
Separate property of wife, see this index **Separate Estate of Wife**
ICE and snow—
Generally, see this index **Ice and Snow**
ILLUSORY tenancy—
Effect—
Protecting against speculative profiteering by tenants of rent controlled apartment. **Land & Ten 278.4(6)**
Summary proceedings to dispossess, right to maintain. **Land & Ten 298(1)**
ILLUSORY tenants—
Entering into sublease in order to evade rent stabilization requirements. **Land & Ten 200.16**
IMPLIED contracts, see this index **Implied Contracts**
IMPLIED covenants. **Land & Ten 45**
IMPLIED tenancy, see this index **Implied Tenancy**
IMPROVEMENTS. **Land & Ten 150–161**
Actions. **Land & Ten 159**
Claims for. **Land & Ten 223(7)**

LANDLORD AND TENANT—Cont'd
IMPROVEMENTS—Cont'd
Compensation. **Land & Ten 157(6–8)**
Damages for failure to make. **Land & Ten 223(6)**
Lien. **Land & Ten 157(10)**
Ownership in general. **Land & Ten 157(2)**
Reimbursing tenant for repair of boiler made at request of tenant. **Impl & C C 40**
Remedy for failure to make. **Land & Ten 159**
Removal. **Land & Ten 157(4)**
INCOME tax, see this index **Income Tax**
INCUMBRANCES. **Land & Ten 145–149**
Reasonable rent, incumbrances as factor in determining. **Land & Ten 200.25**
INDEMNITY against liability for negligence. **Indem 8.1(2)**
INDORSEMENT, extension or renewal on lease. **Land & Ten 89**
INFANT'S property, lease of. **Infants 44**
INJUNCTION—
Assessing tenants nonrefundable rental fees. **Inj 136(2)**
Communication by tenant by signs or notices—
Free speech. **Const Law 90.1(1)**
Covenants as to use of leased premises. **Inj 62(2)**
Disturbance of possession of tenant. **Land & Ten 132(2)**
Preliminary injunction, tenant's consent to sale of building's air rights. **Inj 136(2)**
Summary proceedings. **Land & Ten 299**
Unlawful detainer, action for. **Land & Ten 290½**
Violation of laws relating to suspension of right of reentry and recovery of possession by landlord. **Land & Ten 278.16**
Land & Ten 55(4)
INJURIES—
Land & Ten 139(4)
Dangerous or defective condition. **Land & Ten 162–170**
Mobile home parks, see this index **Trailer Parks or Camps**
Employees of tenant. **Land & Ten 165, 169(5)**
Patrons of lessee—
Liability of lessee. **Land & Ten 167(8)**
Premises. **Land & Ten 140–142**
Eviction. **Land & Ten 176**
Property of tenant. **Land & Ten 166**
trance of trespassers and vandals. **Land & Ten 166(6)**
Property of third persons. **Land & Ten 167(9)**
Reversion. **Land & Ten 55**
Scalding of cleaning woman when steam pipe burst—
Liability of tenant. **Land & Ten 167(2)**
Tenants or occupants. **Land & Ten 164**
INNKEEPERS—
See this index **Innkeepers**

LANDLORD AND TENANT—Cont'd
INNKEEPERS—Cont'd
Membership in metropolitan hotel industry stabilization association. **Inn 2**
INSANE persons, see this index **Mental Health**
INSOLVENCY, termination of lease. **Land & Ten 101½**
INSURANCE—
Covenants to insure. **Land & Ten 156**
Insurable interest. **Insurance 115(4)**
Landlord's liability insurance—
Risks and causes of loss. **Insurance 435.34**
Nature and cause of injury or damage. **Insurance 435.35**
Lessee's good-faith efforts to obtain—
Preventing cancellation of lease. **Land & Ten 103(1)**
Right to proceeds. **Insurance 580(4)**
INTLRFERENCE with—
Possession of tenant. **Land & Ten 131–133**
Relationship. **Land & Ten 19**
Use of premises. **Land & Ten 134(4), 172(2)**
INTERVENTION, see this index **Intervention**
INTOXICATING liquors, see this index **Intoxicating Liquors**
INTRUDER—
Lessor's liability for lessee's injuries inflicted by. **Land & Ten 164(1)**
INVALIDITY as affecting action for unlawful detainer. **Land & Ten 290(4)**
JOINT tenants, implied tenancy between. **Land & Ten 8**
JUDGMENT—
Conclusiveness. **Judgm 684**
Recovery of possession, action for. **Land & Ten 285(6)**
Summary proceedings for possession, post
Unlawful detainer, action for. **Land & Ten 291(17)**
JURISDICTION, see this index **Jurisdiction**
Justices of the Peace
KEY to leased premises, see this index **Keys**
KNOWLEDGE of defects affecting liability for injuries. **Land & Ten 164(6, 7), 165, 166(10)**
LACHES, affecting rescission of lease. **Land & Ten 34(4)**
LANDLORD'S title, estoppel dependent on. **Land & Ten 62(2)**
LARCENY of property from landlord or tenant, see this index **Larceny**
LEASES. **Land & Ten 20–49**
Bankruptcy proceedings. **Bankr 3086–3088**
Farm lease. **Land & Ten 322**
Female tenant's right to possession of apartment though not married to signing tenant—
Civil R 11.5
Land & Ten 43
Nonassignment clauses—
Restraints on alienation, policy against. **Perp 6(17)**
Protection leases—
Nature of. **Mines 56**

Subtopic Heading

Topic Name and Key Number

To select topics, you can review an alphabetical list of the more than 400 digest topics that appears in the front of any West Digest volume.

Just as the topic method should be used with caution to find statutes, it should be used with caution to locate topic names and Key Numbers because you may miss other topics and Key Numbers under which this area of the law may be digested. Because West's *American Digest System* has more than 400 topics, this method should be used only after you have become thoroughly familiar with West's Key Number classification system. Each topic discussion begins with an overview of its coverage as well as an identification of subjects included and subjects excluded, which will help ensure you are searching within the correct topic. See Figure 5-4 for a sample page from the *Ninth Decennial Digest, Part 2*, showing a partial list of Key Numbers within the topic Landlord and Tenant. Once again, you can see that if you need to review cases relating to damage to a tenant's property, West has organized these under the topic name "Landlord & Tenant" and the Key Number 166.

c. Table of Cases Approach

If you know the name of a case, you can look it up in an alphabetically arranged master Table of Cases, which will provide you with the citations to the case (although not in *Bluebook* or *ALWD* form) and a list of the topics and Key Numbers under which it has been classified. For example, if you have the name of the case *DeGracia v. Huntingdon Associates, Ltd.*, and you know it was decided between 1981 and 1986, you can use the Table of Cases in the *Ninth Decennial Digest, Part 2* (which covers the time period 1981-1986). When you look up this case, you will be given all citations to the case, the history of the case (whether it has been affirmed or reversed), and all of the topics and Key Numbers under which it is digested or classified. See Figure 5-5.

Each *Decennial* unit and each volume of the *General Digest* contains its own Table of Cases listed alphabetically by plaintiff. The Table of Cases is usually located after the last volume in a *Decennial* set. Some of West's digests contain an additional Table of Cases, the Defendant-Plaintiff Table, so if you know only the name of a defendant, you can determine the exact case name and parallel citations (although you will not be given topic names and key numbers). This may be useful if you wish to locate other cases involving a certain defendant.

d. "Case on Point" Approach

If you have already located a case on point, its headnotes will display applicable topic names and Key Numbers. If one of these headnotes is relevant to your research, you can then use that headnote to locate other similar cases by inserting your topic name and Key Number into the various units of the *Decennial Digest System*. For example, review pages 111–113 of this text, where the case *State v. Boyd*, 595 S.E.2d 697 (N.C. Ct. App. 2004), appears. Note headnote number 3. given the topic name **Sentencing and Punishment** and the Key Number **98**. If you read the *Coughlin* case and determine that this section of the case relating to damages is

Figure 5-4
Sample Page from *Ninth Decennial Digest, Part 2*

LANDLORD & TENANT ◄ Topic name

VII. PREMISES, AND ENJOYMENT AND USE THEREOF.—Cont'd

(D) REPAIRS, INSURANCE, AND IMPROVEMENTS.

◄150. Right and duty to make repairs in general.
    (1). In general.
    (2). Duty to rebuild on destruction of property.
    (3). Landlord's right of entry to make repairs.
    (4). Rights of subtenants.
    (5). Right of tenant to repair at landlord's cost.
151. Statutory provisions.
152. Covenants and agreements as to repairs and alterations.
    (1). In general.
    (2). Consideration for agreement.
    (3). Construction and operation of covenants in general.
    (4). Nature of repairs included in covenant or agreement.
    (5). Duty to rebuild on destruction of property.
    (6). Right of landlord to notice that repairs are necessary.
    (7). Agreement by landlord to pay for repairs.
    (8). Rights and liabilities of assignees and subtenants.
    (9). Waiver of claims under or stipulations in covenant or agreement.
    (10). Right of tenant to repair and recover cost.
    (11). Alterations by tenant.
153. Mode of making repairs.
154. Remedies for failure to make repairs and alterations.
    (1). Nature and form of remedy.
    (2). Right of action and defenses.
    (3). Pleading and evidence.
    (4). Damages.
    (5). Trial.
155. Maintenance of boundaries and fences.
156. Covenants and agreements as to insurance.
157. Improvements by tenant and covenants therefor.
    (1). Covenant by lessee to make improvements.
    (2). Ownership of improvements in general.
    (4). Right to remove and agreements for removal of improvements.
    (5). Forfeiture or waiver of right to remove improvements.
    (6). Right to compensation in general.
    (7). Covenants and agreements to pay for improvements.
    (8). Liabilities of successors of lessor.
    (9). Mode of termination of tenancy as affecting right to compensation.
    (10). Lien for value of improvements.
    (11). Determination of compensation.
    (12). Actions for compensation.
158. Improvements by landlord and covenants therefor.
159. Remedies for failure to make improvements.
    (1). Actions for breach of tenant's covenant to make improvements.
    (2). Actions for breach of landlord's covenant to make improvements.
160. Condition of premises at termination of tenancy.
    (1). In general.
    (2). Covenants and agreements as to condition of premises on termination of tenancy.

    (3). Duty of tenant to rebuild or replace personal property.
    (4). Actions for breach of covenant.
161. Personal property on premises at termination of tenancy.
    (1). Rights and liabilities as to property on premises in general.
    (2). Care of property left on premises by outgoing tenant.
    (3). Actions to recover property or value.

(E) INJURIES FROM DANGEROUS OR DEFECTIVE CONDITION.

◄162. Nature and extent of landlord's duty to tenant.
163. Mutual duties of tenants of different portions of same premises.
164. Injuries to tenants or occupants.
    (1). Injuries due to defective or dangerous condition of premises in general.
    (2). Injuries due to failure to repair.
    (3). Injuries due to negligence in making repairs.
    (4). Injuries due to unlighted passageways.
    (5). Liability for injuries to subtenant.
    (6). Liability of landlord as dependent on knowledge of defects.
    (7). Notice to or knowledge of tenant as to defects.
165. Injuries to employé of tenant.
    (1). Injuries due to defective or dangerous condition of premises in general.
    (2). Injuries due to failure to repair.
    (3). Injuries due to unlighted passageway.
    (4). Liability of landlord as dependent on knowledge of defects.
    (5). Failure to guard dangerous places.
    (6). Operation or condition of elevators.
    (7). Notice to or knowledge of tenant as to de-

166. Injuries to property of tenant on premises.
    (1). Nature and extent of the duties of landlord and tenant respectively.
    (2). Injuries due to defective condition of premises in general.
    (3). Injuries due to failure to repair.
    (4). Injuries due to negligence in making repairs.
    (5). Injuries due to defective water pipes or drains.
    (6). Injuries due to negligent acts of landlord.
    (7). Injuries due to negligence of third persons in general.
    (9). Injuries due to negligence of cotenant.
    (10). Liability of landlord as dependent on knowledge or notice of defects.

Outline of topics and key numbers listed under "Landlord & Tenant"

    (1). Duties of landlord and tenant to third persons.
    (2). Injuries due to defective or dangerous condition of premises in general.
    (3). Injuries due to failure to repair.
    (4). Failure to light or guard dangerous places.
    (5). Injuries due to openings, defects, or obstructions in walks or streets.
    (6). Injuries caused by fall of snow or ice from roof.
    (7). Injuries due to the negligence of tenant.

Figure 5-5
Sample Page from Table of Cases to
Ninth Decennial Digest, Part 2

References are to Digest Topics and Key Numbers

DeFulmer, People ex rel., v. Scully, NYAD 2 Dept, 487 NYS2d 401, 110 AD2d 671. See People ex rel. DeFulmer v. Scully.

de Furgalski v. Siegel, DCIll, 618 FSupp 295.—Civil R 13.3(1), 13.4(1), 13.5(1), 13.10, 13.12(3); Courts 100(1); Equity 67, 72(1), 84; Fed Cts 425.

DeFusco v. Giorgio, RI, 440 A2d 727.—Judgm 90, 91, 344; Usury 104; Witn 198(2), 205.

DeGarcia v. I.N.S., CA9, 783 F2d 931. See Magallanes-Damian v. I.N.S.

DeGarmo v. State, TexCrApp, 691 SW2d 657, cert den 106 SCt 337, 474 US 973, 88 LEd2d 322.—Crim Law 409(5), 662.-65, 983, 986.2(2), 1134(1), 1144.13(6), 1213.8(1), 1213.8(8); Homic 253(1), 342.

DeGase v. DeGase, MoApp, 690 SW2d 485.—App & E 80(4), 1008.1(5), 1010.-1(6), 1012.1(1); Partners 328(3), 336(3).

De Gasperis v. De Gasperis, NYAD 2 Dept, 469 NYS2d 469, 98 AD2d 758.—Compromise 21.

DeGay v. State, TexApp-Beaumont, 711 SW2d 419, review gr.—Const Law 75; Crim Law 982.9(1).

DeGay v. State, TexApp 9 Dist, 663 SW2d 459.—Ind & Inf 166; Weap 17(4).

Degelos, Succession of, LaApp 4 Cir, 450 So2d 682.—Ex & Ad 92; Spec Perf 106(3).

Degelos, Succession of, LaApp 4 Cir, 446 So2d 412.—Des & Dist 109; Wills 11.

Degen v. General Coatings, Inc., TexApp 14 Dist, 705 SW2d 734.—Courts 81, 85(1); Pretrial Proc 587.

Degenaars v. Degenaars, NJSuperCh, 452 A2d 222, 186 NJSuper 233.—Divorce 87; Infants 18.

Degenaars Co. v. U.S., ClCt, 2 ClCt 482. —U S 70(21), 73(15), 74(11).

Degenaars Co. v. U.S., ClCt, 1 ClCt 129, 555 FSupp 403.—Fed Cts 1101.

Degener, In re Marriage of, IllApp 2 Dist, 75 IllDec 878, 458 NE2d 46, 119 IllApp3d 1079.—Divorce 72, 252.3(4).

Degeneres v. Burgess, LaApp 1 Cir, 486 So2d 769.—Contracts 108(1), 186(3), 205.15(3), 280(3), 322(4), 324(1); Damag 123, 188(1); Evid 445(1); Lim of Act 32(1); Neglig 1; Sales 391(3), 394; Subrog 30; Ven & Pur 3(1).

DeGenova v. Board of Review, Ohio App, 498 NE2d 287, 24 Ohio App3d 125, 24 OBR 196.—Social S 473.

DeGeorge v. First Bank and Trust Co., IllApp 5 Dist, 77 IllDec 238, 460 NE2d 97, 121 IllApp3d 658.—Venue 2, 8(2), 22(1).

DeGette v. Mine Co. Restaurant, Inc., CAColo, 751 F2d 1143.—Lim of Act 95(1).

De Gevulde Hoorn, Matter of, BkrtcyAla, 44 BR 23. See Childers, Matter of.

De Giacomo v. Regan, NYAD, 444 NYS2d 273, 84 AD2d 629.—Offic 101.-5(2).

Degideo v. Com., Unemployment Compensation Bd. of Review, PaCmwlth, 433 A2d 607, 61 PaCmwlth 263.—Social S 728.

DeGidio v. Perpich, DCMinn, 612 FSupp 1383.—Civil R 13.3(1), 13.7, 13.12(6); Fed Civ Proc 172, 181, 186.10; Fed Cts 255, 266, 267, 268, 269; Judgm 567.

DeGier v. Commissioner of Public Safety, MinnApp, 387 NW2d 908.—Autos 144.1(1); Const Law 262.

DeGirolamo v. U. S., DCNY, 518 FSupp 778.—Lim of Act 55(3), 95(1); U S 113, 125(6).

Degiman v. Degiman, SC, 281 SE2d 123, 276 SC 600.—Divorce 235, 240(2), 240(4), 286(3), 287.

Deglopper, In re, BkrtcyIdaho, 53 BR 95.—Bankr 396(5), 399(1); Home 80.

Degnan v. Executive Homes, Inc., Mont, 696 P2d 431.—Contracts 188.-5(1), 205.35(2), 205.40, 322(1); Torts 1.

Degnan v. Monetti, NJSuperAD, 509 A2d 277, 210 NJSuper 174.—Zoning 487, 489, 512, 610, 623, 709.

Degolyer Co., Inc. v. Standard & Poor's Corp., CATex, 672 F2d 433. See Municipal Bond Reporting Antitrust Litigation, In re.

DeGraaf v. General Motors Corp., MichApp, 352 NW2d 719, 135 MichApp 141, appeal den.—Prod Liab 96.5.

DeGrace v. Shelby Tp. Police and Fire Civil Service Com'n, MichApp, 389 NW2d 137, 150 MichApp 587.—Mand

DeGracia v. Huntingdon Associates, Ltd., GaApp, 336 SE2d 602, 176 GaApp 495.—Judgm 185(3), 185.3(14); Land & Ten 164(1).

phone Co., KanApp, 687 P2d 1380.—App & E 930(1), 931(1), 989, 994(1), 1001(1), 1010.1(6); Damag 50, 50.10; Neglig 136(14); Pub Ut 103; Tel 278, 284.

DeGraff, Matter of Compensation of, OrApp, 630 P2d 895, 52 OrApp 1023.—Work Comp 1545.

DeGraff v. Kaplan, IllApp, 65 IllDec 75, 440 NE2d 930, 109 IllApp3d 711.—App & E 984(5); Costs 173(1); Evid 455; Partners 81, 86, 121.

DeGraff's Estate, Matter of, MoApp, 637 SW2d 277.—Ex & Ad 218, 459, 495(3), 496(1), 501; Jury 19(7).

DeGraffenreid v. Curtwright, MoApp, 652 SW2d 310.—Judgm 334.

DeGraffenreid, State ex rel. v. Keet, MoApp, 619 SW2d 873. See State ex rel. DeGraffenreid v. Keet.

de Graffenried v. U.S., ClCt, 2 ClCt 640. —Fed Cts 1112; Pat 203, 292.1(2), 292.2, 328(2).

DeGrand v. Alton Tel. Printing Co., Inc., BkrtcyIll, 15 BR 367. See Alton Tel. Printing Co., Inc., In re.

Degree v. Degree, NCApp, 325 SE2d 36, 72 NCApp 668, review den 330 SE2d 607, 313 NC 598.—Hus & W 279(2), 281; Stip 3.

De Gregorio v. CBS, Inc., NYSup, 473 NYS2d 922, 123 Misc2d 491.—Const Law 90.1(8); Damag 50.10; Libel 6(1); Torts 1, 8.5(6), 8.5(8).

De Gregorio v. Pennsylvania Public Utility Com'n, PaCmwlth, 481 A2d 1241, 85 PaCmwlth 354.—Autos 87, 106; Pub Ut 194.

DeGrio v. American Federation of Government Employees, Fla, 484 So2d 1.—Courts 489(1); Labor 221.

DeGroat v. Ingles, CalApp 1 Dist, 191 CalRptr 761, 143 CA3d 399.—Judgm 181(2), 181(6), 183.

DeGroat v. New York State Higher Educ. Services Corp., NYAD, 456 NYS2d 159, 90 AD2d 616.—Lim of Act 66(11).

Degroot v. State, FlaApp 5 Dist, 489 So2d 1163, review den 496 So2d 142.—Crim Law 986.2(4), 1208.1(3).

DeGreff v. Bethlehem Cent. School Dist., NYAD, 460 NYS2d 630, 92 AD2d 702.—Mun Corp 741.1(8); Schools 112.

DeGroot v. American Legion Post No. 1247, IllApp 1 Dist, 86 IllDec 199, 475 NE2d 5, 130 IllApp3d 735. See Monsen v. DeGroot.

DeGroot v. Arizona Racing Com'n, ArizApp, 686 P2d 1301, 141 Ariz 331. —Admin Law 349, 360, 669, 754, 760, 763, 786, 791; Const Law 287.2(1), 318(1); Theaters 3.10.

DeGroot v. Employment Sec. Com'n, SCApp, 328 SE2d 668, 285 SC 209.—Admin Law 791; Const Law 278.7(3); Social S 584.5, 660.

DeGrow v. DeGrow, MichApp, 315 NW2d 915, 112 MichApp 260.—Divorce 303(6), 303(7); Infants 19.3(6); Parent & C 2(3.4).

De Gryse v. De Gryse, Ariz, 661 P2d 185, 135 Ariz 335.—App & E 982(2); Divorce 163, 165(2), 194, 252.3(4); Hus & W 279(2); Judgm 346.

Deguffroy & Associates, Inc. v. W.C. A.B. (Bianchetti), PaCmwlth, 503 A2d 994, 94 PaCmwlth 566.—Work Comp 504, 1981.

DeHart v. A.C. and S. Co., Inc., DelSuper, 484 A2d 521. See Sheppard v.

DeHart v. Aetna Life Ins. Co., Ohio, 431 NE2d 644, 69 Ohio St2d 189, 23 003d 210.—App & E 962, 1092; Courts 78, 85(1); Pretrial Proc 551.

DeHart v. Diversified Services, NYAD, 442 NYS2d 255, 83 AD2d 685.—Work Comp 1536, 1676, 1939.8.

DeHart v. Moore, DCFla, 424 FSupp 55.—Exchanges 11(11).

DeHart v. Ritenour Consolidated School Dist., MoApp, 663 SW2d 332.—Deeds 144(1); Quiet T 46; Schools 65.

DeHart v. R/S Financial Corp., NCApp, 337 SE2d 94, 78 NCApp 93, review den 342 SE2d 893.—App & E 263(1); Evid 267, 402; Judgm 199(1), 199(3.9); Pretrial Proc 44; Trial 139.1(5), 143, 178; Usury 117.

DeHart v. R/S Financial Corp., NCApp, 311 SE2d 694, 66 NCApp 648, appeal after remand 337 SE2d 94, 78 NCApp 93, review den 342 SE2d 893, 316 NC 376.—Plead 427; Trial 139.1(16), 168, 178; Usury 11, 119.

DeHart v. State, IndApp 3 Dist, 471 NE2d 312, reh den; transfer den.—Const Law 199; Crim Law 150; Health & E 25.5(5), 25.5(5.5), 37, 39, 41; Statut 190.

DeHart v. State, OrApp, 637 P2d 1311, 55 OrApp 254.—Const Law 268.1(6).

DeHart v. U.S., BkrtcyPa, 50 BR 685. See Metropolitan Metals, Inc., In re.

DeHaven v. Dan-Co FS Co-op, WisApp, 383 NW2d 509, 128 Wis2d 472.—Social S 241.

DeHaven v. DeHaven, La, 412 So2d 537. —App & E 185(1); Divorce 387; Hus & W 279(2); Parent & C 3.3(8); Ven & Pur 1.

DeHaven v. DeHaven, LaApp, 401 So2d 418, writ gr 406 So2d 624, rev 412 So2d 537.—App & E 185(1); Courts 37(2), 39, 472.1; Divorce 297, 311.5; Hus & W 279(2); Parent & C 3.1(8), 3.3(8).

DeHaven v. Gant, WashApp, 713 P2d 149, 42 WashApp 666, review den.—App & E 232(2), 241, 754(1); Evid 555.-10; Phys 18.80(8); Trial 388(3).

DeHaven v. Thomas D. Gant, M.D., P.S., WashApp, 713 P2d 149, 42 WashApp 666. See DeHaven v. Gant.

De Hay v. Town of West New York, NJSuperAD, 460 A2d 157, 189 NJSuper 340, certification den 468 A2d 227, 94 NJ 591.—Equity 72(1); Mun Corp 191, 220(8).

Note topics and key number under which case is digested

relevant to your research, you can take the topic name and Key Number **Sentencing and Punishment 98** and insert it into the various *Decennial* units to locate other similar cases.

6.   *Using Digests*

Once you have obtained a topic and a Key Number, such as **Landlord & Tenant 166(1)**, you merely insert this into the various units of the *American Digest System* and you will unlock the door to cases from 1658 until last month, all of which relate to injuries to a tenant's property.

Because the *Decennials* are arranged alphabetically, you simply retrieve the "L" volume in any of the *Decennial* units and look up **"Landlord & Tenant 166(1)."** At this point, West will do more than merely list the digest headnotes in a haphazard fashion. West has carefully arranged the entries, giving you federal cases, first from the highest federal court, the United States Supreme Court, through cases from the United States Courts of Appeal to the lowest federal courts, the United States District Courts. After all of the federal cases have been digested, you will be given the entries for state court cases. Again, West will impose order and list the states alphabetically, making it easy for you to quickly locate cases from Arkansas, Louisiana, Minnesota, and South Carolina. West's listing of cases from South Carolina will be in order of the South Carolina court hierarchy and then in reverse chronological order so you will proceed from the newer South Carolina Supreme Court cases to the older South Carolina Supreme Court cases and then from the newer South Carolina Appellate Court cases to the older South Carolina Appellate Court cases. See Figure 5-6 for a sample page from the *Ninth Decennial Digest, Part 2*, showing the organization of cases.

In inserting your topic and Key Number into the *Decennial* units, you should start with the most recent *Decennial* unit. If you cannot find the cases you need, proceed to the earlier *Decennial* units. You should never exclusively rely on the brief summaries or digests of the cases. While they are usually very clearly and concisely presented, you must read a case in full to really understand it. Similarly, you should *never* cite a digest as legal authority. Its sole function is to locate cases for you, not to serve as support for an assertion you make.

In your review of the various West publications and case reporters, you may have observed that there are diagrams or drawings of "keys" on the spines of many books in the law library. This diagram indicates the volume is a participant in West's Key Number System.

7.   *Other West Digests*

As you have seen, the *American Digest System* is the most comprehensive digest system, with its coverage of all federal and state cases. It is entirely likely, however, that you may not need such extensive coverage. In this regard, there are several specialized digests published by West that will

Figure 5-6
Sample Page from *Ninth Decennial Digest, Part 2,*
Showing Digests of Cases

⬤≈166. **Injuries to property of tenant on premises.**

Library references

C.J.S. Landlord and Tenant § 423 et seq.

⬤≈166(1). **Nature and extent of the duties of landlord and tenant respectively.**

Cal.App. 1 Dist. 1983. Where lessee of storage space was afforded option, by operator of space, of greater monthly payments under lease with insurance or of purchasing insurance elsewhere, and she was not subjected to an adhesive contract under which she had to accept exculpatory clause or forego lease, storage lease did not involve the public interest so as to render exculpatory clause in lease invalid under Civil Code section providing, inter alia, that all contracts which have as their object to exempt anyone from responsibility for his own fraud or willful injury to person or property of another are against policy of the law. West's Ann.Cal.Civ. Code § 1668.—Cregg v. Ministor Ventures, 196 Cal.Rptr. 724, 148 C.A.3d 1107.

Cal.Super. 1982. Apartment building owners and managers had no affirmative duty to secure parking facilities, which they never represented as being protected, merely because they had notice of previous instances of vandalism to parked cars and thus tenant could not recover from owners and managers for destruction by fire of tenant's automobile in building parking area.—Jubert v. Shalom Realty, 185 Cal.Rptr. 641, 135 C.A.3d Supp. 1.

D.C.App. 1983. Exculpatory clause in lease which purported to relieve landlord of liability for personal property damage caused by any source, including defective roofing and plumbing, was ineffective to bar recovery of damages from landlord inasmuch as clause amounted to waiver or modification of tenant's rights under implied warranty of habitability.—George Washington University v. Weintraub, 458 A.2d 43.

Kan. 1982. Landlord, having leased premises in their entirety to tenants, did not have control over portion of premises wherein fire started and had no duty to inspect same, and thus failure of landlord to inspect wiring and failure to discover and correct latent defect on premises could not, as a matter of law, constitute negligence.—Moore v. Muntzel, 642 P.2d 957, 231 Kan. 46.

There were no warranties flowing from landlord to tenants on which liability for fire damage could be predicated.—Id.

La.App. 4 Cir. 1982. Alleged failure of lessee to present evidence of negligence by ultimate building owner or lessor had no effect on her right to recover for loss of personal property destroyed in fire at apartment under statutes which base liability on status, either as owner or lessor, rather than on personal fault. LSA-C.C. arts. 2322, 2695.—Barnes v. Housing Authority of New Orleans, 423 So.2d 750.

Minn.App. 1984. Lease provision exculpating landlords from liability for water damage was not ambiguous, even though contract's reference to "premises" varyingly referred to entire building or to first floor and basement.—Fena v. Wickstrom, 348 N.W.2d 389.

N.Y.A.D. 1982. Where the tenant had notice that water would be turned off in building on a Friday and knew that water would be turned on before he reopened his shop on the following Monday, and where building owner did not have access to tenant's premises, tenant's responsibility to be particularly careful in closing all the faucets, and his failure to do so was proximate and sole cause of flooding.—Arthur Richards, Inc. v. 79 Fifth Ave. Co., 450 N.Y.S.2d 13, 88 A.D.2d 517, reversed 455 N.Y.S.2d 596, 57 N.Y.2d 824, 441 N.E.2d 1114.

Pa. 1986. Exculpatory clause in commercial lease agreement relieving lessor of liability for injury or damage to personal property in premises caused by fire in any part of building of which demised premises was a part, was valid and enforceable; the clause did not contravene any policy of the law, commercial lease related entirely to parties' own private affairs, there was no disparity in bargaining power between parties, and clause, as modified, spelled out intention of parties with particularity.—Princeton Sportswear Corp. v. H & M Associates, 507 A.2d 339, 510 Pa. 189, appeal after remand 517 A.2d 963, 358 Pa.Super. 325.

Pa.Super. 1984. Exculpatory clauses in lease were valid and enforceable where lease was commercial lease, there was no disparity in bargaining power between the parties, exculpatory clauses had been reviewed, negotiated and modified by both parties and their counsel, and clauses, as modified, evidenced clear and unambiguous intent to release landlords from liability for damages caused by fire when such fire was not the result of any negligence on landlords' part.—Princeton Sportswear Corp. v. H & M Associates, 484 A.2d 185, 335 Pa.Super. 381, reversed 507 A.2d 339, 510 Pa. 189, appeal after remand 517 A.2d 963, 358 Pa.Super. 325.

Landlords were not liable for damages tenant suffered as result of fire which damaged building's power center and thereby deprived tenant of heat, electricity and water, where under exculpatory clauses in lease, it was clear that landlords were not liable for any property damage caused by fire in any portion of the building of which demised premises was a part unless such fire was caused by landlords' negligence, power center constituted portion of building in which demised premises was a part, and lower court specifically found that landlords' conduct was not tortious.—Id.

⬤≈166(2). **Injuries due to defective condition of premises in general.**

C.A.La. 1983. Not every defect in leased premises will serve as a basis for a claim of damages against lessor under Louisiana law; instead, vices and defects must be substantial and of such nature as are likely to cause injury to a reasonably prudent individual. LSA-C.C. art. 2695.—Volkswagen of America, Inc. v. Robertson, 713 F.2d 1151.

D.C.App. 1983. While landlords clearly bear burden of maintaining rented premises in compliance with housing code provisions, liability is not imposed upon landlords for losses arising from all conditions that violate the code.—George Washington University v. Weintraub, 458 A.2d 43.

Fla.App. 1 Dist. 1984. Lessee's complaint, which alleged making of lease and lessor's covenant to keep the roof in good repair, the undertaking by lessor through services of a roofing contractor to keep the roof in good repair, a breach of that covenant by reason of the roof collapsing during course of repairs due either to defects in the structure or to overloading of the roof by the contractor, and resulting damages to lessee's property, was sufficient to state cause of action against lessor for breach of contract.—Cisu of Florida, Inc. for Use and Benefit of Aetna Cas. and Sur. Co. v. Porter, 457 So.2d 1118.

Ill.App. 1 Dist. 1985. Under common law, landlord is not liable for injury to property of tenant caused by defects in demised premises absent express warranty as to condition of premises or covenant to repair.—Wanland v. Beavers, 86 Ill.Dec. 130, 474 N.E.2d 1327, 130 Ill. App.3d 731.

Ill.App. 1982. Warranty of habitability implied in lease of building does not give rise to a cause of action for permanent injuries or property damage.—Auburn v. Amoco Oil Co., 61 Ill. Dec. 939, 435 N.E.2d 780, 106 Ill.App.3d 60.

La.App. 1 Cir. 1986. Lessee and its property insurer were not required to show negligence on the part of the lessor in order to recover damages resulting from a fire caused by a defect in the premises. LSA-C.C. arts. 2322, 2695.—Great American Surplus Lines Ins. Co. v. Bass, 486 So.2d 789, writ denied 489 So.2d 245.

Even if lessee assumed responsibility for the electricity, lessor was liable for damages resulting from the destruction of the lessee's property due to a fire caused by a defect in the building's electrical system where there was no proof of negligence on the part of the lessee and where the lessor knew or should have known of the defect. LSA-R.S. 9:3221.—Id.

La.App. 3 Cir. 1985. Under LSA-C.C. art. 2695, lessor is liable to lessee for any losses sustained as result of "vice and defects" in premises, provided they did not arise as result of lessee's fault.—Freeman v. Thomas, 472 So.2d 326.

La.App. 3 Cir. 1984. Mere fact that common wall between premises leased for jewelry store purposes and adjacent premises was constructed of sheetrock and thus susceptible to breach by burglars did not render the condition a "vice" under statute so as to render owner lessor liable to lessees for damages arising out of the burglary. LSA-C.C. arts. 2322, 2703.—Hall v. Park Dell Terrace Partnership, 452 So.2d 342.

La.App. 4 Cir. 1985. Tenant's allegation that security services provided by landlord were inadequate did not provide basis for landlord's liability for arson damage, where all security services promised in lease were provided.—U.S. Fidelity and Guar. Ins. Co. v. Burns Intern. Sec. Services, Inc., 468 So.2d 662, writ denied 470 So.2d 882.

Implied warranty of fitness for intended use and freedom from defects, applicable to leased office building, did not extend to fire damage caused by arson, in light of provisions in lease waiving landlord's liability for damage caused by fire or unauthorized persons.—Id.

La.App. 4 Cir. 1984. Clause in lease clearly and unambiguously transferred liability of lessor to lessee for damage caused by leaks in roof, and thus lessor and its managing partner could not be held liable to lessee for damage which occurred when roof of premises failed under the burden of a heavy rainstorm.—St. Paul Fire & Marine Ins. Co. v. French Eighth, 457 So.2d 35, writ denied 462 So.2d 195 and Oreck v. French Eighth, 462 So.2d 195, reconsideration not considered 462 So.2d 1240, two cases.

La.App. 4 Cir. 1983. Tenants of building destroyed by fire were entitled to recover damages from landlord, despite fact that defect in leased premises was alleged not to have been in building in which tenants leased premises, but within the building, owned by same landlord, next door to tenants' building, unless landlord could exculpate himself. LSA-C.C. arts. 2322, 2695.—Broome v. Gauthier, 443 So.2d 1127, writ denied 445 So.2d 449.

N.J.Super.A.D. 1982. Exculpatory clause in commercial lease which exempted landlord from liability for damage or injury resulting from carelessness or negligence or improper conduct of landlord or others, but did not exclude liability for damage flowing from defective design and construction of major structural aspects of building, did not immunize landlord from liability for water damage to tenant's computer equipment caused by defective design of roof.—Ultimate Computer Services, Inc. v. Biltmore Realty Co., Inc., 443 A.2d 723, 183 N.J.Super. 144, 30 A.L.R.4th 963.

Where exculpatory clause did not expressly exclude intention to exclude liability for injuries resulting from improper construction, landlord, in

For references to other topics, see Descriptive-Word Index

assist you in locating cases from a specific region, jurisdiction, or state, or covering a certain topic. The following digests are kept up to date by annual cumulative pocket parts.

a. *United States Supreme Court Digest*

This digest is published by West and classifies its headnotes according to the Key Number System. As its name indicates, this set provides brief summaries, or digests, only to United States Supreme Court cases. A Defendant-Plaintiff Table of Cases is included.

b. Federal Practice Digests

There are several West digests that serve as casefinders for cases from all federal courts — for example, the United States Supreme Court, the United States Courts of Appeal, and the United States District Courts. Each digest covers a specific time period, similar to the manner in which the *Decennials* each cover a ten-year period.

> *Federal Digest*: Federal Courts (1754-1938)
> *Modern Federal Practice Digest*: Federal Courts (1939-1961)
> *West's Federal Practice Digest 2d*: Federal Courts (1961-1975)
> *West's Federal Practice Digest 3d*: Federal Courts (1975-1987)
> *West's Federal Practice Digest 4th*: Federal Courts (1987-Date)

Thus, if you are interested only in recent cases from the Third Circuit, you could consult West's *Federal Practice Digest 4th* and West's *Federal Practice Digest 3d*. Cases are arranged in groups by court, circuits, and districts, making it easy for you to locate cases from the United States Supreme Court, cases from the Third Circuit, or cases from the United States District Court for the Eastern District of Pennsylvania. All of the *Federal Practice Digests* include a Defendent-Plaintiff Table of Cases.

c. Regional Digests

West has created regional digests for some of its regional geographic units.

> *Atlantic Digest* — digests cases reported in the *Atlantic Reporter*
> *North Western Digest* — digests cases reported in the *North Western Reporter*
> *Pacific Digest* — digests cases reported in the *Pacific Reporter*
> *South Eastern Digest* — digests cases reported in the *South Eastern Reporter*

Thus, if you were interested in locating cases from several neighboring states, you could consult the *North Western Digest*, which would assist you in finding cases from North Dakota, South Dakota, Nebraska, Minnesota, Iowa, Wisconsin, and Michigan. Again, the *Digest* will arrange the cases for you so that under **Criminal Law 1169.1(5)** all of the digest headnotes for Iowa cases are grouped together, all of the digest headnotes for North Dakota cases are grouped together, and all of the digest head-notes for Wisconsin cases are grouped together.

You will note there are no current digests for the *Southern Reporter, South Western Reporter,* and *North Eastern Reporter.* This should not be considered a drawback, however, as cases from states within these repor-ters are included within the all-inclusive *American Digest System* and also in their own respective state digests.

d. State Digests

West publishes digests for 47 of the states and the District of Columbia. Only Delaware, Nevada, and Utah do not have a digest. Additionally, Virginia and West Virginia are combined in one digest, as are North Dakota and South Dakota. Even though there is no separate digest for Delaware, Nevada, or Utah, you may locate cases from these states in the appropriate regional digest (*Atlantic Digest* or *Pacific Digest*) as well as in the comprehensive *Decennial* units, which arrange the digests or summaries of the cases alphabetically by state.

The state digests are all similarly named (*Alabama Digest, Missouri Digest, Tennessee Digest*), and each digest's cases from a particular state according to West's Key Number System. Moreover, these state digests include cases decided by the lower federal courts and the United States Supreme Court that arose in that state jurisdiction, that were appealed from that state, or that pertain to that state's law. The state digests also include a Defendant-Plaintiff Table of Cases.

There is overlap and duplication in the digest entries. For example, a digest entry for a 2000 California case will be located in the *California Digest,* the *Pacific Digest,* and the *Eleventh Decennial Digest, Part 1.* Which digest should you use? Generally, if your issue involves Califor-nia law, start with the *California Digest.* If you do not find helpful cases, perhaps because the issue is one of first impression in California, expand your search by using the *Pacific Digest* and then the *Decennial* units.

e. Specialized Digests

In addition to the digests for federal court cases, the regional digests, and the state digests, West publishes various specialized digests, each of which digests cases relating to a specific topic or from a particular court. The function of each specialized digest is fully described by its name. These specialized digests are as follows:

> *West's Bankruptcy Digest*
> *West's Military Justice Digest*
> *Federal Claims Digest*
> *West's Education Law Digest*
> *United States Merit System Protection Board Digest*
> *West's Veterans Appeals Digest*

———— Practice Tip ————

Digests

• Never quote from a digest. Always read and rely upon the cases to which a digest directs you.
• When researching, think small. Start with the smallest digest unit that will be helpful to you. For example, when researching Oregon law, start with the *Oregon Digest*. If it is not helpful, then review the *Pacific Digest* and the various Decennial units.

---

8. Common Features of West's Digests

a. Uniform Classification

All of West's digests are classified to West's uniform topic and *Key Number System*. Thus, once a legal issue is assigned the topic and Key Number **Landlord & Tenant 166(1)**, later cases that deal with this issue will also be digested under **Landlord & Tenant 166(1)**, whether they appear in a *Decennial* unit, *West's Federal Practice Digest 4th*, the *South Eastern Digest*, or the *Wyoming Digest*.

b. Descriptive Word Indexes

All of West's digests include Descriptive Word Indexes arranged in similar fashion that provide you with topic names and Key Numbers, which you then insert into the pertinent digest. The indexes use words describing facts, places, things, and legal principles from actual cases.

c. Table of Cases

All of the West digests contain a Table of Cases by plaintiff, so you may look up a case by the plaintiff's name and be provided with parallel citations, the topic names, and Key Numbers under which it has been digested, and the subsequent history of the case. Additionally, the *Ninth, Tenth,* and *Eleventh Decennial Digests*, the *United States Supreme Court Digest*, the *Federal Practice Digests*, the state digests, and the specialized digests also contain a Defendant-Plaintiff Table of Cases listing the defendant's name first, so if you know a case only by the defendant's name, you will still be able to locate the case. These tables are usually located after the last volumes in a set.

d. Table of Words and Phrases

Many of the digests (the *United States Supreme Court Digest*, the *Federal Practice Digests*, the state digests, and the specialized digests) contain a

Table of Words and Phrases, which alphabetically lists words and phrases that have been construed or defined by cases. Thus, if you look up the word "conspiracy" in the *Colorado Digest*, you will be provided with citations to all of the cases decided in Colorado that define or interpret this word.

e. Supplementation

The *United States Supreme Court Digest*, the *Federal Practice Digests 3d* and *4th*, the regional digests, and the state digests are kept current by annual cumulative pocket parts and supplemental pamphlets. The *American Digest System*, of course, is supplemented by the *General Digest*. If a pocket part or supplement exists, you must consult it to locate more recent cases and to determine if any new topics have been added. Additionally, the most current information is found in digest pages located in West's reporters (in both the recent hardbound volumes and their advance sheets).

f. Cross-Referencing

Because West's Key Number System is a truly integrated research approach, other West publications will give you topic names and Key Numbers, allowing easy access into the system. Thus, West's encyclopedias (discussed in Chapter 6) *Corpus Juris Secundum* (C.J.S.) and *American Jurisprudence, Second Series* (Am. Jur. 2d) routinely provide you with topic names and Key Numbers. Similarly, West's set *American Law Reports* (discussed below) directs you to relevant topic names and Key Numbers. Finally, the Key Number System is also used in West's online legal research system called Westlaw. Thus, this cross-referencing by West continually helps you gain access to its digests to allow you to find all cases on a similar point of law.

9. *Other Digests*

While West is the largest publisher of digests and while its Key Number System provides easy access to all reported cases relating to a particular legal issue, it is not the only publisher of digests. The best known of the non-West digests is the *United States Supreme Court Digest, Lawyers' Edition*, published by LEXIS Publishing. This digest uses its own classification scheme to direct readers to cases in *United States Supreme Court Reports, Lawyers' Edition* because only West may use its copyrighted Key Number System. Use the descriptive-word approach or table of cases approach to access this digest. Because this digest is published by LEXIS Publishing, it provides references to other LEXIS publications.

There are also a few state digests published by companies other than West. These non-West digests also use their own classification schemes. Nevertheless, the basic system is the same: The researcher locates topics and subtopics and uses those to find citations to relevant cases.

The Final Wrap-Up

Using and Citing Digests

Use: Use digests to help you find all cases from your state, region, jurisdiction, or the entire nation on a similar point of law.

Citation: Never cite to or quote from digests. Retrieve the cases you are directed to by the digests, and cite to these.

B. *American Law Reports*

1. *Introduction*

The *American Law Reports* ("A.L.R.") is a product of West that publishes selected appellate court decisions as well as comprehensive and objective essays relating to the legal issues raised in a case. For this reason, A.L.R. forms a logical bridge between the primary sources (cases, constitutions, and statutes), which have been discussed, and the secondary sources (encyclopedias, law review articles, treatises, and so on), which will be discussed in the next chapters. A.L.R. combines features of primary sources (in that it publishes cases) with features of secondary sources (in that it publishes essays, called "annotations," which explain and expand upon the issues raised by the cases published in A.L.R.).

West's lawyer-editors review both state and federal appellate court decisions from all over the country and publish certain selected decisions that they believe are of widespread significance to legal professionals. You may recall that West's *American Digest System* digests *all* reported cases. A.L.R., on the other hand, does not have such a goal. Its aim is to publish only leading cases rather than cases of purely local interest or those that do not represent a new trend in the law.

The significance of A.L.R. does not lie in the fact that it publishes cases. After all, if A.L.R. selects a recent California Supreme Court case to be published, that case will already be published officially in the *California Reports* and unofficially in both the *Pacific Reporter* and *California Reporter*. The true value of A.L.R. lies in its scholarly and comprehensive articles (the "annotations"), which follow each case A.L.R. selects to publish. Often the case that is published is of average length — perhaps seven or eight pages. The annotation that explains and analyzes the issues raised in the case may exceed 150 pages. Not all annotations are this long, although all are thorough and well researched.

For example, assume A.L.R. elects to publish an appellate court case relating to the liability of a blood bank for providing tainted blood. Immediately following the case is an exhaustive and objective analysis of the development of this area of law and how courts in other jurisdictions are treating this subject. The editors may spend months researching this legal issue and writing the annotation, which in many respects is a scholarly research brief thoroughly examining this area of the law and looking at both sides of the issue. A.L.R.'s thorough coverage includes cases from each jurisdiction that has examined the issue and then arranges these cases according to jurisdiction so you can easily find the cases of interest to you. Each volume of A.L.R. includes about ten cases and their respective ten annotations.

If you are researching a certain area of the law and an A.L.R. annotation has been written regarding your topic, you should immediately retrieve the annotation and view it as "free research," as seldom, if ever, will you have the luxury of being able to devote as much time to an analysis of a legal topic as the A.L.R. editors have in their annotations. In fact, the publisher of A.L.R. reports that A.L.R. is quoted from and cited more often than any other secondary authority.

2.   *A.L.R. Organization*

A.L.R. is published in six series and consists of more than 500 volumes.

   A.L.R.   This set consists of 175 volumes and covers federal cases and state appellate court cases decided between 1919 and 1948.

   A.L.R.2d.   This set consists of 100 volumes and covers federal cases and state appellate court cases decided between 1948 and 1965.

   A.L.R.3d.   This set consists of 100 volumes and covers state appellate court cases decided between 1965 and 1980 and federal court cases decided between 1965 and 1969.

   A.L.R.4th.   This set consists of 90 volumes and covers state appellate court cases from 1980 to 1991.

   A.L.R.5th.   This set was introduced in 1992 and covers state appellate court cases from 1992 to date.

   A.L.R. Federal.   This set was introduced in 1969 and, as its name indicates, exclusively covers federal court cases from 1969 to date. As of late 2004, it included approximately 200 volumes.

As you can see, until A.L.R. Federal ("A.L.R. Fed.") was introduced in 1969, federal court cases were published and analyzed in A.L.R., A.L.R.2d, and A.L.R.3d. A.L.R. Fed. follows the format of the other A.L.R. series: Significant federal court cases are selected for publication and following the case is an annotation, which thoroughly analyzes the legal topics raised in the case and discusses the treatment of this topic by other federal courts.

A.L.R. is not published in advance sheets and the first volumes that appear on the library shelves are hardbound.

3. *Features of A.L.R.*

The following are all current features of the *American Law Reports*. Note, however, that not all features are found in all of the six units that make up A.L.R. The set was recently purchased by West from Lawyers Co-op, and thus newer volumes in the A.L.R. sets direct you to relevant West Digest topic names and Key Numbers and give you tips on using Westlaw, while earlier volumes do not because Lawyers Co-op would never direct its users to a West publication.

Cases. All of the volumes in each A.L.R. series publish contemporary cases illustrating new developments or significant changes in the law. A brief synopsis of the case (called "Summary of Decision") is provided together with headnotes summarizing the issues in the case.

Annotations. Following the representative case, a complete essay or annotation analyzing the case and the issues therein is presented. In A.L.R. 5th, and A.L.R. Fed. after approximately 1992, the cases analyzed are collected together in the back of each volume, following the annotations.

Research References. Before the annotation begins, you will be directed to additional sources relating to the topic to be discussed, including other books, law review articles, form books, encyclopedias, and texts. Additionally, you will be given suggestions for drafting electronic search queries so you can find additional information on Westlaw and LEXIS, the computerized research systems. Finally, you are directed to relevant West topic names and Key Numbers so you can gain access to West's digests to find other similar cases.

Outline. An article outline is presented that shows how the annotation is organized so you can easily locate and read the sections that may be of the most interest to you.

Index. An alphabetical word index is presented for each annotation, which references the various issues and topics discussed in the annotation, enabling you to readily locate the sections of the annotation that are relevant to the issues of most interest to you.

Jurisdictional Table of Cited Statutes and Cases. Because you may be more interested in the manner in which the topic under discussion has been treated in some jurisdictions than in others, you will be provided with a table showing you which sections in the annotation discuss cases and statutes from individual states. Analogous information in A.L.R. Fed. is found in its Table of Cases.

Scope Section. The annotation begins with a section titled "Scope," which briefly describes the matters discussed in the annotation and then refers to earlier annotations discussing the topic that are superseded. You will also be informed what topics are not included in the annotation.

Related Annotations Section. This section directs you to other annotations or other sources such as cases, law reviews, or textbooks dealing with topics related to the annotation.

Summary. A concise and useful summary of the entire annotation is presented, setting the stage for the extensive annotation that follows. Additionally, annotations often contain "practice pointers," which provide practical tips on how to handle a case dealing with the subject matter under discussion.

See Figure 5-7 for features of A.L.R.

4. *Finding A.L.R. Annotations*

a. Index or Descriptive-Word Approach

A multi-volume alphabetical index called *A.L.R. Index* exists that directs you to annotations in A.L.R.2d, A.L.R.3d, A.L.R.4th, A.L.R.5th, and A.L.R. Fed. Using this index is similar to using any other index. Use the descriptive word approach and insert words or phrases that describe the problem or issue you are researching, and you will be directed to the appropriate annotation. The *A.L.R. Index* is another "forgiving" index allowing you to locate an annotation by using various words or phrases rather than requiring you to reduce the legal issue to one perfect word. For example, if your research task is to determine whether an obscene movie constitutes a nuisance, you simply look up the word "nuisance" in the *A.L.R. Index*, and you will be directed to the appropriate annotation. See Figure 5-8 for a sample page from the *A.L.R. Index*. After using the *Index*, check the pocket supplement (updated quarterly) located in the back of each volume of the *A.L.R. Index*, which will provide you with references to more recent annotations.

The *A.L.R. Index* also contains a Table of Laws, Rules, and Regulations directing you to annotations that cite particular federal and state statutes, rules, and regulations. Thus, if you are researching 42 U.S.C.A. § 2487 (West 2003), you can look this up in the Table of Laws, Rules, and Regulations, and you will be directed to any annotation that mentions or discusses this statute.

West also provides a one-volume softcover index called *Quick Index*, which is easy to use and directs you to annotations in A.L.R.3d, A.L.R.4th, and A.L.R.5th. The *Quick Index* does not provide as much detail as the *A.L.R. Index*, but it is a useful starting place for many research problems. A similar index called *A.L.R. Federal Quick Index* will direct you to annotations dealing with the federal law collected in A.L.R. Fed. and is usually shelved after the last volume in A.L.R. Fed.

b. Digest Approach

Multivolume digests for A.L.R. and for A.L.R.2d as well as a combined digest for A.L.R.3d, A.L.R.4th, A.L.R.5th, and A.L.R. Fed. organize areas of the law into more than 400 topics and present them alphabetically. For example, if you look up the topic "nuisance" in the digest to A.L.R.3d,

Figure 5-7
Sample Pages from A.L.R. Annotation
Showing Features of Annotations

(ANNOTATION) ———————————— Annotation analyzes issues raised by leading case

EXHIBITION OF OBSCENE MOTION PICTURES AS NUISANCE

by

Jack W. Shaw, Jr., J.D.

§ 1. Introduction:
    [a] Scope, 971
    [b] Related matters, 971
§ 2. Background, summary, and comment:
    [a] In general, 971
    [b] Practice pointers, 974
§ 3. Applicability of "constitutional" definition of obscenity, 975
§ 4. Procedure or remedy as violation of constitutional guaranties:
    [a] Freedom of speech and press, 977
    [b] Other constitutional guaranties, 981
§ 5. Accessibility of view of motion picture by other than patrons as affecting existence of nuisance, 985
§ 6. Results in particular cases:
    [a] Existence of nuisance found or held supportable, 987
    [b] Existence of nuisance not found, 990

Annotation outline/scheme shows overall organization of annotation

---

TOTAL CLIENT-SERVICE LIBRARY® REFERENCES

4 AM JUR 2d, Amusements and Exhibitions § 37; 50 AM JUR 2d, Lewdness, Indecency and Obscenity § 26

18 AM JUR PL & PR FORMS (Rev ed), Nuisances §§ 1 et seq.

8 AM JUR PROOF OF FACTS 527, Nuisances; 18 AM JUR PROOF OF FACTS 465, Obscenity—Motion Pictures

10 AM JUR TRIALS 1, Obscenity Litigation

ALR DIGESTS, Amusements, etc. § 1; Indecency, etc. § 3

US L ED DIGESTS, Amusements, etc. § 1; Indecency, etc. § 1

ALR QUICK INDEX, Amusements, Exhibitions, Shows and Resorts; Indecency, Lewdness, and Obscenity; Motion Pictures; Nuisances

FEDERAL QUICK INDEX, Amusements and Exhibitions; Lewdness, Indecency, and Obscenity; Motion Pictures; Nuisances

TCSL provides references to other helpful sources (no longer printed)

Consult **POCKET PART** in this volume for later case service

179

Figure 5-7 *(Continued)*

§ 1. Introduction

[a] Scope

Scope section describes topics to be discussed

This annotation collects those cases considering whether the exhibition[1] of motion pictures[2] alleged to be of an obscene, lewd, or indecent nature constitutes a nuisance sufficient to support an action for damages by those injured thereby, or to support a civil action of abatement.[3]

This annotation deals with or states relevant statutory law only insofar as it is reflected in the reported cases which are within its scope, and the reader is advised to consult any applicable statutes of the jurisdiction in which he is interested.

[b] Related matters

Related matters section refers you to other annotations, cases, and sources

Modern status of rules as to balance of convenience or social utility as affecting relief from nuisance. 40 ALR3d 601.

Punitive damages in actions based on nuisance. 31 ALR3d 1346.

Comment Note.—Validity of procedures designed to protect the public against obscenity. 5 ALR3d 1214.

Modern concept of obscenity. 5 ALR 3d 1158.

Drive-in theater or other outdoor dramatic or musical entertainment as nuisance. 93 ALR2d 1171.

Power of municipality in respect of inspection and censorship of motion-picture films. 126 ALR 1363.

What amounts to obscene play or book within prohibition statute. 81 ALR 801.

Constitutionality of regulation of obscene motion pictures—federal cases. 22 L Ed 2d 949.

Constitutionality of federal and state regulation of obscene literature—federal cases. 1 L Ed 2d 2211, 4 L Ed 2d 1821.

§ 2. Background, summary, and comment

[a] In general

Brief summary of annotation

As a matter of federal constitutional law, matter is said to be obscene only if (1) the dominant theme of the material taken as a whole appeals to prurient interest in sex; (2) the material is patently offensive because it affronts contemporary community standards relating to the description or representation of sexual matter; and (3) the material is utterly without redeeming social value.[4]

A nuisance may be broadly defined as that which unlawfully annoys or does damage to another, and anything wrongfully done or permitted which injures or annoys another in the enjoyment of his legal rights; and the term is applied to that class of wrongs which arises from the unreasonable, unwarrantable, or unlawful use by a person of his own property, which produces such material annoyance, inconvenience, discomfort, or hurt that the law will presume a consequent damage.[5]

These concepts must be kept clearly in mind in determining whether the exhibition of an allegedly obscene motion picture constitutes either a public nuisance (one that affects the public at large or such of the public as may come in contact with it) or a private nuisance (affecting the individual or a limited number of individuals only).[6] Since mo-

---

1. Only those cases dealing with the exhibition of such motion pictures, rather than their private possession or their sale, are included herein.

2. Cases involving live theatrical productions and the like are not included herein, as involving potentially different questions.

3. Cases involving criminal prosecutions

for the maintenance of a public nuisance have been included on a merely illustrative basis in the exercise of editorial discretion.

4. 50 Am Jur 2d, Lewdness, Indecency, and Obscenity § 4.

5. 58 Am Jur 2d, Nuisances § 1.

6. 58 Am Jur 2d, Nuisances § 6.

Figure 5-8
Sample Page from *A.L.R. Index*

A.L.R.4th, A.L.R.5th, and A.L.R. Fed., you will be presented with detailed summaries of the various annotations relating to this topic.

c. Miscellaneous Approaches

You will see in Chapter 6 that another of West's publications, its encyclopedia Am. Jur. 2d, often refers readers to A.L.R. annotations. Similarly, when you Shepardize a case either by using conventional print volumes of *Shepard's Citations* or by using LEXIS or check its validity through West's electronic updating service called "KeyCite," as discussed in Chapter 9, you will be informed whether the case has been published in any of the A.L.R. series. If A.L.R. has published a case you are interested in, this is a signal that an exhaustive and analytical annotation will be provided on the general topic discussed in that case.

Westlaw contains the full text of all articles or annotations printed in A.L.R.2d, 3d, 4th, 5th, and A.L.R. Fed. Updates are added weekly, making researching A.L.R. annotations through Westlaw timely and easy. A.L.R. annotations are also available on LEXIS. Computerized legal research is discussed in Chapter 11.

5. *Updating A.L.R. Annotations*

If a case was decided in 1980 and an annotation was prepared that year analyzing that case, it is possible that a case may have been decided after 1980 that has modified or limited the original case or that a newer annotation has been prepared that discusses the changes in the law since 1980. The publisher has developed systems to help you locate newer cases or newer annotations relating to the topic you have researched. In fact, after you have located an annotation, you *must* update it to determine if the annotation remains an accurate interpretation of the law.

A.L.R.   If you have read an annotation in A.L.R. (that is, an annotation written between 1919 and 1948), you update it by checking a source named *A.L.R. Blue Book of Supplemental Decisions*. These volumes are usually located close to the A.L.R. volumes. Thus, if you have read an annotation at 168 A.L.R. 204, you simply look up this reference in the *A.L.R. Blue Book of Supplemental Decisions*, and you will be informed if the annotation has been supplemented or superseded by any later annotation in any A.L.R. series. You will also be directed to cases decided after the date your annotation was published and that relate to the issues discussed in your annotation.

A.L.R.2d   Annotations written between 1948 and 1965 and that appear in A.L.R.2d are updated by a set of books called *A.L.R.2d Later Case Service* and are typically located near A.L.R.2d. If your annotation was located at 80 A.L.R.2d 368, you simply look up that citation in the *A.L.R.2d*

Later Case Service, and you will be directed to cases decided after 80 A.L.R.2d 368 that relate to the issues discussed in that annotation. These cases will be briefly summarized so you may easily determine which cases will be most helpful to you. The *A.L.R.2d Later Case Service* will also direct you to more recent annotations relating to the subject matter discussed by the annotation at 80 A.L.R.2d 368. *A.L.R.2d Later Case Service* is itself updated by annual cumulative pocket parts placed in the back of each volume that must be consulted.

A.L.R.3d, A.L.R.4th, A.L.R.5th, and A.L.R. Fed. Updating annotations in A.L.R.3d, A.L.R.4th, A.L.R.5th, and A.L.R. Fed. is easier than updating annotations in A.L.R. or A.L.R.2d (which require you to use separate books) because these sets are kept current by the more conventional method of updating: annual cumulative pocket-part supplements inserted in the back of each volume. After you read an annotation in A.L.R.3d, A.L.R.4th, A.L.R.5th, or A.L.R. Fed., you simply turn to the pocket part in that volume, which will direct you to more recent annotations and more recent cases relating to the topic discussed by your annotation. See Figure 5-9.

Annotation History Table. The last volume of the *A.L.R. Index* contains the Annotation History Table. This table will inform you whether the annotation you have been researching has been "supplemented," meaning that additional information has been collected in a later annotation, or whether it has been "superseded," meaning that the topics discussed in your annotation have been so significantly changed by later cases that only the new annotation should be relied upon. See Figure 5-10 for a sample page from the Annotation History Table.

Toll-free Number. The front of each softcover pocket-part supplement in A.L.R.3d, A.L.R.4th, A.L.R.5th, and A.L.R. Fed. will provide you with a toll-free telephone number (1-800-225-7488), which you can call to obtain the most recent information regarding annotations.

Figure 5-9
Updating A.L.R Annotations

Location of Annotation	Method of Updating
A.L.R.	*A.L.R. Blue Book of Supplemental Decisions*
A.L.R.2d	*A.L.R.2d Later Case Service*
A.L.R.3d	Pocket Part in each volume
A.L.R.4th	Pocket Part in each volume
A.L.R.5th	Pocket Part in each volume
A.L.R. Fed.	Pocket Part in each volume

Figure 5-10
Sample Page from Annotation History Table

29 ALR3d 1021
Superseded 13 ALR4th 52

29 ALR3d 1407
Superseded 96 ALR3d 195
24 ALR Fed 808

29 ALR3d 1425
§ 3[a], 3[b], 3[g], 3[i] Superseded 100
ALR3d 1205

30 ALR3d 9
§ 6 Superseded 76 ALR3d 11
§ 14.1 Superseded 90 ALR4th 859
§ 16, 19[d] Superseded 67 ALR3d 308
100 ALR3d 10
100 ALR3d 940
§ 19[c] Superseded 99 ALR3d 807
99 ALR3d 1080
§ 25 Superseded 7 ALR4th 308
§ 26[c] Superseded 11 ALR4th 241
§ 29 Superseded 69 ALR3d 1162

30 ALR3d 203
§ 18 Superseded 46 ALR3d 900

30 ALR3d 1352
Superseded 110 ALR Fed 211

32 ALR3d 508
Superseded 22 ALR4th 294

32 ALR3d 1446
Superseded 20 ALR4th 63

33 ALR3d 1417
Superseded 38 ALR4th 538

34 ALR3d 1256
§ 5 Superseded 81 ALR4th 259
§ 6 Superseded 85 ALR4th 19
§ 8, 11, 13, 15 Superseded 74 ALR4th
388
§ 14 Superseded 71 ALR4th 638

35 ALR3d 412-486
§ 19 Superseded 27 ALR4th 568

35 ALR3d 692
Superseded 4 ALR5th 1000

35 ALR3d 1129
§ 3, 4 Superseded 2 ALR5th 475
§ 6 Superseded 12 ALR4th 611

35 ALR3d 1404
§ 10.5 Superseded 8 ALR5th 463

36 ALR3d 405
§ 7, 8 Superseded 85 ALR4th 979

36 ALR3d 735
Superseded 43 ALR4th 1062

36 ALR3d 820
Superseded 74 ALR4th 277

37 ALR3d 1338
Superseded 22 ALR4th 237

38 ALR3d 363
Superseded 61 ALR4th 27

39 ALR3d 222
Superseded 68 ALR4th 294

39 ALR3d 1434
Superseded 1 ALR5th 132

40 ALR3d 856
Superseded 85 ALR4th 365

41 ALR3d 455
§ 3[e, f] Superseded 91 ALR Fed 547

41 ALR3d 904
Superseded 6 ALR4th 1066

42 ALR3d 560
§ 8 Superseded 96 ALR3d 265

44 ALR3d 1108
Superseded 58 ALR4th 402

45 ALR3d 875
§ 13 Superseded 58 ALR4th 559

45 ALR3d 1181
§ 1-4 Superseded 61 ALR4th 615
§ 5-7 Superseded 61 ALR4th 464

45 ALR3d 1364
Superseded 20 ALR4th 136
24 ALR4th 508

46 ALR3d 680
Superseded 50 ALR4th 787

46 ALR3d 733
Superseded 46 ALR4th 220

46 ALR3d 900
§ 11 Superseded 58 ALR4th 902

46 ALR3d 979
§ 7[b] Superseded 35 ALR4th 225

46 ALR3d 1024
§ 5 Superseded 52 ALR4th 18

46 ALR3d 1383
Superseded 53 ALR4th 231

47 ALR3d 909
Superseded 47 ALR4th 134

47 ALR3d 971
Superseded 47 ALR4th 100

47 ALR3d 1286
Superseded 81 ALR3d 1119

49 ALR3d 915
Superseded 97 ALR3d 294

49 ALR3d 934
Superseded 49 ALR4th 1076

50 ALR3d 549
§ 4 Superseded 70 ALR4th 132

51 ALR3d 8
§ 2 [b] Superseded 65 ALR4th 346

51 ALR3d 520
Superseded 65 ALR4th 1155

52 ALR3d 636
§ 9 Superseded 87 ALR Fed 177

52 ALR3d 1289
Superseded 48 ALR4th 229

52 ALR3d 1344
Superseded 76 ALR4th 1025
79 ALR4th 171

53 ALR3d 731
Superseded 4 ALR5th 273

53 ALR3d 1285
Superseded 97 ALR3d 528

53 ALR3d 1310
Superseded 2 ALR5th 396

55 ALR3d 581
§ 9[c,d] Superseded 86 ALR3d 1116

57 ALR3d 584
§ 5 Superseded 86 ALR Fed 866

58 ALR3d 533
Superseded 45 ALR4th 949

59 ALR3d 138
Superseded 76 ALR4th 22

59 ALR3d 321
§ 5, 6, 13 Superseded 83 ALR4th 1056

Indication that annotation at 35 A.L.R. 3d 692 has been superseded or replaced by a later annotation

1180   Consult POCKET PART for Later Entries

The Final Wrap-Up

Using and Citing A.L.R. Annotations

Use: Use A.L.R. annotations to read comprehensive analyses of various topics and to locate other primary and secondary sources.

Citation: You may cite to A.L.R. annotations in memos and court documents. Although the annotations are a secondary source, they are credible and well written. A better approach, however, is to allow the A.L.R. annotations to direct you to binding primary authorities that you then cite in your documents.

———— Practice Tip ————

Pocket Parts

When using sets of books that are updated by pocket parts (such as A.L.R. 2d, 3d, 4th, 5th, and Fed., and *Words and Phrases*), always check the pocket part. It is malpractice not to do so. Don't forget that some books are also updated by softcover supplements placed on the shelves next to them. Check these too.

C. *Words and Phrases*

In the mid-1980s in Southern California, two young men attended a party at which one of them consumed a great deal of an alcoholic beverage. This individual, recognizing he should not drive, asked his friend to drive him home and slid into the passenger side of the vehicle. Before the driver could get into the car, however, the car began rolling down the hill on which it was parked. The passenger grabbed wildly for the steering wheel and managed to move his leg enough to apply the brake. Nevertheless, the car struck another vehicle, and the passenger was issued a citation by the police officer who arrived at the scene for "driving while under the influence of an alcoholic beverage," a violation of the California Vehicle Code.

The entire case depended on the interpretation of the word "driving," for if the passenger was not "driving," he could not be in violation of the statute. The definition of the word "driving" can obviously be found in any dictionary. How this word has been defined and construed in a legal sense by case law can be found in a set of books comprising more than 100 volumes published by West called *Words and Phrases*. It arranges words and phrases in alphabetical order from Volume 1 ("A" to "Accident") to Volume

Figure 5-11
Sample Page from West's *Words and Phrases*

GUARDED

Cross References

Appropriately Guarded

Sufficiently Guarded

GUARDIN ———————————— **Word to be defined**

In general—p. 700

Appointed by court—p. 702

Appointed by will—p. 702

Conservator distinguished—p. 703

Natural guardians—p. 703

Next friend—p. 704

Trustee—p. 704

Cross References ———————— **Cross references**

Action to Remove a Guardian

Agent

Committee

De Facto Guardian

Discharge

Express Trust

General Guardian

Legal Guardian

Legal Representative

Natural Guardian

Next Friend

Occupant; Occupier

Owner

Quasi Guardian

Special Guardian

Trustee of Express Trust

Unsuitable Guardian

Voidable

In general

A guardian is one who is entitled to the custody of the person of an infant. Wilson v. Me-ne-chas, 20 P. 468, 469, 40 Kan. 648.

A guardian is a person upon whom the law imposes the duty of looking after the pecuniary interests of his ward. Sparhawk v. Allen, 21 N.H. 27, 1 Fost. 27.

Judicial definitions of "guardian"

The term "guardian", as defined in statute governing adoptions, embraces within its meaning the custodial guardianship resulting from a final committal of dependent or neg-

186

46 (also called Book 107, "Willfulness" to "Zygoma"), making the set as easy to use as any dictionary. *Words and Phrases* aims at providing the definition of words and phrases as interpreted by cases from 1658 to the present time. *Words and Phrases*, like digests, is thus an excellent casefinder. It contains no narrative treatment as secondary sources do, but rather focuses exclusively on locating cases. It is the last "bridge" to the secondary sources to be discussed in Chapters 6 and 7.

In the case described above, a review of the definition of the term "driving" revealed that "driving" required one to have control of a vehicle. The court hearing the case in California determined that the passenger was not "driving" under the meaning of the California statutes because he had no true ability to control the vehicle. The case was dismissed.

Once again, West will do more than merely list citations for the cases defining words such as "assessment," "clemency," "distress," "guardian," or "petition." *Words and Phrases* will provide you with a brief summary of the cases that have defined these words so you may easily determine which cases you should read in full.

Words and Phrases is kept current by annual cumulative pocket parts. Thus, once you have reviewed the cases in the main volume that define a word—for example, "guardian"—examine the pocket part to determine if newer cases have interpreted or construed the word "guardian." See Figure 5-11 for a sample page from *Words and Phrases*.

The Final Wrap-Up

Using and Citing *Words and Phrases*

Use: Use *Words and Phrases* to help you find cases that have construed and defined terms, words, and phrases, whether those are legal terms or everyday terms.

Citation: Never cite to or quote from *Words and Phrases*. Read the cases to which you are directed, and rely on and cite to these.

D.   Citation Form

Digests and *Words and Phrases* are used solely to locate cases. You may never cite to them. You may, however, cite to an A.L.R. annotation:

The Bluebook: Francine L. Harris, Annotation, *The Battered Spouse Syndrome as a Defense in Manslaughter Cases*, 96 A.L.R.4th 797 (1988).

ALWD: Francine L. Harris, *The Battered Spouse Syndrome as a Defense in Manslaughter Cases*, 96 A.L.R.4th 797 (1988).

Cybersites ▐███████████████████████████████████

Georgetown University Law Library offers a series of online guides and tutorials to teach and explain legal research strategies. Access http://www.ll. georgetown.edu/tutotials/index.cfm for tutorials on the use of the Key Number System, digests, and A.L.R. annotations.

Neither West's digests nor A.L.R. annotations are available on the Internet. Nevertheless, both may be found via computer-assisted legal research.

Westlaw, West's electronic research system, allows you to search for cases using West's topics and Key Numbers. When you see a topic and Key Number in a case you are reading in any of West's reporters, you can immediately locate other cases classified under the same topic and Key Number by running a topic and Key Number search on Westlaw (as opposed to inserting the topic and Key Number into a print digest).

Annotations in A.L.R. are available both on Westlaw and on LEXIS, Reed Elsevier's computerized legal research system. One helpful feature of locating A.L.R. annotations online is that the supplementation is completely integrated with the annotation. Using A.L.R. in conventional print form requires that you supplement and update A.L.R. annotations using either separate books or pocket parts. When you access A.L.R. online, the supplements or updates are included together with the annotation, saving you time and effort.

Words and Phrases is not available on Westlaw, probably because searching for judicial definitions of words is easily accomplished by using key terms inserted in search boxes.

Computer-assisted legal research will be fully discussed in Chapter 11.

Writing Strategies

In any research project, remember the key distinction between primary and secondary authorities: If on point, primary authorities must be followed and are binding, while secondary authorities are persuasive at best. Therefore, you should always cite at least one primary authority to support each of your arguments. Secondary authorities such as A.L.R. annotations should be used only in conjunction with primary authorities, namely, as "extra" support for a contention.

Use some variety in the manner in which you discuss your authorities. If each paragraph begins with the phrase "In [case name] or [authority] , . . ." or if each paragraph discusses one topic and always concludes with a citation, your writing will have one rigid and structured appearance. Introduce citations, paragraphs, and sentences in varying ways. This variety will enhance readability. Your project must not only be right—it must be read.

Assignment for Chapter 5

1. Use the Tables of Cases to the *Eleventh Decennial, Part 1*.
   a. Under which topic and Key Numbers is the following case digested: *Trecom Business Systems, Inc. v. Prasad*?
   b. Give the citation to the case in which the defendant's name is *Derokey*.
2. Use the Descriptive Word Index to the *Eleventh Decennial, Part 1*.
   a. Which topic and key number discuss lethal injection as a mode of execution in death penalty cases?
   b. Look up this topic and key number in the *Eleventh Decennial, Part 1*. Which 1999 case from Arizona discusses this?
3. Use the Descriptive Word Index to the *Tenth Decennial, Part 2*.
   a. Which topic and key number discuss games as nuisances?
   b. Look up this topic and key number in the *Tenth Decennial, Part 2*. Which 1991 Nebraska case discusses this general topic?
   c. Which 1997 Rhode Island case updates this?
4. Use West's set *Federal Practice Digest, 4th Series*.
   a. Which topic and key number discuss a right to a jury trial in employment discrimination cases?
   b. Review this topic and key number. Which 2003 case from the Eighth Circuit ruled on this issue?
   c. Review this case. Was the plaintiff entitled to a jury trial in this matter? Why or why not?
5. Use West's set *United States Supreme Court Digest*. Give the citations to the case *Bayne v. Wiggins*.
6. Use West's *Atlantic Digest*.
   a. Which topic and key number discuss the use of expert witnesses in battered women's syndrome cases?
   b. Review the topic and key number. Give the name of the 1981 Maine case that discusses this issue and tell whether the expert witness testimony was permitted.
7. Use A.L.R. *Quick Index* for A.L.R.3d, A.L.R.4th, and A.L.R.5th. Find and cite the annotations that relate to the following issues:
   a. Liability of a nursery school and day care center for injury to a child attending the facility (specifically, for injury caused by a crib).
   b. Liability of dog owners for emotional injuries sustained by persons frightened by the owners' dogs.
8. Review the above annotations, and answer the following questions:
   a. For 7(a) generally, which is the most recent case from the Georgia court of appeals in which negligence was established and the *res ipsa loquitur* doctrine was not at issue?
   b. For 7(b), cite a 1932 California court of appeals case that generally relates to this topic.
9. Use West's *Words and Phrases*. What cases construe the meaning of the phrase "nurturing parent doctrine"? Give case names only.

State Your Answer

1. Access West's Web site at http://www.west.thomson.com. Select "Product Type" and then "Digests" and locate the digest for your state. Use the format "West's Iowa Digest" if you have difficulty. How often is your state's digest updated?
2. Access the site MegaLaw at http://www.megalaw.com. Use "State Law" to access authorities and information for your state. Review "State Government Information" for your state.
   a. Identify your state's lieutenant governor.
   b. Identify whether your lieutenant is a native of your state.
3. Access West's Web site at http://www.west.thomson.com.
   a. Select "User Guides" and then review a User Guide entitled "Using Secondary Sources." How does West describe A.L.R. on page 1 of this User Guide?
   b. Using the "Search Products" box, search for *Words and Phrases*. Review the product information about this set, specifically its "Summary of Contents." What words and phrases does Volume 37 (also called Book 86) cover?

Legal Research: Secondary Authorities and Other Research Aids

Encyclopedias, Periodicals, Treatises, and Restatements

For centuries, the most important sources of law were not judicial opinions themselves, but treatises that restated the law, such as the commentaries of Coke and Blackstone.

Hart v. Massanari, 266 F.3d 1155, 1165 (9th Cir. 2001)

A. **Encyclopedias**
B. **Legal Periodicals**
C. **Texts and Treatises**
D. **Restatements**
E. **Citation Form**

Chapter Overview

Section I of this text discussed the major primary legal authorities: statutes, constitutions, and cases. Administrative rules and regulations are discussed in Chapter 10. All other sources are secondary authorities. In general, the secondary sources serve to explain, summarize, analyze, and locate primary sources.

If you know a legal question can be answered by a statute, you can and should begin your research in one of the annotated codes by locating and reading the statute and then examining the annotations following it to find cases that interpret and construe the statute. Often, however, when presented with a legal issue, you may not know where to begin. In these instances, many experts recommend that you start your research projects by using a secondary source. Secondary sources provide you with analysis of an issue and then direct you to the relevant primary authorities.

Always keep in mind that primary sources are binding on a court or tribunal. If on point, these primary authorities must be followed. Secondary sources lack this mandatory authority. While often highly respected, the secondary sources are persuasive only. A court may elect to adopt a position set forth in a secondary authority or may reject it. Thus, your goal is always to locate relevant primary sources. The secondary authorities will assist you in this task.

The secondary authorities discussed in this chapter are those most frequently used: encyclopedias, periodicals, treatises, and restatements. The following chapter will discuss miscellaneous secondary authorities, including opinions of attorneys general, dictionaries, directories, form books, uniform laws, looseleaf services, and jury instructions.

A. Encyclopedias

1. Introduction

Just as *Encyclopaedia Britannica* or *The World Book* encyclopedia are reference works that alphabetically arrange topics ostensibly covering all human knowledge, legal encyclopedias exist that alphabetically arrange topics related to legal issues, from abandonment to mortgages to zoning. Legal encyclopedias are easy to use and serve as an excellent introduction to an area of the law. In addition to providing summaries of hundreds of legal topics, encyclopedias will direct you to cases through the use of footnotes. That is, as you read about an area of the law such as corporations, deeds, or trusts, you will be referred continually to cases dealing with these areas of the law. Generally, the narrative statements or summaries of the legal topics will cover the top half of each page in the set, and the bottom half of each page will be devoted to case citations that support the narrative statements of the law.

One of the hallmarks of encyclopedias is their noncritical approach, meaning that encyclopedias explain the law as it is, without any critical comment or recommendations for changes in the law. Many other secondary sources offer critical opinion and suggestions for change in the law.

The treatment of legal topics in encyclopedias is general and somewhat elementary. For this reason, encyclopedias are seldom cited in court documents such as briefs. They are rather most useful for providing an overview of an area of law and sending you to cases that will provide more thorough analysis. They give you the background you need on a legal topic before reading cases. Encyclopedias are excellent casefinders (although the cases you are sent to are often criticized for being older cases) and tools for introducing you to an area of law. Moreover, they are readily available; even small law libraries usually have one, if not both, of the general sets.

It is unlikely that you will need to use both sets. Your choice of which set to use will likely depend upon convenience or habit.

There are three types of encyclopedias: general sets, local sets, and special subject sets.

2. General or National Encyclopedias

A general or national encyclopedia is a set that aims at discussing all of American law, civil and criminal, state and federal, substantive and procedural. That is, a discussion of false imprisonment will include a complete overview of this area of the law, including summaries of the majority and minority views and then send you to federal cases as well as various state cases dealing with this topic.

There are two general or national encyclopedias: *Corpus Juris Secundum* (C.J.S.) published by West, and *American Jurisprudence 2d* (Am. Jur. 2d) previously published by Lawyers Co-op and now also published by West.

a. C.J.S.

C.J.S. is an encyclopedia consisting of more than 150 dark blue volumes, which discusses in excess of 400 different topics of the law. These topics are arranged alphabetically, making it easy for you to locate the discussions on covenants, franchises, or trial.

C.J.S. is an extremely thorough and comprehensive set, which aims at providing you with references to all cases that support any narrative statement of the law. The narrative material is articulately presented and is easy to understand. The cases that support the narrative statements are arranged in the footnotes alphabetically by state so you can readily locate cases from your jurisdiction or from neighboring states. Often, the "leading case" in an area of the law is summarized briefly for you.

Each topic begins with a thorough outline to provide you with quick access to the most pertinent parts of the discussion. Each section within a topic begins with a boldface "Black Letter" summary of the rule discussed in the section. By reading this preview of the section, you can quickly determine whether you should proceed to read the section in full.

As its very name indicates (*Corpus Juris Secundum*, meaning "Body of Law Second"), C.J.S. was preceded by an earlier set, *Corpus Juris*. While many law libraries still maintain *Corpus Juris* (C.J.), it is unlikely you will use this older set, and you should always begin your research in C.J.S. rather than C.J.

C.J.S. contains a multi-volume index, usually found after the last volume in the set, and is kept current by annual cumulative pocket parts, which will inform you if the narrative statement of the law found in the main volume has changed and will refer you to newer cases supporting the text statement. C.J.S. also now includes a Table of Cases so you can readily find a discussion of a case if you know the case name.

Because C.J.S. is a West publication, it is a participant in West's *Key Number System*. As each discussion begins, in a section called "Library References," West provides you with the pertinent topic and Key Number to enable you to locate all cases on this area of the law, particularly the most recent cases, through the use of West's *General Digest*. See Figure 6-1 for a sample page from C.J.S.

b. Am. Jur. 2d

American Jurisprudence 2d (Am. Jur. 2d) consists of more than 100 green volumes, which discuss more than 400 areas of the law. Similar to the arrangement of C.J.S., Am. Jur. 2d arranges its topics (or "titles")

Figure 6-1
Sample Page from C.J.S.

§ 182. Abandonment and Nonuser
   a. Abandonment in general
   b. Nonuser
   c. Miscellaneous acts or omissions
   d. Operation and effect
   e. Evidence

a. Abandonment in General

Summary of rule discussed in section to follow

Trade-marks and trade-names may be lost by abandonment; abandonment requires the concurrence of both an intention to abandon and an act or omission by which such intention is carried into effect.

The title to a trade-mark or trade-name acquired by adoption and user may be lost by an abandonment of such use,[5] although abandonment is not favored.[6] An actual intention permanently to give up the use of a name or mark is necessary to constitute abandonment of it.[7] Abandonment requires the concurrence of both an intention to abandon and an act or omission by which such intention is carried into effect.[8] Abandonment must have been voluntary,[9] and an involuntary deprivation of the use of the name or mark does not in itself constitute abandonment.[10] Failure to affix a trade-mark to goods through inadvertence is not abandonment where no intention to abandon is shown;[11] nor can an undisclosed intention constitute abandonment.[12] Despite the fact that abandonment depends in a large part on the intention of the parties, an ineffective attempt to assign a trade-mark ordinarily results in its abandonment.[13]

b. Nonuser

Nonuser of a trade-name or trade-mark is not of itself an abandonment thereof; however, where intention to abandon is shown by other circumstances and conditions, nonuser is a sufficient act of relinquishment and effectuates the abandonment.

While trade-marks and trade-names may be lost through nonuser,[14] mere disuse, although for a con-

5. U.S.—Greyhound Corp. v. Rothman, D.C.Md., 84 F.Supp. 233, affirmed, C.A., 175 F.2d 893—G. F. Heublin & Bro. v. Bushmill Wine & Products Co., D.C.Pa., 55 F.Supp. 964—Bisceglia Bros. Corp. v. Fruit Industries, D.C.Pa., 20 F.Supp. 564, affirmed, C.C.A., Fruit Industries v. Bisceglia Bros. Corp., 101 F.2d 752, certiorari denied 59 S.Ct. 1043, 307 U.S. 646, 83 L.Ed. 1526.
Ky.—**Corpus Juris cited in** Stratton & Terstegge Co. v. Stiglitz Furnace Co., 81 S.W.2d 1, 4, 258 Ky. 678.
N.Y.—Winthrop Chemical Co. v. Blackman, 268 N.Y.S. 647, 150 Misc. 229.
Wash.—Foss v. Culbertson, 136 P.2d 711, 17 Wash.2d 610—Seattle Street Railway & Municipal Employees Relief Ass'n v. Amalgamated Ass'n of Street Electric Railway & Motor Coach Employees of America, 101 P.2d 338, 3 Wash.2d 520.
63 C.J. p 523 note 17.

6. U.S.—Du Pont Cellophane Co. v. Waxed Products Co., D.C.N.Y., 6 F.Supp. 859, modified on other grounds, C.C.A., 85 F.2d 75, certiorari denied E. I. Dupont De Nemours & Co. v. Waxed Products Co., 57 S.Ct. 194, 299 U.S. 601, 81 L.Ed. 443.

7. Ky.—**Corpus Juris cited in** Stratton & Terstegge Co. v. Stiglitz Furnace Co., 81 S.W.2d 1, 4, 258 Ky. 678.
N.Y.—Neva-Wet Corp. of America v. Never Wet Processing Corp., 13 N.E.2d 775, 277 N.Y. 163.
63 C.J. p 523 note 18.
Letter assuring noncontest
Where plaintiff ordering trade-marked razors from manufacturer sent to lender a letter which consented to manufacturer's pledge of razors as security for loan to manufacturer and which stated that plaintiff would not assert any claims contrary to lender's right to realize on security in event of nonpayment of loan, letter was abandonment of all plaintiff's trade-mark and fair trade rights.—Stahly, Inc. v. M. H. Jacobs Co., C.A.Ill., 183 F.2d 914, certiorari denied 71 S.Ct. 239, 340 U.S. 896, 95 L.Ed. 650.

8. U.S.—E. I. Du Pont De Nemours & Co. v. Celanese Corp. of America, 167 F.2d 484, 35 C.C.P.A., Patents, 1061, 3 A.L.R.2d 1213—Greyhound Corp. v. Rothman, D.C.Md., 84 F.Supp. 233, affirmed, C.A., 175 F.2d 893—Hygienic Products Co. v. Judson Dunaway Corp., D.C.N.H., 81 F.Supp. 935, vacated on other grounds, C.A., 178 F.2d 461, certiorari denied 70 S.Ct. 802, 803, 339 U.S. 948, 94 L.Ed. 1362—Colonial Radio Corp. v. Colonial Television Corp., D.C.N.Y., 78 F.Supp. 546—Coca-Cola Co. v. Dixi-Cola Laboratories, D.C.Md., 31 F.Supp. 835, modified on other grounds, C.C.A., Dixi-Cola Laboratories v. Coca-Cola Co., 117 F.2d 352, certiorari denied Coca-Cola Co. v. Dixi-Cola Laboratories, 62 S.Ct. 60, 314 U.S. 629, 86 L.Ed. 505—Bisceglia Bros. Corp. v. Fruit Industries, D.C.Pa., 20 F.Supp. 564, affirmed, C.C.A., Fruit Industries v. Bisceglia Bros. Corp., 101 F.2d 752, certiorari denied 59 S.Ct. 1043, 307 U.S. 646, 83 L.Ed. 1526—Du Pont Cellophane Co. v. Waxed Products Co., D.C.N.Y., 6 F.Supp. 859, modified on other grounds, C.C.A., 85 F.2d 75, certiorari denied E. I. Dupont De Nemours & Co. v. Waxed Products Co., 57 S.Ct. 194, 299 U.S. 601, 81 L.Ed. 443.

Ky.—Stratton & Terstegge Co. v. Stiglitz Furnace Co., 81 S.W.2d 1, 258 Ky. 678.
Wash.—Foss v. Culbertson, 136 P.2d 711, 17 Wash.2d 610.
63 C.J. p 524 note 19.

9. U.S.—E. I. Du Pont De Nemours & Co. v. Celanese Corp. of America, 167 F.2d 484, 35 C.C.P.A., Patents, 1016, 3 A.L.R. 2d 1213—DuPont Cellophane Co. v. Waxed Products Co., C.C.A.N.Y., 85 F.2d 75, certiorari denied E. I. DuPont De Nemours & Co. v. Waxed Products Co., 57 S.Ct. 194, 299 U.S. 601, 81 L.Ed. 443.

10. U.S.—Fraser v. Williams, D.C.Wis., 61 F.Supp. 763—Reconstruction Finance Corp. v. J. G. Menihan Corp., D.C.N.Y., 28 F.Supp. 920.
Md.—American-Stewart Distillery v. Stewart Distilling Co., 177 A. 473, 168 Md. 212.
Wash.—Washington Barber & Beauty Supply Co. v. Spokane Barbers' & Beauty Supply Co., 18 P.2d 499, 171 Wash. 428.

11. U.S.—Chrysler Corp. v. Trott, Cust. & Pat.App., 83 F.2d 302.

12. Wash.—Olympia Brewing Co. v. Northwest Brewing Co., 35 P.2d 104, 178 Wash. 533.

13. D.C.—Old Charter Distillery Co. v. Ooms, D.C., 73 F.Supp. 539, affirmed Continental Distilling Corp. v. Old Charter Distillery Co., 188 F.2d 614, 88 U.S.App.D.C. 73.

14. U.S.—G. F. Heublin & Bro. v. Bushmill Wine & Products Co., D.C.Pa., 55 F.Supp. 964—Bisceglia Bros. Corp. v. Fruit Industries, D.C.Pa., 20 F.Supp. 564, affirmed, C.C.A., Fruit Industries v. Bisceglia Bros. Corp., 101 F.2d 752, certiorari denied 59 S.Ct. 1043, 307 U.S. 646, 83 L.Ed. 1526.

alphabetically, enabling you to quickly locate the discussion you need. While C.J.S. historically has aimed at directing you to *all* cases that support any legal principle, Am. Jur. 2d will direct you to a representative cross-section of cases that support a legal principle. In fact, its editors have prided themselves on "weeding out" irrelevant, redundant, or obsolete cases and selecting the best cases that support the narrative summaries of the law. As stated in the Foreword in volume one of Am. Jur. 2d, "[W]e do not devote pages to listing multiple citations to mere platitudes which no court would deny or doubt."

Many of the features of Am. Jur. 2d are similar to those seen in C.J.S. That is, the narrative statements of the law are clearly and concisely presented in an easy-to-read manner. The cases you are sent to in the footnotes are often briefly summarized for you. Each topic begins with an outline to allow you to locate readily the parts of the discussion of greatest interest to you.

Am. Jur. 2d is the successor to *American Jurisprudence* (Am. Jur.), which is still in existence but seldom used due to the expanded coverage of Am. Jur. 2d. Am. Jur. 2d contains a multi-volume general index and, similar to C.J.S., is kept current by annual cumulative pocket parts, which describe changes in the law and send you to newer cases than those found in the main hardbound volumes. Like C.J.S., Am. Jur. 2d also includes "Research References," which lead you to other West publications, including the valuable A.L.R. annotations discussed in Chapter 5.

Am. Jur. 2d also features two unique books in its encyclopedia system:

Am. Jur. 2d Desk Book. This book serves as a legal almanac and is a unique collection of miscellaneous legal and historical information. The Desk Book contains the text of the United States Constitution, the Declaration of Independence, the United Nations Charter, and the Monroe Doctrine. Additionally, there are diagrams showing the organization of various federal agencies, such as the Departments of Labor and Transportation, and directories with addresses, telephone numbers, and Web site addresses of the agencies and of the United States Courts of Appeal, United States District Courts, and United States Bankruptcy Courts. Various statistical charts are given, such as suicide rates, life expectancy tables, and marriage and divorce statistics. The Desk Book also contains other miscellaneous tables, data, charts, diagrams, statistics, and glossaries of terms of interest in the legal profession. The Desk Book is updated by pocket parts.

Am. Jur. 2d New Topic Service. The New Topic Service is a looseleaf binder volume of pamphlets designed to provide you with information relating to new and emerging areas of the law, such as the Federal Sentencing Guidelines, the Americans with Disabilities Act, and Real Estate Time-Sharing. The articles discussed in the pamphlets are merged into the appropriate hardbound volumes when volumes are replaced or revised.

See Figure 6-2 for a sample page from Am. Jur. 2d.

Figure 6-2
Sample Page from Am. Jur. 2d

§ 242   DRUGS AND CONTROLLED SUBSTANCES   25 Am Jur 2d

2. CONDUCT RELATED TO FILLING OF PRESCRIPTIONS [§§ 242–244]

§ 242. Generally

A pharmacist has a duty to act with due ordinary care and diligence in the compounding and selling of drugs.[93] In this regard, a pharmacist owes his customers a duty to properly[94] and accurately[95] fill prescriptions. A pharmacist is required to assure that the drug prescribed is properly selected and measured.[96] Indeed, a pharmacist is held to a high standard of care in filling prescriptions[97] and dispensing prescription drugs,[98] and may be held liable in tort for any breach of his duty to properly fill prescriptions.[99] Generally, however, a pharmacist will not be held liable for correctly filling a prescription issued by a licensed physician.[1] In addition, a pharmacist who sells a generic drug as a substitute for the drug specifically prescribed, as authorized by statute and a physician's prescription, is not negligent for injuries resulting from an adverse side effect of a generic drug, unless the pharmacist knew that the generic drug is inferior or defective.[2]

§ 243. Mistakes in preparing, filling, or dispensing prescriptions; dispensing drug other than that prescribed

Liability may be imposed on a pharmacists for negligently misfilling a prescription,[3] or negligently dispensing a drug other than that prescribed[4] or requested,[5] when a druggist negligently supplies a drug other than the drug

249, app den (Tenn) 1990 Tenn LEXIS 362.

93. Ferguson v Williams, 101 NC App 265, 399 SE2d 389, review den 328 NC 571, 403 SE2d 510; Dooley v Everett (Tenn App) 805 SW2d 380.

94. Adkins v Mong, 168 Mich App 726, 425 NW2d 151, app den 431 Mich 880.

95. Nichols v Central Merchandise, 16 Kan App 2d 65, 817 P2d 1131, review den 250 Kan 805; McKee v American Home Products Corp., 113 Wash 2d 701, 782 P2d 1045, CCH Prod Liab Rep ¶ 12399.

96. Murphy v E. R. Squibb & Sons, Inc., 40 Cal 3d 672, 221 Cal Rptr 447, 710 P2d 247, CCH Prod Liab Rep ¶ 10818.

97. Adkins v Mong, 168 Mich App 726, 425 NW2d 151, app den 431 Mich 880.

98. French Drug Co. v Jones (Miss) 367 So 2d 431, 3 ALR4th 259.

99. Adkins v Mong, 168 Mich App 726, 425 NW2d 151, app den 431 Mich 880.

1. Adkins v Mong, 168 Mich App 726, 425 NW2d 151, app den 431 Mich 880.
Forms: Answer—Denial of negligence—No breach of duty. 9 Am Jur Pl & Pr Forms (Rev), Drugs, Narcotics, and Poisons, Form 37.

2. Ullman v Grant, 114 Misc 2d 220, 450 NYS2d 955.

462

3. Boeck v Katz Drug Co., 155 Kan 656, 127 P2d 506.

Annotations: Druggist's civil liability for injuries sustained as result of negligence in incorrectly filling drug prescriptions, 3 ALR4th 270.

Refere[r]
to A.L.[ ]
annota[ ]

Forms: Complaint, petition, or declaration—Against pharmacy and pharmacist—Damages resulting from alteration of prescription by pharmacist. 9 Am Jur Pl & Pr Forms (Rev), Drugs, Narcotics, and Poisons, Form 31.1.

4. Stebbins v Concord Wrigley Drugs, Inc., 164 Mich App 204, 416 NW2d 381; Walgreen, Inc. v Knatt (Tex Civ App Beaumont) 506 SW2d 751.
Practice References: 18 Am Jur Proof of Facts 1, Medication Errors.
Forms: Complaint, petition, or declaration—Injuries sustained as result of negligence in filling drug prescription—Filling prescription with drug other than drug prescribed. 9 Am Jur Pl & Pr Forms (Rev), Drugs, Narcotics, and Poisons, Form 31.
Complaint, petition, or declaration—Allegation—Harmful drug supplied in place of harmless drug ordered. 9 Am Jur Pl & Pr Forms (Rev), Drugs, Narcotics, and Poisons, Form 36.

5. Troppi v Scarf, 31 Mich App 240, 187 NW2d 511 (criticized on other grounds by Bushman v Burns Clinic Medical Center, 83 Mich App 453, 268 NW2d 683) and (criticized on other grounds by Rinard v Biczak, 177 Mich

c. Features Common to C.J.S. and Am. Jur. 2d

The following features are common to both C.J.S. and Am. Jur. 2d:

(i) Both C.J.S. and Am. Jur. 2d discuss more than 400 topics of the law, which are arranged alphabetically (Abandonment, Assault, Banks, Contracts, Deeds, and so forth).

(ii) Only C.J.S. includes an alphabetized Table of Cases. There is no Table of Cases for Am. Jur. 2d.

(iii) While there is some discussion of statutes in the narrative discussions of the law, neither C.J.S. nor Am. Jur. 2d provides indepth analyses of statutes. Detailed discussion of all state and federal statutes on each of the more than 400 areas of the law discussed would make the sets too cumbersome and unwieldy to use. In general, Am. Jur. 2d stresses statutory law more than C.J.S. Each set, however, includes a separate volume usually called "Table of Laws and Rules," which directs you to specific sections within each set that discuss or cite federal statutes, various rules, the *Code of Federal Regulations*, and Uniform Laws.

(iv) The narrative statements of the law are presented concisely in both sets. The style of writing is similar, and the discussion of the law is straightforward. For this reason, it cannot be said that one set is clearly superior to the other. Each set has its advantages, and your choice of which set to use will be based largely on habit and personal preference. While the sets do have some distinguishing features, they are more alike than not, and for most purposes you should research in either C.J.S. or Am. Jur. 2d, but not both. Moreover, now that both sets are published by West, both provide you with West topics and Key Numbers and give references to other West resources.

(v) Each set contains a multivolume general index usually located after the last volume in the set and each of the more than 400 topics or titles begins with its own table of contents or index allowing you to locate quickly the sections of the discussion of greatest interest to you.

(vi) Each topic discussion in both sets begins with a "scope" paragraph, which briefly outlines what will be discussed in the topic and what specific subjects may be treated or discussed elsewhere in the set. These "scope notes" enable you to determine rapidly whether you are researching the correct topic or whether you should direct your attention to some other topic in the set.

(vii) Both sets support the narrative discussion of the law with footnotes that provide citations to cases, although, as discussed previously, C.J.S. generally purports to send you to all cases that support any statement of the law, while Am. Jur. 2d will send you to selected leading cases. You will first be sent to federal cases and then to state cases, listed alphabetically by state to allow easy access to the law of selected states and jurisdictions. When presented with a statement of the law and numerous case citations that support it, there are some techniques you can use effectively to select cases when time or budget constraints prevent you from examining all cases. Select and read cases from your jurisdiction before reading cases from other jurisdictions; review newer cases before older cases; and review cases from higher courts before those from lower courts. Do not misinterpret these guidelines as saying "old cases are bad." Old cases are *not* bad; however, when presented with numerous cases and when pressed for time, you should develop effective research strategies, and these guidelines will help you research more efficiently. After all, it may not be productive to review cases from the 1930s only to discover that the law substantially changed in the 1990s, rendering the earlier cases outmoded or invalid statements of the law.

(viii)   Both sets will refer you to other sources to enhance your understanding of the law. C.J.S. has always included references to topic names and Key Numbers and the new replacement volumes of Am. Jur. 2d do as well. Both sets will refer you to pertinent and useful A.L.R. annotations.

(ix)   Each set is kept current by annual cumulative pocket parts and by replacement volumes when needed. For example, because the law relating to internal revenue and federal taxation changes so often, both C.J.S. and Am. Jur. 2d replace their tax volumes on an annual basis. Moreover, new topics, such as "Pipelines," "Products Liability," and "Energy" are often added to the sets, and these additions necessitate replacement volumes.

(x)   Both C.J.S. and Am. Jur. 2d are available in CD-ROM form and on Westlaw (selected articles only).

(xi)   Both sets are cited in the same manner:
    1A C.J.S. *Actions* § 9 (1985).
    1 Am. Jur. 2d *Actions* § 9 (1994).

d.   Total Client-Service Library

Lawyers Co-op, the former publisher of Am. Jur. 2d, created a number of other sets of books, which it referred to as the Total Client-Service Library (TCSL), which are now published by West. The books in TCSL are designed to be used with Am. Jur. 2d, although they are not encyclopedias. See Figure 5-7 for a reference to TCSL sources. One of the sets in TCSL has already been discussed (the A.L.R. system). Most of the remaining units of the TCSL deal primarily with litigation and trial practice. Many are available in CD-ROM as well as print form (see Chapter 11). These very practical sets routinely refer you to Am. Jur. 2d and are as follows.

(1) Am. Jur. Proof of Facts

This set of more than 130 volumes (*Proof of Facts, Proof of Facts 2d*, and *Proof of Facts 3d*) is designed to assist in the preparation for and proving of facts at trials, both civil and criminal trials. The set is also available on Westlaw and in CD-ROM form. The articles in *Proof of Facts* are kept current by annual pocket parts and the addition of new volumes each year. *Proof of Facts* provides practical information regarding conducting client interviews, preparing witnesses for trial, conducting discovery, negotiating settlements, examining witnesses, and introducing evidence at trial. Each article provides background information regarding certain types of cases, for instance, personal injury, employment discrimination, or real estate litigation, and will then succinctly set forth the elements of such a case, which must be proved to prevail at trial. Sample interrogatories (written questions directed at parties in litigation) and other sample discovery forms will be provided together with model questions for examining witnesses. Each article includes a checklist providing an outline of the essential facts that must be established to prevail in a case or in asserting a defense. Diagrams and drawings that may be suitable for enlargement into poster-size courtroom exhibits are often included.

Access to this useful and practical guide to trial techniques is gained through a multivolume General Index. You only need to think of words that describe the issue or case you are researching and you will be directed to the appropriate article. That is, use the descriptive word approach to gain access to a pertinent article in this set.

(2) Am. Jur. Trials

This set of books consists of more than 80 volumes that focus on trial tactics and strategies. The articles in *Am. Jur. Trials* are authored by experienced litigators and provide a step-by-step approach to trial practice.

The first six volumes of the set, titled "Practice, Strategy, Controls," are devoted to matters common to all trials, such as fee agreements, investigating cases, discovery, settlement, jury selection, and closing arguments. Information is often presented by easy-to-follow checklists, which outline steps to be taken in litigation matters.

The remaining volumes in *Am. Jur. Trials* are titled "Model Trials" and are devoted to specific kinds of cases, such as elevator accident cases, dental malpractice cases, or contact sports injury cases and will analyze in depth the strategy of conducting trials of these specific types of cases, from the first meeting with a client through appeal. The articles in *Am. Jur. Trials* are kept current by annual pocket-part supplements. West states that the articles are authored by "a virtual 'Who's Who' of the American trial bar."

Access to the articles is achieved through the General Index, which is best utilized through the descriptive word approach. To locate a pertinent article, simply look up words or phrases that describe your research problem or trial, and the General Index will direct you to the appropriate volume and page of an article. Remember to use the supplement to the General Index.

Following are examples of actual topics covered by *Am. Jur. Trials*:

- Disputed Paternity Cases
- Stockbroker Liability Litigation
- Pharmacist Malpractice
- Automobile Airbag Malfunction Litigation: Practice and Strategy

West also offers this set on Westlaw and in CD-ROM form.

(3) Am. Jur. Pleading and Practice Forms Annotated

This set of books consists of more than 70 volumes that provide forms for every stage of state and federal litigation, including forms for complaints, answers, interrogatories, jury instructions, motions, and appeals. These forms are extremely useful and serve as excellent "how to" guides for drafting forms. Practical checklists are included to remind you of items to be included in various forms. If your state does not have its own sets of form books, this set will provide several examples of litigation documents, which you can tailor to your state's requirements and a client's needs. If you are asked to prepare a complaint or a set of interrogatories, consult *Am. Jur. Pleading and Practice Forms Annotated*, which contains numerous forms you can use as models. Case notes indicate the proper usage for each form and references to topic names and Key Numbers and other West resources, such as A.L.R. annotations, help you expand your research. More than 36,500 forms are included in this set, which is kept up to date by pocketpart supplements. To locate a form, retrieve the multivolume General Index to the set and then use the descriptive word technique. You will then be directed to the appropriate form. The set is available in CD-ROM form and on Westlaw, enabling you to export forms directly to your word processor and print forms instantly.

(4) Am. Jur. Legal Forms 2d

There are many documents prepared in the legal profession that are not litigation-oriented. These documents are often used in connection with a client's personal or business needs, such as a will, a trust, a lease, or minutes of corporate meetings. *Am. Jur. Legal Forms 2d* provides more than 23,000 such forms together with checklists, tips, and advice for preparing various forms and documents. For example, if you are drafting a lease, *Am. Jur. Legal Forms 2d* will provide you with a list setting forth the elements required for a valid lease. As is the case with *Am. Jur. Pleading and Practice Forms Annotated*, described above, you should feel free to customize the forms you find to comply with the client's needs and your state statutes. Often, optional or alternative clauses are provided, allowing you to pick and choose clauses to construct the best document for the client. A "caution" section is included to help you avoid common errors in document drafting. Tax checkpoints and information are also included. References to West's Key Number system, A.L.R., and other West resources are provided.

As in the other sets in TCSL discussed herein, this set is kept current by the use of pocket parts, which will provide new forms, checklists, or other pertinent material. Locating an appropriate form is accomplished by using the General Index to the set and then inserting words or phrases that

Figure 6-3

Sample Page from *Am. Jur. Legal Forms 2d*

---

§ 87:76　　　　　　　　　　　　　　　　　　　　DEEDS

Cross reference: For form of acknowledgment, see § 7:46. For forms of acknowledgments under the Uniform Recognition of Acknowledgments Act, see §§ 7:281 et seq.

§ 87:77 Connecticut—Quitclaim deed

Quitclaim deed made on __1____, 19_2_. To all people to whom these presents come, greeting:

Know ye, that I, __3____, of __4____ *[address]*, City of __5____, County of __6____, State of __7____, for the consideration of __8____ Dollars ($___) received to my full satisfaction, do remise, release, and forever quitclaim unto __9____, of __10____ *[address]*, City of __11____, County of __12____, State of __13____, his heirs, and assigns forever, all the right, title, interest, claim, and demand whatsoever that I have or ought to have in or to the following premises which are situated in the City of __14____, County of __15____, State of Connecticut: __16____ *[set forth legal description of property]*.

To have and to hold the premises, with all the appurtenances, unto the releasee, his heirs, and assigns forever, so that neither I, the releasor, nor my heirs nor any other person under myself or them shall hereafter have any claim, right, or title in or to the premises or any part thereof, but therefrom I and they are by these presents forever barred and excluded.

In witness whereof, I have hereunto set my hand and seal on the day and year first above written.

　　　　　　　　　　　　　　　　　　　　　　　　　[Signature]

　　　　　　　　　　　　　　　　　　　　　　　　　[Seal]

[Attestation]

[Acknowledgment]

☑ **Tax Notes:**

(See Tax Notes following § 87:61)

☑ **Notes on Use:**

(See also Notes on Use following § 87:61)

Statutory reference: This form reflects generally the provisions of **Conn** Gen S § 47-5. Statutory deed forms have not been enacted in Connecticut.

Text reference: For general discussion of drafting requirements of deeds, see 23 Am Jur 2d, Deeds §§ 18–40.

Cross reference: For form of acknowledgment, see § 7:46. For forms of acknowledgments under the Uniform Recognition of Acknowledgments Act, see §§ 7:281 et seq.

(For Tax Notes and Notes on Use of form, see end of form)

describe the problem or matter with which you are dealing. You will then be directed to the appropriate form. See Figure 6-3 for a sample page from *Am. Jur. Legal Forms 2d.* This set is also available in CD-ROM form and on Westlaw, allowing you to export forms to your word processor for printing and drafting.

e. Research Strategies for Using General Encyclopedias

There are several techniques used in locating the discussion of an area of law in C.J.S. or Am. Jur. 2d. The most commonly used research techniques, the descriptive word approach and the topic approach, are ones you are already familiar with and that you have used before in locating statutes in the annotated codes and cases in the digests.

(1) Descriptive Word Approach

The editors at West have selected certain words and phrases that describe the topics discussed in the encyclopedias and have listed these alphabetically in the multivolume general indexes to C.J.S. and Am. Jur. 2d. To use this approach, simply think of words or phrases that describe the issue you are researching. Look up these words in the volumes of the general index for C.J.S. or Am. Jur. 2d and you will be directed to the appropriate topic and section. You should read the section to which you are referred for the background information relating to your legal issue and then begin reading in full the cases cited in support in the footnotes. Be sure to supplement your research by checking the pocket part to ensure that the narrative statement of the law is correct and to locate cases more recent than those cited in the footnotes in the main volume. See Figure 6-4 for a sample page from an index to Am. Jur. 2d.

Because volumes in Am. Jur. 2d are replaced as needed, and because the replacement volumes may add new sections and discussions, it is possible that the General Index may send you to a section in an older volume that does not exist in a newer replacement volume. In such a case, check the Table of Parallel References found in the front of each volume. This feature is called the Correlation Table in newer volumes and is now found in the back of the hardback volumes. These tables will convert the old section number to the new section you should read in the replacement volume.

(2) Topic Approach

Because the more than 400 legal topics discussed in C.J.S. and Am. Jur. 2d are arranged alphabetically, it is often possible to use the topic approach successfully in locating a discussion of the area of law in which you are interested. To use the topic approach, simply think of the area of law related to your issue, for instance, Corporations, Landlord and Tenant, or Partnerships — and immediately retrieve that volume from the shelf. You should then examine the "scope note" to ensure that the specific issue you are interested in is included in the discussion to follow. The next step is to review the outline of the topic under discussion, which will quickly refer you to the appropriate section.

Figure 6-4
Sample Page from General Index Update to Am. Jur. 2d

GENERAL INDEX UPDATE

JOB DISCRIMINATION —Cont'd
Pregnancy discrimination
    generally, **JobDiscrim** § 135-146
    benefits during pregnancy. Pregnancy benefits, above
    fetal protection plans, selection and screening practices, **JobDiscrim** § 397
    health insurance
        benefits provided, **JobDiscrim** § 709, 710
        pregnancy benefits, above
    maternity leave, above
    no-pregnancy requirement, selection and screening practices, **JobDiscrim** § 396
    sex bias, pregnancy discrimination as, **JobDiscrim** § 138
    sick leave, **JobDiscrim** § 756
    state statutes, pregnancy leave and associated benefits, **JobDiscrim** § 146
    transfers and job assignments, **JobDiscrim** § 801-804
    weight restriction, selection and screening practices, **JobDiscrim** § 435
Preliminary injunctions. Injunctions, above
Preliminary motions
    generally, **JobDiscrim** § 2265-2283
    dismissal, motions for, above
    judgments on the pleadings, **JobDiscrim** § 2279
    more definite statement, **JobDiscrim** § 2280
    sanctions under FRCP 11, motions for, **JobDiscrim** § 2282, 2283
    stay of proceedings, **JobDiscrim** § 2281
    strike, motions to, below
    summary judgment motions, below
President of United States
    Government Employee Rights Act, presidential appointees, judicial proceedings on employment
        determinations, **JobDiscrim** § 1809
    religious discrimination, presidential appointees, prohibition, **JobDiscrim** § 126
Pretext
    generally, **JobDiscrim** § 2505-2510
    attacking employer's credibility, **JobDiscrim** § 2509
    comparison with similarly situated individuals, **JobDiscrim** § 2507
    direct evidence of discriminatory intent, **JobDiscrim** § 2508
    discharge and discipline, **JobDiscrim** § 946, 947
    disparate treatment, standard in individual case, **JobDiscrim** § 2505, 2506
    liquidated damages, **JobDiscrim** § 2669
    pattern and practice cases, **JobDiscrim** § 2510
    retaliation, **JobDiscrim** § 251
Pretrial conferences and orders
    generally, **JobDiscrim** § 2312-2314
    individual cases, **JobDiscrim** § 2313
    pretrial orders, **JobDiscrim** § 2314
    strategic considerations, **JobDiscrim** § 2313
Pretrial pleadings and motions
    generally, **JobDiscrim** § 2220-2295
    admissibility of testimony, summary judgment motions, **JobDiscrim** § 2289
    affirmative defenses in answers, **JobDiscrim** § 2257
    business necessity defense, summary judgment motions, **JobDiscrim** § 2292
    continuance of summary judgment motions, **JobDiscrim** § 2290
    counterclaims, **JobDiscrim** § 2258

(3)   Table of Statutes Approach

Because both Am. Jur. 2d and C.J.S. include a separate volume titled "Table of Laws and Rules," you can use this volume to look up specific statutes, administrative regulations, or Uniform Laws in which you are interested, and you will be directed to the appropriate volume, topic, and section within the encyclopedia set. The Table is usually shelved at the end of the set.

(4)   Table of Cases Approach

Because C.J.S. now includes an alphabetical table of cases (found in softcover volumes shelved after the main volumes in the set), you can readily locate a discussion of a case if you know its name. Am. Jur. 2d does not include a table of cases, so this approach will not work if you are using Am. Jur. 2d.

3.   Local or State Encyclopedias

a. Introduction

You have seen that C.J.S. and Am. Jur. 2d are general encyclopedias that provide a national overview of more than 400 areas of the law. It is possible, however, that you may not need such broad coverage of a topic and are interested only in the law for your particular state. In this instance, you should consult an encyclopedia for your state, *if* one is published for your state. Not every state has its own encyclopedia. Generally, you will find encyclopedias published for the more populous states.

To determine if an encyclopedia exists for your state, check the card catalog in the law library, ask a reference librarian, or simply look at the shelves in the law library devoted to the law of your state. Carefully examine the books you find, as some state encyclopedias label themselves "digests."

Most of the local sets are published by West (either because West was the original publisher of the set or acquired the set when it purchased Lawyers Cooperative). The West sets are arranged much like C.J.S. and include references to other West resources, including A.L.R. annotations and various sets in the TCSL, such as *Am. Jur. Legal Forms*. Many include references to topic names and key numbers, allowing easy access into West's digests. A few sets are published by LEXIS Publishing. If your state does not have a local encyclopedia, use C.J.S. or Am. Jur. 2d and research your state's law by locating cases in the footnotes from your state. See Figure 6-5 for a list of the local encyclopedias and their publishers.

b. Features Common to State Encyclopedias

The following features are common to most state encyclopedias:

  (i)   *Coverage.* The discussion of the law presented will relate only to the law of a particular state, and the cases you will be directed to will be from that state or from federal courts that have construed that state's law.

(ii) *Arrangement.* The various topics covered in a state encyclopedia are arranged alphabetically. The narrative statements of the law are clearly presented, and you will be directed to cases and other authorities through the use of supporting footnotes.

(iii) *Table of Cases.* Unlike Am. Jur. 2d, which does not contain a table of cases, many local sets will contain tables that alphabetically list the cases discussed or cited in the set. Thus, if you know the name of a case in your state, you can readily locate the text discussion of it or the area of law with which it deals by using the Table of Cases.

(iv) *Table of Statutes.* While C.J.S. and Am. Jur. 2d refer you only to selected federal statutes or uniform laws, many state encyclopedias contain a detailed table of statutes, which will direct you to a discussion or reference of a statute in which you are interested. Thus, if you are interested in Section 50 of the California Probate Code, you simply look this up in the table of statutes and you will be referred to any titles and sections in Cal. Jur. 3d where this statute is discussed.

(v) *Indexing.* Most state encyclopedias have a multi-volume general index usually located after the last volume in the set. Additionally, many encyclopedias precede the discussion of a topic with an index or outline of the various subjects discussed within the topic.

Figure 6-5
List of Local Encyclopedias

Encyclopedias Published by West	*Encyclopedias Published by LEXIS*
California Jurisprudence, Third	Illinois Jurisprudence
Florida Jurisprudence, Second	Michigan Law and Practice
Georgia Jurisprudence	Encyclopedia, 2d
Illinois Law and Practice	Pennsylvania Law Encyclopedia
Indiana Law Encyclopedia	Tennessee Jurisprudence
Kentucky Jurisprudence (ceased in 2001)	Michie's Jurisprudence of Virginia and West Virginia
Maryland Law Encyclopedia	
Massachusetts Jurisprudence (ceased in 1998)	
Michigan Civil Jurisprudence	
New York Jurisprudence, Second	
Ohio Jurisprudence, Third	
Summary of Pennsylvania Jurisprudence, Second	
South Carolina Jurisprudence	
Texas Jurisprudence, Third	

(vi) *Supplementation.* State encyclopedias are supplemented or kept up to date in the same manner as the general encyclopedias, C.J.S. and Am. Jur. 2d, that is, by cumulative pocket parts and replacement volumes.

c. Research Strategies for Using State Encyclopedias

The research techniques used to access the state or local encyclopedias are as follows:

(i) *Descriptive Word Approach.* By selecting words and phrases that describe the issue you are researching and then inserting these into the general index, you will be directed to the appropriate topic and section.

(ii) *Topic Approach.* Think of the topic or area of law your issue deals with and then retrieve this specific volume from the shelf. Examine the outline of the topic preceding the narrative discussion of the law to determine the specific section you should read.

(iii) *Table of Cases Approach.* If you are interested in a discussion of a particular case from your state, look up the case name in the table of cases for your set, and you will be referred to the topic and section that discuss it.

(iv) *Table of Statutes Approach.* If you are researching a particular statute in your state, you can look it up in the table of statutes, and you will be directed to the relevant topic and section in the encyclopedia.

Practice Tip

Encyclopedias

When using legal encyclopedias, start small. Use a set for your state (if one is available) before using either of the national sets (C.J.S. or Am. Jur. 2d). Similarly, when presented with a list of cases in footnotes, read the ones from your jurisdiction before reading those from other jurisdictions.

---

4. Special Subject Encyclopedias

The encyclopedias previously discussed, C.J.S., Am. Jur. 2d, and the local encyclopedias, discuss hundreds of areas of the law. There are, however, a few encyclopedias that are devoted to just one area of the law. For example, *Fletcher Cyclopedia of the Law of Private Corporations* contains more than 30 volumes and discusses in depth the law relating to corporations. Check the card catalog at your law library to determine if an encyclopedia exists for a particular subject. Many of these "encyclopedias," however, are more accurately classified as treatises, as discussed in Section C of this chapter. The best research strategy to employ when using a special subject encyclopedia is the descriptive word approach. The encyclopedia will contain either a separate index volume or the index will be found in the last volume of the set. The alphabetically arranged index will contain numerous words and phrases describing topics discussed in the set and will refer you to the appropriate volume and section of the set describing the area of law in which you are interested.

5. *Summary*

Encyclopedias provide excellent introductions to numerous areas of the law as well as easy-to-understand summaries of the law. You must remember, however, to read the primary sources you are directed to by the encyclopedias, as these mandatory authorities *must* be followed by courts, and the encyclopedias are merely persuasive authorities, which *may* be followed. If you are assigned a research project and you are uncertain where or how to begin, begin with an encyclopedia. Be sure this is the beginning, however, and not the end of your research, as the information presented to you in encyclopedias is generally introductory rather than analytical. Encyclopedias generally tell you what the law is, not what it should be. While you may readily rely on encyclopedias to provide an accurate overview of the law, you should not cite an encyclopedia as authority in any brief or project you prepare unless there are no primary authorities or no other more creditable secondary authorities, such as Restatements, treatises, or law review articles on which to rely. Although encyclopedias are helpful resources, they are not sufficiently scholarly to serve as the sole support for an argument you advance. If you remember these guidelines, encyclopedias will serve as excellent starting points for your legal research.

The Final Wrap-Up

Using and Citing Legal Encyclopedias

Use: Use legal encyclopedias to "get your feet wet" and gain background information about a topic. Encyclopedias provide a general overview rather than an exhaustive treatment of a topic. Rely on the cases encyclopedias refer you to rather than on the encyclopedia itself.

(continued)

The Final Wrap-Up *(Continued)*	
Citation:	Do not cite to encyclopedias in any court documents or other legal writings unless there are no primary authorities on which you can rely. A citation to a legal encyclopedia is a signal to a reader that your argument is so weak that there are no mandatory authorities that support your viewpoint.

B. Legal Periodicals

1. Introduction

Just as you might subscribe to a periodical publication such as *Time Magazine, People Weekly*, or *Sports Illustrated*, law firms, legal practitioners, paralegals, law libraries, legal departments of businesses, and agencies subscribe to a variety of publications that are produced on a regular or periodic basis and which discuss a wide range of legal topics.

There are four broad categories of legal periodicals: publications of law schools; publications of bar associations and paralegal associations; specialized publications for those in the legal profession sharing similar interests; and legal newspapers and newsletters. All of these publications are secondary sources. While many of them, particularly the publications of law schools, are very well respected and scholarly, they remain persuasive authorities whose views *may* be followed rather than primary or mandatory authorities that *must* be followed, if relevant.

The legal periodicals typically direct you to primary authorities (cases, statutes, regulations, and constitutions) through the use of extensive footnotes. In fact, sometimes half of each page of a law school periodical consists of footnotes. The footnotes will also direct you to other relevant secondary authorities and practice guides.

The periodical publications serve many functions. Some provide extensive analyses of legal topics; some serve to keep practitioners current on recent developments in the law; and some provide practical information relating to problems and issues facing those in the legal profession.

2. Law School Publications

Most law schools produce a periodical publication generally referred to as a "law review," such as the *Montana Law Review, University of Cincinnati Law Review*, or *William and Mary Law Review*, although a few title their publications "journals," such as the *Emory Law Journal, Rutgers Law Journal*, and *Yale Law Journal*. These are typically published three or more times each year, initially in softcover pamphlet form and later in hardbound volumes. More than 100 law schools publish these reviews, which contain articles on a variety of legal topics. Because the law reviews are published so frequently, they often provide topical analysis of recent cases or recently enacted legislation.

The law reviews are published by law students who have been selected to write for the law review based on academic distinction or writing samples submitted to the board of editors of the law review. These editors are typically second- and third-year law students who bear the primary responsibility for editing and publishing the law review, although faculty members often advise the students. Despite the fact that the law reviews are principally the product of students, they have a high degree of respectability due to the exacting and rigorous standards of the editors. Do not equate these law reviews with the newspapers or newsletters produced at a college. The law reviews provide scholarly analysis of legal topics and are routinely cited with approval by courts. The law reviews differ greatly from encyclopedias, which are noncritical in their approach and usually focus on merely explaining the law. The law reviews offer a critical approach and often advocate reform and change in the law.

A law review usually has several sections:

(i) *Articles.* "Articles" are usually scholarly monographs or essays written by professors, judges, or practicing attorneys. Often exceeding 30 pages in length, an article examines a topic in depth. The topics explored are diverse and may range from an analysis of the California Agricultural Relations Act to a study of discrimination against handicapped persons to an examination of the legal rights of the mentally ill. Despite the fact that these articles are authored by professors, judges, and attorneys, the students on the review's board of editors edit the articles, check the accuracy of the citations in the article, and make suggestions for revisions.

(ii) *Comments* and *Notes.* "Comments" and "Notes" are generally shorter pieces authored by students. These shorter analyses typically examine diverse legal topics, such as warranties in the sale of goods, conflicts of interest for former government attorneys, or tort liability for defective products.

(iii) *Case Comments / Recent Cases / Recent Developments.* This section is also authored by students and examines the impact of a recent case or newly enacted legislation.

(iv) *Book Reviews.* Just as *Newsweek Magazine* reviews recent works of fiction in each issue, most law reviews contain a section that reviews books or texts relating to legal issues, such as *Hazardous Product Litigation, Handbook of the Law of Antitrust,* or *Justice by Consent: Plea Bargains in the American Courthouse.* A critical analysis of the book is provided together with an identification of the publisher and the price of the book.

Almost all law schools publish one of these general types of law reviews; that is, a review containing articles on a variety of topics, such as corporate law, civil law, criminal law, trademark law, and so forth. In addition to these general law reviews, many law schools also provide other law reviews devoted to a specific area, such as international law or civil rights. For example, Boston College Law School publishes the following reviews in addition to its general law review, called the *Boston College Law Review*:

> *Boston College Environmental Affairs Law Review*
> *Boston College International and Comparative Law Review*
> *Boston College Third World Law Journal*

Often law reviews are arranged alphabetically in a law library, so that the *Akron Law Review* is followed by the *Alabama Law Review*, which is then followed by the *Albany Law Review*, and so forth, making the task of locating a law review easy and efficient. Law reviews are cited as follows:

> Article (*The Bluebook* and *ALWD*): Carl L. Vacketta & Thomas C. Wheeler, *A Government Contractor's Right to Abandon Performance*, 65 Geo. L.J. 27 (1976).
> Student Note (*The Bluebook*): Sylvia T. Parker, Note, *Debtors' Rights to Debt Counseling*, 98 Tul. L. Rev. 1604 (1988).
> Student Note (*ALWD*): Sylvia T. Parker, Student Author, *Debtors' Rights to Debt Counseling*, 98 Tul. L Rev. 1604 (1988).

See Figure 6-6 for a sample page of a law review.

3. Bar Association and Paralegal Association Publications

Each state and the District of Columbia has a bar association. Usually an attorney cannot practice law in a jurisdiction without becoming a member of that state's bar association. The dues paid to the association often fund various legal programs such as services for indigents, disciplinary proceedings, and the periodical publication of a journal for the members of the bar. Some bar associations publish monthly journals while others publish every other month. The *ABA Journal* is a very professional-looking publication that is sent to members of the American Bar Association each month.

These publications usually offer a very practical approach to practicing law in a jurisdiction and feature articles on ethics; changes in local court rules, local cases, or local legislation; provide human interest biographies of judges or practitioners in the state; publish lists of attorneys who have been suspended or disbarred from the practice of law; and review books, software, and other publications of interest to practitioners. These journals usually resemble nonlegal publications such as *Time Magazine* or *Newsweek Magazine*. Their size ($8\frac{1}{2}'' \times 11''$) is the same as the popular press publications, and they usually feature a photograph of a judge or lawyer on a glossy front page. A table of

Figure 6-6
Sample Cover from Law Review

Fall 2004   Volume 41 Number 1

CALIFORNIA

WESTERN

LAW

REVIEW

contents is included as well as a variety of advertisements for products and services aimed at the legal profession, such as office furniture, software programs, seminars, and books.

The articles published in these bar association publications are far more practical in their approach than the academic articles published in law reviews. For example, an article in a law review relating to child support might well examine the development and evolution of cases and legislation in that area of the law, analyze the social policies served by child support, and advocate for reform, if needed. In contrast, an article in a bar association publication might be titled "How to Calculate Child Support" and would provide no such scholarly analysis, but rather would focus on the practical aspects of the process of calculating the amount of child support a noncustodial parent should pay.

Just as there are state bar associations, many local jurisdictions will often have city or county bar associations, such as the Bar Association of Montgomery County, Maryland. Many specialized groups may form local associations, such as the Women's Bar Association of the District of Columbia. These associations also produce periodical publications: Some are pamphlets, and others are informal newsletters or flyers. Generally, these publications are very practical and informal in approach. Articles relate solely to local matters, such as changes to the local rules of court, and they often serve to inform the membership of educational or social functions. Job postings are often included.

In summary, the publications of bar associations tend to focus on practical guidelines for law practice. It is unlikely that you would conduct substantive research using these publications. It is far more likely that your use of these publications will be aimed at keeping you current on legal issues facing your jurisdiction. See Figure 6-7 for a sample cover from a bar association periodical.

Just as bar associations are composed of attorneys and produce a periodical publication, there are associations composed of legal assistants that produce periodical publications. For example, the National Association of Legal Assistants publishes a quarterly magazine called *Facts & Findings*. Similarly, the National Federation of Paralegal Associations issues a bimonthly publication called the *National Paralegal Reporter*. Other periodicals and journals exist for paralegals and are published independently of any association. One of the better-known publications is *Legal Assistant Today* (see http://www.legalassistanttoday. com). These publications publish articles of interest to paralegals, such as information on licensing and certification issues; articles offering practical approaches to paralegal tasks such as interviewing, document control, and discovery; and data on average salaries and benefits. Advertisements feature books, software, and seminars. If you belong to a local paralegal association, you will see that its newsletter will undoubtedly contain announcements of job vacancies.

Similar in approach to the journals and periodicals published by bar associations, the journals and periodicals published for legal assistants share a practical focus and are oriented to providing useful information to practicing paralegals.

Figure 6-7
Sample Cover from Bar Association Periodical

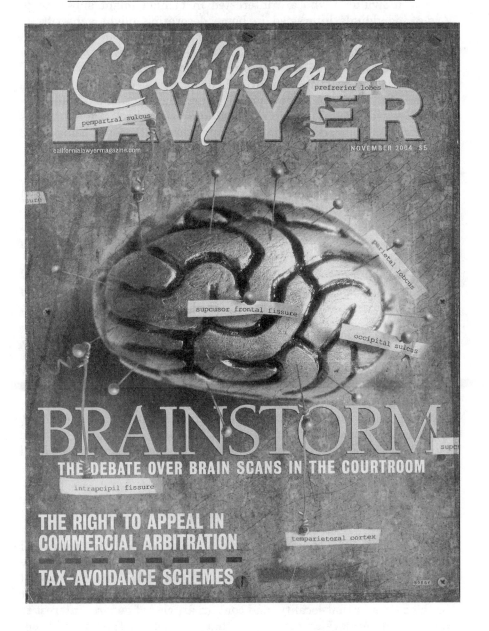

4. Specialized Publications

Just as individuals who are interested in fashion might subscribe to *Vogue*, individuals interested in home decorating might subscribe to *Better Homes and Gardens*, and individuals interested in aviation and defense might subscribe to *Aviation Week & Space Technology*, legal practitioners who have an interest in a specialized area of the law might subscribe to a specialized periodical. Thus, numerous journals and periodicals exist to provide practitioners who focus on a certain area of the law with the information of most interest to them. The numerous specialized periodicals vary in their approach, with some being more analytical and academic, such as the *Computer/Law Journal*, which contains scholarly articles on trade secrets and the protection of proprietary computer software, and others being more practical in approach such as the *Medical Trial Technique Quarterly*, which contains useful articles on topics such as how to cross-examine an expert cardiologist or how effectively to review medical records. Other examples of specialized periodicals are the *American Bankruptcy Law Journal*, the *Human Rights Quarterly*, the *Entertainment and Sports Lawyer*, the *Transportation Law Journal*, the *Trial Lawyer's Guide*, the *Practical Real Estate Lawyer*, and the *Journal of Taxation*. Practitioners interested in keeping current with developments in these fields subscribe to these publications.

Additionally, many periodicals are published for individuals who may share common interests, such as the *Chicano-Latino Law Review*, the *Catholic Lawyer*, the *Women's Rights Law Reporter*, the *National Black Law Journal*, and the *American Indian Law Review*. Some periodicals focus on the interplay between law and other fields of endeavor, such as the *Journal of Health Law*, the *Review of Clinical Psychiatry and the Law*, the *Journal of Law and Politics*, and the *Ecology Law Quarterly*. These journals or periodicals focus on issues that have implications for the legal field as well as some other field.

5. Legal Newspapers and Newsletters

In large cities such as New York and Los Angeles, you will find daily legal newspapers such as the *New York Law Journal* and the *Los Angeles Daily Journal*. These newspapers, published every weekday, contain the text of recent appellate cases from the state, publish the court calendar or docket for the courts in that locality, and contain articles of general interest to lawyers and paralegals practicing in that jurisdiction. They usually contain extensive classified advertisements and serve as a useful source of job announcements and vacancies.

Other smaller metropolitan areas, such as San Diego, often publish a newspaper every weekday that combines information about law with general business information. Thus, the *San Diego Daily Transcript* contains the court docket, information, and articles of interest to those in the legal profession as well as information relating to bankruptcy filings, the recording of mechanics' liens, and bidding dates for various construction projects in the area.

Some legal newspapers do not restrict their coverage to any locality; they are national in scope, such as the *National Law Journal*, which is published weekly. This weekly newspaper for legal professionals includes articles on a variety of legal topics including ethics, law school admissions, and criminal law matters. Additionally, recent state court and federal court decisions are highlighted. Professional announcements such as those relating to law firm mergers or formations and advertisements for career opportunities are included. A weekly newspaper, *Legal Times*, and a monthly newspaper, *The American Lawyer*, are similar in their coverage.

In addition to legal newspapers, more than 2,000 legal and law-related newsletters are published in the United States. Some of these newsletters are one-page bulletins; others are multiple-page newsletters; and others are looseleaf reporting services, which are stored in ringed binders. Some newsletters offer only short articles, while others provide in-depth analysis of legal issues. Examples of these newsletters include *Jury Trials and Tribulations* (published twice per month and containing summaries of civil jury trials in Florida) and *Bank Bailout Litigation News* (a publication reporting on bank closings and related banking matters).

6. *How to Locate Periodical Articles*

While each issue of a law review, bar association publication, specialized periodical, or legal newspaper will contain its own table of contents, it would be extremely ineffective to conduct research by retrieving each of these hundreds of publications and scanning its table of contents in the hope that you will eventually stumble upon an article of interest to you. To locate an article in a periodical publication, you must consult one of several published indexes that will direct you to articles published in periodicals. There are several well-known indexes you can use.

a. *Index to Legal Periodicals & Books*

If you think back to the research you did for high school or college term papers, you may recall using *The Readers' Guide to Periodical Literature*, which directed you to articles in the popular press such as *Time Magazine*, *U.S. News & World Report*, or *Forbes Magazine*. Your technique was to think of words and phrases that described the topic you were researching and look those up in *The Readers' Guide*. You would then be directed to a relevant article in a particular issue of a periodical.

The *Index to Legal Periodicals & Books* is substantially similar in format to *The Readers' Guide*. In fact, both are published by the same company, so if you have used *The Readers' Guide*, you will be comfortable using the *Index to Legal Periodicals & Books* (I.L.P.). I.L.P. indexes articles and books published in the United States, Australia, Canada,

Great Britain, Ireland, and New Zealand. The articles, case notes, and biographies must be at least two pages in length to be included. I.L.P. is initially published in softcover monthly pamphlets that are later bound in hardcover volumes.

To locate an article you may use any of the following techniques:

(i)   *Subject-Author Approach.*   The subject approach calls for you to think of words describing the topic you are interested in, such as bankruptcy, divorce, or emotional distress. Look for these words in I.L.P.'s alphabetically arranged Subject and Author Index. You will then be directed to periodicals that have published articles regarding this topic. Alternatively, if you happen to know that Deborah L. Rhode is an expert on gender bias, you can look up "Rhode" in this Index and you will be directed to articles written by her.

(ii)   *Table of Cases Approach.*   If you want to read articles that have discussed certain cases, such as *United States v. Nixon*, you can look up this case name in I.L.P.'s Table of Cases. Case names can be located by either the plaintiff's or the defendant's name. You will then be directed to pertinent periodical articles written about this case.

(iii)   *Table of Statutes Approach.*   If you are interested in whether any articles have analyzed a particular statute, you can look the statute up in I.L.P.'s Table of Statutes, which will direct you to articles discussing this statute.

(iv)   *Book Review Approach.*   If you are looking for a review of a certain book, locate the title of the book in the Book Review Index in I.L.P., and you will be directed to periodicals that have reviewed this book.

See Figure 6-8 for sample pages from I.L.P.

Because I.L.P. is cumulated on a monthly, quarterly, and annual basis, you may need to check several pamphlets and several bound volumes for the years you are interested in. Thus, if you are interested in nuisances, you may have to check the softcover pamphlets for this year, looking up "nuisance" in each one, and then continue by looking up "nuisance" in last year's bound volume of I.L.P., then the previous year's bound volume of I.L.P., and so forth. While this process may seem a bit time-consuming, it will yield great rewards, as I.L.P. indexes more than 800 periodicals and dates back to 1908. When using I.L.P., start with the current issues and work backward in time.

I.L.P. is also available in CD-ROM. If your library has purchased I.L.P. in CD-ROM, this will make your search easier by eliminating the need to look at several pamphlets or volumes of the set. An online or Web-accessible version of I.L.P. is called "Legal Periodicals & Books." It is updated on a monthly basis and encompasses everything included in I.L.P. since 1983. Researching using the online index is much easier than using the conventional I.L.P. print volumes because the online version is completely cumulative. Once you type in the appropriate search terms

Figure 6-8
Sample Pages from *Index to Legal Periodicals & Books*

Entry by author

Entry by topic

Figure 6-8 *(Continued)*

TABLE OF CASES

(topic, author, case, and so forth) you will be directed to all pertinent articles from 1983 until last month. I.L.P. is also available on LEXIS and Westlaw.

b. *Current Law Index, Legal Resource Index,* and *LegalTrac*

Current Law Index. (C.L.I.) is a comprehensive index of more than 900 legal periodicals from the United States, Australia, Canada, Ireland, New Zealand, and the United Kingdom. C.L.I. is published in monthly softcover pamphlets that are cumulated each quarter and then again at year end. C.L.I. indexes all articles from the periodicals it covers, unlike I.L.P., which does not index shorter articles. There are four approaches to locating articles in C.L.I.

(i) *Subject Approach.* The Subject Index lists entries alphabetically by subject name, such as contracts, franchises, or health insurance. By looking up the subject you are interested in you will be referred to a relevant periodical article.

(ii) *Author-Title Approach.* The Author-Title Index alphabetically indexes articles written by certain authors, such as Laurence H. Tribe. When you look up the author's name, you will be directed to periodicals containing articles by that author. This section also indexes book reviews by title of the book and the author's name.

(iii) *Table of Cases Approach.* If you are interested in cases that have been the focus of an article, you can look up the case in the Table of Cases by either the plaintiff's name or the defendant's name, and you will be directed to pertinent periodical articles.

(iv) *Table of Statutes Approach.* If a statute has been analyzed in depth in an article, you can locate it in the alphabetically arranged Table of Statutes, which will refer you to any article that has concentrated on treating that statute.

The company that publishes C.L.I., Thomson Gale (part of the Thomson Corporation, of which West is also a part), offers on microfilm the same information found in the conventional books that make up C.L.I. as well as articles from legal newspapers and articles in the popular press that are related to law. C.L.I. is also available on LEXIS and Westlaw as "Legal Resource Index." Finally, C.L.I. is available in CD-ROM form and through the Internet as a product called LegalTrac. LegalTrac is an online index to the articles found in C.L.I. together with articles found in business and general interest periodicals. Many law libraries subscribe to Legal-Trac, allowing you desktop computer access so you can easily search for and locate relevant articles by subject matter, author name, or key words. Because LegalTrac is a Web-based product, it is continuously updated.

One of the advantages of Legal Resource Index (or LegalTrac) over C.L.I. has to do with cumulation. C.L.I. (the conventional printed set) is arranged very similarly to I.L.P., thus requiring you to look at several pamphlets and hardbound volumes to find articles of interest to you. Because the microfilm version of C.L.I., Legal Resource Index (and its CD-ROM and Internet version, LegalTrac) is completely cumulative, once you locate the topic, author, case, or subject you are interested in, you will be presented with all relevant articles written since 1980, the year this index was created.

While C.L.I. covers more periodicals than I.L.P., it does have one drawback: It was created in 1980, and therefore its coverage does not extend to any article written before 1980. To locate articles before 1980, use I.L.P. or one of the other indexes discussed herein.

c.   Other Indexes

While I.L.P. and C.L.I. (and their online versions) are the most comprehensive indexes because they send you to hundreds of periodicals, there are several other indexes you should know about that may help you locate periodical articles.

   (i)   *Index to Periodical Articles Related to Law*.   The indexes previously discussed will direct you only to legal publications. It is possible, however, that articles related to law may appear in the popular press such as *Time Magazine, U.S. News & World Report*, or *Fortune*. The *Index to Periodical Articles Related to Law*, published quarterly, will direct you to such articles through its indexes arranged alphabetically by subject and author.

  (ii)   *Index to Foreign Legal Periodicals*.   You may have noticed that I.L.P. and C.L.I. index articles from common law countries. The *Index to Foreign Legal Periodicals* will direct you to periodical articles from countries other than the United States and the British Commonwealth. This index is issued quarterly and indexes articles longer than four pages that relate to international law, comparative law, and the municipal law of non-common law countries. Access is gained through an alphabetically arranged subject index (which is in English), a geographical index, and an index by author. If you are interested in reviewing articles written in foreign countries, the *Index to Foreign Legal Periodicals* is an excellent starting place.

 (iii)   *Current Index to Legal Periodicals*.   This weekly publication provides very rapid access to recent periodical articles.

  (iv)   *Jones-Chipman Index to Legal Periodicals*.   As you know, I.L.P. will index and direct you to periodical articles written since 1908. To locate articles written before 1908, consult this index.

d. Special Subject Indexes

There are numerous other indexes, some of which index articles related to specific legal topics such as the following: *Criminal Justice Periodical Index; Index to Federal Tax Articles*; and *Index to Canadian Legal Periodical Literature*. These indexes typically are arranged alphabetically by subject.

e. Other Finding Techniques

Often you may be directed to a particular law review or periodical article in the course of your research. For example, following a statute in U.S.C.S. is a "Research Guide," which typically recommends various A.L.R. annotations and law review articles relating to the statute you are researching. (See Figure 3-6.) These references to law reviews are found in U.S.C.A. and other annotated codes as well. Similarly, when you Shepardize or KeyCite cases or statutes, you will be directed to periodical articles written about them. Additionally, after you locate an article, you can Shepardize it and be directed to later cases and other articles that have mentioned the article you have read, leading to an ever-increasing collection of legal resources. Shepardizing and KeyCiting are discussed in Chapter 9. Periodical articles can also be located through LEXIS and Westlaw, the computer-assisted research systems discussed in Chapter 11.

Finally, an astounding number of articles are available on the Internet. For example, the University Law Review Project (http://www.lawreview.org) offers links to hundreds of law reviews and periodicals. The site allows searching for journal articles by key words inserted into a search box at the Internet site. Moreover, many law reviews have their own Web sites. For example, the Duke Law Journal offers the full text of each published issue online (at www.law.duke.edu/journals/dlj). Moreover, a number of specialty journals exist only on the Internet, as discussed in Chapter 12.

7. *Summary of Legal Periodicals*

All of the legal periodicals (law reviews, bar association and paralegal journals, specialized periodicals, and newspapers and newsletters) are secondary authorities. A court is not required to adhere to the view expressed in a periodical, though it may be persuaded to do so. Periodicals range in approach from the scholarly law reviews to the more practical bar association and paralegal association journals to brief bulletins and newsletters. Locating periodical articles is best accomplished by using one of the separately published comprehensive indexes such as the *Index to Legal Periodicals* or the *Current Law Index*. You may use the descriptive word approach, the author approach, the table of cases approach, or table of statutes approach to locate relevant articles. Consider using LegalTrac, the online index of legal periodicals since 1980.

Generally, if a periodical article has been written about a topic of interest to you, you should view it as "free research," because the article may well examine the area of law in depth, comparing and contrasting cases in various jurisdictions and analyzing all facets of the topic, thus reducing your research tasks. You can then Shepardize or KeyCite the article to locate newer articles or cases that mention the article you have read. Although periodical publications are not primary authorities, they are frequently cited (especially the authorative academic journal articles) in briefs and court documents to clarify and lend support to primary authorities such as cases.

The Final Wrap-Up

Using and Citing Periodicals

Use: Use legal periodicals to obtain a thorough analysis of a legal topic. Many periodicals (especially the law reviews) are highly regarded and will provide extensive information about a subject you are researching. Legal periodicals can provide a fresh and creative approach and are published more quickly than other books so they can offer information on current developments in the law.

Citation: Although all periodicals are secondary sources, some are highly persuasive. As you gain familiarity in reading cases, you will obtain greater insight into which periodicals are the most credible. Use *Shepard's Law Review Citations* to direct you to cases that cite your periodical with approval. You should primarily cite to the academic law reviews and special subject journals. Avoid citing to bar association publications, newspapers, and newsletters, which you should use to keep current in your field.

C.   Texts and Treatises

1.   Introduction

Texts written by legal scholars that focus on one topic of the law are referred to as treatises. Treatises comment upon and analyze an area of law. They do not include cases or statutes and are thus secondary sources. The authors may be academics or practicing attorneys. Treatises vary a great deal in scope and depth. A treatise may be a one-volume work on a fairly narrow legal topic, such as *Evaluating and Settling Personal Injury Claims*, or an analysis of a newly emerging area of the law, such as *Animal Law*, or an extremely well-known multivolume set on a broader topic, such as the 15-volume set *Collier on Bankruptcy, 15th Edition Revised*.

As you have seen, an encyclopedia typically examines hundreds of topics of law from abandonment to zoning and provides introductory information on these topics. Treatises, on the other hand, are devoted to one area of the law and usually examine it in depth. For example, if you were to read all of the sections of C.J.S. on Contracts, you would be presented with approximately 2,000 pages of material. If you were to review a well-known treatise on contracts, titled *Treatise on the Law of Contracts* by Samuel Williston, you would be presented with more than 30 volumes and approximately 18,000 pages of material.

You may recall that encyclopedias are noncritical summaries of the law, meaning that the information you are given merely summarizes the law relating to that topic. Treatises, however, may be "critical" in the sense that they may boldly criticize case law or question the logic of a judicial opinion. For example, the following language is found in 2 J. Thomas McCarthy, *McCarthy on Trademarks and Unfair Competition* § 18:56 (4th ed. 2004): "A small number of cases appear to have held that a contractual stipulation for quality control is sufficient, even though the licensor failed to exercise the right. In the author's opinion, such cases miss the point that not only must there be a right to control, but that right must be discharged by the licensor." While this comment may not strike you as overly harsh or critical, it is far different in tone from the encyclopedias, which merely present the law without any such disapproving commentary.

The narrative statements found in a treatise are typically more analytical than those found in encyclopedias. One feature treatises share in common with encyclopedias, however, is that they serve as casefinders. The format of most treatises is also similar to that of encyclopedias: Narrative discussions of the law are found on the top portion of each page with case citations located through the use of supporting footnotes in the lower portion of each page. One particular type of treatise is called a "hornbook," a one-volume text devoted to one area of the law, such as contracts, torts, or real property. Hornbooks are primarily designed for use by law students and offer broad and fairly academic coverage of a topic. Cases discussed tend to be the landmark cases in the field.

Remember that texts and treatises come in many forms: from one volume to a multivolume set; from analysis of very narrow topics, such as *Standby and Commercial Letters of Credit*, to analysis of a broader topic, such as criminal law, corporations or bankruptcy; from recently published analysis of newer legal topics, such as *Americans with Disabilities Act Handbook*, to the extremely well-known and respected treatise, *Prosser and Keeton on the Law of Torts*, which was first published in 1941 and is still the premier authority on torts; and from volumes that are in hardbound form to looseleaf binders to softcover pamphlets. Many treatises are now available in CD-ROM form. See Figure 6-9 for a sample page from a treatise.

In fact, if you are unsure what "category" a law book falls in, it is probably a treatise. No matter what kind of treatise it may be, however, it

Figure 6-9
Sample Page from a Treatise

§ 2.12 Determining Number of Business Units To Use in Organizing.

Ordinarily each enterprise or each set of closely related enterprises undertaken by the same group of participants is conducted through a single business organization. The use of a single business unit generally tends to promote efficiency and economy of management and operation by avoiding duplication of personnel, equipment, bookkeeping systems, advertising, incorporation fees and franchise taxes. Not uncommonly, however, a particular enterprise can be operated most advantageously not just as a single corporation or LLC but as several corporations or LLC's, or as a number of those entities and a partnership or two.[1] There may be sound business reasons, for instance, for separating the manufacturing and distribution phases of a business into two different organizations, or for setting up several entities to handle business in widely separated localities.

If a business is to be conducted in several states, organization of a separate corporation in a particular state to handle the business conducted within its borders may be desirable in order to take advantage of laws in that state favoring domestic corporations, or to avoid to some extent a prejudice against absentee ownership. Or the owners of a business may want to limit their liability to the greatest possible extent, and, with that end in view, they may organize a separate corporation for each locality in which they operate.[2]

[Section 2.12]

[1] The tax and nontax factors affecting the use of multiple corporations are considered in Dreher, Federal Income Tax Aspects of Multiple Corporations, 9 Hous L Rev 8, 9–15 (1971). See also Comment, United States v. Vogel Fertilizer Co.: Supreme Court Paves the Way for Avoidance of Brother-Sister Controlled Group Status, 16 Loy LAL Rev 647 (1983); Comment, Corporate Diversity Jurisdiction: Voluntary Multiple Incorporation and the Forum Doctrine, 12 Gonz L Rev 347 (1977); Moldave, Proposed Revision of IRC § 1563(a)(2): A New Definition for Brother-Sister Controlled Groups, 34 Hastings LJ 665 (1983).

For possible advantages, tax and otherwise, of setting up a "holding partnership," that is, of having a partnership (rather than a number of individuals) hold stock in a corporation, see Corneel, Using Partnerships To Solve Close Corporation Problems, NYU 22nd Inst on Fed Tax 629 (1964).

For an interesting discussion of the use of multiple corporations in real estate development, see Note, 19 Sw LJ 389 (1965).

[2] An extreme and unsuccessful example of fragmentation of a business into multiple corporations in order to limit liability is to be found in Walkovszky v. Carlton, 18 NY2d 414, 276 NYS2d 585 (1967); Goldberg v. Lee

remains a secondary authority, meaning that while a court may choose to follow a position advanced by a well-known and highly regarded treatise such as John H. Wigmore's *Evidence in Trials at Common Law*, the court is not required to do so. Courts have, however, cited numerous treatises with approval, and some treatises such as *Prosser and Keeton on the Law of Torts* have been cited hundreds of times, partly because of the caliber of the authors. You should feel free to rely upon and quote from treatises in memoranda and briefs that you prepare so long as you also have at least one "on point" primary authority to support your position. If you are unsure as to the credibility of the treatise, you can consult a source titled *Who's Who in American Law* and review the author's credentials. Alternatively, you can look up the author's name in the *Index to Legal Periodicals & Books* or in the *Current Law Index* to determine if the author has produced other writings on this topic, or you can ask the reference librarians in your law library for their opinions on the expertise of the author and the treatise's overall reputation in the courts. Finally, if the treatise has been published in multiple editions, this is a signal it is widely accepted and used.

Practice Tip

Books and Treatises

Treatises are usually found only in conventional book or print format. They are not available on the Internet (as are cases, statutes, constitutions, and other legal authorities) and unless they are practice guides including lots of forms, they are usually not available on LEXIS or Westlaw.

---

2. *Common Features of Treatises*

Treatises usually share the following features:

(i) *Format*. Treatises are essentially "expert opinions" on one topic of the law. The analysis of the law is presented in narrative form, and readers are usually directed to cases and other authorities through the use of footnotes. Generally, treatises are arranged by chapters and then by sections or paragraphs within those chapters.

(ii) *Index*. An index to the treatise consisting of an alphabetical arrangement of the topics, subjects, words, and phrases discussed in the treatise will be located in the last volume of the set or as a separate index volume after the last volume in the set.

(iii) *Table of Contents*. A table of contents will usually be presented in the front of each volume showing how the discussion of this area of the law is arranged by chapter.

(iv)   *Table of Cases.*   Most treatises contain an alphabetically arranged table of cases so you may readily locate a discussion of a certain case.

(v)   *Table of Statutes.*   Some treatises contain a table of statutes so you can locate the discussion of a certain statute.

(vi)   *Appendices.*   Many treatises include the text of statutes and regulations that are relevant to the area of law covered by the treatise. For example, the appendix to the treatise *McCarthy on the Law of Trademarks and Unfair Competition* includes the full text of the United States Trademark Act.

(vii)   *Updating.*   Most treatises are maintained by the traditional method of updating of legal books: an annual cumulative pocket part. If the treatise consists of looseleaf binders, it will be updated by periodically issued supplements placed in the binder or by replacement pages sent to the law library on a periodic basis. The law library will be provided with a set of instructions to, for example, "replace old page 41 with new page 41 and discard old page 41." Some treatises are kept current by a separate softcover supplement, which will be placed next to the main volume(s) of the treatises. Check the copyright year of any hardback volumes to make sure they are current.

You must *always* check the pocket part or supplement to determine if the narrative statement of the law presented in the main hardbound volume is still an accurate statement of the law and to locate cases and other authorities more current than those found in the footnotes in the hardbound volume.

3.   *Use of Treatises*

While encyclopedias serve as excellent introductions to a wide variety of legal topics, a treatise usually serves as a thorough examination of one area of the law. Although you are discouraged from citing encyclopedias, you are encouraged to cite treatises, particularly those with established reputations. For a comprehensive analysis of a topic with thoughtful evaluation of case law, consult a treatise.

If you are unsure whether a treatise has been written regarding the topic of law you are interested in, you can try various strategies:

(i)   Check the catalog in your law library for your topic (bankruptcy, contracts, trusts, and so forth). The catalog, which may be in print or microfiche format or online, will list every treatise the library contains relating to this topic and will direct you to the particular "stack" where the treatise is located.

(ii)   You can also go directly to the shelves where the books relating to this area of law are maintained. For example, all of the books relating to criminal law are generally shelved together, and all of the books relating to real property are generally shelved together. By skimming the titles of the books in the stacks and randomly inspecting these books, you may well "stumble upon" an excellent treatise.

(iii)   Ask the reference librarian for assistance. Even if your law library does not contain the treatise you need, you may be able to obtain one via an interlibrary transfer, that is, a "loan" from another library.

(iv)   Because many treatises are in high demand, check the reserve room at your law library, which may keep the most frequently consulted treatises on reserve.

4. *Research Strategies for Treatises*

There are several alternative methods you can use to locate a discussion in a treatise on an issue in which you are interested. Most of these are familiar to you.

(i)   *Descriptive Word Approach.*   This method simply calls for you to select a word or phrase describing the issue you are researching and locate this word or phrase in the index. The index will then direct you to the appropriate volume, paragraph, or section in the treatise.

For example, if the index directs you to **4:12**, this is a signal for you to review section 12 of volume 4 of the set. As always, the descriptive word approach is the most reliable research technique for beginning researchers.

(ii)   *Topic Approach.*   If you are relatively familiar with the treatise or subject matter you are researching, you may elect to bypass the index to the treatise and proceed directly to the table of contents. You would then scan the list of chapter titles and subdivisions and proceed immediately to the appropriate chapter.

(iii)   *Table of Cases Approach.*   If you are interested in locating a discussion of a particular case, you can look up the case name in the alphabetically arranged table of cases, which will direct you to that section of the treatise that analyzes, evaluates, and discusses that case. Similarly, if your treatise includes a table of statutes, it will direct you to text discussion of specific statutes.

(iv)   *Other Approaches.*   It is possible that you may be referred to a treatise through another source entirely. Thus, if you are reading a pertinent case on an issue you are researching and the case comments favorably and relies upon a treatise, you should then retrieve and examine the cited treatise. Similarly, other sources (encyclopedias, periodical articles, and library references found in U.S.C.A. and U.S.C.S.) may refer you to a treatise. See Figure 3-6 for references in U.S.C.S. to treatises on patents.

The Final Wrap-Up

Using and Citing Treatises

Use: Use treatises to find detailed and usually scholarly information on one topic of the law. A treatise will explain the law, provide commentary and practice tips, and will refer you to other authorities, generally through the use of footnotes. Use a treatise to obtain more in-depth analysis of a topic than that given by an encyclopedia and to help you locate cases on point.

Citation: Many treatises are highly regarded. In fact, some are so influential that they are known only by an author's name, such as "Prosser" or "Williston," and are given great credence in their respective fields. You may freely cite to treatises so long as you also cite to primary authority for your argument. Thus, cite a treatise to lend additional support to your argument, not as the sole support for your argument.

D. Restatements

1. Introduction

In 1923, a group of law scholars established the American Law Institute, which is composed of judges, law professors, eminent lawyers, and other jurists. The Institute was created in response to the ever-increasing volume of court decisions, which the members of the Institute believed produced both uncertainty and complexity in the law. The Institute's solution to this mass of irreconcilable and ambiguous case law was to "present an orderly statement of the general common law of the United States."

To accomplish this task, legal scholars called "Reporters" were appointed by the Institute for various subject matters such as torts, property, contracts, conflict of laws, and agency. Individuals are selected for membership in the Institute on the basis of their professional accomplishments and their commitment to improving the law. Membership is currently limited to 3,000, with the United States Supreme Court justices and chief judges of all United States Courts of Appeal and highest state courts as ex officio members. Each Reporter, together with his or her assistants and advisors, was assigned to one of these topics of the law to analyze carefully the assigned subject matter and thoroughly examine pertinent cases. Restatements do not exist for all areas of the law but only for selected topics. See Figure 6-10 for a chart of Restatements.

Figure 6-10
Charts of Restatments

Topic	Series
Agency	First* and Second
Conflict of Laws	First* and Second
Contracts	First* and Second
Foreign Relations Law of the United States	Second* and Third
Judgments	First* and Second
Law Governing Lawyers	Third
Property (includes volumes for Landlord & Tenant, Wills and Donative Transfers, Mortgages, and Servitudes)	First, Second, and Third
Restitution	First
Suretyship and Guaranty**	Third
Torts (includes volumes for Apportionment of Liability, Products Liability, and Liability for Physical Harm)	First and Second
Trusts (includes volume for Prudent Investor Rule)	First,* Second, and Third
Unfair Competition	Third
(**Replaces superseded Restatement of Security)	(*The original work on this subject is now out of print and has been replaced by the current series.)

The Reporters then prepared and presented preliminary drafts restating American common law in a terse and nearly rule-like fashion to the Institute. Various revisions to the drafts were made, and ultimately the Institute directed the publications of various final "Restatements," such as Restatement of Torts, Restatement of Contracts, and Restatement of Agency. Some of the Restatements have been updated or newly created in a second or third series, such as Restatement (Second) of Torts, Restatement (Second) of Contracts, and Restatement (Third) of Foreign Relations Law of the United States. For example, the newly created Restatement (Third) of the Law Governing Lawyers (dealing with regulation of the legal profession and the attorney-client relationship) was created in 2000 in its third series with no preceding first or second edition or series. All of the series of Restatements are subject to rigorous drafting and review, making them highly credible and reputable.

The goal of the Institute, to restate American case law in a clear and certain manner, has largely been accomplished due to the authority and repute of the members of the Institute. While the initial focus of the

Institute was merely to restate American case law in an unambiguous manner, the current emphasis is on predicting what courts might do in the future as well as restating what courts have held in the past.

2.   Arrangement of Restatements

Each Restatement typically consists of two to five volumes. Each volume is arranged in chapters, and the chapters are arranged in titles and numbered sections. Each section relates a principle of the law in clear straightforward language printed in bold typeface. These Restatement sections are followed by "comments" and "illustrations." The comments section provides general analysis of the legal principle previously given. The illustrations section exemplifies the legal principle by providing articulately written examples demonstrating the application of the principle. The Reporter's Notes then complete each section by providing general discussion and explanations, together with references to cases that support the Restatement position. Each Restatement includes updating volumes called "Appendix" volumes that direct you to cases that have cited Restatement sections. Recent volumes include cross-references to West's Key Number System and A.L.R. annotations.

The Restatements are updated by pocket parts, cumulative annual supplements, and the Interim Case Citation service, semiannual pamphlets providing Restatement citations more recent than those covered in the current pocket part. See Figure 6-11 for a sample page from Restatement (Second) of Torts.

3.   Research Strategies

To locate a pertinent Restatement provision, you can use either the descriptive word approach or the topic approach. To use the descriptive word approach, consult the alphabetically arranged index to the pertinent Restatement generally found in the last volume of the Restatement set. Look up words or phrases that describe your research problem and you will be directed to the appropriate section of the Restatement. Alternatively, you can use a one-volume index published for all of the Restatements in the First Series (although this is now out of date for Restatements in the Second or Third Series).

To use the topic approach, simply scan the table of contents located in the first volume of any Restatement volume. By quickly viewing the table of contents you will be sent to the pertinent section.

Because there is an alphabetical Table of Cases for the newer Restatements, you can use this to locate pertinent Restatement sections. The Table of Cases is usually located in the Index volume for the relevant Restatement. Look up case names in the Table of Cases and you will be directed to particular Restatement sections that mention or cite those cases.

as a secondary consequence illness or other bodily harm, such as
a miscarriage, by its internal operation upon the well-being
of the other. As to acts which are negligent because they are
intended or likely to cause an emotional disturbance which the
actor should recognize as likely so to affect the action of the
other or a third person as to cause bodily harm to the other,
see § 303. As to acts which threaten bodily harm, but result
in emotional disturbance alone, see § 435 A. As to acts which
otherwise threaten bodily harm, but result in such harm only
through emotional disturbance, see § 436. As to emotional disturbance as an element of damages where there is other harm,
see § 905.

§ 312. Emotional Distress Intended

If the actor intentionally and unreasonably subjects
another to emotional distress which he should recognize
as likely to result in illness or other bodily harm, he is
subject to liability to the other for an illness or other
bodily harm of which the distress is a legal cause,

(a) although the actor has no intention of inflicting
such harm, and

(b) irrespective of whether the act is directed against
the other or a third person.

See Reporter's Notes.

Comment:

a. The rule stated in this Section does not give protection
to mental and emotional tranquillity in itself. In general, as
stated in § 436 A, there is no liability where the actor's conduct
inflicts only emotional distress, without resulting bodily harm
or any other invasion of the owner's interests. The emotional
disturbance is important only in so far as its existence involves
a risk of bodily harm, and as affecting the damages which may
be recovered if the bodily harm is sustained. See § 905.

b. There is a considerable degree of duplication between
the rule stated in this Section and that stated in § 46, which
deals with the intentional or reckless infliction of emotional
distress by extreme and outrageous conduct. In most of the
cases in which the intentional infliction of emotional distress
results in foreseeable bodily harm, the known risk of such bodily
harm is sufficient in itself to make the act one of extreme out-

Alternatively, you may be directed to a Restatement section in the course of your research. For example, a case you may be reading may refer to a Restatement section. In this instance you should review the section mentioned.

Be sure to check the Appendix volume for the section you are researching and the pocket part therein to determine if the Restatement section has been modified or limited and to locate cases supporting the Restatement section.

Finally, the Restatements are available on CD-ROM from West and on LEXIS and Westlaw.

Practice Tip

Restatements

• **At present, there is no one index to all of the Restatements.** To conduct research in the Restatements, you must know which is the pertinent Restatement for your research task.
• **The American Law Institute has now published** *Concise Restatement of Torts* **and** *Concise Restatement of Property*, **one-volume softcover books that include the most critical information from their respective Restatements and which are meant to be especially helpful for students. Check to see if your library has either of these concise Restatements.**

---

4. *Effect of Restatements*

The Restatements are a secondary source. Courts are not required to adopt or follow the Restatement positions. Nevertheless, the Restatements have been cited in cases more than 160,000 times. In fact, to determine if a Restatement section you are interested in has been cited by a court, you can consult a set of books entitled *Restatement in the Courts*, which indicates cases that have cited Restatement sections. However, because citations to cases that refer to the Restatements are now in the pocket parts and Appendix volumes of the individual Restatements, *Restatement in the Courts* is now out of print. For more recent cases, you can also review Shepard's *Restatement of the Law Citations*, which will direct you to federal and state cases, as well as other authorities, that have cited Restatement provisions. Many legal experts believe the Restatements are the most highly regarded of all of the secondary authorities, and you are encouraged to rely upon them and cite to them in research projects you prepare. In fact, in ordering citations to secondary authorities, only the uniform and model codes are cited before the Restatements, according to *The Bluebook* (Rule 1.4(i)), which provides rules for citation form. This preeminence of the Restatements in the order of listing secondary materials confirms their authority.

The Final Wrap-Up

Using and Citing Restatements

Use: Use Restatements to obtain clear and concise statements of the law as well as comments upon and illustrations of those rules of law. Make sure you read the cases the Restatements direct you to, especially those in your jurisdiction.

Citation: Although the Restatements are a secondary authority, they are probably the most highly regarded of the secondary authorities. Thus, you should feel free to cite to them in your research memos and projects.

E. Citation Form

Encyclopedias (The Bluebook and ALWD):
46 C.J.S. *Mechanics Liens* § 121 (1986).
79 Am. Jur. 2d *Trusts* § 42 (1980).

Periodicals (The Bluebook and ALWD):
Stanley L. Paul, *Due Process*, 41 Dick. L. Rev. 1091 (1985).

Treatises:
   The Bluebook: Susan L. Baker, *Federal Sentencing Guidelines* § 12:06 (2d ed. 1988).
   ALWD: Susan L. Baker, *Federal Sentencing Guidelines* § 12:06 (2d ed., West 1988).

Restatements:
   The Bluebook: Restatement (Second) of Torts § 13 (1976).
   ALWD: *Restatement (Second) of Torts* § 13 (1976).

CyberSites

Georgetown University Law Library offers useful guides and tutorials for performing legal research using secondary sources. Use the following sites:

http://www.ll. georgetown.edu	Select "Learn" and then "Research Guides" for information about performing legal research tasks.
http://wwwll.georgetown. edu/tutorials/second/ index.html	These tutorials provide an overview of secondary sources and helpful research tips and strategies on using encyclopedias, treatises, periodicals, and Restatements.

Encyclopedias

Encyclopedias are not available on the Internet. The legal encyclopedia Am. Jur. 2d is available both in CD-ROM form and on Westlaw. Selected articles from C.J.S. are also available on Westlaw. Some state encyclopedias are also available on both LEXIS and Westlaw and in CD-ROM form.

Treatises

Due to their voluminous content, treatises are not generally available either on the Internet or LEXIS or Westlaw. While numerous articles and law-related discussions are available on the Internet, there has been no effort to put comprehensive treatise collections on the Internet, likely due to authors' reluctance to have their materials distributed globally with a concurrent loss of royalty revenue.

Periodicals

Following are Internet addresses that will allow you to retrieve various articles relating to law.

http://www.lawreview.org	The University Law Review Project, a coalition of legal educators, provides links to hundreds of law reviews, legal periodicals, newsletters, and so forth. Searching may be done by key words, topics, and specific journal names.
http://www.findlaw.com	The FindLaw Web site offers access to a wide variety of legal materials. To locate periodicals, select "Students" and then "Law Reviews."
http://www.hg.org/ journals.html	The Web site HierosGamos is a comprehensive law and government portal with links to hundreds of law reviews and journals.
http://www.usc.edu/library/ resources/journals.html	The Web site for University of Southern California Law School provides links to numerous law reviews and journals as well as to ABA journals and newsletters.

(continued)

CyberSites *(Continued)* ▬▬▬▬▬▬▬▬

http://www.ilrg.com/   The Web site of the Internet Legal Research
  journals.html   Group provides access to hundreds of law-related
                             publications and journals.

Restatements

The Restatements are not available on the Internet. All of the Restatements currently in print are, however, available in CD-ROM form from West and on LEXIS and Westlaw. Additionally, the Web site of the American Law Institute (http://www.ali.org) lists the Restatements currently in print and discusses the status of Restatements under consideration and in the drafting or revising process.

Writing Strategies

Writing is neither as mechanical nor as precise as mathematics. You cannot write by formula, assuming that "one primary authority plus one secondary authority equals one winning argument." In fact, constructing a writing using such an approach will result in a rigid and choppy project.

There is no easy answer to the question, "how many authorities are enough?" For some straightforward issues, a reference to one statute may be sufficient. Complex issues will require more in-depth analysis and expanded discussion of authorities.

Vary the authorities you rely upon. If your entire writing consists of references only to the Restatements, the reader will assume you are a lazy researcher who is uninterested in thoroughly researching the issues and content to rely upon one source. Thorough analysis calls for a combination of primary and secondary sources.

If you are relying upon primary sources as well as secondary sources to discuss an issue, analyze the primary authorities first. After you have shown the reader why the statutes, regulations, cases, or constitutional provisions control, enhance your discussion by providing additional support from a periodical, Restatement, annotation, or treatise.

Assignment for Chapter 6

1. Use Am. Jur. 2d.
   a. Which volume, title, and section deal with gambling on sports events?
   b. Review this section. What exceptions exist to the federal statute prohibiting gambling on sporting events?
2. Use Am. Jur. 2d.
   a. Which volume, title, and section deal with chickens as nuisances?
   b. Review this section. Which Massachusetts case held that noises and odors from a chickenhouse and yard maintained in a clean manner are not a nuisance?
3. Use C.J.S.
   a. Use the Table of Cases. Under which topic and section is the case *Albertson v. Leca* discussed?
   b. Which topic and section discuss cruelty as grounds for divorce?
   c. Review the above section. What happens if both parties are guilty of habitual cruel and inhuman treatment?
   d. Give a short summary of the definition of "release."
4. Use *Am. Jur. Proof of Facts (3d)*.
   a. Give the citation to an article relating to the availability of punitive damages in an automobile accident with a school bus.
   b. Review the above section. What South Carolina case(s) discuss(es) this? Give the case name(s) only.
   c. Who authored this article?
5. Use *Index to Legal Periodicals & Books* to answer the following questions:
   a. Cite an article written by Ann Laquer Estin in spring 2002 relating to marriage.
   b. Cite an article written in late 2003 relating to end-stage anorexia and competence to refuse treatment.
   c. Cite an article published in the winter of 2002 about a case in which the defendant's name is *Gilmore*.
6. Use the Subject Index for *Current Law Index* for 2003 and give the citation to an article relating to school busing.
7. Give the title and the authors of the April 2003 law review article located at 81 Tex. L. Rev. 1177.
8. Use *J. Thomas McCarthy on Trademarks and Unfair Competition* (4th ed. 1992).
   a. What section discusses "puffing" as false advertising?
   b. Review the section. Is a claim that a product is "better" than another product false advertising? Why or why not?
9. Use *Williston on Contracts* (Richard A. Lord ed., 4th ed. 1996).
   a. What section discusses rejection of goods for defective quality?
   b. Review this section. May a buyer reject goods for deficient quality where the buyer has failed to provide specifications needed by the seller to determine and meet the alleged quality standards? Provide an answer and cite the best case in support of your answer.

10. Use *Restatement (Third) of Trusts*.
     a. What section discusses the removal of a trustee, generally?
     b. Review this section. How may a trustee be removed?
     c. Review the Reporter's Notes for this section (specifically, comment e). May a trustee be removed for habitual drunkenness in Ohio? Provide an answer and cite the relevant statute in support of your answer.

State Your Answer

1. Access the Web site for Georgetown University Law Center at www.ll.georgetown.edu. Select "Learn" and then "Tutorials." Review the information given on encyclopedias. Which of the two national or general encyclopedias does this site recommend as a starting place? Why?
2. Access the University Law Review Project at www.lawreview.org. Select "General Law Reviews." What law reviews from your state are now available through this site?
3. Access the Washington & Lee Law School study on the most cited legal periodicals at www.wlu.edu.library/research/lawrevs/mostcited.asp. Sort the table by rank. As of 2003, which were the top four most-cited periodicals? How many times was each cited?
4. Access the site of the American Law Institute at www.ali.org and review ALI's annual report for 2004. Review the table that indicates how many times published cases cite to the Restatements.
     a. How many times has your state cited the Restatement of Torts as of March 1, 2003?
     b. What is the most frequently cited Restatement in your state?

Miscellaneous Secondary Authorities

Even trained lawyers may find it necessary to consult legal dictionaries, treatises, and judicial opinions before they may say with any certainty what some statutes may compel or forbid.

Rose v. Locke, 423 U.S. 48, 50 (1975)

A. **Attorneys General Opinions**
B. **Legal Dictionaries**
C. **Directories**
D. **Form Books**
E. **Uniform Laws**
F. **Looseleaf Services**
G. **Jury Instructions**
H. **Summary**
 I. **Citation Form**

Chapter Overview

The previous chapter discussed the most frequently used secondary authorities: encyclopedias, periodicals, treatises, and Restatements. There are, however, several other authorities that are used by legal researchers. These include opinions of attorneys general, dictionaries, directories, form books, uniform laws, looseleaf services, and jury instructions.

These sources summarize and explain the law as well as assist you in locating primary sources. The sources discussed in this chapter are often more practical in their approach and content than encyclopedias, periodicals, treatises, and Restatements. For example, dictionaries help you find the meaning of a word in its legal sense; form books provide information so you can effectively draft complaints, contracts, and other legal documents; and looseleaf services provide an "a" to "z" approach to understanding certain specialized areas of the law.

At the conclusion of this chapter you will be familiar with all of the tools you will need to have in order to locate answers for most research questions.

A. Attorneys General Opinions

1. Introduction

An attorney general is the chief law enforcement officer in a government. The United States attorney general is appointed by the president and is confirmed by the United States Senate. The United States attorney general is the head of the Department of Justice and serves as a member of the president's Cabinet and is the only cabinet member without the title "Secretary." Each of the 50 states also has an attorney general. In most states, the attorney general is elected by the voters. As the chief law enforcement officer, an attorney general issues written opinions on a variety of legal topics, including the interpretation of statutes and the duties and operations of government entities. These opinions typically are written in response to questions by legislators, the executive branch, or other government officials.

For example, the United States attorney general represents the United States in legal matters generally and gives advice and opinions to the president and to the heads of the executive departments of the government when requested. The attorney general may appear in person to represent the government before the U.S. Supreme Court in cases of exceptional importance.

Any large law library in your area will collect the opinions of the United States attorney general. However, your law library will likely collect only the opinions of the attorney general from your state and will not have any of the attorneys general opinions from the other 49 states.

The opinions of attorneys general are secondary authority because they are not cases, constitutions, or statutes. Thus, a court is not required to follow an opinion of an attorney general. Because, however, these opinions are written by the chief legal advisor to the executive branch, whether federal or state, and are usually followed, they are highly persuasive, and you should feel free to rely upon them and cite them in briefs and memoranda that you write because courts view them as respectable and creditable commentaries on case law and legislation. In fact, the opinions carry the weight of law unless a court rules otherwise or legislation changes a statute being interpreted.

2. Research Strategies

Most sets of opinions of attorneys general will have an index, which you can use by the descriptive word approach; that is, by selecting words that describe the issue you are researching, looking up these words in the alphabetically arranged index, and then being directed to the appropriate opinion. Unfortunately, these indexes are often not well-maintained and may be out of date.

It is more likely that you will be directed to a pertinent attorney general opinion by another source you are using. For example, if you are researching a particular statute in U.S.C.A. or U.S.C.S., you will be provided with a reference to any attorney general opinion that has interpreted or construed this statute. Similarly, when you are researching a state statute in your state's annotated code, you may be directed to a state attorney general opinion analyzing this state statute. Additionally, as you will see in Chapter 9, when you Shepardize or KeyCite a case, you will be directed to any attorneys general opinions that have mentioned this case.

Finally, many opinions are now available on the Internet. The assistant attorney general in charge of the Office of Legal Counsel assists the attorney general in his function as legal advisor to the president and all the executive branch agencies. The Office of Legal Counsel drafts legal opinions of the United States attorney general. Many of these can be found at its Web site at http://www.usdoj.gov/olc/opinions.htm. Searching is by date.

Similarly, the vast majority of states now offer their attorneys general opinions through their respective Web sites. Access the site http://www.library.unt.edu/govinfo/law/agopinions.htm#us to link to your state's attorneys general opinions.

B. Legal Dictionaries and Thesauri

Just as you would use a standard dictionary to determine the spelling, pronunciation, and meaning of a word with which you are unfamiliar, you can use a legal dictionary to determine the spelling, pronunciation, and meaning of a legal word or phrase with which you are unfamiliar. Thus, if you need to know the meaning of a word in its legal sense, such as "negligence," or the translation of a Latin phrase such as *damnum absque injuria* ("harm without injury in the legal sense"), or the meaning of a phrase such as "watered stock," you should consult a legal dictionary, which is an alphabetical arrangement of legal words and phrases. Many legal dictionaries will not only provide the definition of a word but will then give you a citation to a case or secondary authority in which the word was defined. So if you look up the word "mistrial" in a legal dictionary, you will not only be given its meaning but often will be directed to a case that defines the word "mistrial." This is another example of a secondary source not only explaining the law but directing you to primary sources. Remember that when you define a word in a research project, cite to the case defining the word rather than the dictionary if the case is relevant and on point.

Perhaps the best known of the legal dictionaries is *Black's Law Dictionary*, a one-volume book published by West, which has been in existence since 1891. *Black's* not only includes more than 40,000 definitions but also provides a guide to pronunciation of Latin terms, a table of common legal abbreviations, a chart showing the composition of the United States Supreme Court from 1789 to date, definitions of legal maxims, a Table of British Regnal Years listing the sovereigns of England for the last 900 years, the text of the United States Constitution, an extensive appendix of legal abbreviations, and references to West's Key Numbers to make researching easier. *Black's Law Dictionary* is available in hardcover, paperback, and on Westlaw. A new edition is released every several years. See Figure 7-1 for a sample page from *Black's Law Dictionary* (6th ed. 1990).

Another of the well-known legal dictionaries is *Ballentine's Law Dictionary*, a one-volume book published by the former Lawyers Co-op, which defines more than 45,000 words and phrases. Like *Black's, Ballentine's* also contains guides to pronunciation of Latin terms. Moreover, because it was formerly a Lawyers Co-op publication, it contains thousands of references to the Lawyers Co-op publications, *United States Supreme Court Reports, Lawyers' Edition*, A.L.R., and Am. Jur. 2d. *Ballentine's*, however, has not released a new edition since 1969, and thus *Black's* is far more current and should likely be consulted in preference to *Ballentine's*.

There are numerous other legal dictionaries that you can use, including specialized dictionaries such as Bryan A. Garner's *A Handbook of Criminal Law Terms*, which provides definitions of criminal law terms. Most legal dictionaries are located in the reference section of the law library, and you should make a point of browsing the shelves in the reference section to discover which dictionaries are available.

You may recall that the set *Words and Phrases* will provide you with definitions of words and phrases. Its coverage, however, is limited to words and phrases that have been defined in cases and therefore you will not be able to find a word in *Words and Phrases* unless it has been the subject of court action. Moreover, because *Words and Phrases* is a multivolume set, it is more unwieldy than the more standard one-volume legal dictionaries such as *Black's* and *Ballentine's*. One of the advantages of *Words and Phrases*, however, is that it is supplemented by pocket parts, easily allowing for the addition of new words that enter the legal field. *Black's* and *Ballentine's* are similar to other traditional dictionaries and are not supplemented on an annual basis.

Many legal dictionaries such as *Black's* publish an abridged softcover version at a moderate price. These dictionaries are excellent resources for beginning researchers.

A legal thesaurus provides synonyms and antonyms for legal words and terms. When writing a letter, memorandum, or legal document, you may become tired of using the same word or may need to think of another way of expressing a legal term. A thesaurus will help you select the right word you need. One of the best known of the legal thesauri is *Burton's Legal Thesaurus* by William C. Burton, which provides more than 7,000 legal terms, synonyms, and definitions. For example, if you wish to find another

Figure 7-1
Sample Page from *Black's Law Dictionary*
(6th ed. 1990)

Unilateral mistake. A mistake by only one party to an agreement and generally not a basis for relief by rescission or reformation.

Mister. A title of courtesy. A trade, craft, occupation, employment, office.

Mistery. A trade or calling.

Mistrial. An erroneous, invalid, or nugatory trial. A trial of an action which cannot stand in law because of want of jurisdiction, or a wrong drawing of jurors, or disregard of some other fundamental requisite before or during trial. Trial which has been terminated prior to its normal conclusion. A device used to halt trial proceedings when error is so prejudicial and fundamental that expenditure of further time and expense would be wasteful if not futile. Ferguson v. State, Fla., 417 So.2d 639, 641. The judge may declare a mistrial because of some extraordinary event (*e.g.* death of juror, or attorney), for prejudicial error that cannot be corrected at trial, or because of a deadlocked jury.

"Mistrial" is equivalent to no trial and is a nugatory trial while "new trial" recognizes a completed trial which for sufficient reasons has been set aside so that the issues may be tried de novo. People v. Jamerson, 196 Colo. 63, 580 P.2d 805, 806.

Misuse. As defense in products liability action, requires use in a manner neither intended nor reasonably foreseeable by manufacturer. Smith v. Sturm, Ruger & Co., Inc., 39 Wash.App. 740, 695 P.2d 600, 604.

Misuser /misyúwzər/. An unlawful use of a right. Abuse of an office or franchise. 2 Bl.Comm. 153.

Mitigating circumstances. Such as do not constitute a justification or excuse for the offense in question, but which, in fairness and mercy, may be considered as extenuating or reducing the degree of moral culpability. For example, mitigating circumstances which will reduce degree of homicide to manslaughter are the commission of the killing in a sudden heat of passion caused by adequate legal provocation. People v. Morrin, 31 Mich.App. 301, 187 N.W.2d 434, 438.

Those that affect basis for award of exemplary damages, or reduce actual damages by showing, not that they were never suffered, but that they have been partially extinguished.

In actions for libel and slander, refer to circumstances bearing on defendant's liability for exemplary damages by reducing moral culpability, or on liability for actual damages by showing partial extinguishment thereof. The "mitigating circumstances" which the statute allows defendant in libel action to prove are those which tend to show that defendant in speaking the slanderous words acted in good faith, with honesty of purpose, and not maliciously. Roemer v. Retail Credit Co., 44 C.A.3d 926, 119 Cal.Rptr. 82, 91.

See also Comparative negligence; Extenuating circumstances; Extraordinary circumstances.

Mitigation. To make less severe. Alleviation, reduction, abatement or diminution of a penalty or punishment imposed by law.

Mitigation of damages. Doctrine of "mitigation of damages," sometimes called doctrine of avoidable consequences, imposes on party injured by breach of contract or tort duty to exercise reasonable diligence and ordinary care in attempting to minimize his damages, or avoid aggravating the injury, after breach or injury has been inflicted and care and diligence required of him is the same as that which would be used by man of ordinary prudence under like circumstances. Darnell v. Taylor, La.App., 236 So.2d 57, 61. Mitigation of damages is an affirmative defense and applies when plaintiff fails to take reasonable actions that would tend to mitigate his injuries. Mott v. Persichetti, Colo.App., 534 P.2d 823, 825. See Restatement, Contracts § 336(1); U.C.C. § 2–603. *See also* Avoidable consequences doctrine.

Mitigation of punishment. A judge may reduce or order a lesser sentence in consideration of such factors as the defendant's past good behavior, his family situation, his cooperation with the police and kindred factors.

Mitior sensus /míshiyər sénsəs/. Lat. The more favorable acceptation.

Mitius imperanti melius paretur /míshiyəs impərǽntay míyl(i)yəs pəríytər/. The more mildly one commands, the better is he obeyed.

Mitter. L. Fr. To put, to send, or to pass; as, *mitter l'estate,* to pass the estate; *mitter le droit,* to pass a right. These words are used to distinguish different kinds of releases.

Mitter avant /mítər əvǽnt/. L. Fr. In old practice, to put before; to present before a court; to produce in court.

Mittimus /mítəməs/. The name of a precept in writing, issuing from a court or magistrate, directed to the sheriff or other officer, commanding him to convey to the prison the person named therein, and to the jailer, commanding him to receive and safely keep such person until he shall be delivered by due course of law. State v. Lenihan, 151 Conn. 552, 200 A.2d 476, 478. Transcript of minutes of conviction and sentence duly certified by court clerk. United States ex rel. Chasteen v. Denmark, C.C.A.Ill., 138 F.2d 289, 291.

Old English law. A writ enclosing a record sent to be tried in a county palatine; it derives its name from the Latin word *mittimus,* "we send." It is the jury process of these counties, and commands the proper officer of the county palatine to command the sheriff to summon the jury for the trial of the cause, and to return the record, etc.

Mixed. Formed by admixture or commingling; partaking of the nature, character, or legal attributes of two or more distinct kinds or classes.

As to mixed Action; Blood relations *(Mixed blood);* Contract; Government; Jury; Larceny; Marriage; Nuisance; Policy; Presumption; Property; Tithes; and War, see those titles.

Note reference to case interpreting "mistrial"

word for "abandon," the thesaurus will suggest "forsake," "abdicate," "retract," and other terms.

A recent trend is publication of glossaries of legal terms on the Internet. For example, the Web site Law.Com offers a legal dictionary at http://dictionary.law.com. As of the date of this text, such online glossaries are not particularly comprehensive. They may, however, be helpful in providing you with a quick understanding of a legal term or Latin phrase.

The Final Wrap-Up

Use and Citation of Attorneys General Opinions, Dictionaries, and Thesauri

Use: Use attorneys general opinions as strong persuasive authorities that often clarify and interpret statutes and regulations. Although they are secondary authorities, they are highly credible. Use dictionaries and thesauri to obtain a quick definition of an unknown legal term.

Citation: Cite freely to attorneys general opinions because of their renown and highly persuasive nature. You may cite to dictionaries and thesauri, but consider citing instead to the primary authorities to which these sources usually direct you.

C. Directories

1. Introduction

A directory is simply a list of lawyers. Some law directories, such as the extremely well-known and highly regarded *Martindale-Hubbell Law Directory*, aim at listing all lawyers admitted to all jurisdictions. Other directories are more limited in coverage and may list only lawyers in a particular geographic region or locality. Still other directories focus on law schools, law libraries, or courts. Law directories are usually kept in the reference section of a law library.

2. Martindale-Hubbell Law Directory

a. Overview of *Martindale-Hubbell*

The best known law directory in the United States is *Martindale-Hubbell Law Directory*, which has been in existence for more than a century. The initial goal of the directory was to publish an address for a lawyer, a banker, and a real estate office in every city in the United States. At present, nearly all major U.S. law firms pay to be listed in *Martindale-Hubbell*. The set is currently published annually in hardbound volumes and is also available on CD-ROM. Additionally, the set is available online through LEXIS and on the Internet. (See Chapter 12.) The CD-ROM discs enable one to find attorneys solely by name without requiring the user to know the city in which the attorney practices. In fact, search criteria can be constructed so that you can readily locate an attorney who graduated from a specific school, such as Yale Law School, is fluent in French, and concentrates in the field of health law. The CD-ROM set costs approximately $1,000 and is updated quarterly. Finally, much of the information in *Martindale-Hubbell* is free on the Internet (http://www. martindale.com).

There are more than 20 volumes in *Martindale-Hubbell*, arranged alphabetically by state. For instance, Volume 1 covers the states Alabama, Alaska, Arizona, and Arkansas. Within the listing for each state, cities are arranged alphabetically from Abbeville, Alabama, to Wetumpka, Alabama. Within each city, law firms and attorneys are arranged alphabetically as well. Thus, if you were interested in locating a firm in Minneapolis, Minnesota, to handle a transaction for you or to refer a case to, you could scan through the law firms located in Minneapolis and select a firm that you believe could best represent the client's interests. See Figure 7-2 for a sample page from the *Martindale-Hubbell Law Directory*.

Each firm that has an entry will list its attorneys and provide biographical information about them. The date of birth, colleges and universities attended, honors awarded, and articles authored by the attorneys in the firm are given. Moreover, the firm's address, phone number, Web site, a sample of its representative clients, and the areas in which it practices will be noted. The firm may also include a firm profile, discussing its achievements and expertise. By reviewing *Martindale-Hubbell* you may be able to select a firm that focuses on a particular practice area such as franchise law, securities litigation, or white-collar criminal defense. Law firms pay a fee for these biographical entries, and therefore not every firm or attorney may elect to participate.

On the other hand, the front of each volume of *Martindale-Hubbell* contains a list of all attorneys licensed to practice in the states covered by that volume. Attorneys are listed in this blue pages section free of charge, and the biographical information given is limited to name, year of birth, address, education, date of bar admission, and the area of practice specialized in by the attorney. *Martindale-Hubbell* also lists corporate law departments by company name and indicates the city and state in which the corporate law department is located. In 1995, *Martindale-Hubbell* began assigning identification numbers to the more than 850,000 attorneys in its database, including former President Clinton and Chief Justice William Rehnquist. These universal numerical identifiers are designed to make it easier to track attorneys disciplined for misconduct. *Martindale-Hubbell* also rates attorneys based on their legal ability and ethical standards. For example a rating of "AV" indicates very high legal ability and very high ethical standards. These ratings are developed by confidential polling of members of the bar.

Figure 7-2
Sample Page from *Martindale-Hubbell Law Directory*

DRATH, CLIFFORD, MURPHY, WENNERHOLM & HAGEN

A PROFESSIONAL CORPORATION

1999 HARRISON STREET, SUITE 1900
OAKLAND, CALIFORNIA 94612-3578
Telephone: 510-287-4000
Telefax: 510-287-4050
Email: dcmwh@msn.com

San Diego, California Office: 600 B Street, Suite 1550. Telephone: 619-595-3060. Fax: 619-595-3066.

Areas of practice
Civil Litigation with an emphasis in the fields of insurance and self-insured defense, insurance coverage analysis, construction, employment, environmental, products liability, personal injury and professional liability defense.

FIRM PROFILE: Drath, Clifford, Murphy, Wennerholm & Hagen is a Martindale-Hubbell Bar Register of Preeminent Lawyers firm.

JOHN M. DRATH, born Portland, Oregon, November 14, 1944; admitted to bar, 1970, California; 1971, Colorado; 1993, Montana. *Education:* University of Washington (B.A., 1965); University of San Francisco (J.D., 1969). *Member:* State Bar of California; Association of Defense Counsel, Northern California (President, 1992-1993); Defense Research Institute; American Board of Trial Advocates; Federation of Insurance and Corporate Counsel. *PRACTICE AREAS:* Professional Liability Defense; Personal Injury Defense; Insurance Coverage; Bad Faith Defense; Complex Litigation. *Email:* dcmwh@msn.com

RICK J. MURPHY, born San Francisco, California, March 26, 1951; admitted to bar, 1976, California. *Education:* University of California at Davis (B.A., cum laude, 1973); University of Santa Clara School of Law (J.D., cum laude, 1976). *Member:* State Bar of California; Association of Defense Counsel; American Board of Trial Advocates. *PRACTICE AREAS:* Insurance Defense; Accident and Personal Injury; Business Litigation. *Email:* dcmwh@msn.com

TRACI E. WENNERHOLM, born Los Angeles, California, July 13, 1960; admitted to bar, 1985, California. *Education:* University of California at Riverside (B.A., 1982); Hastings College of the Law, University of California (J.D., 1985). *Member:* State Bar of California; Association of Defense Counsel; Defense Research Institute. *PRACTICE AREAS:* Construction Law; Personal Injury Defense; Asbestos Defense. *Email:* dcmwh@msn.com

DAVID F. BEACH, born Jackson, Michigan, March 31, 1955; admitted to bar, 1980, California. *Education:* College of San Mateo (A.A., 1975); University of California at Berkeley (B.S., 1977); University of San Diego (J.D., magna cum laude, 1980). *Member:* State Bar of California; American Arbitration Association; Association of Defense Counsel; Defense Research Institute. *PRACTICE AREAS:* Personal Injury Defense; Insurance Coverage; Construction Litigation; Asbestos Litigation. *Email:* dcmwh@msn.com

GRETCHEN W. LATIMER, born Berkeley, California, August 8, 1965; admitted to bar, 1992, California. *Education:* University of Puget Sound (B.A., 1987), Seattle University (J.D., 1992). *Member:* San Francisco Bar Association; Contra Costa County Bar Association. *PRACTICE AREAS:* Construction Defect; Insurance Defense. *Email:* dcmwh@msn.com

Representative clients
REPRESENTATIVE CLIENTS: Allstate Insurance Co.; American Equities Insurance Co.; American States Insurance Co.; Cooper Industries; First Financial Insurance Company; First Mercury Syndicate; Motors Insurance Co.; Nationwide Insurance Co.; Nautilus Insurance Co.; National General Insurance Co.; Northbrook Insurance Co.; Preferred Risk Mutual Insurance Co.; Scottsdale Insurance Co.; Super Computer, Inc,; TOPA Insurance Co.; USS-POSCO Industries, USX Corporation; Unicare Insurance Co.; Willis Corroon.

(For complete Biographical Data on Additional Personnel, see Professional Biographies at San Diego, California)

A separate volume in the *Martindale-Hubbell* set called "Corporate Law Directory" provides information on more than 35,000 in-house attorneys and corporate law departments. Thus, if you needed a list of the attorneys working in-house for Exxon-Mobil, you would consult this volume for their names, biographical information, and current responsibilities.

These features of *Martindale-Hubbell* make it an excellent source of information for career opportunities. You should consider directing a resume to a law firm that focuses on an area of law in which you are interested. There is no point in applying for a position with a law firm that is exclusively engaged in bankruptcy work if you have no interest in this area of law. Similarly, before interviewing with a firm, always review *Martindale-Hubbell* to familiarize yourself with the firm's practice areas, its office locations in other cities, and the general profile of the firm.

Because many law firms now maintain sophisticated Web sites with biographies of their attorneys, some are reconsidering their decision to list with *Martindale-Hubbell*. For example, in early 2000, Chicago's Sidley Austin Brown & Wood, a mega-firm with now more than 1,500 attorneys, decided not to list in *Martindale-Hubbell*, a savings of $110 per attorney per year. The firm decided that its Web site provided identical information and thus did not renew its *Martindale-Hubbell* listing.

Most law firms maintain Web sites with biographies, photos of attorneys, office locations, descriptions of firm practice areas, summaries of recent "wins," and topical articles written by attorneys in the firm. Thus, these Web sites provide more information than is available in *Martindale-Hubbell* and can be readily updated as attorneys leave or join a firm.

Practice Tip

Martindale-Hubbell

Don't ever go on a job interview without doing some homework about your potential employer by using *Martindale-Hubbell*. Find out something about the firm and mention it during your interview to showcase your research skills and professional savvy. Comment about the firm's new European office, its practice areas, or some other item to demonstrate your familiarity with *Martindale-Hubbell* as well as your level of interest in the firm.

---

b. *Martindale-Hubbell* Law Digest Volumes

In addition to *Martindale-Hubbell's* directory list of lawyers, the set contains numerous other features that make it a useful and practical research tool.

(1) State Digests

Martindale-Hubbell contains two volumes providing a brief overview of some of the laws of all 50 states, the District of Columbia, Puerto

Rico, and the Virgin Islands. While *Martindale-Hubbell* will not provide all of the laws of these jurisdictions, it will provide a summary of some of the more common laws of each state together with references to pertinent state statutes. For example, you will be able to determine the fees for creating a limited partnership in a state, how many individuals are needed to witness execution of a will, residency requirements to obtain a divorce, information relating to discovery in litigation actions, what the statute of limitations is for personal injury actions, and other items of information commonly needed. Thus, if a client is interested in incorporating a business in another state and you do not have ready access to that state's code, *Martindale-Hubbell's* Law Digest volumes will provide you with a concise summary of the corporate laws for that state. Moreover, these Law Digest volumes will provide you with forms for documents and instruments commonly used by a certain state, such as a form for acknowledging the veracity of an instrument. See Figure 7-3 for a sample page from the Law Digest volume of *Martindale-Hubbell* for Wisconsin.

(2) *International Law Directory and Law Digests*

The print version of *Martindale-Hubbell* includes three volumes referred to as the International Law Directory. Volumes I and II contain profiles of lawyers and law firms from more than 160 countries, organized alphabetically within major geographic regions. Volume 1 covers Europe, Asia, Australasia, the Middle East, and Africa. Volume 2 covers North America, the Caribbean, and Central and South America. Volume 3 is an index.

Another volume, the International Law Digest, provides summaries or digests of the laws of more than 80 countries, such as Canada, El Salvador, Japan, and Saudi Arabia. Once again, all of the laws of a foreign country will not be provided but rather only those laws that are most likely to be needed by practitioners. Descriptions of the organization of the government and legal systems are also given. See Figure 7-4 for a sample page from the *Mexico Law Digest*.

(3) *International Conventions*

Martindale-Hubbell also provides the text of several international conventions or treaties to which the United States is a party, such as the United Nations Convention on Contracts for the International Sale of Goods, the Convention on the Civil Aspects of International Child Abduction, and the Convention on the Taking of Evidence Abroad in Civil or Commercial Matters.

(4) *Uniform Acts, Rules, and Court Information*

The complete text of some of the better known Uniform Acts is also provided, including the Uniform Commercial Code, the Uniform Arbitration Act, and the Uniform Probate Code.

Figure 7-3
Sample Page from *Martindale-Hubbell Law Digest*

Ref. to
page
24 of
Wisconsin
Law
Digest

WI – 24 MARTINDALE-HUBBELL LAW DIGEST

DEPOSITIONS AND DISCOVERY ... *continued*
pleading; (3) court deems cause sufficient; (4) when required for use on any hearing. Commission must be signed and sealed by clerk. (887.26).

Compelling Attendance of Witnesses.—Nonparty deponent served by subpoena within state and party served with notice may be compelled to give deposition within 100 miles of residence, place of employment, or where nonparty deponent transacts business or at any other place fixed by court order. Plaintiff may also be compelled to give deposition in county of state where action is commenced or is pending. Nonresident defendant may be compelled by subpoena to give deposition in any Wis. county in which he is personally served. (804.05[3]). Witness fees: $5 per day before municipal judge, arbitrator, or any officer, board or committee, $16 per day before any other court and 20¢ per mile travel expense. (814.67).

Examination of Witnesses.—Examination and cross-examination of deponents proceeds as permitted at trial. (804.05[4]). However, it is not grounds for objection that testimony will be inadmissible at trial if testimony appears reasonably calculated to lead to discovery of admissible evidence. (804.01[2]).

Errors in notice for taking of deposition are waived unless written objection promptly served upon party giving notice. Objection to taking of deposition because of disqualification of officer before whom it is to be taken is waived unless made before taking of deposition begins or as soon thereafter as disqualification becomes known or could be discovered through reasonable diligence. (804.07[3]). Objections to competency of witness or to competency, relevancy or materiality of testimony are not waived by failure to make them before or during taking of deposition, unless ground of objection might have been obviated or removed if presented at that time. Similar rule applies as to errors or irregularities occurring in manner of taking deposition, in form of questions or answers, in oath or affirmation, or in conduct of parties and errors of any kind which might be obviated if objection were seasonably made. Errors and irregularities as to completion and return of deposition are waived unless motion to suppress is made with reasonable promptness. (804.07[3]).

Return.—Person recording testimony must certify on deposition that witness was duly sworn by him and that deposition is true record of testimony given by deponent, must then securely seal deposition in envelope endorsed with title of action and marked "Deposition of (here insert name of deponent)" and must promptly serve it upon attorney requesting deposition or send it by registered or certified mail to attorney requesting deposition and give notice of service to all parties and court. (804.05[7]).

Production of Documents and Things.—Any party may serve on any other party request to produce any designated documents for inspection and copying or to inspect any tangible things or to enter land or other property for inspection, provided matter sought to be inspected is within scope of 804.01(2). Party upon whom request is served must respond within 30 days of service. (804.09).

Interrogatories.—Any party can serve on any party written interrogatories, which, unless objected to, must be answered fully under oath within 30 days. Interrogatories may relate to any matter within scope of 804.01(2). When answer to interrogatory can be ascertained from business records and burden of ascertaining answer is same for either party, it is sufficient to specify appropriate records and provide opportunity for inspection and copying. (804.08).

Physical and Mental Examination.—Upon motion by party court can order party whose physical or mental condition is at issue to undergo physical or mental examination. (804.10[1]). In personal injury actions, court may also order claimant to permit any party to inspect X-rays taken in course of treatment or diagnosis and any hospital, medical or other records concerning claimed injuries. (804.10[2]). Evidence obtained pursuant to 804.10 is only admissible if true copies of reports of examination are provided to other party within ten days of receipt. (804.10[3]).

Admissions.—Party may serve on any other party written request for admission of truth of any discoverable matter. Matter is admitted unless answer or objection is served within 30 days of service of request. Matter admitted is conclusively established unless court permits withdrawal or amendment. (804.11). If party fails to admit matter which is subsequently established, requesting party may recover reasonable cost of establishing matter, including attorney's fees. (804.12[3]).

Discovery Sanctions.—Variety of sanctions, including order compelling discovery, order deeming certain factual matters established, striking claim for defenses, dismissal of action, and default judgment, are available under certain conditions for failure to comply with discovery rule. (804.12).

DESCENT AND DISTRIBUTION:

Real Estate.—All property descends as follows: (1) Spouse takes entire estate if no surviving issue, or if surviving issue are all issue of surviving spouse and decedent; if there are surviving issue any one of whom are not issue of surviving spouse, spouse takes one-half of decedent's estate not disposed of by will consisting of decedent's property other than marital property; (2) issue take share of estate not passing to spouse or entire estate if there is no surviving spouse; issue in same degree of kinship take equally but if they are of unequal degree then take by representation; (3) if there is no surviving spouse or issue, property descends as follows: (a) parents or surviving parent; (b) brothers and sisters, descendants of deceased brothers and sisters taking by representation; (c) grandparents; (d) next of kin of equal degree. If potential heir dies within 72 hours of death of decedent, property of decedent passes as if person had predeceased decedent. (852.01). Interest in home is assigned to surviving spouse as part of his or her share unless surviving spouse requests otherwise. (852.09). Person to whom property would otherwise pass may disclaim all or part of property by filing signed declaration of disclaimer with court and serving copy on personal representative or holder of legal title to property within nine months after date of decedent's death. (852.13; 853.40).

Degrees of kindred are computed according to the rules of the civil law. (852.03[2]).

Surviving spouse takes as indicated in subhead Real Estate, supra.

Half Blood.—Kindred of half blood inherit equally with whole blood. (852.03[3]).

Posthumous persons may be heirs if conceived before decedent's death. (852.03[4]).

Nonmarital child inherits from and through mother and also from person who has been adjudged to be father or has admitted in open court or in writing signed by him that he is father. (852.05[1]). If nonmarital child dies intestate without surviving spouse or issue, estate descends as provided in 852.01 except that father and his kindred can inherit only if father has been adjudicated to be father. (852.05[2]).

Adopted Children.—See topic Adoption.

Determination of Heirship.—Upon petition to probate court six years or more after death of intestate, descent of property may be determined. (867.05).

Advancements to an heir are considered as a part of estate of intestate so far as it regards division and distribution among issue and must be taken as part of his share of estate. (852.11). Gift by decedent during life is advancement only if there is writing by decedent so stating or if heir states in court or in writing that gift was advance. If any prospective heir so advanced dies before intestate, leaving issue, advancement is taken into consideration in division and distribution of estate and amount allowed to issue of heir so advanced in like manner as if advancement had been made directly to them. (852.11).

Election.—See topic Wills.

Escheat.—See topics Absentees, subhead Escheat: Banks and Banking, subhead Unclaimed Deposits: Wills, subhead Unclaimed Legacies.

Renunciation.—Heir can disclaim in writing within nine months after decedent's death. (852.13; 853.40).

DESERTION: See topic Husband and Wife.

DISSOLUTION OF MARRIAGE: See topic Divorce.

DIVORCE:

Grounds for Absolute Divorce.—This subject governed by 767.001 et seq. Grounds for divorce exist if marriage is irretrievably broken. Marriage is irretrievably broken if: (1) Both parties by petition or otherwise under oath or affirmation so state; (2) one party so states and parties have voluntarily lived apart continuously for at least one year prior to commencement of action; or (3) if only one party so states and parties have not voluntarily lived apart one year, court either finds no prospect of reconciliation or, after court finds prospect of reconciliation and adjourns hearing, at adjourned hearing either party under oath or affirmation that marriage is irretrievably broke. (767.07; 767.12[2]).

Grounds for Legal Separation.—Grounds for legal separation exist if marriage is irretrievably broken (767.07; 767.12[2]), or if both parties by petition or otherwise state under oath or affirmation that marital relationship is broken (767.12[3]).

Citizenship Requirements.—None.

Residence Requirements.—Either party must have been bona fide resident of state for at least six months and of county in which action is brought for at least 30 days prior to commencement of action for divorce. (767.05[1m]).

Jurisdiction.—Circuit Courts have jurisdiction. (767.01).

Venue.—See topic Venue.

Process.—If one party initiates action, service of summons accomplished as in civil actions. If both parties initiate action, service of summons not required. (767.05[1]; 767.085[3]). See topic Process.

Pleading.—Action is initiated by petitioner or joint petitioners. Responding party is respondent. (767.05[3]). Petition is entitled "In re the marriage of A.B. and C.D." (767.05[5]). Petition must state name, birthdate, and social security number of parties, occupations, date and place of marriage, facts relating to residence of parties, name and birthdate of minor children of parties and other children born to wife during marriage, whether wife is pregnant, if petition not filed under 767.12(3), that marriage is irretrievably broken, or, alternatively, that both parties agree it is irretrievably broken, whether action for divorce or legal separation was ever commenced by either party or is pending, whether either party was previously married, manner in which prior marriage terminated, and if terminated by court judgment, name of court and time and place of judgment, whether parties have entered into any written agreement as to support, custody, visitation of children, maintenance and property division (attach copy of agreement to petition), relief requested and, whenever petition requests order affecting minor children, request that Department of Health and Social Services provide services on behalf of minor children. (767.085[1]). If legal separation requested, petition must state specific reason for request (767.085[1][f]), and if petition filed under 767.12(3) petition must state that both parties agree marital relationship is broken (767.085[1][cm]). Commencement of action affecting minor child constitutes application to Department of Health and Social Services for services on behalf of child. (767.02[3]).

Practice.—All hearings and trials to determine whether judgment shall be granted are before court, except may be before court commissioner when both parties state that marriage is irretrievably broken and that all material issues are resolved or when one party does not participate. (767.12[1]; 767.13[5][a]). Unless nonresidence in state shown by competent evidence, or service is by publication, or court otherwise orders, both parties must appear at trial. Order to that effect must be procured and served by moving party on nonmoving party before trial. (767.125). Each party must, within 20 days after service on other party of petition or pleading or before filing same in court, serve copy on Family Court Commissioner. Commissioner may appear when appropriate and must appear when requested by court (767.14). Commissioner must inform parties of availability of counseling services. (767.081). If both parties agree, court may suspend action for 90 days for reconciliation. (767.082).

Judgment.—Judgment of divorce is effective immediately. Neither party may remarry for six months. (767.37[3]; 765.03[2]).

Overview of divorce laws in Wisconsin with references to Wisconsin statutes

See note at head of Digest as to 1992 legislation covered.

See Topical Index in front part of this volume.

Figure 7-4
Sample Page from Law Digest Volume of
Martindale-Hubbell

MEXICO LAW DIGEST

Revised for 1992 edition by

CURTIS, MALLET-PREVOST, COLT & MOSLE, of the New York Bar.

(Abbreviations used are: C. C., Civil Code of Federal District; Com. C., Commercial Code; C. C. P., Code of Civil Procedure of Federal District. References are to articles of these Codes. See also topic Statutes.)

ABSENTEES: See topic Death.

ACKNOWLEDGMENTS:

Certificates of acknowledgment are unknown in Mexican law, since all documents which in the United States would ordinarily require a certificate of acknowledgment are executed before a notary public who certifies in the instrument itself to the facts which, in the United States, are usually expressed in a certificate of acknowledgment.

Documents executed in the United States should be acknowledged in the usual manner if they are to be used in Mexico. A certificate of the county clerk or other competent official as to the power of the notary to take the acknowledgment should be attached and a certificate of a Mexican consular or diplomatic officer should then be obtained to the effect that the signature of the county clerk or other official is authentic and that he is qualified to act. When the Minister of Foreign Relations of Mexico has attached a certificate regarding the qualifications of the consular or diplomatic officer the document may be recorded in the protocol of a Mexican notary by order of a competent court and is then duly recognized.

ACTIONS:

Actions for Death.—See topic Death, subhead Actions for Death.

Limitation of.—See Prescription.

ADMINISTRATION:

See Executors and Administrators.

ADOPTION:

A person over 25 years of age, free of marriage, and in full exercise of his civil rights may adopt one or more minors or an incapacitated minor or adult; in any case adopting party must be 17 years older than adopted. Individual exercising actual "Patria Potestad" must give his/her consent. Adopting party must prove: (a) Sufficient means to support them; (b) that adoption is beneficial to them; and (c) that he is person of good morals. Adopted party shall have rights and obligations of son. Husband and wife may also adopt when both agree to consider adopted as their own children, and when they are 17 years older than adopted. Adopted persons may use name of adopting party. Adoption can be revoked: (a) When both parties agree to do so, if adopted is over 18 years of age, and (b) in case of ingratitude of adopted. Ingratitude is deemed to exist when: (a) adopted commits intentional crime against adopting party or his family, or (b) if adopted brings criminal action against adopting party. (C. C. 390-410).

ADVERSE POSSESSION: See Prescription.

AGENCY: See Principal and Agent.

ALIENS:

According to Constitution of 1917 aliens have same individual guaranties as citizens. Guaranties are elaborately defined.

Aliens may not intervene in politics, and Federal Executive may require any alien to leave the country immediately and without trial in case his presence in Mexico is deemed undesirable. (Const., art. 33). Ministry of any cult may be exercised only by native Mexicans. (Const., art. 130). Practice of professions is restricted to Mexican citizens by Law of Professions (May 26, 1945; Regulations of Sept. 27, 1945) but not by Constitution. Amparo suit may be filed against law of professions in order to practice. Marriage in Mexico of aliens to Mexicans must be authorized by Department of Interior. Marriage and divorce must be authorized by Ministry of Interior. Entry of aliens is governed by General Law of Population of Dec. 11, 1973, am'd by Decree of Dec. 29 of 1974 and its Regulations of Nov. 12, 1976 as am'd.

Naturalization is governed by Nationality and Naturalization Law of Jan. 20, 1934, as am'd.

Rights of aliens in lands and waters are governed by art. 27 of Constitution and by law of Dec. 31, 1925, and regulations thereof dated Mar. 22, 1926, as am'd Aug. 1, 1939. Only Mexicans and Mexican companies may acquire ownership of lands, waters and their appurtenances, or obtain concessions to develop mines or waters. State may grant same right to aliens, provided they agree before Ministry of Foreign Relations to be considered Mexicans in respect to such property and not to invoke protection of their governments in respect thereto, under penalty of forfeiture of property to nation. No alien may under any conditions acquire direct ownership of lands or waters within a zone 100 kilometers wide along frontiers and 50 kilometers wide along coasts, nor be a member of a Mexican company acquiring such ownership within these zones. Foreigners may acquire use of property in said zone through trust as beneficiaries only. In order to hold interest in Mexican company owning lands, waters and their appurtenances, or concessions to develop mines or waters within Republic, alien must make above mentioned agreement before Ministry of Foreign Relations with respect to his interest. Ministry will not grant permission to alien if result would be to give aliens total interest of over 50% in company holding property for agricultural purposes. Aliens holding 50% or more of capital of any companies owning properties for agricultural purposes prior to Dec. 31, 1925, may retain their interests until their death, in case of physical persons, or for ten years, in case of legal entities. Provisions do not apply to colonization contracts made with Federal Government prior to operation of this law. Rights legally acquired by aliens prior to this law may be held by them until their death. Should alien acquire by inheritance rights, acquisition prohibited to aliens,

Ministry of Foreign Relations will grant permit for acquisition and for registration of corresponding deed. Office of Foreign Relations may also permit alien to hold property, acquisition of which is prohibited by law, if property was acquired in good faith prior to date of law. In both of foregoing cases permission will be granted on condition that rights be disposed of within five years to person authorized to acquire them. Aliens who acquired rights enumerated in this law before law took effect were required to make statement of rights to Ministry of Foreign Relations prior to Jan. 21, 1927, in default of which property is considered to have been acquired after law took effect.

Employment of Aliens.—(Labor Law, effective May 1, 1970). Objective is to obtain equilibrium and social justice in labor-management relations; to work is both right and social obligation. These concepts are to be considered in interpreting law, and in case of doubt, interpretation most favorable to worker takes preference. In every enterprise or business at least 90% of workers must be Mexican. Technical and professional employments requiring special skills not available in country may be filled temporarily by foreign workers, but these may not be more than 10% of total number of workers engaged in each specialization area. Employer and foreign workers must be jointly responsible for training Mexican workers. Doctors on duty in factories or enterprises must be Mexicans. Provisions shall not be applicable to directors, administrators and/or general managers. Employment of aliens for maritime industries is prohibited.

See also topic Corporations, subhead Property.

Legal Rights for Foreigners to Reside in Mexico.—Under Mexican Constitution and laws enacted in accordance with it, every person is accorded right to enter and depart from Mexico, to travel in its territory, and to make changes of residence without need for authorization or documentation of any kind.

In practice, however, exercise of these rights is subordinated to limitations imposed by immigration, population, and public health laws of Republic as well as to authority of Federal Executive summarily to ban or eject from country any foreigner whom government considers to be "persona non grata".

Art. 1 of Constitution of the United Mexican States provides that every person shall enjoy guarantees granted by that instrument; and principle of equality between nations—between Mexican and foreigners—is recognized in specific legislation.

Principle of equality between nationals and foreigners is subject to restrictions and limitations imposed by Constitution, regulatory laws that implement Constitution, and other legislation.

Migration to Mexico or entry for any purpose other than tourism is fraught with restrictions arising from statutes, administrative regulations, and internal policy. Latter, as fixed by Secretariat of Interior (Secretaria de Gobernación), General Bureau of Population (Direccion General de Población), and Department of Immigration (Departamento de Migración), is not always written.

Mexican Immigration Code is Federal in nature, administered and enforced through Secretariat of Interior (Gobernación), which also is charged with responsibility for civil peace and tranquility of nation.

Another important power relating to foreigners stems from Art. 33 of Constitution under which President of United Mexican States is clothed with exclusive authority to deport summarily any alien from national territory without hearing if in judgment of Federal Executive his presence in Mexico is deemed disadvantageous ("inconveniente") for nation. Mexico's Supreme Court has ruled—and after five like decisions by Supreme Court on same point of law it becomes jurisprudence and therefore mandatory on lower courts—that President may act without alien having been granted hearing or without any finding of fact to support his decision.

In contrast Ministry of Interior in moving to expel alien must act on finding of fact and one that falls within causes for expulsion set out in General Law of Population (Ley General de Población). These are that alien has entered country illegally, hidden his previous expulsion (if any); failed to obey previous order from Ministry to leave country; committed illicit or dishonest act; concealed or been accomplice to concealment of alien who has committed any of previously described acts; claimed immigration status different from that actually possessed; or made false declaration in order to enter or remain in Mexico.

Immigration Categories.—Fact that alien is subject to these administrative proceedings points to differences between status of foreigner and that of citizen.

Foreigners are divided into three broad categories for purposes of immigration and according to which documentation is issued to them to legalize their presence in country. Each of these categories is further divided into sub-categories of immigration status.

General Law of Population establishes three general categories under which aliens may enter Mexico temporarily, or reside here as case may be, namely: (a) Nonimmigrant ("no-inmigrante"), (b) immigrant ("inmigrante"), and (c) one who has immigrated ("inmigrado").

Letters and numbers following Spanish designation of each sub-category is pertinent form number used to document status.

Nonimmigrant Status ("No-Inmigrante").—Nine sub-categories included under this general heading are following:

1. Tourist ("Turista" F.M.T.) status is extended to individual who comes to Mexico for pleasure, recreation or health or for activities of scientific, or artistic nature or to participate in sports. Amateur athletes are usually documented as tourists. No person so documented may be remunerated from or by source in Mexico. Maximum life of tourist permit is 180 days.

See Topical Index in front part of this volume.

Martindale-Hubbell also contains the Model Rules of Professional Conduct of the American Bar Association and the Code of Judicial Conduct.

Finally, the set includes a "Buyer's Guide" to help you find expert witnesses, court reporters, private investigators, or other consultants or suppliers to the legal profession.

3. *Local Directories*

Directories may be available for a particular region or locality. For example, some local bar associations may publish a booklet listing members of the association. Other local directories may be published by private publishers. An example of a local directory is the "District of Columbia Bar's Lawyer Directory." Some local directories provide only the attorney's name, address, and telephone number, while others may provide brief biographical sketches and even photographs of the lawyers listed in the directory.

4. *Specialized Directories*

A number of directories provide lists of attorneys who concentrate in specialized practice areas or contain information relating to a certain specialized topic. Examples include the following:

> *Directory of Corporate Counsel* (a directory of personnel of the law departments of corporations, both for-profit and not-for-profit, in the United States).
>
> *Want's Federal-State Court Directory* (a directory of general information about federal and state courts and their personnel).
>
> *American Association of Law Libraries Directory and Handbook* (a directory of information about American law libraries).

5. *Internet Directories*

All of the attorney information found in the conventional hardbound print volumes of *Martindale-Hubbell* can also be located through the Internet at its site "Martindale-Hubbell Lawyer Locator" at http://www.martindale.com/locator/home.html. The site provides free access to comprehensive listings of one million lawyers and law firms in 160 countries around the world. Searching is easily accomplished by name, firm, location, or law school attended.

Another excellent free legal directory on the Internet is provided by FindLaw, West's legal Web site. Access http://lawyers.findlaw.com to search for attorneys by name or practice area. You may also search for corporate and government attorneys. Articles about retaining attorneys and lists of process servers and other legal consultants are also provided.

D. Form Books

1. Introduction

One of the typical tasks performed by paralegals is drafting legal documents. Some of the documents may be for use in litigation, such as forms for complaints, answers, notices of depositions, or interrogatories. Other forms may relate to transactional aspects of law practice, such as leases, partnership agreements, or corporate bylaws. Seldom, if ever, do attorneys or paralegals draft documents "from scratch." Generally they rely on forms or models, which have proven useful in other instances.

If you are asked to draft a legal document, there are several alternatives you can pursue. The office you work in may have a central form file, which contains forms for commonly used documents. In such a case you would review the form provided and modify it to suit your needs. Alternatively, you can ask another paralegal, a secretary, or an attorney if any individual client files might have a comparable form you can use as a guide. If these strategies are not helpful, you can consult a form book (sometimes called a "practice set").

A form book is a single volume or, more typically, a multivolume set that contains forms for use in the legal profession. Some sets of form books contain forms that can be used in any aspect of legal practice and include litigation forms as well as forms used in practice areas not related to litigation. Other books provide forms related solely to one state or to one area of the law. An example of such a specialized set of form books is *Murphy's Will Clauses: Annotations and Forms with Tax Effects*, a multivolume set containing numerous forms used in connection with drafting wills, trusts, and other estate-related forms.

2. Well-Known Form Books

Some of the better known sets of form books are as follows:

> *American Jurisprudence Legal Forms 2d*. This set consists of more than 60 alphabetically arranged volumes of forms and provides forms for contracts, wills, and leases as well as for hundreds of other topics.
>
> *American Jurisprudence Pleading and Practice Forms Annotated*. This set consists of more than 70 volumes of forms and provides more than 36,000 forms relating to litigation, such as forms for complaints, answers, discovery procedures, motions for change of venue, motions for new trial, and appeals.
>
> *Bender's Federal Practice Forms*. This more-than-15-volume set also contains forms for use in federal practice, both civil and criminal.
>
> *Current Legal Forms with Tax Analysis* by Rabkin and Johnson is a multivolume set of forms for general law practice.

Federal Procedural Forms, Lawyers Edition. This set consists of more than 25 volumes and provides forms for use in federal practice.

Bender's Forms of Discovery by Matthew Bender is a multivolume set of forms related solely to discovery matters such as interrogatories, depositions, requests for production and inspection, and medical discovery.

West's Legal Forms 3d. This set of books, consisting of more than 40 volumes, contains a variety of forms for general law practice, such as bankruptcy forms, forms for purchase and sale of real estate, and forms relating to business organizations, including partnerships and corporations.

Some publishers have produced sets of form books devoted strictly to forms for use in that state. For example, a set commonly used in California for business or transactional matters is Matthew Bender's *California Legal Forms: Transaction Guide*. If your state does not have a set of books containing forms specifically tailored for your state, use one of the "general" sets of form books, such as *West's Legal Forms, 3d* or *Am. Jur. Legal Forms 2d*, which are designed to provide forms for use in any state. You may also encounter a set of form books for one specific legal topic, such as trademark forms, bankruptcy forms, and so forth.

There are two recent form books prepared strictly for paralegals: *Personal Injury Paralegal: Forms and Procedures* by Joyce Walden, which contains sample correspondence, forms, checklists, and pleadings related to personal injury practice, and *Paralegal Litigation: Forms and Procedures*, Third Edition, by Marcy Fawcett Delesandri, which includes more than 60 forms, checklists, and procedures for drafting litigation documents.

Another source of forms is treatises, which often contain sample documents and forms. For example, one of the best known treatises on bankruptcy, *Collier on Bankruptcy, 15th Edition Revised*, contains three volumes of forms to complete its thorough analysis of bankruptcy practice. Additionally, the Law Digest volumes of *Martindale-Hubbell* contain some forms for use in various states. Finally, some state annotated codes contain forms. See Figure 7-5 for samples of forms.

The Internet offers thousands of legal forms. As with many offerings on the Internet, however, it is unknown who authored the forms or whether they have been subjected to the rigorous checking and editing that accompanies print publications. Thus, they should be used with extreme caution. Such forms may nevertheless provide a useful starting place. References to Internet sites offering forms are provided at the end of this chapter.

Some states now offer various forms on their official Web sites. For example, all states now provide comprehensive forms banks for organizing, maintaining, and dissolving business entities (such as corporations, limited partnerships, and limited liability companies). The forms can be downloaded and printed for free and are generally available on the home page for the state's secretary of state.

Similarly, many courts now offer free forms on their Web sites. For example, the California Judicial Council offers hundreds of downloadable and electronically fillable forms, from notices of appeal to petitions for

Figure 7-5
Sample Page from Virginia Forms—Criminal Procedure

No. 9-1002. Order Allowing Attorney to Withdraw.

ORDER ALLOWING ATTORNEY TO WITHDRAW

This matter came on this ___ day of _____, 1998, to be heard on the motion of Hope N. Pray, counsel, for leave to withdraw as counsel of record for Daniel Dissatisfied.

Daniel Dissatisfied being present in person in court, the Court heard statements by counsel and defendant.

The Court finding there being good cause and it being proper so to do, it is hereby ORDERED that Hope N. Pray is relieved as counsel of record for Daniel Dissatisfied.

It is further ORDERED that the next attorney on the court-appointed list be assigned this case.

Enter: _____
                            Judge

Date: _____

I ask for this:

_____
Hope N. Pray

Seen and Agreed:

_____
Daniel Dissatisfied

Note: Rules of the Supreme Court of Virginia, Virginia Code of Professional Responsibility, DR 2-108 as to termination representation.

Figure 7-5 *(Continued)*
Sample Corporate Resolutions by Written Consent

Action by Written Consent of Directors

The undersigned, constituting all of the Directors of ___[name]___ (the "Corporation") hereby take the following actions by written consent pursuant to Section 709 of the Business Corporation Law of New York and Article V of the bylaws of the Corporation as if present at a meeting duly called pursuant to notice.

> RESOLVED, the Directors approve the hiring of ___[name]___ as ___[identify position]___ for the Corporation to perform such duties and at a salary and upon terms and conditions as determined by the President of the Corporation.

> RESOLVED, the Articles of Incorporation for the Corporation shall be amended to change the name of the Corporation to ___[name]___ which action shall be voted on by the shareholders of the Corporation pursuant to a special meeting to be called therefor by the President of the Corporation.

> RESOLVED, that the Corporation shall instruct its counsel to ___[identify action]___ against ___[identify person]___ for ___[identify reason]___.

The officers of the Corporation are hereby authorized to take appropriate action to effect the purposes of these resolutions.

Date: _____   _____
                             [Director name and signature]

Date: _____   _____
                             [Director name and signature]

Date: _____   _____
                             [Director name and signature]

changes of name (access http://www.courtinfo.ca.gov/forms). Access your
state's judicial site (see Table T.1 of *The Bluebook*) and see if forms are
offered. Alternatively, access MegaLaw at http://www.megalaw.com and
select "Legal Forms" and then "Government Forms" to see if your state
offers free judicial forms.

3. *Locating Form Books*

To locate form books, check the card catalog in your law library, browse the
shelves, or consult your law librarian. Often form books are located near
other related books. For example, the books containing forms related to
federal practice are usually found near the sets of books containing federal
cases. Similarly, sets of books containing forms for use in criminal law
practice are often located in the "criminal law" section of the law library
or the stack that also contains treatises on criminal law and case books
devoted solely to criminal law cases. Thus, the easiest way to locate form
books is often to browse the stacks devoted to a certain legal topic. Similarly, form books for use in a state are usually located with the cases and
statutes for that state.

4. *Research Strategies*

When you have located a set of form books that is pertinent to the legal
issue you are researching, you can locate the form you need by either the
descriptive word approach or the topic approach.

To use the descriptive word approach, locate the index to the set,
generally found in the last volume of the set. The index is alphabetically
arranged. You should look up words or phrases that describe or relate to the
form you are drafting (contract, trust, complaint, bylaws, venue) and you
will then be directed to the appropriate volume and page for the form
you need.

To use the topic approach, scan the chapter headings and subheadings in the set. You can then examine the particular form that seems most
appropriate.

One of the useful features of many form books is that they are annotated. This means that you will be referred to cases that have approved or
supported language used in the form. Moreover, many form books provide
analysis and commentary on use of the forms and practical aids such as
checklists, providing items to consider in drafting a certain type of form.

Most form books are kept current by pocket parts. Therefore, after
reviewing a form, check the pocket part to determine if language used in
the form has been revised or if new annotations and comment have been
provided.

One of the recent developments in form books is for the publisher to
put the forms on disc for use with various software programs or to offer
them electronically. For example, West offers *Am. Jur. Legal Forms 2d* and
Am. Jur. Pleading and Practice Forms Annotated, in CD-ROM form and on

Westlaw, allowing you to locate forms quickly with a word search, export forms directly to your word processor, and then customize, copy, and print them with a simple keystroke.

5. Summary

Form books provide an excellent starting point for drafting legal documents. You should not view drafting documents as merely an exercise in finding a form and then "filling in the blanks." Carefully review the form to ensure it is appropriate for the document you need to prepare. Feel free to revise the form to make it fit your purposes so long as these revisions are consistent with the law in your jurisdiction. Often you may combine features or elements of several forms to create the best document. Be alert to forms prepared by others in your office as well as other firms and start collecting your own set of forms of documents and pleadings you believe are well drafted and effective. In sum, exercise discretion in using form books. "Cut and paste" until you have a form that is best suited to your needs.

The Final Wrap-Up

Use and Citation of Directories and Form Books

Use:	Use directories to locate information about lawyers and law firms. Use the law digest volumes of *Martindale-Hubbell* to obtain a quick answer to a research question about another state's laws or procedures. Use form books to help you draft forms for both litigation and transactional matters and to give you ideas about how to phrase and structure certain agreements.
Citation:	Do not cite to directories or form books. These books are in the nature of finding tools rather than research tools.

E. Uniform Laws

1. Introduction

You have seen that the Restatements were produced as a result of concern by legal scholars that case law was overly complex and uncertain. At about the same time that the American Law Institute (the "Institute") was formed to produce the Restatements, legal scholars became concerned over the great disparity in state statutes on areas of the law that could be treated similarly or uniformly among the states.

The result of this concern was the formation of the National Conference of Commissioners on Uniform State Laws in 1892. The Conference is composed of more than 300 practicing attorneys, judges, law professors, and other legal scholars who are usually appointed by the governor of each state and meet on an annual basis to draft proposed legislation on various areas of the law. These proposed laws, which are the result of considerable time and effort, are then presented to the legislatures of the 50 states with the hope and expectation that the state legislature will pass the Conference's version of the law on that particular legal topic. The Conference can only propose uniform laws. No Uniform Law is effective until a state legislature specifically enacts it.

For example, after studying statutes relating to partnerships from various states, the Conference drafted its proposed set of partnership statutes, titled the Uniform Partnership Act, and began persuading the various state legislatures in the 50 states to adopt the Uniform Partnership Act in place of their divergent partnership statutes. Once a state adopts a Uniform Law, it is then a primary authority in that state. Until they are adopted, however, Uniform Laws have no such legal effect and thus assume the characteristics of secondary authority. Once adopted, a Uniform Law is published in the state's annotated codes together with other statutes in that state. After printing the text of the Uniform Law, the state code will usually provide you with the text of the Conference's comments about the law and with an explanation as to how the state version of the Uniform Law differs from the original version drafted by the Conference. Cases interpreting the Uniform Law will follow.

Some states, after holding hearings, debates, and other legislative proceedings, just as for any other state law, will adopt the uniform act "as is." Other states may reject the act, while others may revise the act, adding certain provisions and omitting others. Thus, while the goal of the Conference is to produce a statute that will be uniform from state to state, the end result is a statute that nearly always has some variation from state to state. Nevertheless, many of an act's provisions will be retained intact or with only minor revisions so there will be resulting overall uniformity among the states that adopt a uniform act.

The Conference has approved more than 200 uniform laws, ranging from perhaps the best known, the Uniform Commercial Code (relating to commercial practices and sales), which took ten years to complete and has been adopted in whole or in part by every state, to the Uniform Adoption Act, to the Uniform Simultaneous Death Act.

The Conference also drafts proposed legislation known as "Model Acts." While a Uniform Law is one whose adoption is urged in every state by the Conference, a Model Act is one for which uniformity among the states is not as necessary or desirable. An example is the Model Punitive Damages Act, intended to address the need for consistency in awards of punitive damages throughout the nation. While the Model Punitive Damages Act serves as a source to which states can looks for guidance in formulating their laws relating to punitive damages, it is unlikely that all states will adopt identical statutes in this area because the manner in which wrongdoers are punished and damages are awarded is a matter of greatest concern to the jurisdiction where the wrong is committed. In sum, Model Acts are intended as guidelines that states can borrow from or modify when drafting their own legislation while Uniform Acts are intended to be adopted exactly as written. The Conference often works with the Institute in developing uniform and model legislation. For example, the two worked together to prepare the UCC and the Institute drafted the Model Penal Code.

2. *Research Strategies*

Uniform Laws Annotated, Master Edition. To locate the text of the more than 200 Uniform Laws and the Model Acts, you can consult West's *Uniform Laws Annotated, Master Edition.* This multi-volume set not only provides the text of Uniform Laws and Model Acts but also provides official comments of the drafters explaining the intent and purpose of each Uniform Law, a list of the states that have adopted each particular Uniform Law, the date the Law was adopted, brief descriptions of how various states have modified the Uniform Law, references to law review articles regarding the Uniform Law, annotations or brief summaries of cases interpreting the Uniform Law, references to topics and Key Numbers to enable the reader to access West's Key Number System, and references to sections of C.J.S., which discuss that area of the law. The set is kept current by pocket parts and supplements. See Figure 7-6 for a sample page from the *Uniform Laws Annotated, Master Edition.*

While *Uniform Laws Annotated, Master Edition* thus provides an overview of all uniform legislation, it lacks a comprehensive general index or table of contents. The Uniform Laws and Model Acts are, however, grouped together by general subject matter. For example, estate, probate, and related laws are found in volumes 26 through 30 of the set. Additionally, a pamphlet published regularly in conjunction with the *Master Edition,* titled *Directory of Uniform Acts and Codes,* lists all Uniform Laws alphabetically and will direct you to the location of the Law in the *Master Edition.* In effect, this directory serves as an index to the *Master Edition.* The directory also lists each state and the particular Uniform Laws it has adopted. See Figure 7-7 for a sample page from the *Directory of Uniform Acts and Codes.*

Am. Jur. 2d and *C.J.S.* The one-volume "Table of Laws and Rules" in Am. Jur. 2d and C.J.S. will refer you to sections in each of the encyclopedias that discuss Uniform Laws.

Martindale-Hubbell. The complete text of several of the better known and more widely adopted Uniform Laws, such as the Uniform Commercial Code, the Uniform Arbitration Act, and the Uniform Probate Code can be found in *Martindale-Hubbell.*

Westlaw. The text of all uniform and model acts contained in the Master Edition is also available on Westlaw. Some are available on LEXIS.

Figure 7-6
Sample Page from the *Uniform Laws Annotated,*
Master Edition

wife which listed as a possible heir the illegitimate child of appellant. In re Raso's Estate, Fla.App.1976, 332 So.2d 78.

Trial court abused its discretion in denying appellant's motion to vacate default judgment where appellant properly alleged excusable neglect for her failure to timely respond to petition for determination of heirs and where appellant properly alleged a meritorious defense. Id.

Section 2-102. [Share of the Spouse.]

The intestate share of the surviving spouse is:

(1) if there is no surviving issue or parent of the decedent, the entire intestate estate;

(2) if there is no surviving issue but the decedent is survived by a parent or parents, the first [$50,000], plus one-half of the balance of the intestate estate;

(3) if there are surviving issue all of whom are issue of the surviving spouse also, the first [$50,000], plus one-half of the balance of the intestate estate;

(4) if there are surviving issue one or more of whom are not issue of the surviving spouse, one-half of the intestate estate.

COMMENT

This section gives the surviving spouse a larger share than most existing statutes on descent and distribution. In doing so, it reflects the desires of most married persons, who almost always leave all of a moderate estate or at least one-half of a larger estate to the surviving spouse when a will is executed. A husband or wife who desires to leave the surviving spouse less than the share provided by this section may do so by executing a will, subject of course to possible election by the surviving spouse to take an elective share of one-third under Part 2 of this Article. Moreover, in the small estate (less than $50,000 after homestead allowance, exempt property, and allowances) the surviving spouse is given the entire estate if there are only children who are issue of both the decedent and the surviving spouse; the result is to avoid protective proceedings as to property otherwise passing to their minor children.

See Section 2–802 for the definition of spouse which controls for purposes of intestate succession.

Law Review Commentaries

How the family fares. Donald L. Robertson. 37 Ohio S.L.J. 264 (1976).

Modern Wills Act. John T. Gaubatz. 31 U.Miami L.Rev. 497 (1977).

Probate change. 20 Boston Bar J. No. 11, p. 6 (1976).

59

Figure 7-7
Sample Page from *Directory of Uniform Acts and Codes*

DIRECTORY OF UNIFORM ACTS

———

List of Uniform Acts or Codes, in alphabetical order, showing where each may be found in Uniform Laws Annotated, Master Edition.

The designation "Pocket Part" under the page column indicates that the particular Act or Code is complete in the Pocket Part. The designation "Pamphlet" under the page column indicates that the particular Act is complete in a Supplementary or Special Pamphlet. The user should always, of course, consult the Pocket Part or Pamphlet for changes and subsequent material when an Act or Code appears in the main volume.

———

Title of Act	Uniform Laws Annotated Volume	Page
Abortion Act, Revised	9, Pt. I	1
Absence as Evidence of Death and Absentees' Property Act	8A	1
Acknowledgment Act	12	1
Notarial Acts, Uniform Law on	14	125
Administrative Procedure Act, State (1981) (Model)	15	1
Administrative Procedure Act, State (1961) (Model)	15	137
Adoption Act	9, Pt. I	11
Aircraft Financial Responsibility Act	12	21
Alcoholism and Intoxication Treatment Act	9	79
Anatomical Gift Act (1987 Act)	8A	Pocket Part
Anatomical Gift Act (1968 Act)	8A	15
Ancillary Administration of Estates Act	8A	69
Antitrust, State Antitrust Act	7B	711
Arbitration Act	7	1
Attendance of Witnesses From Without a State in Criminal Proceedings, Act to Secure	11	1
Audio-Visual Deposition Act [Rule]	12	Pocket Part
Brain Death Act	12	Pocket Part
Canada—U.S. Transboundary Pollution Reciprocal Access Act	9B	625
Certification of Questions of Law Act	12	49
Child Custody Jurisdiction Act	9, Pt. I	115
Children and minors,		
Abortion Act, Revised	9, Pt. I	1
Adoption Act	9, Pt. I	11
Child Custody Jurisdiction Act	9, Pt. I	115
Civil Liability for Support Act	9, Pt. I	333
Gifts to Minors Act (1966 Act)	8A	181
Gifts to Minors Act (1956 Act)	8A	225
Interstate Family Support Act	9, Pt. I	Pocket Part
Juvenile Court Act	9A	1
Parentage Act	9B	287
Paternity Act	9B	347
Putative and Unknown Fathers Act	9B	Pocket Part
Reciprocal Enforcement of Support Act (1968 Act)	9B	381
Reciprocal Enforcement of Support Act (1950 Act)	9B	553
Revised Abortion Act	9, Pt. I	1
Status of Children of Assisted Conception	9B	Pocket Part
Transfers to Minors Act	8A	Pocket Part

1

Internet. Many Uniform Laws are available on the Internet. The National Conference of Commissioners on Uniform State Laws posts all final acts on its Web site at http://www.nccusl.org/Update. The text of all are given, together with a summary of each act, and legislative facts about the adoption of an act in the various states. See also CyberSites at the end of this chapter.

3. Use of Uniform Laws

If you are researching a state statute that has been adopted as a Uniform Law and there are no cases interpreting it, you should review the Official Comment to the Uniform Law and cases from another state that has also adopted the Uniform Law. As you will recall from Chapter 1, while cases from one state are never binding in another state, cases from another state interpreting Uniform Laws may be highly persuasive inasmuch as such cases would be interpreting statutory provisions that are similar or identical to those enacted in your state.

A Uniform Law or Model Act drafted and approved by the Conference is secondary authority. The official comments of the drafters related to the background, purpose, and effect of a Uniform Law are also secondary authority, and while these comments provide credible insight into the goals of a Uniform Law and the ills it is designed to remedy, they need not be followed by a court. Once a Uniform Law or Model Act is adopted by your state legislature, however, it is primary authority that must be followed in your state.

F.   Looseleaf Services

1. Introduction

You have seen that law books are usually published in a hardbound version or in softcover pamphlets, supplements, or advance sheets. Yet another method of publication is "looseleaf," meaning a ringed binder (or a book with removable covers and pages stacked on posts) with individual looseleaf sheets of paper, which are easily removed and replaced. These are the looseleaf services. The major looseleaf publishers are CCH Incorporated, Bureau of National Affairs, Clark Boardman Callaghan (now part of West), and Matthew Bender (now part of LEXIS Publishing).

The looseleaf services are a variety of treatise and may consist of one volume or several volumes devoted to one topic of the law, such as labor law, securities, environmental law, Social Security compensation, bankruptcy, tax, criminal law, or family law. In general, looseleaf services are used for areas of the law that are subject to frequent change or that are highly regulated, such as securities law. Similarly, revisions are constantly being made to our tax laws. To publish information relating to taxation in hardbound sets of books would not be efficient or cost-effective, as the hardbound volumes would be out of date almost as soon as they would be placed on library shelves. Even frequent updating by pocket parts will not keep pace with our changing tax laws. Therefore, the looseleaf service binder sets are purchased by law firms and law libraries. As changes occur in the law or as new cases are decided, the publisher will send packets of replacement pages to the subscriber with an instruction to remove and destroy certain pages in the set and replace them with the new pages provided by the publisher — an updating technique called interfiling. In this manner, the books are kept current to reflect accurately the status of the law without being cost-prohibitive to the subscriber. Some looseleaf services are updated as frequently as once a week.

Many of the looseleaf services are devoted to rules and regulations promulgated by our federal agencies, such as the service titled Occupational Safety and Health Reporter. These will be discussed in greater detail in Chapter 10. Several of the looseleaf services, however, report on areas of the law for which no particular agency is responsible but for which there is general interest, such as criminal law or family law. There are hundreds of looseleafs covering nearly every legal topic.

A typical looseleaf service will include primary and secondary authorities. Primary authority will be found in the statutes governing a certain area of the law, which are set forth in full text as well as in the court decisions, which are often included. Often summaries or digests of court cases related to this area of the law are given. Secondary authority is found in the commentary and discussion of this topic and of recent developments in this area of the law as well as practice tips and notices of upcoming seminars or meetings of legal professionals or proposed legislation related to this area of law. The looseleafs then function to provide a complete treatment of an area of the law, bringing together all information on a legal topic in one set. Some experts call the looseleafs "minilibraries" because they are comprehensive collections of current legal materials devoted to one of the law and brought together in one source.

Although a treatise may appear in binder or looseleaf form (such as the six-volume binder set, *McCarthy on Trademarks and Unfair Competition*), a true looseleaf service is distinguisable from such a treatise because the looseleaf service will contain primary authority, such as cases, statutes, and administrative regulations as well as secondary authority. A treatise usually includes only comment and analysis of an area of the law with no cases (although statutes may be included in an appendix to the set).

You should feel free to cite a looseleaf service in a memorandum or brief that you prepare. Often, however, the looseleaf services function more as "finding" tools, which provide general background information on a certain area of law and direct you to the primary authorities (statutes and cases) in the field, which you would then cite.

2. *Arrangement of Looseleaf Services*

There is no one uniform pattern for arrangement of looseleaf services. Different publishers arrange the discussion of the law in different ways, and each service is different from another. Often the best way to determine the arrangement of the service to enhance your research efforts is simply to invest 20 to 30 minutes in reading the editor's introduction to the service and then browsing through the set to familiarize yourself with its features and structure.

In general, however, looseleaf services will consist of multiple ringed binders, each of which has several sections, divided by colorful marked tabs. For example, one tab is usually marked "How to Use." This section provides an overview of the service and guidelines for using the set. Other tabs may be marked "Topical Index," "Table of Cases," "State Laws," "Federal Laws," "Cumulative Index," and "New Developments."

3. *Research Strategies*

To determine if a looseleaf service exists for an area of the law you are researching, for instance, labor law, consult the card catalog in your law library or ask the reference librarian. Alternatively, you could locate the stacks in the law library that contain labor law materials and simply scan the shelves to determine if a looseleaf service exists. You also check a publication called *Legal Looseleafs in Print,* which provides information on more than 3,000 looseleafs and will also inform you if the looseleaf is available on the Internet.

Each looseleaf service will have a general index, which will alphabetically list the topics and subjects discussed in the service. Use the descriptive word approach to locate words in the index that describe your research issue. The index will then refer you to the appropriate paragraph or section. Some looseleaf sets have more than one index, so be sure you always check the most current index as well as the "standard" topical index. Alternatively, you can use the table of cases to locate cases reported or discussed in the set. Review the cases to which you are directed.

Note that references in the index are seldom to *pages*. It is typical of looseleaf services that paragraph or section references are used rather than references to pages, as this facilitates the addition of new replacement sheets in the set. Many looseleaf services also use subsections and decimals such as a reference to "¶ 10060.101" to accommodate the insertion of new pages. Thus, it may take you a bit of time to become accustomed to the organization of the looseleaf services. Invest the time it takes to understand how to use looseleaf services because these mini-libraries provide a comprehensive discussion of relevant legal topics.

G. Jury Instructions

1. *Introduction*

At the conclusion of a trial, a judge will "charge" the jury by providing it with instructions for reaching a decision. Preparing instructions for the jury is done by attorneys and paralegals. Until approximately 60 years ago, new jury instructions were developed for each trial. Often the instructions were erroneous statements of the law, and an appellate court would order a new trial due to the improper instruction. For example, if judges were free in criminal trials to develop their own definitions for "reasonable doubt," convictions of criminal defendants would be based upon differing standards.

Recognizing the duplication of effort required in preparing jury instructions for each trial and the waste of time and excessive cost involved in new trials due to erroneous instructions, a movement for pattern or form jury instructions emerged. Just as there are forms for leases, contracts, and motions for change of venue, there are now form books that contain jury instructions.

The jury instructions are typically drafted by committees of legal scholars or bar associations who study cases and then prepare accurate, brief, and easily understood instructions regarding the law. A new development is the drafting of jury instructions in "plain English" to improve jurors' comprehension. In many states, the standard jury instructions are so highly regarded that rules of court for the state recommend or require that the trial judge read the applicable instruction. In other instances, jury instructions may be modified to state the law accurately. For example, in 2003, after six years of study, California adopted new civil jury instructions (the Judicial Council of California Civil Jury Instructions) after determining that the state's then-existing instructions were "simply impenetrable to the ordinary juror." The newly drafted instructions are in "plain English" so they are readily understandable to the average juror. Their use is not mandatory but they are designated "official" instructions, meaning that they are to be used unless a judge determines that a different instruction would more accurately state the law and be understood by jurors. All of the jury instructions, together with commentary, directions for their use, and references to primary and secondary authorities supporting their use are available on the Internet at http://www.courtinfo.ca.gov/jury/civiljuryinstructions.

Paralegals often play a major role in preparing jury instructions. While the primary role of a jury instruction is to provide an accurate statement of the law for a judge to communicate to a jury, a secondary role is to provide research sources. Many sets of jury instructions not only provide the actual text of an instruction but follow it with commentary directing you to cases, statutes, or treatises that support the language used in the instructions or provide additional information relating to that area of the law. This commentary is an excellent secondary authority source. Moreover, the instruction itself is a source of useful information for researchers. For example, if you were writing a memorandum on a contract matter and needed to list the elements of a cause of action for breach of contract, a jury instruction will likely set them forth. That is, when you read the jury instruction relating to contracts, you will see language similar to the following:

> Ladies and Gentlemen, if you find from your consideration of all the evidence that there was an agreement between the parties, that the parties

were legally capable of entering into the agreement, that the defendant without justification or excuse breached the agreement, and that this breach was the cause of damage to the plaintiff, then you should find the defendant liable for breach of contract.

By analyzing the statement, you can easily see that a cause of action for breach of contract arises when three elements exist: an agreement; a breach of the agreement by one party; and damage caused by the breach. Thus, jury instructions serve to provide a quick summary of the key elements of many areas of the law, including contracts, fraud, negligence, infliction of emotional distress, assault, and battery.

2. *Research Strategies*

To locate the jury instructions in your law library, check the card catalog or ask a reference librarian for assistance. Some law libraries keep the materials on trial practice in one section, and in such instances you may be able to locate the jury instructions in that section. Nearly every state has its own sets of jury instructions for both civil and criminal cases. All federal circuits have model or pattern criminal jury instructions and most have approved instructions for civil cases as well.

If there is no set of jury instructions specific to your state, consult the set *Am. Jur. Pleading and Practice Forms, Annotated*. As you will recall from Chapter 6, this multivolume set contains thousands of forms and documents for use in all phases of litigation and also contains standard jury instructions. For federal cases you may consult a set titled *Modern Federal Jury Instructions*, which provides jury instructions for both civil and criminal cases. Some sets are available in both conventional bound volumes, in CD-ROM form, and on LEXIS and Westlaw.

When you have located the books containing jury instructions, consult the general index to the set. As is typical of indexes, it is usually found at the end of the last volume of the set and lists alphabetically the topics covered by the set.

Use the descriptive word approach and locate words describing the issue you are researching, such as burglary, misrepresentation, or perjury. You will then be directed to the instructions used in such cases. Most sets of jury instructions are updated by pocket parts. See Figure 7-8 for sample jury instructions for the definition of intent in international tort cases.

As discussed earlier, many states and courts now offer their jury instructions on the Internet. Search your state's judicial Web site (see Table T.1 of *The Bluebook*) or review the article "What's the Law? Finding Jury Instructions" at http://www.llrx.com/columns/reference19.htm, which includes links to jury instructions for several states.

Figure 7-8
Sample Jury Instruction from *California Civil Jury Instructions*

1320. Intent

[Name of defendant] **acted intentionally if [he/she] intended to** *[insert facts, e.g., "assault [name of plaintiff]," "commit a battery"]* **or if [he/she] was substantially certain that the** *[insert facts, e.g., "assault," "battery"]* **would result from [his/her] conduct.**

— Jury instruction

Directions for Use

This instruction may be used to define intent for other intentional torts, where appropriate.

Sources and Authority

- "In an action for civil battery the element of intent is satisfied if the evidence shows defendant acted with a 'willful disregard' of the plaintiff's rights." (*Ashcraft v. King* (1991) 228 Cal.App.3d 604, 613 [278 Cal.Rptr. 900], internal citation omitted.)

Reference to case supporting language used in instruction

- "As a general rule, California law recognizes that '. . . every person is presumed to intend the natural and probable consequences of his acts.' Thus, a person who acts willfully may be said to intend ' " 'those consequences which (a) represent the very purpose for which an act is done (regardless of the likelihood of occurrence), or (b) are known to be substantially certain to result (regardless of desire).' " ' " The same definition is applied to many intentional torts." (*Gomez v. Acquistapace* (1996) 50 Cal.App.4th 740, 746 [57 Cal.Rptr.2d 821], internal citations omitted.)

Secondary Sources

5 Witkin, Summary of California Law (9th ed. 1988) Torts, § 348

6 California Forms of Pleading and Practice, Ch. 58, *Assault and Battery* (Matthew Bender)

2 California Points and Authorities, Ch. 21, *Assault and Battery* (Matthew Bender)

(New September 2003)

———— **Practice Tip** ————

Jury Instructions

Don't forget to use jury instructions to obtain a quick answer to a straightforward research question. If you need to know the elements of a fraud cause of action or what a plaintiff must prove to prevail in a sexual harassment case, check your state's jury instructions for a quick and concise statement of the law and then a reference to a leading case on the topic.

The Final Wrap-Up

Using and Citing Uniform Laws, Looseleaf Services, and Jury Instructions

Use: Use Uniform Laws adopted in your state as you would any state statute. If your state has no cases interpreting its particular Uniform Law, review cases from other jurisdictions as these may be highly persuasive. Use looseleaf services to locate current primary and secondary sources for highly regulated areas such as tax and securities. Use jury instructions when preparing for trial or to find a quick answer to a research question.

Citation: Cite freely to Uniform Laws. Remember that if adopted by your state, they have the force and effect of any statute. Looseleaf services are highly regarded and enjoy credible reputations, so they may also be freely cited. Cite jury instructions only when submitting them to a court before it charges a jury in a civil or criminal case.

H.   Summary

All of the sources discussed in this and the preceding chapter are secondary authorities, meaning that while you may refer to these sources and cite them in memoranda or briefs, courts are not required to follow them. While secondary authorities are often highly reputable, they remain persuasive at best and lack the force of the primary authorities of cases, constitutions, statutes, and administrative regulations. Keep in mind that some of the secondary authorities such as Restatements and law review articles are highly regarded and often cited, while others, such as encyclopedias, are viewed as elementary in approach and are seldom cited. One of the best indications of the strength of a secondary source is found in Rule 1.4 (i) of *The Bluebook*, which provides the following hierarchical order when string-citing numerous secondary authorities: model acts; Restatements; treatises and books; works in journals, such as law review articles; annotations; magazine and newspaper articles; and electronic sources. Encyclopedias are not listed. *ALWD* Rule 45 is substantially similar. All of the secondary authorities do an excellent job of providing commentary on the law and typically direct you to the primary authorities that you should rely upon and cite in your memoranda and briefs. A summary of the secondary sources is provided in Figure 7-9.

I. Citation Form

You sould never cite to a directory. Other secondary sources are cited as follows:

1. Attorneys General Opinions:

The Bluebook:	46 Op. Att'y Gen. 496 (1997)
ALWD:	46 Op. Atty. Gen. 496 (1997)

2. Dictionaries:

The Bluebook:	*Black's Law Dictionary* 909 (8th ed. 2004)
ALWD:	*Black's Law Dictionary* 909 (Bryan A. Garner ed., 8th ed., West 2004)

3. Uniform Laws:

The Bluebook:	Unif. P'ship Act § 103, 7A U.L.A. 119 (2002)
ALWD:	Unif. Partn. Act § 103, 7A U.L.A. 119 (2002)

4. Looseleaf Services:

The Bluebook:	*In re Stevens Textiles Co.*, 4 Bankr. L. Rep. (CCH) ¶ 16,041 (Bankr. D.N.J. Mar. 10, 2003)
ALWD:	*In re Stevens Textiles Co.*, 4 Bankr. L. Rep. (CCH) ¶ 16,041 (D.N.J. Mar. 10, 2003)

5. Jury Instructions:

The Bluebook:	2 Leonard Sand et al., *Modern Federal Jury Instructions* § 12.04 (2003)
ALWD:	Leonard Sand et al., *Modern Federal Jury Instructions* vol. 2, § 12.04 (Matthew Bender 2003)

Figure 7-9
Chart of Secondary Sources

Secondary Source	Overview	Description of Set	Supplementation	Research Techniques	Research and Use Notes
Encyclopedias	Alphabetically arranged narrative statements of hundreds of areas of the law supported by cases and other authorities found in footnotes	Multivolume general sets: C.J.S. and Am. Jur. 2d Multivolume state sets Special subject sets	Annual cumulative pocket parts	Descriptive word approach Topic approach	Excellent introductory information. Be cautious about citing to encyclopedias, as they are considered elementary in approach.
Legal Periodicals	Publications produced on a periodic basis discussing a wide variety of legal topics	Law school publications Bar association and paralegal association publications Specialized publications Legal newspapers and newsletters	No supplementation. Each periodical issue is complete.	Index to Legal Periodicals & Books Current Law Index Other separately published indexes Online indices	Periodicals range from the very scholarly and well-respected law reviews to the more practical and seldom cited bar association publications and newsletters.

Texts and Treatises	Texts written by legal scholars on one legal topic that discuss cases and statutes in the narrative statements	Multivolume sets that contain thorough and often critical analysis of an area of the law	Annual cumulative pocket parts or softcover supplements	Descriptive word approach Topic approach Table of cases or statutes approach	Many treatises are highly regarded, and you should feel free to refer and cite to them.
Restatements	Statements of the law in clear and unambiguous language	Multivolume sets on selected areas of the law such as torts, agency, or property	Appendix volumes with pocket parts	Descriptive word approach Topic approach	Restatements are probably the most highly regarded of all of the secondary authorities.
Attorneys General Opinions	Written opinions by United States attorneys general and state attorneys general on a variety of legal topics	Multivolume sets for United States attorneys general opinions and opinions of state attorneys general	No supplementation. Each volume is complete.	Descriptive word approach References from other sources	Attorneys general opinions are strongly persuasive and highly respected.
Legal Dictionaries	Books providing definitions of legal words and phrases and references to cases so defining a word	One-volume alphabetical arrangement of words, phrases, Latin and other foreign terms	No supplementation. Each volume is complete.	Alphabetical approach	While many dictionaries are well known and authoritative, you should cite to and rely on the cases you are directed to rather than the dictionary's definition of a word or phrase.

Figure 7-9 (Continued)

Secondary Source	Overview	Description of Set	Supplementation	Research Techniques	Research and Use Notes
Law Directories	Lists of lawyers	General directories such as *Martindale-Hubbell* contain lists of all attorneys and other useful features such as law digests. Specialty directories list attorneys specializing in certain practice areas or certain geographical regions.	Generally, no supplementation. Replacement sets issued annually or as needed.	Alphabetical approach by state, city, attorney's and firm's name	Used primarily to obtain information about attorneys and law firms. *Law Digests of Martindale-Hubbell* provide summaries of laws of 50 states and more than 80 foreign countries.
Form Books	Sets of books containing standard or pattern forms for general use or for use in certain practice areas. Often annotated and containing useful commentary and practice guides.	Multivolume sets of books containing forms for general legal practice or specialty areas such as criminal law, corporate law, etc.	Pocket parts	Descriptive word approach Topic approach	Used primarily to assist in drafting documents. Seldom, if ever cited, though used with great frequency.

Uniform Laws	Drafts of statutes proposed by legal scholars for certain areas of the law.	Multivolume set, *Uniform Laws Annotated, Master Edition*, containing text of *Uniform Laws*, commentary, references to other sources, etc.	Pocket parts and supplements	Use *Directory of Uniform Acts and Codes* to locate a Uniform Law.	Cases interpreting a Uniform Law, even those from another state, may be highly persuasive in your state if your state has also adopted the Uniform Law.
Looseleaf Services	A variety of treatise devoted to one area of the law (usually a frequently changing area) containing both primary and secondary authority	Multivolume sets of books, arranged in ringed binders containing statutes, cases, case digests, and commentary on one topic of the law	Replacement pages	Descriptive word approach Consult "how to use" section	Looseleaf services provide a thorough overview of an area of the law though their arrangement and use can be awkward.
Jury Instructions	Sets of books containing instructions for charging the jury in civil and criminal trials as well as commentary and annotations	One-volume or multivolume sets specific to federal courts, one state, or general in nature	Pocket parts	Descriptive word approach	Useful in obtaining a "snapshot" of an area of the law, though seldom cited in research projects.

CyberSites ▬▬▬▬▬▬▬▬▬▬▬▬▬▬▬▬▬▬▬▬

Attorney General Opinions

http://www.usdoj.gov/ag	The Web site for the United States Attorney General provides a great deal of information about the attorney general's duties as well as the text of speeches but does not provide opinions of the attorney general.
http://www.usdoj/gov/olc/ opinions.htm	The Web site for the Department of Justice's Office of Legal Counsel has posted many opinions of the U.S. attorney general. Search by topic name or key word.
http://www.library.unt.edu/ govinfo/law/ agopinions.htm#us	The University of North Texas provides direct links to the opinions of the U.S. attorney general and to nearly all states' attorney general opinions. Search by key word, year, or citation.
http://www.washlaw.edu	Some states post their state attorney general opinions on their Web sites. This site provides a direct link to the home page for each state attorney general so you can search the site to determine if it offers the attorney general opinions.

Dictionaries

http://www.duhaime.org/ dictionary/diction.aspx	Attorney Lloyd Duhaime offers a law dictionary online.
http://www.nolo.com/ lawcenter/dictionary/ wordindex.cfm	Nolo's legal dictionary is offered at this site.

Directories

http://lawyers.findlaw.com	This Web site offered by West at FindLaw provides a searchable directory of more than one million lawyers and law firms.
http://martindale.com	This Web site offered by Martindale-Hubbell offers a searchable directory of law firms and lawyers in private and public practice.

Forms

http://www.lectlaw.com/ form.html	The Web site of 'Lectric Law Library offers a variety of forms, including many used for litigation, business, real estate, wills, trusts, and corporations.
http://www.megalaw.com	MegaLaw offers a wide variety of legal materials. Select "Legal Forms."

▬▬▬▬▬▬▬▬▬▬▬▬▬▬▬▬▬▬▬▬ *(continued)*

CyberSites *(Continued)*

http://www.washlaw.edu	Washburn School of Law publishes and links to thousands of legal forms, including forms for both state and federal courts. Select "Legal Documents & Forms."
http://exlibris.memphis.edu/ resource/unclesam/ forms.html	The University of Memphis provides a section called "Forms From the Feds" with direct links to numerous useful forms used by government agencies.

Uniform Laws

http://www.nccusl.org	The official Web site of the National Conference of Commissioners on Uniform State Laws provides the text of all final Uniform Laws, information and legislative status on Uniform Laws, and discussion of projects under consideration.
http://www.law.upenn.edu/ bll/ulc/ulc.htm	The Web site of the University of Pennsylvania provides the text of most Uniform Laws and Model Acts and discusses projects currently under consideration.

Looseleaf Services

While there is no one site providing the text of looseleaf services, the University of Illinois College of Law provides a comprehensive list of looseleafs (together with their publishers) at http://library.law.uiuc.edu/sub/looseleaf.htm.

Jury Instructions

There is no one site to locate jury instructions. Some states, however, post their state-specific jury instrucions on their home pages. To locate home pages, access http://www.megalaw.com, then select "State Law" and then select the paricular state in which you are interested. The following sites may be helpful as well.

http://www.llrx.com/ columns/reference19.htm	An article entitled "What is the Law? Finding Jury Instructions" provides links to several sets of jury instructions.
http://netlizard.com/ yourlaw/ juryinstructions.htm	The legal research site NetLizard provides direct links to several sets of federal and state jury instructions, including those from the Seventh and Ninth Circuits and those from California, Idaho, and Mississippi.

Writing Strategies

There is a great temptation in using secondary sources such as *Black's Law Dictionary* or form books to use the very language you are provided. While the use of a definition from a legal dictionary or the use of certain language given in a form book may be technically correct, it may result in "legalese." Legalese produces a document that is difficult for the reader to understand because its meaning is buried in a sea of redundant phrases and archaic word forms.

When discussing the secondary sources explained in this chapter, be on the alert for the following signs of legalese:

archaic words	hereinabove, erstwhile, albeit, opine
Latin or foreign phrases	*inter alia, res gestae*
redundancies	final result, basic fundamentals
nominalizations	"inspection" rather than "inspect," "harassment" rather than "harass," "decision" rather than "decide"
overuse of negatives	"notwithstanding anything to the contrary discussed herein, you are not prohibited from assigning this agreement."

Assignment for Chapter 7

1. Use *Black's Law Dictionary* (8th ed. 2004).
   a. What is the definition of "motion to suppress"?
   b. What topic and key number are you directed to relating to this definition?
   c. What does the legal maxim *fructus pendentes pars fundi videntur* mean?
2. Use the most current edition of *Martindale-Hubbell Law Directory*.
   a. An attorney named Hugh L. Wilcox, Jr. is with the Florence, South Carolina firm of Wilcox, Buyck & Williams. Where and when did Mr. Wilcox attend law school?
   b. Review the Corporate Law Departments volume. What corporation employs Catrina McLean?
   c. An attorney named Philippe Beurier is with the Paris, France law firm Bredin Prat. Where did he receive his law degree?
   d. What is the filing fee in North Carolina for filing articles of incorporation for a corporation?
   e. Review the ABA Model Rules of Professional Conduct. What Rule relates to confidentiality of information?
   f. In China, how long does software copyright protection last?
   g. Review the Uniform Arbitration Act. What does § 13 cover?
3. Use *Am. Jur. Legal Forms (2d)*.
   a. What forms relate to the payment of moving expenses in employment contracts?
   b. Review the first form. What Am. Jur. 2d reference are you given?
4. Use *Am. Jur. Pleading and Practice Forms Annotated*.
   a. What form provides a complaint against a bar or tavern owner for an attack by an intoxicated mob?
   b. Review the complaint. What does paragraph 1 allege?
   c. What form provides a complaint against a cosmetic surgeon for facial disfigurement?
   d. Review the complaint. What does paragraph 7 allege?
5. Use *Uniform Laws Annotated*.
   a. Has Utah adopted the Uniform Probate Code (1969)?
   b. If so, give the citation to Utah's statute.
   c. Review the Uniform Probate Code. What is the general topic of section 2-907?
   d. Review section 2-907. Generally, is a trust for the care of a designated animal valid?

State Your Answer

1. Access the Web site for the National Association of Attorneys General at http://www.naag.org and identify the attorney general for your state.
2. Access the online legal dictionary at http://dictionary.law.com and provide the definition for "nunc pro tunc."
3. Access the Web site for the National Conference of Commissioners on Uniform State Laws at http://www.nccusl.org/update/AboutNCCUSL_desktopdefault.aspx and identify the commissioners from your state.
4. Access MegaLaw at http://www.megalaw.com and select "Legal Forms" and then "Secretary of State Forms." What is the filing fee in your state for filing articles of incorporation (to incorporate a business) for a stock or "for profit" corporation?
5. Access the article "What is the Law? Finding Jury Instructions" at http://www.llrx.com/columns/reference19.htm and determine whether your state's jury instructions are available online.

Legal Citation Form

Citations direct the path of the law; they stabilize and provide guidance.

Carol M. Bast & Susan Harrell, *Has* The Bluebook
Met Its Match? The ALWD *Citation Manual,*
92 Law Libr. J. 337, 337-38 (2000)

Chapter Overview

Paralegals are routinely assigned the task of "cite-checking." Cite-checking comprises two components: verifying that citations given in a project are accurate and in compliance with rules for citation form (sometimes called "bluebooking") and then verifying that the authorities cited in a project are still "good law." The guidelines and rules relating to the form of citations will be discussed in this chapter and the method of ensuring that authorities relied upon are still correct statements of the law, usually called "Shepardizing" or "KeyCiting," will be discussed in the following chapter.

This chapter will review the history of *The Bluebook* and *ALWD*, the best known guides to citation form, and will provide examples of citations for the primary authorities of cases, constitutions, and statutes as well as the secondary authorities of encyclopedias, legal periodicals, treatises, Restatements, and other authorities. Moreover, this chapter will provide information on more intricate citation tasks, such as punctuation, quotations, and the use of signals such as *id., supra,* and *infra*. Note that while numerous examples of citations are provided in this chapter, most are fictitious and are provided solely for the purpose of illustrating citation rules. References to *Bluebook* and *ALWD* rules are given in parentheses. Finally, many examples of citation form are found in other chapters. For example, illustrations of citation form for international materials and court rules are found in Chapter 10, which discusses those subjects.

A.   Introduction to Citation Form

You may have already observed that legal writings are filled with references to cases, statutes, annotations, and numerous other authorities. The reason for this is that statements about the law must be attributed to their sources. You cannot simply make an assertion such as stating that a trial by jury is waived unless it is requested by a party. Such statements must be supported by legal authority; that is, by primary authorities or secondary authorities. These supporting authorities appear as "citations" or "cites" within the body of your work. Moreover, these citations must appear in a standard and consistent format so that any judge, attorney, paralegal, or other reader, upon viewing your citation, will be able to retrieve the legal authority you cited and verify that you have accurately represented the status of the law.

Because citations communicate information to a reader, it is essential that legal professionals communicate using the same "language" or citation form. You should be able to prepare a legal argument and present it to any court in the United States with confidence that a reader will be able to locate the authorities you cite. If legal professionals cited cases, statutes, and other authorities in varying ways, this would not only impede communication but would dilute the strength of your argument. When you present a persuasive argument, you do not want to distract the reader from the argument by using disfavored or incorrect citation form.

Newcomers to the legal field often inquire what will happen if citation form is incorrect in a brief or other document. Improper citation form has an effect similar to spelling errors in a writing: Such errors will not transform an otherwise winning argument into a losing one. Rather, they result in a loss of respect for the author and cause readers to question the integrity and analysis of an argument. Many readers will conclude that if an author cannot be depended upon to cite or spell correctly, the author likely cannot be depended upon to conduct thorough legal analysis.

B.   Citation Manuals

1.   *Introduction*

Citation manuals provide the rules for citing legal authorities. Just as writers routinely consult dictionaries and style guides to ensure their writings are correct, legal writers consult citation manuals to ensure that references to legal authorities are in proper form.

There are two primary citation manuals in the United States (and some lesser-known ones, which will be discussed later in this chapter): *The Bluebook: A Uniform System of Citation* (Columbia Law Review Ass'n et al. eds., 18th ed. 2005) (the "*Bluebook*") and ALWD & Darby Dickerson, *ALWD Citation Manual* (2d ed., Aspen Publishers 2003) ("*ALWD*," pronounced "all wood"). *The Bluebook* is the oldest and best-known citation manual, but the ease of use and readability of *ALWD* have made it highly popular since its inception in 2000. The two manuals are more alike than they are different. This chapter provides separate sections on *The Bluebook* and *ALWD* and gives examples showing citations in both *Bluebook* and *ALWD* form.

2.   *Overview of* The Bluebook

The best-known rules for citation form are found in the small ringed publication known as *The Bluebook*, which is now in its 18th edition. Its front and back covers are bright blue, and it is the most commonly used guide to citation form. *The Bluebook* was originally produced in the 1920s by the editorial boards of the *Columbia Law Review*, the *Harvard Law Review*, the *University of Pennsylvania Law Review*, and the *Yale Law Journal*. As time has passed, the editors of these law reviews have updated *The Bluebook*, and the 18th edition was published in mid-2005 by the same consortium. Questions and comments about *The Bluebook* can be addressed to The Harvard Law Review, Gannett House, 1511 Massachusetts Avenue, Cambridge, Massachusetts 02138. Its Web site is http://www.legalbluebook.com.

Unless you are specifically directed to use some other system of citation rules or unless your jurisdiction has its own system of citation, follow *The Bluebook* because it is the best-known and accepted citation system. If local citation rules exist for your jurisdiction, they must be followed.

Law students, paralegals, and practitioners have long bemoaned the organization of *The Bluebook*, its confusing index, its dearth of sufficient examples, and its lack of articulate explanation of certain citation rules. While each edition of *The Bluebook* attempted to respond to such criticisms, each new edition seemed to create as much confusion as it resolved. The 15th edition, released in 1991, however, reorganized *The Bluebook*, making it easier to use and of more benefit to practitioners, who often believed *The Bluebook* devoted far too much attention to citation form for various obscure publications and far too little attention to citation problems commonly encountered by practitioners. Similarly, the new 18th edition of *The Bluebook* is far more user-friendly than previous editions, and it includes a new section, the Bluepages, that includes numerous examples and is designed to assist practitioners with citation form.

In sum, there are few jurisdictions that require use of *Bluebook* form. For example, the rules of the United States Supreme Court impose requirements for nearly every aspect of documents submitted to the Court, from size of paper used to font size for footnotes, yet are silent on citation form. Use of *The Bluebook* is simply expected and traditional.

One helpful guide in using *The Bluebook* is *Bieber's Dictionary of Legal Citations* (Mary Miles Price ed., 6th ed. 2001), which alphabetically lists hundreds of examples of legal authorities following *Bluebook* rules. It is published by William S. Hein & Co., Inc. of Buffalo, New York ((800) 828-7571).

3. *Overview of* ALWD

In 2000, and as a response to continued criticism that *The Bluebook* was not user-friendly, the Association of Legal Writing Directors, an organization of directors of legal writing programs throughout the nation, released the *ALWD* citation manual, now in its second edition. *ALWD* is about the same size as *The Bluebook* and is also produced in a ringed booklet. *ALWD* is likely easier to use than *The Bluebook*, has numerous examples, and extensively uses color (namely, green) to show spacing, denote examples, and provide headings.

Although *ALWD* actually is longer than *The Bluebook*, most commentators find it far easier to use, and it has been widely accepted since its release. In fact, more than 50 paralegal programs throughout the country teach citation form using *ALWD*. Nevertheless, the legal profession is slow to change, and many judges and attorneys in private practice have never heard of *ALWD* and continue to use *The Bluebook*. Thus, although both *The Bluebook* and *ALWD* attempt to provide a standardized and uniform system of citation, the existence of two well-known citation manuals may well cause confusion for some students who will be taught using one manual and yet expected to know the other "on the job." The good news is that while there are clear differences between *The Bluebook* and *ALWD*, those differences are not so significant that legal writers will have trouble using either or both manuals. This chapter will discuss *Bluebook* citation rules and then *ALWD* citation rules, giving examples of both, but with greater emphasis on *The Bluebook* because — as of the writing of this text — it remains the best-known citation system.

4. *Other Citation Manuals*

In addition to *The Bluebook* and *ALWD*, there are other guides to citation form, the most notable of which is the *University of Chicago Manual of Legal Citation* (2d ed. 2000), usually called the *Maroonbook*, and used primarily in the Chicago metropolitan area. The *Maroonbook*, first published in 1986, is far easier to use than *The Bluebook*. In fact, it is so concise (fewer than 70 pages) and it leaves so many decisions about citation form to the discretion of the writer that it has failed to attract widespread interest beyond the Chicago area.

Additionally, in 1999, the American Association of Law Libraries ("AALL") published its *Universal Citation Guide* to create a set of universal citation rules for American legal authorities, whether those authorities appear in print or electronic form. The *Universal Citation Guide* developed from the work of many groups, including federal and state courts and the American Bar Association. Its full text is available through the ABA's committee on legal technology resources (www.lawtechnology.org) or the AALL site (www.aallnet.org/committee/citation).

Finally, in addition to these citation manuals, there is state variation. For example, legal professionals in Texas and California use their own formats and there is significant variation from one local jurisdiction to another. In fact, California endorses the use of a specific manual published by West, the *California Style Manual* (4th ed. 2000) in citing cases. Cal. R. Ct. 14 advisory cmt. In sum, *The Bluebook* is probably still the best-known citation system with *ALWD* continuing to attract admirers. State-specific rules may require yet different citation formats. Always follow your firm or office practice.

Practice Tip

Citation Form

In citing legal authorities, do not rely on the way books and cases refer to themselves. For example, every volume of U.S.C.A. includes an instruction similar to the following: "Cite This Book Thus: 42 U.S.C.A. §1220." Yet this form is incorrect according to both *The Bluebook* and *ALWD*, which provide the following correct form: 42 U.S.C.A. § 1220 (West 1994). Similarly, many courts in California use the incorrect abbreviation "C.A." rather than the correct abbreviation "Cal. App." to refer to cases from the California appellate courts.

Thus, always rely on the appropriate *Bluebook* or *ALWD* rules rather than the citation forms you may observe in books or case reports.

C. *The Bluebook*

1. *Organization of* The Bluebook

While it would be unnecessarily time-consuming to read *The Bluebook*, you should become familiar with its overall arrangement and read at least the

Bluepages section in the front of the book. *The Bluebook* is composed of six major sections:

> *Preface.*   The Preface provides a summary of the changes initiated in the 18th edition of *The Bluebook.*
>
> *Introduction.*   The Introduction discusses the structure of *The Bluebook* and general principles of citation.
>
> *Bluepages.*   The Bluepages is new to the 18th edition and is a how-to guide for basic legal citation form. It is designed for use by legal professionals and includes numerous useful examples. It also includes two tables, one showing abbreviations for use in court documents and one providing references to local citation rules. References in this chapter to Bluepages will be shown as "B."
>
> *General Rules of Citation and Style.*   This section, printed on white paper, provides general standards of citation and style used for legal writings and then sets forth 21 specific rules of citation for primary authorities (cases, constitutions, and statutes) and secondary authorities (books, periodicals, foreign materials, and so on). References in this chapter to Rules will be shown as "R."
>
> *Tables.*   *The Bluebook* contains 18 tables, most of which are printed on white paper with blue trim for easy access describing how cases and statutes from federal courts and each state court are cited and providing abbreviations for court documents, geographical terms, months, and various periodicals.
>
> *Index.*   An alphabetically arranged Index is found at the end of *The Bluebook.* When you have a question or concern regarding citation form, use the descriptive word approach to access the Index, which will refer you to the pertinent page for the citation rule you need.

2. *Typeface Conventions*

Perhaps the single most important fact you should know about *The Bluebook* is that almost all of the examples given in the white pages of *The Bluebook* show how to cite authorities as if you were writing a law review article. Because your cite-checking work as a paralegal will in all likelihood relate to authorities cited in court documents and legal memoranda, you must convert the examples you are given by *The Bluebook* that relate to law review format to those suitable for practitioners.

The Bluebook includes a special section on light blue paper near the front of the book called the Bluepages, which shows you how to adapt the examples you find in the body of *The Bluebook* to the format needed for court documents and memoranda. For example, if you were citing a text in a law review article, it would appear as follows:

> 1 J. THOMAS MCCARTHY, MCCARTHY ON TRADEMARKS AND UNFAIR COMPETITION § 3:1 (4th ed. 1997).

On the other hand, if you were to cite this same text in a court document or a legal memorandum, it would appear as follows:

1 J. Thomas McCarthy, *McCarthy on Trademarks and Unfair Competition* § 3:1 (4th ed. 1997).

The obvious difference between these two citation forms is that the first, used for law reviews, uses a style of large and small capitals for the author's name and treatise title, while the second format, used by practitioners, uses initial capital letters only. It is customary for law reviews to use large and small capitals for statutes, book titles, periodicals, and other materials. This format, however, is not used by practitioners. In fact, the 18th edition of *The Bluebook* (B13) clearly instructs practitioners, "[l]arge and small caps are never used." Thus, when you see an example given in *The Bluebook* such as the reference to the Florida Law Review as "FLA. L. REV.," you will need to adapt the format to that used by practitioners, namely, "Fla. L. Rev."

Many experts believe that the use of large and small capitals in law reviews is a holdover from the time law review articles were manually typeset. Because documents prepared by practitioners were typed rather than typeset and typewriters could not change fonts to make one capital letter larger than another, practitioners never used large and small capitals (even though the advent of word processing has made this possible). Thus, every time you encounter an example in *The Bluebook*, ask yourself, "Could this format be reproduced on an old-fashioned typewriter?" If not, it is a signal to you that the form is for law reviews, not for practitioners' documents. This dual system of citation (the use of large and small capitals for law reviews and the use of ordinary roman type by practitioners) has continued to exist long past any need for it. Because word processors can readily use a large and small capital format, practitioners could adopt that method of citation, and the dual citation system could be scrapped. Why do two separate systems continue to exist, each with its own rules and requirements? No one knows. One of the nice advantages of *ALWD* is that it eliminates this odd distinction between large and small capitals and ordinary type and requires only the use of "ordinary" type.

Other useful guides to showing you the differences in citation form between law review format and the style used for court documents and legal memoranda are on the inside front and back covers of *The Bluebook*. The inside front cover is titled "Quick Reference: Law Review Footnotes" and gives you several examples for citation form for use for law review footnotes. The inside back cover is titled "Quick Reference: Court Documents and Legal Memoranda" and gives you the same examples for use in legal writings for practitioners.

Be sure to refer often to the inside back cover. Do not become confused and assume that because an example appears in the body of *The Bluebook* it is correct. It may well be correct — but only for law review footnotes. After viewing an example in the body of *The Bluebook*, check the Bluepages and the inside back cover of *The Bluebook* and adapt the typeface for use in a court document or legal memorandum. Remember that practitioners never use large and small capitals.

Another difference you will note between citations shown on the inside front cover (for law review footnotes) and those shown on the inside back cover (for use by practitioners) is that full case names are neither underscored nor italicized in law review footnotes and yet they are always underscored or italicized by practitioners. Moreover, hundreds of examples throughout the white pages in *The Bluebook* show full case names in ordinary roman type (without underscoring or italicization). Do not become confused by the examples shown in the white pages throughout *The Bluebook*. Unless you are preparing footnotes for a law review article, case names will always be underscored or italicized.

3. *Revisions to the 18th Edition of* The Bluebook

The 18th edition of *The Bluebook* retains the same basic approach to citation form as earlier editions. Nevertheless, it does contain some changes, primarily in the rules relating to the situations requiring use of parallel citations and guidance for citing materials in electronic form and on the Internet. While these changes are discussed in detail in the preface to *The Bluebook* and throughout *The Bluebook*, and in this chapter, some of the more significant changes are as follows:

(i)   The Bluepages include two new tables. BT.1 (previously called Table T.8) provides suggested abbreviations for words commonly found in the titles of court documents, such as "Aff." for "Affidavit." BT.2 references some helpful local citation rules and some jurisdiction-specific citation manuals that provide guidance on local citation practices.

(ii) *The Bluebook* now provides spacing guides to show spacing in ellipses. These guides are shown in blue ink to demonstrate how ellipses are presented.

(iii) *The Bluebook* prohibits the use of the word "The" as the first word of a statute's name. Thus, refer to "Patriot Act" rather than "The Patriot Act."

(iv) Rule 18, relating to citation to electronic sources (namely, LEXIS, Westlaw, and the Internet) has been revised, and citation to these electronic sources is simplified, although *The Bluebook* retains its general requirement that traditional printed sources should be used and cited unless the information cited is not available in a traditional printed source or a copy of the printed source cannot be located because it is so obscure that it is practically unavailable. Only in these two narrow instances should citation be made to an electronic source alone.

(v)   Reflecting the increasing cross-border emphasis in legal practice, the rules relating to citation to international materials and Table T.2 (relating to citation to authorities from foreign jurisdictions) have been rewritten and greatly expanded.

D. *Bluebook* Citation Rules and Examples for Primary Authorities

1. *Cases*

a. Introduction

A typical case citation includes the following components:

- Case name
- References to the set(s) of case reports that published the case and the page on which the case begins
- A paranthetical that includes the court and jurisdiction and the year of decision
- The subsequent history of the case, if any (R. 10.1).

Thus, a typical citation to a case cited in a court document in Nevada is as follows:

Smith v. Jones, 329 P.2d 411, 414 (Nev. 1979).

b. Case Names

The Bluebook contains numerous rules regarding case names in citations. Carefully review Bluepages B5.1.1 and Rules 10.2, 10.2.1, and 10.2.2 in *The Bluebook* for a full discussion of these rules. Some of the more common guidelines you should be aware of are as follows:

    (i)   Cite only the last names of the parties to an action.

        Correct: *Talbert v. Carver*

        Incorrect: *Luisa N. Talbert v. Jay Carver*

Note, however, that many corporations use an individual's name as part of the business name. In such a case, include the full name of the business entity.

        Correct: *Ruiz v. Edward N. Pauley, Inc.*

        Incorrect: *Ruiz v. Pauley, Inc.*

    (ii) If more than one party is listed, omit all but the first party.

        Correct: *Hart v. Ward*

        Incorrect: *Hart v. Ward, Schiff, and Newley*

    (iii) If several actions have been consolidated into one decision, omit all but the first listed action.

Correct:	*Marrien v. Jacobson*
Incorrect:	*Marrien v. Jacobson, Taylor v. Reynolds*

(iv) Omit any indication of multiple parties.

Correct:	*Galinda v. Dubek*
Incorrect:	*Galinda v. Dubek, et al.*

(v) Omit indications of legal status or other descriptive terms.

Correct:	*Brumer v. Crawford*
Incorrect:	*Brumer v. Crawford, Executor*
Incorrect:	*Brumer v. Crawford, d / b / a The Green Grocer*
Incorrect:	*Brumer v. Crawford, Defendant*

(vi) Do not abbreviate "United States" in a case name if it is the entire name of a party and omit the phrase "of America."

Correct:	*United States v. Souther*
Incorrect:	*U.S. v. Souther*
Incorrect:	*United States of America v. Souther*
Incorrect:	*USA v. Souther*

(vii) For criminal cases decided by your state, cite as follows:

Correct:	*State v. Eagan*
Incorrect:	*State of Kansas v. Eagan*
Correct:	*Commonwealth v. Nelson*
Incorrect:	*Commonwealth of Pennsylvania v. Nelson*

If the case was not decided by a court in your state (if, for example, the case was later appealed from the Kansas Supreme Court to the United States Supreme Court), cite as follows:

Correct:	*Kansas v. Eagan*
Incorrect:	*State v. Eagan*
Correct:	*Pennsylvania v. Nelson*
Incorrect:	*Commonwealth of Pennsylvania v. Nelson*

(viii) Omit the second "business signal" such as "Inc.," "Co.," or "Corp." if the case name already contains one business signal.

Correct:	*Smith v. Auto Service Corp.*
Incorrect:	*Smith v. Auto Service Corp. Inc.*

(ix) Omit prepositional phrases of location unless they follow the word "City" or a similar word.

Correct:	*Brown v. Board of Education*

Incorrect: *Brown v. Board of Education of Topeka, Kansas*

(x)   When a case name appears in a textual sentence, for example, when it appears as a grammatical component of a sentence, abbreviate only the following words in a case name and widely known acronyms (such as FBI, CIA, and NLRB) (B5.3; Rule 10.2.1(c)):

and	&
Association	Ass'n
Brothers	Bros.
Company	Co.
Corporation	Corp.
Incorporated	Inc.
Limited	Ltd.
Number	No.

When a citation appears or stands alone by itself, rather than functioning as a grammatical component of a sentence, always abbreviate any word in the case name that is listed in Table T.6 of *The Bluebook* (B5.3; Rules 10.2.1. (c) and 10.2.2). The word is abbreviated even if it is the first word in a case name or the only word in a party's name.

Examples

Textual Sentence: In *Franklin Hospital Guaranty Co. v. Southern Division Ltd.*, 780 F. Supp. 91 (W.D. Tex. 1990), the court held that fraud requires a material misrepresentation.

Stand-alone Citation: Fraud requires a material misrepresentation. *Franklin Hosp. Guar. Co. v. S. Div. Ltd.*, 780 F. Supp. 91 (W.D. Tex. 1990).

This rule is one of the least understood rules in *The Bluebook* and requires you to focus on the location of a citation before you determine which words can be abbreviated in a case name. For simplicity, use this rule: If a case name in a citation appears as a textual part of a sentence (meaning the cite is needed to make sense of the sentence), you may abbreviate only widely known acronyms and the eight well-known and commonly used abbreviations provided in Rule 10.2.1., such as "Co." and "Inc." On the other hand, if a citation stands alone in a clause or after the end of a sentence and is not needed to make sense of a sentence, you must abbreviate any of the nearly 170 words listed in Table T.6, even if they are the first word in a party's name or the only word in a party's name. Why? Many experts believe that because readers are unused to seeing abbreviations in the middle of sentences, to abbreviate any words other than very commonly used words would be distracting. On the other hand, if a citation stands by itself, readers will not be disconcerted by seeing abbreviations such as "Indem." or "Sur."

The rule requiring abbreviation of the first word in a party's name that appears as a "stand-alone" citation was introduced in the previous

17th edition and has caused some confusion. For nearly 100 years, practitioners have been firmly instructed, "never abbreviate the first word in a party's name." Thus, the change in the 17th edition has required some effort for existing practitioners to become familiar with, particularly when the citation might read *Allen v. W.*, 520 U.S. 13, 16 (1998).

(xi)   Generally, omit the word "The" as the first word of a party's name.

Correct: *May Co. v. Lorenzi*

Incorrect: *The May Co. v. Lorenzi*

(xii) Entities that are widely known (for example, NAACP, SEC, FCC, FDA) may be referred to as such in case names, without periods.

Preferred: *SEC v. Garcia*

Disfavored: *S.E.C. v. Garcia*
Disfavored: *Securities and Exchange Commission v. Garcia*

The Bluebook (R. 6.1 (b)) gives only a few examples of such entities. Generally, however, if an entity is referred to in spoken language by its initials rather than its full name (for example, one usually says, "He was investigated by the FBI" rather than "He was investigated by the Federal Bureau of Investigation"), it may be used in its abbreviated form without periods.

(xiii) The "v." in a case citation stands for "versus" and always appears in lower case form. While you may see some other form for "versus" in a pleading such as a complaint or answer, in citation form always use a lower case "v" followed by a period.

Correct: *Marksen v. Sigler*

Incorrect: *Marksen V. Sigler*
Incorrect: *Marksen vs. Sigler*

(xiv) Always underline or italicize the name of a case in a citation, including the "v.," and any procedural phrases such as "In re." Use a solid unbroken line. Either underlining (also called "underscoring") or italicizing is appropriate (B2). Years ago, underlining was most popular, as few typewriters were capable of producing italics. With the advent of word processors, which are capable of italicizing, this technique became very popular. Many legal writers, however, continue to prefer underlining because it is very noticeable and dramatic on a white sheet of paper. Moreover, the examples given in the Bluepages section of *The Bluebook* show underlining, indicating a slight preference for such. Note these rules for underlining:

- The line should be unbroken.
- The line should be placed underneath the entire case name, including any periods.

Correct: <u>*Peters v. Swanson & Johnson Co.*</u>

Incorrect: <u>*Peters v. Swanson &*</u> *Johnson Co.*

Whichever method (namely, underscoring or italicizing) you select, be consistent. Check your firm or office practice for preferences.

(xv)   The case name should always be followed by a comma. The comma is not underlined or underscored.

Correct: <u>*Jeffries v. Purvis*</u>,

Incorrect: <u>*Jeffries v. Purvis,*</u>

Practice Tip

Case Citations

- **Note that the correct legal abbreviation for "second" is 2d and the correct legal abbreviation for "third" is 3d, rather than 2nd or 3rd, which are commonly encountered in nonlegal writings.**
- **Note that the first page given in a case citation is the page on which a case begins and is not introduced with an abbreviation such as "p." which is often used in nonlegal writings.**

---

c. Parallel Citations

(1) *Old* Bluebook *Rule*

Until relatively recently, *Bluebook* citation rules required that all citations to all state court cases include all parallel cites; that is, references to the official report and the unofficial reporter(s) that published the case. The parallel citations were provided as a courtesy to the reader because the writer would not know if the reader had access to the official reports or the unofficial reporter(s). The writer would thus provide *all* citations so the reader could easily locate the cited case no matter which set of books or case reports the reader used.

Example

Liston v. Alpha Co., 129 Va. 109, 381 S.E.2d 12 (1980)

This requirement of providing all parallel cites made citation form awkward and difficult for the writer because the writer would have to obtain all parallel cites and then, if quoting from a certain page in the text, would have to indicate the exact page the quote appeared on in each case report. For California, Illinois, and New York cases, which may have three parallel cites, this rule made the difficult task of citation form even more complicated.

(2) *New* Bluebook *Rule*

Bluebook Rule 10.3.1 and Bluepages 5.13 govern parallel citations for state court cases. *The Bluebook* now makes it clear that you need only include a parallel citation if court rules require such. Note that when court rules do require parallel citations, the official citation is given first, followed by the unofficial parallel citation(s). Remember, however, that many states no longer publish their cases officially, and cases from those jurisdictions will have only one citation.

In all other instances, cite to the relevant regional reporter (for example, *Atlantic Reporter* or *Pacific Reporter*) if the case is in that set, and then indicate the name of the court and its geographical jurisdiction (using the abbreviations found in Table T.1) parenthetically with the year of decision. There is, however, one exception to this rule: Do not include the name of the court if the court that decided the case is the highest court of the state. For example, the highest court in nearly all states is called the supreme court, and Table T.1 in *The Bluebook* indicates that for most state supreme courts, the appropriate abbreviation indicates the name of the state and no other information is given. Thus, Table T.1 states that "Cal." indicates a case from the California Supreme Court and "Ohio" indicates a case from the Ohio Supreme Court. Cases from those states' appellate courts are indicated by the following abbreviations (again, respectively, as shown in Table T.1): "Cal. Ct. App." and "Ohio Ct. App."

Thus, consider the following examples:

- *Green v. Hall*, 68 Mich. 2d 802, 310 N.W.2d 604 (1979)
  [This is how the *Green* case would be cited if a court rule required parallel citations.]
- *Green v. Hall*, 301 N.W.2d 604 (Mich. 1979)
  [This is how the *Green* case would be cited in any other instance, including in a court document for a court that does not have local rules requiring parallel citations, in a letter to a client, or in an internal office memorandum. Because Table T.1 of *The Bluebook* tells us that the abbreviation for the Michigan Supreme Court is "Mich.," upon encountering this citation, a reader knows the case is from the Michigan Supreme Court.]
- *Taylor v. Fletcher*, 304 N.W.2d 18 (Mich. Ct. App. 1981)
  [This is how the a case from the Michigan Court of Appeals would be cited in any instance other than for a court whose rules require parallel citations.]

Although *The Bluebook* rule does not require parallel cites in an internal law office memorandum, many practicing legal professionals will include the parallel cite knowing that if the memorandum later becomes the basis for a brief submitted to a court that requires parallel citations, such as a motion for change of venue or a trial brief, the parallel cite would be required for that document. Thus, including it in an earlier memo will save time later by eliminating the need to return to the law library to track down the parallel cite. Follow your firm or office practice.

As you will recall from Chapter 4, 21 states and the District of Columbia no longer publish their cases officially, and cases from those jurisdictions appear only in the relevant regional reporter. If you are citing a case from one of these states decided after the date official publication ceased, the correct citation form will refer the reader only to the regional reporter and will include information about the court that decided the case parenthetically as follows:

Gray v. Donoghue, 704 P.2d 118 (Colo. 1989).

To determine which states no longer publish officially and when those states discontinued their official publications, consult the chart in Chapter 4 herein or Table T.1 of *The Bluebook*, which alphabetically lists all 50 states and provides information about correct citation form for each state.

Some jurisdictions (the District of Columbia, Maine, Montana, Nevada, New Hampshire, Rhode Island, South Dakota, Vermont, West Virginia, and Wyoming) have no intermediate appellate courts. In those jurisdictions, all citations are to the state's highest court, usually called the supreme court, and the parenthetical would always display only the abbreviation of the state (such as "Wyo.") and never any abbreviation that would indicate an appellate court (such as "Wyo. Ct. App.").

Finally, in a few states (including Arizona, Idaho, New Mexico, South Carolina, and Wisconsin), cases from the state supreme court are published in the same volumes as those from the lower intermediate court of appeals. For example, the set *New Mexico Reports* includes cases from the New Mexico Supreme Court and the New Mexico Court of Appeals. Citations to cases from these states may need parentheticals identifying the deciding court. For example, when citing a case from the New Mexico Court of Appeals (assuming local rules require parallel citations), show this as follows: *Cruz v. Harley*, 94 N.M. 861, 729 P.2d 14 (Ct. App. 1993). Without the parenthetical, the reader would assume the case is from the New Mexico Supreme Court. If the case is, in fact, from the New Mexico Supreme Court, the parenthetical need only include the date; it need not include any reference to "S. Ct." Allow the reader to assume it is from the highest court in New Mexico. In sum, if the name of the reporter contains the name of the state, omit the state abbreviation in the parenthetical.

Do not indicate the department, division, county, or district in citing a case from a state court unless that information is of particular importance (R. 10.4(b)).

Preferred: *Crandall v. Brown*, 291 So. 2d 481 (La.
                        Ct. App. 1981)

Disfavored: *Crandall v. Brown*, 291 So. 2d 481 (La. Ct.
                        App. 4th Dist. 1981)

Practice Tip

State Cases: The Bluebook *and* ALWD

Rule 1:   **If the name of the reporter is the same as the name of the
            jurisdiction, you need not give the name of the court in the
            parenthetical with the date.**

    Example: 113 Cal. 3d 118 (1999)
    Explanation: You need not include "California Supreme Court"
         in the parenthetical with the date because Table T.1
         of *The Bluebook* tells you that the name of the
         reporter is identical to the court abbreviation and
         by looking at the citation, the reader can tell what
         court decided the case (namely, the California
         Supreme Court).

Rule 2:   **You must include the name of the court in the parenthetical
            with the date if a reader cannot tell what court decided the
            case from reading the citation.**

    Example: 790 P.2d 989 (Or. 1997)
    Explanation: In reviewing the citation, "P.2d" doesn't tell the
         reader what court decided the case, so the
         parenthetical must indicate such. The "Or." in the
         parenthetical tells the reader implicitly that the
         case is from the Oregon Supreme Court. Otherwise,
         the parenthetical would have indicated "Or.
         Ct. App."

---

(3)   *Neutral Citation Format*

As difficult as *The Bluebook*'s rules are, legal professionals have had,
until recently, only this one source to learn. The proliferation of legal
materials on electronic databases and the Internet, however, is likely to
add further to the confusion already associated with citation form. A controversy currently rages with regard to citation form: how to adapt the
traditional citation systems advanced for more than 70 years by *The Bluebook* to an increasingly technological age.

Current citation rules require citations to conventional print forms,
the majority of which are published by West, requiring legal professionals to
purchase West sets even though cases and other materials are easy and
inexpensive to access on the Internet. Thus, many legal professionals and

consumers advocate the implementation of what is usually referred to as a neutral, public domain, "format-neutral," or "vendor-neutral" citation system, meaning that the citation looks the same whether the reader has accessed the case by conventional print format or by electronic methods, such as CD-ROM, LEXIS, Westlaw, or the Internet. These groups argue that *The Bluebook* rules requiring citation to West sets, such as the *Federal Reporter* and the *Federal Supplement*, give West a near monopoly and discourage other legal publishers from entering the market, which would ultimately lead to increased competition with resulting lower costs for consumers.

While the text of cases and statutes are public domain materials and are thus not subject to copyright protection, when a publisher such as West compiles these materials, adds headnotes, indexes, and other features, it can copyright the resulting product. To end what is perceived as West's unfair market advantage obtained through citation rules requiring or preferring citation to West books, both the American Bar Association and the American Association of Law Libraries as well as numerous professionals support the development of a neutral citation scheme, namely, the *Universal Citation Guide*, discussed earlier.

In February 2003, the ABA passed a resolution committing that it would facilitate discussion with organizations working on legal citation formats to develop a universal American citation system that is equally effective for printed case reports and for case reports published electronically. The ABA is hoping that cooperation among courts, law schools, and others to create a vendor and media neutral citation system will benefit the public and make increasing amounts of information available electronically.

Note that *ALWD*'s approach to neutral citations is similar to that of *The Bluebook* and provides that you should use neutral citations when required by local rule.

At the time of the writing of this text, the following states have adopted a neutral citation format: Arizona, Colorado, Louisiana, Maine, Mississippi, Montana, New Mexico, North Dakota, Ohio, Oklahoma, South Dakota, Utah, Wisconsin, and Wyoming. Other states are considering doing so. With regard to federal courts, only the Sixth Circuit has presently adopted a neutral format for citations to its cases, and its use is optional. Citation to Sixth Circuit cases is discussed later in this chapter, in Section D.1.g. When states adopt a neutral citation format, it is prospective only and effective only after a certain date (clearly indicated in Table T.1 in *The Bluebook*). Citations to cases decided before the date a state adopts a neutral or public domain format would follow the standard citation format previously described in Section C of this chapter.

The Bluebook (R. 10.3.3) requires that for neutral citations, one give the case name, year of decision, that state's two-character postal code, the court abbreviation (unless the court is the state's highest court), the sequential number of the decision, and, if a parallel citation is available, it must be provided. A pinpoint paragraph rather than a pinpoint page is given. If the case is unpublished, a capital "U" should be placed after the sequential number of the decision.

Bluebook Example

Albert v. Tinley, 1998 ME 116, ¶ 3, 710 A.2d 14, 17.

In the above example, the case name is *Albert v. Tinley*, the case was the 116th case decided in 1998 by the Maine Supreme Court, and the relevant information is located in paragraph 3 of the case. The remaining information is the usual unofficial citation. Thus, the neutral citation replaces only the official citation in state court cases. If available, the unofficial or regional citation must be given as well to ensure easy access to the case by readers.

The ABA recommends the following standard form of citation for a decision from a federal court of appeals:

ABA Example

Baker v. Smith, 2004 7Cir 14, ¶ 17, 231 F.3d 123.

In the above example, the year of decision is 2004, "7Cir" refers to the U.S. Court of Appeals for the Seventh Circuit, "14" indicates the citation is to the 14th decision released by the court in 2004, "17" is the pinpoint paragraph in the case, and the remainder of the information is the parallel citation to the *Federal Reporter, Third Series*.

Table T.1 of *The Bluebook* clearly indicates which states have adopted the neutral or public domain citation format, and Rule 10.3.3 provides citation rules. As in all citations, if a jurisdiction has adopted its own rules as to citation form, they supersede *The Bluebook* rules, and the same is true for neutral citation format. *The Bluebook's* Web site (http://www.legalbluebook.com) and the Web site of the American Bar Association (http://www.lawtechnology.org/research/citation/home.html) provide additional information on jurisdictions that have adopted a neutral format. A state's own judicial Web site (see Table T.1 in *The Bluebook* and Appendix 2 of *ALWD*) may provide court rules giving instruction as to citation presenation. There is a great deal of discrepancy among the adopting states as to spacing in the citations so carefully follow the examples you are given.

d. Recent Cases

(1) Official Cite Unavailable

West typically publishes its cases a bit quicker than the official publishers. If you wish to cite to a very recent case and the official report is not yet available, you may cite as follows:

Hunter v. Hoffman, __ Conn. __, 417 A.2d 704 (2005)

The "blank" lines serve as a signal to a reader that an official citation will exist but it is not yet available. This form is not permitted or recognized by *The Bluebook* but is commonly used by practitioners. *ALWD* Rule 12.13 recognizes this citation format.

(2) Slip Form

When a case is not yet reported and is available only in slip or looseleaf form, give the case name, the docket number, the court, and the exact date (Rule 10.8.1(b)).

Correct: *Miller v. Pritchett*, No. 04-201 (N.D. Cal. Dec. 9, 2004)

(3) Cases Available on Electronic Databases (Rule 18.1.1)

A case may be cited to a widely used electronic database such as LEXIS or Westlaw, only if it is not reported (meaning that it is not published in print reporters or in slip form). Provide the name of the case, docket number, identification of the database (with sufficient information to allow a reader to locate the case), name of court, and the full date of the most recent disposition of the case. If screen or page numbers have been assigned, they should be preceded by an asterisk.

Examples

Gruber v. Edwards, No. 04-829 (2004 U.S. Dist. LEXIS 20104, at *3 (D. Utah Oct. 1, 2004)

McKnight v. Walter, No. 04-10426, 2004 U.S. App. LEXIS 4221, at *4 (4th Cir. Apr. 14, 2004)

Thomas v. Bowman, No. 04-6040, 2004 WL 65102 (S.D. Cal. July 17, 2004)

Neely v. Younger, No. 04-4091, 2004 WL 46723, at *3 (D.C. Cir. 2004)

(4) Cases Available on the Internet (Rules 18.2 and 18.2.2)

Although there are now hundreds of thousands of cases available on the Internet, *The Bluebook* requires the use and citation of traditional printed sources, except when the information is not available in a printed source, or if the traditional source is so difficult to find that it is practically unavailable. Only in these two narrow instances should citation be made to an electronic or Internet source alone. Because nearly all cases appear traditional print form within a matter of days after they are decided, *The Bluebook* seems to suggest that citing to the Internet would be exceptional, for example, only for newly released decisions.

If a printed source can be found, a parallel citation to an electronic source or to the Internet as related authority may be provided if it will substantially improve access to the relevant information or case. Thus, the first citation must be to the printed source and then an electronic or Internet source may be given, introduced with the explanatory phrase *"available at,"* (and assuming that the content of the Internet source is identical to the print version) as follows: *Ryan v. Kimball*, 530 U.S. 16

(2005), *available at* http://caselaw.lp.findlaw.com/scripts/getcase.pl?nav-by=case&court=us&vol=520&page=1.

    An Internet source may be cited alone only when the material does not exist in a traditional printed format or on a widely available commercial database such as LEXIS or Westlaw. The Internet Uniform Resource Locator is provided at the end of the citation, as follows: *United States v. Gonzales*, No. 04-1023, slip op. at 10 (U.S. Jan. 10, 2005), http://www.surpemecourtus.gov/opinions/05pdf/04-1023.pdf.

    The Bluebook provides information on citing statutes, books, and journals to Internet locations. Examples of each of these will be found in Section G.9 of this chapter.

e. Abbreviations in Case Citations

Do not assume that you know the correct abbreviations for Colorado, Idaho, or Oklahoma. While you may know the correct abbreviation for a state for purposes of addressing a letter, *The Bluebook* contains some surprising abbreviations for commonly known geographical terms. Review Table T.10 in *The Bluebook* to determine the required abbreviations for the 50 states and for other geographical locations. Similarly, rely upon Table T.12 for the correct abbreviations for months of the year.

f. Spacing (*Bluebook* Rule 6.1(a))

The print in *The Bluebook* is very small, and it can be difficult to simply look at the examples given and determine the appropriate spacing in a citation. Therefore, you must memorize three spacing rules given as Rule 6.1 of *The Bluebook*:

    • Do not put a space between adjacent single capital letters. For purposes of this rule, the abbreviations for "2d," "3d," "4th," and so forth are viewed as single capitals.

Examples

    N.W.2d
    S.W.
    P.2d
    F.3d
    U.S.
    A.L.R.5th

Each of the examples given here shows adjacent single capital letters. Therefore, do not put spaces between them.

    • Multiple letter abbreviations are preceded and followed by a space:

Examples

    So. 2d
    F. Supp. 2d

L. Ed. 2d
Cal. 4th
Ill. App.
S. Ct.

Each of the examples given here includes a multiple letter abbreviation. Therefore, put a space before it and after it.

Practice Tip

Superscripts

Ordinals are numbers that show a series, such as "first" and "fourth." In legal citations, the ordinals are replaced by their appropriate abbreviations, for example, "1st" and "4th." Many word processing programs automatically force abbreviations such as "st" and "th" above other text in superscript, as in "1st" and "4th." Both *The Bluebook* and *ALWD* show ordinal abbreviations "set on line" as follows: "1st" and "4th" so their presentation will be consistent with "2d" and "3d" which are always set on line with other text.

Either disable this automatic setting in your word processor by consulting your "tools" menu bar (select "Tools," then "AutoCorrect," then "Auto Format As You Type," and then uncheck the superscript feature). Alternatively, immediately after a superscript is inserted on your page, click on the "undo" arrow (the backward facing arrow on your menu bar), which will correct the superscript and set the abbreviations on line. *Bluebook* Rule 6.2(b) forbids the use of superscripts.

Correct:	1st, 4th, 8th
Incorrect:	1st, 4th, 8th

• In abbreviations of the names of legal periodicals, close up adjacent single upper case letters except when one or more of the upper case letters refers to a geographical or institutional entity. In this case separate the upper case letter referring to the entity from other adjacent single letters with a space (*Bluebook* Rule 6.1 (a)).

This rule is confusing. Perhaps the best guide when citing legal periodicals is simply to mimic carefully Table T.13 of *The Bluebook*, which provides more than 700 abbreviations for periodicals.

Examples

B.U. L. Rev.

Because the "B.U." in this abbreviation refers to an institutional entity, namely, Boston University, the capital letters for this entity are separated from the other adjacent single letters.

Loy. L.A. L. Rev.

Because the "L.A." in this abbreviation refers to a geographical entity, namely, Los Angeles, the capital letters for such are separated from the next adjacent single letter, "L," which stands for "Law."

Note that Table T.14 shows the abbreviations as "B.U. L. REV." and "LOY. L.A. L. REV.," using large and small capitals, as would be used for law review typeface style. Practitioners should always follow the rules on typeface conventions and convert the large and small capitals to ordinary type, specifically "B.U. L. Rev." and "Loy. L.A. L. Rev."

With regard to presentation of citations within your project, *The Bluebook* does not offer any guidelines whatsoever. Most experts suggest that you "break" your citation from one line to the next at a "natural" break point, that is, one that is pleasing to the eye and doesn't strike the reader as awkward in appearance.

g. Federal Cases (*Bluebook* B5.1.3; Table T.1)

(1)   United States Supreme Court Cases

Despite the fact that cases from the United States Supreme Court are published in permanent hardbound volumes in three different sets of books (U.S., S. Ct., and L. Ed.), *The Bluebook* rule is to cite only to the official set, *United States Reports* (U.S.).

This rule of requiring a single citation to U.S. and ignoring the sets S. Ct. and L. Ed. is the reason "star paging" was developed, namely, to allow a reader to read a case in S. Ct. or L. Ed. and yet cite to the official *United States Reports*. (See Chapter 4 for discussion of star paging.)

> **Correct:**   *Leroy v. Holden*, 368 U.S. 46 (1975).
>
> **Incorrect:**   *Leroy v. Holden*, 368 U.S. 46, 96 S. Ct. 101, 109 L. Ed. 2d 14 (1975).

You may recall that the *United States Reports* have only had that title since 1875 and that before that date, the volumes were named after the individual primarily involved in editing the set (for example, Dallas, Cranch, Wheaton, Peters). Thus, if you see an awkward looking case citation such as *Carter v. Lee*, 4 U.S. (2 Dall.) 16 (1798), you should simply recognize that this is a very old case.

If you cannot cite to U.S. because the official report is not yet available, cite to S. Ct., L. Ed., or U.S.L.W., in that order.

Examples

> *Hogue v. Davidson*, 241 S. Ct. 902 (2005).
> *Hogue v. Davidson*, 289 L. Ed. 2d 101 (2005).
> *Hogue v. Davidson*, 63 U.S.L.W. 1226 (U.S. May 19, 2005).

Remember that you should never give a parallel cite for cases from the United States Supreme Court.

(2)   United States Courts of Appeals Cases

There are no official citations for cases from the United States Court of Appeals; therefore, cases will be cited only to West's *Federal Reporter* (F., F.2d, or F.3d). The reader will need to know the circuit that decided the case. Not only will circuit information confirm the case on point (for example, arguments submitted to the Eighth Circuit Court of Appeals should rely on precedents from the Eighth Circuit), some circuits may have established reputations in deciding certain kinds of cases. Thus, this information must be provided to the reader in the parenthetical with the date. *Bluebook* Rule 10.4 clearly requires that every case citation must indicate which court decided the case unless this information is unambiguously conveyed by the name of a reporter (such as is the case with *United States Reports* or *California Reports*). The information must appear in the parenthetical before the date. Thus, because a reference to "F.2d" tells a reader only that a case is from one of the United States Courts of Appeal, the parenthetical must identify the particular circuit, as follows:

> **Correct:**   *Rose v. Capwell Co.*, 721 F.2d 806 (3d Cir. 1988).

The Sixth Circuit (covering Kentucky, Michigan, Ohio, and Tennessee) has adopted a public domain or neutral citation format for cases after December 31, 1993, but its use is optional in the Sixth Circuit. Table T.1 of *The Bluebook* shows the following example for a public domain citation for a case from the Sixth Circuit:

> *Equal. Found. v. City of Cincinnati*, 1997 FED App. 0318P (6th Cir).

(3)   United States District Court Cases

There are no official citations for cases from the United States District Courts; therefore, cases will be cited only to West's *Federal Supplement* (F. Supp. and F. Supp. 2d). For the same reasons that readers need to know which circuit court decided a case, readers need to know which district court decided a case. Thus, identify the district court (but not the division of the district court).

> **Correct:**   *Simon v. Parker*, 760 F. Supp. 918 (E.D. Ark. 1988).
>
> **Correct:**   *Arnold v. Kenney*, 697 F. Supp. 2d 746 (D. Ariz. 1999).

See Figure 8-1 for abbreviations for our more than 90 district courts.

──────────────── **Practice Tip** ────────────────

Abbreviations for District Courts

Creating the abbreviations for the nation's more than 90 district courts is relatively easy.

- The abbreviation for "district" is "D."
- The abbreviations for the geographical divisions of the courts are as follows:
  - "N." for "Northern" (thus, N.D. stands for "Northern District")
  - "S." for "Southern"
  - "E." for "Eastern"
  - "W." for "Western"
  - "M." for "Middle"
  - "C." for "Central"
- Indicate the geographical division of the court, following the spacing rules given above.
- Indicate the state abbreviation using Table T.10 of *The Bluebook* or Appendix 3 of *ALWD*.

Examples:	D. Alaska
	S.D. Cal.
	D.D.C.
	M.D. Pa.

Figure 8-1
Abbreviations for District Courts

ALABAMA	11th Cir.	HAWAII	9th Cir.
M.D. Ala.		D. Haw.	
N.D. Ala.			
S.D. Ala.		IDAHO	9th Cir.
		D. Idaho	
ALASKA	9th Cir.		
D. Alaska		ILLINOIS	7th Cir.
		C.D. Ill.	
ARIZONA	9th Cir.	N.D. Ill.	
D. Ariz.		S.D. Ill.	
ARKANSAS	8th Cir.	INDIANA	7th Cir.
E.D. Ark.		N.D. Ind.	
W.D. Ark.		S.D. Ind.	

Figure 8-1 *(Continued)*

CALIFORNIA	9th Cir.	**IOWA**	8th Cir.
C.D. Cal.		N.D. Iowa	
E.D. Cal.		S.D. Iowa	
N.D. Cal.			
S.D. Cal.		**KANSAS**	10th Cir.
		D. Kan.	
COLORADO	10th Cir.		
D. Colo.		**KENTUCKY**	6th Cir.
		E.D. Ky.	
CONNECTICUT	2d Cir.	W.D. Ky.	
D. Conn.			
		LOUISIANA	5th Cir.
DELAWARE	3d Cir.	E.D. La.	
D. Del.		M.D. La.	
		W.D. La.	
DISTRICT OF			
COLUMBIA	D.C. Cir.	**MAINE**	1st Cir.
D.D.C.		D. Me.	
FLORIDA	11th Cir.	**MARYLAND**	4th Cir.
M.D. Fla.		D. Md.	
N.D. Fla.			
S.D. Fla.		**MASSACHUSETTS**	1st Cir.
		D. Mass.	
GEORGIA	11th Cir.		
M.D. Ga.		**MICHIGAN**	6th Cir.
N.D. Ga.		E.D. Mich.	
S.D. Ga.		W.D. Mich.	
MINNESOTA	8th Cir.	**OKLAHOMA**	10th Cir.
D. Minn.		E.D. Okla.	
		N.D. Okla.	
MISSISSIPPI	5th Cir.	W.D. Okla.	
N.D. Miss.			
S.D. Miss.		**OREGON**	9th Cir.
		D. Or.	
MISSOURI	8th Cir.		
E.D. Mo.		**PENNSYLVANIA**	3d Cir.
W.D. Mo.		E.D. Pa.	
		M.D. Pa.	
MONTANA	9th Cir.	W.D. Pa.	
D. Mont.			
		RHODE ISLAND	1st Cir.
NEBRASKA	8th Cir.	D.R.I.	
D. Neb.			
		SOUTH CAROLINA	4th Cir.
NEVADA	9th Cir.	D.S.C.	
D. Nev.			

Figure 8-1 *(Continued)*

NEW HAMPSHIRE	1st Cir.	**SOUTH DAKOTA**	8th Cir.
D.N.H.		D.S.D.	
NEW JERSEY	3d Cir.	**TENNESSEE**	6th Cir.
D.N.J.		E.D. Tenn.	
		M.D. Tenn.	
		M.D. Tenn.	
NEW MEXICO	10th Cir.		
D.N.M.		**TEXAS**	5th Cir.
		E.D. Tex.	
NEW York	2d Cir.	N.D. Tex.	
E.D.N.Y.		S.D. Tex.	
N.D.N.Y.		W.D. Tex.	
S.D.N.Y.			
W.D.N.Y.		**UTAH**	10th Cir.
		D. Utah	
NORTH CAROLINA	4th Cir.		
E.D.N.C.		**VERMONT**	2d Cir.
M.D.N.C.		D. Vt.	
W.D.N.C.			
		VIRGINIA	4th Cir.
NORTH DAKOTA	8th Cir.	E.D. Va.	
D.N.D.		W.D. Va.	
OHIO	6th Cir.	**WASHINGTON**	9th Cir.
N.D. Ohio		E.D. Wash.	
S.D. Ohio		W.D. Wash.	
WEST VIRGINIA	4th Cir.	**N. MARIANA**	9th Cir.
N.D.W. Va.		**ISLANDS**	
S.D.W. Va.		D.N. Mar. I.	
WISCONSIN	7th Cir.	**PUERTO RICO**	1st Cir.
E.D. Wis.		D.P.R.	
W.D. Wis.			
		VIRGIN ISLANDS	3d Cir.
WYOMING	10th Cir.	D.V.I.	
D. Wyo.			
		U.S. COURT OF	
		APPEALS FOR	
MISCELLANEOUS		**THE FEDERAL**	Fed. Cir.
		CIRCUIT	
CANAL ZONE	5th Cir.		
D.C.Z.		**U.S. COURT OF**	
(ceased operations in 1982)		**FEDERAL CLAIMS**	Fed. Cl.
GUAM	9th Cir.		
D. Guam			

h. Subsequent History (*Bluebook* B5.1.5; Rule 10.7)

Whenever you cite a case you are required to provide its subsequent history. Do not, however, give history relating to:

- denials of *certiorari* or denials of similar discretionary appeals unless the case (not the denial of *certiorari*) is less than two years old or is particularly relevant; or
- history on remand or any denial of a rehearing unless it is particularly relevant.

The rule instructing writers to omit history relating to denials of *certiorari* (unless the case is less than two years old or particularly relevant) is new since 1996 and has caused some disagreement. Many practitioners take the position that the refusal of the United States Supreme Court to grant "cert" and take a case is always relevant because it confirms that the decision is thus final and not subject to further review. Therefore, many practitioners simply ignore the rule and always note that "cert" has been denied. Consult your firm or office to determine its policy on this much-criticized change.

Correct: *Bernard v. Scott*, 761 F.2d 902 (8th Cir. 1986), *aff'd*, 106 U.S. 921 (1988)

Correct: *Dowell v. Wong*, 629 F.2d 809 (2d Cir. 2003), *cert. denied*, 410 U.S. 466 (2005)

Note that if any subsequent history occurred in the same year as the lower court case was decided, give the year only once, in the last parenthetical (R. 10.5(d)).

Correct: *Walker v. Whiteley*, 701 F.2d 416 (9th Cir.), *rev'd*, 430 U.S. 906 (1985)

A list showing the appropriate abbreviations for subsequent history such as "reversed," "affirmed," "modified," "rehearing granted," all of which must be underlined or italicized, is provided in Table T.8 of *The Bluebook*. You will be informed of the subsequent history of a case when you Shepardize or KeyCite it. Shepardizing and KeyCiting are discussed in Chapter 9.

i. Prior History (*Bluebook* Rule 10.7)

There is no ethical obligation to give the prior history of a case. *The Bluebook* states only that you should give prior history of a case if it is relevant to the issue you are discussing or if the case you are citing does not fully describe the issues (such as a memorandum opinion) and therefore you are relying on the lower court case for a full analysis of the issues involved in the case.

This citation rule is logical and eliminates needless citations. For example, virtually all United States Supreme Court cases get to the Supreme Court from some other court and thus have a prior history. Some, in fact, have three or even four prior histories. To include these citations would be confusing and unnecessary because the decision by the United States Supreme Court is the one that is determinative under our system of stare decisis, as discussed in Chapter 1.

j. Parenthetical Information (*Bluebook* B5.1.4; B11; Rules 1.5, 5.2; and 10.6)

If you are relying upon or quoting from any part of an opinion other than the majority opinion, you must so indicate in your citation. A reader will always assume that you are relying upon the majority opinion unless you indicate otherwise. While it is acceptable to cite a dissent or a concurring opinion, remember that only the majority opinion is binding. Dissents and concurring opinions are persuasive only.

> **Correct:**   *Wu v. Bradley*, 490 U.S. 102 (1985) (White, J., dissenting).

Similarly, if you wish to give more information about the case (for example, 7-2 decision, author of opinion) do so parenthetically as follows:

> *Parker, Inc. v. Simpson*, 504 U.S. 66 (1989) (7-2 decision).

If the citation you rely on quotes from another case, present that information as follows:

> *Costello v. McCarty*, 490 U.S. 102, 106 (1985) (quoting *Lyons v. Wagner*, 488 U.S. 66, 75 (1983)).

Parentheticals must be given in a certain order. Parenthetical information relating to the weight of a decision (whether it is a 6-3 decision or *per curiam* decision) must precede parenthetical information explaining something about the decision, for example, a phrase such as "following the exclusionary rule." Note that explanatory phrases should begin with a present participle (a verb plus an "ing" ending, as in "arguing" or "holding") and a lowercase letter, although they may consist of a quoted sentence or a short statement. Parentheticals should precede any references to prior or subsequent history (Rule 10.6.3).

k. Different Case Name on Appeal (*Bluebook* Rule 10.7.2)

You may recall that if a case is instituted by a plaintiff, Jones, against a defendant, Smith, and Smith loses the case and appeals, some courts reverse the order of the parties and refer to the case on appeal as *Smith v. Jones*. If the parties' names are merely reversed on appeal, retain the original order, here, *Jones v. Smith*.

l. Order of Preference for Citations

Bluebook Rule 10.3.1 provides an order of preference for citing cases: Generally, if a case is not available in an official or preferred unofficial reporter or as a neutral or public domain citation, cite to another unofficial reporter, to a widely used computer database (such as LEXIS or Westlaw), to a looseleaf service, to a slip opinion, to an Internet source, or to a newspaper, in that order of preference.

2. *Statutes*

a. State Statutes (*Bluebook* B6; Rule 12 and Table T.1)

Citations to state statutes must include the name of the code; the section, paragraph, or article number(s) of the statute; and parenthetically the year of the code, as follows: Miss. Code Ann. § 1401 (1986). The "year of the code" is not necessarily the year the statute was enacted but the year that appears on the spine of the volume, the year identified on the title page, or the latest copyright year, in this order of preference (*Bluebook* Rule 12.3.2).

You may recall from Chapter 3 that some states have codes that classify statutes by title, such as an Agriculture Code, a Civil Code, a Corporations Code, an Evidence Code, or a Probate Code. Usually the more populous states have arranged their codes in such titles. The states that have such subject matter codes are California, Kansas, Louisiana, Maryland, New York, and Texas. If your state organizes its statutes in such a manner, you must indicate the name of the title. Otherwise, if you refer to "Cal. § 301," the reader does not know whether to review Cal. Civ. Code § 301, Cal. Evid. Code § 301, or Cal. Prob. Code § 301. The other 44 states and the District of Columbia do not organize their statutes by subject matter, and therefore you follow the standard statute citation rule and identify the name of the code; the section/paragraph/article number; and the date.

Cite to the official code, if possible. If no official code exists, cite to the unofficial or privately published code, but then indicate the publisher parenthetically with the date. If you cite a statute to an electronic database (because the official or unofficial code or privately published session laws are not available), give parenthetically the name of the database (LEXIS or Westlaw) and information relating to the currency of the database as provided by the database itself (Rule 18.1.2).

Example

Cal. Evid. Code § 52 (West, Westlaw through 2004 Sess.).

Table T.1 of *The Bluebook* lists all 50 states alphabetically and gives instruction on how to cite statutes from every state. For those states such as California, New York, Texas, and the others that classify their statutes by subject matter, be sure to properly abbreviate the subject matter according to Table T.1. For example, in Texas, the abbreviation for the Family Code is "Fam.," the abbreviation for the Insurance Code is "Ins.," and the abbreviation for the Property Code is "Prop."

Examples for states that do not have subject matter codes:

Official Codes: Mont. Code Ann. § 1401 (1996).
N.C. Gen. Stat. § 29-104 (1998).
Utah Code Ann. § 6-781 (1996).

Unofficial Codes: Colo. Rev. Stat. Ann. § 5-109 (West 2001).
Fla. Stat. Ann. § 1401.03 (West 1997).
Ohio Rev. Code Ann. § 1609 (West 1999).

Examples for states that organize their statutes by subject matter:

Cal. Fin. Code § 2922 (West 1996).
La. Code Crim. Proc. Ann. art. 1024 (1998).
N.Y. Educ. Law § 1401 (McKinney 1994).

Remember that the examples given in *The Bluebook* show large and small capitals, for example, "TEX. LAB. CODE ANN. § 4.06.002 (Vernon 1996)," the format used for law reviews. As a practitioner, you will need to adapt the style as follows: "Tex. Lab. Code Ann. § 4.06.002 (Vernon 1996)."

b.   Federal Statutes (*Bluebook* B6; Rule 12)

You will recall from Chapter 3 that all federal statutes are published officially in the *United States Code* (U.S.C.) and unofficially in *United States Code Annotated* (U.S.C.A.), published by West, and *United States Code Service* (U.S.C.S.), now published by LEXIS Publishing. The elements of a citation for a federal statute are the number of the title, name of set, section number, and year of the code. Once again, the "year of the code" is the date that appears on the spine of the volume, the date shown on the title page, or the most recent copyright year of the volume, in that order. In most cases, this date will *not* be the date the statute was enacted.

Cite federal statutes to the current official code (U.S.C.) if possible. If you cannot cite the federal statute to the official code because it is not available at your law firm or local law library, cite to the unofficial codes (U.S.C.A. or U.S.C.S.). Cite to the actual set in which you located the statute. That is, do not merely drop the "A" of U.S.C.A. to produce an official cite. When you cite to the unofficial codes, you must identify the publisher in the parenthetical before the year of the code.

Examples

U.S.C.   42 U.S.C. § 1246 (2000).
U.S.C.A.   42 U.S.C.A. § 1246 (West 1996).
U.S.C.S.   42 U.S.C.S. § 1246 (LexisNexis 2000).

If a statute is commonly known by a popular name or such information would assist the reader, you may include the popular name as follows (do not include "The" as the first word of a statute name):

Norris-LaGuardia Act § 161, 29 U.S.C. § 221 (1986).

c.   Miscellaneous Rules Regarding Citation of Statutes

(1)   Spacing

A space should appear between the signal for the section (§) and the number of the statute because the section sign is an abbreviation or replacement for the word "section." A space should also be placed before the parenthetical.

41 U.S.C. § 1982 (1988).

(2) *Internal Revenue Code* (Bluebook *Rule B6.1.5; 12.8.1*)

There are special rules for citing to Title 26 of the *United States Code*, entitled "Internal Revenue." For Internal Revenue statutes, you may drop "26 U.S.C." and replace it with "I.R.C."

Preferred: I.R.C. § 501 (2000).

Disfavored: 26 U.S.C. § 501 (2000).

(3) *Pocket Parts and Supplements* (Bluebook *Rules 3.1 and 12.3.1(e)*)

If the statute appears only in a pocket part or supplement, indicate as follows:

Alaska Stat. § 1401 (Supp. V 1998).
17 U.S.C. § 101 (Supp. III 2003).

If the original statute appears in the hardbound volume and an amendment to it appears in a pocket part or supplement, cite as follows:

17 U.S.C. § 102 (2000 & Supp. I 2001).

(4) *Multiple Sections* (Bluebook *Rule 3.3(b)*)

Because of the often awkward numbering system used for statutes, you must be precise when referring a reader to a group of statutes. For example, if you referred a reader to Tenn. Code Ann. § 1764-66 (1996), the citation is ambiguous. The reader is unsure whether to read sections 1764, 1765, and 1766 or whether there is one particular statute identified as section 1764-66.

While it is common (and, in fact, required) in references to page numbers to drop repetitious digits, do not do so for statutes. If you wish the reader to review sections 1764 through 1766 indicate as follows:

Correct: Tenn. Code Ann. §§ 1764-1766 (1996).

Incorrect: Tenn. Code Ann. §§ 1764-66 (1996).

For clarity, follow these rules:

- When referring a reader to one section, use one section symbol (§).
- When referring a reader to more than one section, use two section symbols (§§) and do not drop any digits.

- When referring a reader to more than one section, do not use the term "et seq.," a Latin term for "and the following." Such a reference is too imprecise as it does not tell the reader when to stop reading. For example, the citation 28 U.S.C. §§ 4201 et seq. (2000), strictly interpreted, tells the reader to read the thousands of statutes in the United States Code following section 4201 of title 28.

*(5)   Section Reference (*Bluebook *Rule 3.4)*

In a citation, use the sign "§" for the word "section." Most word processors include this symbol, so if it is available, use it. Otherwise, use the word "section." However, spell out the word "section" in a narrative discussion of a statute (except when referring to a provision of the U.S. Code) as follows: The court's interpretation of section 1110 was confined to an analysis of the meaning of the term "compensation." (R.6.2(c)).

*(6)   Publisher (*Bluebook *Rule 12.3.1(d))*

While you may be tempted to omit the parenthetical identification of publisher and/or year in citing statutes, and while practitioners commonly omit such information, *The Bluebook* is unambiguous in requiring such information.

Correct:	16 U.S.C. § 141 (2000).
	16 U.S.C.A. § 141 (West 1996).
	16 U.S.C.S. § 141 (LexisNexis 2003).
Incorrect:	16 U.S.C. § 141.
	16 U.S.C.A. § 141.
	16 U.S.C.S. § 141.

Practice Tip

Citing Statutes

While *The Bluebook* and *ALWD* clearly require a parenthetical after any citation to a statute (which parenthetical must include the year of the code and the publisher, unless the set is an official one), practitioners around the country routinely strike the entire parenthetical in citing both federal and state statutes.

Bluebook and *ALWD* style: 11 U.S.C.A. § 509 (West 1998).

Practitioner style: 11 U.S.C.A. § 509.

Note also that individual volumes in U.S.C.A. and U.S.C.S. are replaced only when necessary. Thus, different volumes in a set will have different years in the parenthetical.

3. *Rules* (Bluebook *B6.1.3; Rule 12.8.3)*

Cite rules of evidence and procedure without any section sign or date, as follows:

> Fed. R. Civ. P. 56(a).
> Fed. R. Crim. P. 12.
> Fed. R. Evid. 210.

4. *Constitutions (*Bluebook *B7; Rule 11)*

a. State Constitutions

The correct form for citing a state constitution is shown on the inside back cover of *The Bluebook*. Note that you do not include a date unless the provision you are citing has been repealed, amended, or superseded.

> **Correct:**　　　Cal. Const. art. XXII.

b. United States Constitution

Cite current provisions of the United States Constitution without dates.

> **Correct:**　　　U.S. Const. art. III, § 8.
> U.S. Const. amend. I.

The Bluebook (R.8) requires capitalization of parts of the United States Constitution when they are discussed in textual sentences.

> **Correct:**　　　First Amendment
> Equal Protection Clause
> Fifth Amendment
>
> **Incorrect:**　　first amendment
> equal protection clause
> fifth amendment

E. *Bluebook* Citation Rules and Examples for Secondary Authorities

Examples for citing secondary authorities will be discussed in the order in which those authorities were discussed in Chapters 6 and 7.

1. *Annotations (*Bluebook *Rule 16.6.6)*

For A.L.R. annotations give the author's full name, identify the item as an "Annotation," give the title of the annotation (underlined or italicized), the reference to the volume and page of A.L.R. in which it can be found, and the year it was written. A.L.R. annotations are cited as follows:

> Jack W. Shaw, Jr., Annotation, *Exhibition of Obscene Motion Pictures as Nuisance*, 50 A.L.R.3d 969 (1978).

2. *Encyclopedias (* Bluebook *B8; Rule 15.8(a))*

Because the encyclopedias are weak secondary sources and are used primarily to give you introductory explanations of the law and to help you locate cases, you should not cite encyclopedias in support of a contention unless you have no primary authorities or stronger secondary authorities. The correct citation form is as follows:

> 1 C.J.S. *Abandonment* § 14 (1984).
> 1 Am. Jur. 2d *Abandonment* § 14 (1986).
> 6 Cal. Jur. 3d *Contracts* § 221 (1988).

Be sure to include and underscore the title in your citation (*Abandonment, Contracts, Deeds*). Otherwise a citation to 1 C.J.S. § 14 (1984) leaves the reader wondering whether to read Abandonment § 14 or Administrative Law § 14, both of which titles or topics are found in Volume 1 of C.J.S.

3. *Periodical Materials (* Bluebook *B9; Rule 16)*

For periodical articles, give the author's full name (as he or she does), the title of the article (underscored or italicized), the reference to the periodical in which it appeared (abbreviated according to Table T.13 in *The Bluebook*), the page on which the article begins, and the date of publication. Be sure to convert the law review format form of large and small capital letters you see in Table T.13 to ordinary typeface. *The Bluebook* (R.15) provides special rules on articles written by multiple authors.

> **Law Review Articles (*Bluebook* Rules 16.1, 16.6).**   Steven A. Peterson, *Plea Bargaining in Federal Courts*, 68 Loy. L. Rev. 1421 (1975).
> **Student-written Works.**   Elizabeth A. Brandon, Comment, *Philosophy of Law*, 48 Ariz. L. Rev. 123 (1998).
> **Bar Association Publications.**   Lori B. Andrews, *Surrogacy Wars*, Cal. Law., Oct. 1998, at 42.
> **Special Subject Publications.**   Andrew P. Neil, *Thrift Regulations*, 16 Inst. on Sec. Reg. 411 (1998).
> **Legal Newspapers.**   Joan M. Cheever & Joanne Naiman, *The Deadly Practice of Divorce*, Nat'l L.J., Oct. 12, 1999, at A1.

Note that a comma is used after the title of the article.

4. *Books, Texts, and Treatises* *(Bluebook B8; Rule 15)*

For texts and treatises, give the volume the material appeared in (if there is more than one volume to the set), the author's full name as the author gives it, the title of the text, the page/paragraph/section that the reader should review, and in parentheses the edition (for any edition after the first edition) and date of publication, as follows:

> 2 J. Thomas McCarthy, *McCarthy on Trademarks and Unfair Competition* § 18:18 (4th ed. 2004).

If the book has two authors, give the full names of both in the order they are listed on the publication, separated by an ampersand (&). If there are more than two authors, you may give the first author's name, followed by "*et al.*," or you may list all authors. Always give the full name of any editor or translator, followed by "ed." or "trans." in the parenthetical.

Refer to later editions and pocket parts as follows:

> 6 Daniel R. Donoghue, *Maritime and Admiralty Law* § 7.09 (3d ed. Supp. 1992).

Note that there is no comma after the title of a book, text, or treatise, although a comma is given after the title of a periodical article.

5. *Restatements* *(Bluebook B6.1.3;* *Rule 12.8.5)*

Restatements should be cited to the title of the Restatement, the edition being referred to, the section the reader should review, and the date of publication.

> Restatement (Second) of Torts § 312 (1976).
> Restatement (Second) of Agency § 24 cmt. a (1979).

6. *Uniform Laws* *(Bluebook B6.1.3;* *Rule 12.8.4)*

If you are referring to a Uniform Law as adopted by a state, use the standard statutory citation form for that state, as follows:

> Cal. Com. Code § 2-216 (West 1996).

If you are referring to the actual Uniform Law adopted by the Commissioners, cite as follows:

> U.C.C. § 2-216 (1977).

If you are referring to the set *Uniform Laws Annotated*, cite as follows:

Unif. Com. Code § 2-216 (amended 1988), 10 U.L.A. 109 (1992).

7. *Dictionaries* (Bluebook *B8; Rule 15.8*)

Dictionaries should be cited to the name of the dictionary, the page on which the definition appears and, parenthetically, the edition and year of publication, as follows:

> *Black's Law Dictionary* 679 (8th ed. 2004).
> *Ballentine's Law Dictionary* 415 (3d ed. 1969).

8. *Attorneys General Opinions* (Bluebook *Rule 14.4*)

Cite opinions of attorneys general by title of opinion (if desired), the volume, title of set, first page of opinion, and year, as follows:

> State attorneys general opinions:
>> 64 Op. Md. Att'y Gen. 104 (1995)
>>> or
>> Pharmaceutical Standards, 64 Op. Md. Att'y Gen. 104 (1995).
> United States Attorneys General Opinions:
>> 47 Op. Att'y Gen. 16 (1985)
>>> or
>> Treasury Regulations, 47 Op. Att'y Gen. 16 (1985).

9. *Looseleaf Services* (Bluebook *Rule 19*)

Cite looseleaf services by volume, title of the service (using appropriate abbreviations (see Table T.15)), publisher, section/subdivision/paragraph, and date, as follows:

> 1 Bus. Franchise Guide (CCH) ¶ 3202 (1988).

To cite cases in looseleaf services, cite as follows, unless the case is also published in an official reporter in which case you should cite to it.

> *Anderson v. CFFC Franchise Corp.*, 2 Bus. Franchise Guide (CCH) ¶ 8904 (S.D.N.Y. 1992).

F. The *ALWD* Citation Manual

1. *Introduction*

As discussed earlier, the *ALWD* citation manual was created in 2000 and has drawn a great deal of interest because of its user-friendly format, generous spacing and use of color, and numerous examples.

In many instances, the *ALWD* format for citations is identical to *Bluebook* format. For example, the format for lower federal court cases, most statutes, constitutions, journals and periodicals, and encyclopedias is identical. Rules for spacing and short forms are identical. There are, however, several differences (especially in abbreviations for the names of periodicals). See Figure 8-3 for a chart showing the more significant differences between *ALWD* and *The Bluebook*. Because at the time of writing this text *The Bluebook* is still the best-known citation guide, this section will provide examples of many *ALWD* citation forms but will not provide as much detailed explanation for those forms as the previous section did in discussing *The Bluebook*. The *ALWD* citation manual may be obtained at most school bookstores or from Aspen Publishers at www.aspenpublishers.com. Moreover, a great deal of useful information about *ALWD*, other examples, citation exercises, and a list of schools that have adopted *ALWD* is available at the *ALWD* Web site at www.alwd.org.

In the examples to follow, an asterisk (*) indicates that the *ALWD* citation format is identical to that of *The Bluebook*.

2. **ALWD** *Citation Rules and Examples for Primary Authorities*

a. Citation of Cases (*ALWD* Rule 12)

ALWD's rules for citing cases are very similar to those of *The Bluebook*. In fact, there are only three major differences for conventionally published cases:

- **Information About Divisions for State Court Cases**. *ALWD* Rule 12.6(b) generally requires that when you cite state cases, you must include available information about departments, districts, or divisions that decided the case. *The Bluebook* generally does not permit this information.

  ALWD: *Coffey v. Huntley*, 909 S.W.2d 13 (Ark. App. Div. II 1990)

  Bluebook: *Coffee v. Huntley*, 909 S.W.2d 13 (Ark. Ct. App. 1990)

- **Parallel Citations for Supreme Court Cases**. For U.S. Supreme Court cases, *ALWD* permits parallel citations while

The *Bluebook* prohibits parallel citations when citing U.S.
Supreme Court cases.

ALWD: *Riley v. Harris*, 490 U.S. 909 (2000) or
                 Riley v. Harris, 490 U.S. 909, 218 S. Ct. 78,
                 211 L. Ed. 2d 445 (2000)
Bluebook: *Riley v. Harris*, 490 U.S. 909 (2000)

- **Abbreviations in Case Names.** *ALWD* adopts a permissive
  approach to using abbreviations in case names and states that
  you "may" abbreviate any word in a case name when the case name
  appears as a stand-alone citation, and that it is traditional to spell
  out all words in a case name when it appears in text as part of a
  textual sentence. *The Bluebook* approach is more rigid and requires
  that you spell out all words in a case name when it appears in text
  and requires that you abbreviate words in a case name when it
  appears as a stand-alone citation.

In addition to these significant differences, there are some other
minor differences as well. For example, the abbreviations used in *ALWD*
and *The Bluebook* vary. *ALWD* abbreviates the word "Association" in a
case name as "Assn." while *The Bluebook* uses "Ass'n." Similarly, *The
Bluebook* requires that when the United States is a party to a case, the
case name must read "United States," while *ALWD* (Rule 12.2(g)) provides
that the case name must read "U.S.," as in *U.S. v. Rafferty.* Finally,
abbreviations for names of courts vary. For example, *Bluebook* Table
T.1 shows "Colo. Ct. App." for the Colorado Court of Appeals while *ALWD*
Appendix 1 shows this as "Colo. App."

(1)   Spacing (ALWD Rule 2.2)

ALWD's rules for spacing are identical to those found in *The Bluebook*:

- Close up spaces between adjacent single capitals (as in U.S. or
  N.W.) and treat the ordinal abbreviations as a single capital (as
  in A.L.R.4th);
- Place a space before and after any multiple letter abbreviation (as
  in F. Supp. 2d);
- In legal periodicals, set the abbreviations for an institution or
  geographical entity apart from other capital letters (as in N.M.
  L. Rev.).

(2)   Federal Cases (ALWD Rule 12)

With the exception of the presentation of U.S. Supreme Court cases
(for which *ALWD* permits parallel citations), the presentation of federal
cases for *ALWD* is identical to that for *The Bluebook*:

Example of case from United States Supreme Court:
Carroll Bros. v. Allen Co., 490 U.S. 116 (1995)* or
Carroll Bros. v. Allen Co., 490 U.S. 116, 230 S. Ct. 90,
216 L. Ed. 2d 88 (1995)

Example of case from intermediate court of appeal:
Weber v. Franklin, 38 F.3d 119 (9th Cir. 1999)*

Example of case from district court:
Richardson v. McAfee, 98 F. Supp. 2d 778 (S.D.N.Y. 2000)*

(3) Subsequent History (ALWD Rule 12.8)

ALWD's rules relating to subsequent history are nearly identical to those of *The Bluebook*, namely, you must include the subsequent history for the cases you cite, although you may omit denials of *certiorari* unless the case is less than two years old or if the denial is particularly important.

> ***ALWD* Example:** *Lee v. Nelson*, 109 F.3d 45 (2d Cir. 1998), *aff'd*, 490 U.S. 16 (1998)

Note that *ALWD* provides that when citing a decision with subsequent history in the same year, include the year each time.

b. Citation of Statutes (*ALWD* Rule 14)

(1) Federal Statutes

The presentation of federal statutes is the same in *ALWD* as it is in *The Bluebook*. The rules requiring you to include a date parenthetical for federal statutes and the name of the publisher for the unofficial sets (U.S.C.A. and U.S.C.S.) are also identical, although *Bluebook* uses "LexisNexis" and *ALWD* uses "LEXIS."

Examples:	42 U.S.C. § 2220 (2000)*
	42 U.S.C.A. § 2220 (West 1999)*
	42 U.S.C.S. § 2220 (LEXIS 2003)

(2) State Statutes

Appendix 1 of *ALWD* provides the format for citation for each state's statutes. They are highly similar or identical in form to those shown in *The Bluebook*.

Examples:	Alaska Stat. § 10.2.6 (West 2001)*
	Colo. Rev. Stat. § 12-220 (2001)*
	N.C. Gen. Stat. § 8-014 (2000)*

3. ALWD *Citation Rules and Examples for Secondary Authorities*

Most of the *ALWD* rules relating to citing secondary authorities are identical to those for *The Bluebook*. Following are examples for the most often cited secondary authorities. Again, an asterisk following an example indicates that the format is identical for both *ALWD* and *The Bluebook*.

a. Annotations (*ALWD* Rule 24)

Cite A.L.R. annotations as follows: Kyle A. Smith, *Private Nuisances*, 124 A.L.R.5th 667 (1999).

b. Encyclopedias (*ALWD* Rule 26)

Cite encyclopedias as follows: 45 C.J.S. *Hospitals* § 201 (1996)*
24 Am. Jur. 2d *Easements* § 21 (1994)*

c. Periodical Materials (*ALWD* Rule 23)

Generally, cite periodical articles as follows: Jacob N. Scheib, *The Hearsay Rule*, 35 Tenn. L. Rev. 105 (2001).*

d. Books, Texts, and Treatises (*ALWD* Rule 22)

A key difference in the way citations for treatises are presented under *ALWD* rules is that *ALWD* requires that the publisher of the treatise be identified in the parenthetical with the date. *The Bluebook* does not require this information. Another difference is that *ALWD* requires that the volume number of the treatise be given after the name of the set.

ALWD Example: Penny D. Davis, *Corporate Handbook* vol. 3, § 12:8 (3d ed., West 2002).

e. Restatements (*ALWD* Rule 27)

Cite Restatements as follows: *Restatement (Second) of Torts* § 24 (1995).

G. Special Citation Issues (*Bluebook* and *ALWD*)

1. Introduction

Learning the various citation rules can be difficult, and the task is made even more complicated by the work of integrating citations into your legal writing. While citations for law review and other academic articles appear in footnotes, citations in other legal writings such as legal memoranda or court documents usually appear in the body of your narrative text. Because you will typically be preparing or checking cites appearing in text, the information presented in this chapter relates to citing in text. Citations do not exist alone. They appear as part of sentences that must be correctly punctuated, as support for quotations, and together with certain signals that give readers information about the level of support the citation provides for the assertion of law you have made. This section of the chapter will address these special citation issues such as punctuation, quotations, signals, and short form citations you can use when you have once cited an authority in full and now wish to refer to it again. Examples provided will be shown in the form used by legal practitioners.

2. *Punctuation (* Bluebook *Bluepages 2;* ALWD *Rule 43)*

There are three punctuation marks that may follow a citation: a period; a comma; or a semicolon.

a. Citation "Sentences"

Citations appear in legal writings in two ways: as complete "sentences" or as clauses set off by commas within a sentence. If you have made an assertion about the law, it must be supported by legal authority. You cannot make a statement about the law without attributing it to the appropriate authority. If the statement that you have made about the law is a sentence, the citation that follows the sentence will appear as though it were a "sentence" itself.

Example

Landlords are required to provide written notice to tenants before commencing actions for eviction. *Williams Co. v. Sanders Elec. Enter.*, 428 P.2d 102 (Alaska 1996).

In this example, a statement about the law was made in a complete sentence. The citation that supports this legal assertion also appears as a "sentence" in that it starts with a capital letter and ends with a period. The citation informs the reader that the entire preceding sentence is supported by the case *Williams Co. v. Sanders Elec. Enter.* Note that the words "Electrical" and "Enterprise" have been abbreviated because the citation stands alone.

b. Citation "Clauses"

Authorities that support (or contradict) only a portion of a sentence appear in a citation format set off by commas, which immediately follow the statement they support (or contradict).

Example

While it has been held that landlords must provide notice to tenants before commencing eviction actions, *Williams Co. v. Sanders Elec. Enter.*, 428 P.2d 102 (Alaska 1996), the amount of time provided by the notice may vary from three to ten days, *Hill v. Irwin*, 432 P.2d 918 (Alaska 1997).

This example informs the reader that *Williams Co. v. Sanders Electrical Enterprise* requires landlords to give notice to tenants and that *Hill v. Irwin* provides that the length of time set forth in the notice may vary. Note that because the *Williams* case cite is not needed to make sense of a sentence or clause, it is viewed as a stand-alone cite rather than as part of a textual sentence. Thus, words such as "electrical" and "enterprise" are abbreviated.

Do not place a citation in parentheses or brackets. Try to vary your placement of citations. If your writing consists of a series of sentences each of which is followed by a citation, your project will be choppy. Besides varying citations so that some appear as sentences and some appear as clauses, another technique used by many legal writers to achieve variety and interest in their writing is occasionally to use citations in introductory clauses.

Example

According to *Williams Co. v. Sanders Electrical Enterprise*, 428 P.2d 102 (Alaska 1996), landlords must provide written notice to tenants before commencing actions to evict those tenants.

or

One of the first cases to address the issue of default notices was *Williams Co. v. Sanders Electrical Enterprise*, 428 P.2d 102 (Alaska 1996), which held that landlords must provide written notice to tenants before commencing actions to evict those tenants.

These phrases provide a different technique for introducing citations and add interest to a project. Again, however, do not fall into the lazy habit of always introducing your legal authorities in the same manner. Occasionally students start each and every paragraph in a project with the phrase "In *Williams v. Sanders* . . ." or "In *Hill v. Irwin* . . ." The reader, on looking at the page, is presented with a series of paragraphs each of which commences with the word "in" followed by a case citation, giving the project a rigid look and a style lacking in interest and variety.

ALWD refers to the technique of incorporating a citation into a textual sentence (as shown in the foregoing examples and as in, "In *Jones v. Smith*, 520 U.S. 106, 109 (1998), the Court held . . .") as an "embedded citation" and states that some readers dislike embedded citations because they make sentences more difficult to read.

3. *String Citing* **(Bluebook *B4.5 and*** ***Rule 1.4;* ALWD *Rule 45*)**

a. **Introduction**

Another manner in which citations appear in legal writing is in "strings" or groups of several citations. If you cite more than one authority in support of a proposition, separate each citation from the next by a semicolon and a space and follow the last citation with the appropriate punctuation mark, usually a period.

Example

> Courts from all over the country are in agreement in requiring land-
> lords to provide notice to tenants before commencing actions to evict
> those tenants. *Samson v. Oak Tree Apts., Inc.*, 761 P.2d 118 (Cal.
> 1980); *Allen v. Carwood*, 421 A.2d 181 (N.J. 1976); *Fulton v. Garden
> Apts., Ltd.*, 388 S.W.2d 200 (Tex. 1977).

In general, "string citing" is disfavored. Courts prefer that you select
the best authority that supports a proposition and cite it rather than clut-
tering your writing with citations that do not add anything. In certain
situations, however, string citing is acceptable. Thus, as shown in the
preceding example, if you need to demonstrate to a reader the breadth
and variety of authorities that are in agreement, or if your state has no
authorities for a certain issue and you wish to persuade the court to adopt a
view espoused by several jurisdictions, you may wish to string cite.

b. Order of Citations in String Cites

When you string cite, however, you must place the citations in a certain
order. *The Bluebook* (Rule 1.4) provides that if one authority is more helpful or authoritative than the others, it should be placed first. Except in this
situation, you should list the citations in the following order (see *Bluebook*
Rule 1.4 for complete list):

> (i) Constitutions (list federal Constitution first, then state con-
> stitutions, alphabetically by state).
> (ii) Statutes (list federal statutes first by order of U.S.C. title,
> then state statutes alphabetically by state).
> (iii) Cases (list federal cases first, ordering by United States Su-
> preme Court, United States Courts of Appeal, United States
> District Courts, then state cases, alphabetically by state and
> from highest court to lowest court).
> (iv) Secondary authorities (in this order: uniform and model codes,
> Restatements, books, law review articles, annotations, and
> electronic sources).

If you have several cases from the same state, for example,
Missouri — cite from highest court to lowest court and within each group
from newer cases to older cases.

If you have several cases from the United States Courts of Appeal or
the United States District Courts, cite by date, giving the newer cases first.

Bluebook Example

> Landlords must provide notice to tenants before commencing actions
> for eviction. *Alan v. Anderson*, 421 F.2d 101 (4th Cir. 1985); *Darwin v.
> Balboa Gardens*, 415 F.2d 222 (8th Cir. 1984); *Swanson v. Trudeau*,
> 399 S.W.2d 14 (Ark. 1988); *McNenly v. Trainor*, 346 S.W.2d 606 (Ark.
> 1981); *Harrison v. J.T. Alton, Inc.*, 394 S.W.2d 102 (Ark. Ct. App.
> 1986).

ALWD Rule 45 covers string citing and is nearly identical to *The Bluebook* approach. The order in which authorities are given in the string is also nearly identical to the order directed by *The Bluebook*. Thus, for example, federal cases are given before state cases (which are arranged alphabetically) and cases from higher courts are given before those from lower courts. One difference, however, is that *The Bluebook* states that the most helpful or authoritative source should be given first in the string while *ALWD* has no such approach.

4. *Quotations* (Bluebook *B12 and Rules 3.2 and 5;* ALWD *Rules 5 and 47)*

a. Introduction

You may find in the course of legal writing that you wish to quote directly from a case, treatise, law review article, or other legal authority. Your decision to quote a legal authority rather than merely summarize or paraphrase it may stem from your desire to emphasize a certain point or perhaps your determination that the judge's or author's manner of expressing a legal principle is so articulate that you wish to present the material in its original form rather than weaken its force by summarizing it. Quoting from legal authorities is certainly acceptable so long as it is not overdone and so long as the citation is in correct form.

You must *always* indicate the exact page a quote appears on to allow a reader to review the original source and ensure that you have correctly reproduced the material and have not altered the meaning of the quotation by omitting or adding material. This reference to the exact page on which the quoted material appears is often called a "spot cite," "pinpoint cite," or "pincite," as you are pinpointing the reader's attention to a specific page, or a "jump cite," as you are asking the reader to "jump" from the first page of a legal authority to a specific page within that authority.

The reference to quoted material is placed immediately after the page on which the case or article begins, separated by a comma.

Examples

Case: *Goodman v. Gray*, 429 F.2d 109, 114 (7th Cir. 1979). This informs the reader that the case begins at page 109, and the quoted material is found at page 114.

Article: Susan L. Hoffman, *The Juvenile's Right to Counsel*, 47 N.C. L. Rev. 411, 446 (1985). This informs the reader that the article begins at page 411, and the quotation is found at page 446.

If local court rules require you to give parallel citations, you must inform the reader on which page a quote occurs in each parallel cite. In some instances, you will have to locate the quote in several sources.

Examples

"A landlord must provide a notice to a tenant before commencing an action to evict the tenant." *Tapper v. Savage*, 201 Wis. 2d 191, 196, 299 N.W.2d 47, 52 (1986).

"It is incumbent upon the prosecution to prove defendant's guilt beyond a reasonable doubt." *State v. Harrison*, 262 Cal. 3d 104, 106, 461 P.2d 201, 204, 189 Cal. Rptr. 966, 968 (1979).

If the quote spans more than one page, provide the inclusive page numbers but separate them by a hyphen. Retain the last two digits but omit any other repetitious digits. *Bluebook* (R. 3.2(a)). *ALWD* Rule 5.3, however, allows such page spans to be presented in two ways: by retaining all digits or by retaining the last two digits but dropping other repetitious digits.

Correct **Bluebook** *example*	*Correct* **ALWD** *examples*
320 F.3d 1071, 1074-76	320 F.3d 1071, 1074-76 or
	320 F.3d 1071, 1074-1076

If you are citing from individual scattered pages from a source, indicate the separate pages as follows *Bluebook* (R. 3.2(a); *ALWD* R. 5.4).

Example

Bailey v. Pridewell, 412 F.2d 109, 114, 121 (9th Cir. 1978).

The Bluebook states that pincites are "critical." Thus, always include a pincite whether you are quoting directly from material or you are paraphrasing. This practice is a courtesy to readers to enable them to locate easily that portion of the authority you are discussing. If your research is accurate and the legal authority does in fact say what you claim it does, there is no reason not to provide a reference to a specific page. This is the position suggested by *The Bluebook* (R. 3.2(a)), which states that when referring to "specific material" within a source, one should include both the page on which the source begins and the pinpoint. Similarly, *ALWD* Rule 5.2 requires pinpoints for quoted material and "cited material."

If a point is continually made throughout a source, use *passim*, a Latin word meaning "everywhere" and interpreted as "scattered here and there," as follows *Bluebook* (R. 3.2(a); *ALWD* R. 5.5).

Examples

Bluebook: *Taft v. Alpert*, 429 S.E.2d 616 *passim* (W. Va. 1988).
ALWD: *Taft v. Alpert*, 429 S.E.2d 616, *passim* (W. Va. 1998).

If your specific material appears on the first page of a source, repeat the page number (*Bluebook* B5.1.2 and R.3.2(a); *ALWD* R. 5.2(b)), as follows:

Example

Allison P. Page, *Statutory Construction*, 46 BYU L. Rev. 109, 109 (1998).

b. Indicating Quotations in Text

The Bluebook and *ALWD* rules regarding quotations conform to the rules regarding quotations that you have been familiar with since high school, that is, that quotations of 49 or fewer words appear in the text of your writing while longer quotations of 50 or more words are indented.

(1) Non-Indented Quotations (Bluebook Rule 5.1(b); ALWD Rule 47.4)

Quotations of 49 or fewer words should appear in the body of your text without indentation. Indicate the beginning and ending of the quotation by quotation marks ("/"). If your quote then relies on or incorporates other quoted material, indicate such by a single quotation mark ('). Commas and periods must be placed inside the ending quotation mark. Other punctuation marks such as question marks or exclamation points appear inside the ending quotation mark only if they are part of the matter quoted.

Example

In one recent case, the court ruled that the defendant could properly be found to have been carrying a knife for use as a dangerous weapon and held as follows: "Although appellant was attempting to check the knife when arrested, his statements permitted the inference that he was prepared to use it, should the occasion arise, but prior to entering and, after retrieving the briefcase, immediately upon leaving the Longworth Building." *Monroe v. United States*, 598 A.2d 439, 441 (D.C. 1991).

(2) Indented Quotations (Bluebook B12 and Rule 5.1(a); ALWD Rule 47.5)

Quotations of 50 words or more should be indented (typically ten spaces), left and right, and appear without quotation marks. This "block" quote should be single-spaced. A reader is alerted to the fact that material is being quoted by the indentation itself. Separate the block quote from the text below and above it with a blank line. If your quotation quotes from some other source or authority, indicate such with quotation marks ("/"). That is, retain all punctuation marks and quotation marks as they appear in the original quote. This is quite different from a non-indented quote, which requires you to use a single quotation mark (') when it is quoting from another source.

Note that *ALWD* also allows any quotation to be presented as a block if it exceeds four lines of typed text. Thus, in the example given above, under *ALWD*, the quotation could have been shown as a block quote because it exceeds more than four lines.

To determine whether you should indent a quote and place it in block form, you must count the words in the quote. While this is somewhat time consuming, it must be done. There are, however, a few word processing programs, such as SpellCheck, that will count the words in a quote for you. Again, remember that *ALWD* allows any quotation that exceeds four lines to be presented as a block quote.

Some legal writers indent quotes of fewer than 50 words to emphasize the indented material and make it stand out from the remainder of the narrative. Avoid this practice, as it not only violates *Bluebook* rules but has been overdone, with the result that some readers "skip over" short indented material. Your writing should be sufficiently forceful in itself without resorting to "tricks" to draw emphasis.

One of the mistakes most commonly made by legal writers relates to placement of the citation that supports the quote. The citation does *not* appear within the block indentation. Placement of the citation within the indention indicates that it is part of the quote. The citation should be placed at the left margin on the line of text that follows the quote.

Correct:
XXXXXXXXXXXXXXXXXXXXX
XXXXXXXXXXXXXXXXXXXXX
XXXXXXXXXXXXXXXXXXXXX
XXXXXXXXXXXXXXXXXXXXX

Monroe v. United States, 598 A.2d 439, 441 (D.C. 1991).

Incorrect:
XXXXXXXXXXXXXXXXXXXXX
XXXXXXXXXXXXXXXXXXXXX
XXXXXXXXXXXXXXXXXXXXX
Monroe v. United States, 598 A.2d
439, 441 (D.C. 1991).

After you have placed your citation at the left margin, continue your narrative. If you begin a new paragraph, skip to the next line (or skip two lines if you are double spacing) and indent as usual to show a new paragraph is beginning.

c. Alterations of Quotes (*Bluebook* Rule 5.2; *ALWD* Rule 48)

Anytime you alter a quote in any way, whether by pluralizing a word, inserting a word, capitalizing a word that was not capitalized in the original quote, or some other alteration, you must always alert the reader that you have changed the quote. When you change a letter from lower case to upper case, or vice versa, enclose it in brackets. Similarly, substituted words or letters or other inserted material should be bracketed. If a letter has been omitted, indicate such with empty brackets — for example, "boy[ ] for "boys."

If the original quote was, for example, "The factfinder must consider circumstances surrounding the use of the dangerous weapon," you must indicate an alteration of the quoted material as follows: "The factfinder must consider circumstances surrounding [the possession and] use of the dangerous weapon."

If a mistake or misspelling has occurred in the original material, indicate such by following the mistake by the word *sic*, a Latin word meaning "thus; so; in such manner." For example, if the original quoted material provides, "Defendants was convicted in the Superior Court," indicate the error in the original as follows: "Defendants was [sic] convicted in the Superior Court." Note that *ALWD* Rule 48.5 states that you may retain the mistake, correct it, or use [sic] to show that it appeared in the original quoted material.

d. Adding Emphasis (*Bluebook* Rule 5.2; *ALWD* Rule 48.4)

If the material you are quoting is emphasized in the original by italics, underscoring, or otherwise, retain the original emphasis but do not otherwise indicate such. Thus, do not state "emphasis in original." By including the italicized or underscored word or phrase in the quotation, the reader will assume this emphasis occurred in the original. If, on the other hand, you wish to emphasize something that was *not* so emphasized in the original, you must indicate your alteration of the quote by a parenthetical explanation.

> For example, assume the original quote read as follows:

> "The court refused to hold that merely possessing a dangerous weapon was a violation of the statute." *Franklin v. James*, 681 F.2d 102, 106 (8th Cir. 1988).

> If you wish to emphasize any of the words or phrases in the original material, do so as follows:

> "The court refused to hold that *merely possessing* a dangerous weapon was a violation of the statute." *Franklin v. James*, 681 F.2d 102, 106 (8th Cir. 1988) (emphasis added).

e. Omitting Citations (*Bluebook* Rule 5.2; *ALWD* Rule 49.3(d))

It is possible that the quotation you wish to include is peppered with other citations, resulting in a quote that is disrupted by these intervening cites, weakening the force and effect of the quotation. To eliminate these intrusive citations (or footnotes) and yet remain faithful to the original quoted material, simply indicate to the reader that you have omitted citations.

Example
> The court relied on numerous precedents in refusing to hold that "merely possessing a dangerous weapon was a violation of the statute." *Franklin v. James*, 681 F.2d 102, 106 (8th Cir. 1988) (citations omitted).

> If readers wish to review the other cases whose citations have been omitted, they may easily do so by locating page 106 of the case *Franklin v. James*, located at volume 681 of the *Federal Reporter, Second Series*.

f. Use of Ellipses (*Bluebook* Rule 5.3; *ALWD* Rule 49)

If you omit a word, phrase, or sentence from quoted material, you must indicate this omission by the use of an ellipsis, three periods separated by spaces from each other and set off by a space before the first period and after the last period. An ellipsis signals that words have been omitted from the middle of a quotation or the end of a quotation. Do not use an ellipsis to begin a quotation. If you have altered a word or omitted words at the beginning of a quotation, indicate such by changing the first letter of the word now beginning your quote from a lowercase letter to an uppercase letter and enclosing it in brackets. This will signal the reader that you have altered the beginning of a quote.

For example, assume your quote is as follows:

> "In order to prove a violation of the statute, the prosecution must prove defendant's intent."

If you wish to omit the first part of the quote, do so as follows:

> "[T]o prove a violation of the statute, the prosecution must prove defendant's intent."

g. Omissions from the Middle of a Quote

To indicate that you have omitted language from the middle of a quote, use the ellipsis, three periods separated by spaces:

> Example: "In order to prove a violation . . . the prosecution must prove . . . intent."

h. Omissions from the End of a Quote

To indicate that you have omitted language from the end of a quote, use three periods separated by spaces followed by the final punctuation of your quote, typically a period.

> Example: "Although Appellant was attempting to check the knife when arrested, his statements permitted the inference that he was prepared to use it . . . ."

i. Using Quoted Language as a Phrase

When using quoted language as a phrase or clause incorporated into your sentence rather than as a full sentence, you need not use an ellipsis.

Example

> Justice O'Connor stated that malice and recklessness "will give rise to punitive damages."

j. Paragraph Structure

If you have indented a quote of 50 or more words and this quote commenced a paragraph, indent further to let the reader know that your quote is from the beginning of a paragraph.

Example

       XXXXXXXXXXXXXXXXXXXXXXXXX
XXXXXXXXXXXXXXXXXXXXXXXXXXXXX
XXXXXXXXXXXXXXXXXXXXXXXXXXXXX
XXXXXXXXXXXXXXXXXXXXXXXXXXXXX
XXXXXXX.

If you continue to quote another paragraph, skip a line and once again indent the second quote to indicate it commenced a paragraph.

Only indent your block quote(s) if the original quote began a paragraph. Quotations from the middle of paragraphs appear in block style with no additional indentations.

If you are quoting one paragraph of 50 words or more and then wish to omit or skip an entire paragraph and then continue quoting another paragraph of 50 words or more, use four indented periods on a new line to signal that you have omitted an entire paragraph.

Example

       XXXXXXXXXXXXXXXXXXXXXXXXX
XXXXXXXXXXXXXXXXXXXXXXXXXXXXX
XXXXXXXXXXXXXXXXXXXXXXXXXXXXX
XXXXXXXXXXXXXXXXXXXXXXXXXXXXX
XXXXXXX.

. . . .

       XXXXXXXXXXXXXXXXXXXXXXXXX
XXXXXXXXXXXXXXXXXXXXXXXXXXXXX
XXXXXXXXXXXXXXXXXXXXXXXXXXXXX
XXXXXXXXXXXXXXXXXXXXXXXXXXXXX
XXXXXXX.

To signal an omission at the beginning of a second or subsequent paragraph, use an ellipsis (even though you may never use an ellipsis to begin a quotation). *The Bluebook* (R.5.1) shows a standard ellipsis but *ALWD* (R. 49.4(d)) requires centering of the ellipsis and five to seven spaces between each ellipsis point.

Bluebook Example

       XXXXXXXXXXXXXXXXXXXXXXXXX
XXXXXXXXXXXXXXXXXXXXXXXXXXXX
XXXXXXXXXXXXXXXXXXXXXXXXXXXXX

XXXXXXXXXXXXXXXXXXXXXXXXXXXXXX
XXXXXXXXXXXXXXXXXXXXXXXXXXXXXX
XXXXXXX.

. . . XXXXXXXXXXXXXXXXXXXXXXXX
XXXXXXXXXXXXXXXXXXXXXXXXXXXXXX
XXXXXXXXXXXXXXXXXXXXXXXXXXXXXX
XXXXXXXXXXXXXXXXXXXXXXXXXXXXXX
XXXXXXXXXXXXXXXXXXXXXXXXXXXXXX
XXXXXXX.

5. *Citation Signals (*Bluebook *B4 and Rule* 1.2; ALWD *Rule 44)*

Legal writers often use certain citation signals as a shorthand method of indicating to the reader the manner in which an authority supports or contradicts an assertion. If a citation does anything other than directly state a proposition, identify the source of a quotation, or identify an authority referred to in text, a signal indicating such should be used before the citation. These signals can be very confusing, and often there are only very subtle shadings of difference between one signal and another. Moreover, the use of signals is complicated by the fact that their use and meaning have shifted from one edition of *The Bluebook* to the next. See Figure 8-2.

> (i) *No signal.* If, after having made an assertion, the author immediately cites a legal authority, this indicates the legal authority directly states the proposition, (or "directly supports" the proposition, according to *ALWD*), identifies the source of a quotation, or identifies an authority referred to in the preceding text.
> (ii) *Accord.* The word *accord* is used after one authority has been given and introduces a second authority agreeing with the first.

Example

"Landlords are required to provide notice to tenants before commencing actions to evict tenants." *Li v. Carr,* 420 U.S. 20, 29 (1994); *accord Smith v. Jones,* 681 P.2d 104, 107 (Cal. 1990).

> (iii) *See.* The Bluebook states that the signal *see* is used when the citation clearly supports the proposition. *See* is used when the proposition is not directly stated by the authority you rely upon but obviously follows from it. The use of *see* has shifted over time. See Figure 8-2. *ALWD* states that the signal *see* is used when the cited authority either supports the stated proposition implicitly or contains dicta that support the proposition.

Figure 8-2
The Evolution of Citation Signals in *The Bluebook*

	[No signal]	*See*	*Contra*
Fifteenth Edition (1991-1996)	Citation clearly states the proposition or identifies the source of a quotation or authority referred to in text.	Citation clearly supports the proposition.	Citation directly states the contrary of the proposition.
Sixteenth Edition (1996-2000)	Citation identifies the source of a quotation or authority used in text.	Citation clearly states or clearly supports the proposition.	*Contra* did not exist in the Sixteenth Edition of *The Bluebook*.
Seventeenth Edition (2000-2005)	Citation directly states the proposition or identifies the source of a quotation or authority referred to in text.	Citation clearly supports the proposition.	Citation directly states the contrary of the proposition.
Eighteenth Edition (2005-date)	Same as Seventeenth Edition.	Same as Seventeenth Edition.	Same as Seventeenth Edition.

(iv)   *See also.* This signal is used to show additional legal authorities that support a proposition. *The Bluebook* encourages you to use a parenthetical explaining the relevance of the authorities.

(v)   *Cf.* The signal *cf.*, meaning "compare," is used to indicate legal authority supporting a proposition that is different from the main proposition but that is analogous to the main proposition. *The Bluebook* strongly recommends that when using this signal, the writer explain parenthetically how the cited authority supports the proposition.

(vi)   *Contra.* The signal *contra* indicates contradiction and is used when the cited authority directly states the contrary of the proposition you have made. Like "no signal" and *see*, the use of *contra* has shifted over time, and, in fact, was omitted entirely from the 16th edition of *The Bluebook*. It was revived in the 17th edition.

(vii) *But see. The Bluebook* provides that this signal is used when the legal authority you cite clearly supports a proposition contrary to the main proposition. *ALWD* states that *but see* is used when the cited authority either contradicts the stated proposition implicitly or contains dicta that contradict the stated proposition.

(viii) *But cf.* The signal *but cf.* is used when the legal authority you cite supports a proposition analogous to the contrary of the main proposition. *The Bluebook* strongly recommends a parenthetical explanation as to the relevance of the authority you cite.

(ix) *See generally.* The signal *see generally* indicates that the legal authority you cite provides helpful background material related to the proposition. *The Bluebook* recommends an explanatory parenthetical.

(x) *E.g.* The signal *e.g.* is used to show an example, meaning that the authority you cite is merely an example of several authorities that directly state the proposition but are not cited. The signal *e.g.* may be used with other signals. Note that *The Bluebook* follows the signal *e.g.* with a comma, but *ALWD* does not.

These signals are given before your citation. They may or may not be capitalized, depending on the context in which they are used. Capitalize a signal beginning a citation sentence and do not capitalize a signal that is part of a sentence. The signals are underscored or italicized unless they are used as verbs in ordinary sentences, and an unbroken line is used for signals composed of two words, such as *see generally*.

Most individuals find these signals confusing and very difficult to distinguish. Typically, they are used more often in academic legal writing, such as law review articles, which provide a complete analysis of an issue, including cases in support of a proposition and cases in contradiction to a proposition, rather than in court documents and legal memoranda, which often use citations with no or few introductory signals. Moreover, there are subtle differences in the presentation and meaning of the signals depending on whether you are following *The Bluebook* or *ALWD*. For example, as noted above, *The Bluebook* follows the signal *e.g.* with a comma while *ALWD* does not.

Because the meaning of the various signals can be so nuanced, both *The Bluebook* and *ALWD* recommend that when you use any signal, you include a parenthetical explanation after the cited source to describe the meaning and force of the authority. Generally, both *The Bluebook* and *ALWD* require that explanatory phrases begin with a present participle (a verb plus an "ing" ending, as in "arguing" or "holding") and a lowercase letter unless the parenthetical is a full quoted sentence.

6. Short Form Citations

Once you have cited an authority in full, to save time you may use a short form on subsequent occasions when you refer to it in your writing. *The Bluebook* (B5.2) provides that a short form may be used if it will be clear to the reader which citation has been shortened, the earlier full citation appeared in the same general discussion, and the reader will be able to locate readily the earlier full citation. *ALWD* Rule 11.2 is similar.

a. Cases (*Bluebook* B5.2 and R. 10.9; *ALWD* Rule 12.21)

Assume your full citation is *Singer v. Bryant*, 219 N.E.2d 409, 411 (Ind. 1987). Once you have given this full citation, you may use any of the following short forms:

> *Singer*, 219 N.E.2d at 411.
> 219 N.E.2d at 411.
> *Id.* at 411.

For cases in which a parallel citation is required, such as *Lowell v. Allen*, 204 Ga. 102, 104, 68 S.E.2d 19, 21 (1976), you may use any of the following short forms:

> *Lowell*, 204 Ga. at 104, 68 S.E.2d at 21.
> 204 Ga. at 104, 104 68 S.E.2d at 21.
> *Id.* at 104, 68 S.E.2d at 21.

The Bluebook and *ALWD* also provide that if you have given a full case citation and later refer to the case in the same general discussion, you may use one of the parties' names without including any further citation (*Bluebook* B5.3 and Rule 10.9 (c); *ALWD* Rule 12.21 (c)(2)).

Example
> In *Lowell*, the court also held that punitive damages are recoverable in fraud actions.

Generally, use the plaintiff's name in a short form unless the plaintiff is a common litigant such as the United States, "People" or some government agency, in which case use the more distinctive defendant's name.

b. Statutes (*Bluebook* B6.2(b); *ALWD* Rule 14.6)

Once you have given a full citation to a statute, you may later use any short form that clearly identifies the statute.

> **First reference:**   Ohio Rev. Code Ann. § 101 (West 1988).
> **Later reference:**   Ohio Rev. Code Ann. § 101.

c. Constitutions (*Bluebook* B7; *ALWD* Rule 13.4)

Do not use any short form other than *id.* for constitutions.

d. Books and Periodical Materials (*Bluebook* B8.2 and B9.2; *ALWD* Rule 22.2)

Use *id.* or *supra* to refer to these materials after you have given a full citation to them.

7. Use of Id., Supra, Infra, *and* Hereinafter

a. *Id.* (*Bluebook* Rule 4.1; *ALWD* Rule 11.3)

(1) Introduction

Id. is an abbreviation for *ibidem*, a Latin word meaning "in the same place." You may recall using *ibid.* or *id.* in high school or college term papers to avoid having to repeat information in a footnote and to signal the reader that your material originated from the same source as that indicated immediately before.

Id. functions the same way in legal writing. A short court document or legal memorandum may rely almost exclusively on one case, which you discuss over the course of several pages. To avoid having to repeat and retype the citation each time you make an assertion, you can elect to use the signal *id.* to refer the reader to the immediately preceding authority. Note that while the signal *ibid.* is acceptable in some writings, it is not acceptable in legal writing. Only *id.* may be used.

Id. may be used for any legal authority. That is, *id.* may be used to direct a reader to a preceding case, statute, treatise, law review article, or other legal authority. *Id.* will be capitalized if it "stands alone" or begins a sentence or it will be introduced with a lower case letter if it is part of a citation clause or sentence. If underscoring, underscore the period in *id.* If italicizing, italicize the period in *id.*

If you have cited a case or some other authority and you then wish to direct the reader to that immediately preceding citation, use *id.*

Example

In order to prove a violation of the statute, the government must demonstrate only that the defendant carried a dangerous weapon, and intended to carry a weapon. *Monroe v. United States*, 598 A.2d 430, 439 (D.C. 1991). There is no requirement that a defendant evidence a specific intent to use the weapon for a wrongful purpose. *Id.*

The use of the signal *id.* in the example indicates to the reader that *Monroe v. United States* is the source of the assertion that there is no requirement that the government prove that a defendant had a specific intent to use a weapon for an unlawful purpose. The reader is directed to page 439 of *Monroe*.

(2) "Id. *Plus*"

Use *id.* alone if you wish to direct the reader to the exact source and page/section/paragraph as the preceding citation. If, however, you wish to direct the reader to the preceding source, but to a different page/section/ paragraph within that source, use "*id.* plus" the change:

Example

"A landlord is required to provide written notice to a tenant before instituting an action to evict the tenant." *Jasper v. Schick*, 92 P.2d 106, 109 (Wash. 1984). "This notice must be hand-delivered to a tenant at least three days before the action is commenced." *Id.* at 114.

The reader has been directed to *Jasper v. Schick* but to a different page within that source.

Examples

First reference to a case: *Daly v. Chu*, 661 F.2d 918, 920 (10th Cir. 1986).
Next reference: *Id.* or *Id.* at 921.
First reference to a statute: 42 U.S.C. § 1604 (1986).
Next reference: *Id.* or *Id.* § 1606.
First reference to a treatise: 1 J. Thomas McCarthy, *McCarthy on Trademarks and Unfair Competition* § 18:18 (4th ed. 1997).
Next reference: *Id.* or *Id.* § 18:22.
First reference to a law review article: Carolyn L. Gray, *Tariff Restrictions*, 40 Mo. L. Rev. 161, 166 (1982).
Next reference: *Id.* or *Id.* at 169.

Note that under *Bluebook* rules when you are directing a reader to a different page you use "*Id.* at ___." When, however, you direct a reader to a different section or paragraph, you simply use "*Id.* § ___" or "*Id.* ¶ ___." *The Bluebook* expressly states that the word "at" is not used before a section or paragraph symbol. (Rule 3.3).

Correct:	*Id.* § 314.
	Id. ¶ 14.120.
Incorrect:	*Id.* at § 314.
	Id. at ¶ 14.120.

The *ALWD* approach is different and allows the use of the word "at" before a section symbol, as in *Id.* at § 314 (*ALWD* R. 14.6).

(3) Parallel Citations

Remember that local rules may require parallel citations. This requirement makes the use of *id.* somewhat more complicated because you must use the following form:

First cite	*Garde v. Whetsell*, 209 Ariz. 106, 108, 309 P.2d 309, 311 (1986).
***Id.* reference**	*Id.* at 110, 309 P.2d at 313.

Note that only the official citation is replaced with *id.* The regional reporter citation is repeated. The *ALWD* approach is similar (*ALWD* R. 12.21(f)).

(4)   The Use of "Id." in Footnotes

The signal *id.* may be used to refer to an immediately preceding authority within the same footnote or to an immediately preceding footnote when that preceding footnote contains only one authority. If the preceding footnote or reference contains more than one source, later use of *id.* does not tell the reader which of the preceding sources is being referenced, and thus it may not be used (*Bluebook* B5.2 and R. 4.1; *ALWD* R. 11.3(b)).

b.   *Supra (Bluebook* B8.2, 9.2, and Rule 4.2; *ALWD* Rule 11.4)

(1)   Introduction

Supra means "above" and informs a reader to look at preceding authorities (although not *immediately* preceding sources, for which you should use *id.*) for the information desired. For example, if you are searching an index for entries related to tenants, you may find the following:

Tenant, see Landlord, *supra.*

This is an instruction that the information you need is arranged and presented under the heading "Landlord," which appears "above" or earlier in the volume, rather than being arranged under the heading "Tenant."

Often in a legal writing you may refer to one authority, for example, a treatise, then refer to various other authorities and then wish to refer to the treatise again without repeating the entire citation. In this situation you cannot use *id.* because there are citations that intervene between your first reference to the treatise and your current reference to it. In this instance, use *supra*, which informs the reader that you have given the citation previously in your project, although it was not given immediately preceding.

The Bluebook and *ALWD* are both quite clear that you may not use *supra* when referring to most primary authorities (cases, constitutions, statutes, most legislative materials, or regulations) "except in extraordinary circumstances," such as when the name of the case or other authority is very long (*Bluebook* Rule 4.2). If you have referred to a case, constitution, or statute and then discussed other authorities and then wish to refer again to the case, constitution, or statute, you may not use *supra.* You must use a "short form" citation, discussed previously in Section G.6, *supra.*

This prohibition against using *supra* to refer to previously cited cases is violated by some practicing attorneys and paralegals. Before embarking on such a violation, determine what the common practice is in your firm or agency. Some firms, usually the larger ones, will rigidly adhere to the citation manuals and would view your use of *supra* to refer to a preceding case as an unforgivable gaffe, while other firms would view such a use of *supra* as a practical and effective citation form.

Supra does not "stand alone" like *id.* It must appear with other identification, usually the last name of an author, or, if there is no author, the
title of a work.

Examples

First cite:	Carolyn L. Gray, *Tariff Restrictions*, 40 Mo. L. Rev. 161, 164 (1982).
Intervening cite:	*Powell v. Silvers*, 661 F.2d 918 (10th Cir. 1986).
Supra cite:	Gray, *supra*.

To indicate a variation, use "*supra* plus" the variation, such as *Gray,
supra*, at 166. If you are underscoring, underscore the word *supra* but not
any punctuation following it.

The examples given in *The Bluebook* for practitioners show a comma
after *supra* when the "*supra* plus" form is used to refer a reader to a book or
article such as Gray, *supra*, at 166 (B8.2).

**Bluebook Examples of Short Forms
in a Brief or Court Document**

Page 1.	*Taylor v. Ellis*, 501 U.S. 621, 626 (1994).
Page 2.	*Id.*
Page 3.	*Id.* at 629.
Page 4.	6 Judith N. Hunter, *Intellectual Property* § 104 (3d ed. 1991).
Page 5.	*Id.*
Page 6.	*Id.* § 107.
Page 7.	a. *Taylor*, 501 U.S. at 630 *or*
	b. 501 U.S. at 630 *or*
	c. In *Taylor*, the Court also held . . . .
Page 8.	Hunter, *supra* or Hunter, *supra*, § 108.

*(2) Internal Cross-References (*Bluebook *Rule 3.5;* ALWD *Rule 10)*

Bluebook. It is possible that you may have cited a book or treatise very
early in your project and then wish to refer to it many pages later. If your
only direction to the reader is "Gray, *supra*," the reader may have to thumb
through several pages to find the original citation. As a courtesy to the
reader you may wish to include a reference to the specific page in your
project on which the original citation appeared. Use "p." or "pp." to direct
your reader to the first page in your project on which the full citation
originally appeared.

Examples

Gray, *supra* p. 3

Gray, *supra* p.3, at 168. (This signal directs the reader to page
168 of the article written by Carolyn L. Gray and informs the reader

that the full citation appears on page 3 of your project.) Follow *supra* with a comma when you direct a reader to the page or section of the previously cited legal authority. No comma is used after *supra* when you refer a reader to a previous page or section within your project.

ALWD. ALWD has a slightly different approach to internal cross-references. *ALWD* generally supports referring readers to previous footnotes through the use of the abbreviation "n." as in Ruiz, *supra* n. 4, at 64, meaning that you are being sent to page 64 of a previous book or article written by Ruiz and discussed earlier in your paper at footnote 3. *The Bluebook* uses the word "note" rather than the abbreviation "n." and would display the example as Ruiz, *supra* note 4, at 64.

c. *Infra*

Infra is a Latin word meaning "below" or "beneath." It is used to direct a reader to material that will appear later in a project. For example, if you were directed to review some chapter appearing after this one, the signal would be "Chapter 10, *infra.*" *Infra* is the direct opposite signal of *supra* and you should follow the guidelines discussed previously for *supra* in using *infra*. Note that neither *supra* nor *infra* may be used to refer to the primary authorities of cases, constitutions, statutes, most legislative materials, or regulations.

As you can imagine, *infra* is not used very often in documents or memoranda prepared by practitioners. It makes little sense to state a legal principle and then give the reader the following citation: Gray, *infra*, meaning that you will be giving the full cite to the article by Carolyn L. Gray later in the project. It is more likely that your use of *infra* will relate to directing a reader to a later section in your document. In this case, use the following form: *See infra* Section V.

d. Use of "Hereinafter" (*Bluebook* Rule 4.2 (b); *ALWD* Rule 11.4(d))

If an authority would be difficult to identify repeatedly due to an extremely long name or title, you may identify it in full the first time you cite it and then inform the reader that thereafter you will be referring to it by a shorter name or form.

Earlier editions of *The Bluebook* required that writers identify a session number for a Congress when citing to bills, hearings, committee reports, and other documents. Because astute readers know that the first session of a Congress (1st Sess.) always occurs in odd-numbered years and the second session (2d Sess.) always occurs in even-numbered years, *The Bluebook* no longer requires a reference to a congressional session for any materials published after the 60th Congress in 1907.

Bluebook Examples

First citation: *Proposed Amendments to the Federal Fair Franchising Practices Act of 1992: Hearings on H.R. 5961 Before*

the House Comm. on Energy and Commerce, 102d Cong. 41 (1992)
[hereinafter *Franchising Hearings*]
    Later citations: *Franchising Hearings, supra.*

The *ALWD* approach is similar, but it requires the exact date in the parenthetical, so that in the above example, the parenthetical would appear as follows: (Jan. 14, 1992).

8. *Capitalization in Court Documents and Other Legal Memoranda*

Bluebook Rule 8 and Bluepages 10.6 require that in headings and titles of documents submitted to courts you should capitalize the initial word, the word following a colon, if any, and all other words except articles (a, an, the), conjunctions of four or fewer letters (or, but, and), and prepositions of four or fewer letters (of, up, to). *ALWD* Rule 3.0 is similar, except that *ALWD* does not require capitalization of any preposition, regardless of its length. Additionally, capitalize the following:

- Act — when you are referring to a specific act of a legislature, as in "the Lanham Act."
- Circuit — when you use the word with a circuit name or number, as in "the Eighth Circuit."
- Court — when you name any court in full, as in "the California Supreme Court"
   - —whenever you refer to the United States Supreme Court.
   - —in a court document when referring to the court that is receiving the document, as in "this Court is respectfully urged to grant Plaintiff's motion."
- Party designations — when referring to the parties in a matter that is the subject of the court document, as in "Defendant's argument to this Court misstates the law."
- Judge, Justice — when referring to a specific judge or justice, as in "Justice Smith" or any reference to any of the justices of the United States Supreme Court, as in, "The Justices were unanimous in their decision."
- State — when it is part of the full title of the state, such as "State of Florida"; when the wording it modifies is capitalized, as in "the State Attorney General"; or when referring to a state as a litigant, such as "the State argues for conviction."

9. *Electronic Sources, Databases, and the Internet (*Bluebook *Rule 18;* ALWD *Rules 38-42)*

The Bluebook (R. 18) announces three general principles for citing to electronic media and other nonprint resources, such as LEXIS, Westlaw, and the Internet.

First, because sources in these media often lack the permanence and reliability of traditional printed material, *The Bluebook* requires the use and citation of traditional printed sources, unless (1) the information cited is not available in a traditional printed source; or (2) a copy of the source cannot be found because it is so obscure that it is "practically unavailable." Only in these two narrow instances should citation be made to an electronic source alone.

Second, if a printed source can be located, a parallel citation to an electronic source as related authority may be provided if it will significantly improve access to the relevant information and if the content of the electronic source is identical to that of the printed source. In this case, cite first to the printed source and then give the electronic source, introduced with the phrase *"available at."*

Third, if a source does not exist in conventional print format or on LEXIS or Westlaw, cite solely to the Internet, giving the Internet URL at the end of the citation. Use other *Bluebook* rules for guidance, so that articles on the Internet will be cited similarly to periodical articles, dictionary definitions found on the Internet will be cited similarly to *Black's Law Dictionary*, and so forth.

The *ALWD* approach is similar to that of *The Bluebook*: If a source is available in both print and electronic formats, cite only to the print source if it is readily available to most readers. *ALWD* provides that if it is necessary to cite to the Internet, give the case name and then insert the URL and a parenthetical with the court abbreviation and exact date, as follows: *Kunkle v. Texas*, http://supremecourtus.gov/orders/courtorders/111804/pzr.pdf (U.S. Nov. 18, 2004).

Practice Tip

What Does "Available" Mean?

Neither The Bluebook nor *ALWD* **allow you to cite to electronic sources (such as LEXIS, Westlaw, and the Internet) unless material is not "available" in traditional print sources. What does "available" mean? Does it mean available to the legal community in general? Does it mean available in your office? No one knows.** *ALWD* **Rule 38.1 provides some guidance in stating that you should cite to the print source if it is "readily available to most readers."**

Most cases are available in print form within days or weeks. Thus, it would seem that the window of opportunity for citing to electronic sources is quite narrow: Cite to an electronic source only during the period of time it takes for the print source to "hit the shelves," which is typically quite short.

a. Statutes and Constitutions (*Bluebook* Rule 18.1.2; *ALWD* Rule 14.5)

Statutes and constitutions must be cited first to a traditional source and then to an electronic database (such as LEXIS or Westlaw). If the information is not available in a traditional source or electronic database, one may cite to the Internet.

Bluebook **Example**

> Cal. Prob. Code § 503 (Deering, LEXIS through 1998 Sess.)

ALWD **Example**

> 11 U.S.C. § 105 (available at http://caselaw.lp.findlaw.com/scripts/ts_search)

b. Books, Journals, and Magazines (*Bluebook* Rules 18.1.4 and 18.2.3; *ALWD* Rule 23.1(i))

As always, cite books, journals, and magazines first to a traditional source and only to the Internet when the information is not available in a traditional format or electronic database. Very few books are available in their entirety on the Internet, but there are now a variety of journals and articles that are published exclusively online and are not available in print form.

Bluebook **Example**

> **Article available only on the Internet:** Vicki L. Gregory, *UCITA: What Does It Mean for Libraries?*, 25 Online 1, ¶ 3 (2001), http://www.infotoday.com/online/OL2001/gregory1_01.html.

According to *ALWD* Rule 23.1(i), use the following format for an article appearing solely on the Internet: Vicki L. Gregory, *UCITA: What Does It Mean for Libraries?*, 25 Online 1, ¶ 3 (Jan. 2001), http://www.infotoday.com/onlie/OL2001/gregory1_01.html.

At this time, no one is entirely certain what direction legal citation form will take. In general, practitioners are in favor of the speed and lower costs associated with locating and citing cases to electronic sources such as the Internet, while many judges prefer the traditional method of citation. The ABA Standing Committee on Technology and Information Services, the American Association of Law Libraries, and the Judicial Conference's Committee on Automation and Technology continue to meet and discuss citation form in the digital age. As of now, however, cases are relatively easy to locate on the Internet but hard to cite to in legal documents.

See Figure 8-3 for a chart showing the more significant differences between *ALWD* and *The Bluebook*.

H. Tips for Effective Cite-Checking

Whenever you are presented with a cite-checking assignment, there are several practical tips you should consider to ensure you perform your task accurately and efficiently.

(i)   Ask the individual who assigned the project to you when the deadline is so you can be sure you do the cite-checking in a timely fashion. Often cite-checking is one of the last tasks performed in legal writing projects, and you may need to start working immediately on the project so it can be filed timely.

(ii)   Highlight all citations in the document as soon as it is given to you and while you are fresh, so you will readily be able to find citations and check them even after several hours have passed and your energy level is low. It is easier to locate citations when they are underscored rather than when they are italicized. Thus, highlighting italicized citations will help you find these citations when your energy levels are flagging.

(iii) If the document is being filed with a court, you must obtain a copy of the court rules so you can determine whether the court requires a specific citation form. Some courts insist that documents follow non-standard citation form. For example, some courts in California require that papers submitted show citations in the following format, even though it is unsupported by *The Bluebook* or any other guideline: *Atwell v. Jay* (1985) 142 Cal. 2d 109. If court rules dictate a specific format, you must adhere to that format. To obtain a copy of the rules of the court, call the court clerk and inquire. Alternatively, most states and courts publish their court rules on the Internet. For rules for the United States Supreme Court, access http://www.supremecourtus.gov. For lower federal courts, access http://megalaw.com. For state court Web sites, Table T.1 of *The Bluebook* provides a reference to each state's judicial Web site. *Bluebook* Table BT.2 references some helpful local rules and several jurisdiction-specific manuals that provide guidance on local citation practices. Appendix 2 of *ALWD* contains local citation rules. If no court rules exist with regard to citation form, use *Bluebook* form unless directed otherwise.

(iv)   You will quickly learn that some writers are more exacting than others. It is possible that the document you are cite-checking contains complete citations and you need only compare each cite against *The Bluebook* to ensure compliance with *Bluebook* rules. It is equally possible that the document you are given has several omissions and you need to go to the law library or log on to LEXIS or Westlaw to obtain dates of decisions, pages of quotes, and so forth. Therefore, as you

Figure 8-3
Differences in *ALWD* and *Bluebook* Citation Formats

Topic	*ALWD Format*	Bluebook *Format*
Typeface	Ordinary roman type is always used. *ALWD* eliminates use of large and small capital letters.	Practitioners use ordinary roman type. Materials in law reviews appear in large and small capitals.
Capitalization in Headings	Do not capitalize prepositions or conjunctions.	Capitalize prepositions and conjunctions of more than four letters.
Parallel Citations for United States Supreme Court Cases	*ALWD* permits parallel citations for United States Supreme Court cases.	*The Bluebook* does not permit parallel citations for United States Supreme Court cases.
Case Names	• Words in case names are only abbreviated if the citation appears as a stand alone and not as part of a textual sentence. • If the United States is a party, cite as "U.S."	• Words in case names are only abbreviated if the citation appears as a stand alone and not as part of a textual sentence. • If the United States is a party, cite as "United States."
Treatises and Dictionaries	Publisher is included in parenthetical with date.	Publisher is not included in parenthetical with date.
A.L.R. Annotations	The word "Annotation" is omitted from the citation.	The word "Annotation" is given after the author's name.

Miscellaneous

- When giving pinpoints, one may retain all digits (example: 1014-1019).
- One must use the word "at" before any pinpoint, even a section sign or paragraph symbol (example: *Id.* at § 14).
- There are many differences in abbreviations used in *ALWD* and *The Bluebook* (for example, *ALWD* abbreviates "Publishing" as "Publg." while *The Bluebook* abbreviates it as "Publ'g" (with no period following)).
- *ALWD* includes local citation rules and forms.

- *ALWD* uses "LEXIS" in the parenthetical with the date for federal statute citations in U.S.C.S.

- When giving pinpoints, drop repetitive digits (example: 1014-1019).
- The word "at" cannot be used before a section sign or paragraph symbol (example: *Id.* at § 14).
- There are many differences in abbreviations used in *ALWD* and *The Bluebook* (for example, *ALWD* abbreviates "Publishing" as "Publg," while *The Bluebook* abbreviates it as "Publ'g" (with no period following)).
- *The Bluebook* does not include local citation rules and forms, although Bluepages Table BT.2 references some local rules.
- *The Bluebook* uses "LexisNexis" in the parenthetical with the date for federal statute citations in U.S.C.S.

review the document, use different colored pens, sticky flags, or different symbols to indicate which cites have been checked and are accurate, which need further information supplied, and those for which you have questions. Determine if the author of the document has any preferences as to format, such as preferring underscoring of case names and signals rather than italicizing. Similarly, determine if the author has any special conventions as to format you should follow in lieu of *Bluebook* format. In the absence of instruction, assume *Bluebook* rules govern.

(v)   When you find an error, make the correction by interlineating or crossing out the error and inserting the correct information. You may wish to note in the margin which *Bluebook* rule governs your correction as authors can be notoriously defensive about recognizing errors, and you should be ready to support and defend your correction. Because you may not be preparing the final version of the document, write legibly so that support staff can correctly insert your edits.

(vi)   Because the document may be evolving as you work on it, and other attorneys and paralegals may be continuing to edit the document, make sure each version is clearly marked with the date and the time it is printed. This will help you ensure you are working on a current version, not one superseded by a later version.

(vii)   If the document contains quotations, check each one for accuracy. Quotations must be faithfully reproduced. If alterations and omissions are made, make sure those are indicated by brackets and ellipses. You must also verify that the citation includes the pinpoint page of a quote.

(viii) Pay attention to short form citations, and verify that the author's use of short forms, *id.*, and *supra* are correct. Because the document may be subject to revising and editing at the eleventh hour, you must always check the accuracy of signals in the final version of the document.

(ix)   Make sure that you look beyond the body of the document and also check the cites in any appendices, footnotes, table of contents, or index of authorities.

(x)   Be consistent. If you underscore case names, underscore book titles and signals such as *id.* and *supra*. If you italicize case names, italicize book titles and signals.

(xi)   Allow LEXIS and Westlaw to help you locate pinpoints, verify the spellings of case names, and check the accuracy of quotations. Remember, however, that only you can determine when to use a short form, when you may abbreviate words in a case name, and when to use a citation signal.

(xii) After the document is resubmitted for revision and correction, review to ensure that your corrections were incorporated.

(xiii) Validate all primary authorities listed in the document, either manually or online (see Chapter 9).

Practice Tip

What To Do if Your Corrections Are Overruled

In many instances, attorneys are thrilled that you are detailed enough to catch errors in their citation form. In other instances, they may become defensive. In still other instances, they may simply say, "I don't care what *The Bluebook* (or *ALWD*) requires, I want to cite the case this way."

What should you do if you know your cite checking is correct but the attorney overrules you? Give in. The author of a document always has the right to control authorship. You have done what you were asked to do, namely, correct citation errors, and you were overruled. If you find that certain attorneys are routinely submitting briefs with numerous citation errors, and you are concerned that the firm's reputation for accuracy may be impaired, raise the issue with your paralegal coordinator or mentor and ask for help.

It is possible that the author might wish you to do more than simply correct errors in citation format and might ask that you confirm the accuracy of the author's conclusions. Thus, if the author has cited *Jones v. Smith*, 421 A.2d 91 (Pa. 1986), for the proposition that a landlord is required to provide notice to a tenant before commencing an action to evict the tenant, you will have to review this case to verify that it does in fact support the author's conclusion. Similarly, checking citation signals such as *see, cf.*, and *accord* requires that you read the cited source to confirm the author has used the correct signal. This extensive type of cite-checking is less common than the usual cite-checking assignment, which typically requires you only to correct errors in citation form and then to Shepardize or KeyCite. Unless you are directed otherwise you should assume that if someone asks you to cite-check a document you are expected only to verify that the citations are in correct form and to Shepardize.

I. Quick Reference for Citations (*Bluebook* and *ALWD* Form)

1. *Cases*

Following are examples of the most commonly cited authorities showing both *Bluebook* and *ALWD* form. If only one example is given, the example complies with both *Bluebook* and *ALWD* rules.

(i) State Cases (*Bluebook* and *ALWD*)

Sidley v. Steinman, 201 N.C. 118, 429 S.E.2d 16 (1984) [if local rules require parallel citations].
Sidley v. Steinman, 429 S.E.2d 16 (N.C. 1984) [in all other instances].

(ii) Federal Cases

United States Supreme Court:

LaPointe v. Sullivan, 98 U.S. 396 (1984). [Note that *ALWD* permits parallel citations.]

United States Courts of Appeals:

Lawrence v. Mather, 691 F.2d 114 (8th Cir. 1984).

United States District Court:

Blakely v. Yost, 742 F. Supp. 908 (D.R.I. 1986).

2. *Statutes*

(i) State

Ga. Code Ann. § 10-04.01 (1998).

N.Y. Gen. Bus. Law § 308 (McKinney 1988).

(ii) Federal:

17 U.S.C. § 101 (2000).

17 U.S.C.A. § 101 (West 1996).

17 U.S.C.S. § 101 (LEXIS 2000). [*ALWD* form]

17 U.S.C.S. § 101 (LexisNexis 2000). [*Bluebook* form]

3. *Constitutions*

   ()   **State:**   N.M. Const. art. III.
   (i)   **United States:**   U.S. Const. amend. X.

4. *Encyclopedias*

   68 C.J.S. *Trusts* § 302 (1988).
   54 Am. Jur. 2d *Trusts* § 114 (1989).

5. *Law Review Articles*

   Allan A. Sanders, *The Juvenile's Right to Counsel*, 46 Colum. L. Rev. 891 (1988).

6. *Texts and Treatises*

   Bluebook: Joy N. Hildebrand, *Securities Review* § 421 (2d ed. 1991).
   ALWD: Joy N. Hildebrand, *Securities Review* § 421 (2d ed., West 1991).

7. *Restatements*

   Bluebook: Restatement (Second) of Contracts § 112 (1992).
   ALWD: *Restatement (Second) of Contracts* § 112 (1992).

8. *Dictionaries*

   Bluebook: *Black's Law Dictionary* 1172 (8th ed. 2004).
   ALWD: *Black's Law Dictionary* 1172 (Bryan A. Garner ed., 8th ed., West 2004).

9. *Attorneys General Opinions*

Bluebook: **State:**   65 Op. Cal. Att'y Gen. 104 (1995).
                     United States: 49 Op. Att'y Gen. 918 (1988).
ALWD: **State:**   65 Cal. Atty. Gen. Op. 104 (1995).
                     United States: 49 Op. Atty. Gen. 918 (1988).

10.   *Summary of Special Citation Issues*

() **Quotations**: Always give the page of a quotation. As a courtesy to readers, always include a pinpoint cite even for material paraphrased. Quotations of fewer than 49 words should appear in text with quotation marks. Place periods and commas inside quotation marks. Quotations of 50 words or more should appear indented or in "block" form without quotation marks. Retain the original paragraph structure of a block quotation. Remember that *ALWD* also allows indenting of a block quote if the quotation exceeds four lines of typed text.

(i) **Short forms**: Once you have cited a case in full you may use a short form.

First cite: *Parsons v. Geneva*, 92 U.S. 104, 109 (1982).
Short forms: *Parsons*, 92 U.S. at 111.
                         92 U.S. at 111.
                         Id. or *Id.* at 114.
                         In *Parsons*, . . .

(iii) ***Id.***:   Use *id.* or "*id.* plus" to refer a reader to the immediately preceding cite.

(iv) ***Supra***:   Use *supra* to refer the reader to a previous cite that is not the immediately preceding cite. *Supra* may not be used to refer to cases, constitutions, statutes, most legislative materials, or regulations. *Supra* must appear with the name of an author or title of a work.

11.   *Internet Citation Form*

Bluebook:

Article available solely on the Internet: Wendi L. Weinstein, *The European Design Patent Has Arrived!*, 3 Outs & Ins 3 (2004), http://www.burnsdoane.com/pubs/weinstein/cfm.

ALWD:

Article available solely on the Internet: Wendy L. Weinstein, *The European Design Patent Has Arrived!*, 3 Outs & Ins 3 (accessed Nov. 21, 2004), http://www.burnsdoane.com/pubs/weinstein/cfm.

CyberSites

http://www.legalbluebook.com	This Web site of *The Bluebook* provides an overview of changes to the 18th edition of *The Bluebook*, asks for comments and corrections, allows ordering of *The Bluebook*, and provides introductory material about *The Bluebook*.
http://www.alwd.org	The Web site of the Association of Legal Writing Directors offers information about *ALWD*, charts and appendices, updates to *ALWD*, information about citing to tax materials, and a list of schools that have adopted *ALWD* as their citation manual.
http://www.uchastings.edu/?pid=2527	Hastings College of Law provides a chart showing the differences between *ALWD* and *Bluebook* rules.
http://lexisnexis.com/icw	LEXIS offers an "interactive citation workstation" allowing users to quiz themselves on both *ALWD* and *Bluebook* citation formats.
http://www.abanet.org/tech/ltrc/research/citation/home.html	The American Bar Association Web site has information devoted to neutral, public domain, or universal citation form and provides the ABA resolution regarding this issue as well as lists of states that have adopted public domain citation formats and those considering adoption.
http://www.law.cornell.edu/citation	Educator Peter W. Martin of Cornell Law School offers a complete citation primer based on the 17th edition of *The Bluebook*. *Bluebook* rules are explained and numerous examples are provided.
http://www.ualr.edu/~cmbarger/shortfrm.htm	This Web site provides basic information about constructing and using short form citations.
http://www.citeit.com	The Web site of CiteIt! provides a free tutorial showing how its citation formatting system works.

Citation Software Programs

At this time, there is no absolutely reliable way to put your citations in proper *Bluebook* or *ALWD* form other than for you to do the task the old-fashioned way: manually. Nevertheless, LEXIS offers a service called CiteRite II, which will put your citations in proper *Bluebook* or California citation format. While it is unclear whether CiteRite II can understand all of the idiosyncracies of citation form (such as when you can abbreviate the word "Surety" in a case name and when you cannot), it is clear that CiteRite II will notify you of improper underlining in a cite, missing parallel cites, or improper punctuation (such as the failure to put a period after the word "Supp.").

(continued)

CyberSites   *(Continued)* ██████████████████

Additionally, computer-assisted legal research offers some quick approaches to ensure that at least the name and numbers in a case cite have been reproduced accurately.

Use LEXIS's CheckCite to verify the accuracy of the name of a case and the volume and page numbers you have indicated. You will be informed whether *Shepard's* agrees with you or whether it reports different volume numbering or pagination for a case. Westlaw's KeyCite citation research service also provides citation verification information such as correct case name and parallel citations.

A company in Massachusetts, Sidebar Software, has created a software program called CiteIt!, which purportedly formats all citations to *Bluebook* rules or *ALWD* rules. When you wish to enter a citation into your document, you choose a citation source and then select the appropriate citation from ones displayed. Even such a system, however, presupposes some familiarity with *The Bluebook* or ALWD; otherwise, how would one be able to select the "correct" citation when several are given? Law firms can purchase separate individual licenses, which are approximately $180 each. Although there is some special pricing, a law firm with 100 legal professionals could expect to pay approximately $18,000 for licenses, all of which may be outdated with the next edition of *The Bluebook*. Contact http://www.citeit.com for additional information.

Writing Strategies

When citing authorities in a brief, avoid "string citing" (citing more than one authority to support a contention). Too many citations clutter your project and disrupt the flow of your narrative. Moreover, string cites must be in a specific order according to *The Bluebook* and *ALWD*, making string citing even more difficult.

Similarly, avoid footnotes in writing projects. Upon encountering footnotes, most readers will either stop reading the narrative while they jump to the footnote or will skip over the footnote entirely. Neither result is desired; the first causes a disruption of your argument, while the second renders your research ineffective. Some experts contend that if something is not significant enough to be included in the main body of a text, it should be omitted, and thus there is never a need for footnotes.

To some extent, the overuse of quotations may also result in the reader skipping over them. Use quotations sparingly, in those situations in which what the court has said is so authoritative and persuasive that paraphrasing the statement would dilute its impact. Judicious use of quotations adds drama and variety to your project. Overuse of quotations may cause the reader to wonder if you have taken the easy way out by simply reproducing another's words rather than analyzing those words.

Assignment for Chapter 8

CITATION FORM

There is at least one thing wrong with each fictitious citation below. Correct the citations using the current edition of *The Bluebook* or *ALWD*. You may need to supply missing information such as dates. Punctuation is not needed after the citations. Assume you are preparing a memorandum in your office and unless otherwise indicated, assume that the citations appear in textual sentences rather than as "stand alone" citations. There is no need to include "pinpoints," unless otherwise directed.

1. Vincent Amato, Jr. v. Randall F. Cochran, a 1990 Rhode Island Supreme Court case found in volume 601 at page 224 of the relevant reporter.

2. Anderson General Construction Company v. Candy Benner, a Michigan Supreme Court case decided in 2001, located in volume 664 at page 14.

3. Michael J. Finnegan versus Teresa Finnegan, a 1994 case from the Georgia Court of Appeals, located in volume 607 of the relevant reporter, page 903, with quoted material on pages 914 to 916.

4. Douglas Consolidated Corporation vs. Flynn Brothers, 502 United States Reports 16, 329 Lawyers' Edition (Second Series) page 789, 319 Supreme Court Reporter page 906.

5. Federal Communications Commission v. Anne Griffin, Richard Garcia, and Diana Francois, 145 Federal Reporter (Third Series) 886.

6. USA v. Mark Gage, Trustee, 114 Federal Supplement (Second Series) 423, decided in the District Court for the District of Columbia.

7. Gunther Association v. Andrea Chu, a 2003 Supreme Court case.

8. Title 42, United States Code, Sections 2244 through 2248.

9. Title 15, U.S.C.A. Section 109.

10. Title 35 U.S.C.S. Section 1561(a).

11. Section 15-455 of the Idaho Code.

12. Section 22-013 of Maryland's Health Occupations Code.

13. Fourth Amendment to the United States Constitution.

14. Section 3-211 of Restatement (Second Series) of Contracts.

15. An article by Kelly Gray and Richard P. King entitled "Calculating Loss of Consortium," published in volume 42 of the South Carolina Law Review, at page 1054, with a quotation from pages 1062 through 1068.

16. Volume 6, Section 14:10 of the second edition of the treatise authored by Kevin Bidwell entitled "A Practitioner's Guide to Family Law."

17. Assume the following case is cited in a brief to a Massachusetts state court that requires parallel citations: Reynolds v. Patty

Shaw, 309 Massachusetts Appeals Court 109. Give the correct citation.

18. Assume the following citation appears as a "stand alone" citation: the 2004 United States Court of Appeals case from the Third Circuit entitled Reynolds Restaurant Division Inc. v. Northern Maintenance Management Company. Give the correct citation.

19. The definition of "negligence" appearing on page 450 of the current edition of *Black's Law Dictionary*.

There are numerous errors in the fictitious citations in the following brief memorandum. Correct citation errors using the current edition of *The Bluebook* or *ALWD*. You may need to supply missing information.

MEMORANDUM

The general rule is that shareholders of a corporation receive dividends when and if declared by the board of directors acting in its discretion. Allen Association v. Taylor Corporation, 523 U.S. 16 (1998). Thus, the determination to distribute dividends is a discretionary decision subject to the business judgment of the directors. Id., on 23. The directors may properly decide that dividends should not be paid so that the corporation can build up a "war chest" to acquire another corporation, for purposes of growth and expansion, or for the purpose of investing its profits. Sanderson v. Bailey Brothers Corp., 29 F. 3d 250, 251-254 (2nd Cir. 2001) affirmed at 530 U.S. 62 (2001). The mere fact that the corporation has sufficient funds from which to pay a dividend does not entitle the shareholders to a dividend. ID.

The articles of incorporation may provide for a fixed dividend to one class or series of shares. Calif. Corporations Code § 8023. In such a case, the directors will be required to declare the agreed-upon dividend when legally available funds exist. Catherine Leonard, *Corporate Investment*, § 36-41 (third edition 1999). If the dividends are cumulative, any arrearages must be paid for prior years in which the corporation did not pay dividends, before any dividends can be paid to other (usually common) shareholders. California Corporations Code § 8023.

Courts are reluctant to interfere with the management of corporations, and, therefore, unless the shareholders can clearly prove bad faith or an abuse of discretion by the directors, the directors cannot be compelled to pay dividends. Leonard, id. This is yet another example of the business judgment rule, which protects directors who make business decisions in good faith. Id. As a practical matter, however, directors who fail to declare dividends when profits permit may well find themselves out of a job.

State Your Answer

1. Review the Universal Citation Guide Version 2.1 at www.aallnet.org/committee/citationucg/index.html. Review paragraph 29. In what way do the AALL Proposal and the ABA model for universal citation forms differ?

2. Access the ABA site relating to universal citation form at www.abanet.org/tech/ltrc/research/citation/home.html and review ABA Citation History.
   a. When was the first draft report on citation reform submitted?
   b. What did this report recommend?

3. Access the ABA site relating to universal citation form and review the information related to Wisconsin. What action has Wisconsin taken with regard to universal citation form?

4. Access the site of the Association of Legal Writing Directors at www.alwd.org. Select "ALWD Citation Manual" and review Chart 12.7.
   a. List the divisions of your state's appellate courts.
   b. Are decisions of one court binding on other intermediate courts?

Updating
and Validating
Your Research

The process of "Shepardizing" a case is fundamental to legal research and can be completed in a manner of minutes, especially when done with the aid of a computer.

Meadowbrook, LLC v. Flower, 959 P.2d 115, 120 n.11 (Utah 1998)

Chapter Overview

The task of cite-checking has two components: ensuring that the format of the citations meets *Bluebook, ALWD*, or local standards and then verifying that the primary authorities cited are still valid. This second component of updating and validating your authorities can be conducted manually, using *Shepard's Citators* (published in conventional print form and available online through LEXIS, the owner of *Shepard's* database of more than 146 million references) or using KeyCite, West's online citation service. Additionally, Loislaw, an online legal research service, offers GlobalCite, which updates the cases and authorities in Loislaw's databases (see later discussion in this chapter and in Chapter 11). Validating your authorities through the use of *Shepard's* products is called "Shepardizing."

Until recently, the only method of updating authorities was Shepardizing. In the late 1990s, however, West lost the right to use *Shepard's* database and launched its own online citation service, called KeyCite. In sum, there are now two major methods of updating and validating your research: using *Shepard's* (in print or online) or using KeyCite (offered exclusively online). In this chapter, *Shepard's* and KeyCite will be referred to as "citators" because they both provide citations to other authorities that update, validate, and comment on the sources you cite.

This chapter focuses on techniques for effective and efficient Shepardizing and KeyCiting as well as the use of these citators as research tools. Once you thoroughly understand the technique of Shepardizing or KeyCiting, you will readily see why a citator is much more than a merely mechanical way to check that primary authorities are still "good"; it is also an excellent way to expand your research and locate other references dealing with the issue you are researching.

This chapter will initially discuss Shepardizing cases and will then explain the procedure of Shepardizing statutes, constitutions, and ordinances. You will also be introduced to other citators produced by the publishers of *Shepard's* for specialized research needs. Updating authorities online is far more common than using conventional print forms of *Shepard's*. Thus, this chapter will address updating through the use of *Shepard's* online and through KeyCiting. However, a thorough grounding in the way the conventional print versions of *Shepard's* work will enhance your understanding of the techniques and value of online updating. Thus, it is discussed first.

A. Introduction to Updating and Validating

In the course of your research efforts thus far, you may have noticed that there are often several alternative paths you can follow to obtain an answer to a research issue. That is why there are so few "rules" for legal research. You may, however, recall one inflexible rule from Chapter 3: Whenever a book has a pocket part or a supplement, it must be examined. Neglecting a pocket part or supplement might cause you to rely on outdated law. For example, the pocket parts to U.S.C.A. and U.S.C.S. inform you of changes in statutes, whether those changes are amendments to a statute or a complete repeal of a statute. Moreover, the pocket part will direct you to cases interpreting a statute that are more recent than those annotated in the main volume.

Even if you rely on cases from the most recent issue of a pocket part, however, it is still possible that the case may have been overruled or reversed or somehow limited since the pocket part was published. You must therefore determine the current status of every primary authority on which you rely. To do this, you can use sets of books called *Shepard's Citations*. The technique of using *Shepard's* to check whether the authorities you wish to cite are still "good law" is called "Sheppardizing." *Shepard's Citations* are now the product of LEXIS and were first introduced more than 100 years ago. They have developed from gummed stickers solely devoted to Illinois cases to hundreds of bound volumes as well as online services devoted to cases and other legal authorities from every jurisdiction. Alternatively, you can use West's product, KeyCite, available exclusively online.

If the first inflexible rule of legal research is to check the pocket parts, the second is that you must update every primary authority you cite. Updating and validating must be done not only for briefs that you file with a court but for internal office memoranda, letters to clients, and other writings.

You cannot simply validate most of the cases in a brief, or only older cases, or gamble that the cases you refer to are still good. You must validate each and every case, statute, regulation, and constitutional provision. You should assume that your adversary will be validating the authorities you cite to ensure that your brief or argument is valid. It would not only be an acute embarrassment to rely on an outdated case and have this called to your attention by an adversary or a judge, it would be a clear breach of the duty imposed on legal professionals to represent a client's interests adequately by performing accurate legal research. According to at least one judge, "without belaboring the point, we remind the bar that, as this case so dramatically shows, cases must be Shepardized. ...." *Glassalum Eng'g Corp. v. 392208 Ontario Ltd.*, 487 So. 2d 87, 88 (Fla. Dist. Ct. App. 1986). Numerous other cases include similar statements by judges clearly indicating there is a legal duty to check the validity of the authorities one cites.

Another advantage of updating is that *Shepard's* and KeyCite can be used as additional research tools. These citators will provide you with parallel citations and references to other sources in the law library that mention or discuss your case, statute, regulation, or constitutional provision, such as law review articles, annotations, and attorneys' general opinions. While some individuals view updating solely as a means to determine whether authorities are still valid, you should remember this other function of a citator: It will serve as an excellent research finding tool by directing you to numerous authorities that discuss your case, statute, regulation, or constitutional provision.

B. Sheppardizing Cases

1. *Locating* Shepard's Citations

Assume the case you are interested in updating is *Gose v. Monroe Auto Equipment Co.*, 409 Mich. 147, 294 N.W.2d 165 (1980), and you have decided to Shepardize it using conventional print sources. Before you can begin the actual task of Shepardizing, you must gather the volumes of *Shepard's* that you need. There is a set of *Shepard's Citations* for each set of case reports. Thus, there are sets called *Shepard's Arizona Citations, Shepard's Idaho Citations, Shepard's Massachusetts Citations*, and *Shepard's Washington Citations*. Moreover, there are sets of *Shepard's* for cases reported in West's regional reporters, such as *Shepard's Atlantic Reporter Citations, Shepard's Northwestern Reporter Citations*, and *Shepard's Southern Reporter Citations*. Similarly, there are sets of *Shepard's* for federal cases such as *Shepard's United States Citations* (covering United States Supreme Court cases), and *Shepard's Federal Citations* (covering cases from the United States courts of appeal, published in the *Federal Reporter* and cases from the United States district courts, published in the *Federal Supplement*).

Most law libraries place the volumes of *Shepard's* immediately after the last volume in a set of case reports. Thus, the volumes of *Shepard's New Jersey Citations* are usually located after the final volume of the *New Jersey Reports*; the volumes of *Shepard's Pacific Reporter Citations* are usually located after the final volume of the *Pacific Reporter*; and the volumes of *Shepard's United States Citations* are usually located after the final volume of the *United States Reports*.

Some law libraries, however, maintain all of the volumes of *Shepard's* in one central location. In such a case, the volumes may comprise several stacks. Many law libraries, realizing the critical importance of Shepardizing, keep duplicate sets of *Shepard's* on reserve. If you cannot find the volumes you need, ask a law librarian for help.

Often locating the appropriate volumes of *Shepard's* is more difficult in a law school library than it would be in a law firm or other office. This is because many law students will be using *Shepard's* and they may be somewhat careless with the *Shepard's* volumes, leaving them in a study room or carrel. In a law firm, however, more care will be taken, and the volumes of *Shepard's* will seldom leave the confines of the firm's library. The volumes of *Shepard's* are typically quickly used and then returned to the shelves. They are not meant to be perused or read at a leisurely pace.

You will usually be using two or three hardbound volumes of *Shepard's* and one or two softcover advance sheets. All of the hardbound volumes of *Shepard's* are deep maroon in color. The softcover advance sheets or supplements are white (issued approximately every six weeks), bright red (issued quarterly), or gold (issued annually or semi-annually). *Shepard's* also issues blue "express" supplements for federal authorities. Eventually, the softcover supplements are accumulated into hardbound volumes, and new supplements will be issued to provide the treatment of the case you are relying on by recently decided court decisions.

To be sure that you have all of the volumes of *Shepard's* you need, look at the most recent softcover supplement. The front of each supplement displays a box or notice labeled "What Your Library Should Contain," which lists the volumes of *Shepard's* you will need to complete your task. If the supplement you are using is more than three months old (dates are provided at the top of each supplement), consult a reference librarian as there should always be a *Shepard's* volume marked with a date within the past calendar quarter. You cannot simply proceed to Shepardize assuming that it is sufficient if you have most of the volumes you need. Incomplete Shepardizing is the equivalent of not Shepardizing at all. See Figure 9-1 for a sample cover sheet from *Shepard's*.

Figure 9-1
Sample Cover Sheet from *Shepard's*

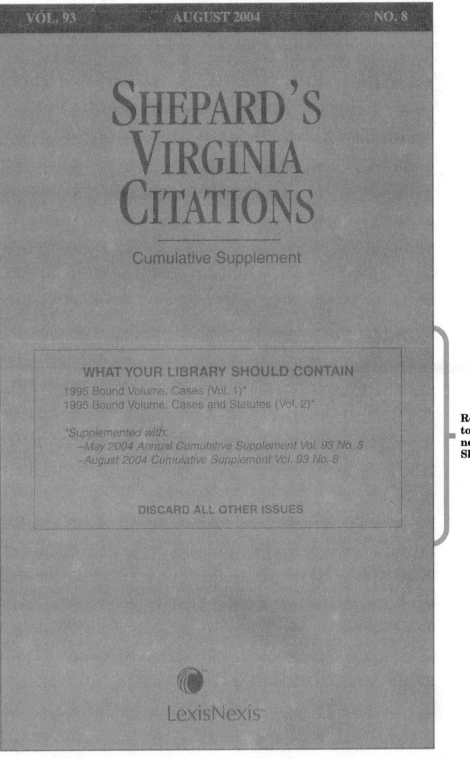

VOL. 93   AUGUST 2004   NO. 8

SHEPARD'S
VIRGINIA
CITATIONS

Cumulative Supplement

WHAT YOUR LIBRARY SHOULD CONTAIN

1995 Bound Volume, Cases (Vol. 1)*
1995 Bound Volume, Cases and Statutes (Vol. 2)*

*Supplemented with:
    —May 2004 Annual Cumulative Supplement Vol. 93 No. 5
    —August 2004 Cumulative Supplement Vol. 93 No. 8

DISCARD ALL OTHER ISSUES

Reference
to volumes
needed to
Shepardize

LexisNexis™

2. *Locating* Shepard's *References to Your Case*

Because the case you are Shepardizing is a Michigan case, you will need to locate the volumes of *Shepard's Michigan Citations*. Open the first volume of *Shepard's Michigan Citations* and scan the upper corners of each page looking for a reference to **Vol. 409**, the volume in which *Gose v. Monroe Auto Equipment Co.* is reported. This process is similar to looking at the guide words in the upper corners of each page in a dictionary or telephone directory to determine which page will contain the word or name you need.

When you have located the page or pages for **Vol. 409**, scan this page looking for the black boldfaced typed reference - **147** - because this is the page on which *Gose v. Monroe Auto Equipment Co.* begins. There are three possibilities:

(i) There may be no reference at all to - **147** -. There may be a reference to - **126** -, followed by a reference to - **217** -. Lack of a reference to your page is an indication that during the period of time covered by that issue of *Shepard's*, no case or other authority mentioned *Gose v. Monroe Auto Equipment Co.* in any manner. For instance, assume you are looking in one of *Shepard's* gold yearly supplements. If no entry for - **147** - is found, it merely means that during this one-year period, *Gose v. Monroe Auto Equipment Co.* was not discussed or referred to in any way, either favorably or unfavorably. If this occurs, close this volume of *Shepard's* and examine the next volume, once again looking for a reference to **Vol. 409** in the upper corners of each page and then scanning the page for a reference to - **147** -.

(ii) There may be citations appearing in parentheses immediately below - **147** -. These are parallel cites for *Gose v. Monroe Auto Equipment Co.* You may recall from Chapter 4 that if you have an official cite and wish to obtain an unofficial cite (or vice versa), you can consult the Table of Cases in your state digest or the *National Reporter Bluebook* (or a *State Blue and White* book) or you can Shepardize your citation. *Shepard's* will provide you with parallel citations for your case, and provides perhaps the easiest and most efficient way of locating parallel citations. You will be given a parallel citation in the first volume of *Shepard's* published after the parallel cite becomes available. To save space, the parallel cite will not be repeated in subsequent volumes or supplements.

If your case has been selected by the publishers of A.L.R. as a leading case about which an annotation has been written, this will be indicated by a reference to A.L.R. in parentheses immediately below the parallel cite also given in parentheses. When you see such a reference, consider stopping further research until you read the annotation; it may provide you with a thorough review of a legal topic, eliminating the need for you to conduct much of your own research.

(iii) There may be cites below - **147** - that do not appear in parentheses. These are references to the history and treatment of *Gose v. Monroe Auto Equipment Co.* as it has traveled through the courts and to sources that have mentioned, discussed, or commented upon *Gose v. Monroe Auto Equipment Co.* in any manner whatsoever.

Practice Tip

Using the First Volume of Shepard's

In recent years, the editors at *Shepard's* have added a new feature: The first time a case is cited in any volume of *Shepard's* the case name and date of decision are shown with its parallel citation (if any). In subsequent volumes, only the reference to the page (for example - 89 -) will appear.

---

3. *Analysis of References in* Shepard's

a. Abbreviations

You may have already observed that the presentation of citations in *Shepard's* is not in *Bluebook* format. In fact, the citations given you by *Shepard's* have a uniquely peculiar appearance such as follows:

38LE106

132Az991

2
182NW282

These examples are correctly interpreted as follows:

38 L. Ed. 106
132 Ariz. 991
182 N.W.2d 282

Because *Shepard's* is tasked with presenting so much information as efficiently as possible, it has developed its own "shorthand" references for cases and other legal authorities. You will quickly learn how to interpret correctly the citations given you by *Shepard's*. If you have any difficulty, each volume of *Shepard's*, whether a hardcover volume or a softcover supplement, will contain a Table of Abbreviations placed in the front of each volume decoding these abbreviations. Cases that have not yet been published in a case reporter are temporarily identified by a condensed LEXIS citation, as in "2004 Mich LX 14."

b. History References

Shepard's will provide you with a history of *Gose v. Monroe Auto Equipment Co.*, meaning that you will be informed whether a rehearing of *Gose v. Monroe Auto Equipment Co.* has been denied, whether *certiorari* was denied, whether *Gose v. Monroe Auto Equipment Co.* has been affirmed, or whether it has been reversed.

The first references provided by *Shepard's* under - **147** - (after the parallel citations) relate to the direct history of *Gose v. Monroe Auto Equipment Co.*, that is, how this case has been dealt with as it has progressed through the courts. Often this history must be included in your citation because *The Bluebook* (Rule 10.7) and *ALWD* (Rule 12.8) may require that the subsequent history of a case be included in its citation.

For instance, if upon Shepardizing *Jones v. Smith*, 681 F.2d 911 (4th Cir. 1986), you discover it was reversed on appeal to the United States Supreme Court, you are obligated to indicate this in the citation, as follows:

Jones v. Smith, 681 F.2d 911 (4th Cir. 1986), *rev'd*, 482 U.S. 601 (1988).

Shepard's provides you with this information relating to the history of *Gose v. Monroe Auto Equipment Co.* by means of an identifying abbreviated letter placed immediately before the citation. Most of the letters are easy to understand. For example, "a" means "affirmed"; "r" means "reversed"; and "m" means "modified." If, however, you cannot remember the meaning of a history letter, each volume of *Shepard's* contains a Table of Abbreviations identifying each letter and providing a brief explanation. History references always include an abbreviation letter. See Figure 9-2 for the most common abbreviations relating to the history of a case.

c. Treatment References

Shepard's Michigan Citations will not only inform you how *Gose v. Monroe Auto Equipment Co.* has been dealt with by higher courts but will also refer you to every other case as well as selected law review articles, annotations, and attorneys general opinions that discuss or even mention *Gose v. Monroe Auto Equipment Co.* in passing. *Shepard's* does more than merely refer you to these authorities. These sources have been thoroughly analyzed, and *Shepard's* will inform you how *Gose v. Monroe Auto Equipment Co.* has been treated by other sources, namely, whether it was followed by a later case, mentioned in a dissenting opinion, or criticized or questioned by a later authority.

Shepard's provides you with this information relating to the treatment of *Gose v. Monroe Auto Equipment Co.* by means of an identifying abbreviation letter placed immediately before the reference. Once again, most of the letters are easy to interpret (such as "o" for "overruled" or "f" for "followed"), but each volume of *Shepard's* will provide you with a Table of Abbreviations, which will decode the abbreviations. See Figure 9-3 for the most common abbreviations relating to treatment of cases.

Pay careful attention in examining the treatment of a cited case. If the case you are relying on is continually being questioned or criticized, you

Figure 9-2
Abbreviations for History of Case

a	(affirmed)	Your case has been affirmed on appeal by a higher court.
cc	(connected case)	The citing case is related to your case in some way. Either it involves the same parties or arises out of the same subject matter.
D	(dismissed)	A case that has been appealed to a higher court has been dismissed or discontinued without further hearing.
Gr	(granted)	The citing case grants review in the case you are Shepardizing.
m	(modified)	The lower court's decision is modified in some way. For example, a lower court decision that is affirmed in part and reversed in part is shown as "modified."
Nu	(nullified)	Your case has been designated as without precedential value or effect.
r	(reversed)	Your case has been reversed on appeal to a higher court.
ReG	Reh./Recon. granted	The case you are Shepardizing has been granted a rehearing or reconsideration.
ReD	Reh./Recon. denied	The case you are Shepardizing has been denied a rehearing or reconsideration.
s	(same case)	The case is your case, although at a different stage of proceedings.
S	(superseded)	A subsequent opinion has been substituted for your case.
v	(vacated)	Your case has been rendered void and has no precedential force or effect.
W	(withdrawn)	Your case has been withdrawn by either the court or the publisher.
US cert den		The United States Supreme Court has denied *certiorari* for your case.
US cert dis		The United States Supreme Court granted *certiorari* and then dismissed cert.
US reh den		The United States Supreme Court has denied a rehearing of your case.
US reh dis		The United States Supreme Court granted a rehearing of your case and then dismissed it.
US app pndg		An appeal of your case is pending before the United States Supreme Court.
US cert gran		The United States Supreme Court has granted *certiorari* for your case.
lv app den		Leave to appeal has been denied to your case.

may wish to reevaluate your research strategies and attempt to locate a case that is more authoritative. Conversely, if the case you are relying upon has been followed by later cases on a number of occasions, this indicates the opinion has a certain amount of precedential weight and you may wish to inform a reader of this significance. If your case is mentioned in dissenting opinions, you should review these. If your case is the view of a bare majority and dissenting justices are challenging it, a change in the composition of the court could result in your case being overruled.

The difference between the *history* of a case and the *treatment* of it is readily illustrated by comparing "reversed" (relating to the history of a case) with "overruled" (relating to the treatment of a case). Assume *Smith v. Jones* was decided in 1990 by the United States District Court for the Southern District of Georgia. If Smith loses the case and appeals the decision to the Eleventh Circuit Court of Appeals, which decides that an error of law was committed at the trial, it may *reverse* the case. On the other hand, it is possible that in 2004, several years after *Smith v. Jones* is decided, the Eleventh Circuit, in hearing an entirely unrelated case titled *Gray v. Hill*, may decide that the reasoning in *Smith v. Jones* was erroneous and *Gray v. Hill* may *overrule Smith v. Jones*. Thus, a reversal refers

Figure 9-3
Abbreviations Relating to Treatment of a Cited Case

c	(criticized)	The court is disagreeing with the soundness of the opinion in your case.
d	(distinguished)	The case cited is significantly different from your case, either in the fact or issues involved.
e	(explained)	Your case is being explained or interpreted in a significant manner.
f	(followed)	Your case is being relied upon as controlling or persuasive authority.
h	(harmonized)	The cases differ in some way. Nevertheless, the court has found a way to reconcile or harmonize the differences.
j	(dissenting opinion)	Your case is mentioned in a dissenting opinion.
L	(limited)	The court restricts the application of the opinion in your case. Generally, the court finds that the reasoning in your case applies only in specific instances.
o	(overruled)	The court has determined that the reasoning in your case is no longer valid, either in part of in its entirety.
q	(questioned)	The soundness of your case is being questioned.
~	(concurring opinion)	Your case is mentioned in a concurring opinion.

to later history of a case, that is, what was decided by a higher court relating to that very case. An overruling refers to how a case was treated by some entirely different case, perhaps years after the original case was decided. For example, *Brown v. Board of Education*, 347 U.S. 483 (1954), overruled the much earlier case of *Plessy v. Ferguson*, 163 U.S. 539 (1896).

Shepard's has recently added a few abbreviations. Moveover, the abbreviations may vary in some states. For example, the following abbreviations are found in *Shepard's California Citations:*

GP   Review granted and case ordered published.

RE   Republished (Reporter of Decisions directed to publish opinion previously ordered not published).

\#   Citing reference may be of questionable value as precedent because review was granted by California Supreme Court or case was ordered depublished.

d. No Indication of Treatment

You may have observed that several of the references listed in *Shepard's* have no letters whatsoever preceding them. In fact, it is far more common for entries to appear without identifying letters than for letters related to treatment to be included. The absence of an identifying letter before a reference means that the later case has mentioned your case in some fashion, but the editors at *Shepard's* have not made any judgment as to the effect of this later case on your case.

4. *Arrangement of Later Cases*

The references in *Shepard's* to cases mentioning your case will be arranged in a fashion similar to the following:

    226P2108
    231P2414
    239P2106
    239P2109
    239P2111
    246P2901

These are all references to cases in the *Pacific Reporter, Second Series,* that have mentioned your case. These references are arranged in chronological order so you are first sent to earlier cases mentioning your case and then to more recent cases. If a later case mentions your case on several different pages, *Shepard's* will direct you to each and every page within that case on which your case is discussed. Although *Shepard's* does not provide a date for the later cases that discuss your case, by carefully examining the entries you can easily select more recent cases. You will also be directed to cases from the federal courts that mention your case.

You will recall that a standard case citation always directs you to the page on which a case begins. *Shepard's* references, however, are precise and direct you to the very page within a case on which your case is being discussed. This is far more efficient than merely being directed to the page on which a lengthy case begins, which you might have to read through to locate the reference to your case. If you retrieve one of the cases listed in *Shepard's* and you cannot locate a reference to your case on the page *Shepard's* directed you to, check any footnotes that appear on the page because it is possible that the discussion or mention of your case is not in the main body of the later case but instead is in a footnote.

5. *Other Identifying Letters*

When Shepardizing you may come across two lowercase letters placed after an entry. A lowercase "n" placed at the end of an entry indicates that the reference to your case appears in an A.L.R. annotation or an annotation in *United States Supreme Court Reports, Lawyers' Edition*. A lowercase "s" placed at the end of an entry indicates that the reference to your case appears in a supplement (either a pocket part or a softcover supplement) to an annotation.

6. *References to Headnotes*

You will recall from Chapter 4 that when a case is reviewed by editors at a publishing company, they will assign headnote numbers for each legal issue in the case. For example, if the case deals with 11 different issues, there will be 11 headnotes; if the case deals with six different legal issues, there will be six headnotes.

It is possible that you are relying on only a portion of a case in a brief or argument you have written. That is, you may be referring to a case only with reference to the issue discussed in headnote 4 of that case. *Shepard's* will not only provide you with information relating to the treatment by later cases of your case, it will focus on cases that have discussed specific headnotes of your case.

These references are accomplished by small elevated or superscript numbers placed immediately after the name of the case reporter. For example, when Shepardizing *Gose v. Monroe Auto Equipment Co.*, you observe one of the *Shepard's* entries is 125McA[4]474. This indicates that page 474 of Volume 125 of the *Michigan Court of Appeals Reports* discusses the point of law discussed in headnote 4 of *Gose v. Monroe Auto Equipment Co.* This feature of *Shepard's* allows you readily to locate later cases discussing the specific points of law discussed in your case.

Thus, if you relied solely upon the issue discussed in the second headnote of *Gose v. Monroe Auto Equipment Co.*, you could quickly run your finger down the column of *Shepard's* entries looking for elevated "2s" because these will direct you to later cases that mentioned *Gose v. Monroe Auto Equipment Co.* with regard to the point of law discussed in its headnote 2. Similarly, if, when you Shepardize, you discover that only headnote 4 of *Gose v. Monroe Auto Equipment Co.* has been criticized or questioned, and you are relying solely upon the point of law discussed in headnote 3 of *Gose*, you may be able to bypass those references with elevated number 4s. Because some cases have been mentioned or discussed by subsequent cases on hundreds of occasions, you can use this feature of *Shepard's* to save time and eliminate cases that are not relevant to the particular issue you are researching.

It is possible that some entries in *Shepard's* contain no elevated or superscript numbers. This is an indication that a later case discusses *Gose v. Monroe Auto Equipment Co.* only in some general fashion rather than focusing on a specific legal issue discussed in any particular headnote.

7. *References to Sources Other than Cases*

In addition to validating the case you rely on, *Shepard's* will direct you to a wide variety of other sources that mention or discuss your case. Thus, *Shepard's* functions as a finding tool to expand your research efforts. *Shepard's* state citators will direct you to decisions from any federal court that mentions your case and to selected law reviews and annotations that mention your case.

a. Attorneys General Opinions

When you Shepardize a case in one of the state sets such as *Shepard's Illinois Citations*, after *Shepard's* directs you to every case that has mentioned or discussed your case, it will refer you to the specific page of any opinion of that state's attorney general that mentions your case.

b. Law Review Articles

When you Shepardize a case in one of the sets of *Shepard's* for state cases, you will be provided not only with a list of every case from your state decided after your case that mentions or discusses your case, you will be provided with references to leading law review articles or periodicals that mention your case (such as the *Columbia Law Review, Stanford Law Review*, or *Yale Law Journal*). References are given to the specific page of an article that mentions your case.

You should read any article that discusses your case because it may well provide a thoughtful and complete analysis of your case or the issues presented in your case, saving you precious research time.

c. Annotations

The state *Shepard's* will also direct you to any A.L.R. annotations that mention your case and will indicate if your case has been selected by the publisher of A.L.R. as a "leading" case about which an annotation has been written. This is accomplished by a reference to A.L.R. in a parenthetical immediately following the parenthetical for the parallel cite. Remember that a small "n" appearing after the A.L.R. citation indicates that your case has been cited in an annotation. A small "s" appearing after the A.L.R. citation indicates that your case is mentioned in a pocket part or softcover supplement. See Figure 9-4 for a sample page from *Shepard's Michigan Citations*.

8. *Using* Shepard's

As you can see, *Shepard's* provides a vast amount of information about your case, from its history as it progresses through the court system, to its treatment by later cases that mention or discuss it, to other sources such as attorneys' general opinions, law review articles, and A.L.R. annotations that mention your case. It is possible that a controversial or well-known case such as *Brown v. Board of Education*, 347 U.S. 483 (1954), has been mentioned hundreds of times by other cases and by attorneys' general opinions, law review articles, and A.L.R. annotations.

Beginning researchers typically wonder whether they are required to read each and every one of these cases or other references that mention a case they have updated. The answer to this question is a typical legal response: It depends. If you have been specifically directed by your supervisor to retrieve and review every case or other reference that mentions your case, you must do so. If you are pleased with your research project and you believe the cases cited in your writing clearly and articulately support the arguments you have made, Shepardizing can be reduced to the fairly easy task of simply locating the entries in *Shepard's* for your case and looking for "bad" letters, such as "r" (reversed), "m" (modified), "o" (overruled), "L" (limited), "c" (criticized), or "q" (questioned). If your updating does not disclose any such negative history or treatment of your case, your task is complete and you need not read and analyze the entries that refer to your case. Conversely, if your case is being consistently followed by later cases, you may wish to read a few of these and mention this in your document as a means of further enhancing the strength of your arguments and conclusions.

It is possible, however, that you are not entirely pleased with the cases you have located. Perhaps the cases are a bit older than you would prefer, or from your state appellate court rather than from your state supreme court, or the legal principles in your case are not clearly stated. In this case, use *Shepard's* as a research tool to locate newer cases, cases from a higher court, or cases that more clearly or articulately explain a legal issue. When you Shepardize, look for such newer cases or cases that have followed your case. Remember to use the elevated numbers to locate only those cases dealing with the issues presented in the relevant headnotes from your case.

If the issue you are researching is an uncertain area of the law or a newly emerging legal topic, you should probably read some of the cases listed in *Shepard's* to obtain better insight into this area of the law.

9. *Analyzing Negative Letters*

If your Shepardizing reveals one of the "negative" letters, especially "r" (reversed), "m" (modified), "c" (criticized), "o" (overruled), "L" (limited), or

Figure 9-4
Sample Page from *Shepard's Michigan Citations*

Volume number → **Vol. 409**

Page number →

Parallel citation →

e148McA[6]224
j148McA7
d149McA647
f149McA[24]
[647
149McA[14]648
d149McA[16]
[650
151McA[2]168
Cir. 6
564FS355
61MBJ558
61MBJ563
27WnL972
28WnL915
29WnL815
30WnL707
ICD§ 6.03
28Æ551s
20Æ1112n
23Æ19n
23Æ46n
25Æ20n
25Æ58n
28Æ424n
30Æ181n
30Æ183n
30Æ194n
—67—
(293NW315)
s409Mch1102
j409Mch868
f409Mch883
j412Mch892
106McA[2]223
115McA[10]786
28WnL703
28WnL1153
29WnL419
29WnL1034
—110—
(293NW588)
s406Mch1009
s86McA5
410Mch884
e418Mch[6]
j418Mch126
99McA[2]559
f101McA471
107McA280
107McA[4]742
111McA[4]743
118McA690
119McA[5]557
131McA[2]674
27WnL428
27WnL665
28WnL707
28WnL745
—126—
(293NW332)
s403Mch845
s406Mch1008
s77McA411
e409Mch[6]736
410Mch[6]864
410Mch920
411Mch852
411Mch[6]858
f411Mch946
414Mch952
d416Mch[1]244

416Mch[6]587
d416Mch[7]600
99McA[6]741
d101McA[5]582
d103McA[3]713
d105McA[6]638
108McA[6]627
j108McA631
110McA[1]289
110McA346
111McA[6]49
112McA[2]649
d112McA[6]787
f115McA[1]437
115McA[6]438
e125McA[6]110
e126McA[1]299
e127McA[6]639
139McA[7]804
d139McA[6]809
d143McA[5]583
143McA[3]589
150McA[2]747
Cir. 6
741F2d[6]838
741F2d[6]838
27WnL666
28WnL746
30WnL450
31WnL444
—147—
(294NW165)
s80McA190
412Mch[2]583
414Mch112
414Mch[3]589
101McA[2]160
105McA[2]130
114McA[2]383
115McA[2]747
116McA392
118McA[2]49
119McA[3]478
120McA[1]151
123McA[2]439
125McA[4]474
125McA[3]670
126McA[2]572
133McA[2]789
135McA[2]263
136McA[2]394
d139McA[2]181
147McA[2]75
j147McA76
f148McA[2]753
149McA[2]350
Cir. 6
758F2d[1]1145
512FS[1]1165
512FS[2]1165
564FS[2]1301
611FS[2]854
631FS1520
64MBJ1093
28WnL1195
29WnL407
30WnL335
31WnL347

—217—
(293NW341)
409Mch913
417Mch[1]1050
99McA[6]786
100McA[1]743
104McA[1]112
e117McA135
f129McA[1]282
143McA312
147McA[6]421
28WnL484
28WnL642
28WnL661
31WnL635
—231—
(293NW594)
s405Mch826
s405Mch827
s83McA207
409Mch887
414Mch10
418Mch[6]647
418Mch[6]662
f100McA172
103McA[6]439
110McA[4]137
115McA679
118McA[1]808
121McA771
125McA[1]125
134McA194
137McA699
137McA811
139McA[1]61
154McA[6]327
1983MiAG53
28WnL918
27Æ178n
—262—
(293NW346)
409Mch1102
61JUL58
—271—
(294NW827)
s403Mch832
90McA399
419Mch[2]926
119McA582
Cir. 6
s653F2d[3]269
754F2d168
1567FS[6]65
64MBJ174
28WnL936
—279—
(294NW571)
s83McA153
409Mch916
411Mch[1]705
411Mch709
d110McA569
118McA[1]445
128McA[2]576
Cir. 6
551FS[1]1282
28WnL1133
88Æ926s

—299—
(294NW578)
s406Mch1011
s89McA564
410Mch868
410Mch876
414Mch647
422Mch[1]90
101McA[3]397
f103McA[4]783
111McA444
142McA[3]717
146McA[1]420
151McA[1]695
151McA[2]695
1981MiAG
1981MiAG
[494
[757
59JUL117
64MBJ1067
64MBJ1068
27WnL855
28WnL969
22Æ1118n
—346—
(294NW197)
s407Mch873
s409Mch1102
s93McA579
84McA87
116McA[1]419
122McA273
d143McA778
28WnL761
29WnL551
—356—
(294NW202)
410Mch[6]899
109McA[3]311
d113McA[6]624
118McA[1]249
125McA[2]234
125McA[3]234
28WnL882
—364—
(294NW827)
s402Mch926
420Mch[12]161
420Mch[3]171
e420Mch[11]171
f107McA[4]481
113McA[1]61
113McA[2]61
113McA[6]61
113McA[6]61
114McA[1]478
27WnL425
28WnL713
RLPB§ 4.13
48Æ1436s
—401—
(295NW50)
s409Mch1116
s79McA639
135McA[1]250
414Mch[25]573
416Mch[25]224
416Mch[1]225
j416Mch231
420Mch[16]260

420Mch[11]263
421Mch136
422Mch[2]600
422Mch[7]600
422Mch[6]600
422Mch[12]601
422Mch[13]604
422Mch[1]620
422Mch[13]620
423Mch572
f100McA[6]688
f100McA[7]688
f100McA[6]689
f100McA[3]689
f100McA[6]690
j100McA842
102McA[2]647
102McA[7]649
e103McA[11]
[348
f103McA[11]
[515
104McA[10]68
104McA[6]72
107McA[12]451
f110McA[3]423
110McA[6]511
f111McA[7]149
114McA[1]182
114McA[3]182
f116McA[12]
[119
117McA706
118McA[6]629
119McA[6]236
j119McA542
120McA[1]217
120McA[2]218
f121McA[1]21
f121McA[2]23
121McA[1]733
123McA[6]171
f123McA[6]524
f123McA[10]
[525
f123McA[11]
[525
f123McA[15]
[525
f123McA[4]525
f123McA[2]526
f123McA[3]526
j123McA528
124McA[2]268
e124McA[4]476
e124McA[6]476
124McA[4]476
125McA[11]249
127McA[2]458
128McA[11]70
f129McA[1]216
f129McA[5]216
f129McA[1]216
f132McA[11]
[106
f134McA[2]606
d135McA598
138McA[7]432
f139McA[13]
[606
141McA[1]112

141McA[11]621
141McA[1]682
f142McA[1]635
f142McA[2]635
e143McA[11]
[425
e143McA[13]
[426
146McA[2]498
150McA[20]754
151McA[11]636
152McA[11]121
Cir. 3
570FS[2]620
Cir. 6
695F2d[12]234
716F2d[2]388
741F2d[1]877
f772F2d276
503FS[11]845
503FS[11]1059
f506FS[6]636
f506FS[7]636
f506FS[6]636
510FS348
f510FS[2]349
f517FS[2]224
564FS[1]358
d576FS[2]543
f576FS[10]544
583FS[1]355
635FS[2]1467
642FS[1]336
24BRW159
36BRW[1]438
f36BRW[2]439
Cir. 7
568FS[11]553
Cir. 10
784F2d[2]1057
60JUL120
60MBJ257
60MBJ654
60MBJ745
61MBJ624
62MBJ773
63MBJ599
64MBJ174
27WnL651
27WnL837
28WnL735
29WnL930
29WnL399
29WnL514
29WnL808
30WnL439
30WnL468
33CLA1586
70Cor838
69VaL304
ICD§ 6.36
LPIB§ 3.21
47Æ314s
38Æ1010n

419Mch310
f105McA[1]659
e107McA[1]338
f107McA[1]466
107McA[1]741
e108McA[1]469
f108McA[1]596
111McA[1]52
114McA[1]669
j115McA542
117McA[2]526
120McA652
120McA[1]772
121McA335
d122McA[1]590
128McA550
129McA[1]474
f131McA[1]629
140McA[1]232
f141McA[1]625
142McA200
142McA575
154McA[1]21
27WnL747
30WnL468
18Æ3259s
—468—
(295NW813)
134McA674
28WnL1209
—474—
(295NW482)
US cert den
in449US1101
s77McA357
j109McA742
d110McA[3]610
d110McA[6]610
d110McA[6]610
d110McA[6]610
j110McA613
f111McA[6]51
113McA541
f124McA[2]787
f124McA[6]787
133McA635
134McA[1]156
27WnL429
28WnL809
—495—
(296NW813)
s96McA276
106McA589
112McA[6]12
116McA787
c118McA22
119McA83
119McA411
62MBJ429
HCC§ 3.14
—500—
(297NW876)
s79McA63
s80McA721
s116McA791
f421Mch[6]283
113McA[3]438
113McA865
e411Mch1044
123McA[13]121
125McA[4]348
130McA713
149McA[4]741
150McA[6]81

64MBJ289
28WnL706
28WnL766
30WnL408
77NwL496
5Æ866s
—552—
(297NW115)
s127McA716
416Mch[3]261
f120McA697
121McA[1]496
130McA[3]151
141McA[3]164
143McA448
—564—
(297NW120)
s92McA427
419Mch[2]307
119McA[2]729
e119McA[2]781
d121McA[2]329
d126McA[2]713
e135McA[2]194
f150McA[2]444
1982DCL909
27WnL659
28WnL752
28WnL764
30WnL460
31WnL455
—569—
(297NW544)
s77McA357
28WnL82
28WnL691
—639—
(297NW387)
s402Mch828
s420Mch463
s74McA237
s96McA92
s88LÆ223
s89LÆ294
s92LÆ504
s106SC224
s106SC1175
s106SC3129
cc54USLW
[5037
410McA[10]249
410Mch[1]257
410Mch[1]275
413Mch632
120McA320
131McA769
1981MiAG
[617
1985DCL
[1031
28WnL1165
62Æ314s
63Æ388s
—672—
(299NW304)
s116McA791
(13Æ1180)
s396Mch843
s402Mch938
s403Mch821
Continued

922

"q" (questioned), you should be extremely alert and exercise great caution. It may be premature, however, to assume that your entire project is now incorrect and useless.

In *all* instances, retrieve and read the cases that have been assigned one of these negative abbreviations. It is possible that only a portion of your case has been criticized or overruled and that the remainder of the case is still authoritative. Carefully examine the elevated numbers because it is also possible that only headnote 8 of your case is being criticized or questioned or only the issue discussed in headnote 10 has been modified. If you are relying solely on headnote 6 from a case, this negative history and treatment is serious but not devastating. Read the cases listed in *Shepard's* to determine whether your case may still be relied upon.

If the portion of the case you are relying upon is still valid and some other portion has been reversed, you may still cite your case, but you must disclose to the reader the later history as follows:

> *Smith v. Jones*, 418 P.2d 945, 950 (N.M. 1984), *rev'd on other grounds*, 419 P.2d 109, 115 (N.M. 1985).

10. *Shepardizing Using a Regional Shepard's*

Because many cases are published in both an official report as well as in a West regional reporter such as the *Atlantic Reporter* or the *Pacific Reporter*, you may elect to Shepardize such a case either in a state or regional *Shepard's*. For example, assume your case is cited as follows: *Gose v. Monroe Auto Equipment Co.*, 409 Mich. 147, 294 N.W.2d 165 (1980). You may Shepardize this case using *Shepard's Michigan Citations*, as discussed previously, or by using *Shepard's Northwestern Reporter Citations*.

The process of Shepardizing a case is always the same whether you Shepardize your case in a state *Shepard's* or in a regional *Shepard's*. For example, to use the regional *Shepard's*:

(i) Locate the volumes of *Shepard's Northwestern Reporter Citations*.

(ii) Examine the box or notice labeled "What Your Library Should Contain" to ensure you have all of the *Shepard's* volumes necessary.

(iii) Open a volume of *Shepard's* and examine the upper left and right corners of each page to find a reference to **Vol. 294**.

(iv) Scan down the page looking for a boldface **- 165 -**.

(v) Examine the entries listed.

The first entry given will be the parallel citation to *Gose v. Monroe Auto Equipment Co.* and will be placed in parentheses.

The next entries will be references to the history of the case and then to other cases in the *Northwestern Reporter* that mentioned or discussed *Gose v. Monroe Auto Equipment Co.* First you will be directed to cases from

Michigan, the state that decided *Gose v. Monroe Auto Equipment Co.* You will then be sent to federal cases and then to cases from other states whose cases are reported in the *Northwestern Reporter*, such as Minnesota, North Dakota, and Wisconsin. Next you will be given citations to cases from other units of the *National Reporter System*, such as the *Pacific Reporter* and *Southern Reporter*, and then you will be directed to any A.L.R. annotations discussing *Gose v. Monroe Auto Equipment Co.*

One of the advantages of Shepardizing *Gose v. Monroe Auto Equipment Co.* in *Shepard's Northwestern Reporter Citations* rather than *Shepard's Michigan Citations* is that you will be directed to cases from states other than Michigan that have mentioned or discussed *Gose v. Monroe Auto Equipment Co.* If you Shepardize *Gose v. Monroe Auto Equipment Co.* in *Shepard's Michigan Citations*, you will only be directed to cases from Michigan (and federal cases) that mention or discuss *Gose v. Monroe Auto Equipment Co.*

A disadvantage, however, is that the regional *Shepard's* will not direct you to law review articles or attorneys general opinions that mention *Gose v. Monroe Auto Equipment Co.* If *Gose v. Monroe Auto Equipment Co.* has been overruled, reversed, limited, and so forth, however, you will be provided this information whether you Shepardize in *Shepard's Michigan Citations* or in *Shepard's Northwestern Reporter Citations*. You will be directed to annotations in A.L.R. no matter which set of *Shepard's* you use.

Are you required to Shepardize the same case in both *Shepard's Michigan Citations* and in *Shepard's Northwestern Reporter Citations*? For the most complete treatment of *Gose v. Monroe Auto Equipment Co.*, you should Shepardize in both sets, as the state *Shepard's* will direct you to law review articles and attorneys' general opinions, and the regional *Shepard's* will direct you to cases from states other than Michigan that have mentioned *Gose v. Monroe Auto Equipment Co.* In practice, however, most legal professionals will Shepardize in the state *Shepard's* or the regional *Shepard's*, but not both. Because the most critical information provided by *Shepard's* is the history of a case (whether it has been affirmed, reversed, or so forth), and both sets give you this information, Shepardizing in one set rather than both is sufficient for these purposes. Updating electronically eliminates this concern.

After some experience in Shepardizing, you may develop a preference for one method over another. Unless you have a compelling reason otherwise, you should probably Shepardize in the companion *Shepard's* to your case. That is, if you read a case in the *Kansas Reports*, Shepardize it in *Shepard's Kansas Citations*. If you read this same case in the *Pacific Reporter*, Shepardize it in *Shepard's Pacific Reporter Citations*. This procedure will enable you to most effectively use the elevated (superscript) numbers given by *Shepard's* to pinpoint later discussion of the headnotes from your case. That is, because the publisher of the official report may use a different headnote numbering system than West will use when it reports the same case in its regional reporter, Shepardizing is most effective when you use a set of *Shepard's* that will pinpoint the particular headnote of your case that is treated by later cases. See Figure 9-5 for a sample page from *Shepard's Northwestern Reporter Citations*.

Figure 9-5
Sample Page from *Shepard's Northwestern Reporter Citations*

Volume number

Vol. 294

NORTHWESTERN REPORTER, 2d SERIES

Page number

Parallel cite

```
25Æ58n
30Æ181n
30Æ194n
ICD§6.03
- 165 -
(409Mch147)
s263NW329
300NW¹481
306NW¹421
317NW¹4
319NW¹353
321NW¹799
323NW413
323NW³915
324NW¹777
326NW¹415
327NW272
328NW¹22
332NW¹570
336NW³31
337NW¹267
337NW¹582
349NW²547
351NW¹921
357NW¹54
512FS²1165
564FS¹1301
- 194 -
(409Mch271)
s270NW1
s282NW8
f326NW568
355NW²110
e653F2d⁵269
d567FS¹65
- 197 -
(409Mch346)
s286NW909
312NW¹620
323NW425
332NW¹466
- 202 -
(409Mch356)
311NW⁶761
d318NW⁶497
324NW¹502
336NW³455
336NW⁵455
- 205 -
(96McA510)
309NW²577
309NW⁵582
f311NW¹756
d311NW⁶758
e313NW347
f316NW³430
j316NW431
f325NW⁵560
329NW497
84Æ375s
- 209 -
(96McA524)
v306NW103
j308NW464
60Æ226s
- 215 -
(96McA708)
```

```
- 218 -
(96McA714)
44Æ1156s
- 221 -
(96McA726)
(19Æ361)
311NW³738
328NW⁴618
f328NW¹619
f346NW⁴54
Ariz
676P2d622
Wash
685P2d626
86Æ1443s
- 224 -
(96McA763)
r309NW174
c304NW¹540
q311NW¹373
335NW115
343NW³186
502FS¹731
q502FS¹732
- 228 -
(97McA5)
a327NW783
324NW⁵338
324NW613
336NW⁸833
f348NW¹⁰709
NY
469S2d555
26Æ672n
26Æ687n
- 236 -
(97McA33)
US cert den
in104SC3537
r341NW92
cc244NW619
318NW³669
- 241 -
(97McA44)
312NW¹425
- 243 -
(97McA50)
- 246 -
(97McA56)
261NW215
299NW¹⁰374
304NW¹⁰578
323NW⁷532
357NW⁸814
- 249 -
(97McA92)
e309NW⁴255
350NW⁴269
Fla
435So2d391
Colo
679P2d1067
- 253 -
(97McA122)
cc241NW260
299NW¹²397
300NW³542
318NW¹482
323NW⁷519
```

```
326NW837
j338NW403
339NW⁷498
339NW⁸498
96Æ768s
15Æ715n
- 262 -
(97McA287)
e308NW⁷197
e308NW⁸197
351NW³907
86Æ722s
39Æ1000s
- 266 -
(97McA340)
r307NW682
- 269 -
20Æ988s
75Æ616s
- 271 -
356NW⁴849
NM
680P2d609
- 275 -
296NW¹380
- 280 -
295NW²101
295NW¹546
j295NW547
297NW²288
299NW²738
302NW¹31
305NW²342
306NW²118
349NW²296
350NW926
- 286 -
d313NW¹433
d321NW¹890
68Æ37s
- 288 -
d298NW³356
f309NW⁷44
354NW⁸118
354NW⁵470
716F2d1215
- 297 -
f307NW²³772
e336NW²152
336NW²²53
343NW²³709
351NW¹⁸379
352NW¹⁸807
d353NW557
355NW²²302
356NW²¹741
356NW²³742
512FS941
- 312 -
348NW375
73Æ1238s
24Æ939n
```

```
- 320 -
313NW¹388
325NW¹642
- 321 -
354NW451
- 322 -
Md
439A2d6
Tenn
654SW414
61Æ293s
- 324 -
319NW34
357NW²149
17MJ503
45Æ958s
- 327 -
cc270NW758
330NW104
336NW³53
- 330 -
(206Neb516)
f330NW²744
- 334 -
(206Neb559)
e303NW⁶310
321NW428
328NW³179
334NW²449
334NW³449
343NW⁴758
343NW⁴758
343NW⁴758
- 338 -
(206Neb578)
- 341 -
(206Neb587)
- 343 -
(206Neb599)
320NW¹102
320NW¹104
- 347 -
(206Neb615)
333NW¹404
333NW²404
6Æ1244s
42Æ13s
81Æ456s
- 350 -
(206Neb619)
328NW³773
96Æ745s
- 354 -
(206Neb625)
300NW²23
300NW³23
301NW¹342
336NW²604
76Æ163s
- 357 -
(206Neb630)
d295NW273
j304NW677
```

```
318NW⁶744
5Æ1033n
- 363 -
(206Neb639)
73Æ1238s
24Æ942n
- 369 -
(206Neb651)
318NW⁴727
329NW101
- 372 -
(206Neb655)
352NW²601
- 374 -
(206Neb658)
333NW¹909
335NW537
352NW¹585
- 376 -
(206Neb662)
f316NW⁶602
- 379 -
(206Neb666)
cc262NW187
319NW⁴442
15Æ684n
- 382 -
(206Neb670)
s300NW194
d294NW⁴871
357NW⁴205
NH
480A2d186
NY
444S2d415
- 386 -
s261NW399
s264NW888
- 391 -
310NW739
312NW¹363
d313NW735
336NW²112
61Æ1390s
- 397 -
325NW¹215
Fla
428So2d366
18Æ1376s
- 404 -
302NW⁴783
311NW⁸184
315NW⁴680
315NW⁷681
f315NW⁸681
316NW⁷96
322NW²464
e328NW³218
e329NW³³376
331NW²17
e340NW²175
343NW³366
351NW¹96
82LÆ326
104SC⁶3144
```

```
Fla
400So2d1000
Mass
438NÆ63
25Æ1407s
31Æ565s
- 411 -
301NW⁴398
576FS⁵809
ICD§6.02
- 416 -
313NW²468
328NW259
334NW²489
337NW²813
346NW²307
350NW²610
e356NW472
53Æ1102s
- 419 -
303NW¹356
303NW²356
304NW¹109
304NW⁵111
304NW¹122
304NW¹714
310NW²785
315NW¹499
315NW²499
329NW⁴888
329NW⁸888
f330NW⁵544
- 426 -
(14Æ5773)
Me
461A2d1059
3Æ1072s
- 431 -
504FS²1092
- 435 -
f318NW¹9
f318NW²9
338NW¹292
- 437 -
(97W260)
(13Æ61)
s284NW120
f293NW⁵901
j293NW908
297NW²499
297NW¹⁶500
307NW903
308NW³²408
311NW⁵223
340NW¹⁴219
340NW³⁴496
342NW⁸54
342NW²⁸54
342NW443
344NW³⁰519
347NW²603
355NW563
75LÆ646
103SC²1636
655F2d2658
665F2d²⁹208
686F2d¹⁵467
```

```
686F2d¹⁸467
686F2d²469
717F2d⁵834
717F2d³839
727F2d527
727F2d⁹529
e746F2d1241
746F2d
[³³]1241
512FS¹¹1280
520FS⁵161
526FS⁵900
536FS467
548FS²²376
572FS³³119
f572FS³121
572FS⁴121
576FS201
576FS³⁴202
Iowa
347NW410
347NW²411
Colo
684P2d215
Conn
472A2d312
Fla
403So2d467
426So2d1109
428So2d247
438So2d194
438So2d1068
Ill
427NÆ616
450NÆ1207
Ind
460NÆ184
Kan
666P2d713
NJ
471A2d438
472A2d583
NY
481S2d971
Pa
469A2d662
469A2d671
25Æ31416s
10Æ949n
11Æ1262n
- 473 -
(97W332)
s282NW637
f297NW²76
f297NW²376
e298NW⁶104
d298NW106
298NW410
300W²69
302NW¹¹508
d306NW¹297
f309NW⁵12
314NW⁸323
e314NW⁸324
324NW¹443
f325NW⁵318
327NW¹61
327NW²61
327NW⁵63
329NW²241
331NW⁹607
334NW²583
f337NW²191
```

```
338NW⁵488
f339NW¹336
348NW¹153
348NW³153
f349NW100
351NW⁴163
535FS666
74Æ984s
- 485 -
(97W485)
in449US994
296NW741
298NW555
325NW²⁴689
342NW¹⁴407
348NW¹⁴562
587FS²⁴1481
W Va
314SÆ398
314SÆ400
- 501 -
(97W521)
a301NW156
340NW²²927
508FS¹⁸222
539FS917
11Æ39s
18Æ310s
18Æ388s
51Æ3981s
12Æ108n
13Æ326n
- 528 -
(97W627)
298NW³413
313NW¹⁰823
326NW¹119
334NW¹688
345NW¹514
- 534 -
(97W638)
r303NW608
10Æ22s
11Æ39s
18Æ310s
18Æ3170s
12Æ180n
- 540 -
(97W654)
a307NW881
e321NW¹314
Ind
443NÆ70
- 547 -
(97W699)
j306NW697
Wash
688P2d149
- 551 -
(97W669)
315NW³370
- 555 -
s242NW702
304NW³235
322NW¹302
f322NW⁴308
Continued
```

1229

11. *Shepardizing Neutral or Public Domain Citations*

As you know from reading Chapter 8, several states now assign public domain numbers to cases as they are released, such as "1998 MT 1" for the first Montana case in 1998. These can be Shepardized in the state *Shepard's* in a separate section devoted to public domain opinions as well as in the regional *Shepard's*. Thus, 1998 MT 1 can be Shepardized in *Shepard's Montana Citations* and in *Shepard's Pacific Reporter Citations*.

12. *When to Shepardize*

When to perform the task of Shepardizing is left to your discretion. You may find that if you have been assigned the task of cite-checking someone else's project, you may be Shepardizing after the final draft has been completed and just before the document is delivered to court or to the adverse party. The obvious hazard of Shepardizing so late in the research process is that you run the risk of discovering that a key case cited in the document has been overruled or reversed, causing a last-minute crisis.

If the project is your own writing, you should consider Shepardizing fairly early in the research process for two reasons: first, to eliminate any possibility of a devastating eleventh hour surprise; and, second, to locate other sources to support your argument.

Many legal professionals Shepardize almost concurrently with performing legal research. That is, as they locate cases that appear promising, they immediately Shepardize them so as not to invest time and effort in reading, analyzing, and writing about cases only to discover later they are no longer valid. The other advantage of early Shepardizing is that you will be directed to law review articles, A.L.R. annotations, and attorneys' general opinions. These sources may provide a thorough analysis of the very subject you are researching and can serve as "free research." If you wait to Shepardize until a project is completed, you may miss these valuable research leads.

━━ Practice Tip ━━

Keeping an Eye on the Adversary

When you receive a brief or other document prepared by your adversary, consider Shepardizing it so you can spot weaknesses in his or her case. Your opponent may be relying on questionable or outdated authorities, in which event you will want to draw the court's attention to this fact.

13.   *Shepardizing Federal Cases*

a.   United States Supreme Court Cases

Use *Shepard's United States Citations* to Shepardize cases from the United States Supreme Court. The technique used to Shepardize United States Supreme Court cases is identical to that used to Shepardize state cases.

Assume you are Shepardizing the case *Rabeck v. New York*, 391 U.S. 462 (1968). The first entries *Shepard's* will provide you are parallel references to your case, that is, the references to 20 L. Ed. 2d 741 and 88 S. Ct. 1716. *Shepard's* will then give you references to the history of the case *Rabeck v. New York*, and then entries relating to the treatment of *Rabeck v. New York* by later United States Supreme Court cases and lower federal court cases. These entries are arranged by circuit and state allowing you to easily locate cases from the Ninth Circuit, Fifth Circuit, Alaska, or Connecticut. You will next be sent to annotations that discuss or mention *Rabeck v. New York*.

Shepard's now offers separate sets to Shepardize cases from the United States Supreme Court. Thus, cases published in the official *United States Reports* are Shepardized using one set of *Shepard's*, while cases published in West's *Supreme Court Reporter* are Shepardized using a separate set of *Shepard's*, and cases published in LEXIS's *United States Supreme Court Reports, Lawyers' Edition*, are Shepardized using still another set of volumes.

See Figure 9-6 for a sample page from *Shepard's United States Citations*.

b.   Lower Federal Court Cases

Use *Shepard's Federal Citations* to Shepardize cases that appear in the *Federal Reporter, Federal Supplement*, or *Federal Rules Decisions*. The technique used to Shepardize cases from the United States courts of appeal and the United States district courts is exactly the same as that used to Shepardize any case.

When you Shepardize a lower federal court case, *Shepard's* will provide you with references to federal cases relating to the history of your case and then cases relating to the treatment of your case. Once again, entries will be arranged by circuit and state so you can readily locate cases from a specific circuit or state that discusses your case. *Shepard's* will also direct you to annotations and law reviews that mention or discuss your case. See Figure 9-7 for a sample page from *Shepard's Federal Citations*.

14.   *How Many Volumes to Use When Shepardizing*

You have seen that Shepardizing may require you to use more than one volume of *Shepard's*. Often you may need to use one or two hardbound volumes and one or more of the softcover supplements. While you can

Figure 9-6
Sample Page from *Shepard's United States Citations*

427NYS2d682	Cir. 3	48Wis2d615	Cir. 3	**—363—**	396US372
Ohio	431F2d472	99Wis2d583	441FS1155	Federal Power	j) 397US131
300S2d119	d) 441F2d565	148Wis2d547	Cir. 4	Com. v Pan	398US61
~) 300S2d128	Cir. 5	155Wis2d397	429F2d611	American Petro-	e) 399US263
480S2d387	404F2d913	164NW518	313FS49	leum Corp.	j) 400US247
283NE155	413F2d323	180NW708	324FS262	1968	403US18
~) 283NE160	426F2d144	299NW638	Cir. 5	(20LE638)	403US224
358NE621	505F2d915	436NW291	434F2d939	(88SC1664)	d) 405US458
P R	518F2d892	455NW650	j) 434F2d954	s) 389US1002	j) 405US467
122DPR302	534F2d610	49NYL863	285FS774	s) 376F2d161	408US101
1988JTS119	296FS1343	65VaL1319	293FS952	5LE1000s	408US184
100PRR809	Cir. 6	5A4969n	296FS179	**—364—**	409US114
R I	454F2d346	**—359—**	311FS107	Branigin v	j) 409US128
104RI312	j) 515F2d493	Seferi v Ives	311FS659	Duddleston	j) 411US100
111RI253	Cir. 9	1968	316FS372	1968	j) 413US103
~) 111RI266	432F2d496	(20LE640)	320FS671	(20LE641)	j) 413US234
244A2d252	467F2d960	(88SC1665)	321FS891	(88SC1666)	415US586
302A2d70	316FS347	s) 155Ct580	326FS1263	s) 385US455	j) 415US599
~) 302A2d77	Cir. 10	s) 236A2d83	329FS1328	s) 390US932	416US410
S D	431F2d382	Conn	Cir. 6	s) 255FS155	j) 417US858
429NW35	f) 434F2d1233	164Ct258	432F2d339	s) 284FS176	d) 418US409
Tex	552F2d915	180Ct39	j) 432F2d346	Cir. 5	420US495
j) 4SW732	Cir. DC	180Ct585	432F2d535	189FS2d553	422US211
Utah	513F2d447	255A2d841	312FS1122	Cir. 6	422US934
858P2d1016	522F2d1338	320A2d827	448FS338	38FS2d529	d) 424US16
910P2d1188	398FS965	428A2d801	Cir. 8	Cir. 7	j) 425US148
Vt	15LE904s	430A2d1287	302FS1400	435F2d363	425US771
141Vt439	17LE1026s	**—359—**	312FS28	12LE1282s	427US78
450A2d341	**—353—**	North American	314FS37	**—365—**	d) 427US363
Wash	Zwicker v Boll	Van Lines, Inc.	Tenn	California v	429US265
99Wsh2d859	1968	v United States	491SW83	Phillips Petro-	430US713
664P2d1238	(20LE642)	1968	49NYL863	leum Co.	430US716
W Va	(88SC1666)	(20LE646)	15LE904s	1968	431US93
164WV637	s) 270FS131	(88SC1665)	8ARF479n	(20LE639)	431US94
264SE855	Cir. 1	s) 277FS741	**—361—**	(88SC1664)	433US467
Wis	309FS726	105MCC185	Jackson v	s) 377F2d278	433US476
d) 269Wis2d	331FS716	**—360—**	Nelson	s) 405F2d6	435US786
[274	Cir. 2	Goldblatt v	1968	**—366—**	436US428
d) 674NW601	288FS356	Dallas	(20LE648)	Brooklyn Union	j) 442US283
80CaL745	295FS185	1968	(88SC1671)	Gas Co. v	446US90
1975LF305	Cir. 3	(20LE646)	US reh den	Standard Oil	j) 446US132
Citing 65VaL909	324FS796	(88SC1666)	392US947	Co.	447US462
cases 22LE876n	329FS1204	s) 279FS106	**—362—**	1968	d) 447US540
arranged 22LE889n	441FS1155	Cir. 5	Walker v Cali-	(20LE640)	450US469
by 46LE913n	Cir. 4	386FS213	fornia	(88SC1665)	452US69
18A4673n	324FS263	Cir. 6	1968	s) 391US9	453US65
circuit 28A41134n	Cir. 5	179F3d438	(20LE648)	s) 376F2d578	j) 453US559
96A5332n	285FS774	**—360—**	(88SC1672)	**—367—**	456US226
and	296FS180	Howard v	US reh den	United States v	458US912
then **—352—**	329FS1328	Ohio	392US947	O'Brien	j) 459US950
state Wilson v Port	Cir. 6	1968	**—362—**	1968	460US580
Lavaca	432F2d339	(20LE647)	Rubeck v New	(20LE672)	460US586
1968	Cir. 7	(88SC1671)	York	(88SC1673)	461US216
(20LE636)	286FS852	**—361—**	1968	US reh den	f) 466US804
(88SC1502)	288FS206	Brooks v	(20LE649)	393US900	j) 466US824
s) 409F2d1362	307FS402	Briley	(88SC1672)	s) 376F2d538	468US293
s) 285FS85	309FS1343	1968	s) 28NYAD	j) 393US57	j) 468US308
393US84	310FS297	(20LE647)	[1208	393US113	j) 468US689
395US827	311FS770	(88SC1671)	s) 286NYS2d	j) 393US250	j) 468US703
404US2	314FS812	s) 274FS538	[217	394US594	468US847
414US806	318FS631	Cir. 1	Cir. 6	j) 394US616	469US76
419US100	322FS1276	343FS903	179F3d439	j) 394US652	f) 470US611
419US812	327FS1387	Cir. 2		395US455	471US228
Cir. 1	Cir. 8	321FS679			f) 472US688
309FS1336	302FS1402				j) 473US822
Cir. 2	Wis				j) 474US1072
435F2d1250	41Wis2d508				*Continued*
436F2d1293					

Figure 9-7
Sample Page from *Shepard's Federal Citations*

FEDERAL SUPPLEMENT

Vol. 446

Citing cases arranged by circuit and then state

—120—
j446US466
j64LE433
j100SC1785
Cir. 2
596F2d[3]1100
Cir. 5
j597F2d430
Cir. 8
624F2d826
Cir. 10
535FS[2]528
Ill
117Il2518
452NE1388
Minn
280NW25
59ARF840n
59ARF854n
14ARF849s

—124—
j446US466
j64LE433
j100SC1785
Cir. 5
j597F2d430
14ARF849s

—129—
23ARF637s

—131—
s595F2d1209
s646F2d563
60LE[3]936
99SC[2]2330
Cir. 4
500FS[2]782
Cir. 8
579F2d[3]1087
72ARF438n

—136—
f471FS[4]962
471FS[1]963
565FS[3]1548
Cir. 7
d581FS[2]657
d581FS[5]657
N Y
85NYAD926
446NYS2d
[770
Cir. DC

—141—
a577F2d723
cc585F2d7
Cir. 3
555FS[1]693
Cir. 11
68BRW[5]227
68BRW[7]228
P R
109DPR828

—149—
a593F2d1372

—153—
a589F2d39

—160—
(199PQ466)
a599F2d1126
Cir. 2
452FS444
452FS[5]446
469FS680
512FS982
Cir. 7
635FS[2]611

—165—
(201PQ242)
s463FS232
Cir. DC
477FS[5]947
Cir. 3
f482FS[5]17
495FS[5]540
f503FS[5]211
503FS[4]213
509FS[5]351
533FS[5]20
Cir. 11
644FS[5]547

—171—
Cir. DC
f516FS[3]1259
d538FS[4]895
Cir. 4
724FS[4]378
Cir. 7
565FS414
Cir. 9
652F2d[3]917
AgD§ 17.53
Cir. 4
500FS[5]782

—175—
Cir. 2
604F2d794

—178—
r581F2d172
s553F2d51
Mo
cc530SW457
S D
272NW311

—181—
US cert den
in444US926
in100SC265
a598F2d310
Cir. DC
655F2d361
729FS7
Cir. 1
d695FS[8]638
Cir. 2
475FS[7]934
Cir. 5
659F2d[3]709
Cir. 10
595F2d[1]538
716F2d1351
D C
462A2d14
Haw
1HA212
616P2d1030
Ky
598SW471
Mo
643SW14

N J
189NJS574
461A2d190
N C
42NCA228
256SE479
35ARF461s

—186—
Cir. 1
562FS[3]227
Cir. 2
497FS[4]1071
Mo
618SW452
13ARF145s
28ARF266s
28ARF534s

—191—
Cir. 8
d510FS[1]1060
Cir. 9
537FS[1]979
73ARF357n

—193—
US reh den
in449US1028
in101SC601
D449US808
D66LE11
D101SC55
s489FS1248
cc392US83
cc20LE947
cc88SC1942
cc271FS1

—195—
Cir. 2

—196—
Cir. 3
66BRW[1]395
Cir. 6
15BRW[1]754
59BRW[1]844

—199—
Cir. 6
550FS[5]431
550FS[6]431

—206—
(197PQ903)
649FS[5]343
649FS[7]345
Cir. 3
495FS[4]317
495FS[6]317
527FS[8]740
539FS[4]161
539FS[5]161
539FS[6]161
d583FS523
632FS[1]0[2]
704FS[5]545
718FS[10]344
Cir. 7
575FS[5]1424
12ARF502s

13ARF323s

—209—
Cir. 2
461FS[1]135
601FS[1]725
Cir. 11
666F2d[1]523
Md
54MdA144
458A2d457
64ARF683n
20ARF731s

—210—
Cir. 2
511FS1186
549FS[3]1141
556FS[3]560
Cir. 3
657F2d[3]35
Cir. 6
c500FS[3]1154
Cir. 8
627F2d[3]850
471FS[1]464
e471FS[2]465
e471FS[3]465
627FS[3]850
Cir. 11
533FS[2]88

—212—
Cir. 1
752F2d[1]8
655FS[2]743
Cir. 2
462FS[4]700
562FS824
639FS[3]320
673FS[2]91
696FS[9]61
710FS461
Cir. 9
719FS1517
Cir. 10
520FS[4]1198
Colo
626P2d691

—216—
Cir. DC
q683F2d449
526FS[7]822
Cir. 2
555FS[7]268
Cir. 4
476FS[10]801
Cir. 7
f25BRW267
25BRW[3]268
Ark
266Ark536
588SW694
Colo
42CoA391
595P2d273
61ARF848n
11ARF815s
27ARF602s

—221—
a585F2d22
Cir. 2
488FS[1]516
488FS[4]517
Cir. 9
d815F2d[1]1274

Cir. 6
c864F2d[16]424

—226—
Cir. 10
457FS1016
474FS[3]443
480FS[2]262

—232—
Mo
654SW334
29A281n

—236—
a588F2d90

—242—
ML
446FS1268
448FS[1]273
458FS[1]225
483FS[1]825
MFP§ 6.20

—244—
v687F2d14
s636F2d480
s453FS648
s464FS949
cc768F2d1263
cc533FS703
cc89FRD695
539FS[24]838
13MJ884
16MJ892
22MJ74
75TCt15
669F2d[2]949
Cir. 8
720F2d[1]535
720F2d[2]535
Cir. 11
704F2d588
Calif
132CA3d926
183CaR501
Conn
180Ct105
429A2d816
D C
422A2d1285
Haw
60Haw245
589P2d520
Ill
68Il2385
385NE853
Ind
441NE472
Iowa
834F2d6
Cir. 3
505FS[32]1228
729FS[12]1482
88FRD562
Cir. 4
800F2d440
814F2d956
493FS602
495FS[11]565
592FS[25]441
728FS1273
Cir. 5
722F2d1198
508FS1202
508FS1203
508FS1204
561FS697

f503FS[9]797
f503FS[10]797
f503FS[11]797
f503FS[12]797
Cir. 7
d607F2d785
803F2d[36]279
521FS[5]121
521FS[5]221
532FS[50]1133
546FS[88]1140
688FS[35]1323
Cir. 8
633F2d[36]84
633F2d[37]85
641F2d598
c771F2d1120
779F2d[38]436
d779F2d[39]439
88FRD[88]348
Cir. 9
500FS[66]428
502FS[9]866
Cir. 10
570FS[7]1519
575FS340
Cir. 11
704F2d[49]1538
541FS1350
Cir. 4
669F2d[2]949
Alk
700P2d1307
718P2d141
Ariz
134Az348
656P2d637
—248—
ML
464FS[1]966
470FS[1]866
487FS[1]1354
—252—
Cir. 1
470FS[1]859
Calif
87CA3d760
151CaR433
GMS§ 2.05
PLPD§ 2.37
TT§ 15.08
La
425So2d759
Md
296Md686
296Md707
306Md328
48MdA390
55MdA468
427A2d1046
463A2d293
464A2d1037
464A2d1047
508A2d983
Mass
377Mas202

381Mas734
15MaA402
17MaA708
20MaA120
385NE519
412NE343
446NE91
462NE331
478NE753
Mich
432Mch110
123McA317
175McA765
333NW267
437NW613
438NW659
Minn
292NW769
Mo
609SW434
N J
432A2d91
N M
97NM686
643P2d250
99NYM871
100NYM388
105NYM845
107NYM233
109NYM77
117NYM754
118NYM237
136NYM736
417NYS2d
[648
419NYS2d
[426
433NYS2d
[542
435NYS2d
[463
437NYS2d
[1020
459NYS2d
[540
460NYS2d
[883
474NYS2d
[987
519NYS2d
[318
N C
315NC85
337SE840
N D
337NW147
Ohio
169A283
475NE810
Ore
309Ore116
786P2d153
W Va
358SE200
Wyo
638P2d1282
674P2d725
674P2d729
HHb§ 6.01
2LE1686s
15AE1152s
5A3763s

5A3819s
37A3612s
19A21213n
48ARF454n
55ARF695n
57ARF960n
60ARF532n
85ARF61n
25ARF723s

—329—
35LE735s

—330—
Cir. DC
579FS[2]166
Cir. 2
d465FS[11]602
493FS740
497FS[12]1086
529FS[8]229
534FS[3]330
582FS[1]1524
609FS[1]79
628FS733
658FS[8]813
83FRD448
20BRW[2]806
[465
N M
93NM117
597P2d302
100NYM388
105NYM845
107NYM233
109NYM77
117NYM754
118NYM237
38A31102s

—342—
Cir. 5
755F2d[4]1167

—348—
Cir. 2
478FS[1]1064
602FS[5]514
602FS[5]514
603FS[13]373
49ARF403n
72ARF109n
27ARF407s

—357—
s469FS54
s83FRD112
Cir. 5
634F2d[1]290
Cir. 6
f598F2d[1]1024
Cir. 3
489FS1283
49ARF397n

—361—
a588F2d61
Cir. DC
813F2d430
Cir. 1
677F2d[9]161
Cir. 3
630F2d[6]90
474FS[1]1261
483FS[10]341
Cir. 3
q466FS[18]1227
472FS[4]1328
Cir. 4
q454FS1083

Continued

certainly look up your case citation in each and every one of the *Shepard's* volumes, both hardcover and softcover, that may not be necessary. The front cover or the spine of the *Shepard's* volumes may provide you with information that your case is not covered by that volume. For example, assume the case you need to Shepardize is *Pillsbury Co. v. Conboy*, 459 U.S. 248 (1983). When you retrieve the volumes of *Shepard's*, you may note that the spine or the front of the first hardcover volume states, "Cases to 420 U.S." This would be an indication that your case is not covered by that volume. You would then proceed to examine the next volume of *Shepard's* and determine whether your case will be Shepardized by that volume.

Another tip as to which volume to start in is that *Shepard's* will provide you with a parallel citation in parentheses only the first time your case is cited. After that, the parallel citation will not be repeated in subsequent volumes. Thus, when you find the parallel citation in parentheses, you know that you should Shepardize in that volume and in volumes published thereafter. Similarly, when you Shepardize, if you are never provided with a parallel citation, this should serve as a signal that one of the volumes of *Shepard's* is missing, unless there is no parallel citation for your case.

It does not matter whether you start with the more recent softcover supplements and work backward to the older hardbound volumes or whether you start Shepardizing by using the hardbound volumes and work forward to the recently issued softcover supplements. Use the approach that works best for you so long as you check all the volumes that cover the period of time after your case was decided.

Remember that *Shepard's* volumes are not always cumulative. You cannot examine the most recent volume or supplement and assume it covers every case decided since your case was decided. Each volume of *Shepard's* relates to a separate and distinct period of time. For example, the most recent softcover supplement for *Shepard's Maryland Citations* will list only those cases decided in the past six weeks that have mentioned or discussed certain cases. Thus, you may need to examine several volumes of *Shepard's*. As a rule of thumb, the older your case is, the more volumes of *Shepard's* you will need to examine.

Practice Tip

Daily Updating

The print volumes of *Shepard's* are updated about every six weeks. To make sure that nothing has happened in the past six weeks that negatively affects your case, use *Shepard's* Daily Update service. Call (800) 899-6000 to determine what has happened to your case since your last print supplement arrived.

15. *Troubleshooting*

There are several events that should serve as hints that something has gone wrong in the Shepardizing process.

(i)   If you never find a parallel cite for your case, this may indicate that one of the volumes of *Shepard's* is missing. Do not forget, however, that lower federal court cases have no parallel cites and that many states no longer publish officially. Thus, there are no parallel cites for these cases. Check the box or notice labeled "What Your Library Should Contain" to be sure you have all of the volumes you need.

(ii) If you never see any entry for your case, it is possible that the citation is incorrect. Check to make sure you have not transposed numbers in the citation. It is also possible that you are attempting to Shepardize in the wrong series. This is a common mistake. For example, if your citation is *Jones v. Smith*, 141 Ill. App. 3d 499, 349 N.E.2d 809 (1986), and you are Shepardizing using *Shepard's Illinois Citations*, make sure you have located the pages that Shepardize Volume 141 of *Illinois Appellate Reports, 3d Series*, rather than *Illinois Appellate Reports, 2d Series*, or *Illinois Appellate Reports. Shepard's* will contain a Table of Contents directing you to the appropriate pages for the series in which you are interested.

(iii) If the entries in the book look completely unfamiliar to you, it is likely that you have retrieved the volumes of *Shepard's* for statutes rather than cases.

(iv) If one or two of the *Shepard's* volumes do not list your case, this may mean that during the period of time covered by that issue no case or other source mentioned or discussed your case. This is not a cause for concern.

(v)   Remember that *Shepard's* is entirely self-correcting. To reassure yourself that your Shepardizing technique is correct, retrieve one of the cases listed by *Shepard's* and verify that it mentions your case. Once you have verified that you are Shepardizing correctly, you will soon feel more confident about your technique.

16. *Using* Shepard's *to Find Parallel Citations*

While there are usually alternative ways to find a parallel cite for a case (see Chapter 4), Shepardizing is probably the easiest and most efficient. If you have only a single citation to a case and your law library or law firm does not purchase this set, or the volume you need is missing from the shelf, you should immediately Shepardize the citation and obtain the parallel cite, which is given in parentheses. This will enable you to readily locate the case you need. See Figure 9-8 for steps in Shepardizing cases.

Figure 9-8
Steps in Sheparding a Case

- Locate the volumes of *Shepard's* you need (state *Shepard's*, regional *Shepard's*, or federal case *Shepard's*).
- Examine the front cover of the most recent issue of *Shepard's* and read the box labeled "What Your Library Should Contain." Make sure you have all of the volumes needed.
- Select the volumes of *Shepard's* that contain citations to cases decided after your case was decided.
- Examine the upper right and left corners of the pages in *Shepard's* to locate the volume number of the case you are Shepardizing.
- Scan down the page looking for the bold page number identical to the page on which your case begins.
- Carefully examine the entries listed, paying particular attention to the parallel citation, the history of the case as it progressed through the court system, its treatment by other cases, and any other sources, such as annotations and law review articles that discuss your case.
- If desired, verify that you are Shepardizing correctly by checking one or two cites listed by *Shepard's* to ensure your case is, in fact, mentioned by these cites.
- Repeat, as needed, in other volumes of *Shepard's*.
- Examine and analyze troublesome entries, including later cases that criticize or question your case.

C. Shepardizing Statutes

1. *Locating* Shepard's *for Statutes*

Just as you must Shepardize a case to determine whether it is still "good law," you must Shepardize a statute to determine its history and how it has been treated by later court decisions. The technique of Shepardizing statutes is substantially similar to Shepardizing cases.

You must make sure you have the volumes of *Shepard's* for statutes rather than cases. Some states, usually those with a rich body of case law, such as California, have volumes of *Shepard's* for cases and then entirely separate volumes devoted solely to statutes. Other states have combined the references for cases and statutes in one volume. In these books, the *Shepard's* case citations are given first, followed by the statute citations. Within the volumes or sections for statutes are also citations for a state's constitution and usually citations to local ordinances as well as court rules and jury instructions.

Be sure to check the section on the front cover of the latest issue of *Shepard's* entitled "What Your Library Should Contain" and retrieve all of the volumes you need, both hardcover and softcover. Most law libraries

maintain the volumes of *Shepard's* for statutes immediately next to the
volumes of *Shepard's* for cases. All of the *Shepard's* volumes are usually
located immediately after the last volume of reports for state or for federal
cases.

2.   *Locating* Shepard's *References to Your Statute*

If your state arranges its statutes solely by number, as most states do, open
one of the volumes of *Shepard's*, check the upper left and right corners of
each page and look for a reference to your statute or one numerically close
to it. Then scan down the page looking for a boldfaced reference to your
statute.

If your state arranges its statutes by title, as do California, Maryland,
New York, and Texas, locate the title you need by looking at the upper left-
and righthand corners of each page. When you have located your title
(Agriculture, Corporations, or Education), scan down the page to locate
the boldfaced reference to your statute. Be sure you are checking the right
title and that when you want to Shepardize Education Section 5201,
you are not mistakenly Shepardizing Elections Section 5201 or Finance
Section 5201.

3.   *Analysis of References in* Shepard's

Similar to the way *Shepard's* provides you with information about a case
through the use of various abbreviations, it also indicates the history and
treatment of a statute you are Shepardizing by the use of abbreviations
placed before the entries listed. Do not be concerned that you will not be
able to remember or memorize all of the abbreviations. Each volume of
Shepard's Citations for Statutes will contain a Table of Abbreviations
placed near the front of the volume. See Figure 9-9 for the most common
abbreviations for history and treatment of statutes.

a.   History References

The first entries given will relate to the history of your statute, namely,
how it has been treated subsequently by the *legislature*. It is possible that
your statute has been amended, repealed, or suspended. *Shepard's* will
provide this information to you through the use of identifying letters. For
example, a reference to "A1990C37" would mean that your statute had
been amended and you would find the amending language in Chapter 37 of
your state's session laws for 1990.

b.   Treatment References

Following the entries related to the history of your statute in the legislature, you will be given entries related to the treatment of your statute by
cases. Perhaps a court in your state or a federal court case has interpreted

Figure 9-9
Abbreviations Relating to Statutes

History in Legislature

A	(amended)	Statute amended
Ad	(added)	Addition of new section
E	(extended)	Provisions of a statute extended to a later statute or additional time allowed for performance of duties required by a statute within a specific time
L	(limited)	Provisions of a statute not extended to a later statute
R	(repealed)	Repeal of an existing statute
Re-en	(re-enacted)	Statute re-enacted
Rn	(renumbered)	Existing sections of a statute renumbered
Rp	(repealed in part)	Repeal of part of an existing statute
Rs	(repealed and superseded)	Repeal of an existing statute and substitution of new legislation
Rv	(revised)	Statute revised
S	(superseded)	Substitution of new legislation for an existing statute not expressly repealed
Sd	(suspended)	Suspension of statute
Sdp	(suspended in part)	Suspension of part of statute
Sg	(supplementing)	Addition of new matter to an existing statute
Sp	(superseded in part)	Substitution of new legislation for part of an existing statute not expressly repealed

Judicial Treatment

C	(constitutional)	Statute declared to be constitutional
U	(unconstitutional)	Statute declared to be unconstitutional
Up	(unconstitutional in part)	Statute declared to be unconstitutional in part
V	(void or invalid)	Statute declared to be void or invalid
Va	(valid)	Statute declared to be valid
Vp	(void or invalid in part)	Statute declared to be void or invalid in part
f	(followed)	Case follows or relies upon statute
i	(interpreted)	Case interprets or construes statute
j	(dissenting opinion)	Statute mentioned in dissenting opinion
na	(not applicable)	Case finds statute not applicable
rt	(retroactive/ prospective)	Case discusses retroactivity or prospective application of statute

your statute and determined it is unconstitutional or void. This treatment is indicated by letters placed before the citation. For example, if you have Shepardized a statute and you are presented with the entry "U577A2d784," this signifies that your statute was held unconstitutional, and the determinative language is located on page 784 of Volume 577 of the *Atlantic Reporter, Second Series*. If no identifying letters are given, this is simply an indication that a case has mentioned your statute in some generalized fashion.

c. No References to Your Statute

One of the detailed features of Shepardizing a statute is that you will be directed to the history and treatment of each particular subsection of a statute. For example, if you have cited Section 5201(b) of your state's code, generally you need only examine the references for subdivision (b) of Section 5201. If other portions of the statute have been repealed or ruled unconstitutional, you may still be able to rely upon and cite your particular subdivision. Moreover, you can readily locate cases interpreting the subdivision in which you are interested and bypass the cases or other authorities that mention or discuss other portions of the statute.

If you are Shepardizing your statute in a volume of *Shepard's* and your statute never appears, it is possible that during the period of time covered by that volume of *Shepard's* the legislature did not deal with that statute and no cases or other sources mentioned or discussed your statute. You may then close that volume of *Shepard's* and proceed to examine the next volume.

d. Other References

Just as *Shepard's Citations* for cases will direct you to law review articles, attorneys general opinions, and annotations that mention or discuss a case you are Shepardizing, *Shepard's Citations* for statutes will direct you to law review articles, attorneys general opinions, and annotations that mention your statute. Additionally, *Shepard's* will cite administrative decisions that have mentioned your statute.

4. Advantages of Shepardizing Statutes

You may recall from Chapter 3 that statutes are typically updated by cumulative pocket parts or statutory supplements, which will provide you with any changes or amendments to a statute as well as references to newer cases interpreting that statute. Most publishers issue these pocket parts on an annual basis and the supplements on a quarterly basis. Because *Shepard's* issues its new supplements every few weeks, it can offer you the most up-to-date information on your statute. For example, if a case declares your statute unconstitutional, *Shepard's* will usually provide you with a reference to this case well before a new pocket part or supplement to the annotated code is issued.

5. *Analyzing Negative Letters*

If you encounter "negative" letters when you Shepardize your statute (such as "R" for repealed or "U" for unconstitutional), exercise great caution. Carefully examine the *Shepard's* entries. It is possible that only a portion of the statute or some other subdivision of the statute has been repealed or ruled unconstitutional. In all instances, retrieve and read the negative entries listed in *Shepard's* to determine the exact status of your statute. See Figure 9-10 for a sample page from *Shepard's Virginia Citations for Statutes*.

6. *Shepardizing Federal Statutes*

The process of Shepardizing a federal statute is virtually identical to that of Shepardizing a state statute. Assume that you are interested in Shepardizing 29 U.S.C. § 216 (2000). Locate the volumes of *Shepard's* entitled *Shepard's Federal Statute Citations*. Examine the section entitled "What Your Library Should Contain" to ensure you have all of the volumes of *Shepard's* you need. Look in the upper right- and left-hand corners of the pages for references to Title 29. Then scan down the page to locate a boldfaced reference to Section 216.

You will now be presented with references to the history of this statute (for example, what treatment it has received from the United States Congress), references to the treatment of this case by federal cases (arranged by circuits and districts), references to annotations, and to articles, texts, and treatises that have mentioned this statute. See Figure 9-11 for a sample page from *Shepard's Federal Statute Citations*.

7. *When to Shepardize*

Just as you have seen with regard to Shepardizing cases, the decision when to Shepardize statutes is left to your discretion. Shepardizing fairly early in the research process, however, may save you time by alerting you to any problems with your statute and may provide you with valuable research sources by referring you to cases, annotations, and law review articles that discuss your statute.

8. *How Many Volumes to Use When Shepardizing a Statute*

There are usually fewer volumes of *Shepard's* for statutes than for case citations. When you first begin Shepardizing a statute, use all volumes. As you become more experienced, you may be able to skip some volumes by

Figure 9-10
Sample Page from *Shepard's Virginia Citations for Statutes*

§ 1-1 et seq.
1962C345
1964C625

§§ 1-1 to 1-18
85McL649

§ 1-2
192Va518
198Va824
65SE575
97SE5

§ 1-3
193Va47
67SE923

§ 1-4
1962C520
A 1971C14
189Va847
193Va47
55SE49
67SE923

§ 1-7
202Va979
121SE516

§ 1-10 et seq.
1960p418
1960p498
1962p1232
1966p1332

§ 1-10
189Va1
194Va165
197Va169
201Va829
211Va530
212Va191
213Va102
214Va93
216Va470
218Va473
219Va287
221Va623
221Va977
226Va594
227Va395
232Va353
244Va65
248Va282
4VCO311
6VCO15
8VCO232
12VCO445
29VCO427
33VCO192

34VCO511
52SE135
72SE321
89SE23
113SE875
178SE506
183SE200
189SE678
197SE205
220SE245
237SE900
247SE400
272SE444
275SE631
311SE410
315SE849
350SE623
418SE864
448SE628
Cir. 4
439F2d940
845F2d88
979F2d990
221FS185
529FS625
538FS606
624FS472
726FS646
755FS693
875FS1175
98BRW247
Cir. 8
439F2d229
14RIC157
15RIC250
15RIC283
27RIC908
52VaL35
57VaL1511
58VaL220
76VaL1516
42W&L435
13W&M253
24W&M730

§ 1-11
221Va623
272SE444
Cir. 4
7F3d390
2W&M388
13W&M253

§ 1-12
A 1971C49
A 1981C329
219Va143
219Va658
246SE613
250SE739
Cir. 4
640F2d502
391FS463

Subsec. A
Cir. 4
829F2d1326

§ 1-13 et seq.
13VCO466

§ 1-13
A 1950C18
1954C271
214Va425
21VCO277
201SE777
Cir. 4
330FS351

§ 1-13.1 et seq.
1954C697
1958C373 §1

§ 1-13.1
Ad 1950C18
201Va514
112SE137
46VaL1664

§ 1-13.1:1
Ad 1977C156
237Va487
378SE827

§ 1-13.2
Ad 1950C18
A 1971C49

§ 1-13.3
Ad 1950C18
A 1987C92
2VaA39
5VCO371
6VCO15
6VCO344
10VCO487
15VCO312
17VCO164
17VCO299
18VCO358
22VCO55
25VCO193
27VCO149
32VCO438
341SE214
Cir. 4
895F2d142
145BRW224
44VaL506
98AE1428n

§ 1-13.3:1
Ad 1962C284
A 1977C93
A 1986C166
7VCO89
10VCO488

12VCO135
17VCO165
25VCO193
32VCO438
Cir. 4
567F2d263
895F2d142
145BRW224
17RIC35

§ 1-13.4
Ad 1950C18
R 1986C155
199Va665
101SE631

§ 1-13.5
Ad 1950C18
197Va123
87SE806

§ 1-13.5:1
Ad 1971C49
57VaL1566

§ 1-13.6
Ad 1950C18

§ 1-13.7
Ad 1950C18
227Va288
20VCO31
315SE385

§ 1-13.8
Ad 1950C18

§ 1-13.9
Ad 1950C18
208Va700
213Va545
216Va25
230Va484
9VaA334
12VaA764
14VaA1087
13VCO376
160SE563
193SE671
215SE637
339SE543
387SE794
406SE917
421SE865
Cir. 4
550FS1030

§ 1-13.9:1
Ad 1993C308

§ 1-13.10
Ad 1950C18

§ 1-13.11
Ad 1950C18
R 1981C228
219Va1084
254SE108
Cir. 4
979F2d990

§ 1-13.12
Ad 1950C18
197Va861
91SE441
Cir. 4
547FS108

§ 1-13.13
Ad 1950C18

§ 1-13.14
Ad 1950C18

§ 1-13.15
Ad 1950C18

§ 1-13.16
Ad 1950C18

§ 1-13.17
Ad 1950C18
195Va844
195Va1084
196Va177
203Va182
212Va693
215Va231
221Va206
222Va236
223Va763
233Va449
3VaA582
4VCO316
5VCO156
20VCO29
27VCO16
27VCO258
30VCO306
34VCO135
80SE605
81SE587
83SE397
122SE911
187SE168
208SE51
269SE362
279SE161
292SE383
352SE13
357SE202

§ 1-13.18
Ad 1950C18

§ 1-13.19
Ad 1950C18
1954C645 §2
1954C669
1954C693 §2
1956p1064
1956C677
1962p537
1964C480
A 1988C36
203Va182
203Va522
209Va383
210Va138
214Va425
217Va595
217Va699
10VCO118
122SE911
125SE169
164SE676
169SE440
201SE777
231SE309
233SE120
299SE347
299SE620
Cir. 4
943F2d1385
330FS351
424FS291
800FS343
28RIC1151
48VaL1193
55VaL1605

§ 1-13.20
Ad 1950C18
197Va861
91SE441

§ 1-13.21
Ad 1950C18
A 1971C49
Cir. DC
507FS986

§ 1-13.22
Ad 1950C18
1954C295
A 1958C330
A 1966C78

§ 1-13.22:1
Ad 1954C295
Rn §1-13.10:1

§ 1-13.23
Ad 1950C18

§ 1-13.23:1
Ad 1954C543

Continued

621

Figure 9-11
Sample Page from *Shepard's Federal Statute Citations*

UNITED STATES CODE   **TITLE 29 § 216**

Cir. 5	2003USDist LX23830	314FS2d1257△2004	Cir. 5
2004USDist LX16298	[*2003	342FS2d1133△2004	2003USDist LX20681
[△2004	i) 2005USDist LX2274	ClCt	[△2003
Cir. 7	[△2005	2005USClaims LX74	2004USDist LX14965
296FS2d916△2003	Cir. 4	[△2005	[△2004
Cir. 8	337F3d427△2003	2005USClaims LX74	2004USDist LX20477
2005USDist LX2559	344FS2d952△2004	[*2000	[△2004
[△2005	Cir. 5		2004USDist LX23568
Cir. 9	363F3d572△2004	**§ 215(a)(5)**	[△2004
345F3d744△2003	2005USDist LX2221	Cir. 1	2005USDist LX2903
Cir. 11	[△2005	1991USDist LX21853	[△2005
333FS2d1371△2004	2005USDist LX2903	[△1991	2005USDist LX3753
	[△2005	Cir. 7	[△2005
§ 215(a)(2)	2005USDist LX3323	296BRW167△2003	244FS2d685△2002
Cir. 5	[△2005	Cir. 8	318FS2d449△2004
2005USDist LX2221	252FS2d367△2003	287FS2d984△2003	319FS2d754△2004
[△2005	286FS2d802△2003	Cir. 10	Cir. 6
Cir. 6	318FS2d375△2004	1980USDist LX17856	292FS2d954△2002
328FS2d834△2004	Cir. 6	[△1980	312FS2d972△2004
Cir. 7	355F3d563△2004		Cir. 7
296BRW167△2003	119Fed Appx778△2005	**§ 216**	1993USDist LX21446
Cir. 8	2002USDist LX26129	**et seq.**	[△1993
287FS2d984△2003	[△2002	Cir. 2	2003USDist LX7275
Cir. 10	2003USDist LX10700	364F3d72△2004	[△2003
360F3d1185△2004	[△2003	2004USDist LX14516	2003USDist LX13759
365F3d1203△2004	259FS2d654△2003	[△2004	[△2003
1980USDist LX17856	341FS2d762△2004	Cir. 11	2004USDist LX23753
[△1980	Cir. 7	289FS2d1370△2003	[△2004
Cir. 11	2005USApp LX4557		268FS2d1009△2003
347F3d1243△2003	[△2005	**§ 216**	Cir. 8
302FS2d1319△2004	2000USDist LX22587	Cir. DC	2003USDist LX19058
303FS2d1274△2004	[△2000	j) 396F3d1218*1960	[△2003
	2003USDist LX14698	Cir. 1	2004USDist LX4556
§ 215(a)(3)	[△2003	1991USDist LX21853	[△2004
Cir. DC	2003USDist LX16459	[△1991	341FS2d1090△2004
2004USDist LX27084	[△2003	252FS2d9△2001	Cir. 9
[△2004	i) 2004USDist LX3283	312FS2d116△2004	87Fed Appx26△2003
338FS2d130△2004	[△2004	Cir. 2	2001USDist LX25344
Cir. 1	2004USDist LX8476	2005USApp LX4935	[△2001
375F3d102△2004	[△2004	[△2005	2003USDist LX25500
2004USDist LX21997	2004USDist LX19194	2003USDist LX16706	[△2003
[△2004	[△2004	[△2003	2004USDist LX20377
2005USDist LX3270	2004USDist LX19452	2003USDist LX21227	[△2004
[△2005	[△2004	[△2003	2005USDist LX4269
257FS2d502△2003	2004USDist LX19562	2003USDist LX23763	[△2005
Cir. 2	[△2004	[△2003	Cir. 10
2005USApp LX4935	2004USDist LX19854	2004USDist LX12816	347FS2d994△2004
[△2005	[△2004	[△2004	347FS2d997*1970
390F3d757△2004	302FS2d883△2004	2004USDist LX14811	214FRD627△2002
75Fed Appx36△2003	Cir. 8	[△2004	Cir. 11
2003USDist LX16706	396F3d1034△2005	2004USDist LX25646	349F3d1297△2003
[△2003	Cir. 9	[△2004	377F3d1245△2004
2003USDist LX18341	2004USDist LX15233	237FS2d509△2002	2003USDist LX8158
[△2003	[△2004	246FS2d174△2002	[△2003
2003USDist LX23230	255FS2d1064△2003	224FRD343△2004	2005USDist LX574
[△2003	300FS2d1068△2004	Cir. 3	[△2005
2004USDist LX1334	Cir. 10	2005USApp LX5225	216FRD556△2003
[△2004	365F3d1201△2004	[△2005	Cir. Fed.
2004USDist LX12816	272FS2d1218△2003	357F3d372△2004	350F3d1226△2003
[△2004	347FS2d996△2004	2003USDist LX21010	ClCt
267FS2d300△2003	Cir. 11	[△2003	2005USClaims LX74
302FS2d135△2003	345F3d906△2003	2004USDist LX2640	[△2005
344FS2d405△2004	2003USDist LX14036	[△2004	
220FRD230△2003	[△2003	2004USDist LX15716	**§ 216(a)**
Cir. 3	236FS2d1299△2002	[△2004	Cir. 4
2003USDist LX23830	243FS2d1373△2003	Cir. 4	314FS2d604△2004
[△2003	296FS2d1307△2003	314FS2d604△2004	

Citing cases arranged by circuit

37

realizing that a newly enacted statute will only appear in the most recently issued softcover *Shepard's* supplements.

9. *Troubleshooting*

If you Shepardize a statute and you never find any entries to it, this may indicate that your statute has never been subsequently dealt with by the legislature or any later cases. It may also indicate a problem in the Shepardizing process. If this occurs:

   (i)   Examine your citation to make sure you have cited it correctly and have not transposed any numbers.

  (ii)   Examine the box on the most recent softcover supplement labeled "What Your Library Should Contain" to ensure you have all of the appropriate volumes.

 (iii)   Review the entries in *Shepard's* to verify that you are Shepardizing Probate Code Section 52 rather than Public Utilities Section 52, if your statute is cited by a title as well as a number.

See Figure 9-12 for steps in Shepardizing statutes.

Figure 9-12
Steps in Sheperdizing a Statute

- Locate the volumes of *Shepard's* you need (*Shepard's [State] Citations for Statutes, Shepard's Federal Statute Citations*).
- Examine the front cover of the most recent issue of *Shepard's* and read the box labeled "What Your Library Should Contain." Make sure you have all of the volumes needed.
- Examine the upper right and left corners of the pages in *Shepard's* to locate the article or title of the statute you are Shepardizing.
- Scan down the page looking for a boldfaced entry for the particular section in which you are interested. If your statutes are arranged by title, exercise caution to be sure you are Shepardizing the correct title.
- Carefully examine the entries listed, paying particular attention to the history of the statute by the legislature, its treatment by cases, and any other sources, such as law review articles and annotations that cite your statute.
- If desired, verify that you are Shepardizing correctly by checking one or two cites listed by *Shepard's* to ensure your statute is in fact mentioned by these other cites.
- Repeat the process in all volumes of *Shepard's*.
- Analyze troublesome entries.

D. Shepardizing Constitutions

1. Shepardizing Provisions of State Constitutions

The volumes of *Shepard's* that enable you to Shepardize statutes from your state will also contain references to the history and treatment of provisions of your state's constitution. To Shepardize provisions of your state's constitution, retrieve all of the volumes of *Shepard's Citations* for statutes for your state. Remember that some states have separate volumes of *Shepard's* for cases and for statutes. Other states will combine the citations for cases and statutes in the same volumes. Check the Table of Contents in the front of each volume of *Shepard's* which will direct you to the appropriate pages containing references to the state constitution.

Examine the upper left- and right-hand corners of each page for references to specific articles or amendments to the state constitution. Scan down the page looking for boldfaced references to specific provisions of your constitution. A typical entry would appear as follows:

> Art. 3
> § 9
> 741FS341
> 576A2d517
> 68TxL982

When you locate the specific provision of the constitution in which you are interested, you will be provided with the history of that provision (for example, whether it has been amended or repealed) and then with citations to state cases, federal cases, attorneys general opinions, law review articles, and annotations that have cited, mentioned, or discussed that provision of the constitution. You should then read and analyze the references as needed.

2. Shepardizing Provisions of the United States Constitution

Citations to the United States Constitution appear in the volumes of *Shepard's* that contain citations to our federal statutes, that is, *Shepard's Federal Statute Citations*. After you make sure you have all of the volumes you need, check the Table of Contents in the front of each volume so you will know on which page the citations to the United States Constitution begin. Check the upper right- and left-hand corners of each page for references to the articles or amendments you are Shepardizing and then scan down the page to find the particular provision in which you are interested. When you locate the pertinent provision you need to Shepardize, you will be presented with references to United States Supreme Court cases, lower federal court cases, and annotations that have cited, mentioned, or discussed that particular provision of the United States Constitution. Read and analyze these references, as needed. See Figures 9-13 and 9-14 for sample pages showing citations to the United States Constitution.

E. Sheparding Administrative Regulations

Chapter 10 discusses the enactment and publications of regulations of administrative agencies such as the FDA, FCC, and FAA. It is possible to Sheparding administrative regulations published in the *Code of Federal Regulations* by using *Shepard's Code of Federal Regulations Citations*. This set will also enable you to research presidential proclamations and executive orders.

The technique of Sheparding a federal regulation is substantially similar to Sheparding a case, statute, or constitutional provision. Retrieve the appropriate volumes and check the Table of Contents to be directed to the page on which references to the regulations begin. Locate the pertinent administrative regulation by examining the upper right- and left-hand corners of the pages and then scan the boldfaced entries on that page. When you locate the entry for your regulation, you will be provided with citations to cases, periodicals, and annotations that discuss your regulation.

F. Sheparding Restatement Provisions

All of the American Law Institute's Restatements (for example, the Restatements of Contracts, Property, Torts, Trusts, and so forth) can be Sheparded by using a set called *Shepard's Restatement of the Law Citations*. Thus, if you are relying upon a Restatement section in a document you are preparing, you can Shepardize the section, and you will be referred to the following authorities that mention your Restatement provision: U.S. Supreme Court cases, lower federal court cases, state court cases published in regional reporters, articles in selected significant law reviews, and A.L.R. annotations. Because the Restatements are likely the most persuasive of all of the secondary authorities, this *Shepard's* tool is a valuable research resource.

The set also includes citations to the Model Code of Evidence, allowing researchers to Shepardize a provision in the Model Code of Evidence and find all cases that have cited the particular provision.

Figure 9-13
Sample Page of Citations to United States Constitution

Preamble	313BRW143	Cir. 8	60FedCl 135	i) 158LE575	Cir. 5
Cir. 9	316BRW118	326F3d949	61FedCl 734	123SC1445	2005USDist
j) 328F3d576	Cir. 3	2003USDist	62FedCl 793	j) 123SC1458	[LX2412
	350F3d398	[LX14500	63FedCl 209	124SC685	265FS2d710
Art. 1	241FS2d480	274FS2d1097	59MJ152	124SC1773	298FS2d462
537US198	271FS2d715	Cir. 9	60MJ206	i) 124SC1792	i) 298FS2d463
538US464	285FS2d602	2004USApp	60MJ786	Cir. DC	j) 298FS2d516
541US272	334FS2d765	[LX9545	123TCt31	386F3d1154	Cir. 9
155LE640	343FS2d369	j) 328F3d582	123TCt97	340FS2d29	331F3d1027
158LE554	2001Bankr LX	399F3d1146	118.ÆS260n	Cir. 2	Cir. 10
j) 158LE786	[2112	2004USDist		394F3d94	265FS2d1267
158LE835	295BRW535	[LX11353	**§ 1**	2004USDist	Cir. 11
158LE896	319BRW388	243FS2d1137	j) 159LE43	[LX21341	330FS2d1280
j) 159LE45	Cir. 4	258FS2d1136	j) 124SC2274	2004USDist	340FS2d1300
159LE480	329F3d364	300FS2d976	Cir. DC	[LX25431	**Cl. 3**
123SC1672	365F3d305	302FS2d1183	251FS2d775	Cir. 3	Cir. DC
124SC1773	382F3d468	300BRW499	Cir. 1	2004USDist	375F3d1179
j) 124SC1920	j) 387F3d369	300BRW771	323F3d143	[LX21694	2005USDist
124SC1944	2001USDist	315BRW131	398F3d32	241FS2d482	[LX524
124SC1987	[LX25781	Cir. 10	290FS2d186	Cir. 4	2005USDist
j) 124SC2276	240FS2d572	389F3d1056	Cir. 2	2003USDist	[LX4309
124SC2589	244FS2d603	2003USDist	352F3d714	[LX25805	Cir. 2
Cir. DC	267FS2d525	[LX17787	2004USDist	2004USDist	2004USDist
321F3d1137	279FS2d692	2003USDist	[LX7500	[LX10835	[LX5559
373F3d1309	Cir. 5	[LX25298	Cir. 4	276FS2d538	Cir. 5
374F3d1167	2005USDist	2005USDist	2004USApp	Cir. 5	298FS2d461
j) 374F3d1172	[LX3926	[LX4266	[LX16730	2001USDist	i) 298FS2d462
2005USDist	330F3d364	241FS2d1301	327F3d360	[LX25424	Cir. 11
[LX1236	344F3d473	277FS2d1093	368F3d394	2001USDist	300FS2d1353
251FS2d713	378F3d432	295FS2d1270	j) 387F3d366	[LX25427	Cir. Fed.
257FS2d249	390F3d363	299FS2d1182	Cir. 5	237FS2d729	363F3d1293
272FS2d42	101Fed Appx4	317FS2d1242	352F3d204	298FS2d463	**Cl. 4**
297FS2d229	2003USDist	289BRW757	Cir. 7	Cir. 6	Cir. 1
303FS2d14	[LX13589	j) 294BRW161	367F3d655	368F3d651	346FS2d302
321FS2d112	2003USDist	294BRW789	2003USDist	j) 385F3d651	Cir. 6
Cir. 1	[LX26247	301BRW94	[LX16044	Cir. 9	385F3d644
377F3d109	2005USDist	Cir. 11	2004USDist	j) 328F3d576	j) 385F3d651
398F3d34	[LX4067	~) 2005USApp	[LX6933	375F3d821	**Cl. 5**
2004USDist	j) 298FS2d516	[LX5073	259FS2d793	Cir. 10	Cir. DC
[LX287	328FS2d658	384F3d1268	Cir. 8	265FS2d1259	309FS2d36
309FS2d182	2004Bankr LX	j) 387F3d1231	314FS2d949	345FS2d1261	**§ 3**
338FS2d276	[598	391F3d1305	Cir. 9	Cir. 11	Cir. DC
Cir. 2	289BRW834	394F3d922	335F3d937	327F3d1184	386F3d1154
344F3d97	307BRW564	395F3d1228	j) 364F3d1028	300FS2d1322	Cir. 2
352F3d713	Cir. 6	2003USDist	302FS2d1178	306FS2d1195	378F3d223
j) 352F3d727	326F3d730	[LX25575	Cir. 10	Cir. Fed.	Cir. 3
361F3d766	368F3d651	236FS2d1363	334F3d1212	363F3d1295	288FS2d704
368F3d97	381F3d528	294FS2d1341	348F3d1216	ClCt	Cir. 4
397F3d117	388F3d968	2003Bankr LX	345FS2d1262	57FedCl 502	305FS2d594
2004USDist	391F3d820	[1386	Cir. 11	58FedCl 189	325FS2d658
[LX6248	93Fed Appx25	2003Bankr LX	364F3d1270	60MJ790	Cir. 6
2004USDist	271FS2d940	[1458	233FS2d1348	**Cl. 1**	341FS2d1000
[LX6591	352FS2d785	Cir. Fed.	58MJ763	538US280	Cir. 7
2004USDist	130BRW499	322F3d1367	**§§ 2 to 3**	155LE432	2004USDist
[LX9134	293BRW130	344F3d1350	Cir. 11	123SC1445	[LX19657
2004USDist	308BRW805	363F3d1297	243FS2d1379	Cir. 1	Cir. 9
[LX17698	314BRW362	88Fed Appx	**§ 2**	338FS2d276	342F3d1079
2004USDist	314BRW685	[396	538US280	Cir. 10	Cir. 11
[LX19658	Cir. 7	ClCt	j) 538US305	265FS2d1259	381F3d1082
2004USDist	323F3d515	2003USClaims	540US187	**Cl. 2**	60MJ790
[LX24808	339F3d585	[LX394	541US272	Cir. 3	**Cl. 2**
242FS2d171	345F3d453	2004USClaims	i) 541US305	351F3d96	Cir. 11
298FS2d305	348F3d609	[LX202	155LE432	361F3d211	387F3d1227
299BRW262	90Fed Appx	57FedCl 236	j) 155LE448	76Fed Appx	j) 387F3d1231
300BRW188	[955	57FedCl 438	157LE575	[469	
	308FS2d924	57FedCl 769	158LE554		
	314FS2d817	58FedCl 381			

Citing cases arranged by article and clause

3

G. Shepardizing Court Rules

Rules of Court are discussed in Chapter 10. You can Shepardize these court rules to locate cases, law review articles, and annotations that refer to these rules, such as Rules of the Supreme Court of the United States, Federal Rules of Evidence, or the Federal Rules of Civil Procedure. To Shepardize state court rules, use the volumes of *Shepard's* for your state's statutes. To Shepardize federal court rules, use *Shepard's Federal Statute Citations*. The technique of Shepardizing a court rule is analogous to Shepardizing cases, statutes, and other sources.

H. Specialized Citators

There are several other sets of books published by *Shepard's* that cover more specialized topics. Among the more commonly used sets are the following:

    (i)   *Shepard's Acts and Cases by Popular Name—Federal and State.* If you know a federal or state statute or a federal or state case by its popular name, for example, the Lemon Law or the Macaroni Case, you can look up the statute or case in the alphabetically arranged lists in this book, which will then provide you with the correct citation to the statute or case.

    (ii)   *Shepard's State Case Name Citators.* *Shepard's* has developed a state case name citator for each state. For example, there is a *Shepard's Florida Case Name Citator* and a *Shepard's Wisconsin Case Name Citator*. These citators arrange cases from your state alphabetically by plaintiff and defendant. If you need to locate a Colorado case and all you know is the plaintiff's name or the defendant's name, look it up in *Shepard's Colorado Case Name Citator* and you will be provided with the citation(s) to the case, the date of decision, and an identification of which court in Colorado rendered the decision. *Shepard's* also publishes regional case name citators, such as *Shepard's Pacific Reporter Case Name Citator*.

    (iii) *Shepard's Federal Case Name Citators.* *Shepard's* has developed books that contain tables of all lower federal court cases since 1940 and all United States Supreme Court cases since 1990. If all you know about a federal case is the plaintiff's name or the defendant's name, the full citation can be located in the alphabetically arranged Table of Cases. There are separate *Federal Case Name Citators* for each of the 11 numbered circuits and for the Federal Circuit and District of Columbia Circuit. Each citator is updated four times a year with supplements. See Figure 9-15 for a sample page from *Shepard's Federal Circuit Case Name Citator*.

Figure 9-14
Sample Page of Citations to United States Constitution

2004USDist	313BRW752	~) 159LE760	89Fed Appx	214FRD30	2003USDist
[LX1461	Cir. 7	160LE541	[280	215FRD1	[LX8957
2005USDist	2004USApp	160LE587	2001USDist	216FRD136	2003USDist
[LX113	[LX15981	j) 160LE591	[LX25302	217FRD45	[LX11451
250FS2d54	340F3d458	160LE846	2002USDist	217FRD264	2003USDist
251FS2d1117	2004USDist	j) 160LE848	[LX26324	225FRD49	[LX12664
254FS2d344	[LX21403	j) 161LE49	2002USDist	Cir. 1	2003USDist
267FS2d327	301FS2d897	123SC1843	[LX27673	325F3d51	[LX13023
283FS2d650	Cir. 8	123SC1891	2002USDist	326F3d295	2003USDist
283FS2d813	358F3d1027	123SC2004	[LX27730	329F3d280	[LX14034
296FS2d487	Cir. 9	j) 123SC2014	2002USDist	337F3d104	2003USDist
298FS2d315	354F3d1113	124SC523	[LX27746	~) 338F3d26	[LX15850
321FS2d397	2002USDist	124SC799	2004USDist	j) 338F3d35	2003USDist
219FRD229	[LX26497	124SC888	[LX7339	338F3d71	[LX17799
313BRW140	2003USDist	i) 124SC889	2004USDist	338F3d80	2003USDist
Cir. 3	[LX18808	124SC1287	[LX25101	341F3d96	[LX17924
357F3d340	2003USDist	j) 124SC1295	2004USDist	344F3d40	2003USDist
362F3d221	[LX18809	124SC1584	[LX27171	346F3d18	[LX18852
2003USDist	2003USDist	124SC2129	2005USDist	347F3d332	2003USDist
[LX20665	[LX25613	124SC2455	[LX1236	348F3d285	[LX18969
2004USDist	256FS2d1129	j) 124SC2464	2005USDist	349F3d12	2003USDist
[LX5257	271FS2d1220	124SC2610	[LX5013	350F3d165	[LX19186
272FS2d471	Cir. 11	j) 124SC2616	2005USDist	350F3d199	2003USDist
334FS2d537	2005USDist	124SC2628	[LX5020	350F3d228	[LX20439
346FS2d800	[LX685	124SC2716	2005USDist	350F3d240	2003USDist
300BRW229	260FS2d1342	124SC2768	[LX5037	350F3d258	[LX20775
319BRW79	273FS2d1325	~) 124SC2771	2005USDist	351F3d24	2003USDist
Cir. 4	340FS2d1274	125SC591	[LX5185	354F3d61	[LX20910
321FS2d675	Cir. Fed.	125SC597	2005USDist	356F3d36	2003USDist
Cir. 5	378F3d1370	j) 125SC601	[LX5192	356F3d132	[LX21670
2003USApp		125SC837	2005USDist	358F3d71	2003USDist
[LX8138	**amend. 4**	j) 125SC838	[LX5357	359F3d21	[LX23488
344F3d441		j) 125SC1215	2005USDist	359F3d26	2003USDist
2002USDist	2005US LX	Cir. DC	[LX5412	359F3d76	[LX24895
[LX27365	[2755	2005USApp	2005USDist	360F3d10	2003USDist
2002USDist	~) 2005US LX	[LX3254	[LX5652	361F3d57	[LX24896
[LX27594	[2755	631F2d917	979FS15	362F3d62	2003USDist
2003USDist	538US627	321F3d1140	239FS2d2	j) 362F3d71	[LX24897
[LX17579	538US706	331F3d983	254FS2d54	365F3d2	2003USDist
2003USDist	538US773	333F3d160	254FS2d104	365F3d10	[LX24901
[LX21330	j) 538US792	334F3d16	257FS2d1	367F3d7	2003USDist
2003USDist	540US33	j) 334F3d21	257FS2d252	367F3d41	[LX24914
[LX22688	540US369	334F3d1162	260FS2d24	369F3d596	2003USDist
2004USDist	540US421	j) 334F3d1173	261FS2d7	j) 373F3d208	[LX25338
[LX18395	i) 540US424	336F3d1052	263FS2d40	375F3d14	2003USDist
2004USDist	540US553	348F3d261	267FS2d7	375F3d27	[LX25953
[LX18738	j) 540US566	351F3d1240	271FS2d98	377F3d54	2004USDist
2004USDist	541US150	351F3d1267	276FS2d148	380F3d543	[LX282
[LX25449	155LE818	353F3d25	279FS2d25	385F3d106	2004USDist
249FS2d771	155LE940	355F3d664	284FS2d149	386F3d9	[LX363
256FS2d565	155LE998	357F3d80	285FS2d35	388F3d13	2004USDist
Cir. 6	j) 155LE1010	360F3d1340	293FS2d23	391F3d28	[LX830
330F3d750	157LE350	365F3d23	293FS2d32	391F3d40	2004USDist
332F3d986	157LE774	365F3d1088	297FS2d13	391F3d337	[LX1080
352F3d1033	157LE849	365F3d1126	297FS2d239	392F3d56	2004USDist
115Fed Appx	i) 157LE851	370F3d1195	298FS2d37	393F3d59	[LX2329
[807	157LE1076	371F3d826	298FS2d43	393F3d66	2004USDist
115Fed Appx	j) 157LE1084	371F3d844	310FS2d13	394F3d56	[LX3429
[815	158LE314	~) 371F3d846	313FS2d3	71Fed Appx78	2004USDist
2001USDist	158LE910	374F3d1326	315FS2d54	78Fed Appx	[LX3663
[LX25461	159LE299	385F3d787	323FS2d39	[138	2004USDist
2004USDist	j) 159LE310	386F3d1150	326FS2d127	79Fed Appx	[LX4412
[LX7773	159LE525	387F3d904	328FS2d67	[451	2004USDist
219FRD122	159LE655	394F3d927	332FS2d38	108Fed Appx3	[LX4542
293BRW175	j) 159LE662	395F3d461	332FS2d224	2002USDist	2004USDist
302BRW253	159LE677	396F3d413	338FS2d55	[LX26280	[LX5240
307BRW606	159LE756		340FS2d12		*Continued*

43

(iv) *Shepard's Citations to Annotations*. If you are relying upon an annotation in A.L.R.3d, A.L.R.4th, A.L.R.5th, or A.L.R. Fed., you can Shepardize the annotation. You will be referred to federal and state cases as well as other authorities, including leading law reviews, that have mentioned or cited one of these A.L.R. annotations.

(v) *Shepard's Law Review Citations*.   If you have read an interesting law review article, you can locate cases and other law review articles that have mentioned or cited your law review article by Shepardizing it in *Shepard's Law Review Citations*.

I. Miscellaneous Citators

Shepard's publishes nearly 200 different citators whose titles describe their coverage. Among them are the following:

Bankruptcy Case Names Citator
Bankruptcy Citations
Code of Federal Regulations Citations
Criminal Justice Citations
Federal Energy Law Citations
Federal Occupational Safety and Health Citations
Federal Rules Citations
Federal Tax Citator
Immigration and Naturalization Citations
Intellectual Property Law Citations
Medical Malpractice Citations
Military Justice Citations
Partnership Law Citations
Products Liability Citations
Professional and Judicial Conduct Citations
Uniform Commercial Code Citations
United States Administrative Citations

J. *Shepard's* Daily Update Service

Law firms, agencies, and law libraries that subscribe to any of *Shepard's* citators may take advantage of a unique service offered by *Shepard's* titled "Daily Update Service." This service provides up-to-the-minute information on cases and statutes you may be Shepardizing, so you can find out what has happened to your authority since the last softcover supplement was published. Information may be as current as 24-48 hours

Figure 9-15
Sample Page from *Shepard's Federal Circuit Case Name Citator*

K

Cases
arranged
alpha-
betically
by
plaintiff
and
defendant

Kaasa v Mekler 97 F.2d 612, 25 C.C.P.A. 1303, 38 U.S.P.Q. 107, 1938 C.D. 718 (1938)

Kaase, In re 140 F.2d 1016, 31 C.C.P.A. 932, 60 U.S.P.Q. 565, 1944 C.D. 271 (1944)

Kabushiki Kaisha Wako, Wagner Shokai Inc. v 699 F.2d 1390, 217 U.S.P.Q. 15, 217 U.S.P.Q. 98 (Fed. Cir. 1983)

Kachurin Drug Co. v United States 26 C.C.P.A. 356, C.A.D. 41 (1939)

Kachurin Drug Co., United States v 39 C.C.P.A. 36, C.A.D. 459 (1951)

Kachurin Drug Co. v United States 39 C.C.P.A. 223 (1951)

Kacprowicz v Office of Personnel Management 740 F.2d 1552 (Fed. Cir. 1984)

Kacprowicz v Office of Personnel Management 769 F.2d 756 (Fed. Cir. 1985)

Kademann v Bollmann 421 F.2d 1372, 57 C.C.P.A. 907, 164 U.S.P.Q. 630 (1970)

Kadin Corp. v United States 782 F.2d 175 (Fed. Cir. 1986)

Kagawa & Co., United States v 5 C.C.A. 388, Treas. Dec. 34934 (1914)

Kaghan, In re 387 F.2d 398, 55 C.C.P.A. 844, 156 U.S.P.Q. 130 (1967)

Kahlen v United States 2 C.C.A. 206, Treas. Dec. 31947 (1911)

Kahn v Phipard 397 F.2d 995, 55 C.C.P.A. 1284, 158 U.S.P.Q. 269 (1968)

Kahn & Co., United States v 13 C.C.A. 57, Treas. Dec. 40881 (1925)

Kaisling, In re 44 F.2d 863, 18 C.C.P.A. 740, 7 U.S.P.Q. 134, 1931 C.D. 35 (1930)

Kalart Company Inc. v Camera-Mart Inc. 258 F.2d 956, 46 C.C.P.A. 711, 119 U.S.P.Q. 139, 1958 C.D. 432 (1958)

Kalich, W. B. Roddenberg Co. v 158 F.2d 289, 34 C.C.P.A. 745, 72 U.S.P.Q. 138, 1947 C.D. 79 (1946)

Kalman v Kimberly-Clark Corp. 713 F.2d 760, 218 U.S.P.Q. 781 (Fed. Cir. 1983)

Kalm, In re 378 F.2d 959, 54 C.C.P.A. 1466, 154 U.S.P.Q. 10 (1967)

Kalter, In re 125 F.2d 715, 29 C.C.P.A. 858, 52 U.S.P.Q. 483, 1942 C.D. 302 (1942)

Kalter, In re 316 F.2d 747, 50 C.C.P.A. 1191, 137 U.S.P.Q. 347, 1963 C.D. 441 (1963)

Kalter Mercantile Co., United States v 11 C.C.A. 540, Treas. Dec. 39680 (1923)

Kamal, In re 398 F.2d 867, 55 C.C.P.A. 1409, 158 U.S.P.Q. 320 (1968)

Kamikawa Bros. v United States 15 C.C.A. 12, Treas. Dec. 42130 (1927)

Kamlet, In re 185 F.2d 709, 38 C.C.P.A. 776, 88 U.S.P.Q. 106, 1951 C.D. 95 (1950)

Kamm, In re 452 F.2d 1052, 59 C.C.P.A. 753, 172 U.S.P.Q. 298 (1972)

Kamp v Houghtaling 376 F.2d 971, 54 C.C.P.A. 1354, 153 U.S.P.Q. 634 (1967)

Kamrath, In re 67 F.2d 928, 21 C.C.P.A. 787, 20 U.S.P.Q. 61, 1934 C.D. 128 (1933)

Kanamaru, Griffith v 816 F.2d 624, 2 U.S.P.Q.2d 1361 (Fed. Cir. 1987)

Kander, In re 312 F.2d 834, 50 C.C.P.A. 928, 136 U.S.P.Q. 477, 1963 C.D. 180 (1963)

Kangaroos U.S.A. Inc. v Caldor Inc. 778 F.2d 1571, 228 U.S.P.Q. 32 (Fed. Cir. 1985)

Kanmak Textiles Inc. v Carnac Inc. 189 F.2d 1006, 38 C.C.P.A. 1148, 90 U.S.P.Q. 105, 1951 C.D. 467 (1951)

Kansas Jack Inc. v Kuhn 719 F.2d 1144 (Fed. Cir. 1983)

Kanter, In re 399 F.2d 249, 55 C.C.P.A. 1395, 158 U.S.P.Q. 331 (1968)

Kanthal Corp., United States v 554 F.2d 456, 64 C.C.P.A. 89, C.A.D. 1188 (1977)

Kaplan Bros. v United States 12 C.C.A. 586 (1925)

Kaplan Bros. v United States 21 C.C.P.A. 87, Treas. Dec. 46396 (1933)

Kaplan, In re 110 F.2d 670, 27 C.C.P.A. 1072, 45 U.S.P.Q. 175, 1940 C.D. 410 (1940)

Kaplan, In re 789 F.2d 1574, 229 U.S.P.Q. 678 (Fed. Cir. 1986)

Kaplan Products & Textiles Inc. v United States 51 C.C.P.A. 2, C.A.D. 828 (1963)

Karlson, In re 311 F.2d 581, 50 C.C.P.A. 908, 136 U.S.P.Q. 184, 1963 C.D. 71 (1963)

Karnofsky, In re 390 F.2d 994, 55 C.C.P.A. 940, 156 U.S.P.Q. 682 (1968)

Karoware Inc. v United States 564 F.2d 77, 65 C.C.P.A. 1, C.A.D. 1197 (1977)

243

399

from the time of decision from the courts. Subscribers can call *Shepard's* and ask for the most recent history and treatment of statutes or cases being Shepardized. Call (800) 899-6000 for the "Daily Update Service." The service is also available on the Internet.

K. Electronic Updating of Legal Authorities

1. *Introduction to Electronic Updating*

For nearly one hundred years, legal researchers updated their legal authorities through the use of conventional print versions of *Shepard's*. Electronic updating, however, provides more up-to-date validation of legal authorities and is easily accomplished. There is no need to learn quirky abbreviations. Negative history, such as reversal of a case, appears in plain English. Electronic updating eliminates the worry that you do not have all of the print volumes in a set of *Shepard's* because all of the citing references to your case or statute appear in a single location. Moreover, there is no need to gather together numerous bulky sets of *Shepard's* if your document cites federal cases, federal statutes, California cases, California statutes, and Nevada cases. You need not worry that you should check the status of a Michigan case in both *Shepard's Michigan Citations* and in *Shepard's Northwestern Reporter Citations* because all of the authorities that mention your Michigan case will be consolidated in a single result online. Updating and checking your opponent's citations are easily accomplished. Finally, references are available online far more quickly than the print versions of *Shepard's* are published, thus directing you to the most recent treatment of your authorities. Consequently, updating electronically is the preferred method for most legal professionals. In fact, a number of law firms and law libraries no longer subscribe to the print volumes of *Shepard's* and all updating is accomplished electronically, through the use of *Shepard's* online (offered by LEXIS) or through West's online product, KeyCite.

One of the newest developments in electronic updating is updating and validating by wireless access. Both *Shepard's* and KeyCite are available through handheld PDAs (personal digital assistants), such as Palm devices. Users can review the full history, negative history, or citations to legal authorities, making updating and validating easier and entirely portable. Legal professionals can now update their cases in their cabs on the way to the courthouse!

2. *Shepardizing Online*

a. How to Shepardize a Case Online

Assume the case you are updating and validating is *United States v. Falstaff Brewing Corp.*, 332 F. Supp. 970 (D.R.I. 1973) (hereinafter called *Falstaff*). If you are viewing the case online using LEXIS, there will be a *Shepard's* signal indicaor displayed on the screen. If you click it, *Falstaff* will be immediately Shepardized. If you are not currently viewing *Falstaff* on your screen but are instead perhaps validating a written brief that mentions *Falstaff*, follow these steps:

- Sign on to lexis.com.
- Click the *Shepard's* tab at the top of your screen.
- Type in your citation (332 fs 970) in the open field.

Figure 9-16
Shepardizing Online

Research Steps for Cases

This case is on point for your issue: *McNeil v. Economics Laboratory, Inc.*, 800 F.2d 111 (7th Cir. Ill. 1986). Is *McNeil* still good law? Are there additional cases that discuss the same issues discussed in *McNeil*? You can *Shepardize* 800 F. 2d 111 to find out.

There are two ways to *Shepardize* a citation through the LexisNexis research system. If you are not viewing the case, click the **Check a Citation** tab. If you want to *Shepardize* the document you are viewing, click the *Shepardize* **link**.

Since you are not viewing 800 F. 2d 111,

Here's what you do:

1. Establish an Internet connection and sign on to **the LexisNexis research system.**
2. Click the **Check a Citation** tab at the top of the screen. *Shepard's* (the default setting) is ready for your citation.
3. **Type your citation** (e.g., *800 f2d 111*) in the open field. Make sure to choose *Shepard's* for Research (FULL) to see the complete universe in which your case has been cited. Then click **Check** at the bottom right corner to start your research.

Click **Check a Citation.**

Type 800 f2d 111 in the open field.

Click **Check** *to start your research.*

If you are unsure of the correct format for your citation, click **Citation Formats.**

- Select one of the following options: "*Shepard's* for Research" also called "FULL," which will list every authority that mentions *Falstaff*) or "*Shepard's* for Validation" (also called "KWIC," which will provide you with negative history only, rather than all authorities that mention *Falstaff*).
- Click the word "Check" at the bottom of your screen. (See Figure 9-16.)

You are now ready to interpret your results. You will be informed, in plain English, whether *Falstaff* has been distinguished, criticized, followed, and so forth. If you are interested in one of these references, you simply click on it, and you will be immediately transported to that reference, thereby eliminating the need for you to run around the library collecting authorities that distinguish, criticize, or follow *Falstaff.*

Shepard's uses "Signal Indicators" to inform you at a glance of the precedential status of your case. These signal indicators appear at the top of your *Shepard's* results. A graphic is given along with citations. The following signal indicator graphics are used:

- Red stop sign: A warning that the case has strong negative history or treatment (for example, your case has been reversed or overruled).
- Yellow yield sign: An indication that there may be some negative history or treatment (for example, your case has been criticized or questioned).
- Green plus sign: Your case has positive history, such as being affirmed or followed.
- Letter "A" in a blue circle: Your case has been analyzed in a neutral manner, such as being explained.
- Letter "I" in a blue circle: Other citation information is available for your case, such as law review articles that mention your case.

These signal indicators make Shepardizing online extremely easy because they tell you at a glance that either your citation is in trouble or it is cleared for your use. You can immediately retrieve the authorities that accompany the signal indicators by clicking on them. *Shepard's* cautions that if you are given a red warning indicator, it does not necessarily mean that your case is no longer good law; it simply means that your case has received some negative treatment that you need to explore and analyze.

When *Shepard's* lists other cases that mention *Falstaff*, they will be organized by jurisdiction and court, and sorted by date, with the most recent decisions appearing first in each category. (See Figure 9-17.)

b. Features of *Shepard's* Online

Shepard's provides a number of tools that help you maximize your research efforts.

- Full citation. *Shepard's* will list the full citation for your case, including all parallel citations.

Figure 9-17
Reviewing *Shepard's* Results

Interpreting Your *Shepard's* Results

Shepard's unique combination of expert editorial analysis and powerful navigational tools helps you organize, prioritize and narrow your research. These tips for interpreting *Shepard's* results use *McNeil v. Economics Laboratory, Inc.*, 800 F.2d 111 (7th Cir. Ill. 1986).

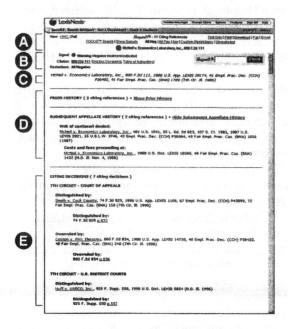

Ⓐ Shows the number of **citing references** for the current viewing mode (**All Neg** for *McNeil*) and provides links to Custom Restrictions, FOCUS search and other navigational tools. Also gives the short-form citation for the authority you are *Shepardizing*.

Ⓑ Shows *Shepard's* **Signal indicator** (graphic and descriptive text), which indicates that the information contained in the report for *McNeil* includes strong negative history. Click on the underlined citation to remove any restrictions; click **Get this Document** to display the full text of *McNeil*. Move to check the cases that *McNeil* based its logic upon by clicking **Table of Authorities**. The restrictions field tells you if there are any restrictions (e.g., **All Negative**). To *Shepardize* another citation, enter a citation in the *Shepard's* box and click **Check**.

Ⓒ Lists the **full citation**, including parallel citations, for *McNeil*.

Ⓓ Provides the **Prior and Subsequent Appellate History**. Click the underlined links to show or hide these fields. Always be sure to check the case history before using Custom Restrictions to preview and narrow citing references that are not part of the direct history.

Ⓔ Shows **citing references outside the direct history chain** of your case. Citing decisions are organized by jurisdiction and court, and sorted by date with more recent decisions appearing first in each category. Also included are citations from secondary sources, including law reviews and annotations. Treatment analysis codes assigned by a *Shepard's* legal editor (distinguished, followed, overruled, etc.) precede the citation. Click on a case name, *Coston v. Plitt Theatres*, for example, to link to the first place in the full text of a

- FULL. Selecting the FULL option will provide you with all of the prior history of your case, all subsequent appellate history, every citing reference to your case (including cases, law reviews, periodicals, statutes, treatises, and A.L.R. annotations), and the ability to do a "FOCUS" search (described below). Thus, FULL helps you find other sources to assist with your research efforts.
- KWIC. Selecting the KWIC option provides a quick answer to the question, "Is my authority still valid?" You will not be directed to law reviews and annotations that mention your authority; you will only be given subsequent appellate history and the ability to do a FOCUS search. Use KWIC when you are satisfied with your research efforts and only want to confirm that your authority is still good law.
- Summary. Begin your analysis with *Shepard's* Summary, which presents a readable synopsis showing why your case received a signal indicator. For example, you might be informed that your case was been distinguished six times, followed twice, and mentioned in nine law reviews.
- FOCUS. By clicking "FOCUS Search" at the top of your screen, you can find authorities dealing with the issues or facts confronting you. For example, if you are interested in locating other authorities that discuss whether it is legal malpractice to neglect a statute of limitations, you can type in your search terms ("legal malpractice," "statute of limitations"), click FOCUS, and you will then be provided with authorities dealing with this issue. The terms you have searched, such as "legal malpractice," will appear highlighted on the screen for ease of review.
- Custom Restrictions. *Shepard's* allows you to tailor the results you desire by selecting groups of citations to review. For example, you can elect to see only those cases that explain *Falstaff*, only those cases from the Third Circuit that mention *Falstaff* after 1990, or only law review articles that mention *Falstaff*.
- Table of Authorities. Assume the *Falstaff* case relied upon and cited ten cases. *Shepard's* new validation tool called Table of Authorities analyzes those ten cases cited in *Falstaff*, allowing you to revaluate the cases upon which *Falstaff* relied. If their validity or authority is weakened or in doubt, *Falstaff* may also be suspect. To activate this feature, click the Table of Authorities tab at the top of your screen.

c. **Sheardizing Statutes and Regulations Online**

Sheardizing statutes and regulations online is similar to Sheardizing cases online. To Shepardize 18 U.S.C. § 2124 (2000), follow these steps:

- Sign on to lexis.com.
- Click the *Shepard's* tab at the top of your screen.
- Type in your citation (18 usc 2124) in the open field (there is no need to use a section sign or the word "section" or "sec" before the section number).

- Select one of the following options: "*Shepard's* for Research" (also called "FULL," which will list every authority that mentions your statute) or "*Shepard's* for Validation" (also called "KWIC," which will provide you with negative history only rather than all authorities that mention your statute).
- Click the word "Check" at the bottom of your screen.

You will now be informed whether your statute has been held unconstitutional by a later case, amended by the legislature, and so forth. Just as with cases, you can use Custom Restrictions to narrow your results, such as to review only legislative materials that amend your statute or only authorities that mention your statute after a certain date. Similarly, you can use the FOCUS feature to locate authorities dealing with your particular issues and facts. The graphic signal indicators used with cases (the stop sign, and so forth) are not used with statutes.

Sheperdizing a regulation and other materials is accomplished much the same way as Shepardizing a case or statute. Directions are easy to follow, and the *Shepard's* Daily Update Service is available to find the most recent authorities that mention the case or legal authority you are citing in your document.

d. Other *Shepard's* Products

(1) *Automatic Citation Validation Through CheckCite*

One of the most significant advances in validating citations is software programs that automatically check whether legal authorities you rely on and cite are still good law. Consider the task of checking the validity of 25 separate citations in a 50-page brief. Although Shepardizing online will be considerably faster than manual Shepardizing (especially if you use KWIC to determine whether the authorities are still valid), keying in 25 separate entries and examining the screen for 25 separate results can be time-consuming.

Shepard's offers a software program called CheckCite, which automatically checks all citations in your brief, without the necessity of your keying in a single citation. The program "reads" your brief, locates your citations, checks them, and then provides you with the results of the citation-checking either on the screen or in a separate printed report. You can customize the results so your citations can be fully Shepardized or merely KWIC cited. CheckCite also checks your quotations for accuracy and locates discrepancies in case names, dates, and page numbers. CheckCite is also useful for checking your adversary's documents, allowing you to spot weaknesses in the opponent's arguments.

(2) *CiteRite II*

CiteRite II is a citation-checking software program that checks your citations for proper form using *The Bluebook* rules (or the *California Style Manual*). You will be provided with parallel cites and informed of errors in punctuation (such as neglecting the period after "Cal"), incorrect reporter abbreviations, improper underscoring, and other errors. In addition to checking the format of case cites, statutes, books, and law review articles, signals and short forms can also be checked. It is unclear, however, whether CiteRite II can thoroughly master the intricacies of citation form, such as when you may abbreviate "Western" and when you may not. Nevertheless, it is a valuable tool for checking citation form errors in both primary and secondary authorities. It does not, however, validate your authorities by telling you whether they are still "good law."

3. *KeyCite*

a. How to KeyCite Cases

KeyCite is West's service, launched in 1997, that updates and validates your legal authorities. KeyCite can be accessed through WestMate software or on the Internet at www.westlaw.com. Although there are some differences between Shepardizing online and KeyCiting online, the services are probably more alike than different. Assume you want to KeyCite the *Falstaff* case. If *Falstaff* is presently displayed on your screen, you will be given a KeyCite status flag at the top of the case (red, yellow, or blue) or the word "update" and you simply click it to access KeyCite. Alternatively, there will be a "KC" displayed in the tool bar. Click it to access KeyCite. If you are not presently viewing a case to KeyCite it, follow these steps:

- Sign on to westlaw.com.
- Click the KeyCite button on the toolbar. Type in your citation in the box displayed and click "GO." Alternatively, you may type a citation in the "KeyCite this citation" text box that is displayed on many tabbed pages and click "GO" or select "KeyCite" from the Services menu.

You are now ready to interpret your results. The first thing that appears is any history of the case. Like *Shepard's* online, KeyCite uses graphics to instantly convey information to you about the status of the case.

- Red flag: Warning that the case is no longer good law for at least one of the issues it discusses (it has likely been reversed or overruled).
- Yellow flag: Indicates that the case has some negative history, such as being criticized or limited.
- Blue "H": The case has some history, such as being explained, affirmed, or having *certiorari* granted.
- Green "C": Indicates that the case has been cited in some references but there is no direct history or negative indirect history.
- No flag or signal: Indicates that there is no direct history or negative indirect history for the case.

You can easily jump to cases that mention *Falstaff* by double-clicking on them. (See Figure 9-18.)

Figure 9-18
Sample KeyCite Screen

Access KeyCite by clicking
KeyCite on the toolbar.

Type a citation in the
KeyCite this citation text
box

b. Features of KeyCite

KeyCite offers the following features to assist you with your citation updating and validating:

- Full citation. KeyCite will provide you with the full citation to the case, including all parallel cites.
- Citation history options. You can customize your KeyCite results to display different types of case history for your case. By clicking on "Show Full History," you will be given the complete history of your case; by selecting "Negative History Only," you will be provided only the subsequent history that negatively affects your case; finally, you can select "Omit Minor History," to suppress minor procedural history of your case.
- Citations to the Case. By clicking on the wording "Citations to the Case," you will be able to retrieve the citing references to *Falstaff*, namely, cases, law review articles, helpful Am. Jur. 2d references, and A.L.R. annotations that mention *Falstaff*. The citations that are most likely to be helpful are listed first. Thus, the cases that might negatively affect *Falstaff* are given first, followed by those that treat *Falstaff* positively.
- Limit Citations. By selecting the "Limit Citations" button, you can restrict the number of citing references KeyCite will give you. You can elect to view only those authorities that explain *Falstaff*, only Ohio cases that mention *Falstaff*, those cases that discuss headnote 2 of *Falstaff*, those that mention *Falstaff* after a certain date, those that discuss *Falstaff* in a dissenting opinion, and so forth.
- Depth of treatment stars. As KeyCite lists the cases that mention *Falstaff*, a number of green stars will be displayed above each citation. These stars tell you the extent to which a citing case discusses *Falstaff*. Four green stars means that the case examines *Falstaff* in depth; three stars indicates that there is significant discussion of *Falstaff*, two stars means that there is some very brief discussion of *Falstaff*, and one star indicates that *Falstaff* was mentioned in passing, probably in a string citation. See Figure 9-19.
- Quotation marks. If KeyCite displays quotation marks (") after a case citation, it means that the case quotes from *Falstaff*.
- Headnote references. *Falstaff's* headnote references are clearly displayed. Thus, a reference to "HN2" means that the case discusses the point of law discussed in headnote 2 of *Falstaff*.
- KeyCite Alert. KeyCite Alert is a clipping service that automatically notifies you of any changes in the treatment of *Falstaff*. You can restrict its coverage so that, for example, you are only notified of later negative treatment of *Falstaff* rather than every time *Falstaff* is later mentioned by some other authority. You can elect to be notified daily, weekly, and so forth.

Figure 9-19
Sample KeyCite Screen Showing History of Case

KeyCite history of a case

── Practice Tip ──

Using KeyCite Alert

KeyCite Alert can deliver information to you about the status of your cases, statutes, and other authorities to several destinations, including your e-mail address, fax machine, or your personal digital assistant, allowing you to determine the validity of your authorities while on the way to the courthouse.

---

c. KeyCiting Statutes and Regulations

If you are viewing a statute on Westlaw, the upper left corner of the screen is labled "Update." You may select this to update your statute. Alternatively, your statute may appear with a red or yellow flag, indicating there is negative treatment of your statute. Click on the flag to be directed to the negative history.

If you are not presently viewing a statute on the screen, update the statute by taking the following steps:

- Sign on to westlaw.com.
- Click the KeyCite button on the toolbar (labeled "KC"). Type in your citation in the box displayed and click "GO." Alternatively, you may type a citation in the "KeyCite this citation" text box that is

displayed on many tabbed pages and click "GO," or select "KeyCite" from the Services menu.

After you enter your statute citation in KeyCite, the history of the statute is displayed, including links to recent session laws that amend or repeal your statute and historical and statutory notes describing the legislative changes affecting your statute.

After viewing the history of the statute, click the "KC Citing Ref" tab to view citations to cases, administrative materials, and secondary sources that mention your statute. You can use KeyCite Alert to automatically notify you of any changes in the statute. KeyCiting regulations in C.F.R. is accomplished in the same manner as KeyCiting statutes.

You can limit your results by selecting specific jurisdictions that have issued cases citing your statute, selecting documents mentioning your statute during certain time periods, and so forth. KeyCite provides status flags for statutes as well, using a red flag to warn you that the statute has been amended, repealed, or held unconstitutional; a yellow flag to indicate that the statute has been limited or received some negative treatment from a court; and a green "C" to show that various authorities cite your statute.

d. Other West Products

(1) *Automatic Citation Validation Through WestCheck and WestCheck.com*

Similar to LEXIS's CheckCite, West offers a software program called WestCheck, which automatically extracts citations from your document, checks their validity, and produces a printed report with the results of the check. The advantage of using WestCheck rather than KeyCite is that WestCheck automatically "reads" and validates your citations, thus saving you the time of keying in each citation you wish to check.

The process is easily accomplished. Once the software is "loaded" onto your computer, you merely open your brief or other document that contains the citations you wish to check and then click the WestCheck button on your toolbar. WestCheck is launched and automatically extracts the citations. The extracted citations will be displayed on the screen. Click "Verify" to determine that the case law citations in the list are valid.

You may customize the results you desire by directing WestCheck to KeyCite the results (limiting or restricting options as you desire), or by using a companion service called "QuoteRight," you can ensure your quotations are accurate. Launch these services by selecting "Run." WestCheck can also be used to create a table of authorities (see Chapter 18), listing all authorities cited in your brief or other document.

Westlaw now offers a Web-based version of WestCheck, called WestCheck.com, available to anyone with Internet access. This product eliminates the need to load software into your computer. You simply attach your Word or WordPerfect document and run it through WestCheck.com, which will automatically extract and check your citations to ensure they are still good law. An easy-to-read online report (using KeyCite flags and symbols) is provided. Access http://westcheck.com to use the service or take a training tutorial.

(2) Table of Authorities

While KeyCite lists cases that mention your case, West's product "Table of Authorities" lists the cases cited by your case. Thus, if *Falstaff* relies upon six federal cases, Table of Authorities will list them, display depth of treatment markers showing how extensively those cases are discussed by *Falstaff*, and inform you whether they are subject to negative history or treatment. Table of Authorities is useful for finding weaknesses in cases relied upon by an adversary as well as in the cases you rely upon.

4. Comparing Shepardizing Online with KeyCite

In most instances, researchers elect to Shepardize online because they are most familiar with *Shepard's* or LEXIS, or they select KeyCite because they are most familiar with Westlaw. Costs are approximately equivalent, and it is impossible to make absolute statements as to pricing and fees. Most large law firms afford desktop access to both LEXIS and Westlaw, realizing their legal professionals have distinct preferences. Moreover, these firms have negotiated pricing schedules with LEXIS and Westlaw, often "in bulk," so that everyone in the firm could be signed on to LEXIS or Westlaw all day long and the fee would be the same. Nevertheless, fees for Shepardizing online or KeyCiting are usually assessed on a per-case basis. Generally, it costs about $4 to check any one citation. Thus, in a document with 25 citations, the cost merely for accessing the databases will be $100. Additional fees will be charged to the client for your time in performing the updating and reviewing results and for the attorney's time as well. Because fees are roughly equivalent, a decision whether to Shepardize online or KeyCite is not usually based upon cost.

Beginning researchers often wonder, "Which service is better?" Advertising material for *Shepard's* clearly touts its superiority, while that for KeyCite does the same. Both offer many of the same features: rapid and easy citation validating; the use of easy-to-understand, colorful graphics (signs and flags) to tell you at a glance that your citation is in trouble; the ability to limit or restrict your results; and the ability to immediately jump to an authority that mentions your case or statute. Both services offer automatic citation updating so you need not key in citations. West's product KeyCite Alert is valuable for notifying you of later changes in your case or statute. While *Shepard's* does not offer a similar service, it does offer its Daily Alert Service, which allows you to check the status of a citation by a toll-free telephone number. *Shepard's* also offers CiteRite II, its service that assists in putting citations in *Bluebook* format. West-Check also verifies case citations to ensure they are accurate (although it does not verify that your citations are in *Bluebook* form). Thus, each provider offers some unique products.

A recent advertisement for KeyCite announced that in an independent head-to-head review of KeyCite and LEXIS's *Shepard's*, KeyCite was named the better citator. On the other hand, the home page for *Shepard's* directs readers to a study showing that *Shepard's* is more current and complete than KeyCite. In sum, the use of *Shepard's* online or KeyCite is usually a matter of habit, convenience, or preference. Additionally, because deciphering the reports generated by *Shepard's* and KeyCite can be somewhat difficult (primarily because so much information is given on each screen), legal researchers tend to stick with one service after they have become familiar with its formatting and layout. It is possible, however, that one service may identify some authorities that the other does not. For critical cases or projects, you may wish to consider using both *Shepard's* online and KeyCite. Alternatively, ask your supervisor whether using both services is necessary. For most citation updates and validation purposes, however, the systems are equally proficient.

5. *Other Services*

Although LEXIS and Westlaw are the giants in computer-assisted legal research systems, three other systems provide citation updating: Loislaw of Arkansas; JuriSearch.com of California; and VersusLaw Inc., of Washington. Loislaw, JuriSearch, and VersusLaw generally aim their services at smaller firms or sole practitioners and charge reasonable fees, but they offer much smaller databases than LEXIS or Westlaw. In fact, JuriSearch's focus is primarily on California and Florida law. Loislaw's citator is called GlobalCite and JuriSearch.com's citator is called Check-Mate. Their use is similar to that of Shepardizing or KeyCiting online, but, in general, they offer fewer enhancements and features for customization. VersusLaw offers only rudimentary updating.

L. Summary

Updating and validating your primary authorities is the second component of cite-checking. After you have corrected citations in a document so they conform to *Bluebook*, *ALWD*, or local form, you must verify that the primary authorities you rely on are still "good law." While the foremost function of updating is to check the status of your primary authorities, a related function is to allow you to tap into additional legal research by providing you with references to cases, periodicals, attorneys general opinions, and annotations that mention or cite the authority being updated.

The determination of when to perform the task of updating is a matter of individual discretion, although updating early in the research process will not only alert you to an invalid or weakened case, statute, or constitutional provision but also enhance your efforts by directing you to additional research sources.

If you elect to update manually after a project is completed using *Shepard's Citations* in print, you may want to arrange the authorities in some order before you begin. On a separate piece of paper, list all cases from the same jurisdiction together so that you update all United States Supreme Court cases and then move on to update lower federal court cases, then state court cases, and so on. This will enhance your efficiency and save you from constantly running around the library from one set of *Shepard's* to the next. Update statutes and constitutional provisions in the same ordered fashion.

Most researchers prefer the ease and convenience of updatng electronically, either by using *Shepard's* online by LEXIS or by using KeyCite online, offered by West. These services provide easy and very recent validation of legal authorities. Moreover, the new software programs offered by LEXIS and West, CheckCite and WestCheck, respectively, offer automatic updating, eliminating the necessity of keying in any citations. Thus, many law firms and legal departments no longer subscribe to the print versions of *Shepard's*, and there are numerous working paralegals who have never updated "manually" ; they have only checked their authorities using *Shepard's* online or by KeyCiting online. Thus, at some point, the print versions of *Shepard's* may be relics.

Once you have Shepardized or KeyCited a few times, you will quickly get the hang of it and will find that while it is a routine task, it is quickly accomplished. Do not assume that because Shepardizing and KeyCiting are easy and routine that they are unimportant. On the contrary, updating is one of the most critical aspects of legal research, and no project is complete until every reference to a case, statute, or constitutional provision has been updated and validated.

CyberSites

http://www.lexisnexis.com/ shepards	The Web site for *Shepard's* fully explains all of its products, both print and other versions; describes new products; and offers free tutorials.
http://helpcite.shepards.com	This reference desk, provided by *Shepard's* (for print products only) will inform you of the most current supplement available from *Shepard's* so you can ensure your library has complete sets of *Shepard's.*
http://west.thomson.com	The Web site of West provides information about its products, including KeyCite and WestCheck, and often offers free tutorials.
http://west.thomson.com/ westlaw/training	Westlaw offers numerous training programs, online demonstrations, and user guides at this site.
https://westcheck.com	Information about WestCheck.com and an interactive tutorial are available at this site.
http://www.loislaw.com	The Web site of Loislaw describes its citation service, called "GlobalCite."
http://www.JuriSearch.com	The Web site of JuriSearch describes its citation service, CheckMate.
http://www.versuslaw.com	The Web site of VersusLaw describes its databases and fees and provides basic information about updating cases.
http://www.lectlaw.com/files/ lwr17.htm	This Web site of the 'Lectric Law Library offers an excellent description on "How to Shepardize."

Writing Strategies

Be sure to update any citations in an adversary's written project. It is possible that while the cases cited may still be "good law," they may have lost some of their strength by being criticized or questioned. You will then be able to point this out in your project or response as follows: "While Plaintiff relies upon *Caldwell Co. v. Baldwin Emporium Inc.*, 688 F. Supp. 101 (S.D.N.Y. 1990), that case has been subject to increasing criticism . . . ."

Similarly, if a case cited by an adversary is limited to its own particular facts, point this out to the reader: "The case relied upon by Plaintiff, *Ellers v. McGrath*, 692 F. Supp. 946 (D. Mass. 1991), has been specifically limited to written lease agreements. *Warren v. Chesterton*, 719 F.2d 101 (1st Cir. 1992). Because the present case involves an option to purchase real property and not a written lease, Plaintiff's reliance on *Ellers* is misplaced."

Use updating as a way of enhancing your own writing. If a case you rely on is followed by a later case, bring this to the reader's attention: "In *Satterly v. Jespersen*, 718 F.2d 906 (9th Cir. 1992), the court [noted with approval] or [endorsed] or [followed] the test for defamation set forth in *Handler v. Jacobson*, 689 F. Supp. 614 (C.D. Cal. 1990)."

Assignment for Chapter 9

In this assignment, you will Shepardize cases, statutes, and other sources using the print volumes of *Shepard's*. Provide the answer as *Shepard's* gives it to you. You need not use *Bluebook* or *ALWD* form. Assignments requiring you to Shepardize or KeyCite electronically all are found in Chapter 11.

1. Shepardize 620 A.2d 485.
   a. Give the parallel citation.
   b. Review the abbreviations in the front of this volume. What does "NJL" stand for?
2. Locate *Shepard's* first reference to 179 N.W. 81.
   a. Give the parallel citation.
   b. What is the first case that follows headnote 3 of 179 N.W. 81?
   c. What is the most recent A.L.R. annotation in this volume that mentions this case?
   d. Review the abbreviations in the front of the volume. What does "CoLR" stand for?
3. Shepardize 692 N.E.2d 369.
   a. Give the parallel citations.
   b. Has this case ever been questioned? If so, give the citation.
4. Locate the first time *Shepard's* discusses 331 S.E.2d 846.
   a. Give the parallel citation.
   b. What negative treatment is given for this case in this volume?
5. Locate the first time *Shepard's* discusses 736 P.2d 161.
   a. Give the name of the case.
   b. Give the citations to the denial of *certiorari* for 736 P.2d 161.
   c. What case was connected with 736 P.2d 161?
6. Use *Shepard's Southwestern Citations, Cases and Case Names* (hardbound volume, volume 2, part 6, for 2001). Locate the entries for 842 S.W.2d 704.
   a. Give the name of the case.
   b. What negative history is given for the case?
   c. Review the entries for 842 S.W.2d 580 in this volume. Was this case cited in a concurring opinion? If so, give the citation.
7. Use *Shepard's Federal Citations* (hardbound supplement, volume 2 for 2003-2004. Locate the entries for 127 F.3d 632.
   a. Give the name of this case.
   b. What Sixth Circuit case followed headnote 3 of this 1997 case?
8. Use *Shepard's Federal Citations* for the first time *Shepard's* mentions 831 F. Supp. 1111.
   a. Was this case affirmed? If so, give the citation to the affirming case.
   b. Retrieve the volume for the case that affirmed 831 F. Supp. 1111. Was this affirming case published?
9. Use *Shepard's United States Citations* for the first time 529 U.S. 765 is mentioned and Shepardize 529 U.S. 765 in this volume. What A.L.R. Fed. annotation discusses this case?

10. Use *Shepard's United States Citations* for the first time 468 U.S. 491 is mentioned and Shepardize 468 U.S. 91 in this volume. What was the first case to explain this case?

11. Use *Shepard's Federal Statute Citations* for 1996-2001, volume 3, hardbound supplement, and Shepardize 36 U.S.C. § 5703. Give the negative history for this statute.

12. Use *Shepard's Federal Statute Citations* for 1996-2001, volume 1, hardbound supplement, and Shepardize 15 U.S.C. § 1052(f).
    a. Which Tenth Circuit case mentions this statute?
    b. What does the delta symbol (Δ) in the citation mean?

13. Use *Shepard's Federal Statute Citations* for 2001-2003, volume 1, hardbound supplement, for the U.S. Constitution. What is the first Fourth Circuit case to discuss clause one of Article Six?

14. Use *Shepard's Federal Statute Citations* for 1996, for Tariff Schedules, Statutes at Large, and so forth.
    a. Shepardize Volume 23 of U.S. Treaties and Other International Agreements 3693. Give the history.
    b. Shepardize Rule 33 of the Rules of the Supreme Court of the United States. What Seventh Circuit case discusses this rule?

15. Use *Shepard's Acts and Cases by Popular Name (Federal and State)*, 1999, Pt. 3.
    a. Give the citation to the Happy Thought Case.
    b. Give the citation to the Sickle Cell Disease Detection Act.

State Your Answer

1. Access http://lexisnexis.com/shepards and select "Shepard's Citations in Print," and then "Features" and "Specialized Citators Table." What does *Shepard's* Federal Circuit Table do?

2. Access http://lexisnexis.com/shepards and select "Features." What two report formats can you select when you Shepardize online?

3. Access http://lexisnexis.com/shepards and then "Features" and then "Product Literature." Review William L. Taylor's article about *Shepard's* and KeyCite.
    a. What is the title of this article?
    b. Review paragraph 29 of the article. What is Mr. Taylor's conclusion?

4. Access www.westlaw.com and locate information on WestCheck.com. What three tasks does WestCheck.com perform automatically?

Special Research Issues

The only thing that was authoritatively adopted for sure was the text of the enactment; the rest is necessarily speculation.

United States v. R.L.C., 503 U.S. 291, 308 (1992)
(Scalia, J., concurring)

A. **Legislative History**
B. **Executive Materials**
C. **Administrative Law**
D. **International Law**
E. **Municipal Research**
F. **Rules of Court**
G. **Citation Form**

Chapter Overview

Most legal research problems can be solved by examining and analyzing the conventional sources of primary authorities and secondary authorities. There are, however, a few types of legal research tasks that lie outside those usual approaches to legal research and that involve sources arranged and published differently from the typical primary and secondary authorities.

This chapter will examine these special research issues and will provide information on legislative histories, presidential documents, administrative law, international law, local and municipal law, and court rules. Although research in many of these unique areas will not be required often, should you need to do any especially thorough research project or should you be employed by a firm concentrating on international or administrative law, you will use the research techniques described herein. A brief introduction to these specialized tasks is needed so you will be able to conduct research efficiently and effectively in these areas if you are asked to do so.

A.   Legislative History

1.   Introduction to Federal Legislative History Research

It is possible that in the course of your research of an issue you realize that the statute relating to the issue is unclear. Usually you would then read and analyze the cases interpreting the statute to determine its meaning. Not all statutes have been subject to court interpretation, however, and you may still be faced with an ambiguous statute and no guidance in determining its meaning. It is equally possible that the cases interpreting the statute are contrary to the position you need to assert on behalf of a client.

In these instances, you should examine the various documents that reflect the activity of the legislature that enacted the statute to assist you in determining the intent of the legislature. This process is referred to as preparing or compiling a legislative history. By examining the various versions of the bills, the testimony given before the committee, the committee report, and the debates, you may be able to resolve ambiguities in a statute or argue that a court's prior interpretation of a statute is contrary to the intended purpose of a statute.

While a well-constructed argument relating to a legislative history and the legislature's intent and purpose may be useful and instructive to a court, a court is not required to adopt an interpretation of a statute based upon the legislature's intent in enacting the law. In fact, many courts view legislative history arguments with skepticism. Typically, courts will not examine the legislative history of a statute if the meaning of the statute is clear or "plain" from a reading of it. Only when a court cannot determine the plain meaning of a statute will it resort to reviewing the legislative history of the statute. Supreme Court Justice Antonin Scalia is vehemently opposed to relying on legislative history. He prefers that legislative intent be determined from the plain meaning of a statute itself.

Alternatively, you may be monitoring a piece of legislation as it progresses in order to better assist clients or your employer. This section will first discuss legislative histories for federal statutes and then legislative histories for state statutes. You may wish to review Chapter 3, which discusses the process by which legislation is enacted. In brief, a bill is introduced, referred to a committee, which hears testimony and issues a report, and then the bill is voted on after debate. This procedure is then duplicated in the second chamber of a legislature.

There are three excellent published guides explaining and describing the background of legislative histories, the documents to be examined when compiling a legislative history, and the actual process of assembling a legislative history. Review the following for introductory information and links to relevant materials and Web sites:

- Carold D. Davis, *How to Follow Current Federal Legislation and Regulation*, CRS Report for Congress 96-473, May 20, 1996,

http://www.house.gov/rules/96-473.htm.
- Richard J. McKinney & Ellen A. Sweet, Law Librarians' Society of Washington, D.C., Inc., *Federal Legislative History Research: A Practitioner's Guide to Compiling the Documents and Sifting for Legislative Intent*, Jan. 2003, http://www.llsdc.org/source-book/fed-leg-hist.htm.
- University of Michigan Documents Center, *Legislative Histories — United States Congress*, Nov. 27, 2004, http://www.lib.umich.edu/govdocs/legishisnew.html.

2. Documents Composing Federal Legislative History

There are several documents you may analyze in the process of compiling a legislative history. Each one of these documents may help you achieve your goals of determining the purpose and intent of a statute.

a. Versions of a Bill

One of the steps in compiling a legislative history is examining the various versions of a bill. By studying the evolution of a statute, you may be able to make certain inferences about the intent of the legislature in enacting a law. For example, assume a bill as introduced allows certain benefits for veterans, their spouses, and dependents. Its first amendment limits the benefits to veterans and their spouses, and its second amendment limits the benefits solely to veterans. You may be able to argue that the legislature considered extending the benefits to various groups of people but then narrowed the groups, and therefore the benefits should be limited solely to the veterans themselves and not to the spouses, dependents, or ex-spouses of the veterans. That is, comparison of the language of the various versions of the bill as it proceeds through the enactment process may enable you to draw certain conclusions regarding the intent and purpose of the law. Additionally, the bill may include a preamble or introductory section that explains its purpose and intent.

b. Transcripts of Committee Hearings

You will recall that after a bill is introduced it is assigned to a committee, which holds hearings and receives testimony regarding the proposed legislation. Usually a transcript of the testimony is prepared and published. Keep in mind that while some of the individuals who testify may be neutral and independent consumers, scientists, or experts, others may be celebrities or may be lobbyists paid to advance a particular viewpoint persuasively. Thus, while the testimony received by the committee may influence the legislators, courts often view the testimony given at committee hearings with a certain amount of skepticism. You may wish to conduct additional research to determine the credibility and reputation of a party who testified before a committee before you advance an argument based on that person's testimony.

c.   Committee Reports and Prints

After the committee has concluded the hearings, it will issue a report with its recommendations and its reasons therefor. The committee report is published and reflects the views of the majority of committee members after a thorough analysis of the bill and after the often lengthy hearing process. A committee may also rely on reports and studies prepared by consultants or staff members. These publications, called committee prints, may include statistical material or legislative analysis. The committee report usually includes the text of the legislation, an abstract of it, and the committee's findings and recommendations. A committee report is viewed by courts as considerably more credible than transcripts of committee hearings. Those members of the committee who disagree with the majority may issue a minority report, which will provide a different point of view on the subject of the legislation. If the bill was sent to a conference committee, it will also issue a report, including the text of the compromise legislation and an analysis of how the compromise was reached.

d.   Debates

If debate is held on a bill, the remarks of the speakers will be published in the *Congressional Record*, a publication prepared for each day Congress is in session. It is possible that the sponsor of the legislation may discuss the intent or purpose of the bill or that interested parties may explain certain provisions of the legislation. These remarks, published in the *Congressional Record*, form part of a legislative history and may be used to persuade a court as to the intent of the legislature when it enacted a statute. Remarks and statements made by sponsors of legislation may carry more weight than remarks made by other legislators, who may enter material into the *Congressional Record* for purely political reasons.

Moreover, the use of debates as a guide to legislative intent is subject to criticism because members of Congress have the right to "revise and extend" their remarks by altering the *Congressional Record*. Although the intent of this right is to allow members to "dot their i's" and "cross their t's," to eliminate minor errors, in some instances members have made more substantive changes, resulting in a *Congressional Record* that is not a verbatim transcript but a revised version of proceedings on the floor of the House and Senate. For example, in April 2004, Representative Jim McDermott (D. Wash.) omitted the words "under God" when he handled the morning duty in the House of reciting the Pledge of Allegiance. After an inquiry, the presiding officer of the House stated that the words "under God" would appear in the day's *Congressional Record* whether they were spoken or not.

3.   *The Process of Compiling a Legislative History*

Many researchers have difficulty compiling a legislative history because the documents are diverse and are seldom located together. Often you will be required to search many sources. This is especially true because a statute may have been enacted one year and then amended on several occasions thereafter. You may have to compile a legislative history for each version of the statute. Moreover, the material is voluminous. Congress's committees produce more than 500,000 pages of material each year. During the 108th Congress, 6,842 bills and resolutions were introduced in the House and 3,630 were introduced in the Senate. Do not be shy asking a reference librarian for help. Reference librarians are aware that conducting legislative history research can be difficult and that few researchers are familiar with the various sources to be used. There are, however, several steps you can take to gather the documents you need.

a. Examining the History of a Statute and Getting a Public Law Number

After you read a statute in U.S.C., U.S.C.A. or U.S.C.S., you will be provided with historical notes giving information about the enactment of the statute. For example, immediately following a statute in U.S.C.A., you will be provided with information such as the following:

> Pub. L. 106-78, Title I, Oct. 22, 1999, 113 Stat. 1139.
> In the section immediately beneath the statute, called "Historical and Statutory Notes," you are directed to "see 1999 Cong. and Adm. News, p. 198."

Thus, in addition to telling you the public law number of your statute, its date of enactment, and its citation in *United States Statutes at Large*, West also refers you to its publication *United States Code Congressional and Administrative News Service* (USCCAN), a monthly pamphlet that is later compiled into hardbound volumes, which includes the public laws recently enacted, the legislative history of selected bills, a summary of pending legislation, some committee reports, presidential signing statements, presidential proclamations and executive orders, various federal regulations, and court rules. Perhaps the most important information you are given is that the statute in question was introduced as Public Law 106-78, that is, it was the 78th bill enacted by the 106th Congress. This public law number will assist you in tracking the legislative history of your statute. You are also informed that the legislation was enacted October 22, 1999, and can be found at 113 *United States Statutes at Large* 1139.

If U.S.C.A. directs you to USCCAN, immediately review the materials you are directed to because they are generally excellent sources of legislative intent and nearly always include committee reports and presidential signing statements. Although only U.S.C.A. sends you directly to the pertinent legislative material in USCCAN, U.S.C. and U.S.C.S. will provide you with the public law number for the statute you are researching. The public law number appears immediately following the statute. You can then use the public law number to access USCCAN and the other sources discussed below. U.S.C. and U.S.C.S. also provide a citation to *United States Statutes at Large*. The popular name tables in U.S.C.A. and U.S.C.S. also provide public law numbers.

If for some reason you do not have or know the public law number for a particular statute but you know the general subject matter of a statute, you should use the subject matter index for USCCAN for the congressional session during which the statute was enacted. Look up the subject matter of the statute (environment, crimes, social security) and you will be given the public law number and other important legislative information pertaining to this statute, which you can then use to locate legislative history materials in USCCAN.

b. Using a Public Law Number

Once you have obtained the critical public law number, you can locate the documents comprising legislative history by using a variety of sources.

(1) USCCAN

At the end of a congressional session, the monthly USCCAN pamphlets are cumulated into bound volumes. USCCAN is subscribed to by many law firms and is readily available at almost all law libraries.

Use USCCAN's Table of Legislative History (known as Table 4) and insert the public law number of the statute you are researching. Remember to obtain your public law number from the end of the statute you are researching. The easy-to-read Table 4 will inform you what bill number was originally assigned to the statute when it was introduced, such as H.R. 289, meaning the 289th law introduced in the House of Representatives, or S. 741, meaning the 741st bill introduced in the Senate. You will then be given a reference to which committee report to examine as well as the dates the House of Representatives and Senate considered and passed the bill. You can use these references to locate the pertinent committee reports as well as the debates published in the *Congressional Record*. USCCAN will provide you with the dates of consideration and passage for each public law. Official committee reports, conference reports, and statements by legislative leaders on major bills are provided, explaining the background, history, and purpose of the legislation. Presidential signing statements are also included, which often explain the intent of the legislation. Read the materials provided to determine legislative intent. Some material that is duplicative or unnecessary is omitted from USCCAN. Nevertheless, USCCAN usually provides excellent legislative history materials, including discussion of the background and purpose of the legislation in question.

(2) Congressional Information Service

Congressional Information Service (CIS), part of the LEXIS family, is published in monthly pamphlets, which are ultimately cumulated in three bound volumes for each year. Many experts consider CIS the most thorough source for compiling a legislative history because it will refer you to all the documents needed for a complete legislative history. One of the volumes is titled *CIS Annual Abstracts of Congressional Publications*; one is called *CIS Annual Legislative Histories*; and the third is an annual Index to the yearly set.

Each CIS yearly set includes a comprehensive index, which allows you to access documents through a variety of methods. You can look up materials by subject matter (environment, crimes, social security), by name of any witness who testified at committee hearings, by bill number, by popular name of a statute, and by the name of a committee chairperson. The indexing by witness name allows you to check the credibility of a witness by determining other hearings at which the witness has testified.

The CIS index will then refer you to the appropriate pages in the CIS Annual Abstracts volume, which contains summaries or "abstracts" of the bill as introduced, the testimony given at committee hearings, the committee reports, and references to the particular days debates were held so you can readily locate these in the *Congressional Record*. Not only will you be provided with these abstracts, you will be given references or citations to the exact documents you will need (for example, "House Report 106-451") so you may obtain and analyze the document in full, if desired. CIS's annual volume, titled *CIS Annual Legislative Histories*, is arranged by public law number. By "plugging in" your public law number (found immediately after your statute in U.S.C., U.S.C.A., and U.S.C.S.), you will be directed to a brief summary of the law and references to the documents you need to compile your legislative history. For example you will be directed to House and Senate Reports, committee hearings, and the debates that appear in the *Congressional Record*.

CIS then publishes these documents in microfiche in its CIS/Microfiche Library so you can easily locate the documents you need. CIS also makes its database available through LexisNexis, on CD-ROM, and on the Internet through its source called LexisNexis Congressional. This Web-based tool offers more than 25 years of congressional information. Searching is easily done by bill number, subject matter, committee name, or public law number. Seamless linking is made to the full range of legislative resources, including bills, hearing transcripts, committee reports, and the *Congressional Record*. Most materials created since the mid-1980s are available. Additional information about LexisNexis Congressional can be found at http://www.lexisnexis.com/academic/1univ/cong/default.asp.

In the event that your law library does not maintain the CIS/Microfiche Library, CIS will provide you with the stock number of the Government Printing Office documents so you can contact the GPO ((202) 512-1800) and order the documents you need. Alternatively, orders can be placed through the GPO online bookstore at http://bookstore.gpo.gov/index.html. In this way, CIS is a complete reference tool for compiling a legislative history.

(3) CCH Congressional Index

CCH Incorporated (CCH) is the publisher of *Congressional Index*, a looseleaf service, which issues weekly pamphlets. A two-volume set of binders is available for each congressional session. Each set contains an index to all public laws introduced in that session. This set will direct you to the specific documents you need to examine but does not itself reproduce them in the set. You can access the index by public law number, name of the law, subject matter, or the name of the legislator who sponsored the bill. If you need to obtain a bill number, use the Subject Index to the set.

When you have a bill number, you can look it up in the section called "Status of House Bills" or "Status of Senate Bills." You will then be given a chronological record of actions taken on the bill, including the date it was introduced, when it was referred to a committee, when hearings were held, when amendments were adopted, when it was passed, and when it was sent to and signed by the president. You will also be informed of the bill's public law number and its citation in *United States Statutes at Large*. You can also take your bill number and insert it into a section called "House Bills" or "Senate Bills," which gives a brief description of the legislation, identifies its chief sponsor and the committee to which it was sent. The *Congressional Index* also includes a variety of other information, such as membership rosters for House and Senate committees and subcommittees, information relating to presidential vetoes, and the voting records relating to bills. Moreover, *Congressional Index* is useful in tracking pending legislation.

Congressional Index does not provide references to the *Congressional Record*, meaning that you will be unable to locate debates through the use of *Congressional Index*.

4. *Using Electronic Sources and the Internet to Compile a Legislative History*

The ability to conduct research electronically has had a significant effect on the way in which legislative history research is conducted. It is no longer necessary to run around a law library collecting documents, mail requests for documents to the Government Printing Office, and call congressional representatives for assistance. Using LEXIS, Westlaw, THOMAS, or GPO Access, researchers can easily find the documents they need by searching by bill number or key words and then link to related documents, enabling them to assemble a legislative history far easier than in the past.

a. LEXIS

The computerized legal research system LEXIS offers easy access to legislative information. After you sign on, select the LEXIS database or "Library" called "Legis." You can search by Congress number (such as the 104th Congress), by a bill number, public law number, topic of the legislation, committee report number, and so forth. You will then be given the full text of the bill, selected hearing transcripts, committee reports, the *Congressional Record* since approximately 1985, and compiled legislative histories for selected legislation of widespread public interest. LEXIS provides hypertext links that allow you to jump from one source or document to another.

Alternatively, after you sign on, you can click on "Get a Document" and then enter the citation to your bill number, the public law number, or to the reference to the *Congressional Record*. You will then be immediately linked to the relevant document.

b. Westlaw

Westlaw, West's computerized legal research system, operates nearly identically to LEXIS. Westlaw offers compiled, full legislative histories for some statutes and other acts of public interest, such as the Family and Medical Leave Act. After you sign on, select the pertinent database. For example, Billcast (enter "BC") provides information on current bills in Congress. Billcast Archives (enter "BC-OLD") provides information on public laws introduced in previous sessions of Congress. The database BILLS provides the full text of bills pending in Congress. The *Congressional Record* (enter "CR") is available since 1985, and legislative history for selected statutes (for example, legislative histories compiled for certain statutes such as the Family and Medical Leave Act or the USA Patriot Act) is available by accessing the database called Arnold & Porter Collection-Legislative Histories.

c. THOMAS

Although LEXIS and Westlaw are easy to use and provide extensive legislative materials, they are fee-based subscription services. Since 1995, it has been possible to obtain many items of legislative history for free, 24/7, through a source called THOMAS. In 1995, the Library of Congress initiated THOMAS, its online database of congressional information and materials named for Thomas Jefferson and located at http://thomas. loc.gov. THOMAS provides a wealth of information, including the following:

- Descriptions of how our laws are enacted.
- Historical documents (including the Federalist Papers, Declaration of Independence, and the U.S. Constitution).
- House and Senate Directories (alphabetical lists of House and Senate members, including their addresses, phone numbers, links to their Web pages, and lists of their committee assignments).
- Committee home pages (providing information about the composition and work of House and Senate committees).
- Committee schedules and calendars of upcoming hearings.
- Direct links to other legislative agencies, including the Government Printing Office, Library of Congress, and others.

More important, THOMAS offers easy access to many documents of legislative history. When you access THOMAS, you may select "Legislation," "Congressional Record," or "Committee Information." If you elect to search "Legislation," you may search by keyword, bill number, or public law number. You will then be given access to the exact text of the bill or public law, a summary of it, and its status (such as the date when it was introduced, when it was referred to a committee, when it was voted upon, and when it was sent to and signed by the president).

If you do not know or have a bill number or public law number, you can search by word or phrase (such as "patent infringement") or by popular name (such as "Family and Medical Leave Act"). In general, searching is done by particular congressional sessions (104th, 105th, 106th, and so forth). Thus, searching can be a bit time-consuming if you do not know in which congressional session legislation was introduced. THOMAS also provides references to the *Congressional Record*.

THOMAS allows one to view, download, and print the entire text of a bill or *Congressional Record* article.

THOMAS provides the following legislative history coverage:

- Bill Summary & Status: a summary of all bills since 1973 is available.
- Bill Text: the full text of all bills since 1989 is available.
- Transcripts of Committee Hearings: selected hearing transcripts are available for some House committees since 1997. At the time of writing of this text, transcripts of Senate hearings were not yet available.
- Committee Reports: the full text of nearly all House and Senate Committee Reports since 1985 is available, and the Reports are searchable by word/phrase, report number, bill number, and committee name.
- *Congressional Record*: the full text of the daily edition of the *Congressional Record* is available since 1989, searchable by member of Congress, date of debate or remarks, or word/phrase.

THOMAS offers an easy, free, and highly reliable way to compile a legislative history, particularly for legislation enacted in the past five to ten years. Once you locate the bill you are interested in, you can track its progress, locate committee reports, and find references to it in the *Congressional Record* through easy-to-use hyperlinks. Simply click on the topics and documents in which you are interested, and you will be immediately transported to that information. THOMAS is updated several times each day, making the information extremely current. Generally, information about a bill's summary and status is available 24 to 48 hours after any action is taken on the bill. THOMAS has proven to be wildly popular with the public, as witnessed by the fact that nearly 118 million files were transmitted by THOMAS in 2003. (See Figure 10-1 for a sample page from THOMAS.)

d. GPO Access

The Government Printing Office offers numerous official publications through its comprehensive and easy-to-use Internet site, called "GPO Access," at http://www.gpoaccess.gov. Congressional bills, transcripts of hearings, committee publications, the *Congressional Record*, and public laws are available, together with a great deal of other congressional and legislative history information. Most materials since the early 1990s are available. Searching is easily done by bill number, public law number, key words or subject titles, or *United States Code* citation. Questions or comments can be directed to a toll-free number at (866) 512-1800.

Figure 10-1
Sample Page from THOMAS

In the Spirit of
Thomas Jefferson,
a service of
The Library of Congress

Congress Now: House Floor This Week | House Floor Now | Senate Schedule: Majority Minority

Search Bill Text 109th Congress (2005-2006)

[   ]   Search

⦿ Enter keywords   ◯ Enter bill number

Search
box for
current
bills

Quick Links: House | House Clerk | House Directory | Senate | Senate Directory | GPO

LINKS	LEGISLATION	*CONGRESSIONAL RECORD*	COMMITTEE INFORMATION
About THOMAS	**Action Yesterday**	**Latest Daily Digest**	**Committee Reports**
THOMAS FAQ	**Search Bills and Resolutions**	**Browse by Date or Keyword**	**House Committees**
Congress & Legislative Agencies	**Public Laws**	**Search Congressional Record**	**Senate Committees**
How Congress Makes Laws: House | Senate		**Roll Call Votes**	
Résumés of Congressional Activity			

Days in Session
Calendar

Appropriations Legislation

U.S. Code

Presidential Nominations

Executive Branch

Treaties

Judicial Branch

State Resources

Historical Documents

The Library of Congress   Contact Us   Please Read Our Legal Notices

---

Practice Tip

Online Legislative History Research

Although THOMAS and GPO Access offer the ability to locate
thousands of legislative history documents, their databases are
relatively current, meaning that you cannot obtain older documents
from these services. Nevertheless, the fact that you cannot perform
legislative history research for older statutes using these free services
is not a significant drawback, because legislative history is usually
performed for newer statutes. Once a statute has been in existence for
several years, there will likely be judicial analysis of the statute and
cases discussing it, rendering the use of a legislative history far less
important.

---

5. *Obtaining Documents Needed for Legislative Histories*

a. Bills and Their Amendments

You can obtain the text of bills and later amendments to bills in committee
reports or in the microfiche collection of CIS titled "Congressional Bills on
Microfiche" or through THOMAS or GPO Access.

b. Transcripts of Committee Hearings

Transcripts of the hearings held by congressional committees and subcom-
mittees are available in pamphlet form as well as in microfiche through
CIS/Microfiche Library. Some are available through THOMAS or GPO
Access.

c. Committee Reports and Prints

Congressional committees and subcommittees issue their reports in conventional pamphlet form. These reports are published in a bound set of
books called the *"Serial Set."* USCCAN also reprints selected committee
reports. CIS produces committee reports in microfiche in its CIS/Micro-
fiche Library. Finally, reports since 1995 are available through THOMAS
and many are available through GPO Access.

d. Debates

Debates are published in the *Congressional Record*, a "newspaper" issued
daily when Congress is in session. The *Congressional Record* is initially
issued in pamphlet form and is finally published in bound volumes at the
end of a congressional session. CIS also publishes the *Congressional Record* in microfiche. If you do not already know the date any debates occurred,
look up the bill number in the *Record's* History of Bills and Resolutions.

This will cite the date of any debate on the bill that you are researching. The spine of each volume clearly indicates the dates covered by the volume, making it very easy to access the set. Once you know the date debate occurred, you simply match this date with the date appearing on the spine of a volume of the *Congressional Record*. The full text of the *Congressional Record* since 1989 is available through THOMAS and since 1994 is available through GPO Access. THOMAS allows searching by word, phrase, member of Congress name, or date.

Committee prints are not generally announced for public distribution because they are usually viewed as internal background publications. They are available in the CIS/Microfiche Library, on LEXIS, and online through GPO Access since 1995.

6. *Alternate Methods of Obtaining Legislative History for Federal Statutes*

a. Compiled Legislative Histories

A compiled legislative history is a "pre-packaged" legislative history. That is, it is possible that a legislative history may already have been compiled on the statute in which you are interested, thereby eliminating the need for you to perform the task of legislative research yourself. USCCAN provides legislative histories for selected federal laws in its monthly pamphlets.

To determine whether a compiled legislative history exists for the statute you are researching, consult Nancy P. Johnson, *Sources of Compiled Legislative History: A Bibliography of Government Documents, Periodical Articles, and Books*, a book that lists by public law number any published legislative histories and includes citations to articles that discuss and interpret the legislative history of particular statutes. Consult the card catalog at your law library to determine whether these sources are available. Generally, compiled legislative histories exist for legislation that is well known or is of public importance. As discussed earlier, both LEXIS and Westlaw offer some compiled legislative histories, especially for significant legislative enactments.

b. Legislative History Worksheets

Recognizing that legislative history can be difficult and time-consuming, some law libraries have worksheets for you to use that provide a step-by-step approach and clear instructions for compiling a legislative history. Ask the reference librarian at your law library if the library provides such a worksheet.

c. Commercial Services

There are several commercial services that will assist you in obtaining documents or in monitoring legislation. Check your local phone book or local legal directory to obtain information about private companies that will obtain government documents for you for a fee. Following is a partial list of some of these companies or services:

(i)   BNA Plus, a division of the Bureau of National Affairs, Inc., in Washington, D.C., will obtain bills and congressional testimony as well as court opinions, agency decisions, or foreign treaties. The toll-free telephone number is (800) 372-1033, or visit http://www.bna.com/products/docs.htm.

(ii)   Washington Document Service of Washington, D.C., will locate various federal and regulatory documents for a moderate fee. The address is 1023 15th Street NW, 12th Floor, Washington, D.C., 20005. The toll-free number is (800) 728-5201, and the Web site is http://www.wdsdocs.com.

(iii)   StateNet, a well-known company that recently acquired Legi-Slate, another leader in the field of providing legislative information, will provide legislative materials for Congress and all 50 states. Contact its office at 444 N. Capitol Street, N.W., Suite 725, Washington, D.C., 20001. The telephone number is (800) 726-4566, and the Web site is http://www.legislate.com.

(iv)   Legislative Intent Service, a well-known company established in 1974, will obtain federal legislative history as well as legislative history for any state. This service also provides expert analysis of materials obtained. Call (800) 666-1917, or visit the Web site at www.legintent.com.

d.   Reference Assistance

Legislative history research is a unique and specialized method of attempting to determine the intent of the legislature when it enacted a statute by reviewing the documents that are part of the legislative process. A bill may be introduced in one congressional session and not enacted and then may be re-introduced the next congressional session with a different bill number. A bill may be reported out of a committee, voted upon, and then referred to conference if the House of Representatives and Senate pass differing versions. Amendments may be made to the statute in several different years.

These complexities make legislative history research a difficult task, especially to the uninitiated. If you encounter difficulty, ask a law librarian for assistance. Large law libraries and law firms often designate an individual to field inquiries and offer assistance in the area of legislative history research. Law librarians are well aware of the complex nature of gathering the documents needed to compile a legislative history and will not be surprised if you ask for help.

e.   Congressional Assistance

Members of the House of Representatives and Senate have office staff assistants whose job it is to perform a variety of tasks, including responding to requests for information by constituents. Call the office of your congressional representative and ask for copies of the bill, the committee report, or other pertinent materials. If you cannot recall the name of your representative, check your telephone directory, as this information is often provided in the first few pages of telephone books. Alternatively, check the House and Senate rosters in THOMAS. Often you will be mailed copies of the materials needed within a few days. If you do not receive the materials you need, call and ask again.

House of Representatives: If you have a bill number, call (202) 226-5200 to check on availability. You may mail a request for a copy of a bill to:

U.S. House of Represenatives
Office of the Clerk
Legislative Resource Center
B-106 Cannon House Office Building
Washington, D.C 20515

United States Senate: If you have a bill number, call (202) 224-7860 to check on availability. You may request a bill online by e-mailing orders@sec.senate.gov or mail a request for a copy of a bill to:

Senate Document Room
B-04 Hart Senate Office Building
Washington, D.C. 20510

If you are looking for a bill but do not have a bill number, call the Congressional Legislative Office at (202) 225-1772 and provide as much information about the statute as possible, such as subject matter, sponsor's name, and date introduced. Alternatively, review the site "How to find bill numbers" provided by the U.S. Senate at http://www.senate.gov/reference/common/faq/how_to_numbers.htm.

f. Law Reviews and Annotations

It is possible that a law review or A.L.R. annotation has already performed the task of legislative history research for you. That is, a law review or other periodical publication may contain a thorough analysis of the statute you are researching and already may have examined the bill, the transcripts of the committee hearings, the committee reports, and the debates and may summarize this legislative history for you.

The best way to determine if an article or annotation discusses your statute is to Shepardize or KeyCite your statute. If *Shepard's* or KeyCite identifies a law review article or annotation as discussing the pertinent statute, examine these sources to determine if they have deduced the intent of the legislature in enacting the statute by examining all of the documents that comprise a legislative history.

Alternatively, you could examine the "Table of Laws, Rules and Regulations" in A.L.R.'s Index to Annotations. This table will direct you to annotations in A.L.R. that cite or analyze federal statutes.

```
┌─────────────────────── Practice Tip ───────────────────────┐
│                                                             │
│ Legislative History Research: Three Easy (and Free) Steps   │
│                                                             │
│ There are many places for you to locate the documents that  │
│ make up a legislative history. Consider simplifying the     │
│ process by following these three steps:                     │
│                                                             │
│ 1. Obtain a public law number by looking at the end of your │
│    statute in U.S.C.A. or U.S.C.S.                          │
│ 2. Insert the public law number (or a key word or phrase    │
│    related to the statute) into THOMAS (http://thomas.loc.  │
│    gov).                                                     │
│ 3. Read and analyze the pertinent documents, linking to     │
│    other related documents as needed.                       │
│                                                             │
└─────────────────────────────────────────────────────────────┘
```

g. Web-based Tutorials

A number of Web sites offer information, guidance, and tutorials on conducting legislative history research for federal statutes. Following are three of the best sites:

- Boston College Law Library's Federal Legislative Histories (www.bc. edu/schools/law/library/research/researchguide/leghist) provides an excellent overview of the legislative history research process with tips on how to compile a legislative history and charts on how to find public law numbers, bill numbers, and so forth.
- Chicago-Kent College of Law's Federal Legislative History (http:// library.kentlaw.edu/Resources/leghist%20Tutorial/Intro.htm) is a multimedia tutorial on the legislative history research process and includes exercises as well as excellent information on legislative history research.
- The Law Librarians' Society of Washington, D.C.'s Federal Legislative History Legislative Source Book (http://www.llsdc.org/ sourcebook/fed-leg-hist.htm) is subtitled "A Practitioner's Guide to Compiling the Documents and Sifting for Legislative Intent." It provides a thorough overview of the research process and numerous links to excellent sources.

7. *Introduction to State Legislative History*

You will recall that the process of enacting state statutes is substantially similar to that of enacting federal statutes. Just as there may be ambiguity in a federal statute that would result in a need to research the intent of the United States Congress in enacting a federal law, there may be ambiguity in a statute enacted in your state. If there are no cases interpreting the state statute, you may wish to perform state legislative history research to determine the intent of your state legislature when it enacted the statute.

The process of compiling a legislative history for a state statute is substantially similar to that for federal statutes. Unfortunately, collecting the actual documents involved can be frustrating because many of them are not published and some are available only at the state capitol.

8. Documents Composing State Legislative History

The documents involved in compiling a legislative history for a state statute are identical to those needed for compiling a legislative history for a federal statute: the original bill, together with any of its later versions, transcripts of committee hearings, committee reports, and floor debates.

9. The Process of Compiling a State Legislative History

After you have read a state statute, carefully examine the historical notes following it to determine the derivation of the statute. For instance, you may be presented with information such as the following:

> *Derivation*   Stats. 1996, c. 141, p. 621

This would indicate the statute was enacted in 1996 and was initially published at Chapter 141 of the state's session laws and can be found at page 621 of the session laws for 1996.

Consult your law librarian to determine if a legislative service exists for your state. Such a legislative service will operate similarly to USCCAN, CIS, or CCH *Congressional Index* in that it will provide you with a bill number for your state statute and information regarding the committee that considered the bill.

Once you have a bill number or the name of the committee that considered the bill, you can contact the chairperson of the committee or a legislative staffer at your state capitol and ask for copies of the pertinent documents. Unfortunately, many states do not maintain many of the documents needed for state legislative histories. While the bill and its versions will be available, the proceedings of committee hearings are rarely transcribed, committee reports are rarely published, and debates are rarely reported. Thus, in many states, the only documents available to you in preparing a legislative history are the various versions of the bill as it proceeds through the state legislature.

To determine what documents are available in your state, consult the following: William H. Manz, *Guide to State Legislative and Administrative*

Materials (2002). This source provides a state-by-state outline of the documents available for each of the 50 states and the District of Columbia.

10. *Alternate Methods of Obtaining Legislative History for State Statutes*

Due to the difficulties in compiling a legislative history for state statutes, you may find that the following alternate methods of legislative history are the most effective.

> *Compiled Legislative Histories.* Some well-known state statutes may already have been the subject of a legislative history. Your law librarian may assist you in locating these.
>
> *Legislative History Worksheets.* Check with your law librarian to determine if a worksheet or checklist has been prepared to assist individuals compiling legislative histories of state statutes.
>
> *Commercial Services.* There may be private companies that will perform state legislative history for you. Because many of the documents are available only at the state capitol, these private companies are often located in the capital city of a state.
>
> Due to the difficulty of compiling a legislative history for a state statute, making arrangements with a private company to obtain the needed documents may well be the most effective way of obtaining a complete legislative history. Often the fees charged by these companies are moderate, and you may be provided with the documents you need within a matter of days.
>
> To determine if such a company exists in your state, check with a reference librarian, consult a directory of legal services, call directory information at the capital city, or contact an attorneys' service.
>
> Following are some fee-based commercial services that provide state legislative history information and documents:

- LegAlert, a state legislative history service provided by NETSCAN iPublishing, provides all proposed state legislation, enacted legislation, and related documents for all 50 legislatures, Committee reports are also available from some states. Contact NETSCAN iPublishing, Inc., at 803 W. Broad Street, Suite 110, Falls Church, VA, 22046. The toll-free telephone number is (800) 982-2177, and the Web site is http://www.legalert.com.
- StateNet, located in California and at 444 N. Capitol Street, N.W., Suite 725, Washington, D.C., 20001, provides legislative materials for all 50 states. Its telephone number is (202) 638-7999 or (800) 726-4566, and its Web site is http://www.statenet.com.
- LEXIS and Westlaw both provide bill text and bill tracking for all 50 states.

> *Web-based Tutorials.* There are a number of Web sites that will greatly assist you in compiling legislative history for state statutes.

Following are some of the best:

- Southern Illinois University's Finding State Legislation, A Web Tutorial (http://mccoy/lib/siu.edu/legis/trace), offers an excellent overview of the process of compiling a state legislative history.
- The Law Librarians' Legislative Source Book (http://www.llsdc.org/sourcebook/state-leg.htm) links to state laws and regulations and includes valuable Web site links and phone numbers.
- A research guide and bibliography to finding state legislation is offered through Cornell University Library at http://www.library.cornell.edu/olinuris/ref/statedocs.html.
- The Web site of the National Conference of State Legislatures (http://www.ncsl.org) is a gateway to state legislative sites, allowing direct linking to the legislative site in each state. Although the site is designed as a source for lawmakers and their staffs, it also provides public users with many reports, meetings schedules, links to the home pages for each state's legislative body, and a method of ordering publications.

Reference Assistance. Be sure to ask your law librarian for assistance if you encounter difficulty in locating the documents you need. You should also check the card catalog at your law library to determine if there are any books or publications that will provide guidance in compiling a state legislative history.

Legislative Assistance. Contact your state legislators or representatives and ask for assistance or for copies of documents.

Law Reviews and Annotations. Shepardize or KeyCite the particular statute you are researching to determine if it has been the subject of any law review article, A.L.R. annotation, or attorney general opinion. If *Shepard's* or KeyCite directs you to any of these sources, review them because they may provide a convenient summary of the information you need.

Internet Tutorials on Legislative History Research

There are two excellent tutorials that provide guidance on compiling federal and state legislative histories. They are, respectively, located at the following sites: http://library.kentlaw.edu/resources/leghist%20Tutorial/Intro.htm; and http://law.indiana.edu/library/services/sta_leg.shtml.

---

11. Tracking Pending Legislation

You may need to track and monitor pending legislation for clients who must keep abreast of emerging laws that could affect their business. Clients must prepare for changes before the measure becomes a law. The process of bill tracking to monitor the progress of proposed legislation is different from reviewing the legislative history for statutes already enacted. Following are some sources that will help you monitor pending legislation:

- CCH *Congressional Index* (discussed earlier in this chapter) describes action on a bill and provides weekly updates, allowing you to track when action is taken on pending legislation. Once you have a bill number (easily obtained from the Subject Index to the set), you can "plug it in" the sections called "Status of House Bills" or "Status of Senate Bills" to determine the most recent action taken on the legislation.
- LexisNexis's Congressional provides bill tracking.
- LEXIS's service, called "Eclipse," will provide you with daily, weekly, or monthly updates on your legislation. You can be notified by e-mail or view the results online. A database entitled Billtrack (enter "BLTRCK") will also provide bill tracking and a report for you.
- Westlaw's database, called US-Billtrack (enter "US-BILLTRK"), provides tracking of pending legislation.
- THOMAS does not automatically alert you to changes in legislation in which you are interested, but by routinely checking the status and summary of a bill, you can determine the progress it is making through Congress. Search by bill number or by word/phrase and then select "Bill Summary and Status."
- StateNet, the commerical service described earlier, will provide bill tracking service for a fee and alert you by e-mail whenever legislative action is taken on a bill you are monitoring.

To track the progress of state legislation, use LEXIS, Westlaw, or StateNet. Alternatively, some states automatically provide you with e-mail updates on the status of pending legislation. For example, in California the legislature provides a bill status updating service to keep you informed as bills you are interested in move through the legislature. The free tracking service (located at www.leginfo.ca.gov) automatically e-mails you when there are changes in the bill or changes in its status.

12. *Summary of Legislative History Research*

The primary purpose of compiling a legislative history is to aid a court in interpreting an ambiguous statute that has not yet been the subject of judicial interpretation. If there are no cases interpreting a statute, you may wish to compile a legislative history to present to a court as evidence of what the legislature intended the statute to accomplish.

The use of legislative history to interpret statutes is often criticized. Perhaps one of the most vocal critics is United States Supreme Court Justice Antonin Scalia. Justice Scalia has stated that using legislative history is "not merely a waste of research time and ink [but] a false and disruptive lesson in the law." *Conroy v. Aniskoff*, 507 U.S. 511, 519 (1993) (Scalia, J., concurring). Moreover, Justice Stevens has remarked that the use of "frankly partisan statements" by lawmakers can and should in no way be viewed as reflective of some consensus in Congress. Demanding that legislatures draft statutes more clearly, many judges believe that when courts go beyond the plain meaning of a statute by relying on legislative history they exceed their function as interpreters of the law and are in danger of making law, which is the exclusive province of legislatures.

Keep in mind that, at best, a legislative history is a secondary source. It is not a case, constitution, regulation, or statute, which are binding on a court and which therefore must be followed. A court may elect to follow the recommendation of a committee report or the sponsor of the legislation in determining the purpose or effect of the statute. Some courts, however, are reluctant to rely on legislative history and view many of the documents as the product of a political process rather than a careful and reasoned analysis of the statute. That is, remarks made at committee hearings or at debates may be the result of political bias or may be made by legislators who are not totally familiar with the legislation. In such cases, over-reliance on legislative history may be misplaced. Nevertheless, if you have no other argument to advance, you should definitely perform the research needed for a legislative history, present it to the court as clearly and persuasively as possible, and hope for the best. With no other guidance to interpret an ambiguous statute, a court may be persuaded to rely upon legislative history as evidence of the purpose or intent of a statute.

Practice Tip

Hierarchy of Legislative History Documents

While there is some disagreement, most experts conclude that the documents making up legislative history can be ranked in the following order, from strongest to weakest:

- Conference and committee reports are usually viewed as the strongest evidence of legislative intent because they reflect the view of experienced members of Congress after careful study of the bill and analysis of testimony at hearings.
- Versions of the bill and its amendments as it progresses through the legislature are considered highly persuasive.
- Statements by a bill's sponsors may show evidence of legislative intent (whether made at a hearing or during debate).
- Floor debates by those other than a bill's sponsors are somewhat weak because legislators may use the opportunity to debate for any number of political or personal reasons.
- Statements made by various individuals (other than bill sponsors) at committee hearings are weak evidence of legislative intent because many are made by paid lobbyists or persons with political agendas.

B.   Executive Materials

1. Introduction

The conventional view of the three branches of our government is that the legislative branch makes our laws, the judicial branch interprets our laws, and the executive branch enforces our laws. The executive branch, however, does issue certain directives and documents that affect all of us, although they are of varying legal effect.

2. Proclamations

A proclamation is a statement issued by the president that has no legal effect. Proclamations are often issued for ceremonial, public relations, or public awareness reasons. For example, Presidential Proclamation No. 6459 declared a certain week to be Lyme Disease Awareness Week. Other proclamations are Presidential Proclamation No. 6461, announcing Buffalo Soldiers Day, and Presidential Proclamation No. 7347, announcing National Disability Employment Awareness Month. Although usually used for ceremonial purposes, proclamations can be used for more substantive statements (such as President Lincoln's Emancipation Proclamation of 1862). See Figure 10-2 for a sample Presidential Proclamation.

Presidential proclamations generally have no legal effect because they do not command or prohibit any action, and no punishment or liability accrues as a result of any "violation" of a presidential proclamation. Proclamations are published in a number of sources:

- USCCAN.
- *Federal Register*, the daily weekday newspaper published by the Office of the Federal Register.
- Title 3 of C.F.R. (the annual codification of the *Federal Register*).
- *Weekly Compilation of Presidential Documents*, a weekly pamphlet containing all messages and statements released by the White House.
- U.S.C.S. advance pamphlets.
- *United States Statutes at Large*, the bound volumes containing all public and private laws passed by the United States Congress.
- LEXIS and Westlaw.

Title 3 of C.F.R. (since 1994) and *Weekly Compilation of Presidential Documents* (since 1993) are both available for free, on the Internet, from the Government Printing Office at the following Web site: http://www. gpoaccess.gov/nara/index.html. Searching can be done by inserting key words in search boxes or by browsing through tables of contents.

Figure 10-2
Sample Presidential Proclamation

Week Ending Friday, January 21, 2005

Proclamation 7862—Martin Luther King, Jr., Federal Holiday, 2005
January 14, 2005

By the President of the United States of America

A Proclamation

Dr. Martin Luther King, Jr., was a visionary American and a dedicated leader who believed deeply in liberty and dignity for every person. His faith and courage continue to inspire America and the world. We honor his life and his work.

Growing up in Atlanta, Georgia, Dr. King witnessed firsthand the injustice of a segregated society. He realized that change was necessary to ensure the full promise of our Constitution for all Americans, and his charismatic leadership awakened the conscience of America.

Dr. King's dream inspired our Nation with what he called "a certain kind of fire that no water could put out." Since Dr. King's involvement in the civil rights movement in the 1950s and 1960s, Americans have witnessed the power of the law to prevent injustice and encourage the finest qualities of our Nation. Last year, we celebrated the 40th anniversary of the Civil Rights Act of 1964. Once this landmark legislation was signed into law, Americans could no longer be denied a room in a hotel or a table at a restaurant because of their race.

Our Nation has accomplished much over the past 40 years. Our journey toward justice and equality has not always been an easy one, and it is not over. However long the journey, our destination is set: liberty and justice for all. Dr. Martin Luther King, Jr., believed in the good that exists in all men and women. We will remember the work of Dr. King as we continue striving to meet the founding ideals of our great Nation.

Now, Therefore, I, George W. Bush, President of the United States of America, by virtue of the authority vested in me by the Constitution and laws of the United States, do hereby proclaim Monday, January 17, 2005, as the Martin Luther King, Jr., Federal Holiday. I encourage all Americans to observe this day with appropriate activities and programs that honor the memory and legacy of Dr. King.

In Witness Whereof, I have hereunto set my hand this fourteenth day of January, in the year of our Lord two thousand five, and of the Independence of the United States of America the two hundred and twenty-ninth.

George W. Bush

3. *Executive Orders*

An executive order has more legal effect than a proclamation. Executive orders are regulations issued by a president to direct government officials and agencies. These executive orders have the force of law (unless, of course, a court rules to the contrary) and require no action by Congress. An example of an executive order is Executive Order No. 13354 for the establishment of a National Counterterrorism Center. Executive orders can be located in the same sources as proclamations, including through GPO Access at http://www.gpoaccess.gov/nara.index.html, except they are not located in *United States Statutes at Large*.

The National Archives and Records Administration provides executive orders and information about executive orders for all presidents since Franklin D. Roosevelt at the following Web site: http://www.archives.gov. As discussed above, GPO Access also provides Title 3 of C.F.R. and *Weekly Compilation of Presidential Documents* on its Web site, and both of these include executive orders.

4. *Weekly Compilation of Presidential Documents*

One of the best sources for materials relating to the executive branch is a set of books entitled *Weekly Compilation of Presidential Documents*. This weekly publication of the Office of the Federal Register contains the following presidential items:

(i)   addresses and remarks such as remarks made at luncheons or ceremonies, press releases, speeches, and press conferences

(ii) announcements such as those recognizing certain programs

(iii) appointments and nominations such as one announcing the assistant secretary for science and education for the Agriculture Department

(iv) bill signings, bill vetoes, and communications to the United States Congress

(v)   communications to federal agencies

(vi) executive orders and proclamations

(vii) interviews with news media

Access to the *Weekly Compilation* is gained through a regularly published index. See Figure 10-3 for a sample page from the *Weekly Compilation of Presidential Documents. Weekly Compilation of Presidential Documents* is also available for free online from GPO Access. Documents since 1993 are available. Searching is usually done by key words or search terms entered in search boxes. Access the following site: http://www.gpoaccess.gov/wcomp/index.html.

Numerous other sources provide executive materials. Browse the shelves in the reference section of your law library. Alternatively, consult

Figure 10-3
Sample Page from *Weekly Compilation of Presidential Documents*

Digest of Other
White House Announcements

The following list includes the President's public schedule and other items of general interest announced by the Office of the Press Secretary and not included elsewhere in this issue.

December 30

The President and Hillary Clinton went to Camp David, MD.

The White House announced that the President directed the Department of Health and Human Services to release $300 million in Low Income Home Energy Assistance Program emergency funds to all States facing substantial increases in home heating fuel prices. °

January 1

The President and Hillary Clinton returned to Washington, DC.

January 2

In the afternoon, the President met with Chairman Yasser Arafat of the Palestinian Authority in the Oval Office.

January 3

In the afternoon, the President attended the swearing-in ceremony for the U.S. Senate class of 2001.

The President announced the recess appointment of James H. Atkins as Chair and member of the Federal Retirement Thrift Investment Board.

The President announced the recess appointment of Allen Carrier as a member of the Board of Trustees of the Institute of American Indian and Alaska Native Culture and Arts Development.

The President announced the recess appointment of Edward Correia as a member of the National Council on Disability.

The President announced the recess appointment of Gerald S. Segal as a member of the National Council on Disability.

The President announced the recess appointment of Dennis Martin Devaney as

---

°This item was made available by the Office of the Press Secretary on December 29 but was embargoed for release until 10:06 a.m., December 30.

Commissioner of the U.S. International Trade Commission.

The President announced the recess appointment Ross Edward Eisenbrey as a member of the Occupational Safety and Health Review Commission.

The President announced the recess appointment of Jayne G. Fawcett as a member of the Board of Trustees of the Institute of American Indian and Alaska Native Culture and Arts Development.

The President announced the recess appointment of Sheryl R. Marshall as a member of the Federal Retirement Thrift Investment Board.

The President announced the recess appointment of Yolanda Townsend Wheat as Chair of the National Credit Union Administration.

The President announced the recess appointment of Hsin-Ming Fung as a member of the National Council on the Arts.

The President announced the recess appointment of Robert M. Lyford as a member of the Board of Directors for the Overseas Private Investment Corporation.

January 4

In the morning, the President and Hillary Clinton traveled to Syracuse, NY, and in the afternoon, they returned to Washington, DC.

January 5

In the morning, the President went to Camp David, MD, and later he returned to Washington, DC, where he met with former Chairman of the Joint Chiefs of Staff Gen. John M. Shalikashvili, USA (Ret.), in the Oval Office.

In the afternoon, the President attended a Preserve America's Forests event at the National Arboretum. Later, he traveled to Arlington, VA, where he attended an Armed Forces Presidential Tribute at Fort Myer. Later, he returned to Washington, DC.

The President announced his intention to appoint Ginger Ehn Lew as a member of the Advisory Commission on Asian American and Pacific Islanders.

The President declared a major disaster in Oklahoma and ordered Federal aid to supplement State and local recovery efforts in the area struck by a severe winter ice storm

Public Papers of the President of the United States, available online at http://www.gpo.gov/nara/pubpaps/srchpaps.html, which provides access to presidential papers, speeches, nominations, proclamations, executive orders, and other presidential documents since 1992. Searching is done by key words and phrases.

C.   Administrative Law

1.   *Introduction to Federal Administrative Law*

In the first half of the 20th century, it became evident that Congress' lawmaking ability could not keep pace with the demands of modern society. As a result, Congress delegated certain tasks to agencies, each created to administer a body of law. For example, the use of air waves to communicate information by radio led to the creation of the Federal Communications Commission in 1934.

You will recall that the typical view of our system of government is that each of the three branches of government (legislative, judicial, and executive) exercises one function (making law, interpreting law, and enforcing law, respectively). The administrative agencies are an apparent contradiction to this principle of separation of powers in that the agencies act quasi-legislatively (like a legislature) in enacting their own rules and regulations and also act quasi-judicially (like a court) in settling disputes.

Despite these seeming sweeping powers, there are some constraints on the agencies' powers: Congress, in creating an agency, typically enacts legislation directing how the agency should operate and also exercises some oversight and supervision of the agency to ensure it properly fulfills its function and does not exceed its authority as set forth in the enabling statute that created the agency. The Administrative Procedure Act (5 U.S.C. §§ 500-584 (2000)) is the federal law under which the agencies create and enforce rules.

Each agency administers or regulates a body of law. For example, the Federal Aviation Administration (FAA) regulates aviation, the Federal Communications Commission (FCC) regulates communication, and the National Labor Relations Board (NLRB) regulates labor practices. Note that agencies have different titles, with some being referred to as "Administrations," some referred to as "Boards," and others "Agency," "Commission," "Service," or "Corporation."

While you may be under the impression that these agencies are far removed from you and exercise only a minor role in your daily life, in actuality these agencies affect you every day in numerous ways. For instance, every time you listen to a radio or watch television, the FCC is playing a role. For every item of food you eat or aspirin you take, the FDA (Food and Drug Administration) is playing a role. Perhaps the most pervasive agency and the one that affects you in a dramatic way each and every day is the IRS (Internal Revenue Service), a branch of the Department of Treasury.

The individuals who head the agency as well as members of their staffs are usually experts in the area of law that the agency regulates, such as aviation, communication, or securities. The agency heads are selected by the president, are approved by the United States Senate, and serve for a specified term of office.

Because legal practitioners tend to specialize and because administrative law research is highly technical, it is possible that you will never need to conduct administrative law research. On the other hand, you may work for one of the administrative agencies or for a company that engages in a highly regulated field, such as the environment, franchising, or securities. You may be employed by a law firm that specializes in communications law or labor law. In such instances, you will likely become highly familiar with the agencies, their rules and regulations, and the books that publish administrative law. In any event, all legal professionals should be able to conduct competent legal research in the field of administrative law to respond to client or employer needs.

You will need to become familiar with the terminology of administrative law in order to conduct research efficiently in this field of law. The term administrative law refers to the body of law created by administrative agencies in the form of rules, regulations, decisions, and other related actions. While the product of a legislature is a "law" or "statute," the product of an administrative agency is a "rule" or "regulation." These terms are synonymous. 1 C.F.R. 1.1 (2004). Rules or regulations are issued by an agency to implement and carry out the policies and tasks assigned to the agency by the enabling statute. They are subject to review by Congress and the president. Violation of a rule or regulation can subject one to punishment just as can violation of a statute. Administrative agencies are often referred to as "regulatory" bodies due to the fact that the function of each agency is to administer or regulate a body of law. Agency rules and regulations are primary law. Some government agencies, including the Internal Revenue Service, issue advisory opinions in response to questions by requesters. The advisory opinion will generally state whether it is legally binding.

2. *Publication of Federal Administrative Law*

Until 1936, there was no official publication of the rules and regulations of administrative agencies. For example, while radio stations were subject to the regulations of the Federal Communications Commission (FCC), the regulations were published sporadically, making it nearly impossible for those companies regulated by the agencies to determine if they were in compliance with the agency's regulations. Moreover, agencies would each publish their own regulations in seperate publications.

This confusing situation reached a climax with the famous case *Panama Refining Co. v. Ryan*, 293 U.S. 388 (1935), in which the defendant company was prosecuted for violation of an administrative regulation. It was not until the case reached the United States Supreme Court that it was discovered that the regulation Panama Refining Company was accused of violating had been revoked before the original prosecution was commenced.

To rectify this situation, the United States Congress enacted the Federal Register Act, which provided for the publication of the *Federal Register*. The *Federal Register* is a pamphlet published weekdays and distributed by the United States Government Printing Office. No agency rule will have legal effect unless it is first published in the *Federal Register*. Thus, the *Federal Register* provides an organized system for making agency regulations available to the public. It contains proposed, interim, and final rules. The *Federal Register* does more than merely recite the language of the agency regulations. It provides a summary of the regulation, its effective date, a person to contact for further information, and background material relating to the regulation. Additionally, as discussed earlier, the *Federal Register* includes various presidential documents. See Figure 10-4 for a sample page from the *Federal Register*.

Because each daily issue of the *Federal Register* is roughly the same size as an issue of *Time Magazine*, and it is published daily, resulting in publication of approximately 50,000 pages each year, researching the *Federal Register* is a daunting task. Therefore, just as our federal statutes published in the *United States Statutes at Large* were better organized or codified into the 50 titles of the United States Code (U.S.C.), so also has the *Federal Register* been codified to better enable researchers to access administrative regulations. In fact, the *Federal Register* has been codified in 50 titles in a set entitled *Code of Federal Regulations* (C.F.R.). These 50 titles represent the areas subject to federal regulation and roughly correspond to the 50 titles of U.S.C. For example, Title 29 of both U.S.C. and C.F.R. is "Labor," while Title 27 of the U.S.C. is "Intoxicating Liquors" and Title 27 of C.F.R. is "Alcohol, Tobacco Products and Firearms." Each of the 50 titles in C.F.R. is divided into chapters. Chapters are further subdivided into "parts" covering specific regulatory areas.

C.F.R. is a softcover set revised annually with one-fourth of the volumes in the set issued on a quarterly basis. Thus, revision of the set is staggered with one-fourth of the set updated or revised each calendar quarter. Titles 1 through 16 are issued each January 1; Titles 17 through 27 are issued each April 1; Titles 28 through 41 are issued each July 1; and Titles 42 through 50 are issued each October 1. The volumes of C.F.R. are always issued in softcover pamphlet form. Each year the pamphlets are published in a color different from the previous year's pamphlets (except Title 3, containing various presidential materials, which is always white or black) so you can readily locate the issues for the year you need. For example, the 2004 edition of C.F.R. was bright pink, while the 2003 edition was royal blue. See Figure 10-5 for a sample page from C.F.R.

Figure 10-4
Sample Page from *Federal Register*

SUMMARY: This document makes a correction to Airworthiness Directive (AD) 2004–19–04. That AD applies to Rolls-Royce plc (RR) RB211–22B, RB211–524, and RB211–535 series turbofan engines. That AD was published in the **Federal Register** on September 22, 2004 (69 FR 56683). In the amendatory language, under § 39.13 [Amended], the amendment number for the AD was inadvertently omitted. This document corrects that omission. In all other respects, the original document remains the same.

EFFECTIVE DATE: Effective September 30, 2004.

FOR FURTHER INFORMATION CONTACT: Christopher Spinney, Aerospace Engineer, Engine Certification Office, FAA, Engine and Propeller Directorate, 12 New England Executive Park, Burlington, MA 01803–5299; telephone (781) 238–7175, fax (781) 238–7199.

SUPPLEMENTARY INFORMATION: A final rule AD, FR Doc. 04–21173 that applies to RR RB211–22B, RB211–524, and RB211–535 series turbofan engines, was published in the **Federal Register** on September 22, 2004 (69 FR 56683). The following correction is needed:

§ 39.13   [Corrected]

■ On page 56684, in the second column, under § 39.13 [Amended], in the fifth line, "2004–19–04 Rolls-Royce plc: Docket No." is corrected to read "2004–19–04 Rolls-Royce plc: Amendment 39–13798. Docket No.".

Issued in Burlington, MA, on September 23, 2004.

Francis A. Favara,

Acting Manager, Engine and Propeller Directorate, Aircraft Certification Service.

[FR Doc. 04–21912 Filed 9–29–04; 8:45 am]

BILLING CODE 4910-13-P

DEPARTMENT OF HEALTH AND HUMAN SERVICES

Food and Drug Administration

21 CFR Part 862

[Docket No. 2004P–0354]

Medical Devices; Clinical Chemistry and Clinical Toxicology Devices; Classification of Sirolimus Test System Devices

AGENCY: Food and Drug Administration, HHS.

ACTION: Final rule.

SUMMARY: The Food and Drug Administration (FDA) is classifying the sirolimus test system device into class II (special controls). The special control

that will apply to the device is the guidance document entitled "Class II Special Controls Guidance Document: Sirolimus Test Systems." The device is intended to measure sirolimus levels in whole blood as an aid to managing therapy for transplant patients receiving sirolimus, an immunosuppressive drug. The agency is classifying the device into class II (special controls) in order to provide a reasonable assurance of safety and effectiveness of the device. Elsewhere in this issue of the **Federal Register**, FDA is publishing a notice of availability of a guidance document that is the special control for this device.

DATES: This rule becomes effective November 1, 2004. The classification was effective July 28, 2004.

FOR FURTHER INFORMATION CONTACT: Avis Danishefsky, Center for Devices and Radiological Health (HFZ–440), Food and Drug Administration, 2098 Gaither Rd., Rockville, MD 20850, 301–594–1243, ext. 161.

SUPPLEMENTARY INFORMATION:

I. Background

In accordance with section 513(f)(1) of the Federal Food, Drug, and Cosmetic Act (the act) (21 U.S.C. 360c(f)(1)), devices that were not in commercial distribution before May 28, 1976, the date of enactment of the Medical Device Amendments of 1976 (the amendments), generally referred to as postamendments devices, are classified automatically by statute into class III without any FDA rulemaking process. These devices remain in class III until the device is classified or reclassified into class I or II, or FDA issues an order finding the device to be substantially equivalent, in accordance with section 513(i) of the act, to a predicate device. The agency determines whether new devices are substantially equivalent to previously marketed devices by means of premarket notification procedures in section 510(k) of the act (21 U.S.C. 360(k)) and part 807 (21 CFR part 807) of FDA's regulations.

Section 513(f)(2) of the act provides that any person who submits a premarket notification under section 510(k) of the act for a device that has not previously been classified may, within 30 days after receiving an order classifying the device in class III under section 513(f)(1) of the act, request FDA to classify the device under the criteria set forth in section 513(a)(1) of the act. FDA shall, within 60 days of receiving such a request, classify the device by written order. This classification shall be the initial classification of the device. Within 30 days after the issuance of an order classifying the device, FDA must

publish a document in the **Federal Register** announcing such classification (section 513(f)(2) of the act).

In accordance with section 513(f)(1) of the act, FDA issued a document on June 15, 2004, classifying the Microgenics CEDIA Sirolimus Assay in class III because it was not substantially equivalent to a device that was introduced or delivered for introduction into interstate commerce for commercial distribution before May 28, 1976, or a device which was subsequently reclassified into class I or class II. On June 16, 2004, Microgenics Corp. submitted a petition requesting classification of the Microgenics CEDIA Sirolimus Assay under section 513(f)(2) of the act. The manufacturer recommended that the device be classified into class II.

In accordance with 513(f)(2) of the act, FDA reviewed the petition in order to classify the device under the criteria for classification set forth in 513(a)(1) of the act. Devices are to be classified into class II if general controls, by themselves, are insufficient to provide reasonable assurance of safety and effectiveness, but there is sufficient information to establish special controls to provide reasonable assurance of the safety and effectiveness of the device for its intended use. After review of the information submitted in the petition, FDA determined that the Microgenics CEDIA Sirolimus Assay can be classified in class II with the establishment of special controls. FDA believes these special controls, in addition to general controls, will provide reasonable assurance of safety and effectiveness of the device.

The device is assigned the generic name sirolimus test system and is identified as a device intended to quantitatively determine sirolimus concentrations in whole blood. Measurements are used as an aid in management of transplant patients receiving therapy with sirolimus.

FDA has identified no direct risks to health related to use of sirolimus test systems. However, FDA has identified improper patient management, which involves failure of the test to perform as indicated or error in interpretation of results, as an indirect risk to health related to use of this device. For example, a falsely low sirolimus measurement could contribute to a decision to raise the sirolimus dose above that which is necessary for therapeutic benefit. This could result in increased risk in the form of thrombocytopenia, leukopenia, anemia, or hyperlipidemia. A falsely high sirolimus measurement could contribute to a decision to decrease the dose below

Figure 10-5
Sample Page from C.F.R.

have not developed throughout the entire cheese.

[55 FR 6795, Feb. 27, 1990]

PART 135—FROZEN DESSERTS

Subpart A—General Provisions

Sec.
135.3 Definitions.

Subpart B—Requirements for Specific Standardized Frozen Desserts

135.110 Ice cream and frozen custard.
135.115 Goat's milk ice cream.
135.130 Mellorine.
135.140 Sherbet.
135.160 Water ices.

AUTHORITY: 21 U.S.C. 321, 341, 343, 348, 371, 379e.

Subpart A—General Provisions

§ 135.3 Definitions.

For the purposes of this part, a pasteurized mix is one in which every particle of the mix has been heated in properly operated equipment to one of the temperatures specified in the table in this section and held continuously at or above that temperature for the specified time (or other time/temperature relationship which has been demonstrated to be equivalent thereto in microbial destruction):

Temperature	Time
155 °F	30 min.
175 °F	25 sec.

[42 FR 19132, Apr. 12, 1977]

Subpart B—Requirements for Specific Standardized Frozen Desserts

§ 135.110 Ice cream and frozen custard.

(a) *Description.* (1) Ice cream is a food produced by freezing, while stirring, a pasteurized mix consisting of one or more of the optional dairy ingredients specified in paragraph (b) of this section, and may contain one or more of the optional caseinates specified in paragraph (c) of this section subject to the conditions hereinafter set forth, one or more of the optional hydrolyzed milk proteins as provided for in paragraph (d) of this section subject to the conditions hereinafter set forth, and other safe and suitable nonmilk-derived ingredients; and excluding other food fats, except such as are natural components of flavoring ingredients used or are added in incidental amounts to accomplish specific functions. Ice cream is sweetened with safe and suitable sweeteners and may be characterized by the addition of flavoring ingredients.

(2) Ice cream contains not less than 1.6 pounds of total solids to the gallon, and weighs not less than 4.5 pounds to the gallon. Ice cream contains not less than 10 percent milkfat, nor less than 10 percent nonfat milk solids, except that when it contains milkfat at 1 percent increments above the 10 percent minimum, it may contain the following milkfat-to-nonfat milk solids levels:

Percent milkfat	Minimum percent nonfat milk solids
10	10
11	9
12	8
13	7
14	6

Except that when one or more bulky flavors are used, the weights of milkfat and total milk solids are not less than 10 percent and 20 percent, respectively, of the remainder obtained by subtracting the weight of the bulky flavors from the weight of the finished food; but in no case is the weight of milkfat or total milk solids less than 8 percent and 16 percent, respectively, of the weight of the finished food. Except in the case of frozen custard, ice cream contains less than 1.4 percent egg yolk solids by weight of the food, exclusive of the weight of any bulky flavoring ingredients used. Frozen custard shall contain 1.4 percent egg yolk solids by weight of the finished food: *Provided, however,* That when bulky flavors are added the egg yolk solids content of frozen custard may be reduced in proportion to the amount by weight of the bulky flavors added, but in no case is the content of egg yolk solids in the finished food less than 1.12 percent. A product containing egg yolk solids in

3. Research Techniques for Administrative Law

a. C.F.R.

Because C.F.R. is revised annually, with new volumes issued quarterly, any rule or regulation promulgated a year or more ago can best be located in C.F.R.

There are several methods or indexes you can use to locate information in C.F.R. In many instances you will be directed to the pertinent reference in C.F.R. after you read a federal statute in U.S.C.A. or U.S.C.S. Carefully examine the notes that follow the wording of federal statutes in U.S.C.A. or U.S.C.S. to see if you are directed to sections of C.F.R.

(1) C.F.R. Index and Finding Aids

C.F.R. contains an index volume entitled "C.F.R. Index and Finding Aids." This one-volume index is revised annually and can be accessed by subject matter (pesticides, wildlife management) or by the name of an agency (Agricultural Marketing Service, Atomic Energy Commission). The index will direct you to one of the 50 titles of C.F.R. and then to the part within that particular title. There is also a separate index for each of the 50 titles of C.F.R. located immediately after the last part of each of the 50 titles.

The C.F.R. Index and Finding Aids volume also contains a table entitled "Parallel Table of Authorities and Rules" (Table I). If you know the citation to the enabling statute that created the agency or by which authority the agency issues its regulations, you can look up this citation in Table I. Because of the similarity in the organization between C.F.R. and our federal statutes, this research approach is easy and effective. You will then be directed to the appropriate title and part of C.F.R. A list of all 50 C.F.R. titles, chapters, and parts is also found in this index, together with an alphabetical list of agencies. See Figure 10-6 for a sample page from the C.F.R. Index.

(2) Index to the Code of Federal Regulations

The *Index to the Code of Federal Regulations* is an annual index privately published by Lexis and which is designed to provide access to C.F.R. by subject matter and by geographic location. Thus, you can look up items by subject matter (port safety, textiles, oil pollution) or by geographic location (California, Boston, Appalachia, Yellowstone National Park). You will be directed to a title and part of C.F.R.

b. The *Federal Register*

Because C.F.R. is issued annually it will not contain newly promulgated rules and regulations, which are published in the *Federal Register*. To access the *Federal Register*, use the *Federal Register Index*, which is issued

Figure 10-6
Sample Page from C.F.R. Index

Tobacco products, cigarette papers and tubes, exportation without payment of tax or with drawback of tax, 27 CFR 290

Turbine engine powered airplanes, fuel venting and exhaust emission requirements, 14 CFR 34

Ultralight vehicles, 14 CFR 103

Water resource development projects administered by Chief of Army Engineers, seaplane operations, 36 CFR 328

Aircraft pilots
See Airmen

Airlines
See Air carriers

Airmen

Air safety proceedings, practice rules, 49 CFR 821

Air taxi operators and commercial operators of small aircraft, 14 CFR 135

Airplane operator security, 14 CFR 108

Alien airmen

    Arrival manifests, lists, and supporting documents for immigration, 8 CFR 251

    Landing, 8 CFR 252

    Parole, 8 CFR 253

Aviation maintenance technician schools, 14 CFR 147

Certification

    Airmen other than flight crewmembers, 14 CFR 65

    Flight crew members other than pilots, 14 CFR 63

    Pilots and flight instructors, 14 CFR 61

Certification and operations

    Airplanes having a seating capacity of 20 or more passengers or a maximum payload capacity of 6,000 pounds or more, 14 CFR 125

    Domestic, flag, and supplemental air carriers and commercial operators of large aircraft, 14 CFR 121

    Scheduled air carriers with helicopters, 14 CFR 127

Customs declarations and exemptions, 19 CFR 148

Reference to C.F.R. title and part

Federal Aviation Administration, representatives of Administrator, 14 CFR 183

Foreign air carrier or other foreign person, lease of aircraft with crew, 14 CFR 218

General aircraft operating and flight rules, 14 CFR 91

Ground instructors, 14 CFR 143

Medical standards and certification for airmen, 14 CFR 67

Pilot schools, 14 CFR 141

Airplanes
See Aircraft

Airports

Air Force Department, aircraft arresting systems, 32 CFR 856

Air traffic control services and navigational facilities, establishment and discontinuance criteria, 14 CFR 170

Airplane operator security, 14 CFR 108

Airport aid program, 14 CFR 152

Airport noise and access restrictions, notice and approval, 14 CFR 161

Airport security, 14 CFR 107

Certification of airmen other than flight crewmembers, 14 CFR 65

Construction, alteration, activation, and deactivation of airports, notice, 14 CFR 157

Customs Service, air commerce regulations, 19 CFR 122

Defense Department, air installations compatible use zones, 32 CFR 256

Environmental criteria and standards, HUD assisted projects in runway clear zones at civil airports and clear and accident potential zones at military airports, 24 CFR 51

Expenditures of Federal funds for nonmilitary airports or air navigation facilities, 14 CFR 169

Federal aid, 14 CFR 151

Foreign quarantine, 42 CFR 71

General aircraft operating and flight rules, 14 CFR 91

Highway engineering, 23 CFR 620

Land airports serving certain air carriers, certification and operations, 14 CFR 139 monthly in cumulative form. Thus, the *Federal Register Index* for June contains all of the information for the previous five months. Entries in this Index are arranged alphabetically by agency (Agriculture Department, Air Force Department, and National Science Foundation).

At the back of each issue of each daily *Federal Register* is a section called "Reader Aids." This section lists any C.F.R. parts affected during the month that issue was published, provides reminders of the rules going into effect that day and within the next few days, identifies the next week's due dates for comments for pending rules, and provides general information for customers needing service and assistance.

Additionally, the United States government periodically offers three-hour free lectures in various locations throughout the United States describing the regulatory process, the relationship between the *Federal Register* and C.F.R., and how to use the *Federal Register*. For dates, locations, and times, check either the inside front or back covers of a few issues of the *Federal Register*.

4. *Updating C.F.R. Regulations*

Because agency rules and regulations are revised or revoked so frequently, you must always check the current status of any regulation you have found. Updating C.F.R. regulations is a two-step process.

a. *List of C.F.R. Sections Affected*

To bring any regulation up to date, consult a publication titled *List of C.F.R. Sections Affected* ("LSA"). LSA is a monthly softcover publication designed to inform researchers of amendments or changes in any regulation found in C.F.R. By looking up the C.F.R. title and section you are researching, you will be provided a short explanation such as "amended" or "revised" and you will then be directed to the appropriate page of the *Federal Register* on which the amendatory language or other change is found. See Figure 10-7 for a sample page from LSA.

b. C.F.R. Parts Affected

After you have used LSA (which will update the regulation only through the end of last month), you must further check a regulation by determining its status as of today's date. This is accomplished by reviewing the section titled "Reader Aids" at the back of the most recent issue of the *Federal Register*. Each issue of the *Federal Register* includes a section within "Reader Aids" titled "C.F.R. Parts Affected," which will inform you of any changes to any C.F.R. regulations for the period after the most recent issue of LSA. Just as with LSA, you will be directed to the particular page of the *Federal Register* that contains the revisions to a regulation. If you do not locate any entries for your C.F.R. title and part in either LSA or C.F.R. Parts Affected, this means there are no revisions to your regulation during the period covered.

Figure 10-7
Sample Page from LSA

30   LSA—LIST OF CFR SECTIONS AFFECTED

CHANGES APRIL 1, 2003 THROUGH FEBRUARY 27, 2004

TITLE 20 Chapter III—Con.

416.1231 (b)(9) amended **53509**
416.1242 (d) amended **53509**
416.1245 (b)(5) amended **53509**
416.1247 (b) amended **53509**
416.1320   Redesignated   from
  416.1321 ....**53509**
416.1321—416.1340   (Subpart   M)
  Authority citation revised **40124**
416.1321 Redesignated as 416.1320;
  new 416.1321 added **53509**
416.1328 Removed...............................**40124**
416.1335 Amended................................**53509**
416.1337 (b)(3)(ii) amended.................**53509**
416.1403 (a)(18) and (19) amended;
  (a)(20) added **74184**
416.1429 Regulation at 68 FR 5219
  confirmed......................................**69009**
416.1436 Regulation at 68 FR 5220
  confirmed......................................**69009**
416.1438 Regulation at 68 FR 5220
  confirmed......................................**69009**
416.1450 Regulation at 68 FR 5221
  confirmed......................................**69009**
416.1618   (d)(3)(i),   (ii)   and   (iv)
  amended **53509**
416.1701 Amended................................**40124**
416.1715 Removed................................**40124**
416.2040 (b) revised **40124**
416.2201—416.2227 (Subpart V) Au-
  thority citation revised............**40124**
416.2201 Revised **40124**
416.2202   Introductory   text
  amended; (f) revised...................**40124**
416.2203 Amended...............................**40125**
416.2209 (c) removed; (d) through
  (h) redesignated as new (c)
  through (g) **40125**
416.2213 Removed................................**40125**
416.2216 (c) removed............................**40125**
416.2217 Introductory text and (f)
  revised **40125**
422.104 Revised **55308**
422.107 (a) and (c) revised.................**55308**
422.401—422.445   (Subpart   E)
  Added **74184**
422.505 Revised........................**499**
433 Added..**28712**
436 Added.............................**66544, 66578**
436.440 Added **66579**
437 Added..**28729**
438 Added..**28745**
439 Added.............................**66557, 66579**
439.510 (c) amended **66580**
439.605 (a)(2) amended **66580**

Reference to revision of C.F.R. section

Chapter   IV—Employees'   Compensation Appeals Board, Department   of   Labor   (Parts
500—599)   Chapter
V—Employment   and   Training
Administration, Department of
Labor (Parts 600—699)

604 Removed **58549**

Chapter VI—Employment Standards   Administration,   Department of Labor (Parts 700—799)

718.2 Revised......................................**69935**
725.2 (c) revised..................................**69935**
725.459 (b) revised; (d) removed
  ....**69935**

Chapter IX—Office of the Assistant Secretary for Veterans' Employment and Training, Department   of   Labor   (Parts
1000—1099)

1001.150—1001.152   (Subpart   F)
  Added; interim **39002**

Proposed Rules:

220..34341
321..63041
404.........**24897, 40213, 45180, 47877, 50985,**
         55323, 61162, 62670,
  307
408 ....**55323, 62670**
416.........**24897, 40213, 45180, 55323, 61162,**
         62670
  ....307, 554
422..69978
641..22520
667..56386

TITLE 21—FOOD AND DRUGS

Chapter I—Food and Drug Ad-
ministration,   Department   of
Health   and   Human   Services
(Parts 1—1299)

1 Authority citation revised...........**58960**
  Meeting...**61340**
  Technical correction....................**63017**
  Policy statement...........................**69957**
  Policy statement **1675, 7347**

NOTE: **Boldface page numbers indicate 2003 changes.**

5. Electronic and Online Methods of Administrative Law Research

LEXIS and Westlaw both include the full text of the *Federal Register* and C.F.R. in their easy-to-use and search databases. Both of these services, however, charge a fee for their use. The Government Printing Office now offers for free both the *Federal Register* (since 1994) and C.F.R. (since 1996) on the Internet. Access http://www.gpoaccess.gov and select either *Federal Register* or *Code of Federal Regulations*. Searching the *Federal Register* can be done by subject or keyword, agency name, citation, or by browsing tables of contents. Searching C.F.R. can be done by keyword, citation, or by browsing your choice of C.F.R. titles or volumes.

Just as a C.F.R. citation located in print must be updated by using LSA and C.F.R. Parts Affected, a C.F.R. section located online must also be updated. In fact, some information is available electronically prior to publication in the monthly print issue of LSA. First, select "List of C.F.R. Sections Affected" (located at http://www.gpoaccess.gov/cfr/index.html). You can then enter your C.F.R. section in the search box. Second, access "Current List of CFR Parts Affected," which lists C.F.R. Parts affected by changes since the last monthly issue of LSA. It is updated daily. Simply scan down the list of parts affected to see if your specific C.F.R. citation has been changed, amended, revised, and so forth.

Internet Tutorial on Administrative Law Research
Review the following Web site for an excellent tutorial on performing administrative law research: http://lib.law.washington.edu/ref/admin.html.

6. Decisions

As discussed earlier, in addition to issuing rules and regulations (acting in a quasi-legislative manner), administrative agencies interpret and enforce their rules and regulations through the process of issuing decisions (acting in a quasi-judicial manner). For example, the Federal Communications Commission issues rules and regulations relating to radio broadcasts. If a radio personality such as Howard Stern allegedly violates those regulations, the FCC will hold a hearing and issue a decision relating to this matter. The hearing held by the agency is somewhat less formal than a trial conducted in a courtroom, but its basic function — to determine facts and render a decision — is the same. There is no jury, and the individual who renders the decision in the proceeding (called an "adjudication") is an administrative law judge ("A.L.J.") who is an expert in this field. Alternatively, the agency can prosecute violators in court, often by referring the matter to the Department of Justice for prosecution. Thus, the

Environmental Protection Agency can ensure compliance with its regulations by instituting a civil or criminal action. There are approximately 1,300 A.L.J.s assigned to more than 30 federal agencies.

These decisions rendered by the administrative agencies will be published so you may gain access to them and review them. There is no one set of books containing the decisions of all of the agencies; however, the United States Government Printing Office does publish sets containing decisions for each agency. Table T.1 of *The Bluebook* identifies more than 40 official administrative publications, from *Decisions and Orders of the National Labor Relations Board* to the *Federal Power Commission Reports*. While these publications are official, the sets lack a uniform approach. Indexes are often difficult to use, and the updating can be sporadic. As a result, private publishers such as CCH, BNA, and Matthew Bender have published sets that report agency decisions. Typically, these sets are in looseleaf format (see Chapter 7), and decisions are located through alphabetically arranged Tables of Cases or through the subject matter index for the set, which will direct you to a narrative discussion followed by annotations to cases. To locate the actual case, use the citation given in the annotation. These cases are often published in separate bound volumes that contain both agency decisions and court decisions. Table T.15 of *The Bluebook* identifies more than 100 of these services, from *Aviation Cases* to the *Environmental Law Reporter*. Many services are also identified in *ALWD*'s Appendix 8, available online at http://www.alwd.org.

If a decision has been rendered by an agency, you can check its current status, namely, Shepardize it, by using *Shepard's United States Administrative Citations*, which provides update information for decisions reported in more than 30 reporters published by federal administrative departments, boards, courts, and commissions. Thus, you can Shepardize an administrative decision or order and ensure it is good law and find other decisions that discuss your case. Alternatively, you can KeyCite the case through Westlaw to make sure it is still good law.

Practice Tip

Administrative Law

Use *Shepard's Code of Federal Regulations Citations* to locate state and federal cases, law review articles, and annotations that interpret or mention C.F.R. regulations, presidential proclamations, and executive orders.

---

7. *Review of Agency Decisions*

If a party is dissatisfied with the decision rendered by the A.L.J., in most instances the matter may be reviewed at a higher level within the agency and then appealed to the federal court. The enabling statutes dictate the type of review afforded to agency decisions. Because a "trial" has already occurred at the agency itself, the aggrieved party often appeals the agency decision to the United States Courts of Appeal, the intermediate level of court in our federal system, bypassing the United States District Courts, which function as trial courts in our federal system. Further appeal may be made to the United States Supreme Court, assuming certiorari is granted. See Figure 10-8 for a chart showing the appeal process for most federal agency decisions. In some cases, however (such as those heard by the Social Security Administration), after the agency itself has reviewed the decision of an A.L.J., a dissatisfied party may file a civil suit in a federal district court.

8. *Locating Federal Cases Reviewing Agency Decisions*

There are several techniques you can use to locate federal cases that have reviewed federal agency decisions. You can Shepardize the agency decision in *Shepard's United States Administrative Law Citations*. This will give you the subsequent history of the agency decision by providing you with the appropriate citations to U.S. Supreme Court cases and lower federal court cases that affect or mention your agency decision.

Because you are now interested in locating cases from lower federal courts of appeal and United States Supreme Court that have reviewed

Figure 10-8
Appeal of Agency Decisions

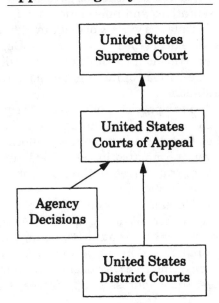

agency decisions, you can also rely on the standard sources you would use to locate federal cases on any topic: digests and annotations.

For all federal court cases, use *West's Federal Practice Digest, 4th Series* (or, if needed, any of the earlier series). To locate United States Supreme Court cases, use West's *United States Supreme Court Digest*. To locate annotations on agency matters, use A.L.R. Fed.

You can check the Web sites of the agencies themselves to see if they provide their decisions. For example, when you access the site of the National Labor Relations Board (http://www.nlrb.gov), you can immediately link to decisions (since 1984) and search by key word. Similarly, LEXIS and Westlaw offer decisions of numerous agencies (although fees are charged to access their databases).

9. The United States Government Manual

One book of particular relevance to administrative law is *The United States Government Manual*, referred to as the "Official Handbook of the Federal Government." This softcover book is prepared annually by the Office of the Federal Register and provides thorough and detailed information on the agencies (such as the Federal Communications Commission), quasi-official agencies (such as the Smithsonian Institution and the Legal Services Corporation), and international organizations in which the United States participates.

For each agency, the *Manual* provides a list of the principal officials, a summary of the agency's purpose, a brief history of the agency, including a reference to the statute that established it, and a description of the activities engaged in by the agency. The *Manual* also provides miscellaneous information about the three branches of government, such as a list of senators and representatives and information about the federal judicial system. The *Manual* displays a variety of diagrams showing the organization of various executive departments, such as the Department of Homeland Security and Department of Justice, making the division of authority and organization of the various offices and divisions within each department readily understandable.

Finally, the *Manual* provides information regarding terminated agencies. For example, when you attempt to find information relating to the Civil Aeronautics Board, you are promptly informed that most functions of the Board were terminated in 1981, 1983, and 1985, and its remaining functions were transferred to the transportation secretary, the FAA, and United States Postal Service.

Since 1995 the *Manual* has been offered for free online by the Government Printing Office at its site, GPO Access. Access http://www.gpoaccess.gov/gmanual/index.html. Searching can be done by entering keywords or search terms in the search box provided. Using the *Manual* online is an easy and free way to gain information about various government agencies, their addresses, appointees, staff members, and functions.

10. State Administrative Law

There are agencies in most states, the actions and activities of which often parallel federal agencies. For example, one of the better known federal agencies, the Occupational Safety and Health Administration ("OSHA"), is patterned after the California Division of Occupational Safety and Health ("Cal-OSHA"). While the federal OSHA agency regulates health and safety measures on a national basis, the state OSHA agency may impose additional standards for ensuring that work environments and public buildings are safe. Similarly, many state agencies issue regulations for the practice of certain occupations in the state, such as standards for beauticians, barbers, and real estate agents.

One of the best examples of a state agency is your state department of motor vehicles. While your state statute will set forth the age at which one may drive, testing and licensing procedures as well as other regulations related to the activity of driving typically are determined by the department of motor vehicles.

Some states, usually the more populous ones, publish their agency's rules and regulations in a fashion similar to the publication of administrative law at the federal level; that is, in separate sets of books devoted solely to agency regulations and titled "Administrative Codes." These generally have indexes, which are arranged similarly to other indexes and are easy to use. Simply look up the word or phrase that describes the issue you are researching, and you will be directed to the pertinent administrative code section.

You may also find that after you read a statute in the state code, you are referred to an administrative regulation in the cross-references or library references that follow the statute. In other instances, in the course of reading a case or a local encyclopedia, you may come across a reference to an administrative regulation. In any of these cases, carefully review the administrative regulations, as they typically provide detailed rules, which are subject to strict compliance.

Some state agencies issue decisions. With the exception of tax and unemployment compensation decisions, these are rarely published. Some agencies, however, publish newsletters or other publications that briefly review and summarize their decisions and other activities. These newsletters may be available for subscription or may be available at your law library or through the agency itself.

Both LEXIS and Westlaw offer state agency rules and some state agency decisions. Agency rules and decisions may also be available for free on the Internet. Start with your state's home page and look for links to administrative agencies, rules, and decisions. Your state's home page can be accessed by starting with Megalaw at http://www.megalaw.com and then selecting "State law." For example, all of California's administrative regulations can be accessed this way, or by accessing http://www.washlaw.edu and then selecting your state's name from the list provided.

For further information contact the pertinent agency. Usually, the main division or office for an agency is located in the state capital. You should begin your search for information and materials there.

D.   International Law

1.   Introduction

"International law" is broadly defined as the law relating to relations among sovereign nations. While most individuals regard international law as the exclusive province of international lawyers and as an area of law that has no relevance to their daily lives, international law does impact your everyday existence. For example, the fish you order in a restaurant or the tuna fish you may purchase in a supermarket may have been caught in another country's "economic fishing zone" and is available here pursuant to a treaty. Similarly, individuals in the legal profession who practice near Canada or Mexico often need to become familiar with various aspects of international law. The General Agreement on Tariffs and Trade ("GATT") and the North American Free Trade Agreement ("NAFTA") will have implications for those doing business in foreign countries. Moreover, with more and more companies "going global" and the Internet allowing worldwide communication and commerce, it is important for legal professionals to have a basic understanding of international law research.

One often hears that there are two branches of international law: public and private. "Public" international law is what we typically view as international law: the conduct and regulation of nations, usually called the "law of nations." "Private" international law is an older and more archaic term, used primarily in Europe to describe an area of law more properly classified as "conflict of laws." For example, assume a store in your city ordered a shipment of vases from France that arrived broken. The issue as to which jurisdiction's law would apply, that of France or that of your jurisdiction, is a matter of "private international law." Many contracts include a choice of law clause that governs what law applies and where venue will lie.

While it is true that international law is a specialized field of law and that most paralegals will not be involved in this practice area, you should become sufficiently familiar with international law sources and research procedures so that, if needed, you can adequately perform a basic research task in this field.

2.   Sources of International Law

International law is derived from four sources:

(i)   International conventions (for example, treaties), which set forth rules for conduct expressly recognized and voluntarily agreed to by signatory nations

(ii)   International custom; that is, some general practice accepted as law or believed to be obligatory

(iii)   General principles of law accepted by civilized nations

(iv) Judicial decisions and the teachings of international law experts

3. Overview of International Law Research Procedure

If you are presented with an international law research task, you should use the following procedure unless you know the exact source for the answer to your issue or problem: You should first "get your feet wet" by reading some basic or introductory information relating to your issue. This familiarization process will save you time by ensuring that you do not head off in the wrong direction due to a lack of understanding of the issues involved. After you have familiarized yourself with the issue by reviewing some basic materials and sources, you should determine whether a treaty covers this issue and provides a definitive answer to your question. If so, you will need to review the treaty and then determine if it is still "good law," that is, if it is still "in force." Finally, you will need to read analyses and cases interpreting the treaty.

To follow this research process, you need to know which sources to consult. This section of the chapter will provide you with the names of the sets of books you should consult in order to perform international law legal research.

4. Basic Texts and Sources

There are several sources to consult to obtain introductory information and background on international law. Law libraries usually collect all international law materials together. You should browse the shelves in this section for other useful materials. Some of the better known general texts and guides relating to international law are as follows:

> Claire M. Germain, *Germain's Transnational Law Research: A Guide for Attorneys* (1991)
> Green H. Hackworth, *Digest of International Law* (1940)
> John B. Moore, *A Digest of International Law* (1906)
> Marjorie M. Whiteman, *Digest of International Law* (1963)

These digests all provide excellent information relating to international law. In many ways, they resemble an encyclopedia in that they are multivolume sets that contain articulate narrative statements of the law and citations to cases that are located in footnotes.

Thus, you are not only provided with a description or summary of an issue, but you are directed to cases as well. Access is gained through the alphabetically arranged index found in the last volume of each set.

You should also consult Restatement (Third) Foreign Relations Law of the United States. This Restatement focuses on international law as it applies to the United States and is an excellent starting place for international law research. The Restatement provides general information on international law, international agreements, and international jurisdiction, judgments, and remedies. The Restatement will also provide you with citations to cases that have interpreted treaties. Additionally, a set of books titled *Foreign Relations of the United States* provides a historical overview of significant foreign policy decisions and diplomatic activities of the United States. Volumes since about 1945 are available online at the State Department Web site (http://www.state.gov).

Finally, you should consult an excellent periodical, the *American Journal of International Law*. This quarterly publication contains thoughtful and analytical articles relating to various international law topics. Use the index for the set or use the *Index to Legal Periodicals & Books* (see Chapter 6) to determine if an article has been written relating to the issue you are researching.

5.   *Treaties*

Once you have gained some background information relating to your research problem, you need to determine if a treaty governs this issue. A treaty is a formal agreement, usually written, between two or more countries. Treaties may be bilateral (between two parties) or multilateral (among several parties). The history of treaty-making goes back thousands of years. Some treaties have ended wars, others have resolved boundary disputes, and still others deal with trade or economic issues. One type of treaty is referred to as a "convention" and usually relates to a formal multilateral agreement with numerous parties, such as "The Geneva Convention Relative to the Treatment of Prisoners of War." While treaties may have been signed and agreed to by representatives of the countries involved, they are not effective until they are ratified or officially approved by each government.

In the United States, treaties are initiated by the executive branch and then negotiated by individuals selected by the president, often foreign service officers employed by the Department of State. They are entered into by the president with the "advice and consent" of the Senate. Two-thirds of the United States Senate must approve a treaty. There are, however, types of agreements called "executive agreements" that can be entered into by the president without Senate approval. There is often a great length of time between the date a treaty is signed by the representatives of the countries and the date it is formally ratified. For example, in 1954 the United States signed a treaty called, in part, "The Hague Convention for the Protection of Cultural Property in the Event of Armed Conflict." As of the date of writing of this text, the treaty had not been approved. In some cases, years pass between signing and ratification, and it is quite difficult to obtain the text of a treaty during this interim stage.

According to the Constitution, "all Treaties made, or which shall be made under the Authority of the United States shall be the supreme Law of the Land; and the Judges in every state shall be bound thereby, any Thing in the Constitution or Laws of any State to the Contrary notwithstanding." U.S. Const. art. VI. Thus, treaties are "primary" law in that they must be followed.

6.   *Sources for Treaties*

a.   Pre-Ratification

During the time between signing of a treaty and approval by the United States Senate, treaties can be located in a series entitled *Senate Executive Documents*. Because the United States Senate, namely, the Committee on Foreign Relations, will hold hearings on a treaty and issue a report much the same way hearings are held and reports are issued for legislation, you can review the report by consulting *Congressional Information Service* (CIS) *Index* (see Sections A.3 and A.5 of this chapter). Additionally, CCH's *Congressional Index* contains a table reflecting the status of treaties pending before the United States Senate. Finally, access the Web site of the Senate Committee on Foreign Relations (http://foreign/senate.gov/ legislation.html) to locate information on pending treaties and links to legislation relating to foreign relations.

b.   Post-Ratification

Since 1945, all treaties and executive agreements to which the United States is a party are published as pamphlets in a set titled *Treaties and Other International Acts Series* (T.I.A.S.). Since 1950, all of the pamphlets published in T.I.A.S. are then published in hardbound volumes called *United States Treaties and Other International Agreements* (U.S.T.). To locate treaties in either of these sets, use the index *United States Treaties and Other International Agreements Cumulative Index*. This Index is easily used. You may locate a treaty by country name (Brazil, Canada, Senegal, United States of America) or by topic (health care, extradition, trademarks, navigation).

Another collection of treaties is the *United Nations Treaty Series* ("U.N.T.S."), which publishes treaties filed, registered, or recorded with the Secretariat of the United Nations. Thus, this collection contains numerous treaties to which the United States is not a party. A cumulative index to U.N.T.S. provides access by country and by topic. U.N.T.S. expands at the rate of more than 100 volumes per year.

Until 1950, treaties and executive agreements were also published in *United States Statutes at Large*. A few well-known treaties to which the United States is a party are published in *Martindale-Hubbell Law Directory* in the last International Law Digest volume.

Many treaties are now available on the Internet. The United Nations Treaty Collection offers access to more than 40,000 treaties and international agreements and complete access to U.N.T.S. Access http://untreaty. un.org/English/treaty.asp (or http://www.un.org). Unfortunately, this is no longer a free service. To obtain access to the entire database, law firms and companies pay a moderate fee, but some treaties and information on the status of certain treaties are available for free viewing and downloading. The United Nations site also offers a glossary of terms relating to treaty actions.

Perhaps the best source for recent treaties to which the United States is a party is THOMAS (http://thomas.loc.gov/home/treaties/treaties.htm). THOMAS includes the full text of treaties since 1996 (and title and status of treaties since 1968). Searching may be done by treaty number, word or phrase, or type of treaty.

More than 20 treaties related to intellectual property are available for free through the Web site of the World Intellectual Property Organization at http://www.wipo.org, and many recent treaty documents can be located for free through GPO Access. Access the site at http://www.gpoaccess.gov. serialset/cdocuments/index.html, select a Congress (such as the 106th), select "Senate Treaty Documents," and then enter either search terms (such as "hazardous waste") or country name (such as "Canada"). You will then be provided with a summary of the treaty as well as its full text.

7. *Determining the Current Status of Treaties*

After you have read and reviewed a treaty, you should determine whether it is still in force. Sometimes the treaty itself will specify the date until which it will be in force. For example, the treaty might provide as follows: "The treaty enters into force 30 days after ratification and remains in force for a period of 10 years and continues in force thereafter unless terminated by either party by giving one year's written notice to the other." You should also check an annual publication of the State Department entitled *A Guide to the United States Treaties in Force*, which identifies all of the treaties and executive agreements still in force. *Treaties in Force* is easy to use as it is organized both by country and by topic.

Perhaps the easiest way to determine whether a treaty involving the United States is still in force is to access the Office of the Legal Adviser of the State Department at www.state.gov/s/l, which provides a link to *Treaties in Force* (with a complete table of contents, allowing easy online searching by country name or treaty topic) as well as to treaty actions and other valuable information.

Until 1989, the State Department issued a monthly publication titled *Department of State Bulletin*. The *Bulletin* provided a monthly update to *Treaties in Force* to provide current information on the status of treaties. For information after 1989, use the weekly *U.S. Department of State Dispatch*. Review the section called "Treaty Actions" to obtain the most current information on treaties. Alternatively, you may consult a private publication called *Foreign Policy Bulletin*. Because *Treaties in Force* is issued only annually, you must check either the weekly *Dispatch* or the bimonthly *Foreign Policy Bulletin* to obtain current information on the status of treaties.

Hardbound distribution of *Dispatch* ended in December 1999. All access is now done via the Internet. Access *Dispatch* through the United States State Department Web site at http://www.state.gov/www/ publications/dispatch/index.html. You can look up country names or specific treaties in each year's Index and then link to the appropriate issue of *Dispatch* online. For example, when you review the 1999 Index, you can look up "Egypt." You will then be directed to the August/September 1999 online issue of *Dispatch*, which informs you that the Egyptian Investment Incentive Agreement was signed at Washington, D.C., on July 1, 1999, and entered into force that same day.

8. *Interpreting Treaties*

To assist you in interpreting treaties, use both secondary sources and primary sources. For secondary sources that have construed treaties, review the digests and the *American Journal of International Law*, described in Section D.4 of this chapter.

To locate primary sources, for example, cases that have interpreted treaties, check the following two sources:

Shepard's Federal Statute Citations. Be sure you have obtained *Shepard's* for statutes rather than the volumes for cases. Locate the section called "United States Treaties and Other International Agreements." By inserting the volume and page of the U.S.T. citation and using the same technique for Shepardizing cases and statutes, you can locate judicial decisions and A.L.R. annotations that have mentioned, discussed, or interpreted your treaty. See Figure 10-9 for a sample page from *Shepard's Federal Statute Citations*.

U.S.C.S. U.S.C.S. contains a separate volume titled "Notes to Uncodified Laws and Treaties," which will provide you with annotations to judicial decisions interpreting treaties.

Once you have located cases construing your treaty, be sure to Shepardize or KeyCite these cases to ensure they are still good law and to help you locate additional pertinent cases.

Internet Tutorials on International Law Research

The following sites provide excellent tutorials for performing international law research: http://www.asil.org/resource/treaty1.htm and http://www.lib.berkeley.edu/doemoff/gov_trtygde.html.

Figure 10-9
Sample Page from *Shepard's Federal Statute Citations*

Vol. 1	**—34—**	A 10UST1857	**Subsec. 1**	7UST2175	5UST161
	5UST138	A 10UST997	3UST2705	12UST269	A 11UST2680
	5UST2111	A 11UST2246	A 3UST581	TIAS7445	13UST241
—1—	6UST5971	A 12UST1420	5UST197	TIAS7536	14UST114
3UST4529	8UST1604	A 15UST1952	5UST2867	TIAS9026	14UST2
3UST5248	8UST354	A TIAS7412	7UST170		TIAS9644
5UST2320	8UST4559		7UST2551	**Art. 1**	
5UST2412	9UST1450	**Annex E**	7UST3499	6UST3920	**—188—**
6UST496	9UST72	**Art. b**	8UST2213		3UST3720
8UST687	11UST2333	6UST4000	9UST1113	**—145—**	3UST4660
11UST1368	12UST1424	**Art. c**	10UST1687	2UST1315	3UST5348
12UST1175	12UST3132	6UST4000	11UST2094	2UST2569	3UST54
A 16UST1157	TIAS6130		12UST392	3UST3874	8UST202
A TIAS6047		**—88—**	13UST1900	3UST4525	E 10UST1303
A TIAS6229	**Art. 1**	3UST4185	14UST1499	3UST5042	
A TIAS6509	**Subsec. 1**	3UST4633	15UST1821	3UST5300	**—199—**
A TIAS6729	5UST142	6UST1159		9UST1345	E 4UST2212
A TIAS6899	9UST1453	6UST2188	**Annex C**		7UST929
A TIAS7140		6UST926	A 3UST2705	**—148—**	A 11UST1507
A TIAS7381	**—50—**	10UST1334	A 5UST197	2UST647	
A TIAS7695	3UST4613	11UST2017	A 5UST2866	3UST4554	**Art. 2**
A TIAS7866	5UST2506	12UST180	A 7UST170	3UST5056	4UST2213
A TIAS8145	5UST2618	TIAS9144	A 7UST2551		
A TIAS8430	6UST3798		A 7UST3499	**—151—**	**Art. 3**
	10UST1985	**Art. 1**	A 8UST2213	2UST1173	4UST2213
Art. 1	10UST336	**Subsec. 1**	A 9UST1113	3UST4559	
Subsec. 1	11UST1912	6UST1161	A 10UST1687	3UST5048	**Art. 4**
5UST2414	12UST641	12UST188	A 11UST2094	4UST2037	11UST1507
11UST1371	TIAS7434		A 12UST1279		
12UST1175		**Annex E**	A 12UST392	**—154—**	**Art. 9**
	Art. 1	5UST2033	A 13UST1900	2UST1317	A 11UST1507
Art. 5	5UST2830	**Art. b**	A 14UST1499	3UST4577	
Subsec. 1	6UST3798	6UST926	A 15UST1821	5UST167	**Art. 10**
10UST1458	**Subsec. 1**	**Art. c**	A TIAS7448		11UST1508
10UST1465	5UST2508	6UST926		**—157—**	
	5UST2619		**—126—**	2UST1906	**Art. 12**
Annex B	10UST336	**—106—**	3UST4159	6UST572	11UST1508
A 4UST2260	11UST1915	3UST4639	3UST4665		
A 6UST3961		A 5UST2866	4UST151	**—160—**	**Art. 13**
A 6UST787	**Annex G**	5UST620	5UST1294	2UST1169	11UST1508
A 8UST687	**Art. 2**	5UST831	6UST1168	3UST4613	
A 10UST1458	5UST2227	6UST6151	8UST835	4UST117	**Art. 14**
A 10UST1465	**Art. 3**	6UST6153	9UST197	5UST2223	11UST1508
A 10UST2033	5UST2227	6UST800	13UST1318	6UST587	
A 11UST2659		7UST170	13UST241		**Art. 15**
A 12UST3127	**—69—**	7UST3499	14UST1178	**—163—**	R 11UST1507
A 13UST2635	3UST4003	9UST971		2UST2149	
A 15UST247	3UST4627	11UST1796	**Art. 1**	3UST4627	**Art. 18**
	5UST1526	11UST2105	**Subsec. 1**		11UST1508
Annex E	8UST761	12UST101	5UST1296	**—166—**	
5UST1321	A 16UST1939	12UST1279	6UST1167	2UST1289	**Art. 19**
	A TIAS6235	A 16UST1174	13UST1321	3UST4246	11UST1508
—19—	A TIAS6499	A TIAS6096		3UST4639	
3UST4554	A TIAS6738	A TIAS6376	**Art. 2**	4UST110	**Art. 20**
9UST271	A TIAS6922	A TIAS6587	8UST835		11UST1508
10UST939	A TIAS7162	A TIAS6764		**—169—**	
11UST1440	A TIAS7705	A TIAS7025	**Art. 3**	2UST1298	**Art. 21**
11UST148	A TIAS8497	A TIAS7237	8UST837	3UST4648	11UST1508
	A TIAS8498	A TIAS7740		4UST1438	
Art. 1	A TIAS8842	A TIAS7975	**Art. 5**		**Art. 25**
Subsec. 1		A TIAS8280	**Subsec. 1**	**5**	11UST1508
11UST1443	**Art. 5**		8UST837	A 4UST1597	
	Subsec. 1	**Art. 1**			**Art. 28**
Annex B	8UST1733	**Subsec. 1**	**Annex B**	**7**	11UST1508
Art. b	10UST997	5UST833	8UST836	¶ 4	
9UST147		11UST2108		A 4UST1438	**—212—**
Art. c	**Annex B**		**—137—**		E 4UST2215
9UST147	A 8UST1733	**Art. 4**	3UST4619	**—184—**	7UST929
	A 8UST761	12UST1279	6UST19	2UST1292	A 11UST1507
			6UST3920	3UST4665	
				4UST1529	**Art. 2**
				4UST1540	4UST2216

464

9. *Citation Form*

The Bluebook (Rule 21.4) provides that a citation to a treaty or other international agreement should include the name of the treaty, the parties to the agreement (although if there are more than three parties, their names need not be given), the particular subdivision of the treaty relied upon (if applicable), the date it was signed, and the source(s) in which the treaty is located.

For agreements to which the United States is a party, cite to U.S.T. or T.I.A.S., in that order.

Example

Treaty on Health Care, U.S. — Can., June 29, 1991, 41 U.S.T. 621.

If there are three or more parties to the treaty (including the United States), cite to one of the following sources: U.S.T, *United States Statutes at Large*, or T.I.A.S. in that order. Rule 21.4.5 also provides some other treaty sources that may be cited.

Example

Treaty on Navigational Waterways, U.S. — Can., Apr. 14, 1986, 38 U.S.T. 1421.

ALWD citation form for treaties differs from *Bluebook* form in that the treaty title should be italicized and the date appears differently as follows: *Treaty on Navigational Waterways* (Apr. 14, 1986), 38 U.S.T. 1421. See *ALWD* Rule 21.

10. *International Tribunals*

There are a variety of methods available to nations to resolve disputes. Often one country will agree to act as an informal mediator in a dispute between two countries. For example, in the dispute over the Falkland Islands between Great Britain and Argentina, the United States attempted to avoid the outbreak of hostilities by acting as a mediator or liaison between the two nations.

The Permanent Court of Arbitration was established in 1899 at The Hague, Holland's royal city. Members of this court serve not as judges but as arbitrators, and the court offers a broad range of services, including mediation, arbitration, and fact-finding, for resolving international disputes. It is the oldest institution dedicated to international dispute resolution.

In 1920, the League of Nations established the Permanent Court of International Justice, also at The Hague. This court was renamed the International Court of Justice in 1946 when the United Nations accepted responsibility for its operations. It is often called the "World Court." This court has 15 judges elected for nine-year terms by the United Nations Security Council and the General Assembly voting independently. The World Court also provides advisory opinions upon request of the six principal organs or 15 specialized agencies of the United Nations. In addition, any United Nations member may bring a dispute before the Court. The Court renders its decision by majority vote. Its decisions are final, and there is no appeal. While the World Court has rendered a number of decisions, including those dealing with war reparations and a ruling that Iranian militants had violated international law by taking 52 American diplomats as hostages, its decisions have often been ignored by the offending nation.

There is no uniform method of enforcing these decisions of the World Court. The United Nations General Assembly may, if the Security Council fails to act on a threat to peace or act of aggression, recommend collective measures, including use of armed force, to maintain or restore peace. The United Nations itself has no permanent police force to resolve international conflicts and will send peacekeeping forces when nine members of the Security Council decide and the disputing countries agree. If any one of the five permanent members of the United Nations (including the United States) votes against the proposal, it fails. Since 1948, there have been 59 peacekeeping operations. At the time of the writing of this text, 16 were currently underway.

One of the better known examples of United Nations action occurred subsequent to the invasion of the Republic of Korea by Communist forces from North Korea. The United Nations Security Council agreed to a "police action," and 16 member nations of the United Nations countries sent armed forces to South Korea, with South Korea and the United States providing most of the supplies and troops.

11. *International Organizations*

There are thousands of international organizations. The best known is the United Nations, established in 1945 and located in New York City. The United Nations now has 191 member nations, including its original 51 member nations.

Other well-known international organizations include the Organization of American States, the oldest regional international organization in the world, composed of 35 North, Central, and South American nations, Caribbean nations, and the United States; the African Union (formerly the Organization of African Unity), an association of 53 African nations; the Council of Europe, composed of 46 members; NATO (North Atlantic Treaty Organization), an alliance of 26 countries from Europe and North America, the European Union, composed of 25 democratic European countries, and the G8, a group comprising the major industrial democracies (Britain, Canada, the European Union, Federal Republic of Germany, France, Italy, Japan, Russia, and the United States) that meets annually to discuss major economic and political issues.

Links to hundreds of international and regional organizations can be found at the following two Web sites:

- Stanford University Library (http://www.standford.edu/group/Jonsson/igourl.html)
- Hieros Gamos, an online legal research source (http://www.hg.org/unitednations.html#other)

E. Municipal Research

1. *Introduction*

Often a legal question may arise that is entirely of local concern. For example, if a client wishes to install a swimming pool in a backyard, he or she will need to know what requirements are imposed by the local jurisdiction with regard to fencing around the pool. A client who has a two-acre parcel of land may wish to maintain horses on his or her property and will need to know if this is permissible. Similarly, a client may desire to put an addition onto a house, bringing the structure within a few inches of a neighbor's boundary line. These and other similar issues are determined by referring to the requirements imposed by the local jurisdiction or municipality rather than the code of the state. To determine the answer to such questions of local concern, you need to know how to conduct municipal or local legal research.

The following is an example of a city code section. "It shall be unlawful to sell or offer for sale any food, beverage or merchandise on any sidewalk within the Central Business District without obtaining a permit pursuant to section 18-547." Richmond, Va., Code § 18-546 (2003).

2. *Terminology*

Most municipalities operate under a document called a "charter," which sets forth the powers and activities in which the municipality may engage. A charter for a city is similar to a constitution for a state or the articles of incorporation for a corporation.

Just as your state passes statutes that are the laws for your state, municipalities also engage in lawmaking. These local laws are usually called "ordinances" or "resolutions." Ordinances are passed by the local governing body. This may be a city council, a city council acting with a mayor, a county board of supervisors, a county executive who supervises a board, or some other local legislative body.

In smaller communities, proposed ordinances are published in the local newspaper, setting forth the text of the proposed ordinance and the time and date of the meeting scheduled to consider and vote on passage of the ordinance. If the measure is passed, its text will also be published in the local newspaper. In larger municipalities, information relating to proposed ordinances and the text of approved ordinances is usually published in a separate journal.

At both the federal and state level, after statutes are passed, they are organized into codes, that is, they are codified. This same process occurs for municipal legislation. The ordinances passed by the local legislature are organized or "codified" so that all of the zoning ordinances are together, all of the health and safety measures are brought together, all of the animal control ordinances are organized together, and so forth.

3. *Municipal Research Materials*

One of the most difficult tasks in performing municipal research is finding an up-to-date version of the city or county code. Often the law library in your area will maintain the codes for the surrounding municipalities. You can also check your public library, which will usually have the codes. Unfortunately, public librarians are not as familiar with updating and supplementing materials as are law librarians, and the code at the public library may be outdated.

The best place to review a code may be at the appropriate government office: city hall, city clerk's office, county counsel's office, or city attorney's office. These codes should be current and complete.

Practice Tip

Locating Municipal Codes on the Internet

Hundreds of city and county municipal codes are published for free on the Internet by various publishers and local governments. Following are some of the best sites to locate municipal codes on the Internet:

- **Municipal Code Corporation (http://www.municode.com)** provides codes for more than 1,000 local governments. Searching is easily accomplished: Select a state, select a locality, and search by key word or by reviewing an index or chapter.
- **The National Association of Counties (http://www.naco.org)** offers hundreds of county codes, arranged by subject, state, and county.
- **LexisNexis Municipal Codes Web Library (http://www.bpcnet.com)** provides links to numerous municipal codes from all over the country. Searching can be done by key word or by viewing chapter headings.
- **eCode, offered by General Code (http://www.generalcode.com/ webcode2.html)** provides numerous city and county codes that are easily searched by key word or chapter.

---

4. *Municipal Research Procedure*

Once you have found the code for your municipality, the research techniques used to locate ordinances are similar to the research techniques used to locate federal or state statutes. The most common method of locating ordinances is the descriptive word approach.

Codes are usually maintained in looseleaf binders that contain all of the municipality's ordinances organized according to topic, such as elections, business regulations, and fire protection. An index is provided at the end of the binder. You use this index to locate ordinances just as you would any other kind of index. Think of words and phrases that describe the problem you are researching, look these up in the alphabetically arranged index, and you will be directed to the appropriate ordinance. Most codes also contain the city or county charter.

5. *Interpretations of Municipal Ordinances*

Municipal codes are rarely annotated. That is, after you read the ordinance relating to the issue you are researching, you are seldom directed to cases interpreting this ordinance. Each ordinance is usually followed only by a brief historical note indicating when the ordinance was enacted. Thus, conducting research on municipal law is very difficult. In many cases, researchers contact their local planning board or city attorney to inquire if there are any cases interpreting municipal ordinances.

Perhaps the best way to locate cases interpreting ordinances is though LEXIS or Westlaw. You can Shepardize local ordinances through LEXIS. Alternatively, you can insert the name or number of your local ordinance into the search boxes offered by LEXIS and Westlaw and you will be directed to cases that have mentioned or cited the particular provision in which you are interested. These cases may provide guidance on how the ordinance has been interpreted or construed.

Moreover, West publishes volumes titled *Ordinance Law Annotations*, which direct you to cases that interpret or apply ordinances. This set is arranged by topic (loitering, taxation, towing, satellite dishes) and will provide digests or brief summaries of all cases that have interpreted ordinances relating to these topics. Thus, if you were to look for ordinances relating to satellite dishes, you would be directed to cases from a variety of states that have interpreted ordinances dealing with this topic.

Practice Tip

Conducting Municipal Research on the Internet

Researching local law on the Internet may well be just as complete and current as performing this research using conventional print volumes. Because the print volumes containing local ordinances are rarely annotated (meaning they seldom direct you to cases), reviewing the local ordinances on the Internet may offer the same information as that which can be found in a law library.

F. Rules of Procedure and Court Rules

1. Introduction

As you know, there is an explosion of litigation in this country. If litigants could file their pleadings with courts whenever they liked and in any format they liked, on any type of paper they liked, the backlog in cases would be even more severe than it presently is. To promote efficient operation, courts are usually empowered to enact certain rules relating to various procedures and administrative matters, such as the correct size of paper to be used, when papers must be filed, and the format of papers presented to the court. In addition to rules relating to such procedural matters, there are rules of evidence, rules of appellate procedure, and rules of criminal procedure.

There are several sets of rules of procedure that might be binding in a jurisdiction. For example, all federal district courts follow the Federal Rules of Civil Procedure (FRCP), which contain rules on pleadings, motions, discovery, and civil trials. In addition, the district courts may make their own rules governing practice in their courts. Thus, the United States District Court for New Hampshire follows the FRCP and also has its own rules relating to the maximum length of memoranda submitted to the court.

Similarly, nearly all states have modeled their own civil procedural rules after the FRCP, and in addition have local or court rules governing practice before the courts. For simplicity, this discussion will refer to the more significant rules (such as the FRCP) as *rules of procedure* and the more local rules, which generally govern less significant matters (for example, the format of documents) as *court rules*.

Courts usually insist on strict compliance with all of their rules and will refuse to accept pleadings submitted that are not in conformance with these rules promulgated for the orderly administration of justice.

2. Federal Rules of Procedure

The Federal Rules of Civil Procedure (FRCP) became effective in 1938 and govern the conduct of all litigation in the United States District Courts. Many states have patterned their own state rules on the FRCP. Thus, there is often a great deal of uniformity between the FRCP and rules adopted by the various states. The FRCP govern all trial-related matters from the commencement of an action, through the pleadings allowed, to motions and discovery practice, to the trial itself. Appellate practice in the federal courts of appeal is governed by the Federal Rules of Appellate Practice. Finally, the United States Supreme Court has its own set of rules, composed of more than 70 pages of materials relating to matters such as the time allowed for oral argument, the necessity of a table of contents for briefs in excess of five pages, and the required color for the covers of briefs submitted to the Court (for example, white for petitions for writs of certiorari and yellow for reply briefs).

The rules of civil procedure for federal courts are set forth both in U.S.C.A. and U.S.C.S. In U.S.C.A., the Federal Rules of Civil Procedure are located in volumes following the statutes in Title 28, and the Federal Rules of Criminal Procedure are located in volumes following the statutes in Title 18. In U.S.C.S., there are separate unnumbered volumes for the Federal Rules of Civil Procedure, the Federal Rules of Evidence, and for the Federal Rules of Criminal Procedure, which follow Title 50. After you read the pertinent rule, you will be directed to relevant cases through the use of annotations.

You can locate a pertinent rule by any of the standard research techniques used for locating statutes: the descriptive word approach, the topic approach, or the popular name approach. Once you have located the rule in which you are interested, you can examine the historical notes, library references, and then the annotations after the rule. The annotations will direct you to cases interpreting or construing the rule. Moreover, West's set titled *Federal Rules Decisions*, discussed in Chapter 4, focuses on United States District Court cases that have interpreted the Federal Rules of Civil Procedure or Federal Rules of Criminal Procedure. Articles commenting on the federal rules are also included.

All of the major federal rules (the Federal Rules of Civil Procedure, Federal Rules of Criminal Procedure, Federal Rules of Appellate Procedure, and Federal Rules of Evidence) are available on the Internet at http://www.uscourts.gov/rules/newrules4.html. Additionally, commentary and background information on the rules are provided together with the text of proposed amendments.

Don't forget to Shepardize the federal rules. Use *Shepard's Federal Statutes Citations* to locate cases, articles, and annotations that have mentioned or interpreted the federal rules.

For ready and convenient access to applicable rules, many attorneys and paralegals rely on deskbooks, one-volume paperbacks that contain a complete set of the federal rules (although they do not include annotations to direct you to cases). The deskbooks are replaced every year to ensure their currency.

Several sets of books are useful in interpreting the federal rules, such as *Federal Rules Service, 3d*, which includes the text of the federal rules and will direct you to cases interpreting the rules. Perhaps the two best-known secondary sources for interpreting and analyzing federal rules are the following treatises:

- *Moore's Federal Practice*, a 33-volume set including the full text of the federal rules together with extensive commentary and analysis; and
- *Federal Practice and Procedure* by Charles Alan Wright (often referred to as "Wright and Miller" for the co-author of some of its volumes, Arthur R. Miller), a 61-volume set of books with full coverage and analysis of all aspects of federal civil, criminal, and appellate procedure, as well as relevant forms.

Forms for use in connection with litigation in the federal courts can be found in *Federal Procedural Forms*, a multivolume set that provides step-by-step assistance in drafting forms (such as complaints, answers, motions for new trials, and so forth) for proceedings before federal courts. Checklists, "how to" guides, and other information make this an invaluable resource. An alternative source for forms is *Bender's Federal Practice Forms*, a multivolume set including a comprehensive range of litigation forms needed by those who practice in any federal court.

3. Federal Rules of Court

In addition to the significant and substantive federal procedural rules that govern practice in our nation's federal courts, the lower federal courts themselves are free to enact their own more local rules of court.

That is, each of the 94 federal district courts and the 13 circuit courts have rules specific just to that court. Often these rules are administrative and relate to matters such as the maximum length of a brief or citation form. Other rules are more substantive and might impose a duty upon counsel to meet and confer regarding disputed issues or to attend a status conference or settlement conference. No matter what the nature of the rule and no matter how insignificant it may seem to you, the court will expect and demand strict compliance with its rules.

With 94 district courts and 13 circuits, determining the specific rules for each court can be a daunting task. One excellent source you should consult is *Federal Rules Service, 3d* (mentioned above), which arranges all the rules alphabetically by state.

All of the "local" court rules of the lower federal courts are now available on the Internet at http://www.uscourts.gov/rules/newrules8.html. Simply point and click on the particular lower federal court in which you are interested and you will be immediately linked to its local rules. Finally, *Bluebook* Bluepages Table BT.2 now references some local rules and manuals that provide guidance on local citation practices.

Practice Tip

Interpreting Federal Rules

Use the Shepard's set *Federal Rules Citations* to direct you to federal and state cases, law review articles, and A.L.R. annotations that interpret or mention federal rules (whether they are the Federal Rules of Civil Procedure, Federal Rules of Criminal Procedure, Federal Rules of Appellate Procedure, or Federal Rules of Evidence). You will also be directed to cases and sources interpreting the rules of the Supreme Court and the local rules of the lower federal courts.

---

4. State Rules of Procedure and Court Rules

To promote efficiency in litigation, states have also adopted rules of procedure and rules of court.

Many states have modeled their rules of civil procedure after the Federal Rules of Civil Procedure. These rules are often published together with the state's statutes. For example, in California, the Civil Procedure statutes follow the Civil Code and precede the Commercial Code. You will be provided with historical notes, library references, and annotations, just as for other state statutes. Additionally, many states now publish their rules on their Web sites. See Table T.1 of *The Bluebook* for each state's judicial Web site.

In addition to these rules governing statewide practice, courts within the state may also issue specific or local rules governing practice before those courts. These local rules tend to be more administrative than substantive and often address such matters as the size and weight of papers accepted by the court, what time the clerk's office closes, whether pleadings are accepted by facsimile transmission or electronically, and the format of citations. Failure to follow the local rules regarding even such minor matters as the type of paper to be used may result in rejection of documents and pleadings. If your pleading is rejected for nonconformance with local rules and the time limit for filing the pleading expires before you can submit an acceptable pleading, the client's rights may be jeopardized, and your firm may be subjected to a claim of professional negligence.

To obtain a copy of the local rules, contact the clerk of the court and arrange to purchase a set of the rules. The fee for obtaining local rules is usually nominal. Changes in local rules are often announced and published in your local legal newsletter or other publication. To ensure you are using a current set of rules, call the court clerk on a periodic basis to inquire if there have been any amendments or revisions to the rules since the time you obtained your set. Alternatively, access MegaLaw at http://www.megalaw. com/rules.php, which will link you to many local court rules for each state. Review *Bluebook* Bluepages Table BT.2 for references to local rules on citation form.

G. Citation Form

1. Legislative Materials (*Bluebook*):
   Bill: H.R. 1026, 106th Cong. (1999).
   Committee Hearing: *Child Care Costs: Hearings on H.R. 1249 Before the Subcomm. on Labor*, 105th Cong. 94-96 (1998).
   Committee Report: H.R. Rep. No. 94-506, at 6 (1987), *as reprinted in* 1976 U.S.C.C.A.N. 109.

   Legislative Materials (*ALWD*):
   Bill: H.R. 1026, 106th Cong. (Jan. 14, 1999).
   Committee Hearing: H.R. Subcomm. on L Lab, *Child Care Costs: Hearings on H.R. 1249*, 105th Cong. 94-96 (July 15, 1998).
   Committee Report: H.R. Rpt. 94-506 at 6 (Feb. 12, 1987).

2. Presidential Materials (*Bluebook*):
   Proclamation No. 6361, 3 C.F.R. 906 (1999), *reprinted in* 3 U.S.C. § 469 (2000).
   Exec. Order No. 7125, 3 C.F.R. 477 (1981-1985), *reprinted in* 3 U.S.C. § 297 (2000).

President's Message to Congress Transmitting Nominations, 16
   Weekly Comp. Pres. Doc. 768 (Feb. 26, 1989).

Presidential Materials (*ALWD*):
Exec. Procl. 6361, 3 C.F.R. 906 (1999).
Exec. Or. 7125, 3 C.F.R. 477 (1981).
George Bush, *Message to Congress Transmitting Nominations*,
   16 Wkly. Comp/ Pres. Docs. 768 (Feb. 26, 1989).

3. Administrative Materials (*Bluebook*):
   Water Pollution Standards, 47 Fed. Reg. 8076 (proposed Mar. 13,
      1995) (to be codified at 38 C.F.R. pt. 47).
   25 C.F.R. § 1592 (1999)

   Administrative materials (*ALWD*):
   Water Pollution Standards, 47 Fed. Reg. 8076 (Mar. 13, 1995).
   25 C.F.R. § 1592 (1999).

4. International Materials (*Bluebook*):
   Convention on Nuclear Proliferation, U.S. — Can., art. 14, Oct.
      18, 1989, 46 U.S.T. 107, 119.

   International Materials (*ALWD*):
   Convention on Nuclear Proliferation (Oct. 18, 1989), 46 U.S.T.
      107, 119.

5. Local and Municipal Materials (*Bluebook*):
   Boise, Idaho, Code § 1409 (1996).
   Baltimore, Md., Code § 7-149 (1988).

   Local and Municipal Materials (*ALWD*):
   Boise Code (Idaho) § 1409 (1996).
   Baltimore Code (Md.) § 7-149 (1988).

6. Court Rules (*Bluebook* and *ALWD*):
   Fed. R. Civ. P. 12(b).
   Cal. Sup. Ct. R. 56.
   Sup. Ct. R. 21.

CyberSites

http://www.gpoaccess.gov/index.html	GPO Access, offering access to C.F.R., the *Federal Register*, public laws, the *United States Government Manual*, the *Weekly Compilation of Presidential Documents*, and United States Congress information
http://www.senate.gov	Web site of the United States Senate
http://www.house.gov	Web site of United States House of Representatives
http://www.whitehouse.gov	Web site of White House
http://thomas.loc.gov	THOMAS, offering text of bills, public laws, committee information, the *Congressional Record*, and other information about the United States Congress
http://www.lib.umich.edu/govdocs/legishisnew.html	Excellent information about legislative histories with links to relevant materials
http://www.llsdc.org/sourcebook/fed-leg-hist.htm	Guide to federal legislative history research
http://www.house.gov/rules/96-473.htm	Guide to following current federal legislation and regulations
http://legintent.com	Web site of Legislative Intent Service, which provides federal and state legislative histories for a fee
http://www.statenet.com	Web site of State Net, a commercial service that provides monitoring and information about federal and state legislation
http://www.wdsdocs.com	Web site of Washington Document Service, which retrieves documents for a fee
http://www.bna.com/bnaplus/docs/doclists.html	Web site of BNA Plus, which retrieves documents for a fee
http://www.washlaw.edu/doclaw/executive5m.html	Washburn School of Law provides direct links to most executive and independent agencies
http://www.gpoaccess.gov/ecfr	GPO Access offers a demonstration project for locating updated C.F.R. provisions. Select a title of the C.F.R. and press "Go."
http://www.un.org	Web site of United Nations, offering text of some treaties, glossary of treaty terms, and links to other information and sites related to international law
http://www.lib.uchicago.edu/~llou/forintlaw.html	Primer on conducting international law research on the Internet with links to treaties and Web sites of major international organizations

(continued)

CyberSites *(continued)* ▬▬▬▬▬▬▬▬▬▬▬▬▬▬▬▬

http://www.gpoaccess.gov/ serialset/cdocuments/ index.html	Select "Senate Treaty Documents" to obtain text of treaties
http://www.state.gov/s/l/	The Office of the Legal Adviser of the State Department provides links to treaty actions and the current edition of Treaties in Force.
http://thomas.loc.gov/home/ treaties/treaties.htm	THOMAS provides treaty status information beginning with the 94th Congress. Search by treaty number, type of treaty, or key word.
http://www.municode.com	Site of Municipal Code Corporation, providing text of many municipal codes
http://www.uscourts.gov/ allinks.html#all	Site offering direct links to federal circuit and district courts

Table T.1 of *The Bluebook* provides each state's judicial Web site and Bluepages Table BT.2 provides references to local citation guides.

Writing Strategies

When writing about the "special" research projects discussed in this chapter, use the following techniques:

Legislative History: To lend credibility to your legislative history results, always use full titles. Refer to *Senator* Joseph Biden, not Joe Biden. Refer to "the United States Senate Committee on Labor" rather than "the Committee."

Administrative Law: In discussing agency decisions, omit personal pronouns. Do not discuss an agency decision by saying, "he decided . . . ." Instead, state that "the National Labor Relations Board decided . . . ."

International Law: Because treaties are usually cited by their names and those names are often lengthy, unclutter your writing by giving the full name of the treaty only once and then giving it a short descriptive title by saying "hereinafter 'Nuclear Waste Treaty.' "

Municipal Law: Do not use personal pronouns in discussing the entity that enacted municipal legislation. Do not say "*our* ordinance provides . . . ." but rather say "County of Fairfax ordinance 12,345 provides . . . ." or "the relevant City ordinance states . . . ."

Assignment for Chapter 10

LEGISLATIVE HISTORY

1. Use the CIS Annual Index for 2000.
   a. What public law relates to Internet false identification and prevention?
   b. Locate the CIS "Legislative History" volume for this public law.
      (i) When was it approved?
      (ii) What was its designation in the Senate?
      (iii) What days did debate occur in the House and in the Senate?
2. Use the CIS Index for 2003.
   a. For what piece of legislation did Maria C. Lehman testify?
   b. Review the CIS Abstracts for 2003. What day did Ms. Lehman testify?
   c. Who is Ms. Lehman?
3. Use *United States Code Congressional and Administrative News*.
   a. To what topic does Public Law 108-110 relate?
   b. Use Table 9 for the 108th Congress, 1st Session. Locate information relating to the Authorization of Substitute Checks (Check Clearing for the 21st Century) Act.
      (i) Give the House Bill number.
      (ii) Give the date the bill was reported from the House.
      (iii) Give the date the bill was passed by the House.
      (iv) Give the date the bill was passed by the Senate.
      (v) Give the date the bill was approved.
      (vi) Give the Public Law Number for this legislation.
4. Review the legislative history in *United States Code Congressional and Administrative News* for the above-identified Public Law.
   a. According to House Conference Report 108-291, page 19, what is the general purpose of this bill?
   b. What volume of the *Congressional Record* includes debates relating to this legislation?
5. Review the *Congressional Record* for January 25, 2005.
   a. Who led the pledge of allegiance in the House?
   b. Which chaplain offered the prayer in the Senate?
   c. What anniversary was remembered in the Senate that day?

ADMINISTRATIVE LAW AND PRESIDENTIAL DOCUMENTS

6. Use the most recent C.F.R. Index and Finding Aids volume.
   a. What C.F.R. title and part deal with school breakfast programs?
   b. What C.F.R. title and part deal with meat inspection, specifically, disposal of diseased carcasses?
      (i) Review this provision and its subparts. What happens if a carcass is affected by brucellosis?
      (ii) Must anemic carcasses be condemned?
7. Use the CCH *Blue Sky Reporter*.

    a. Use the Index. What section deals with the filing of proxy statements in annual reports?

    b. Review this section. When must copies of annual reports be furnished to the SEC?

    c. Use the Table of Cases. What section discusses *Lasker v. Burks*?

    d. Review the section discussing *Lasker v. Burks*. What proposition does the case stand for?

8. Use *Weekly Compilation of Presidential Documents*.

    a. Whose death was acknowledged on July 5, 2002?

    b. Review the "Exchange with Reporters" that occurred in Kennebunkport, Maine on July 6, 2002. Whose birthday was it that day?

INTERNATIONAL LAW

9. Use the Cumulative Index, Volume 29/30 for volumes 1601-1700 for the United Nations Treaty Series. Find the treaty that deals with friendship and delimitation of the maritime boundary between the United States and the Cook Islands. When and where was the agreement signed?

10. Use the Index for volumes 1301-1350 of the United Nations Treaty Series and find the agreement between Brazil and Argentina relating to animal health in the frontier area.

    a. Give the citations to the agreement.

    b. When did the agreement enter into force?

    c. When and where was the agreement signed?

    d. Who signed the agreement for each party?

    e. How long will the treaty remain in force?

11. Use Hackworth's *Digest of International Law*.

    a. What volume and page discuss hauling down or capture of a flag?

    b. Review this section.

        (i) Must a ship be fired upon or boarded to be captured?

        (ii) When is a vessel taken as a prize?

12. Use Whiteman's *Digest of International Law*.

    a. What volume and page provide the definition of "shipwreck"?

    b. Give the definition for "shipwreck."

13. Use U.S. Treaties and Other International Agreements. What is the general subject matter of 35 U.S.T. 1917 (T.I.A.S. 10769)?

14. Use *Resolutions and Decisions Adopted by the General Assembly* for the first part of the 52nd Session of the United Nations in 1997.

    a. What is the general subject matter of the Resolution?

    b. Was the Resolution adopted with or without a vote?

State Your Answer

1. Access http://www.findlaw.com and review California Code of Civil Procedure § 1859. What does it provide regarding how statutes are to be interpreted?

2. Access the GPO Access Web site and locate the *Weekly Compilation of Presidential Documents* for August 23, 2004 (volume 40, number 34). Whose death was recognized by President Bush in a statement? Where did the individual work during World War II?

3. Review the Web site of the Internal Revenue Service. Who is the current Commissioner of the IRS and where did he receive his bachelor's degree?

4. Review title 314 of the State of Washington Administrative Code at http://www.leg.wa.gov/wac. What is the definition of "liquor"?

5. Review the Web site for the United Nations.
   a. When was the Czech Republic admitted as a member state or nation?
   b. How are peacekeepers compensated?

6. Access the site for the Municipal Code Corporation (http://www.municiode.com). What does Chapter 606 (specifically section 606-3) of the Cincinnati Code of Ordinances require?

7. Access the site http:///www.uscourts.gov and locate the rules for the First Circuit. What does Local Rule 32(a) require?

The Digital Library: LEXIS, Westlaw, and Non-Print Research Sources

Technology is so much fun but we can drown in our technology. The fog of information can drive out knowledge.

Daniel J. Boorstin, Librarian of Congress, 1983

A. **Microforms**
B. **Sound Recordings and Videocassettes**
C. **Floppy Disks and CD-ROM**
D. **Computer-Assisted Legal Research**
E. **Other Competitors in Commercial Electronic Research**
F. **Dead-Tree Publishing**
G. **Citation Form**

Chapter Overview

Legal research can be accomplished by means other than using the conventional sources of bound books and journals. There are several methods that enable you to conduct research efficiently and accurately by using new technology. This chapter will introduce you to the digital library: microforms, sound recordings and videocassettes, floppy disks, CD-ROM, and computer-assisted legal research. Legal research using the Internet is discussed in Chapter 12, which is devoted solely to Internet legal research. Being a competent researcher requires use and familiarity with all media, including traditional print sources, CD-ROM, computer systems, and the Internet, to find the best answer to a legal question in the most efficient manner and at the lowest cost to the client.

A. Microforms

Microforms (sometimes called microtext) are based on the principle of microphotography: Images are reduced and placed on rolls or sheets of film. A microfilm reader is then used to review the images recorded on the film. The readers resemble a television screen and are usually equipped with printers so you may obtain a photocopy of the material you have viewed.

There are three principal types of microforms: microfilm, microfiche, and ultrafiche.

1. Microfilm

Microfilm is a reel of film that you thread or insert into a reader. The reader enlarges the images on the film and displays them on the screen before you. The film is usually either 16 or 35 millimeters. Because copying the information displayed on the screen is painstaking, most microfilm reader machines are equipped with printers, which enable you to obtain a photocopy of the image or material displayed.

Older versions of microfilm required you to actually thread the film into the reader. Because it was often difficult to thread the film, users would cut or clip a section of the film so they would have a clean, crisp edge to thread. This continual clipping led to the loss of valuable information recorded on the cut film, so the makers of microfilm, for the most part, have converted to cartridges or cassettes, which you simply insert into the reader and which thread themselves, much the same way a cassette tape is played in the tape deck of your car.

Most readers have written instructions for their use attached to them enabling convenient use of the microfilm. Once you have inserted the cassette of film into the reader you may fast-forward or rewind the film to the image you desire. The image displayed on the screen can be fuzzy or grainy, depending on the quality and age of the microfilm and the reader. Some users complain that the fast-forwarding and "jumpiness" of the image can lead to headaches if frequent breaks are not taken.

While microfilm certainly saves storage space, it has not been used to any great extent in the legal world. It is, however, widely used for government records and documents, bank records, and other commercial records and nonlegal publications.

Many counties maintain their records of land transactions on microfilm. If you needed to determine the owner of a parcel of property on a certain date, you would likely examine the chain of title by reviewing the county records on microfilm. Similarly, marriage, birth, and death records are often maintained on microfilm. This not only saves storage space but allows easy access without destroying the original documents.

Public libraries typically preserve older books, journals, magazines, and newspapers on microfilm. If you do estate work you may need to prove the value of stock as of a certain date. To accomplish this, simply go to a public library and ask for the newspaper for the date in question. In most cases, you will be given a microfilm cassette containing the newspaper for a certain time period. After you locate the information you need, obtain a certified copy of it and you may then attach this as an exhibit to whatever document you are submitting to the court. If the reader is not equipped with a printer, ask the librarian or other curator to obtain a copy of the pertinent page. Much of this information and these records are now also available on the Internet (see Chapter 12).

Some courts also preserve their older files on microfilm, and if you need to review a criminal, civil, probate, or family law file you may be directed to a microfilm section. Seldom, however, are conventional legal research sources such as U.S.C.S., Am. Jur. 2d, or A.L.R. maintained on microfilm.

2. *Microfiche*

The word "fiche" means a card or strip of paper or film used in cataloging or archiving documents. Microfiche is a microform displayed on a thin transparent celluloid flat sheet rather than on a roll of film. The sheet is usually four inches by six inches and greatly resembles the negatives you receive when you have film developed. Its color is usually either an orange-brown or a bluish-gray-green. The images on the sheet of microfiche are arranged in a block or grid type of pattern. Each sheet of microfiche may contain images of up to 400 pages.

Like microfiche, microfiche is not as widely used for legal sources as it is for nonlegal materials. Some libraries have replaced their conventional card catalog, consisting of drawers with small index cards, with microfiche. Each sheet of microfiche will cover certain sections of the alphabet. To determine if the library has a copy of a certain book or publication, insert the sheet of fiche into a reader, which will display the enlarged image on the screen.

It can take a bit of time to get used to using the reader for microfiche because when you move the card to the right, the image on the screen shifts to the left, and vice versa. Many users are not particularly careful when using the microfiche cards or sheets and often neglect to replace them in their specific slots, making searching difficult and time-consuming.

One well-known use of microfiche is the publication through Lexis's Congressional Information Service (CIS) of *Congressional Bills, Resolutions & Laws on Microfiche*. This set is used for compiling a legislative history and provides copies of bills and their amendments in microfiche. You will recall from Chapter 10 that the CIS system includes all of the documents you need to compile a legislative history (bills, committee reports, transcripts of committee hearings, and debates) in microfiche. Moreover, the *Federal Register* and the *Code of Federal Regulations* are also on microfiche.

3. *Ultrafiche*

Ultrafiche, or ultramicrofiche, as it is sometimes called, is a sheet of film that is the same size as a sheet of microfiche ($4'' \times 6''$) but that holds a great many more images. As many as 1,800 pages of text can be held on a single sheet of ultrafiche. West has reproduced its National Reporter System in ultrafiche, with each sheet replacing one hardbound volume of the *Atlantic Reporter, Pacific Reporter*, and others.

Viewing ultrafiche is identical to viewing microfiche. Simply insert the sheet of ultrafiche into the reader, which will display the image or case on the screen. Most readers are equipped with printers, enabling you to obtain a copy of the case if needed.

4. *Summary of Microforms*

All of the varieties of microform (microfilm, microfiche, and ultrafiche) perform the valuable function of saving storage space. While their use for nonlegal purposes has been broad, their role in legal research has been a bit slower to take hold. Most researchers believe it is easier to simply grab a volume of the *Federal Supplement* from the shelf (or use one of the legal research computers to locate a case) than to retrieve the correct sheet of fiche and insert it into a reader. A notable exception is the use of microfiche for the materials comprising a legislative history.

Even though certain materials and sources may be available in microform, your particular law library may not have purchased the microforms. That is, the fact that microforms are published does not mean that they will be available at your law library. Ask your law librarian what materials are available in microform at your law library.

To determine what materials are published in microform, consult *Guide to Microforms in Print*, which is a cumulative list of more than 200,000 journals, books, government publications, newspapers, and other materials currently available from micropublishing organizations. Micro-publications are listed in the *Guide to Microforms in Print* alphabetically by title and by author. Each listing will identify the publication, the publisher, the price, and the particular type of microform.

Many libraries maintain their microforms in a separate section of the law library. This is usually an attempt by the library to control access as well as to preserve the microforms by regulating temperature, humidity, and other conditions that may affect them.

You may wonder whether microforms will continue to be available in the Internet era. In fact, a great number of records and documents continue to be placed on microforms because they provide inexpensive, reliable, and long-term storage. The equipment needed to view and print microform images is simple, and microfilm has a life expectancy of hundreds of years. In contrast, digital images consist of numerous machine codes that require complex computer hardware and software to be visible. Moreover, digital images must be periodically reformatted. Therefore, microforms will likely continue to be popular. In fact, the National Archives and Records Administration continues to place a great number of government records and documents on microfilm.

B. Sound Recordings and Videocassettes

Many continuing legal education programs are offered for those in the legal profession. The programs or seminars are usually held in hotel conference or meeting rooms. Some law firms prefer to purchase a sound recording, videocassette, or CD-ROM of the program, which will then be available for use by all of the professionals in the firm, rather than send just one person to a seminar. Your firm or office may maintain a library of these sound recording cassettes, videocassettes, or CD-ROMs, which you can take home and review at your leisure.

Some law libraries also maintain a library of tapes, both audio and video, which you can check out and review. These tapes cover a variety of subjects from estate planning to recent changes in the tax laws to how to handle a real estate condemnation action. You may also notice advertisements for audio and videotapes for sale in legal journals, newspapers, and other publications.

Most of the sound recordings and videotape presentations are elementary and introductory in their approach. All, of course, are secondary sources in that they explain, describe, or summarize the law rather than provide a verbatim recitation of a statute, case, or constitution.

There are a few other uses of videotape. Some law firms videotape mock questioning of clients before a trial. This helps sharpen the attorney's skill as an advocate as well as perhaps point out certain characteristics of the client that may affect his or her credibility as a witness, such as fidgeting or refusing to answer directly.

Other firms use videotape presentations to introduce the client to certain routine matters, such as providing the client with basic information about having a deposition taken, the trial process, or the basics of will-drafting. This saves time for the attorneys and paralegals because they do not have to repeat the same information over and over for clients and thus saves the clients' money.

Videotapes are often used at trials as well to show the jury an accident scene, for example, or the layout of a building or for criminal prosecutions when the crime itself (bank robbery, shoplifting) has been videotaped.

C. Floppy Disks and CD-ROM

1. Floppy Disks

In addition to their use in a law office for word processing purposes, floppy disks are also used for legal research. Some publishers now offer books on various areas of practice and research on floppy disks. Often the sets available on floppy disks are very practical in their approach and provide forms as well. Thus, you can load the disks into your computer, read about a certain area of the law such as wills, and then begin drafting the will with the aid of the forms provided.

The use of disks is decreasing due to the ease of use of CD-ROMs.

2. CD-ROM

One of the significant technologies available to researchers is CD-ROM (compact disc, read-only memory). These CDs look substantially like any other CD and can contain more than 200,000 pages of text. They offer distinct advantages, however, in that they provide full coverage for a variety of legal topics and yet take up little valuable office or library space.

Martindale-Hubbell Law Directory (see Chapter 7) is now available on CD-ROM. More than one million lawyers and law firms worldwide can be located using two discs. Locating the information you need can be incredibly easy. You can locate attorneys by name, firm name, state, city, county, law school, languages, field of law, and several other criteria. For example, if you need to locate an attorney in Raleigh, North Carolina, who speaks Arabic and is engaged in banking law, you type in these criteria and you will be presented with a list of attorneys who fit the criteria you selected. It is also possible to obtain a print of the information shown on the screen. The CD-ROM version of *Martindale-Hubbell* is more expensive than the print version (about $1,000 compared to about $500).

Several major publishers, including West and Lexis, make cases, statutes, and practice guides available on CD-ROM. Some sets offer only civil cases, while others offer civil and criminal cases. These compact discs save space and provide easy access to cases. One disc can take the place of several bound volumes, making it easy to Shepardize cases and statutes. Various journals and publications, such as the most widely read legal periodical in the United States, *The Business Lawyer*, are also available on CD-ROM. All issues of the *Harvard Law Review* are now avaliable on one searchable CD-ROM. One of the best-known treatises, *Collier on Bankruptcy*, is available on CD-ROM from Lexis. Various bankruptcy forms are included as well.

As discussed in Chapter 6, LegalTrac is a CD-ROM version of the *Legal Resource Index*, which provides you with access to legal periodicals.

Check with your law librarian to determine what sources are available on CD-ROM. CD-ROM not only offers the advantage of saving space by making thousands of pages available on one wafer-thin disc but also saves money, as there are no online charges. Once the CDs are purchased they can be used with no further costs, although replacement discs will need to be purchased for updating.

The CD can be used with a portable laptop computer and small printer, enabling legal professionals to perform valuable research at home or while commuting or traveling. Their use at trial can be extremely valuable. If adverse counsel cites an unfamiliar case or statute, you can use a computer disc and laptop computer to find and read the case and immediately point out exceptions or limitations. Because compact discs containing cases or statutes need to be updated, most publishers will issue you new discs (for a fee) and take back your old ones at monthly or quarterly intervals. In general, the cost for CD-ROM products is about the same as for their print counterparts.

West offers a wide variety of legal materials in a CD-ROM format. Searching can be done by plain language. Hypertext links allow you to jump within a product. Among the publications offered on CD-ROM by various publishers are the following:

Am. Jur. 2d, the legal encyclopedia covering all American law.

Am. Jur. Pleading and Practice Forms, including forms related to federal and state trial practice.

Am. Jur. Trials, a step-by-step guide through all stages of civil and criminal trials.

A.L.R.3d, 4th, and 5th, including leading cases from state appellate courts and annotations on issues raised by those cases.

A.L.R. Federal, providing case law analysis on federal questions of law.

United States Supreme Court Reports, Lawyers' Edition, reporting United States Supreme Court cases in full.

U.S.C.A., providing full coverage of all federal statutes and annotations to cases interpreting those statutes.

C.F.R., containing the entire *Code of Federal Regulations* on disk.

Federal Register, providing full coverage of administrative agencies, proposed regulations, agency notices, and executive orders.

Some products offered by West in CD-ROM include the Restatements, the American Digest System, *Federal Reporter, Federal Supplement*, and various practice sets and treatises such as *Couch on Insurance 3d* and *McCarthy on Trademarks and Unfair Competition*.

D. Computer-Assisted Legal Research

1. *Introduction*

There are two major competing computer-assisted research services: LEXIS, now provided by Reed Elsevier, Inc. (and formerly owned by Mead Data Central, Inc., of Dayton, Ohio) and Westlaw, provided by West Group of Eagan, Minnesota. Other systems, such as FLITE (Federal Legal Information Through Electronics) and JURIS (Justice Retrieval and Inquiry System), are designed for use primarily by federal government employees. Although there are other systems available (which will be discussed later in this chapter), LEXIS and Westlaw remain the best known and most often used computerized legal research systems. LEXIS and Westlaw operate in essentially the same manner. Most users, however, develop a preference for one or the other.

These research systems provide access to a tremendous variety of cases, statutes, administrative regulations, and numerous other authorities, which a law firm, agency, or other employer may not otherwise be able to afford or otherwise be able to set aside shelf space for. Moreover, you can often locate the information you need very rapidly. The more familiar you become with LEXIS or Westlaw, the more efficient you will be at locating the information you need.

Both systems consist of a personal computer, a keyboard used to type in words for searching and locating the information you need, a video display screen, which will display information for you to review, and a printer, which will print the case, statute, or other information you desire.

Each service consists of thousands of databases. The databases include the cases, constitutions, statutes, administrative regulations, and other materials for you to access. LEXIS and Westlaw continually add information and authorities to their databases to bring you as much information as possible.

In general, research using LEXIS and Westlaw is similar. Both allow easy retrieval of cases, statutes, and other materials when you already have a citation. You merely type the citation into an open field and press "Go" or a similar button. When you do not have a citation, you will usually access the appropriate database (such as federal cases or state cases) and then formulate a search question by using Boolean terms and connectors or by using natural language. Neither system is case-sensitive, thus allowing you to use either lowercase or capital letters.

To determine the information contained in a database, you can consult printed lists published by Reed Elsevier and West, which contain all of the sources contained in the databases, for example, Iowa Court of Appeals cases from 1977, the *Environmental Law Reporter*, and federal bankruptcy and tax materials. Your law librarian will usually have a copy of these printed database lists. Alternatively, you can consult the online directory for each system. As soon as you sign on to either service, you can select a directory listing all of the sources and authorities available. Fees and charges are usually assessed as soon as you sign on, so you may want to become as familiar as possible with the printed list of the database rather than relying on the online directories.

The services are both accessible through the Internet. Typically, fees are assessed for each minute online, thus requiring you to research as efficiently as possible. Many law firms and companies, however, pay fixed fees, allowing unlimited access for one fee.

While these computerized research services can provide rapid access to numerous useful authorities, they cannot replace you. It is always your analysis and interpretation of the legal authorities the services provide that is valuable to the client. The computer cannot analyze, evaluate, or consider alternate strategies to achieve a client's goals — only you and your fellow legal professionals can do this.

While it is important to have a basic understanding of the two computerized legal research systems, the best way to learn how to perform computerized legal research is to do it. There is no substitute for "hands on" experience. Both LEXIS and West offer training courses and written materials describing their systems. Online tours and tutorials are also available. Contact:

LexisNexis
P.O. Box 983
Dayton, Ohio 45401
24-hour toll-free customer
  service:
1 (800) 543-6862
http://www.lexisnexis.com/
  custserv/training

West Group
610 Opperman Drive
Eagan, MN 55123
Toll-free customer service:
1 (800) Westlaw
http://www.west.thomson.com/
  westlaw/training

It is entirely possible that your employer may not subscribe to LEXIS or Westlaw. Conventional legal research methods are *always* acceptable to obtain answers to research questions. Computerized legal research is simply an alternative tool you can use to find the information you need — it is not the only tool.

The continual updates to the LEXIS and Westlaw databases, the modifications of search strategies, the frequent addition of new features and screens to these computer-assisted legal research ("CALR") systems, make it nearly impossible to provide current information relating to LEXIS or Westlaw. Legal researchers should therefore review publications and materials issued by LEXIS, and West as well as advertisements and articles in legal publications to keep informed of new developments in the field of CALR.

2. *LEXIS*

a. Introduction and Organization

LEXIS, introduced in 1973 by Mead Data Central, Inc., was the first computerized legal research service. Its database contains more than 3.2 billion searchable documents. LEXIS is part of LexisNexis Group, with LEXIS focusing on legal materials and NEXIS focusing on business and news services.

LEXIS's database consists of a series of "sources" (sometimes called "libraries") — materials relating to particular areas of the law, such as the source titled "FEDSEC," which contains cases, statutes, and rulings on federal securities legislation, or the source titled "HEALTH," which contains materials on health issues, or the source titled "GENFED," which contains materials related to general federal matters.

Within each source are "files." For example, the GENFED source contains separate "files" for cases from the United States Supreme Court, cases from the U.S. Courts of Appeals, the *Federal Register*, C.F.R., and files for other federal materials.

Getting started usually requires you to sign on to either LEXIS or Westlaw and to type in the identification and password assigned to you by your school or employer. When performing research on the job, you will usually enter a client name or number so that the client can be billed for the time spent conducting the research. LEXIS is usually provided by law firms to their legal professionals through a software package allowing desktop computer access.

After you access LEXIS (which can also be accessed through the Web, at http://www.lexis.com), the first screen provides the following research options at the top of your screen:

- Search. Clicking on the "Search" tab allows you to explore sources such as federal authorities, state authorities, secondary authorities, public records, and news.
- Search Advisor. Selecting the "Search Advisor" tab allows you to learn about an area of law and locate cases by legal topic.
- Get a Document. Use the "Get a Document" tab when you know the citation to a case, statute, regulation, or law review.
- Check a Citation. Use "Check a Citation" to Shepardize your primary authorities. (See Figure 11-1.)

b. Constructing a Search

There are two ways to seach for materials on LEXIS if you do not have a citation: the traditional search using Boolean connectors or the newer plain English search method called "Freestyle," or "Natural Language."

Figure 11-1
Sample LEXIS Screen

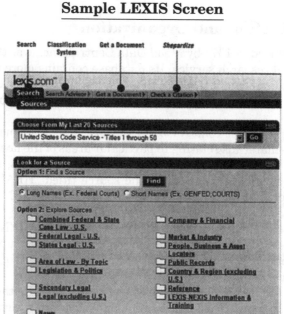

Boolean Searching

"Boolean searching" is the term used to describe searches on computers using symbols, word fragments, and numbers rather than plain English.

You will find that the computer is extremely literal. You may believe that the words "tenant" and "lessee" mean essentially the same thing, but to the computer, these are two entirely separate concepts. If you instruct the computer to search for "tenant," it will do so and will not provide you with information relating to a lessee. Thus, you need to know some basic rules of how LEXIS operates so you can search efficiently. First, LEXIS is not sensitive to capital letters unless you specify in your search request that capital letters be read as such. For basic searching, use all lowercase letters.

(1) Plurals

If a word forms its plural by adding "es" or "s" or by changing "y" to "ies," LEXIS will automatically find both forms for you. Thus, if you are searching "tenant" or "baby," LEXIS will automatically search for "tenants" and "babies" as well. LEXIS will not, however, automatically find the plural of irregular plural forms such as "knives" for "knife."

(2) Possessives

LEXIS will also automatically search for singular and plural possessives of a word. If you enter "defendant," LEXIS will search for defendant, defendant's, and defendants'.

(3) Universal Symbols

Because a search for cases containing the word "explode" would not include "exploding" or "explosion," LEXIS offers two universal characters (usually referred to as "wildcards" or "root expanders") to help you expand your search:

- An *asterisk* (*) substitutes for any character. An asterisk can be used at the middle or end of a word. Thus, "m*n" will search for "men," "man," or a word containing any other letter that might appear where the asterisk is placed.
- An *exclamation point* (!) substitutes for any number of additional letters at the end of a word. Thus, "expl!" will locate "explode," "exploded," "exploding," or "explosion." Remember, however, that it will also locate "explore," "explored," and "exploring," "explain," and any other word beginning with "expl." The "!" may only be used at the end of a word segment, not at the beginning or the middle.

(4) Connectors

Because many concepts are expressed in different ways, LEXIS uses words and symbols called "connectors" to help you locate needed documents. The most common connectors are "or," "/n," "and," and "and not."

- The connector *or* joins words that are synonyms so that a search will locate both words. For example, a search for "tenant or lessee" will locate documents containing either or both of these words. Likewise, a search for "shareholder or stockholder" will locate documents containing either or both of these words.
- The connector */n* (where "n" means any number between 1 and 255) instructs the computer to find documents that contain words appearing within a specified number of words of each other. For example, the search instruction "tenant or lessee /50 evict!" instructs LEXIS to locate documents in which the words tenant or lessee appear within 50 words of the word "evict," "eviction," or "evicting." You may select intervening words from 1 to 255. When counting words, LEXIS ignores what it refers to as "noise words," that is, common words such as "the," "and," "of," "is," "are," and "to."
- The connector *and* instructs LEXIS to locate documents containing certain words no matter how far apart those words are. Thus, the search instruction "tenant and default" instructs LEXIS to locate documents in which the words tenant and default occur anywhere in the same document.
- The connector *and not* instructs LEXIS to exclude certain documents. For example, a search for "negligen! and malpractice and not medical" instructs LEXIS to retrieve documents in which the terms "negligence" (or "negligent") or "malpractice" occur, and excludes documents if they also contain the word "medical."
- The connector */s* finds words in the same sentence. Thus, a search for "alter /s ego" would locate documents in which the words "alter" and "ego" appear in the same sentence.
- The connector */p* locates words in the same paragraph. Thus, a search for "copyright /p infringement" would locate documents in which "copyright" and "infringement" appear in the same paragraph.

While there are other connectors, the four described herein are the most commonly used. For an explanation of the other connectors, consult any of the published descriptions of LEXIS. Multiple connectors may be used in one search request.

Connectors help you limit your search and make it more manageable. If you simply entered "first amendment," LEXIS would locate thousands of documents containing this phrase. A more effective search would be "first amendment /50 free! and press." This instructs LEXIS to locate only documents that contain the phrase "first amendment" within 50 words of the words "freedom" or "free" and "press."

Constructing a proper search is the most important part of computerized legal research and requires thought and planning before you sign on and start incurring charges. Use a pen and paper and play around with the universal characters and connectors to frame the most efficient search instruction.

If your search does not reveal sufficient results or, conversely, provides you with an abundance of documents, it is possible to modify your search. Simply press "m" and modify your search by using additional connectors such as "or," "/n," or "and." Thus, if your search for "landlord /20 tenant and default" discloses hundreds of cases, press "m" and continue by adding "/20 evict! and rent."

Plain English Searching

Recognizing that many individuals find working with Boolean connectors awkward, LEXIS has introduced "Freestyle," a method of searching that allows researchers to use plain English rather than connectors or root expanders. Freestyle allows you simply to type in your search inquiry in plain English and locate documents that respond to your search request. Click inside the open circle on your screen marked "Natural Language" to select this research format. Then type in your search terms. For example, to locate cases relating to adoption of children by unmarried individuals, first select a library or source from the "Source" menu (such as "Federal Legal-U.S." for all federal cases or "States Legal-U.S." for state sources only). Type your search the way you might describe it to another, for instance, "When can unmarried or single individuals adopt children?" To modify your search, press "m." To conduct a new search, press ".ns." To switch to Boolean searching, click inside the open circle marked "Terms and Connectors." (See Figure 11-2.)

Figure 11-2
LEXIS Search Form

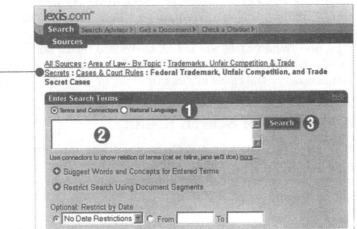

————— Practice Tip —————

Boolean or Plain English Searching?

For the most efficient research, Westlaw suggests that you use Boolean terms and connectors in the following circumstances:

- You are searching for particular terms;
- You are searching for a particular document; or
- You are looking for all documents containing specific information, such as all cases classified under a particular topic and key number.

Westlaw suggests that you use plain English or natural language when:

- You are searching for broad concepts; or
- You are a new or infrequent Westlaw user or you are unfamiliar with Boolean language.

---

c. Search Advisor

A new service offered by LEXIS, Search Advisor, is designed for research in a known area of law. Search Advisor is an ideal place to begin researching an issue because it assists you in selecting a legal topic and a jurisdiction and will suggest terms and words to search.

To use Search Advisor, click on "Search Advisor" at the top of your screen and then either choose a legal topic (such as antitrust, bankruptcy, or contracts) from the menu or type in your legal topic in the open search box. You will be presented with a list of more specific subtopics that you can select to explore. Continue clicking and selecting until you are presented with the specific topic you desire. You can select a jurisdiction and then determine whether you prefer to search using Terms and Connectors (Boolean searching) or Natural Language. Click "Search." When documents are retrieved, you can view the full text of a document or case presented or only a portion. When cases are listed, their core terms (key terms used in the case, such as "debtor" or "arrest") will be presented with their citations so you can select the cases of most interest to you. (See Figure 11-3.)

d. Display of Search Results

It is possible that your search may disclose numerous documents that respond to your search instructions. LEXIS contains several features that allow you to review these documents quickly to weed out the ones that will not be helpful to you.

- KWIC (type in ".KW" or select "KWIC" from the top of your screen). If you use the command "KWIC," the search terms you used will be highlighted and surrounded by 25 words on either side of your search terms. This feature allows you to review at a glance that portion of the document that displays your search terms and determine if the document should be bypassed or studied in greater detail.

- FULL (type in ".FU" or select "Full" from the top of your screen). The command "Full" instructs LEXIS to display the full text of the document containing your search terms.
- CITE (type in ".CI" or select "Cite" from the top of your screen). By selecting "Cite," LEXIS will display the citations to the documents

Figure 11-3
LEXIS Search Advisor

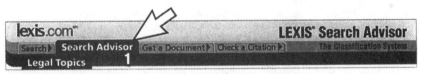

Starting a research project and not sure where to begin?

Search Advisor links treatise articles, law reviews, news, and case law materials within a specific area of law. The following example shows how to use LEXIS Search Advisor to research a summary judgment ruling in a trademark infringement case:

1. Click the *Search Advisor* tab to display a list of practice areas, such as Administrative Law, Bankruptcy Law, Trademark Law, etc.

2. Click *Trademark Law* to display a list of subtopics for trademark law. (See illustration.)

3. Click *Infringement.*

4. Click *Summary Judgment.*

5. Click into relevant treatises, law reviews or legal news on the topic of trademark infringement and summary judgment.

   OR

6. Type search terms in the open field to search on the topic of trademark infringement and summary judgment in case law.

To complete your search, type and select the appropriate information in the fields of the LEXIS Search Advisor template shown below.

Trademark Sub-Topics (Step 2)

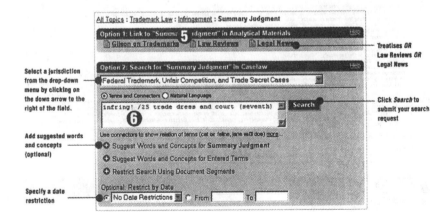

or cases containing your search terms. Each document is assigned a number. To review any of these cases, type the number of the document and "transmit." You will then be shown the text of that case in KWIC format (that is, a 25-word band around your search terms).

(See Figure 11-4.)

e. Searching for Statutes

If you know the precise citation for a statute, you can find it readily by using and clicking the "Get a Document" tab at the top of your screen. Click on the "Citation" tab. Type in your citation (such as "35 uscs 101") in the open

Figure 11-4
Viewing LEXIS Results

Viewing Results

Cite—displays a bibliographic list of the citations in your answer set

KWIC™—displays 25 words of text around your search terms

Full—displays the full text of your document

Powerful Cite List

1. Case Summaries—for an overview of the procedural posture, legal issues, holding, and outcome of the case

2. Core Terms—for a snapshot view of the case

3. Show Hits—displays each sentence where your terms appear in the case

4. Tag Docs—quickly check the cases you want to print/download

5. *Shepard's*® Signals— click on the warning, caution, or positive treatment signal to *Shepardize* the case

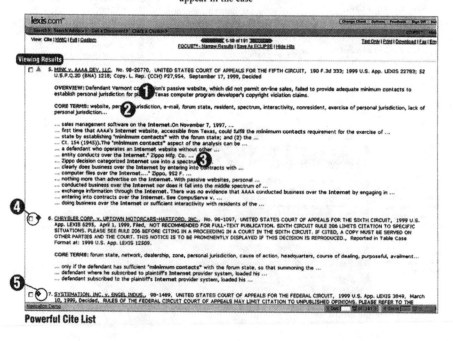

Powerful Cite List

field. Click "Get." This feature, often called LEXSTAT, allows you immediately to locate the statute you need without having to select a library and file.

After you have reviewed the particular statute in which you are interested, you can browse through preceding and consecutive sections to determine whether they are of any use to you just as you would browse pages in a book. To browse, click on "Book Browse" at the top of your screen.

To locate statutes when you do not have a specific citation but know or believe the matter is covered by a statute (such as determining how many days a defendant in Ohio has to answer a complaint or locating federal statutes relating to sex discrimination), you must select a library or source and then construct a search combining descriptive words with root expanders and connectors. For example, to locate the Ohio statute, select or click on "States Legal-U.S." and then "State Statutes" then "Ohio." You might then enter "complaint and defendant /25 answer" to locate Ohio statutes containing the word "complaint" and "defendant" within 25 words of the word "answer."

To find the federal statutes relating to sex discrimination, select or click on "Federal Legal-U.S." and then "USCS Materials." You might then wish to enter "sex! and discriminat!" to locate statutes containing both these terms.

Once you have located a statute, you may browse through preceding or succeeding statutes by selecting "Book Browse."

f. Searching for Constitutions

Searching for constitutional provisions is similar to searching for statutes. If you know the citation to a specific constitutional provision, use the "Get a Document" tab and then type in its citation.

If you do not know the citation, select a library and a file and then use the search techniques discussed above. For example, to find the provision of the United States Constitution that allows freedom of assembly, select or click on "Federal Legal-U.S." and then "USCS Materials." You might then enter "fre! and assemb!"

For state constitutional provisions, select the appropriate state library and file and use the standard search techniques, root expanders, and connectors to help you locate the article or section of the provision you need.

g. Searching for Cases

If you know the citation to a case, you can use the "Get a Document" tab. Enter the citation and click "Get." Even if you do not have the page number on which a case begins, this feature, often called LEXSEE, will locate a case when all you have is a jump cite to a page within the case. Similar to LEXSTAT, LEXSEE allows you to view the case without having to select a source. Simply sign onto LEXIS, click the "Get a Document" tab, click on the "Citation" tab, type in your citation (such as "420 US 104") in the open field, and click "Get."

If you know only the name of the case or even the name of one of the parties, search as follows: Click on the "Get a Document" tab, click on the

"Party" tab, type in the party name(s) in the open fields, and select a jurisdiction. Click "Search."

One of LEXIS's newer features is "Case Brief," which provides a brief snapshot of a case in an easy-to-read format that includes a case summary and other helpful features. To get a LEXIS Case Brief, select "Get a Document," enter your case citation in the open field, make sure the "Case Brief" button is selected, and click "Get."

To locate cases when you do not have a citation, use LEXIS's "Search Advisor," discussed above. One of the advantages of using LEXIS over conventional research methods is the rapid access it affords to newly decided cases. Often cases are available online within hours after they are decided. Contrast this with the several weeks it usually takes to obtain advance sheets.

h. Shepardizing

As fully dicussed in Chapter 9, Shepardizing is easily accomplished on LEXIS. Use the "Check a Citation" tab at the top of your screen and enter the citation to be checked. Click "Check" at the bottom of the screen. Review your results, paying attention to the signal indicators (red for strong negative history, yellow for cautioning you of possible negative treatment, and so forth). Use "Custom Restrictions" to narrow your results, for example, to find out which Fifth Circuit or Iowa cases mention your case.

i. CheckCite and CiteRite II

CheckCite, a new software program, now allows you to validate automatically all of the cases in an entire brief. The program "reads" your document and locates all case citations. Your citations are then KWIK cited or fully Shepardized, depending upon your instructions. Results are printed in a report, which you can then review to determine the subsequent history and treatment of your cases. CheckCite thus instantly and automatically verifies the validity of all of your cases, saving you from the time-consuming task of inputting each citation separately. CheckCite can also verify the accuracy of quotations from cases, statutes, and law reviews.

Due to the ease of checking the validity of cases online, many law firms have ceased subscribing to the print versions of *Shepard's* and rely exclusively on computer-assisted cite-checking.

CiteRite II, a citation-checking software program provided by LEXIS, checks your citation format against that of *The Bluebook* or California citation form. You will be provided with parallel cites, informed of errors in punctuation (such as a failure to place a period after "Mich"), errors in underlining, and errors in the names of reporters.

j. Segment Searching

Segment searching on LEXIS allows you to find segments or parts of documents. LEXIS has divided documents into segments that reflect naturally occurring parts of the document. For example, you can search cases by names of the parties, the court deciding the case, the judge who wrote the opinion, or the date of the document. Similarly, you may wish to restrict your search to a specific time period, for example, cases after 1990.

When the "Enter Search Terms" signal is displayed after you select a source, click on "+ Restrict Search Using Segments." A drop-down menu will allow you to select terms such as "dissent," "concur," or "court" to narrow your research. You can also use date restrictions to locate cases from a certain year or before or after a certain date. A menu is provided so you can select your desired time period.

These features allow you to isolate cases and retrieve only those from certain courts within specified time periods.

k. Law Reviews

LEXIS contains several libraries or sources of particular interest to researchers, particularly the libraries containing law review and journal articles. LEXIS includes the text of articles from more than 700 journals and law reviews. Use the "Get a Document" feature if you have a citation to an article. If you do not have an article citation, select "Search Advisor" and type in key words about the issue you are researching in the open field. Click "Find." Select the topic that looks like the closest match and select "Law Reviews" and review the sources given.

l. Administrative and Legislative Materials

The GENFED library contains files for C.F.R. and for the *Federal Register* since 1980. If you know the citation to a C.F.R. or *Federal Register* provision, select "Get a Document" and type in the citation. If you do not have a citation, select "Search" at the top of your screen, and then enter "genfed;cfr" (or "genfed;fedreg" for *Federal Register* materials) in the open field called "Look for a Source." Click "Short Names" and then "Find." In the search box presented, select "Terms and Connectors," type in your search terms, and then click "Search."

LEXIS includes public laws, *U.S. Statutes at Large*, transcripts of congressional hearings, conference and committee reports, and the *Congressional Record*. If you have a citation, use " 'Get a Document" to obtain the record you wish. If you do not have a citation, follow the steps discussed above for retrieving C.F.R. and *Federal Register* materials. LEXIS also provides bill-tracking reports to show the chronological history of a bill and includes some materials relating to state administrative law.

m. Other LEXIS Features

LEXIS includes a wide variety of other features to make researching easy and customizable, including the following:

- KWIC. Displays 25 words of text in a band around your search terms
- Full. Displays the full text of your document

- Core Terms. Provides a snapshot view of a case by listing the key terms discussed in a case
- Case Summaries. Gives an easy-to-read overview of the procedural background, legal issues, holding, and result of a case
- Show Hits. Displays each sentence where your terms appear in a case
- FOCUS. Narrows your results and pinpoints words within your search results by allowing you to type in words in a FOCUS terms box
- More Like This. Allows you to find other cases or authorities similar to the one you have identified as central to your research efforts

n. Affiliated Services

LEXIS offers a variety of services that are complementary to LEXIS and that are frequently used by legal professionals.

NEXIS. The NEXIS library offers the full text of thousands of general news, business, and financial publications. Select the "News" link under "Explore Sources" and then "Major Newspapers" and "Natural Language." Type in "Bill Gates" and you will be provided with hundreds of articles in which Mr. Gates is mentioned. You may wish to use a date restriction on some NEXIS searches so you are not overwhelmed with articles.

COMPANY DOSSIER. LEXIS's "Company Dossier" provides basic and in-depth business information on more than 35 million companies worldwide, including company overviews, financials, and information on company executives.

COMPANY ANALYZER. This service reviews public records relating to judgments, liens, corporate records, bankruptcy filings, and so forth and then creates a due diligence report.

ACADEMIC. The Academic service offers full-text documents from more than 5,6000 news, business, legal, medical, and reference publications.

ECLIPSE. The ECLIPSE (Electronic Clipping Service) feature allows you to follow the development of a topic automatically. The service automatically runs searches and provides updates to you on legal or business topics.

BANKO. The BANKO library provides information and document retrieval for bankruptcy petitions, dismissals, and discharges from most districts of the United States Bankruptcy Courts.

o. Delivering Documents

There are multiple options for the delivery of documents viewed on LEXIS. They can be printed, downloaded, e-mailed, or faxed to yourself or others. See Figure 11-5 for quick review of LEXIS.

3. *Westlaw*

a. Introduction and Organization

Westlaw, West Group's computer-assisted legal research system, was introduced in 1975, slightly after LEXIS. Initially, Westlaw contained only headnotes and case synopses of cases rather than the full text of cases. Shortly after Westlaw was introduced, however, West began to include the full text of court decisions. Westlaw includes nearly 15,000 databases, more than 1 billion public records, more than 6,800 news and business publications, and more than 700 law reviews.

The information in Westlaw is contained in "databases" (analogous to LEXIS's "libraries" or "sources") and "files." Within each database there may be several files. For example, within the database called "Federal Materials" are files for federal cases and federal statutes.

Generally, to locate materials, either you can use the "Find a Document" feature when you know a citation, or you can construct a search by accessing an appropriate database and entering your search inquiry using Boolean connectors or natural language.

You can access Westlaw through the Internet at http://www. westlaw.com.

b. Getting Started

When you sign on to Westlaw, the first screen will provide you with three choices:

- Find. Enables you to find a case, statute, or other document when

Figure 11-5
Quick Review of LEXIS

Getting Started

1. Turn on the computer.
2. Type in your LEXIS user number, identification number, and password.
3. Type in the client or billing number.
4. If you know a citation to a case, statute, law review article, or federal regulation, select "Get a Document" at the top of your screen, enter the citation, and click "Get."
5. Use "Search Advisor" when you either do know an area of the law (for example, securities) or don't know the area of law relating to your issue. Click on topics until you reach the most relevant topic, select a jurisdiction or click to select analytical materials, type key words into the search boxes, and click "Search" to pull together relevant cases, treatises, and law review materials.
6. Examine entries given. Shepardize all primary authorities. Sign off LEXIS.

you have its citation by typing the citation in a search box and
clicking "Go"
- KeyCite a Citation. Allows you to enter a citation, click "Go," and
update your citation for validity
- Search a Database. Allows you to enter a database identifier (such
as ALLFEDS for all federal cases) and access that database for
searching

If you do not know your database identifier, click "Directory" on the
toolbar for access to Westlaw's list of databases. Once you have accessed a
database, select a search method (either "Terms and Connectors" or "Natural Language"), type your search terms, and click "Search."

Practice Tip

Selecting the Right Database on Westlaw

**Westlaw has introduced "Find a Database Wizard" to walk you
through the process of picking the right database to meet your
research needs. You will be asked a series of questions about what
you are trying to find and the "Wizard" will suggest and help you
select the right database.**

---

c. Constructing a Search

To access information in Westlaw when you do not have a citation, you need
to construct a search or, in West's terms, formulate a "query." As soon as
you access a database by typing a specific database identifier (such as
ALLFEDS or USCA), Westlaw will instruct you to enter your query.
You may select to search either by "Terms and Connectors" or "Natural
Language." The use of Terms and Connectors will be discussed first.
Just as when you perform legal research with conventional sources, or
when you are using LEXIS, think of words and phrases that describe
the research issue that will form the basis of your query. Similar to LEXIS,
Westlaw automatically searches for plural words (boys) if you enter a
regular singular word (boy), and if you enter a nonpossessive word (landlord) Westlaw automatically searches for the possessive forms (landlord's
or landlords').

(1) Universal Symbols

Westlaw uses certain universal symbols to help you expand your query.

An *asterisk* (*) may be placed anywhere in a word and substitutes for a
letter. For example, if you enter "franchis*r," Westlaw will retrieve
"franchisor" and "franchiser."

An *exclamation point* (!) is used at the end of a word to retrieve all forms of a word. For example, "valu!" would retrieve value, valued, valuation, and so forth.

These symbols, sometimes called universal characters, are identical to those used for LEXIS.

(2) *Connectors*

Westlaw uses certain connectors to help you expand your query. The most common connectors are "or," "and," "/p," "/s," "/n," and "but not."

The *or* connector, represented by a single space, will help you search for alternative terms. Thus, the query "landlord lessor" will retrieve documents containing either or both the terms "landlord" or "lessor."

The *and* (or "&") connector will retrieve documents containing two terms. Thus, the query "landlord and lessor" will retrieve documents containing both terms.

Westlaw features two grammatical connectors. The connector /p requires search terms to appear in the same paragraph. Thus, a query for "landlord lessor /p evict!" will result in the retrieval of documents that contain either the word "landlord" or "lessor" within the same paragraph as the words "evict," "evicting," or "eviction." The connector /s requires search terms to appear within the same sentence. For example, a query for "landlord lessor /s evict!" would retrieve documents in which the word "landlord" or "lessor" appear in the same sentence as "evict," "evicting," or "eviction."

The numerical connector /n requires search terms to appear within a specific number of words of each other. You may select any number between 1 and 255. Thus, a query for "rescission /25 contract agreement" would retrieve documents in which the word "rescission" appears within 25 words of the terms "contract" or "agreement." When searching for words, Westlaw, unlike LEXIS, counts "stop words" such as "and," "to," "but," and "the."

You can exclude terms by using the "but not" connector ("%"). For example, a query such as "divorce dissol! % custody" instructs Westlaw to retrieve documents containing the words "divorce" or "dissolution" but to exclude such documents if they also contain the word "custody."

Once again, invest a bit of time in formulating your query. The time you spend in planning and constructing your query is time well spent because your aim is to retrieve documents quickly that are the most useful in helping you research your issue. (See Figure 11-6.)

Just as you can modify your search in LEXIS, you can edit your query in Westlaw. If you discover that your query resulted in too few documents or too many documents, you can click "Edit Search" on the toolbar and modify your search.

d. WIN

Since 1992 Westlaw has provided a legal research method called WIN (an acronym for "<u>W</u>estlaw <u>Is</u> <u>N</u>atural"). WIN allows you to enter your issue in plain English and eliminates the need for root expanders, connectors, or other such commands. Using WIN, you need only enter your question in plain English. For example, if the issue you are researching relates to the liability of a tobacco company for injuries caused by smoking, the typical Boolean search query might be as follows: "liab! negligen! /100 tobacco smok! /100 injur! death." With WIN, however, you could simply type the following: "Is a tobacco company liable for injuries or deaths caused by smoking?" While experienced searchers are comfortable constructing searches using root expanders and connectors and can easily construct a search, less experienced users may find WIN far less intimidating and awkward than Boolean searching. Similar to LEXIS's plain English searching through "Freestyle," this natural language search method greatly simplifies the search process.

e. Display of Search Results

There are several methods to use to browse the documents you retrieve to determine if they are on point. On the left side of the screen, a list of citations to cases that respond to your query will be listed. Select as desired. The right side of the screen displays the full text of the cases selected. The terms in your query, such as "landlord" or "evict," will be displayed in bold type. To move to the next occurrence of your search terms, click the "Term" arrow on your screen. (See Figure 11-7.)

You can also search the document for a particular term, whether or not that term was part of your query. Thus, if your search results in 50 cases and you wish to see if any of the cases also contain the word "option," select "Locate in Result" from the menu at the top of the screen and type in "option." Westlaw will then locate any of the cases that contain the word "option."

Figure 11-6
Sample Westlaw Query Screen

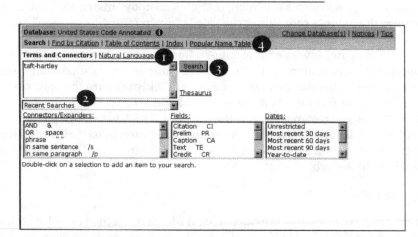

Cases displayed on the screen are presented in "full-text plus" format. That is, you will be given the full text of the case plus West's editorial feature such as a synopsis of the case, headnotes, and topic names and key numbers.

f. Searching for Statutes

There are two ways to locate statutes. If you know the citation, select the tab "Find a Document," type the citation in the "Enter a Citation" box, and click "Go." Thus, you could enter "35 usca 105" to retrieve that statute.

If you do not know the citation to a statute, you will need to select a database. For example, for federal statutes, select the database "USC" or "USCA." You will then need to select a search method by clicking "Terms and Connectors" or "Natural Language." Type your search in the search box and click "Search." To retrieve library references or annotations relating to a statute, enter "re" or "an," respectively. You will then be able to view references to secondary sources discussing your statute or annotations to cases construing your statute.

Westlaw recently introduced "StatutesPlus," which provides links to other sources (including cases, other statutes, and administrative code references) that discuss your statute. You will also be immediately provided with KeyCite flags to warn you if the statute has been repealed or amended or if pending legislation may affect it. Moreover, through "Past-Stat Locator," you can review the exact version of a statute as it existed when a client's legal matter occurred.

g. Searching for Cases

There are two primary methods to locate cases through Westlaw. If you know the citation, select the "Find a Document" tab, enter your citation in

Figure 11-7
Viewing Westlaw Results

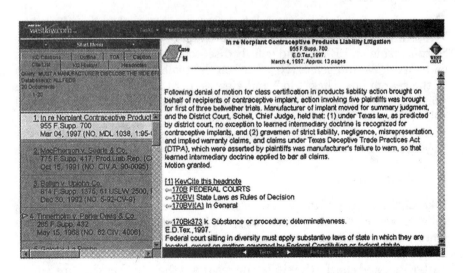

the search box, and click "Go." If you do not know the citation to a case, select an appropriate database and then formulate a query using natural language descriptive words or universal characters and connectors. For federal cases, you may select specific databases ("SCT" for Supreme Court cases, "DCT" for district court cases), or select ALLFEDS, the database containing federal cases from the United States Supreme Court, United States courts of appeal, United States district courts, and other federal courts.

For state cases, you may select state-specific databases ("AZ-CS-ALL" for Arizona cases, "LA-CS-ALL" for Louisiana cases) or ALL-STATES, which will retrieve cases from all 50 states and the District of Columbia. You can also select one of West's regional reporters, such as the *North Eastern Reporter*. Because cases reported in West's National Reporter System are unofficial, Westlaw includes star paging to inform you of the page number you would be on if you were reading the case in an official report.

Like LEXIS, Westlaw offers rapid access to recently issued cases, enabling you to locate cases within hours after they are decided. Because these recent cases are not yet reported, they are in slip form and do not display the editorial fields of synopses, or topics or key numbers.

Westlaw offers a service called "ResultsPlus" to expand your research efforts. References to additional resources are automatically displayed in a list with your search results when you perform case law research on Westlaw. You may be offered links to A.L.R. annotations, Am. Jur. 2d articles, and other useful sources.

One of Westlaw's most recent and popular innovations is the display of cases on a computer screen exactly the way they appear in printed books. Westlaw has been scanning cases to allow you to view them just as they would appear in conventional print volumes. If an image is available for a case you are viewing, a "West Reporter Image PDF" link will appear. Click on this link to view cases in an easy-to-read format and to print the image.

h. KeyCiting

The method of updating and validation of primary authorities offered by Westlaw is called "KeyCite." The service and process are fairly similar to Shepardizing on LEXIS, and is fully discussed in Chapter 9. In brief, sign on to Westlaw and select "KeyCite" on the toolbar. Type in your citation in the search box, click "Go," and view your results, noting the warning graphics (for example, red flags to indicate strong negative history and yellow flags to indicate caution). Alternatively, if you are viewing a case on the screen, simply click on the KeyCite icon on the screen to access KeyCite.

i. WestCheck

Like LEXIS's CheckCite, Westlaw's software program called WestCheck relieves you of the time-consuming and tedious task of inputting each citation in a brief or document to determine whether it is still valid. WestCheck automatically extracts citations from a document or table of authorities and checks the cites. The results of the cite-checking are sent to your choice of a stand-alone printer, attached printer, or computer. See Chapter 9 for additional information about WestCheck.

j. Field Searching/Restrictions

Like LEXIS, Westlaw allows you to retrieve only part of a document or to view documents by name or date. LEXIS refers to this as "segment searching," while Westlaw refers to this as "field searching" or "restrictions." You must select a database before you search for certain "fields" on Westlaw. For example, if you know that a federal case is titled *Anderson v. D'Antonio Co.*, select a database such as ALLFEDS and enter "ti" (for "title") followed by your search terms in parentheses: "ti (Anderson & D'Antonio)." This instructs Westlaw to search for all federal cases in which the names Anderson and D'Antonio appear in the title.

Using these fields or restrictions to limit your search allows you to search by court, date, judge, or attorney. When your search results are displayed on the screen, a "Restrictions" box is provided. Select and click on the restrictions you desire.

You can also limit your search by date so as to retrieve documents before or after a specific date. Thus, by entering "da" followed by a date you can obtain documents restricted by date. For example, if your query is "landlord tenant /20 default da (aft 1990)" Westlaw searches for cases decided after 1990 containing the words "landlord" or "tenant" within 20 words of the term "default."

k. Additional Databases

Westlaw contains several additional databases that are extremely useful in conducting legal research. These databases include the following:

American Law Reports. Westlaw includes A.L.R. annotations since 1965. To access this database, enter "ALR."

Texts and Periodicals. Westlaw includes selected articles from over 700 law reviews and bar journals. To access this database, enter "TP-ALL."

Index to Legal Periodicals. The Index to Legal Periodicals indexes more than 500 legal periodicals and is updated weekly. To access this database, enter "ILP."

Restatements of the Law. Westlaw includes all of the Restatements. To access the Restatements, type in "REST."

Legal Resource Index. The *Legal Resource Index* will refer you to more than 850 legal publications. To access this, enter "LRI."

Black's Law Dictionary. To determine the correct spelling of a legal word or phrase or to check the definition of a legal word, use *Black's Law Dictionary*, which can be accessed by entering "DI."

Jury Verdict and Settlement Summaries. Westlaw includes a variety of jury verdict and settlement summaries.

Legal Newspapers. Westlaw's legal newspapers database ("LEGAL-NP") provides access to a variety of legal newspapers, including *The National Law Journal, Chicago Lawyer*, and the *New York Law Journal.*

Texts and Treatises. Westlaw includes a wide variety of materials, form books, and treatises. Punch in "TEXTS" to access this database.

Congressional Quarterly Weekly Report. Enter "ConGQTWR" to gain access to congressional and presidential actions.

Practice Tip

Reviewing LEXIS's and Westlaw's Databases

• **You can search LEXIS's directory online to get details on any sources in its database at http: //web.nexis.com/sources.**
• **You can review a list of Westlaw's databases (together with their identifiers) at the following Web site: http: //directory. westlaw.com/?tf=90&tc=11.**

Once you access any of these databases, and select the button indicating you wish to use Natural Language (or Terms and Connectors, if you prefer). Type in your query in the search box and click "Go." You will then be directed to the appropriate Restatement, A.L.R. annotation, law review articles, and the like. In some instances (such as for A.L.R. annotations and law review and journal articles), you can search by author's name or title of an annotation or article.

l. Administrative and Legislative Materials

Like LEXIS, Westlaw offers a variety of administrative materials. You can access the *Federal Register* by entering "FR" or access C.F.R. by entering "CFR." If you know the citation to a C.F.R. regulation, you can use the feature "Find a Document" and enter the citation. For example, type "28 cfr 10102" or "38 cfr 2.20." For tracking pending federal regulations, use the database "US-REGTRK." If you do not have a citation to C.F.R. or the *Federal Register*, you will need to formulate a query using descriptive words, universal characters, and connectors. For example, to locate C.F.R. regulations relating to licensing requirements for airline pilots, you could formulate a query similar to the following:

airline pilots /50 licens! test! examin!

Westlaw would then search C.F.R. regulations that included the terms "airline" or "pilots" within 50 words of any form of the words "license," or "test," or "examination."

Westlaw also includes a variety of documents relating to legislative history. For example, Billcast ("BC") provides information on public bills introduced in the current session of the United States Congress.

BILLCAST ARCHIVES ("BC-OLD") provides information on public bills introduced in previous sessions of the United States Congress. "BILLTRK" provides current data for tracking pending bills before Congress or any state legislature. The *Congressional Record* ("CR") since 1985 is also available. Moreover, legislative history for selected provisions of the United States Code since 1948 is available by accessing Legislative History ("LH"). The database LEGIS-ALL provides state legislative information from all 50 states.

m. Affiliated Services

Westlaw offers a wide variety of other publications and services relating to business and economic issues as well as popular press articles and information of general interest to legal professionals. Among these specialized materials are the following:

> Business Information and News: This is a comprehensive collection of news, business, and financial information with more than 8,000 news and business sources, allowing you to access most of the top 50 daily newspapers, business magazines, company profiles for more than 450,000 companies, stock quotes, and filings made with the SEC.
>
> Dow Jones Major Newspapers ("NPMJ"): This database provides access to more than 40 major newspapers from across the country.
>
> Dow Jones News Service ("DJNS"): This service provides business and economic news, general news, the text of the *Wall Street Journal, Barrons*, and 1,500 other publications as well as stock market quotations.
>
> Dun & Bradstreet Business Records PLUS ("DUNBR"): This service provides financial information on over 70 million businesses throughout the world.
>
> ExpertNet ("EXPNET"): ExpertNet provides biographical information on experts in the medical malpractice and personal injury field who are available to serve as consultants or expert witnesses.
>
> WestClip: Westlaw's clipping service enables you to stay informed by monitoring topics, people, litigation, and companies of interest to you. Select "WestClip" from the "More" drop-down menu at the top of any screen.
>
> Westlaw Litigator: This service provides invaluable assistance for litigators. Litigator allows you to profile and get information on attorneys, judges, and experts in cases; investigate criminal records of parties; access jury instructions; search collections of briefs to help you develop arguments; access court rules; draft pleadings, forms, and motions; valuate damages; and monitor litigation trends in certain practice areas.

n. Document Delivery

Westlaw allows you to print documents on a printer attached to your computer or to send them to a stand-alone printer or fax machine.

The documents can also be downloaded for saving in your word processor or e-mailed to yourself or another. Click on the "Westlaw Print/Download" button to display options for document delivery.

o. KeySearch

You will recall from Chapter 5 that West has classified more than 400 areas of the law by topic name (liens, rescue, trespass), each of which is further subdivided by the use of key numbers. Westlaw has assigned a number to each topic name (for example, "liens" is 239, "rescue" is 337, and "trespass" is 386). By entering an appropriate query, you can retrieve all cases classified under certain topics, names, and key numbers.

Access KeySearch by clicking "KeySearch" on the toolbar. Browse the list of numerous topics and subtopics and select one to search. Then choose a source containing the type of document you wish to review (for example, "Cases" or "Law Reviews"). KeySearch formulates a query based on the topics and subtopics you select and any other search terms you add. Click "Search."

If you have identified a topic and key number during the course of your research, you can run a search using the topic and key number to quickly access cases involving the same legal issue. Select "Key Numbers & Digest" from the "More" drop-down list on the toolbar. The West digest topic and key number outline is displayed on the "Custom Digest" page. Once you find the topic and key number relevant to your issue, access a case law database and insert the topic and key number as your query. See Figure 11-8, for a quick review of Westlaw.

Figure 11-8
Quick Review of Westlaw

Getting Started

1. Turn on the computer.
2. Enter your Westlaw password.
3. Identify the client billing information and press ENTER.
4. At the first screen, select "Find" (if you know a citation) and press "Go" to retreive the document.
5. If you do not know a citation and you are searching for cases by issue, you must select an appropriate database. If you do not know which database to search, use the online Westlaw Directory. Browse the databases and click on the desired database. Use either natural language or terms and connectors to formulate a search query in the query text box. Click Search. Review the materials presented and KeyCite all primary authorities.
6. Sign off typing "off." After you sign off, you will be informed of the elapsed time you spent online.

4. *Final Pointers on Computer-Assisted Legal Research*

a. When to Use LEXIS or Westlaw

Some tasks are best performed by using conventional legal research tools, for example, books, while others are best performed by using LEXIS or Westlaw. Still other tasks might call for you to use conventional tools together with a computer-assisted legal research service. Knowing which method to use requires an analysis of many factors, including the complexity of the task, the costs involved, and time constraints.

If you are called upon to provide an answer to a legal question and you know which statute or case to consult, it may be more efficient for you to simply grab the book containing the statute or case and quickly review it.

On the other hand, if you do not have access to all the books or publications you need and it would be time-consuming to travel to a larger law library to review certain materials computer-assisted legal research will undoubtedly save you time and provide you access to publications a law firm could neither afford to purchase nor have room to shelve.

Both LEXIS and Westlaw are extremely current. They often provide access to materials within minutes after their release or publication. Moreover, the materials are available 24/7 and are never "off the shelves." Small firms may be the biggest beneficiaries of CALR, which provides immediate access to a wide array of materials that small firms and sole practitioners could not otherwise afford. Back issues of materials do not need to be retained or shelved, thereby freeing up valuable office space. Law firms can open up branch offices without investing in duplicate sets of books.

LEXIS and Westlaw enable you to rapidly locate cases that would take hours to find using conventional methods. For example, computer-assisted research allows you to quickly locate cases from the Eleventh Circuit decided between 1975 and 1990, authored by Judge Allen Little and dealing with trespass on federal property. Locating such cases using conventional techniques would be either impossible or so time-consuming as to be grossly inefficient.

Perhaps the best caution regarding computer-assisted legal research is that you should never simply sign on and begin working on formulating your search. Once you are "online," charges may be accruing, and time wasted in working on a query is a costly disservice to an employer or client. Therefore, before you sign on to LEXIS or Westlaw, spend some time getting familiar with your subject. Review C.J.S. or Am. Jur. 2d for background information on your topic and to familiarize yourself with the legal issues involved in your problem. Then take a piece of paper and write out your query. Have a "back-up" plan in mind in case your query does not yield the desired results so you can quickly modify or edit the query and try again. Select the smallest relevant database to eliminate irrelevant documents.

Do not spend valuable time reading the screen. Print your results or jot down citations and review them when you are no longer online. This is not only less costly but will be easier on your eyes, because a screen is never as easy to read as a printed page.

The more you use LEXIS or Westlaw, the more familiar you will become with their features, thus enabling you to research rapidly and effectively. If you find that your search is not providing results, go off-line and think through the steps you took, trying to decide on an alternative strategy.

Finally, do not become so wedded to either conventional research methods or computer-assisted legal research techniques that you will be unable to use an alternative method if you change jobs.

With practice, you can become extremely proficient at computerized legal research. Nevertheless, there are numerous tasks that can be performed as rapidly and more cost-effectively by using conventional techniques. Many researchers prefer to use books for most of a task and then switch to LEXIS or Westlaw to look for other perhaps less-known authorities, to verify the results of their searches, and to Shepardize or KeyCite their primary authorities.

To build confidence when you are first learning CALR, you may wish to re-research an issue to which you already know the answer. By going online, using Boolean terms or connectors, or plain English, and attempting to locate previously known cases, statutes, or other authorities, you will easily be able to verify that your CALR techniques are effective.

b. LEXIS or Westlaw

As you have seen, research strategies are substantially similar for LEXIS and Westlaw. The process of constructing a search or query either in Boolean terms or connectors or natural language is nearly identical, and both services allow you to browse documents, readily locate cases and statutes if you have a citation, Shepardize or KeyCite to validate your authorities, and print the results of your search.

Each service has some advantages over the other. LEXIS, as the owner of Matthew Bender & Co., offers a number of treatises, texts, form books, and practice sets. Westlaw offers A.L.R. annotations and its key number system. Both offer federal and state cases and statutes, administrative and legislative materials, selected law review articles, United States Attorney General Opinions, and numerous other publications and documents.

You may find that due to habit or convenience you prefer one service over the other. Researchers often develop a preference for the service on which they were trained or to which they were first introduced. Just as some people prefer U.S.C.A. over U.S.C.S., and vice versa, some people prefer LEXIS over Westlaw, while others feel equally strongly that Westlaw is preferable to LEXIS. Because both services contain substantially the same materials, it is impossible to declare that one service is superior to the other. The one that is "best" is the one that is best for you.

c. New Developments in LEXIS and Westlaw

LEXIS and Westlaw have both recently been making additional efforts to make their services affordable and attractive to sole practitioners and law firms, which often cannot afford the high costs usually associated with CALR. LEXIS has therefore launched "lexisONE" (http://www.lexisone. com), which offers free access to some of the materials available through the fee-based LEXIS service. Users can search federal and state statutes and recent federal and state cases. To access older cases or to Shepardize, the user must switch to LEXIS and pay a fee. A variety of other practice materials, such as forms, are also available. LEXIS hopes that once users become familiar with the new service they will wish to subscribe to LEXIS. Both LEXIS and Westlew now offer "a la carte" or "pay as you go" research plans, allowing you to access their databases without a formal subscription, paying by credit card.

The other new development offered by LEXIS and Westlaw is availability of some of their legal materials in wireless electronic formats accessible through personal digital assistants, such as Palm Pilots or Black Berrys. Both LEXIS and Westlaw offer cases, statutes, and updating (through Shepardizing or KeyCiting), thus allowing legal professionals on the run immediate access to most materials. For example, Westlaw Wireless provides access to the same content found on Westlaw.com, including cases, statutes, regulations, and news. You may search databases using terms and connectors or natural language and then KeyCite your primary authorities to ensure they are still good law.

Practice Tip

When to Use LEXIS and Westlaw

Georgetown Law Center advises using LEXIS or Westlaw when:

- **You are researching a new or evolving area of the law;**
- **Your fact situation is unique;**
- **You know a distinctive phrase from a case or other authority or a topic and key number;**
- **You know the citation to a case or other authority, or you know the name of a party, attorney, or judge;**
- **You need the most current information available; or**
- **You need to Shepardize or KeyCite your primary authorities.**

Use books when:

- **You need to familiarize yourself with an area of law;**
- **Your research topic is complex or your search terms are common (such as "negligence" or "punitive damages" that would produce too many hits in a computer database);**

(continued)

Practice Tip   (*Continued*)

- **Your research search terms include numerous synonyms for
  each other (because the computer will not recover all relevant
  documents); or**
- **You are researching statutory law (because examining the
  annotations and references to cases that follow the statutes is easier
  accomplished in print than on a screen).**
  (List reproduced in part from http://ll.georgetown.edu)

---

d. Limitations of Computer-Assisted Legal Research

There are some limitations to computer-assisted legal research. These can
be briefly summarized as follows:

(1) *Literalness*

Computers are extremely literal, and if you instruct LEXIS or Westlaw
to search for "attorney," it will do so, to the exclusion of "lawyer" or "coun-
selor." This literal approach requires that you construct your search or query
as carefully as possible so as to make the most effective use of the computers.

(2) *Cost*

There are so many pricing variations for LEXIS and Westlaw that it is
impossible to summarize them. Special pricing schemes exist for both
small firms (to encourage their access to materials they otherwise wouldn't
have) and large firms (to obtain the high volume of business generated by a
firm with hundreds of legal professionals). Flat rate or subscription pricing
exists whereby a firm pays a flat annual or monthly rate for CALR services,
allowing unlimited use of CALR materials and enabling firms to have fixed
and predictable costs. Hourly pricing can range from $10 to $800 per hour,
depending upon the files accessed and the time of day the service is used,
with higher fees charged during peak hours.

Another variety of pricing is "transactional" pricing, whereby the
user is assessed a per-search charge to work in a file without regard to
online time (although flat fees are also assessed for certain adjunct services, for example, $5.00 for each case or statute located, and $2.50 printing
charge per document. Both LEXIS and Westlaw usually assess a connection fee merely to connect to the system.

If your time is billed to the client at $50 per hour, the client may pay a
total of approximately $250 per hour for each hour you are online ($50 for
your time and $200 for the time online). This $250 equates to five hours of
your time if you were engaged in conventional legal research. On the other
hand, if you stumble around in the law library or spend valuable time
traveling to a larger library, it may well be more cost-effective to research

using LEXIS or Westlaw. As you gain experience and familiarity with LEXIS and Westlaw, you will be better able to gauge which technique works best for each particular research issue.

(3) *Database Limitations*

While the number of publications and documents in the LEXIS and Westlaw databases is truly staggering and while both LEXIS and Westlaw add to their databases every day, there are some limitations to computer-assisted legal research. For example, LEXIS and Westlaw both provide the text of the *Federal Register*, but only since 1980. Similarly, both provide access to the *Congressional Record*, but only since about 1985. While both provide cases from all states, coverage is similarly limited. For example, LEXIS and Westlaw provide cases from the North Carolina Court of Appeals since only about 1968. To determine the date limitations of publications and materials, consult the database lists published by LEXIS and Westlaw, which will clearly outline the scope and coverage of each database. Alternatively, you may review the coverage of the LEXIS and Westlaw databases online at the following sites, respectively: http://web.nexis.com/sources and http://directory.westlaw.com/?tf=90&tc=11.

While these restrictions may not significantly hamper your research, you should not make the mistake of thinking either service is a perfect substitute for a large, well-equipped law library.

e. Getting Help

Both LEXIS and Westlaw are extremely cooperative in training and assisting researchers. Both provide toll-free numbers, which you can call 24 hours a day to ask for help.

Both LEXIS and Westlaw offer free, Web-based interactive training and tutorials (as well as useful print products) to help you sharpen your research skills and to introduce you to their new products and features.

- LEXIS: For interactive training, select "Take a Tour" when you access the site http://www.lexis.com. Alternatively, access the LEXIS-NEXIS Knowledge Base at http://support.lexis.com, which offers research assistance, sample searches, links to product literature, and training programs. Training materials may be located and downloaded at http://www.lexisnexis.com/literature.
- Westlaw: For interactive training, access http://west.thomson.com/westlaw/training/online/ and select the training module desired. For user guides and reference materials, including excellent information on Westlaw and the free 104-page booklet *Research Guide for Paralegals*, access http://west.thomson.com/westlaw/guides.

Both LEXIS and Westlaw publish numerous materials and publications, including database lists, which fully describe and explain their services. You can obtain these materials by calling or writing LEXIS or West or by reviewing the materials on their respective Web sites.

Finally, both LEXIS and Westlaw offer training classes, including initial introductions to the systems, refresher courses, and advanced classes. The classes are usually free and are held at training centers or law firms. Call LEXIS or West (at (800) 262-2391 or (800) 344-5008, respectively) to inquire about these training classes and to find out if they are offered in your locality. Often the attendees at the classes are offered the opportunity to conduct free research, and instructors are available to assist with research problems.

E. Other Competitors in Commercial Electronic Research

While LEXIS and Westlaw are the acknowledged giants in the field of computer-assisted electronic research, a number of other companies have begun offering access on a fee basis to legal materials through the Internet. Most charge moderate fees and appeal to small firms and sole practitioners. Among the newcomers are the following:

- VersusLaw (http://www.versuslaw.com). VersusLaw provides access to federal and state court opinions, statutes, and other legal materials for a low monthly fee of approximately $12 per attorney or user. Federal statutes, all federal cases, and cases from each state's higher courts are available.
- Loislaw (http://www.loislaw.com). Loislaw offers case law, statutes, constitutions, administrative law, and court rules for all states and the federal courts. Loislaw offers a more comprehensive database than most of the other services described in this section, including all federal and state primary materials as well as treatise libraries for a wide variety of secondary sources, including antitrust, evidence, real estate, and securities laws. Moreover, Loislaw offers GlobalCite, a service similar to Shepardizing, which refers you to cases that mention or discuss the case you are researching. Searching is easily accomplished, either through Boolean terms or through a "find" feature if you know a citation. Low monthly flat fees are charged.
- JuriSearch (http://www.jurisearch.com). JuriSearch specializes in California law but offers Florida, Massachusetts, and federal materials as well. Fees are moderate.
- American LegalNet (http://www.americanlegalnet.com). American LegalNet specializes in litigation-related forms and California law and provides its services for about $30 per month. All California court opinions since 1934 are available, as well as court rules, court forms, and other materials. Some federal materials are also available.

F. Dead-Tree Publishing

The publishing of legal materials in conventional print form is often referred to as "dead-tree" publishing. On occasion, experts ponder whether the new virtual libraries will ultimately replace conventional law libraries with their dead-tree collections. In brief, the more reasoned conclusion is that while the emerging information technologies, especially the Internet, provide excellent tools, they are unlikely to replace books. Consider the following:

- Several years ago, CD-ROMs were touted as the technological marvel that would replace the printed page. Now, most experts recognize their value as complementary sources to conventional printed materials. Many experts view CD-ROMs as interim products whose use is likely to decrease as Internet legal research becomes more familiar to legal professionals.
- Libraries are permanent archives of materials, while the Internet is a temporary host continually being updated, and even replaced, with earlier versions of information sometimes lost forever.
- Certain materials, especially articles, texts, and treatises, are copyrighted and are thus unlikely to appear on the Internet. Their copyright owners, the authors, cannot receive needed royalties if their works are disseminated globally with the touch of a keystroke.
- The Internet is often described as "information chaos," meaning that numerous and sometimes even thousands of "hits" appear in response to certain queries, forcing researchers to undertake the painstaking task of separating useful information from that which is irrelevant.
- While people often read hundreds of pages at a sitting, research shows that most people only read three screens of information before printing it out.

In sum, become familiar with the newly emerging technologies of CD-ROM, CALR, and the Internet. Clients are entitled to the most efficient and accurate research at the lowest cost. These new information technologies, however, should be used in addition to, not in place of, conventional research using print sources. Effective researchers will consider a client's needs carefully and then determine the best approach. If all you need is a copy of a statute, it is far easier and far less expensive to obtain it on the Internet rather than drive to a law library several miles away. On the other hand, if a problem is more complex, you will need to review a variety of sources using a variety of methods: conventional research, computer-assisted research, and the Internet. Be flexible. Be prepared to switch research methods when you reach a dead end. No one method is best. Combine the best features of each approach to best serve a client's needs.

G. Citation Form

Bluebook:

Videotape:	Videotape: Sheparizing Made Easy (Shepard's/McGraw-Hill, Inc., 1994) (on file with Georgetown University Law Center).
LEXIS:	*Bailey v. Carpenter*, No. 96-1402, 1997 U.S. Dist. LEXIS 4098, at *4 (W.D. Tex. Feb. 14, 1997).
Westlaw:	*Franklin v. Darling*, No. 97-176, 1997 WL 26197, at *1 (E.D. Va. Oct. 13, 1997).

ALWD:

Videotape:	*Sheparizing Made Easy* (Shepard's/McGraw Hill, Inc. 1994) (videotape).
LEXIS:	*Bailey v. Carpenter*, 1997 U.S. Dist. LEXIS 96-1402 at *4 (W.D. Tex. Feb. 14, 1997).
Westlaw:	*Franklin v. Darling*, 1997 WL 26197 at *1 (E.D. Va. Oct. 13, 1997).

In summary, computer-assisted legal research is a valuable tool. The computer-assisted research services such as LEXIS and Westlaw provide rapid access to a wide range of materials that no law firm could afford to purchase or shelve. Many tasks such as Shepardizing and KeyCiting are simplified on computer. Nevertheless, computer-assisted legal research may be expensive and will only produce useful results if you understand how to make the system work effectively for you. This takes practice and experience. Neither conventional research nor computer-assisted legal research should be used exclusively. Effective researchers will use a combination of the two methods and employ selectivity to decide which method will yield the best results for a given task.

Strategies and Tips for Using CALR

Use CALR when:

- You already have a citation to a known case or statute.
- You are looking for cases involving a known party, attorney, or judge.
- The area of law is new or evolving.
- You are researching a unique area of law of unique fact situation.
- You are looking for the most current information available.
- You are updating or verifying your primary authorities (such as by Shepardizing or KeyCiting).

(continued)

Strategies and Tips for Using CALR (Continued)

Use books when:

- You need to familiarize yourself with an area of law.
- You are researching a complex area of law.
- You are researching statutes and wish to review the annotations that follow them.
- The search terms in your issue are so commonly used that numerous "hit" would be produced using CALR.

Tips for Efficient Use of CALR

- Construct your search or query before you sign on and start incurring costs.
- You need not memorize all of the commands and root expanders. A quick reference sheet is usually provided at each terminal.
- Do not waste time by reading long cases or law review articles on the screen. Such a practice causes strain to the eyes and the wallet. Either print the document or jot down its citation so you can locate it later.
- To save money, use a smaller file or database rather than a larger one. For example, if you are interested only in California cases, use the database just for California ("CA") rather than one for all 50 states ("ALLSTATES").
- Because CheckCite and WestCheck can check cites from a table of authorities, check the cites in an adversary's brief to ensure that the cases relied upon by the adversary are valid and have not been weakened.
- Use the clipping services to track information about clients and then send the clients articles that mention them. Clients are thrilled when their legal team expresses a personal interest in their business.

CyberSites ▰▰▰▰▰▰▰▰▰▰▰▰▰▰▰▰▰▰▰▰

http://www.westlaw.com   West's home page provides information about
                                  West products and services, including Westlaw

http://www.lexis.com   LEXIS's home page provides information about
                                  LexisNexis

West also provides three options to obtain documents easily, including cases, statutes, court briefs, and so forth:

- West Document Retrieval. This service provides public records, court documents, and so forth by overnight delivery, e-mail, or fax. Call 1-877-DOC-RETR.

- Westlaw by Credit Card.   If you are not a Westlaw subscriber, you may access this service and receive copies of cases, statutes, and court briefs or KeyCite a citation, paying by credit card. Access http://creditcard.westlaw.com.

- WestFind&Print. This service provides a quick way to retrieve copies of cases, statutes, and other documents by merely entering the citation. You may also KeyCite a document. You may download the resulting documents, have them sent to a printer, or e-mail them to yourself and others. The cost is about $12 for each document and $4 for each citation that is KeyCited. Access https://findprint.westlaw.com.

Writing Strategies

While computer-assisted legal research is somewhat mechanical, writing about the results you locate online is not. Because the reader of every project you write will be busy, and some readers may be highly critical, you need to produce a written project that is readable.

To enhance interest in your writing:

- Use the active voice because it is more forceful than the passive voice.

- Use lists and quotations to "break up" long narrative passages and add visual drama to your page.

- Use verbs ("conclude") rather than nominalizations ("drew a conclusion") to create interest.

- Use strong words ("unique" rather than "somewhat unusual").

- Use concrete words ("your lease") rather than vague terms ("your situation").

- Use placement to enhance interest by placing stronger arguments at the beginning and end of your project where they will have more force.

- Use "graphics" such as high-quality paper, headings, and white space to capture the reader's interest.

Assignment for Chapter 11

PART I. LEXIS

1. Select "Get a Document" and "Get by Citation." Retrieve the case located at 534 U.S. 316.
   a. What is the LEXIS citation?
   b. How many pages are in the case?
   c. Select and click on the yellow triangle shown for this case. What does the yellow triangle mean? How many times has the case been distinguished by later cases?
   d. Which 2004 case from the First Circuit Court of Appeals cited this case?

2. Select "Search" at the top of the toolbar and then select the topic "Trademarks." Select "Federal and State Trademark Cases." Using natural language, locate cases relating to scandalous trademarks.
   a. Retrieve the 1993 case with the docket number 93-1464. What is the case name?
   b. Select and click on the yellow triangle shown for this case. Is there any subsequent appellate history for this case?

3. Select "Get a Document" and "Get by Citation." Enter the citation 519 U.S. 2.
   a. What is the name of this case?
   b. Select "More Like This" and then "Search." What is the first case you are directed to?
   c. Return to your original case at 519 U.S. 2. Select "Shepardize."
      (i) List the four categories of citing references that Shepard's indicates.
      (ii) Locate the 2001 law review article that mentions the case located at 519 U.S. 2. Where is the case mentioned in this law review article?

4. Select "Get a Document" and "Get by Citation." Enter 18 U.S.C.S. § 509.
   a. What does this statute relate to, generally?
   b. What Am. Jur. 2d reference are you directed to?
   c. Retrieve this Am. Jur. 2d reference. What Sixth Circuit case are you directed to for the definition of "counterfeiting"?

5. Select "Search" on the toolbar. Select "California" within "States Legal — US" and then select "Deerings California Codes Annotated." In the search box, use natural language and locate the Business and Professions Code statute relating to what paralegals' business cards should include.
   a. Give the citation for this statute.
   b. When was this statute added?

6. Select "Get a Document" and then "Party Name" and locate a United States Supreme Court case in which the plaintiff's name is A. Elliott Archer.
   a. What is the citation for this case?
   b. What is the LEXIS citation for this case?
   c. What was the disposition of this case?

7. Select "Search Advisor" on the toolbar. Explore the legal topic of "Cyberlaw." Explore "Defamation." What three legal topics are listed?

8. Select "Shepard's" on the toolbar. Using the KWIC format, Shepardize 105 N.E.2d 685.
   a. What is the name of the case you are Shepardizing?
   b. What kind of treatment does Shepard's indicate for this case by the use of its icon?

9. Select "Get a Document" and then "Docket Number." Locate the case from the United States Court of Appeals with the docket number 73-1050.
   a. What Seventh Circuit case are you directed to?
   b. Retrieve this case and then Shepardize it. What A.L.R. Fed. annotation are you directed to?
   c. Who wrote the A.L.R. Fed. annotation?

10. Select "Search" from the toolbar and then "Secondary Legal" and then "Law Reviews & Journals." Use natural language and locate U.S. articles relating to the Sarbanes-Oxley Act of 2002.
    a. What 2003 Albany Law Review article are you directed to?
    b. Review this law review article. Whom does footnote 2 quote?

11. Select "Search" and then "Find a Source." Locate the source titled "A Dictionary of Modern Legal Usage." What is a "put" in securities law?

12. Select "Search Advisor" and then "Family Law." Select "Child Custody" and then "Awards." Locate Connecticut family law cases relating to this topic. Give a brief overview of the 2005 Connecticut case in which the plaintiff's name is Denardo.

13. Select "Get a Document" and "Get by Citation." Retrieve Wash. Rev. Code § 26.10.160.
    a. What does this statute deal with, generally?
    b. Shepardize this statute. What treatment was this statute given by the United States Supreme Court?

14. Select "Search" and then "Secondary Legal" and "Restatements." Select the Restatement (Second) of Contracts (case citations). Using natural language (and date restrictions to locate cases after January 1, 2000), locate the case discussing the prison mailbox rule.
    a. What is the name of the case?
    b. According to this case, when is a prisoner's petition deemed filed?
    c. Review Restatement (Second) of Contracts § 63. What is the title of this Restatement provision?

PART II. WESTLAW

1. At the initial Westlaw screen, in the "Find this document by citation" box, enter 568 N.W.2d 585.
   a. What is the name of this case?
   b. How many pages is the case?

    c. Select "West Reporter Image." What is the first word on page 588?

    d. Return to the case in its original format. What A.L.R. reference are you directed to?

    e. On the left side of the screen, select "KeyCite" and KeyCite this case. How many documents are listed (including this case)?

    f. Give the citation for the history of this case, namely, the appeal after remand.

2. Select "Directory" from the toolbar and select "Directories, Reference." Select *Black's Law Dictionary* (8th ed. 2004) and locate the definition for "mistrial." What is another term for mistrial?

3. Select "Directory" and continue selecting the appropriate databases to search Colorado cases. Use natural language and develop a query to locate cases from Colorado dealing with the liability of ski resorts for skiing injuries.

    a. What 1994 Colorado case are you directed to?

    b. Retrieve this case. On the left side of the screen, select "Table of Authorities." How many cases are cited in the 1994 Colorado case?

    c. Return to the case. On the left side of the screen, select "Am. Jur. Proof of Facts." What section in this article discusses the rescue duty of ski patrol?

    d. Return to the case. What KeyCite icon is displayed?

    e. KeyCite this case. What is the subsequent history of this case?

4. Select the appropriate databases for federal statutes. Using natural language, locate the federal statute relating to copyright rights of attribution.

    a. What is the first statute you are directed to?

    b. Select this statute. Give the citation to the 1996 law review article by Geri J. Yonover that comments on the statute.

    c. Select this law review article.

      (i) How many pages is this law review article?

      (ii) What does Section IA of the article discuss?

5. Select "Directory" and the appropriate databases to use the U.S.C.A. Popular Name Index.

    a. Give the citation for the "Blue Star Mothers of America Act."

    b. Review the Act. May a corporation contribute to a political party? What section within the Act governs your answer?

6. Select "Find" on the toolbar and enter the citation 350 F.3d 810.

    a. What is the name of the case?

    b. Review headnote 3 and select or click on the KeyCite icon. What message is displayed?

    c. Return to the case located at 350 F.3d 810. At the left of the screen, select "Petitions, Briefs, and Filings." Review the appellee's brief.

      (i) What does the Corporate Disclosure Statement state?

      (ii) Review the Table of Authorities in the brief. Select the *Anderson* case. Select or click on this case. What KeyCite icon is displayed?

      (iii) Select the KeyCite icon. What case declined to follow *Anderson*?

      (iv) How many green stars are displayed?

      (v) Review the KeyCite box at the left of the screen. What summary is provided for you relating to the current status of this case as good law?

7. Select "Find" and locate the case published at 898 S.W.2d 30. Select or click on the first name identified with a blue hyperlink. Identify this individual and give his or her phone number.

8. Select "Directory" and select "Administrative Material" within the "U.S. State Materials" database. Locate the attorney general opinions for California. Using natural language, search for opinions relating to smoking bans in public places.

    a. Select the opinion from October 1999. What was the question addressed to the attorney general?

    b. What answer was provided by the attorney general?

    c. What California statute was construed in the opinion?

9. Select "Directory" and "Litigation." Select "Jury Verdicts, Settlements, & Judgments" and then "Andrews Minnesota Jury Verdicts." Using natural language, retrieve information relating to medical malpractice cases decided after January 1, 2000. Select the August 2004 case relating to a teenager's death from meningitis. What was the settlement breakdown?

10. Select "KeyCite" from the toolbar and KeyCite the case located at 537 U.S. 79. Review the negative indirect history. Why didn't *Scott v. First Union Securities* follow the case located at 537 U.S. 79?

11. Select "Directory" from the toolbar and then "A.L.R." Using natural language, locate annotations relating to liability for injuries to trespassers. Select the annotation published in 70 A.L.R.3d.

    a. What Idaho case is discussed in this annotation?

    b. Review § 2 of the annotation. What is the discernable trend in this area of law?

12. Select "Find" from the toolbar and then select "Find by party name." Locate a federal case in which one of the party's names is "Grokster." When did the U.S. Supreme Court grant *certiorari* for this case?

13. Select "Find" from the toolbar and then select "Find this document by citation." Locate 42 U.S.C. § 1201. What does this statute relate to, generally?

14. Select "KeySearch" from the toolbar. Select "Corporations" and then "Piercing the Corporate Veil." Select Florida federal and state cases (with West headnotes) and "Search."

    a. What November 2003 case are you directed to?

    b. What key numbers appear in the yellow bands?

    c. Review the November 2003 case and KeyCite it. What occurred on January 14, 2004?

15. Select "Find" and then select "Find this document by citation" to locate the case published at 660 So. 2d 1165. Select "C" at the top of the screen. Give the name of the 1999 Florida case you are directed to.

16. Select "Find" and then "Find a case by party name." How many federal cases are there in which a party's name is "Grainer"?

17. Select "Directory" and then A.L.R. Using natural language, locate an annotation in A.L.R.4th that relates to inhalation of asbestos (and product liability).
    a. Give the citation to the annotation.
    b. Who is the author of the annotation?
    c. What section of the annotation discusses sophisticated users of asbestos products?

18. Select "Find" and then select "Find this document by citation" to locate the document designated as 2003 WL 23004289. What is this document?

State Your Answer

1. Access LEXIS's Directory of Online Sources at http://web.nexis.com/sources. Use the field titled "Geography" and select your state. Determine LEXIS's coverage for your state's attorney general opinions.

2. Access Westlaw's Database Directory at http://directory.westlaw.com/?tf=90&tc=11.
    a. Give the appropriate database identifier for cases from your state's courts.
    b. Give the appropriate database identifier for annotated statutes from your state.
    c. Give the appropriate database identifier for the George Mason Law Review.

E-Research: Legal Research Using the Internet

On the Internet, nobody knows you're a dog.

Peter Steiner, cartoon in *The New Yorker*, July 5, 1993

A. Introduction
B. Glossary of Terms
C. Conducting Legal Research Online
D. Strategies and Tips for Internet Legal Research
E. Ethical Concerns Regarding Use of the Internet
F. Surf's Up: The Best Internet Legal Research Sites
G. Cautionary Notes on Internet Legal Research
H. Citation Form

Chapter Overview

The best legal researchers know how to use a combination of conventional research methods with computerized and electronic research methods to achieve results. While one need not be a computer guru to satisfy one's duty to perform legal research competently, legal professionals should be sufficiently proficient in using the Internet that they can quickly find a case or statute. The Internet affords researchers the ability to find and review cases, statutes, and a vast array of other materials at no cost, 24 hours each day. Every year more and more materials are available on the Internet. While the Internet will never replace conventional research methods and while there are some significant drawbacks to Internet legal research, it is an extremely efficient and timesaving method for some research tasks.

Although this chapter provides a glossary of Internet-related terms, one need not be conversant with the jargon of computers to be an effective researcher. In fact, the most useful strategy in conducting Internet legal research is to have one good starting place and then use this to branch out to other sites of interest.

This chapter provides a glossary of Internet terms, tips and strategies on conducting legal research on the Internet, and some cautionary notes about over-relying on the Internet. The chapter also provides the "best of the best" sites for various legal research tasks as well as some sites for non-legal research.

A.   Introduction

Today's legal professionals have at their fingertips vast amounts of information that is free and available 24 hours each day. Until just recently, a researcher wanting to review a newly issued Supreme Court decision had only two options: drive to a law library or subscribe to a costly computerized legal research service such as LEXIS or Westlaw. The advent of the Internet has dramatically changed legal research, allowing professionals immediate access to cases, statutes, federal regulations, forms, legislative materials, treaties, journal articles, and much more. In some instances, cases are posted to the Internet within hours after their release by the clerk of the court. While the good news is that there is a vast array of legal materials available for your use, the bad news is that the information is so voluminous that making sense of the materials offered can be difficult and confusing.

The Internet was originally developed in the 1970s for military and government use, primarily to provide a secure method of communication in the event of nuclear attack. Use then expanded to the scientific and educational communities and, starting in the late 1980s, people began realizing the Internet' potential for enhancing communication. Use rapidly spread to the commercial sector, which quickly worked to develop the Internet' ability to promote the sale of goods and services. The Internet is now used in nearly every possible field of endeavor, from the military, to the government, to educational institutions, to not-for-profit organizations, to commercial enterprises. Nearly every business, including nearly all large law firms, has a presence on the Internet. In fact, a 2002 survey by the American Bar Association's Legal Technology Resource Center disclosed that every responding law firm with 50 or more lawyers maintained a Web site.

Legal professionals typically use the Internet for the following purposes:

- Communication. Legal professionals use the Internet to communicate with each other and with clients. Through electronic mail ("e-mail"), clients can be kept informed of the progress of their cases. Legal professionals can become involved in "listservs" to keep apprised of topics of interest to them and to continue their legal education. In many instances listservs or newsgroups will automatically e-mail newsletters or bulletins to subscribers, enabling legal professionals to keep current in their fields of interest.
- Marketing. Most law firms have a Web site, which is a marketing brochure about the firm that is published electronically rather than

in print form. The site will typically describe the firm, its professionals, areas of expertise, and locations, and may provide articles or newsletters on legal topics. State bar ethics codes regulate advertising. Thus, firms need to ensure their Web sites are in compliance with those regulations.

- Commerce. Legal professionals can order books, publications, and other materials from publishers and other vendors.
- Research. Legal professionals can use the Internet to conduct research, including legal research. One can determine an adversary's address, a client's exact corporate name, when a company's stock "went public" and who its officers and directors are, and a variety of other research tasks. The Internet can also be used for legal research, including finding cases, statutes, regulations, locating forms, reviewing legal journals and periodicals, and locating legislative documents. This chapter will focus on the use of the Internet to conduct legal research.

Although legal research on the Internet can seem awkward and intimidating to the novice, all legal professionals should strive for some degree of familiarity with Internet legal research. The general duty imposed on legal professionals to have a sufficient level of competence to represent their clients is broad enough to require competence in new and emerging technologies, including the Internet. According to at least one case, a lawyer must "discover those additional rules of law which, although not commonly known, may be readily found by standard research techniques." *Baird v. Pace*, 752 P.2d 507 (Ariz. 1987). Using the Internet will soon be viewed as a standard or common method of conducting research. In fact, the American Association for Paralegal Education states that to be a successful paralegal, one must possess the "core competency" of being able to use both print and electronic sources of law to locate applicable primary and secondary materials. Moreover, employers and clients are increasingly technologically proficient and will justifiably expect their legal team to be equally proficient, so that clients can be kept apprised of the status of their matters by e-mail, relevant cases can be sent electronically to co-counsel, and others in the firm can be provided immediate access to files and records pertaining to a client' case.

Not only is there a nearly overwhelming amount of information available on the Internet, the technology surrounding Internet legal research continues to develop rapidly. For example, access to certain West materials is now available through wireless communications devices, such as Palm devices, allowing users to retrieve a wide variety of legal materials such as cases and then to KeyCite them to check their continued validity. Similarly, LEXIS offers access to cases, statutes, and Shepardizing through personal digital assistants. In order to best serve their clients, legal professionals need to be conversant with all methods of research, from conventional print materials, to microforms, to CD-ROMs, to computerized legal research systems, to the Internet.

There is, of course, some danger in relying too much on the Internet, primarily because not all legal materials are available online.

Nevertheless, learning good Internet research techniques will save you a great deal of time. In most instances, Internet legal research should complement your other research techniques — namely, conventional book research and research using LEXIS and Westlaw.

Finally, be aware that there is an astounding amount of non-legal information on the Internet. Use the Internet as a tool to track clients' stock prices, determine the weather at the client's headquarters, and obtain basic information about clients' industries. Read the press releases issued by clients. Clients will be pleased and flattered that you took the time and effort to do some homework about their business, location, and financial status.

B. Glossary of Terms

Many otherwise confident professionals are intimidated by the Internet, in many cases because terms commonly used when discussing the Internet, such as "browser," "URL," and "hyperlink," are entirely new to them. While this section of the chapter provides you with some basic Internet terms, practically speaking, there is little need to know a great deal about how the Internet works or how specific terms are defined. Most of us have no idea how our cell phones and microwave ovens work and yet are entirely comfortable using these appliances. The Internet should be viewed the same way: It is nice to know some of the terms commonly used, but it is not totally necessary in order to be able to conduct legal research competently.

Following are some of the terms frequently encountered in the electronic world:

Blog: Abbreviation for "Web log," an online journal or diary where a "blogger" posts his or her thoughts, often on a daily basis. The entries, called "postings," are usually arranged in chronological order, with the most recent additions listed first. Blogs devoted to law topics are often called "blawgs."

Browser: Software that helps access and review information on the Internet and translates HTML-encoded files into text and images that one can read and view. Netscape and Microsoft Explorer are examples of browsers.

Cable modem: A cable line used to connect to the Internet allowing faster connection than a telephone line.

Chat room: A location in cyberspace fostering real-time communications among several people.

Cyberspace: The electronic or computer world in which vast amounts of information are available; sometimes used as a synonym for the Internet.

Domain name: The name that identifies an Internet site, such as "www.ibm.com." Domain names have two parts: the "generic toplevel domain," which is the last part of the domain, such as "com," or "gov," and which usually refers to the type of provider of the information, and the "secondary domain," which is more specific and is to the right of "www," such as "ibm" in the above example.

Download: Transferring files or information from the Internet to your personal computer files.

E-mail: Electronic mail or messages sent through the computer rather than in physical form (which is often called "snail mail").

Extranet: An internal company or law firm Intranet that provides access to selected outsiders on a case-by-case basis.

FAQ: "Frequently asked questions," often included on Web sites and that respond to the most commonly asked questions about the site or about the information provided by the site.

FTP: File transfer protocol, a common method of moving files or communicating between two Internet sites or computers.

Home page: The first or main page you are sent to when accessing a person' or business's Web site.

HTML: Hypertext markup language, a standard language of computer code.

HTTP: Hypertext transfer protocol, a common method of moving files or communicating between two Internet sites.

Hyperlink: A method of instantaneous transport to another destination. Hyperlinks are often underscored or appear in different color on the computer screen; by clicking the colored line, you will be immediately transferred to that particular site or page.

Internet: A collection of worldwide interconnected computer networks originally developed for defense purposes and linked together to exchange information; the Internet is not owned by any one person or company.

Internet Service Provider (ISP): A company that provides Internet access, such as America Online or Roadrunner, for a monthly fee.

Intranet: A private network inside a company or law firm that provides access only for internal use to those in the company or firm and not to outsiders; for example, a law firm's intranet could be used only by those in the firm and could not be accessed by any member of the general public.

Link: See "Hyperlink."

Listserv: A system that allows groups of people to e-mail each other and participate in group discussions, usually about a topic of common concern. For example, a listserv comprising law students may automatically send one message to all others in the group.

Log-in: (n.) An account name used to gain entry to a computer system. Unlike a password, it is not secret. Also called a "user name"; log in: (v.) the method of accessing a computer system.

Modem: A device that connects to your computer and to a telephone line or cable TV line allowing the computer to communicate with other computers much the way telephones allow humans to communicate with each other.

Netiquette: The code of etiquette or conduct for the Internet.

Network: The connecting of two or more computers so that they can communicate with each other and share resources, files, and infor-mation.

Newsgroup: An online forum for sharing information and commu-nications. Users view messages, post their own messages, and reply to others.

Online: The process of being connected to the Internet through electronic communication.

Password: The secret code used to gain access to a computer system.

PDF: Portable document format, a format that duplicates on a com-puter screen what a conventional print source looks like.

Posting: Entering information or messages into a network — for example, cases are "posted" to the Web site of the United States Supreme Court, and legal professionals "post" messages on a listserv.

Search box: An initially blank box on a computer screen in which you type or key in the word or terms you are interested in researching.

Search engine: A particular service that helps one locate useful information on the Internet, usually through the use of keywords; common search engines are "Yahoo," "Google," "Lycos," and "Alta-Vista." A search engine is a Web site that looks for and retrieves other Web sites. Search engines look for words in the millions of Web pages on the Internet and direct you to pages that include the search words or keywords you enter in a search box.

Server: A computer or software package that provides or serves information to other computers.

Spamming: Sending blanket unsolicited messages to others; similar to "junk mail."

Surfing the 'Net: The process of moving or linking from one site to another in the course of reviewing information.

URL: Uniform resource locator, one's address on the Internet. Most Internet addresses begin with "www" or "http://www." The URL of IBM is "www.ibm.com."

User name: See "Log-in" (n).

WWW: World Wide Web, commonly used to refer to the entire collec-tion of resources that can be accessed in cyberspace through the Internet.

Web: See "WWW."

Web page: A particular file or "page" included in a Web site.

Web site: A collection of Web pages; for example, IBM's Web site (www.ibm.com) will consist of numerous Web pages, each of which is devoted to a specific topic. A Web site always begins with a "home page," which is the first screen viewed when the Web site is accessed.

Glossaries of Internet terms can also be found at http://www.matisse. net/files/glossary.html and http://www.sharpened.net/glossary.

C. Conducting Legal Research Online

1. *Getting Started*

Following are the steps in accessing the Internet so you can begin conducting legal research. In brief, you will be using your modem and telephone or cable line to connect to the server of your Internet service provider. When the communication between your computer and the Internet has been established, you will type in a request or click a link, and your browser will send a request for information to the server. The server will send the information to you, and you will view it in your browser. You will "surf the 'Net" by clicking on hyperlinks and jumping to other sites of interest. You may download files or information for later viewing or printing.

- Turn on your computer and proceed to log in, using your log-in identification (sometimes called your "user name") and your password.
- Look for the icon that identifies your Internet service provider, such as AOL.
- Double click on the icon.
- Enter any identifying log-ins or passwords to access your account.
- Type in the word or term you are researching in the search box (if you are in a general search engine such as http://www.yahoo.com). Alternatively, in the address "box" at the top of the page, type in your favorite starting page, such as http://www.google.com; http://www.washlaw.edu; or http://www.findlaw.com. Use this page as your jumping-off point and begin double clicking on the links that interest you. (See Figure 12-1.)
- Note that while most Internet addresses begin with "http://www" you may not need to type in the initial "http" information. Some browsers are configured to recognize "www" by itself. Similarly, in most instances the Internet is not "case-sensitive," meaning that you can often type in either upper- or lower-case letters and they will be recognized and read.

2. *Using a Good Start Page*

There is probably no better tip for conducting legal research on the Internet than to always begin your project with one good "start page." Your start page should be reliable and easy to use. It should be formatted in a user-friendly manner so that you can easily read the print on the screen and locate the information you need without confusing graphics, pictures, and distracting scrolling announcements, advertisements, or pop-ups. The advantage of always beginning at the same place or start page is that you will quickly become comfortable and familiar with

Figure 12-1
Home Page for FindLaw

Legal News   For Legal Professionals   For Students   **FindLaw**®   For The Public   For Business   For Corporate Counsel

| Find a Lawyer | Search FindLaw | Search News | Search Cases & Codes | ▶ More Search Options |

City or Zip: [   ] State ▾ [Find Lawyers!] Name Search / Advanced Search

FindLaw.com Named Best Legal Web Site in Ninth Annual Webby Awards. Learn more.   Old homepage

For The Public   More Topics

Accident & Injury	Lawsuits & Lawyers
Adoption	**Living Wills**
Bankruptcy & Debt	Marriage & Prenuptials
Car Accidents	Medical Malpractice
Child Custody	Mesothelioma & Asbestos
Child Support	Mold
Criminal Law	**Personal Injury**
Construction Accidents	Probate & Estates
Dangerous Products	Product Recalls
Divorce & Separation	Real Estate
DUI/DWI	Securities & Stocks
Elder Law & Aging	Traffic Violations
Employees' Rights	Truck Accidents
Estate Planning	Workers' Compensation
Family Law	Wills
Immigration Law	**More Topics...**

Find a Lawyer
Search FindLaw for the Public

For Small Business   More Topics

Bankruptcy	Forms & Contracts
Business Operations	Immigration Law
Business Organizations	Incorporation
Business Laws	Intellectual Property
Collections	Starting a Business
Employment Law & HR	Taxes
Finance & Banking	**More Topics...**

Find a Lawyer
Search FindLaw for Small Business

For Students   More Topics

Law Schools	Outlines & Exams
Law Reviews	Course Pages
Law Student Resources	Employment
Pre-Law Resources	The Bar

@Justice.com Email

For Legal Professionals

US Law: Cases & Codes
  Federal, States, CA, NY ...
Browse by Jurisdiction
  Federal, Int'l, CA, NY, TX ...
Browse by Practice Area
  Litigation, IP, Labor ...

Thomson Legal Record
Legal Career Center
Legal Forms
Newsletters-Case Summaries

Legal Market Center
  Software, Court Reporters
  Expert Witnesses, more ...

NEW! Thomson Legal Record
View Attorney Litigation Records,
Published Articles, and More!

For Corporate Counsel

Browse by Practice Area
  IP, Corp. Gov., Securities ...
Thomson Legal Record
Research Tools
  Law Firm Articles
  Corporate Contracts

Services for Lawyers
Website Development
Advertising Opportunities
Secure Extranets
Local Resources
@Justice.com Email
CLE

MY FindLaw
  Sign in! or Register

Latest News   Go ▶

◆ **N.Y. Times Reporter Ordered Jailed Over Source**
  - The Plame Leak Inquiry
  - The First Amendment

◆ **Rapper Lil' Kim Gets One Year In Jail For Perjury**
  - Read Her Indictment
  - What Is Perjury?

◆ **49 At Air Force Base Face Immigration Charges**
  - Employers & Immigration

Legal Analysis   Go ▶

Justice O'Connor's Retirement
Why It's Acceptable To Retire In Order To Care For An Ill Spouse
By Edward Lazarus

AND Carol A. Entelisano On The Woes of Wal-Mart: A Lesson In Independent Contractor Practices And Immigration Law (Non)Compliance

More Analysis

Marketplace

◆ Submit Your Legal Issues for Free If you need a lawyer, we're here to help.

◆ Westlaw Cases For $12 Use your credit card to access Westlaw® and KeyCite®.

◆ Boston Lawyers Find important local resources.

Advertise with Us - Link to FindLaw - Send Comments
Help - Disclaimer - Privacy - Jobs - About Us

Copyright © 1994-2005 FindLaw, a Thomson business

the page and it will serve as an excellent jumping-off place for your research tasks.

While there are many start pages from which you can begin your research, following are some well-known legal favorites:

- http://www.law.cornell.edu. The Legal Information Institute at Cornell University Law School is one of the best-known legal sites. It offers overviews of legal topics such as bankruptcy and corporations and allows direct linking to federal and state cases, statutes, court rules, and administrative regulations. The site is highly respected and credible.
- http://www.ll.georgetown.edu. This Web site for the Georgetown Law Center will direct you to cases, statutes, journals, and numerous other legal materials. It offers several tutorials and research guides. The site has a pleasing appearance and is easy to use, and because it is the site of an educational institution rather than that of a commercial enterprise, it is highly credible.
- http://www.washlaw.edu. This site of Washburn University School of Law lists legal materials, courts, and states, making it very easy to locate material of interest. Once again, because it is a site offered by an educational institution, it is highly regarded. Its appearance is plain, nearly stark, without any distracting graphics. (See Figure 12-2.)
- http://www.findlaw.com. This site, offered by FindLaw, a commercial enterprise, is another one of the best-known legal sites. It directs users to a vast array of legal materials, including cases, statutes, forms, reference materials, and legal periodicals. Links to hundreds of sources of interest to legal professionals are provided, including links to each state's bar association, special links for law students, links to help locate attorneys, experts, and consultants, and numerous other links to legal resources. Although FindLaw is a commercial site, it is highly reliable and easy to use. It is the highest-trafficked legal Web site. FindLaw is a specialized legal search engine. You can type in a term in which you are interested in a search box and you will be led to sites that display or use that term. In early 2001, West acquired FindLaw. In recent years, the site has developed a more cluttered appearance and many search requests lead to numerous advertisements, making the site somewhat less user-friendly than others. (See Figure 12-1.)
- http://www.megalaw.com. MegaLaw is a commercial site offering links to thousands of useful law-related sites. The site is easy to navigate and offers ready access to federal and state cases, statutes, court rules, legal forms, and more.

Once you choose a "start page" that you are comfortable with, begin your research task with this page and progress from there. After some time, you may encounter other sites that are of more use to you. If you are a beginner in Internet legal research, however, this method of consistently

Figure 12-2
Home Page for Washburn University School of Law

WashLaw
Legal Research on the Web

- Add Site
- Law Library
- Services

- Search
- Contact Us
- Site Index

- Catalog & Resources
- Check Email

Washburn
School of Law

State Law

All States Information
City Codes

Alabama	Kentucky	North Dakota
Alaska	Louisiana	Ohio
Arizona	Maine	Oklahoma
Arkansas	Maryland	Oregon
California	Massachusetts	Pennsylvania
Colorado	Michigan	Rhode Island
Connecticut	Minnesota	South Carolina
Delaware	Mississippi	South Dakota
District of Columbia	Missouri	Tennessee
Florida	Montana	Texas
Georgia	Nebraska	Utah
Hawaii	Nevada	Vermont
Idaho	New Hampshire	Virginia
Illinois	New Jersey	Washington
Indiana	New Mexico	West Virginia
Iowa	New York	Wisconsin
Kansas	North Carolina	Wyoming

Search for People

All Directories
Area Codes (United States)
Area Codes (International)
Discussion Groups
Experts/Consultants & Investigators
Judges
Law Firms

Libraries, Books, & Reference

American Asso. of Law Libraries (AALLNet)
Books, Magazines, & Newsletters
· Publishers
Freenet and Hytelnet
Indexes
Law Discussion Groups
Legal Dictionaries
Legal Humor
Law Journals
Law Library Catalogs
Legal Software
Legal Vendors
Maps
Politics
Radio
Reference–Legal
Research & Study Guides
Research & Writing
State, Court, County Law Libraries
Stock Market
Television
Travel
Video Conferencing

International Law

Foreign & International Law

Federal Law

Agencies
Armed Services Board of Contract Appeals
Caselaw
Circuit Court Opinions
Code of Federal Regulations
Congressional Bills
Congressional Record
Court Current Awareness
Court of Appeals for Veterans Claims
Court of Appeals for the Armed Forces
Court Rules
Executive Law
Executive Orders
Federal Register
Government Documents
· See complete listing in left column under "Legal Documents."
Legislation & Statutes
Statutes–At–Large
U.S. Code
  · U.S. Code via U.S. House of Representatives
  · U.S. Code via Cornell University
U.S. Constitution
U.S. Court of Appeals
U.S. Court of Federal Claims
U.S. Court of International Trade
U.S. Government Stucture
U.S. Supreme Court
U.S. Tax Code
U.S. Tax Court

Circuits:1st 2nd 3rd 4th 5th 6th 7th 8th 9th 10th 11th D.C.

Law School Information

Course Materials
Graduate Law Programs
Law Professors
Law Schools
Prelaw Students
U.S. Law Schools News Brief

Washburn Law
  · Business and Transactional Law Center
  · Center for Excellence in Advocacy
  · Children and Family Law Center
  · Washburn Centers for Excellence
  · Washburn Law Catalog
  · Washburn Law Library
  · Washburn Study Abroad – Netherlands

Kansas

Kansas Web
  · Kansas Bankruptcy
  · Kansas Decisions
Topeka

beginning any Internet legal research task with your "one good start page" is the best way to gain expertise on the Internet.

Practice Tip

Learning How to Conduct Internet Research

One of the best sites to learn how to conduct research on the Internet is The Virtual Chase (http://www.virtualchase.com), offered by the law firm Ballard Spahr Andrews & Ingersoll, LLP. Subtitled "Teaching Legal Professionals How to Do Research," it provides articles and tips relating to performing legal, factual, and business research. Numerous tips and guides are offered. Don't miss this site!

D. Strategies and Tips for Internet Legal Research

It is far easier to get distracted when researching on the Internet than when researching using conventional print volumes. A site piques your interest so you click on it. When you access that site, another site looks promising and you click on it. When you access that site, yet another intriguing link appears. Before you know it, you are no longer researching search and seizure articles but have begun reviewing stock quotes, checking the weather in Seattle, or perusing movie reviews. The vast amount of information on the Internet is a constant source of diversion and distraction. Staying focused is a continuing campaign.

Understand that when you enter a term in a search box — for example, "patent infringement" — and a list of relevant sites is given, the sites are usually listed in order, specifically, in order of how many times your term, "patent infringement," appears on the site, even in coded or hidden form. Thus, the first site identified is not necessarily the best; it is merely the one that uses or displays the term "patent infringement" most often. Because terms can be hidden in Web sites, you may be directed to a site that offers little or no substantive information about patent infringement. In some instances, you are directed to law firm Web sites and you must wade through marketing material before you can locate substantive material on patent infringement. Other sites, notably Google (http://www.google.com), list the most relevant and useful sites first, making research easy and productive.

Why use the Internet rather than LEXIS or Westlaw? While search strategies using LEXIS and Westlaw are generally more focused and produce more targeted results, LEXIS and Westlaw are fee-based services, while the Internet offers free legal research 24/7. LEXIS and Westlaw, however, have far more complete databases. For example, state court cases are available on the Internet only for the past few years, while LEXIS and Westlaw offer access to nearly all state court cases. Moreover, there is no way to check the validity of a case you locate on the Internet, while LEXIS offers Shepardizing and Westlaw offers KeyCiting to determine whether your case is still "good law."

Following are some tips and strategies to help ensure that your Internet research is as efficient and effective as possible:

1. Take notes. Rather than jumping or linking from site to site, jot down the sites that appear promising. You can access other sites after you have come to a dead end in your present research efforts. Moreover, it is possible that you will get disconnected from the Internet. If you have jotted down sites of interest, you will be able to locate them later.

2. Use the history lists. When you research, you will use links to jump from site to site. To return to the immediately previous site, select the "back" arrow at the top of your toolbar. By continually selecting the "back" and "forward" arrows, you can move through the sites you have visited. Alternatively, you can review the sites you have visited by clicking on the "history" button or on the down arrow at the top of your page that displays the URL of the site you are currently visiting. A drop-down menu will be displayed that identifies the most recent sites you have visited. Select the site in which you are interested and you will be transported there.

3. Use bookmarks. When you determine that there are certain sites you continually visit or that provide you with useful information, "bookmark" them so you can readily return to them. When you are at the Web site of interest, select "Favorites" from the top of your toolbar. This site will be bookmarked as your personal favorite. Once you add a bookmark, the page name appears whenever you click the "Favorites" or "bookmark" icon.

4. Do not spend too much time reading the screen. Reading material on a computer screen is very tiring and causes eyestrain. If a long article or case appears promising, print it and read it in hard copy form.

5. Be aware of gaps in the information available on the Internet. While a law library and LEXIS and Westlaw offer all federal court cases, the Internet presently offers only all the United States Supreme Court cases; lower federal cases are often available only for the past several years. Thus, research on the Internet cannot be a complete substitute for research using conventional print sources or the computerized research systems LEXIS or Westlaw.

6. Evaluate the credibility of Internet sources. Understand that books published in conventional print form have been subject to rigorous fact-checking and editing and that the authors are usually experts in their field. On the Internet, it is nearly impossible to judge credibility. Articles often neglect to identify

an author or date. Contributors to listservs or newsgroups are anonymous. Consider the following in evaluating credibility:

- Some sites are considered more reliable than others. For example, the "gov" (government) sites are probably most authoritative, followed by the "edu" (educational) sites, followed by the "com" (commercial) and "org" (organization) sites.
- Articles posted on the Internet may become quickly stale. Examine the site to determine if material has been recently updated.
- Well-known experts like to get paid for their work; thus, "free" articles on the Internet may not be authored by the best-known experts in a field.
- If the site is a commercial one, its content may be influenced by its owner or publisher. Review advertising on commercial sites to determine if there is bias.

7. Never completely rely on the Internet. While the Internet provides some excellent information and is often the easiest and cheapest way to find a case or statute, it is not a substitute for a law library. Relying solely on the Internet for legal research will result in a research project that lacks in-depth analysis. The best way to find cases interpreting statutes is still the old-fashioned way: reviewing the annotations following statutes in U.S.C.A., U.S.C.S., or the state codes. The Internet, however, is an excellent tool for locating a quick answer to questions such as, "What is the statute of limitations for medical malpractice actions in California?" or "What is the definition of 'copyright' in federal law?" or "What is the citation to the United States Supreme Court case *Brown v. Board of Education*?" To complete a research project, you will need to supplement your Internet legal research efforts with conventional research methods or with computerized services such as LEXIS and Westlaw.

8. Subscribe to a listserv. Consider subscribing or signing up to receive news bulletins or updates from a law-related Web site. You will then be provided with daily or periodic updates related to topics of interest to you. Be cautious: While many of the update or listserv services (such as those offered through www.findlaw.com) are excellent, subscribing to too many listservs or newsgroups will only result in duplication of materials and a clogged inbox.

9. Consider disclaimers. Review the disclaimer section of a Web site. It will tell you the limitations of the site and will usually indicate if you are permitted to reproduce the material on the site. Unless otherwise indicated, material on a private, educational, or commercial Web site is protected by copyright law, and you cannot copy and use it any more than you could photocopy a well-known treatise and then use it. The "gov" sites, however, including

THOMAS, publish materials in the public domain, and any material on these sites is freely available for printing, using, downloading, or other purposes.

E.   Ethical Concerns Regarding Use of the Internet

One of the many uses of the Internet is facilitating communication, or e-mail, between legal professionals and their clients. Additionally, in many instances documents are sent to clients for review. Such messages to clients travel over a variety of networks in an essentially open environment. One concern regarding such communications is that of privacy. Legal professionals owe ethical duties to clients to maintain their information in confidence. Electronic communications are vulnerable to interception, misuse, and alteration. Thus, law firms using e-mail must ensure that the means used to communicate information to clients are secure so that the attorney-client privilege is not inadvertently waived. While not every communication between legal professionals and clients needs to be encrypted, some communications may be so sensitive that they should not be sent unless they are protected by encryption software. Before communicating electronically with clients, determine what your firm or office policy is. At a minimum, communications to clients should be accompanied by the type of notice common on facsimile cover sheets, namely, that the communication is intended only for the recipient; it is private and confidential; if it is received in error it should be returned to the sender and may not be copied or disclosed; and so forth. Law firms that market themselves as knowledgeable about the Internet and cyberlaw may be held to a higher standard of care regarding electronic communications.

A number of individuals have considered whether sending unencrypted e-mail over the Internet violates a client's right to confidentiality. In 1999, the ABA resolved the issue in its Formal Opinion 99-413, which concluded that e-mail communications pose no greater risk of interception or disclosure than other methods of communication (such as regular mail) commonly relied upon as having a reasonable expectation of privacy. Thus, sending client material by e-mail does not violate the ethical duty to maintain a client's information in confidence.

Another ethical concern that has arisen regarding use of the Internet by legal professionals is whether law firm marketing materials constitute advertising and solicitation. In one instance, a law firm sent an advertisement for its immigration services to thousands of different newsgroups, raising the question whether the advertisement was improper client solicitation. State bar regulations regarding attorney advertising must be carefully reviewed to ensure that all materials posted by a firm on the Internet or sent out to newsgroups is in compliance with state codes regulating advertising and client solicitation. Law firm Web sites are usually viewed as communications or "advertisements" rather than as unlawful solicitations; thus, so long as their content is neither false nor misleading, they are permissible. Many law firms include disclaimers on their Web sites that a person's visit to the site does not constitute an attorney-client relationship.

Similarly, legal professionals should be circumspect about providing any information on the Internet that could be viewed as legal advice. The Web sites of most law firms include broad disclaimers that state that information posted on the site is not legal advice, does not create an attorney-client relationship, and is provided for general information purposes only.

F.   Surf's Up: The Best Internet Legal Research Sites

At the end of each chapter in this text, pertinent Web sites have been given to assist you in your research efforts. As you have noticed, there are hundreds of Web sites available, so many that research using the Internet can seem overwhelming. For example, federal cases can be located through at least ten different Web sites. This section of this chapter will give you brief descriptions of some of the best sites for legal and non-legal research.

1.   Best Legal Start Sites

As mentioned earlier, the best way to conduct efficient legal research on the Internet is to have a reliable and user-friendly starting place. Among the best starting places are the following:

• http://www.law.cornell.edu	Excellent starting place for legal issues, many tools, and links to sites.
• http://www.ll.georgetown.edu	Site serving as a gateway or portal to numerous other sites providing primary and secondary law.
• http://www.washlaw.edu	Site offering direct links to cases, statutes, journals, international materials, regulations, and numerous other legal resources by easily arranged links for efficient access.
• http://www.findlaw.com	Commercial site, devoted to legal topics, offering easy and direct linking to cases, statutes, journals, and a wide variety of other law-related materials, including bar associations, codes of ethics, directories of lawyers, legal reference materials (such as dictionaries), and numerous other law-related sources.
• http://www.lexisone.com	Free cases, forms, articles, headline legal news, links to law-related sites, all offered by LEXIS.

- http://www.hg.org   Hieros Gamos, a global legal site with great links to legal and non-legal sites.

- http://www.ilrg.com   Internet Legal Research Group, a meta-index of more than 4,000 Internet legal sites.

- http://www.catalaw.com   Catalog of law resources; easy to use.

- http://megalaw.com   Excellent and easy to use site with hundreds of valuable links to legal materials

2. Best Sites for Locating Cases

- http://www.supremecourt.us   United States Supreme Court site allowing searching by party name, citation, or docket number and providing schedules of arguments, the Court's calendar, and Court rules.

- http://www.uscourts.gov   United States federal courts home page and gateway to federal courts and their cases, briefs, and rules.

- http://www.findlaw.com/ casecode/supreme.html   Site offering searches of United States Supreme Court cases by citation, party name, or keyword.

- http://supct.law.cornell.edu/ supct   Site offering access to United States Supreme Court cases since 1990 and other important historical Court decisions.

- http://www.ll.feorgetown.edu/ find/index.cfm   Site providing easy "point and click" access to federal court opinions and related federal sites.

- http://www.law.emory.edu/ FEDCTS   Map of United States allowing immediate linking to federal court decisions.

- http://www.fjc.gov   Federal Judicial Center home page offering directory of offices, phone numbers, and links to federal courts.

3. Best Sites for Locating Statutes

- http://guide.lp.findlaw.com/ casecode   Site offering direct linking to the Constitution, the United States Code, and statutes from all states.

- http://guide.lp.findlaw.com/ casecode/uscodes   Site offering searching of United States Code by citation, keyword, or popular name.

• http://www.law.cornell.edu/ uscode	Site offering access to U.S. Code. Searching may be done by citation or popular name. Easy browsing of all titles provided.
• http://www.megalaw.com	MegaLaw offers direct access to the U.S. Code as well as all state statutes.
• http://www.law.cornell.edu/ ucc/ucc.table.html	Uniform Commercial Code.
• http://www.nccusl.org	Web site of National Conference of Commissioners on Uniform State Laws offering text of uniform laws.

4.   *Best Sites for Government Materials*

In many instances, you can "guess" at Web site addresses for government agencies. For example, the Web site of the Internal Revenue Service is http://www.irs.gov, and the Web site of the Federal Trade Commission is http://www.ftc.gov. Following are some useful sites for locating federal and state government materials:

• http://www.firstgov.gov	The U.S. government's official Web portal is a gateway to all government information, including federal executive, legislative, and judicial materials, information about agencies, and links to state government home pages.
• http://thomas.loc.gov	THOMAS, offering United States legislative information, bills, voting records, public laws, and other legislative information. (See Figure 10-1.)
• http://www.gpoaccess.gov/ index.html	Providing direct links to the Code of Federal Regulations, *Federal Register*, public laws, *United States Government Manual, Weekly Compilation of Presidential Documents*, and other government materials.
• http://www.fedworld.gov	Guide to federal government resources and reports and links to top government Web Sites.
• http://www.senate.gov	Home page of United States Senate.
• http://www.house.gov	Home page of United States House of Representatives.
• http://www.whitehouse.gov	Home page of White House.

5.   *Best Sites for Locating Forms*

| • http://www.lectlaw.com/ form.html | Forms for litigation, business, real estate, wills, trusts, corporations, and other areas. |

• http://findlaw.com	FindLaw site; select "Legal Forms."
• http://www.washlaw.edu	Select "Legal Forms."
• http://www.megalaw.com	MegaLaw site; select "Legal Forms" for numerous free forms and links to other sites offering forms.
• http://www.allaboutforms. com	All About Forms provides more than 2,000 free legal forms.

6. Paralegal Sites

• http://www.paralegals.org	Site of the National Federation of Paralegal Associations, with networking and career opportunities, code of ethics, professional development information, and links to numerous other law-related sites.
• http://www.nala.org	Site of the National Association of Legal Assistants, with information about the paralegal profession, code of ethics, and links to numerous law-related sites.
• http://hg.org/assistants-assoc.html	Listing of national and state paralegal associations.
• http://www. paralegalmanagement. org	Site of International Paralegal Management Association (formerly Legal Assistant Management Association), which promotes development of paralegal managers.
• http://office.microsoft. com/en-us/ FX011385131033. aspx	Microsoft Office offers tips, tools, and strategies for paralegals.

7. Best Specialty Sites

Note that two sites provide extensive and reliable coverage of numerous law topics: Access Cornell University Law School's site at http://www.law. cornell.edu/topics to select numerous topics such as criminal law, employ-ment law, and family law; access MegaLaw's site at http://megalaw.com and select "Law Topic Pages" to review more than 230 law topics from aboriginal law to zoning law.

Following are some sites for specialized legal topics:

Americans with Disabilities Act Site

• http://www.doj.gov/ crt/ada/adahom1.htm	Home page for ADA; information and links relating to the Americans with Disabilities Act.

Attorneys and Ethics Sites

- http://www.abanet.org

  Web site of American Bar Association.

- www.martindalehubbell.com

  Lawyer locator offered by Martindale-Hubbell.

- http://www.legalethics.com

  Comprehensive site providing ethics information and links to other ethics-related sources.

- http://www.law.cornell.edu/ethics

  Links to ethics materials for each state.

Corporate, Business, and Securities Sites

- http://www.sec.gov

  Web site of the Securities and Exchange Commission, offering full text of filings made by public companies.

- http://securities.stanford.edu

  Securities law and information.

- http://www.hoovers.com

  Profiles of more than 12 million public companies.

- http://www.nass.org/sos/sos.html

  Web site of National Association of Secretaries of State, with direct links to each state's corporations division for access to state forms, filing fees, and more for corporations, LLPs, and so forth.

- http://biz.findlaw.com/states__new.html

  Practical business tools including model business documents.

- http://www.megalaw.com/top/corporate.php

  Numerous corporate links, including links to text of laws and regulations and recent cases.

Environmental Sites

- http://www.epa.gov

  Web site of the Environmental Protection Agency.

- http://www.megalaw.com/top/environmental.php

  Environmental Law Center.

- http://www.law.cornell.edu/topics/environmental.html

  Links to statutes, regulations, federal and state agencies, and recent cases.

Intellectual Property Sites

- http://www.uspto.gov

  Official site of the United States Patent and Trademark Office, offering the text of statutes relating to patents and trademarks, forms, general overviews of trademark and patent procedure and law, and a fully searchable database allowing one to search for registered trademarks and patents.

- http://www.copyright.gov

  Web site of the Copyright Office, offering forms, detailed information on copyright law, and links to other resources related to copyright law.

- http://www.ipmall.fplc.edu

  Web site of Pierce Law Center IP Mall, providing in-depth coverage of intellectual property law and numerous links to other sites and documents.

International Sites

- http://www.un.org

  Web site of the United Nations, offering treaties and resolutions.

- http://www.wipo.org

  Web site of World Intellectual Property Organization, offering text of various treaties.

Labor and Employment Sites

- http://www.dol.gov

  Site of United States Department of Labor.

- http://www.osha.gov

  Comprehensive site of Occupational Safety and Health Administration.

- http://www.law.cornell.edu/
  topics/employment_
  discrimination.html

  Links to employment discrimination cases and statutes.

Legal Research and Writing Sites

- www.ll.georgetown.
  edu/guides/index.cfm

  Providing guides describing how to conduct legal research.

- www.ualr.edu/-cmbarger

  Site providing research, writing, and advocacy resources and links.

- http://www.gpoaccess.gov/
  stylemanual

  U.S. Government Printing Office Style Manual, the authoritative guide to writing, spelling, grammar, and so forth.

- http://press-pubs.uchicago.
  edu/garner

  Exercises and information on legal writing from Bryan A. Garner.

- http://www.nara.gov/fedreg/
  dldhome.html

  Office of the Federal Register's guide to legal writing.

- http://www.bartleby.com/
  index.html

  Providing links to many sources, including portions of *The Elements of Style*, the classic guide to good writing.

- http://www.virtualchase.com

  Site providing numerous articles regarding legal and factual research on the Internet.

Reference Materials Sites

- http://aallnet.org   Site of American Association of Law Libraries.

- http://www.bartleby.com   Featuring dictionaries, *Bartlett's Familiar Quotations*, and a wide variety of reference materials.

- http://www.dictionary.com   Dictionary and thesaurus.

- http://dictionary.law.com   Legal dictionary, searchable by word or phrase.

Tax Sites

- http://www.irs.gov   Site of Internal Revenue Service providing information, forms, and links to other resources.

- http://www.taxprophet.com   Valuable information and links to other tax sites.

8. *Best Non-Legal Sites*

While it is helpful to have a repertory of law-related sites at your fingertips, you also need to be familiar with some basic information sites, so you can determine the weather in the city where tomorrow's deposition will be taken, directions to the client's office, or the last price at which the client's stock was sold. Following are some basic information and reference sites.

- http://starlingtech.com/quotes   Offering quotes (for speeches).

- http://www.tollfree.att.net/tf/html   For looking up toll-free 800 numbers.

- http://www.usps.com   Providing zip codes in the United States.

- http://www.refdesk.com   Offering encyclopedia or thesaurus information.

- http://www.mapquest.com   For obtaining a map and directions to a location.

- http://times.clari.net.au   Offering local time around the world.

- http://www.2docstock.com/res-travel.html   Travel resources, including currency converter, maps, weather information, embassy links, and international dialing codes.

- http://www.intellicast.com   For obtaining weather in a given city.

- http://www.superpages.com   Nationwide yellow pages for finding businesses in the United States and Canada.

• http://www.cnn.com	Providing links to current news, weather, and stories.
• http://www.nationalgeographic.com	Home page of National Geographic Society, offering maps.
• http://www.nyse.com	Providing stock quotes for companies listed on the New York Stock Exchange; offering a ticker symbol "look up."
• http://www.nasdaq.com	Providing stock quotes for companies listed on the NASDAQ Exchange; offering a ticker symbol "look up."

9.   *Where to Start When All Else Fails*

General search engines can provide excellent information and leads. Whether you start with Google, Yahoo!, or some other site, you merely type key words into a search box and you will then be given a list of Web sites that respond to your search terms. In the past few years, Google (http://www.google.com), with its references to more than 8 billion Web sites and its ranking of results by relevance, has become increasingly popular. Google's search engine is so intuitive that you can enter terms such as "17 usc 101" and be referred directly to 17 U.S.C. § 101.

Two new features of Google bear mentioning: You may now install Google on your toolbar so that you may do a Google search at any time from any Web site (access http://toolbar.google.com and follow the directions); Google also provides a variety of special features such as a calculator, stock quotes, ability to track UPS packages, check airline flight status, and more at the address http://www.google.com/help/features.html.

Other general-purpose search engines include the following:

- http://www.ask.com
- http://www.yahoo.com
- http://www.altavista.com
- http://www.excite.com
- http://www.hotbot.com
- http://www.go.com
- http://www.lycos.com
- http://www.metacrawler.com
- http://www.snap.com

10.   *Listservs, Newsgroups, and Blawgs*

Listservs, newsgroups, and law-related web logs (called "blawgs") help legal professionals keep current on cutting-edge legal issues and share information. Technically, listservs are different from newsgroups in that listservs operate through e-mail. For example, the listserv system automatically sends everyone on the mailing list a message at the same time. In a newsgroup, anyone with an Internet connection may view the messages, post their own, or reply to other messages. A blawg is an online journal or web log related to legal topics.

To find out more about law-related listservs and newsgroups, review the site Law Lists Info at http://www.lib.uchicago.edu/~llou/lawlists/info. html, which provides information about law lists, instructions on subscribing and unsubscribing, and a comprehensive list of law-related newsgroups.

You can also subscribe to various newsletters to keep current on law-related topics. One of the best newsletters is published by FindLaw, and once you subscribe, a newsletter will be delivered to your e-mail inbox each weekday. Subscribe at http://newsletters.findlaw.com/ index.html.

Perhaps the best place to review blawgs is at BLAWG (http://www.blawg.org), a site that will link you to well-known blawgs, including May It Please The Court. Another interesting blawg is Feed Me Legal at http://www.feedmelegal.com, with links to numerous other blawgs. Finally, review QuackTrack at http://www.quacktrack. com, an index to more than 100,000 blogs, including more than 1,000 related to law.

G. Cautionary Notes on Internet Legal Research

Many researchers confuse locating information on the Internet with researching. Retrieving a case is not the same as analyzing it. Locating a statute or a case is just the beginning of a research task. Cases that interpret the statute must be analyzed; treatises and restatements should be reviewed; and periodicals, looseleaf services, and other materials should be consulted.

Moreover, much of the material that appears on the Internet is anonymous. Thus, you do not know the credibility or reputation of the author. Just as you would not take medical advice from a stranger on the corner, you should not take legal "advice" from strangers on the Internet corner. Most experts prefer to be paid for their work authoring texts and then to receive royalties based on sales of the material. Those who post materials on the Internet may well be reliable experts. Then again, they may not be; there is no way to know for sure.

There are obviously tremendously valuable research materials on the Internet, particularly the *United States Code*, the *Code of Federal Regulations*, state statutes, and federal and state court cases. Note that all of these materials share one thing in common: They are all materials in the public domain. The well-known legal publishers, such as West and LEXIS, have not posted their valuable databases on the Internet, and you should not expect that these materials will be made available for free.

Finally, always consider that even the most reputable-seeming sites can be subject to abuse. The CIA's and Department of Justice's sites have both been hacked. Thus, at any given moment, the materials you review on the Internet may be false.

As long as you remember these cautionary notes, the Internet remains a valuable and efficient tool for beginning your research project. It can never be a substitute for a full, in-depth analysis of legal materials, such as those you find in a law library or through the well-known and reliable computer research services, such as LEXIS or Westlaw.

Fast Facts: Print Libraries and Digital Libraries

The American Bar Association 2002 Legal Technology Resource Center Survey Report disclosed the following:

- Lawyers spend about as much time using conventional print resources as they do using fee-based online tools such as LEXIS and Westlaw.
- The respondents spent slightly more time using online fee-based sources for federal and state primary law but preferred to use print materials for law reviews, periodicals, and treatises.
- About one-third of all lawyers use e-mail discussion lists for legal research.
- Of the more than 90 percent of lawyers who reported using the Internet to conduct research of any type, more than half (53 percent) favored Google as their general search engine.
- Legal publishers reported that print materials remain their dominant format and noted a strong attachment to print products by legal professionals.

H.   Citation Form

As discussed in Chapter 8, *The Bluebook* and *ALWD* require the use and citation of traditional printed sources, unless the information is not available in such traditional print form or the traditional print source is so obscure that it is practically unavailable. Only in these two narrow instances should citation be made to an electronic source alone. Rule 18 of *The Bluebook* and *ALWD* Rule 3 contain numerous rules for citing to the Internet, some of which are quite complicated. Following are some *Bluebook* examples. Additional examples and examples for *ALWD* format are found in Chapter 8.

- Source available in traditional print format but Internet content is identical, and citation to the Internet will substantially improve access

    Allen v. Dorsey, 520 U.S. 118 (2001), *available at* http://www2. law. cornell.edu/cgi-bin/foliocgi.exe/520+US+118.html.

- Source found exclusively on the Internet

  Jason Newbold, *Cyberspace Law Issues*, 3 N. Va. Tech. J. 16, ¶ 8 (2004), http://www.findlaw.com/articles/1109-019-45.html.

Net Tips

Some advantages of using the Internet:

- Access to Internet sources is available 24 hours a day, from anywhere in the world.
- The Internet provides free access to a wide array of legal materials.
- E-mail, chat rooms, and newsgroup postings allow you to ask colleagues for assistance and information.
- The Internet provides access to many private materials. For example, some paralegals have posted their case briefs on the Internet and invited others to print and use them. Similarly, law firms often publish memoranda on selected legal topics.
- The Internet provides direct access to invaluable legal materials including cases, statutes, and regulations.
- Office space for library books and binders is expensive. The Web stores incredible amounts of information at no cost.

Some drawbacks to using the Internet:

- Many unpublished cases find their way onto the Internet. On the Internet, with its vast virtual space, no one edits out the "dog" cases. Some courts prohibit citations to unpublished decisions. Thus, exercise care and look carefully for the words "published" or "unpublished" at the beginning of a case.
- The Internet is transient. Sites appear, then vanish with no explanation. According to one expert, the average life span of a Web page is 100 days.
- The Internet is anonymous. The "experts" providing advice via e-mail or chat rooms are unknown and unproved.
- Accessing the law is far different from understanding and analyzing it.

Writing Strategies

Be careful not to fall into the trap of thinking that everything on the Internet is in the public domain and can be used without permission. Thus, avoid excessive quoting from Internet sources unless attribution is given or permission is received. In many instances, you can directly e-mail the author of an article or piece and ask for permission to reproduce the material. Consider the credibility of the source before relying on it in your writings.

Be cautious in using terms of art when discussing materials found on the Internet. Provide definitions for terms such as "browser" or "server" and use jargon sparingly so as not to confuse or intimidate readers.

When setting up Internet citations, ensure that the often long string of numbers and letters in the URL break at a natural point at the end of a typed line. Proofread carefully to ensure readers can locate the material you cite. It is easy to transpose numbers and letters in long URL strings.

Assignment for Chapter 12

1. Access THOMAS.
   a. Select "Public Laws" and select for the 108th Congress. What is the purpose of P.L. 108–126?
   b. Review the text of this law. When was it approved?
2. Return to THOMAS and locate information relating to the House Agriculture Committee.
   a. When was the committee created?
   b. How many subcommittees does the Committee include?
3. Return to THOMAS and access the Senate Directory. Obtain information relating to Senator DeWine from Ohio.
   a. When was Senator DeWine born?
   b. How many children does Senator DeWine have?
   c. When was Senator DeWine first elected to the Senate?
4. Return to THOMAS and select "Historical Documents."
   a. Select the Declaration of Independence. When was it drafted?
   b. Select the Federalist Papers. Who is the author of the General Introduction? Who is the author of the 41st paper relating to powers conferred by the Constitution?
5. Access the FirstGov site and select "A-Z Agency Index." Select the American Battle Monument Commission and review information relating to the cemetery in Normandy, France. How many graves of American military dead are in the cemetery?
6. Return to the A-Z Agency Index for FirstGov. Select the Patent and Trademark Office.
   a. Select "Trademarks" and conduct a "basic user search" to locate the trademark "You Deserve a Break Today." When was this mark registered?
   b. Select "Patents" and search for the following patent: No. 6,004,596. What is the invention patented?
   c. For the above patent, select "Images." What is shown on the screen?
7. Access the site MegaLaw and select "Entertainment law." Select ASCAP and then select "ACE Title Search." By selecting "writer," locate the songs written by Billy Joel.
   a. How many songs are identified?
   b. Select "Shameless." Who are identified as performers of the song?
8. Access the site www.uscourts.gov and select information relating to the U.S. Bankruptcy Courts. Review "Bankruptcy Basics." What is a Chapter 7 bankruptcy?
9. Return to www.uscourts.gov and identify the address of the U.S. District Court for the Western District of Texas (San Antonio division).

10.   Access the site for the U.S. Supreme Court (www.supremecourtus. gov) and select "Public Information." Review the Chief Justice's Year-End Report on the Federal Judiciary for 2004.

   a.   Review Section II. Which circuits have not had any new judgeships for twenty years?

   b.   Review Section IV. Why was there an 11 percent increase in civil filings?

11.   Access FindLaw and select for federal laws. In the appropriate search boxes, search for 35 U.S.C. § 101. What does this statute provide?

12.   Return to FindLaw and select for U.S. Supreme Court cases.

   a.   In the citation search box, search for 525 U.S. 121. What is the defendant's name?

   b.   In the party name search box, enter "Bush" and search for *Bush v. Gore*. Who delivered the opinion of the Court? Which justices dissented?

13.   Access the site for GPO Access. Select the *Federal Register*, and browse the table of contents for 2004. Select the *Federal Register* table of contents for Wednesday, December 29, 2004. Review the material for the Education Department.

   a.   Generally, what proposed rule is set forth?

   b.   Review the proposed rule. When must comments be received by the Department of Education on this proposed rule?

State Your Answer

1.   Access either FindLaw or MegaLaw. How many witnesses are needed in your state when a will is executed?

2.   Access the site for the National Association for Secretaries of State (http://www.nass.org). Who is the secretary of state for your state?

3.   Access the site Hoover's at http://www.hoovers.com. Locate information for Delta Air Lines, Inc.

   a.   What is the ticker symbol for Delta?

   b.   What is the company's phone number?

   c.   When is the company's fiscal year-end?

   d.   Who are the company's top competitors?

4.   Access the site FirstGov. Select "State Government" and then "State Legislatures." Locate your state's constitution. What is the title of Article 1 of your state's constitution?

5.   Access Google. Enter "rcw 4.16.005." What are you referred to? What does this section provide?

6. Use Google and locate the home page for Oklahoma Association of Wine Producers.
   a. Who established the first successful winery in Indian Territory?
   b. What was the value of wines in 1996?
   c. Review the copyright notice at the end of the site. What message are you given?

Overview of the Research Process

[R]esearch is never completed . . . around the corner lurks another possibility . . . .

Catherine Drinker Bowen (1959)

A. **How to Begin**
B. **Working with the Authorities**
C. **When to Stop**

Chapter Overview

Among the most difficult tasks in performing legal research are beginning and ending the project. It is easy to become so overwhelmed at the task ahead of you that you become paralyzed at the thought of how and where to commence your legal research. Part of the difficulty lies with the tremendous mass of legal publications: millions of cases, volumes of codes, and so many secondary authorities, including encyclopedias, periodicals, treatises, attorneys general opinions, looseleaf services and other sources, that a researcher does not know where to turn first. LEXIS, Westlaw, and the Internet add another layer of complexity to the research process.

Similarly, once you have begun delving into these authorities, you cannot decide when to stop. It seems there is always one more case to read or source to check. This chapter will offer some practical guidelines on beginning your research task and knowing when to end it.

A. How to Begin

1. Introduction

There are few inflexible rules in legal research. It is not nearly so precise as mathematics, which provides step-by-step logical guidelines to enable you to systematically reach a solution to a problem. In legal research you are asked to provide an answer to a legal question. To reach that answer, there are a number of strategies available to you. While the sheer number of authorities available to consult offers great flexibility, they can also produce great uncertainty. Where do I begin? How do I begin? These are often the questions that so intimidate legal researchers that they are unable to begin the task itself. Moreover, researching is rarely a straight line but often involves backtracking and revisiting sources, requiring patience and flexibility.

While this chapter will offer you some guidelines and strategies on getting started, the best approach, as always, is the one that works best for you. If everyone you know prefers to consult an annotated code first but you like to become comfortable with a topic by reviewing an encyclopedia before you start, then that is the best approach.

You should view legal research as a process. While the answer to a question is the destination you are traveling toward, there are many roads you can follow to reach that destination. Which road you choose to take is not important. In fact, while the number of sources you can examine may be staggering, this in itself is one of the benefits of our system of legal publishing. If you cannot locate a case or statute using one research technique, there are many alternatives available to help you find those authorities.

In fact, there are really only two "rules" that you must follow when you perform legal research: First, if the book you are reviewing has a supplement or pocket part, you *must* check it; and, second, you *must* Shepardize or KeyCite all primary authorities. As long as you always perform these two tasks, you have tremendous freedom in accomplishing your goal of solving the research problem presented to you.

2.   *Thinking Things Through*

While it is tempting to run to the library and start grabbing volumes of books as soon as you are given a research task, the time you spend thinking about a project before you begin is time well spent.

It may be helpful to write the issue on a piece of paper. This will help you "frame" the issue and in and of itself may impose some structure on the project and suggest certain approaches to follow. After you write out the issue, develop a list of descriptive words and phrases. Because almost all legal authorities are accessed by alphabetically arranged indexes and the descriptive word approach is usually the most efficient method of using an index, jot down the words that initially occur to you in examining the issue. These will be the words you will use in examining the indexes or online sources.

After you have selected the most obvious words, facts, and phrases, expand your list by thinking of related words, such as synonyms and antonyms. If you cannot think of any such related words right away, consult a dictionary or thesaurus. Consider the following questions, which will help you develop a list of descriptive words or phrases:

> **Who** is involved?
> **What** is the issue being considered?

Where did the activity take place?
When did the activity take place?
Why did the issue develop?
How did the problem arise?

The former Lawyers Co-op recommended that researchers use the "TAPP Rule" in determining which words to insert into an index:

T Consider the Thing involved in the problem
A Consider the Act committed or the cause of Action (or defense) a party would assert
P Consider the Persons involved in a problem
P Consider the Place involved

By focusing on these four areas, you may be able to determine words you can insert into a descriptive word index so you can be directed to relevant authorities.

Once you have given some initial thought to your project and prepared a list of some key descriptive words and phrases, expand your list by adding legal concepts. Consider the following five issues.

- **Criminal or Civil Law.** You must first determine whether the action is a criminal one brought by the federal government or your state government for a wrong done to society or is a civil one, brought by a private party for a wrong done to him or her. The legal authorities, burdens of proof, and punishments and remedies are far different in criminal cases from those in civil cases.
- **Jurisdiction.** You must consider which jurisdiction's authorities you will examine. In other words, is the issue one of Minnesota law enabling you to limit your research strictly to Minnesota authorities or is the issue one of federal law? If the issue is one of federal law, narrow the focus again by considering which district or circuit is involved. If your question relates to a lawsuit filed for violation of the United States Trademark Act and the lawsuit was filed in the United States District Court for the Northern District of Texas, you should initially consult other district court cases from the Northern District of Texas. Because Texas is in the Fifth Circuit, you should look for other cases from the Fifth Circuit. Similarly, when performing research related to a specific state, restrict your search to authorities from that state. Expand your search to other states only if your state lacks authorities. Remember that your jurisdiction need not follow or adopt the viewpoint of another jurisdiction. While authority from outside your jurisdiction may be persuasive, it is never binding.
- **Action.** Once you have identified the issue as being civil or criminal and state or federal and have identified the particular jurisdiction (for example, specific state or district and circuit), you need to consider the legal issues involved in the case. Ask yourself what the plaintiff would allege in a lawsuit based upon this issue. Would the plaintiff's action be for breach of contract? Personal injuries

arising out of a car accident? Trespass to his property? Improper search of her house by police officers?

- **Defenses.** Once you have considered the plaintiff's "gripes," put yourself in the place of the defendant and ask how the defendant would best defeat the plaintiff. What defenses would a defendant assert? Would the defendant allege that there was no agreement or, if there was an agreement, he fully performed its terms? That the plaintiff's failure to wear a seat belt rather than the defendant's conduct caused the injuries suffered by the plaintiff in the automobile accident? That the plaintiff invited the defendant to come onto the plaintiff's property? That the police were acting pursuant to a proper search warrant?

- **Remedies.** After you look at the issue from the perspective of both parties, consider what remedies the plaintiff is seeking. Is the plaintiff asking for money damages for a breach of contract or injuries sustained in an accident or does the plaintiff want to compel the defendant to repair damage caused to his property by the trespass? If you are unsure as to the theories on which the plaintiff would claim relief, what defenses the defendant would assert, or what remedies the parties desire, consult West's list of more than 400 topics of the law (see Figure 5-2). Use this as a "menu" and pick and choose the words and topics that fit your problem.

Examining these issues will not only help develop a list of descriptive words and phrases that you can look up in the indexes you will be using, it will help ensure that you have the "big picture" focus, which is critical in the legal profession. After all, it is deadly to think that because you have examined an issue from the plaintiff's perspective, you are finished. The plaintiff may, in fact, have a cause of action enabling her to recover substantial money damages. Nevertheless, the defendant may have a perfect defense, which would completely defeat the plaintiff's action. If you examine questions only from one party's side, you will be sure to miss critical issues.

To develop your list of descriptive words, facts, and phrases, use any approach that works best for you. Perhaps rough notes jotted down on a legal pad are sufficient. You may prefer to use index cards or a word processor. It is not the technique you use that matters at this juncture—far more important is the thinking process and analytical skill you will develop by examining these legal issues in a precise fashion.

Figure 13-1 provides an approach that you may wish to follow to help develop the working outline described herein, that is, the road map you use in reaching your destination. This outline will also help you develop words to use in formulating a search using LEXIS or Westlaw. Feel free to copy and use this outline for each project you research.

3.   Tackling the Project

Once you have formulated the descriptive words, facts, and phrases that you will insert into an index, you need to decide with which sources to start.

Figure 13-1
Research Project

Client Name: _____

Client/Billing No.: _____

Name: _____

Assigning Attorney or
Supervisor: _____

Date Given: _____

Date Due: _____

ISSUE/QUESTION/TASK _____

_____

_____

_____

Law Category	Jurisdiction	Descriptive Words/Facts	Synonyms	Antonyms	Plaintiff's Action	Defenses	Remedies
Civil ____ Criminal ____ Administrative ____ International ____ Municipal ____ Other ____	State ____ Federal ____ District ____ Circuit ____						Money Damages ____ Compensatory ____ Punitive ____ Other ____ Equitable Relief ____ Injunction ____ Other ____

There are two categories of books you can consider: primary authorities (cases, constitutions, statutes, and administrative regulations) and secondary authorities (everything else).

Some research questions will immediately suggest or even dictate the source to consult. For example, if the question is what the statute of limitation is for an action by a patient against a doctor for professional negligence, how many days a defendant has to answer a complaint, or the number of people required to witness a will, the answer will undoubtedly be found in a statute. In such cases, you should proceed directly to an annotated code, look up your descriptive words in the index, read the statute to which you are referred, and examine the library references and annotations following the statute to review how courts have interpreted the statute.

It is altogether likely, however, that you will not know which source to consult initially. In such instances, consider the following strategy.

a.   Familiarization

When you are unsure where or how to start a research project, invest an hour or so in becoming familiar with the general area of law involved (contracts, property, wills). The best place to "get your feet wet" is an encyclopedia, which will offer you introductory information on an area of the law. If you live in one of the more populous states that publishes its own encyclopedia, start with this. If your state does not have a local encyclopedia, familiarize yourself with the topic by reviewing C.J.S. or Am. Jur. 2d.

If you read C.J.S., a West publication, and you locate a particularly relevant section, make a note of the topic name and key number (**Partnership** 14, **Negligence** 121, **Contracts** 42) as this will unlock the door to other authorities.

If, on the other hand, you are reviewing Am. Jur. 2d, look for relevant annotations in A.L.R., which can provide extremely useful information to you.

Consider also using specialized treatises for your issue. For example, if the question involves corporations or bankruptcy, browse those sections of the law library to see if a treatise exists for that topic. Treatises provide excellent analyses of legal topics as well as references to supporting case law and other authorities.

b.   Consult Primary Sources

After you have begun to feel comfortable with the subject matter, consult the primary authorities: constitutions, statutes, and cases (and, if applicable, administrative regulations).

(1)   Constitutions

If your issue is a federal one, it may be governed by the United States Constitution. Both U.S.C.A. and U.S.C.S. contain the text of the United States Constitution as well as annotations referring you to cases interpreting constitutional provisions. If your issue is not federal but may involve your state constitution, consult your state's annotated code, which will contain the state constitution as well as annotations to cases construing provisions of your constitution.

(2) *Statutes*

Always examine an annotated code because under the American common law theory of stare decisis, it is not merely the language of a statute or law that controls, but the interpretation of that language by a court.

For federal statutes, consult U.S.C.A. (West's publication) or U.S.C.S. (the LEXIS publication), insert your descriptive words into the indexes to U.S.C.A. or U.S.C.S., and read the statutes to which you are referred. After you read applicable statutes, review the library references and cases to determine how the statute is interpreted by courts.

For state statutes, examine your state's annotated code, insert the relevant descriptive words into the index to the code and review the statute to which you are referred, followed by an examination of the library references and cases construing the state statute. Once you have a reference or citation to a specific statute, consider consulting the Table of Statutes construed in an encyclopedia or treatise, which will direct you to a discussion of treatment and interpretation of the specific statute in which you are interested.

Always check pocket parts or supplements to a code to determine if a statute has been amended or repealed and to find cases more current than those in the hardbound volume.

(3) *Cases*

If a review of the annotations for a constitutional or state statutory provision has not yielded any cases on point, use digests, which function as case finders.

Many experts believe that finding "one good case" solves many research problems. If you can find one good case, you can use its topics and key numbers to locate other cases in the Amerian Digest System (if the case is published in a West reporter) and you can Shepardize or KeyCite the case to find other authorities that mention or discuss your case, thereby leading you to a host of other relevant sources. Note that the advice involves finding one *good* case, not one *perfect* case, because there likely is no such thing as the perfect case for a legal issue.

(a) Federal Issues

For a global approach, use the decennial digest system. For a more focused approach, concentrate on West's federal practice digests (*Modern Federal Practice Digest, West's Federal Practice Digest 2d, West's Federal Practice Digest 3d, West's Federal Practice Digest 4th*). Use the Descriptive Word Index for any of the digests. Insert your descriptive words, facts, or phrases and allow the Index to provide you with a topic name and key number (**Venue** 42, **Larceny** 106, **Zoning and Planning** 123). Look up these topic names and key numbers in the appropriate digest and out will spill the cases you need. Focus on the particular state, district, or circuit you need. All of the West's digests organize the cases according to state or district and circuit, so you may easily locate cases on point.

(b) State Issues

If the issue is governed by state law and you wish to find cases from a particular state, the best case finders are digests. West has published a digest for every state but Delaware, Nevada, and Utah (these states use a regional digest such as the *Atlantic Digest* or *Pacific Digest*). Use the Descriptive Word Index available for each set and look up the words, facts, and phrases listed on your research outline. You will be provided with a topic name and a key number such as **Wills** 56. Insert this topic name and key number into your state digest, and you will be provided with other cases from your state dealing with this same issue.

Figure 13-2 provides a chart showing the sets to review when conducting legal research using primary authorities (in any area other than federal administrative law, in which case you should consult C.F.R.'s Index and any looseleaf services published for that specific topic).

c. Consult Secondary Sources

After you have reviewed the pertinent primary authorities (constitutions, statutes, and cases), consult the secondary authorities to fill in the gaps. Many secondary authorities will refer you to cases, thus ensuring that you find all of the case law relating to your topic. The most commonly consulted secondary authorities are A.L.R. annotations, encyclopedias, periodicals, Restatements, texts and treatises, and law dictionaries.

There are several secondary sources, and you should examine the list of secondary authorities shown in Figure 13-3 and ask yourself if your

Figure 13-2
Chart of Primary Authorities

I. *Constitutions*

Federal: Consult U.S.C.A. or U.S.C.S.

State: Consult your state's annotated code

II. *Statutes*

Federal: Consult U.S.C.A. or U.S.C.S.

State: Consult your state's annotated code

III. *Cases*

Federal: Consult digests (American Digest System or Federal Practice Digests)

State: Consult your state's digest or a regional digest

IV. *Regulations*

Federal: Consult C.F.R.

State: Consult your state's administrative code

Figure 13-3
Chart of Secondary Authorities

Secondary Authority	Coverage	To Use
Encyclopedias		
C.J.S.	All U.S. law	Consult alphabetically arranged index
Am. Jur. 2d	All U.S. law	Consult alphabetically arranged index
State-Specific sets	Law of one state	Consult alphabetically arranged index
A.L.R. Annotations		
A.L.R. Fed.	Federal issues	Consult Index to A.L.R.
A.L.R., A.L.R.2d, 3d, 4th, & 5th	State & common law topics	Consult Index to A.L.R.
Texts and Treatises	Law related to one topic	Consult alphabetically arranged index or table of contents
Legal Periodicals	Various topics	Consult *Index to Legal Periodicals & Books* or *Current Law Index*
Restatements	Various topics	Consult alphabetically arranged index to each Restatement
Attorneys General Opinions		
U.S.A.G. Opinions	Federal topics	Consult alphabetically arranged index
State A.G. Opinions	State topics	Consult alphabetically arranged index
Dictionaries	Legal words and phrases	Look up alphabetically arranged words or phrases
Martindale-Hubbell Law Digests	International and state law	Consult list of states and countries arranged alphabetically
Form Books	Various topics	Consult alphabetically arranged index
Uniform Laws	Various topics	Consult *Uniform Laws Annotated, Master Edition* and *Directory of Uniform Acts and Codes*
Looseleaf Services	Various topics	Consult alphabetically arranged index
Jury Instructions	Federal or state	Consult alphabetically arranged index

issue would be addressed by the particular authority in question. If so, review the authority. You need not examine every secondary authority for every issue you research. It is possible that a review of a treatise and an A.L.R. annotation may provide you with such useful information as well as sufficient references to cases that you need not examine other secondary authorities.

d.   Miscellaneous Research Guides

In addition to the primary and secondary authorities discussed above, there are a few other sources that you may wish to consult when performing research. Consider using *Shepard's Citations* or KeyCite not only to let you know whether the authorities you rely upon are still good law, but to lead you to other sources. *Shepard's* and KeyCite will refer you to law review articles, opinions of the attorneys general, and annotations that mention your case, statute, or constitutional provision. It is possible that these authorities have so thoroughly examined an issue that for you to conduct additional research would be "reinventing the wheel."

Do not forget to use common sense. If the question can be easily answered by an individual or organization, call or write. Thus, if your question relates to zoning in your county, contact your county supervisor or the county zoning officer. If your question relates to the current minimum wage, contact a local employment agency. Many basic questions can be answered by Internet legal research techniques.

Browse the library for useful materials. For example, if your issue deals with bankruptcy, locate the section of the law library containing books related to this topic. Scan the shelves for helpful sources. When you come to a dead end, ask your law librarian for assistance.

Use the Research Game Plan shown in Figure 13-4 to ensure you have consulted all applicable sets of books. Fill out the plan as you perform your research to verify that your research has been thorough and has focused on both primary and secondary authorities. Identify the particular source you consult and then rate its helpfulness or value to you on a scale of 0-10, with 10 being the highest. If you later have only a vague recollection of a source that provided valuable information, the Research Game Plan may jog your memory. It also serves as a reminder to check all pocket parts and to Shepardize or KeyCite all primary sources.

e.   Strategies for Effective Research

Following are eight hints to ensure your research is sufficiently thorough:

(i)   Always examine the statutes. Use an annotated code because it will refer you to cases.

(ii)   Use encyclopedias (C.J.S., Am. Jur. 2d, or a local set for your state) to obtain introductory information about the issue you are researching.

(iii) If you cannot locate cases through an annotated code (because the issue is not dealt with by statutes), use digests: The decennial digests can be used for a global approach; the federal

Figure 13-4
Research Game Plan

Source	Specific Source & Section Consulted	Date Consulted	Rating
Encyclopedia	_____	_____	_____
Constitutions	_____	_____	_____
Codes/Statutes	_____	_____	_____
Annotations following statutes	_____	_____	_____
Disgests (topic _____, Key Number _____)	_____	_____	_____
A.L.R. Annotations	_____	_____	_____
Texts/Treatises	_____	_____	_____
Legal Periodicals	_____	_____	_____
Restatements	_____	_____	_____
Attorneys General Opinions	_____	_____	_____
Dictionaries	_____	_____	_____
Martindale-Hubbell	_____	_____	_____
Form Books	_____	_____	_____
Uniform Laws	_____	_____	_____
Looseleaf Services	_____	_____	_____
Jury Instructions	_____	_____	_____
Experts Consulted	_____	_____	_____
Law Librarian Assistance	_____	_____	_____
Computer-Assisted Legal Research	_____	_____	_____
Internet	_____	_____	_____
All Pocket Parts and Supplements Checked	_____	_____	_____
All Primary Sources Shepardized or KeyCited	_____	_____	_____

practice digests can be used for federal cases; and state and regional digests can be used to locate cases from a particular state or region.

(iv)   If there is a well-known treatise or text on this topic, examine it because it will provide excellent analysis as well as references to cases.

(v)   For a complete overview of a topic, consult A.L.R. (or A.L.R. Fed. for federal issues).

(vi)   For discussions of new or controversial issues or a thorough examination of an issue, find legal periodicals through the *Index to Legal Periodicals & Books* or *Current Law Index*.

(vii)   If a looseleaf service is devoted to the topic you are researching, examine it; it will provide an exhaustive treatment of the topic.

(viii)   Use *Shepard's Citations* or KeyCite to locate other cases, legal periodical articles, attorneys general opinions, and A.L.R. annotations.

━━━━━━━━━━   Practice Tip   ━━━━━━━━━━

Just Ask!

Georgetown Law Center recommends considering the acronym JUST ASK before you start any research project.

J   **Consider the *jurisdiction*. Federal? State? Administrative agency?**

U   **Follow *useful* leads by asking experts and colleagues for help.**

S   **What is the *scope* of your project? Is your teacher or supervisor looking for in-depth analysis or a quick review?**

T   **What *terms of art* apply to the project? What terminology do people use when discussing the problem?**

A   **Be sure you know the meaning of any *acronyms* used by others in describing the research issue.**

S   **Ask what *sources* might be of help, such as journals, looseleaf services, and online databases.**

K   **Consider the *key money constraints*. How many hours can be billed to the project?**

(from http://www.ll.georgetown.edu/lib/guides/just_ask.html)

B.   Working with the Authorities

1. *Note-Taking*

As you begin to read the primary and secondary authorities, you need to develop some focused plan for taking notes. Ultimately, the results of your research must be communicated to someone either by way of a letter to a client, an internal office memorandum, or a brief submitted to a court, and the notes you take will form the basis for your written project. There is nothing more frustrating than beginning to write your project, having a vague recollection that some source provided a perfect analysis or quote, and then being unable to find a reference to it in your notes. Equally frustrating is having to go back to the law library or go online at additional expense to a client to obtain complete citations because your notes do not reflect the date of a case or the page of a quotation.

These time-consuming tasks can be avoided by effective note-taking during the research process. This way you do not have to waste time later by retracing your steps to locate information you should have obtained earlier. Effective note-taking requires some practice and is often developed through trial and error. Once you neglect to include the page of a quotation in your notes, thus necessitating another trip to the law library, you will not make the same mistake twice.

Notes that can be used to help you write your project are more than scribbling on a legal pad. If you simply jot down phrases, parts of cases, and isolated sentences on pages in a pad, you will find they are a muddle when you later try to use these notes to construct a written project, with information relating to one issue being hopelessly intertwined with information relating to entirely separate issues.

a. Organizing Your Notes

You should develop a system for taking and organizing notes during your research efforts so you can effectively use these notes to write your project. One of the best approaches is to use a looseleaf notebook that is divided into separate sections through the use of tabs or dividers. You can devote each section to a particular issue. For example, you could use the first section to reflect information relating to the standard of care of physicians, the second section to record information relating to conduct constituting a breach of that standard, the third section to contain notes relating to defenses the doctor could assert, and the fourth section to relate to damages for injuries caused by the physician's breach of his duty of care or malpractice. Consider leaving at least one section untitled for a while because you will invariably discover issues during the course of your research that you had not originally considered.

As you research you may discover that each of these major issues comprises sub-issues. Either insert new tabs or dividers so you can compile information relating to these newly discovered sub-issues, or assign a number or letter to each sub-issue and reflect that in the margin next to any notes relating to it.

If you find that some authorities or cases discuss more than one issue, take notes in one section and in the other(s) simply insert a reminder to review the authority, such as the following: "For discussion of damages in malpractice action, see *Jones v. Smith*, 421 N.E.2d 609, 614 (Ind. 1989), Tab I." Alternatively, you can photocopy the case and "cut and paste" it by placing certain portions of it in your Tab I section and other portions in your notes for Tab III. An advantage of using a looseleaf notebook is that you can shuffle sections of your argument around. If you decide Section II should be discussed after Section IV, it is easy to switch the pages in your notebook.

Some students prefer to use looseleaf sheets (rather than a binder or spiral notebook), label each sheet with a topic name (Duty of Care, Breach of Duty, Damages), and then record information relating to these topics on the appropriate pages. Often students will use different colors of looseleaf paper for different issues so that white sheets relate to the issue of Duty of Care, pink sheets relate to Breach of Duty, and blue sheets reflect notes relating to Damages for such breach.

Other individuals find index cards useful and label each card with a topic name (Duty of Care, Breach of Duty, Damages) and devote a separate card to each case, law review article, A.L.R. annotation, or other authority, briefly summarizing the case, article, or annotation. Some individuals prefer using different colored index cards for different issues. This system allows immediate recognition and retrieval of the sections you later desire to review.

The advantage to any of these techniques is obvious: When your research is completed, it is already partly organized and prepared for the writing stage. All of your information relating to Duty of Care, Breach of Duty, or Damages is in one place rather than hopelessly scattered among numerous pages.

Another advantage of keeping notes related to separate issues in separate sections is that you can take your separate sheets of paper or index cards and shuffle them around so that you can physically organize the results of your research and determine the order in which you will discuss the cases relating to damages or some other topic. For this reason, try to keep your notes about any one case, law review article, annotation, or other authority to one page or one index card. The purpose of taking notes is to record only the critical portions of a case, not to write out the entire case in longhand.

You can always photocopy the case itself so you will have it to refer to when writing your project, but for note-taking purposes, be brief and keep notes to one page or one index card per authority. If you are photocopying cases, invest a bit of time and always maintain them in alphabetical order. Then, when you need to refer to them when writing your project, you will be able to locate the case you need easily. Many individuals prefer to photocopy almost all cases they intend to rely upon (and, in fact, some attorneys insist that finished research projects be accompanied by copies of all cases cited therein).

If you photocopy cases, you will invariably mark or highlight the significant portions of the case so when you review it later you can readily locate its relevant sections. Once again, consider imposing some order on this process by using different color pens or highlighters to reflect different issues so that the portions of the case dealing with a physician's standard of care are highlighted with yellow while the portions of the case relating to damages are highlighted in pink. When you later review the case, you will then be able to quickly locate the portions you need. Do not be afraid to record your own thoughts and reactions on your copies of cases.

An interjection such as "perfect" or "oops" may later jog your memory as to the value of a case you read days earlier. You should consider rating the cases on a scale of 1 to 10 so you will have an easier time of weeding out weaker authorities.

New software packages allow students to simulate highlighting, bookmarks, and sticky notes as they take notes on their laptops while in the law library. This form of electronic note-taking is easy and convenient, and hyperlinks to cases and authorities of interest can be inserted in the notes. Any kind of text can be stored in your "infobase," including cases you have downloaded, class notes, or other materials. You can insert notes wherever you like, just as you would attach sticky notes to a text you read. You can highlight portions of text. Finally, you can search the entire text of your infobase, thereby allowing you to locate immediately your notes and information on "jurisdiction" or "venue."

No one method of note-taking is superior to another. The method that works best for you is the best method. For those students who are decidedly "low tech" or "technologically challenged," do not despair: If a great number of judges in the country do not need computers to do their work, it is likely you can succeed as they do and as legal professionals have done for hundreds of years — with pen and paper.

b. Contents of Notes

If your notes are to be of any assistance to you in constructing your written project, they will need to be more than random words or isolated phrases. The best approach for taking notes on cases is to brief the cases. You will recall from Chapter 4 that briefing a case is, in fact, described as taking notes on a case. Thus, any sheet or index card relating to a case should be a brief of the case and should include the following elements:

- complete citation
- brief overview of facts
- procedural history
- issue(s)
- reasoning
- holding

It is not necessary that your sheet of paper or index card be perfect. It should contain only the most important and relevant information. You can "fill in the gaps" when writing your project by referring to your photocopy of the case itself. The sheet of paper or index card is only for reference purposes. Do not expect to be able to put your project together by simply assembling your sheets of paper or organizing your index cards and turning them over to a word processor or secretary. Your notes provide only the framework for your project. They are not the project itself.

For taking notes on other authorities such as law review articles or A.L.R. annotations, simply summarize the most relevant points. While these authorities may be quite lengthy and often exceed 20 pages, they are secondary authorities, and thus you should not rely too much on them. Such authorities serve as great backups to the cases you rely upon and, because your project will not solely depend upon these authorities, you should be able to record the information you need on one or two pages or index cards. Often, in fact, these authorities are used to introduce you to an area of the law or provide an overview of a topic. While they may be of invaluable help in educating you on a topic, you may decide not to cite these authorities at all in your project, preferring instead to rely upon the primary authorities to which they referred you.

c. Complete Notes

Your notes will be of little help to you if you are constantly returning to the library or going online to obtain additional information. Your goal upon completion of the research phase of your project is to return to your office to write the results of your research, having everything you need in your notes. If you need to return to the library or log-on again during the writing phase to get a parallel cite or the name of the author of a law review article, your note-taking was ineffective.

It is a great temptation when researching simply to jot down part of a citation and then start taking notes, figuring you will obtain the complete cite later. Resist this temptation and always include all of the information you will need for citation purposes in your notes. Follow *Bluebook* or *ALWD* form. This will save time later.

For cases, record the complete name of the case, parallel citations, and date. If your notes contain a quote from the case, indicate the page of the case on which the quote appeared so you can later include this pinpoint in your citation.

When taking notes, clearly identify whether your notes reflect a quote or are merely paraphrasing the judge's or author's statements. It is nearly impossible to remember days after you performed the research whether a statement in your notes that "physicians are liable for the harm to their patients proximately caused by their negligent or intentional wrongful acts" is a quotation or your own summary of a case unless your notes remind you. Any system is sufficient so long as it works for you. You may use quotation marks only for direct quotes and then any material not in quotes is a paraphrase; you may label each statement in your notes with a "q" or a "p"; or you may elect to use a different color pen to show a quotation.

It is wise to record the page even a paraphrase occurs on because you may wish later to review the original language in the case or you will likely include in your citation a reference to specific pages and pinpoints, whether or not the statement is a direct quote. Including pinpoints for paraphrasing is expected professional courtesy. Similarly, if your quotation appeared in headnote 6 of a case or you are relying primarily on headnote 6 of a case, indicate this in your notes as **[6]**. When you later Shepardize or KeyCite, you will be able to focus on the treatment of this portion of the case by later authorities and will not waste time reading later cases relating to headnote 12 when you were not relying on that portion of the case.

Your notes should reflect whether you have checked the pocket part or supplement to the authority and whether any information was found therein as this may need to be included in your citation. Similarly, notes relating to primary authorities should record that they have been She-pardized or KeyCited and are still "good law." You can simply include a "box" on each page or index card and complete it as follows:

PP/Supp ___x___

Info in main vol. ___yes___ or p.p./supp. ___no___

Shep. ___x___ on ___2/6.___ Problems/concerns ___**None.**___

2. *Staying Focused*

One of the most difficult tasks in performing legal research is staying focused on a specific issue or question. Students commonly report that as they are in the process of researching an issue such as negligence and reading a pertinent case, they come across a reference to what appears to be a promising law review article. Without completing the reading of the case, they then grab the law review article, which refers to two other cases. These new cases are then pulled from the shelves, and they also refer to other promising authorities. At the end of a full morning of research, the student is surrounded by a pile of books, none of which has been thoroughly analyzed and some of which, when later re-read, are a mystery as to their relevance because they discuss topics completely unrelated to the original issue of negligence.

This hopscotch approach to research will invariably lead you away from your answer rather than toward it. The reason it occurs so frequently is that it is incredibly tempting to interrupt your analysis of an issue with the thought that the "perfect" authority is the next one, or that if you do not grab the authority now you will forget about it later.

Train yourself to stay focused on each specific issue. If you are researching a problem, for example, whether a physician is liable for injuries sustained by a patient during surgery when the patient consented to the risks of surgery and violated the doctor's orders prior to surgery, devote yourself to one topic at a time. Decide that the first morning you will only research the general duty of care required of a doctor. If you come across cases or references that relate to the consent issue or the issue of damages, jot these down in the sections of your notebook corresponding to those topics so you can review them later, but do not interrupt your research on the assigned issue.

After you are thoroughly satisfied that you understand a physician's general duties, assign yourself the issue of whether the patient's consent was valid; that is, whether it is wrong for a doctor to obtain, in effect, a release prior to surgery for acts that occur during surgery, and whether the patient had any choice but to sign a written consent without which the doctor would not perform the surgery. If, during the course of research related to these consent issues, you come across other references to the physician's duty of care or damages recoverable in malpractice actions, write them down for future reference, but do not allow yourself to be side-tracked from the consent issue on which you are working. With any luck, when it is time to research your last issue, the question of damages, you will already have a list of promising cases and other authorities to review, thus eliminating the need for you to start at the beginning with encyclopedias, codes, or digests.

The hopscotch effect also occurs during Shepardizing or KeyCiting. For example, in the middle of Shepardizing one case, you may find a reference to a later case that explains your case. Avoid the temptation to leave your Shepardizing and obtain that case. Once again, jot down the reference and then look it up after you have completed your review of all of the volumes of *Shepard's*. If you interrupt your Shepardizing to read a case, you may forget where you are in the Shepardizing process. Thus, when you return to the task, you may assume you completed Shepardizing the original case when in reality you only examined some rather than all of the requisite volumes of *Shepard's*. The exception to this is in computer-assisted Shepardizing or KeyCiting, which allow you to quickly flip back and forth between *Shepard's* or KeyCite and the authorities that mention or discuss your case.

C. When to Stop

One of the most difficult tasks in legal research is knowing when to stop. No one will come up to you in the law library, tap you on the shoulder, and inform you that time is up and your task is complete. Moreover, it seems as if some issues can be researched endlessly. If you read a landmark case, it may refer to five other cases, which you may also decide to read. When it is time to Shepardize or KeyCite these six cases, you may discover that each of the six cases has been mentioned or discussed in ten other cases (as well as numerous law review articles, opinions of attorneys general, and A.L.R. annotations). You now have 60 other cases that could be examined, each of which refers to other authorities and each, when Shepardized or KeyCited, is in turn discussed by other cases and authorities. This process could continue indefinitely and is a bit like a funnel that gets wider and wider. Eventually, you need to call a halt to your research.

1. *Practical Considerations*

Sometimes there is a practical reason for stopping your research. It is possible that the client's claim is for $40,000. You cannot possibly afford to expend $20,000 in legal research and then present the client with a bill after the trial that charges the client $20,000 for legal research and $10,000 for other costs and attorneys' fees, leaving the client with a mere $10,000 recovery. Thus, in many cases, economics will dictate how thorough your research will be. When the client's budget dictates the amount of research that can be performed, you will have to be as efficient and streamlined as possible. Keep track of your hours as you go along and after a few hours report back to your supervisor on your progress and estimate how much longer you think will be required. Before you commence the project, discuss the budget with your supervisor and agree on a strategy and a time to meet and discuss your efforts. When you are given the project, your supervisor may expressly tell you that you should allot five to six hours for research and might even suggest a specific statute or case as a beginning point.

This balance between the duty to research adequately and the economic realities of a case is a delicate one. It is the attorney's task to resolve this issue and give you proper guidance. If you do not receive any instruction, take the initiative and state that for time-management purposes, you would like to inquire as to the date the project is due (this in and of itself may give you a clue as to how thorough the project is to be) and a range of time the attorney estimates for the research.

Research as efficiently as possible. If your research efforts produce a number of potentially relevant cases, all of which look promising but the reading of which would be impractical and time-consuming, adopt a strategy that will produce the best results in the least amount of time. For example, read newer cases before you move on to older cases, read cases from higher courts before those from lower courts, and read cases from your forum jurisdiction before those from a foreign jurisdiction.

If you find that the project is far more complex than you and your supervisor originally anticipated and that the authorities are unclear or conflicting, stop your research and go back to your supervisor, explain your progress thus far and why the issue is more complex than anticipated, and ask for direction. Your supervisor would much prefer to find out after six hours of research that you are having difficulty rather than after 30 hours, which cannot be billed to the client.

Do not be embarrassed to ask for direction or acknowledge that you are having difficulties. If the answer to a question was so easy, everyone would already know it and there would be no need to research it.

Attorneys are always interested in economic efficiency, and if you present your question in a manner that shows you are aware of the economics of a law practice, you will be commended rather than criticized. For example, instead of telling your supervisor, "I can't find any authorities on this, so I'm quitting," state "I haven't yet been able to find any authorities on point. If I can't turn up some leads in the next hour, let's meet and discuss our next step." Alternatively, you can report, "I've spent the six hours you suggested and because the circuit courts are in conflict on this issue, I believe I need two to three more hours. Will the client approve this additional time?"

2. Complex Projects

If the project is complex, you may find yourself in the "funnel position," that is, the situation in which there is an ever-expanding list of authorities that could be reviewed. Knowing when to stop researching this type of project is difficult. It is hard to know if you have gotten the "right answer." Seldom, if ever, is there one perfect case or authority that is directly responsive to your research task. It is far more likely that you find numerous cases that are somewhat responsive and that you must patch together to arrive at an answer.

One clue that your research is complete is that you keep bumping into the same authorities. For example, assume that in the course of reading a 1982 case entitled *Jones v. Smith* you make note of a 1970 case referred to therein called *ABC v. XYZ*. When you later read *ABC*, it discusses the same principle discussed in *Jones*. When you Shepardize or KeyCite *ABC*, you are referred to *Jones* and a 1985 case entitled *Henderson v. Powell*. A reading of *Henderson* reveals the same general discussion you read in the earlier cases. When you Shepardize *Henderson*, you are referred to a 1990 case called *O'Connell v. Rowe*. A reading of *O'Connell* discloses a discussion of the previous cases, *Jones* and *Henderson*.

These references to the same authorities are a signal that the principle originally set forth in *ABC* has been continually repeated by later cases. If nothing significant or new is added by the line of cases decided after your "best" case, and Shepardizing or KeyCiting reveals that the cases you rely on are still valid, stop researching. This circular procedure is a hint that your research is complete. You may want to "flesh out" your research by reviewing a law review article or other secondary authority, but if these confirm the results of your earlier research, you will know you have been sufficiently thorough.

Often beginning researchers lack the confidence to stop researching and are convinced there is one perfect case that they will find if they can only devote enough time to the effort. This is a fallacy. Seldom, if ever, is a perfect case sitting on the shelves — for the reason that no two cases are exactly alike. You will find cases that are similar to yours, and you will be able to argue that because the cases are similar the reasoning in the reported cases should apply to your particular problem. It is highly unlikely, if not impossible, however, to find an identical case, so do not waste your time looking for one. Once you have cases "on point" (similar legal issues as your case, similar facts as your case, from the highest courts in your jurisdiction, and that are still valid) this is sufficient.

Another sign of lack of confidence in beginning researchers is their unshaken conviction that they cannot be right and there must be some case hidden in the library that will render meaningless their efforts. If you have examined the statutes (and, if applicable, constitutional provisions) from your jurisdiction as well as the cases interpreting the statutes and have updated the statutes by checking the pocket parts and Shepardizing or KeyCiting the statutes and cases, and the authorities are in agreement, your research is concluded. It is only when you neglect to review the cases interpreting a statute or fail to update by checking pocket parts and Shepardizing or KeyCiting that your research is an unexploded mine field.

After you gain confidence in your research skills through practice, you will be able to trust your instincts and say, "I'm finished," rather than thinking, "I can't possibly have found the right answer even though 22 cases all say the same thing so I'll continue to look for something to prove me wrong."

3. Quick Questions

Often your research task is specific and well-defined. You may be asked to check how many days a defendant has to provide answers to interrogatories propounded by a plaintiff or what the statute of limitations is to sue for breach of contract in your state.

Such specific questions are easily answered by examining your state's annotated code. Review the statute and a few cases construing it. Update and Shepardize or KeyCite the authorities to determine they are still valid. Generally, this approach will be sufficient to answer questions that are straightforward.

4. Established Issues

If your research task relates to an established area of the law, such as the elements of a cause of action for breach of contract, a landlord's duty to provide habitable premises to a tenant, or the damages recoverable in fraud actions, you may find a multitude of authorities. Some of the authorities may be decades old, and there may be numerous cases, periodical articles, A.L.R. annotations, and discussions in texts and treatises. These authorities, however, may reflect remarkable unanimity. That is, researching an issue related to an established area of law usually results in numerous authorities in agreement.

Determining when to stop researching will be relatively easy because the authorities will begin referring to each other over and over again. Once you update and Shepardize or KeyCite to ensure that the primary authorities are still valid, your task is complete.

Conversely, research in newly emerging areas of law can be frustrating because there will often be substantial conflict among courts as judges grapple with a difficult issue and try to establish rules of law. Thus, research relating to the liability of an Internet service provider for defamatory statements made on a Web site or research relating to contracts for hiring a surrogate parent will be fraught with conflict. Often periodical articles or A.L.R. annotations will be most helpful because they will offer an overview of new topics and attempt to explain and reconcile conflicts. Update a law review article with *Shepard's Law Review Citations* and update A.L.R. annotations through the use of pocket parts. Remember computer-assisted legal research, which has the ability to locate hundreds of documents if you carefully formulate the search query.

Research for these newly developing legal topics is difficult because often you cannot find one single right answer. If this is the case, you simply need to follow the standard research techniques and realize that your conclusion may well be that the authorities are uncertain and conflicting.

5. Issues of First Impression

Often the most difficult research task is the one that yields no results whatsoever. Thus, after hours of research, you may not have found any authorities. There are two conclusions to draw from this occurrence: "There are no authorities relating to this issue" or "I must be doing something wrong because I can't locate any authorities." Beginning researchers will always draw the second conclusion and refuse to stop researching even though they are retracing their steps over and over again.

It is possible that an issue is one of "first impression," that is, one not yet considered in your jurisdiction. Unfortunately, there is no foolproof way to determine this. There is no list produced by the legislature or courts of "topics not yet considered." There are, however, two techniques you can use to assure yourself that it is not your research strategy that has resulted in a total lack of authorities.

First, select a populous and varied jurisdiction such as California or New York, which has a rich body of law. Use the same research techniques, sets of books (annotated codes, digests), and descriptive words that you used in your home jurisdiction. If you obtain results, you will know that your strategies, choice of books, and descriptive words were sound and that the lack of authorities in your jurisdiction is the result of an issue of first impression, not misguided research efforts.

Second, computer-assisted legal research, with its ability to search for thousands of documents that contain specific terms, will help verify your research techniques. If your search query is "blood and product and infect! and HIV or AIDS/50 bank" and after you have selected the database for all Utah statutes and cases you obtain no references whatsoever, you should feel more confident that Utah has simply not yet considered this issue. To achieve a final comfort level, contact the service representatives for LEXIS or Westlaw and ask for assistance in formulating a search.

6. How Many Authorities Are Enough?

Beginning researchers usually want to know how many cases or authorities should be cited in a brief or project. There is no answer to this question. As a general rule, however, you will need fewer authorities to support a well-established principle and more authorities to discuss an emerging area of law or one in conflict.

Is one citation enough? It is possible that a single citation may suffice to answer a quick question. Thus, the question of how many days a defendant has to answer interrogatories propounded in a federal court action can be responded to as follows: A party served with interrogatories has 30 days after the date of service to answer or object to the interrogatories. Fed. R. Civ. P. 33(a). A further review of the Federal Rules of Civil Procedure, however, discloses that the answering party has three extra days to respond if served by mail and that if the last day is a Saturday, Sunday, or holiday, the party has until the next business day. Fed. R. Civ. P. 6(a), (e). More complex questions, such as whether a landlord may turn off the heat of a tenant who has not paid rent, may require careful reading of several statutes, cases, and other authorities.

Remember the weight of authorities: Primary authorities (cases, constitutions, and statutes) must be followed by a court. Secondary authorities (encyclopedias, periodical articles, annotations, and so forth) are persuasive only. Thus, you should always aim to have at least one primary authority to support each of your arguments. Do not make the mistake of assuming, however, that if there are 12 cases from your jurisdiction, all of which state that punitive damages are recoverable in fraud actions, you should discuss and cite all 12. Courts are impatient with string citing or repetitive arguments. Exercise discretion and select the most articulate case or the one most similar to your case. Consider selecting the landmark case in this area and then one recent case from your highest court. See Figure 13-5.

Cite secondary authorities if they provide a concise analysis of a topic or if the author is a well-respected and renowned authority in that legal field. Consider combining primary authorities with a secondary authority to support your argument. Do not, however, believe that legal research is like a recipe and that if you always cite two cases and a law review article your argument will win. Different topics require different levels

Figure 13-5
A Blueprint for Legal Research

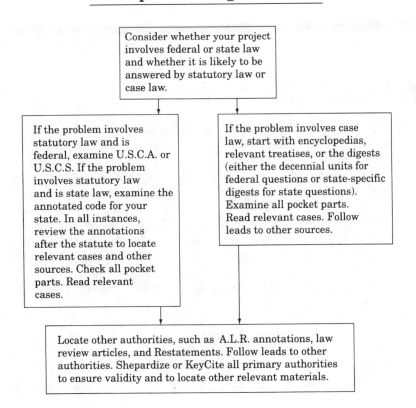

Consider whether your project involves federal or state law and whether it is likely to be answered by statutory law or case law.

If the problem involves statutory law and is federal, examine U.S.C.A. or U.S.C.S. If the problem involves statutory law and is state law, examine the annotated code for your state. In all instances, review the annotations after the statute to locate relevant cases and other sources. Check all pocket parts. Read relevant cases.

If the problem involves case law, start with encyclopedias, relevant treatises, or the digests (either the decennial units for federal questions or state-specific digests for state questions). Examine all pocket parts. Read relevant cases. Follow leads to other sources.

Locate other authorities, such as A.L.R. annotations, law review articles, and Restatements. Follow leads to other authorities. Shepardize or KeyCite all primary authorities to ensure validity and to locate other relevant materials.

of analysis, and you will need to exercise your own discretion to determine how many authorities are enough.

Practice Tip

When to Stop Researching

Although there is no perfect rule when to stop conducting legal research, consider that it is time to stop when:

- **You keep bumping into the same authorities and their commentary is much the same;**
- **You have read the same point in a number of different sources, with nothing new added;**
- **The same citations keep showing up; and**
- **Your Shepardizing or KeyCiting reveal no changes to the law.**

CyberSites

http://www.ualr.edu/ ~cmbarger/Research.htm	This site includes numerous links to sites to enable you to conduct legal research.
http://comp.uark.edu/ ~ksampson/ research2.html	This "legal research libarary" includes good links to state and federal sources as well as a research outline.

Ten Tips for Effective Research

1. ***Be prepared.*** The time you spend thinking about a project before you begin is time well spent. Give yourself a few minutes to plan your research strategies.
2. ***Be flexible.*** If the books you need aren't on the shelf or if your efforts are not yielding results, switch to another set of books.
3. ***Be thorough.*** Check all pocket parts and supplements to be sure you have the most recent materials. Shepardize or KeyCite all primary authorities to make sure the law is still "good." Take complete notes. Be serupulous in transcribing citations to avoid backtracking. Consider a variety of research methods (print sources, CALR, and the Internet) to achieve the best results.
4. ***Be patient.*** Research can be a difficult process. Expect some roadblocks.
5. ***Be organized.*** Tackle one topic or issue at a time. Do not allow yourself to get sidetracked on a minor issue or diverted in another direction. Address each research issue with a laser, not a buckshot, approach.

(continued)

Ten Tips for Effective Research *(Continued)*

6. **Be efficient.** Gather together all the materials you need so you don't waste time wandering around the library.
7. **Be creative.** If all of your colleagues are beginning their research in one set of books, begin in another to avoid the crowd as well as the crowd mentality. Try contacting agencies and individuals and asking for assistance rather than depending exclusively on the books in the stacks.
8. **Be wary.** Make sure you approach your problem from all angles. Play devil's advocate. What will the adversary argue?
9. **Be resourceful.** Look for law review articles and annotations on your legal topic. If someone has already written a through analysis of an issue, why reinvent the wheel?
10. **Be Calm.** If you get stuck, ask a librarian for help. That's what they're there for.

Writing Strategies

As you prepare to write, invest time in "brainstorming." On a piece of paper, jot down anything that comes to mind relating to the project. You can later omit any ideas or topics that are not useful. The mere process of starting to write something will get your creative juices flowing, and some ideas that you originally believe are farfetched may later develop into a creative line of reasoning.

If you initially think of more than one way to express a thought, write down both expressions. Later you can decide which to omit or perhaps you will find a way to combine both ideas.

If an argument occurs to you during the research process, write it down as clearly and completely as possible. You may later be able to "lift" these notes intact and place them verbatim into the written project. That is, the more complete your note-taking is, the easier it will be for you to write the project. In some instances, your notes will almost be the equivalent of a first draft. If your "note-taking" consists merely of photocopying cases and passages of writings, however, you will need to devote far more time to the initial draft as much work needs to be done to develop what is in those cases and writings into a reasoned and concise project.

State Your Answer

1. Access the site http://www.ll.georgetown.edu/lib/guides/cost.html. What is the last tip provided to help keep research costs under control?
2. Access the "Research Steps Tutorial" at the site http://www.lawschool. cornell.edu/lawlibrary/Finding_the_Law. What is the beginning stage of legal research?
3. Access the site http://www.lectlaw.com/study.html and review "Ten Easy Steps to Legal Research." What is the final step?

Legal Writing

Back to Basics

The writer who neglects punctuation, or mispunctuates, is likely to be misunderstood . . . .

Edgar Allan Poe (1848)

A. The Mechanics of Writing
B. Grammar, Spelling, and Punctuation

Chapter Overview

The goal of legal writing is to communicate. The style of the communication may simply be informative, for example, to inform the reader of certain facts or events, or it may be persuasive, for example, to persuade the reader to adopt a certain point of view. No matter what style or form legal writing takes, its mechanics (grammar, spelling, and punctuation) must be correct. Failure to use good grammar results in cloudy and incomprehensible writing. Incorrect spelling casts doubt on your skill and credibility. Improper punctuation results in an unclear project.

This chapter will review these basics of writing so your final product will effectively communicate to its intended audience, whether it is a client, an adverse party, or a court.

A. The Mechanics of Writing

Even if your research is flawless and you have found primary authorities "on point," these will do you no good unless you can communicate your results to a reader. Flaws in the communication process, such as improper spelling, awkward word usage and sentence construction, and errors in punctuation distract your reader from your message, making the reader doubt your abilities and reflect on your carelessness.

Some legal professionals have strong writing backgrounds and are comfortable with grammar, spelling, and punctuation. Others have more scientific or technology-oriented backgrounds and are unused to writing. Even those individuals who have done a great deal of writing in college or on the job may be unfamiliar with the strictures of legal writing. For example, typical undergraduate writing is marked by more flexible punctuation. Punctuation in legal writing is considerably more rigid because a misplaced or omitted comma can change the meaning of a statement. There is vigorous debate among grammarians regarding some punctuation marks and usages. Select a well-known text such as *Chicago Manual of Style* or the U.S. Government Printing Office *Style Manual* (available online at http://www.gpoaccess.gov/stylemanual) and use it to support your position, if necessary.

After years of communicating primarily by telephone, many people in the business fields are now communicating more in writing. Thanks to e-mail, electronic chat rooms, and blogs, people are writing more now than ever before. Unfortunately, communicating via computer is often so informal that careless errors are perpetuated. Thus, while many of us may be writing more, we're also writing worse, with less attention to spelling, punctuation, and proofing. Do not be seduced into thinking that because e-mail to your supervisor or colleagues is easy and informal, it can be incorrect. The way you communicate communicates a message about you. Invest the time and effort in producing a clear and well-written document or message every time you write and no matter what the means of communication. A final word of caution about e-mail: Most law firms and businesses have strict policies about the use of e-mail for business purposes only. Moreover, the security of e-mail is open to question. Many employers monitor e-mail use. Therefore, do not use e-mail for anything other than business reasons and do not say anything you wouldn't want your boss to read.

While there are many guides to grammar, perhaps the best known and easiest to understand is *The Elements of Style* by William Strunk, Jr., and E.B. White. First introduced in 1919, *The Elements of Style* (now in its fourth edition) sets forth in clear and concise fashion principles of usage and composition with illustrative examples. Some writing instructors recommend a cover to cover re-reading of "the little book" each year to refresh one's understanding of the fundamentals of English style. Portions of *The Elements of Style* are available online at http://www.bartleby.com. Additionally, most dictionaries include sections on grammar, spelling, and punctuation together with useful examples. Finally, any bookstore's reference section will include numerous books on writing and style. Invest in a few reference tools and keep them near you when you write.

Don't let the rules of grammar and its incomprehensible terms (such as "pluperfect" or "subjunctive") intimidate you. You do not need to know all of the parts of speech to be a good writer, just as you do not need to know all of the parts of a microwave oven to be a good cook.

This chapter will discuss the rules most commonly misunderstood or violated by legal writers.

B. Grammar, Spelling, and Punctuation

1. Grammar Do's and Don't's

Rules of grammar are used so that we can communicate clearly. Following are some of the most common grammatical errors made by beginning and even experienced writers.

a. Subject-Verb Agreement

A verb must agree in number with the subject of a sentence. That is, if the subject of a sentence is singular, the verb must also be singular. Similarly, if the subject of a sentence is plural, the verb must also be plural. Most problems in subject-verb agreement occur when a subject is used that has more than one word, when the subject is an indefinite pronoun, collective noun, or when several words or a prepositional phrase intervene between the subject and the verb.

(1) Multiple Word Subjects

Examples

Incorrect	*Correct*
Compound Subject: The judge and jury was unpersuaded by Smith's testimony.	The judge and jury were unpersuaded by Smith's testimony.

Because the subject of the sentence in the preceding example consists of two words connected by "and," it is plural, and thus a plural verb (were) is needed.

If the subject is composed of singular words connected by "or" or "nor," use a singular verb.

Incorrect	*Correct*
Neither the defendant nor his counsel were prepared.	Neither the defendant nor his counsel was prepared.

If the subject is composed of a singular and a plural word, the verb should agree with the noun or pronoun nearer to the verb, as in "The jurors and the judge has left."

Often confusion regarding subject and verb agreement arises when a word that ends in -one or -body, such as "someone" or "everybody," or a word such as "each," "either," "neither," or "no one" is used. These indefinite pronouns are considered singular, and a singular verb must be used. Moreover, a singular pronoun (he, she, it) must be used with these words.

While it is common to use plural pronouns in speaking or informal writing, legal writing is more formal and one must be scrupulous in using singular pronouns with such words.

Incorrect	*Correct*
Everyone in the courtroom were seated.	*Everyone* in the courtroom *was* seated.
Each of these incidents involve a consumer who mistakenly purchased one product when they intended to purchase another.	*Each* of these incidents *involves* a *consumer* who mistakenly purchased one product when *he* intended to purchase another.
Somebody forgot to file their papers.	*Somebody* forgot to file *his* or *her* papers.

While the correct examples above show proper usage, you may wish to avoid the words "his" or "he" if they strike you as sexist. As discussed later in this chapter, there are several ways to remedy sexist language. In the first example, you could rewrite the sentence as follows: "Does everyone have *a* ticket to the movie?"

(2) *Collective Nouns*

Collective nouns (nouns that stand for a group of people or items) such as committee, crowd, court, and jury are usually singular. Watch for the word "the" before a noun because it is often a signal that the word to follow is singular.

Incorrect	*Correct*
The jury have adjourned to deliberate the defendant's guilt.	The *jury has* adjourned to deliberate the defendant's guilt.
The court are discussing the plaintiff's right to a speedy trial.	The *court is* discussing the plaintiff's right to a speedy trial.
The board of directors have met.	The *board of directors has* met.

If you wish to discuss the individuals composing the unit, for the sake of clarity use the following form:

Correct
The *jurors have* adjourned to deliberate the defendant's guilt.
The *members* of the court *are* discussing the plaintiff's right to a speedy trial.

(3) *Intervening Words*

Subject-verb agreement problems often occur when several words or a phrase intervenes between a subject and a verb.

Incorrect	*Correct*
The remainder of the goods to be distributed are in storage.	The *remainder* of the goods to be distributed *is* in storage.
The purpose of the will left by the decedents are to provide for their children.	The *purpose* of the will left by the decedents *is* to provide for their children.

In the preceding examples, the subjects are "remainder" and "purpose." Both of these words are singular and therefore they require the singular verb "is." Focus on the subject of the sentence and ignore intervening words.

(4) *Prepositional Phrases*

Prepositional phrases that intervene between a subject and a verb often confuse writers who may be tempted to match the verb with the noun in the prepositional phrase rather than with the subject of the sentence.

Incorrect	*Correct*
One of the best teachers are available.	*One* of the best teachers *is* available.
The deposition, along with many exhibits, show the defendant was speeding.	The *deposition*, along with many exhibits, *shows* the defendant was speeding.

In summary, always carefully scrutinize your writing to identify the subject. Once you have located the subject, classify it as singular or plural and then select the appropriate verb form, ignoring any intervening words or extraneous words.

Practice Tip

Achieving Subject-Verb Agreement

- Try mentally replacing multiple word subjects (such as "the plaintiff and the defendant are present) with the word *they* to determine the correct verb, as in *"They are present."*
- Watch for the word *the* before a noun because it is often a signal that the word should be singular, as in *The board has declared a dividend.*

b. Sentence Fragments

Sentence fragments, or incomplete sentences, are caused by a failure to include a subject and a verb in each sentence. Often a sentence fragment occurs because the writer has assumed that a dependent clause, that is, one that cannot stand on its own, is a sentence by itself. Sentence fragments can often be avoided by correcting the punctuation or by making the dependent clause into a complete sentence.

Incorrect	*Correct*
I gained two valuable lessons. First, the importance of being bilingual. Second, the need to understand a different culture.	I gained two valuable lessons: first, the importance of being bilingual and, second, the need to understand a different culture.
	or
	I gained two important lessons. The first lesson was the importance of being bilingual, and the second was the need to understand a different culture.

c. Run-on Sentences

In many ways, a run-on sentence is the opposite of a sentence fragment. A run-on sentence combines two sentences into one. Run-on sentences can usually be corrected by inserting the proper punctuation or by dividing the run-on into two separate sentences.

Incorrect	*Correct*
The members of the jury were deadlocked, they could not reach a verdict.	The members of the jury were deadlocked; they could not reach a verdict.
	or
	The members of the jury were deadlocked. They could not reach a verdict.

d. Modifiers

The incorrect placement of a modifier (a word that limits, describes, or qualifies another word or group of words) causes ambiguity. Place modifiers next to or as close as possible to the words they modify. For example, the sentence "Ginny agreed only to lend her sister money" is capable of two interpretations. Does it mean that Ginny agreed to lend her sister money and no other item? Or does it mean Ginny will lend her sister money and will not lend money to anyone else? It may be necessary to add words to a sentence with a modifier in order to achieve clarity. Either of the following two sentences will reduce ambiguity:

> Ginny agreed to lend her sister only money and nothing else.
> Ginny agreed to lend money only to her sister and not to anyone else.

Modifiers such as "almost," "ultimately," "frequently," "immediately," "eventually," "finally," and "only" are notorious causes of ambiguity. Exercise caution in using these words.

The typical modifiers are adverbs and adjectives. Once again, try to place these modifiers adjacent to the words they modify.

Confusing	*Better*
He almost argued two hours.	He argued almost two hours.

e. Split Infinitives

An infinitive is the word *to* with a verb, as in *to run* or *to plead*. An infinitive is said to be "split" when a word (usually an adverb) is inserted between the word *to* and the verb, as in *to quickly run* or *to convincingly plead*.

Most writing experts now recognize that there is no formal rule against splitting an infinitive, and split infinitives are commonly seen in nonlegal writing, including newspaper articles; however, legal readers tend to be conservative and may be annoyed or distracted by a split infinitive. Because most split infinitives are so easily corrected (by merely moving the adverb that cases the "split" after the infinitive), correct then when you can and avoid splitting an infinitive unless you want to place emphasis on the adverb.

Awkward	*Better*
The attorney asked me *to thoroughly review* the pleadings.	The attorney asked me *to review* the pleadings thoroughly.

Do not insert "not" or "never" in an infinitive because the result is awkward and incorrect.

Incorrect	*Correct*
She agreed to not examine the witness.	She agreed not to examine the witness.

f.　Dangling Participles

A present participle is a verb ending in *-ing*, as in *arguing* or *entering*. It is said to "dangle" when it does not modify the subject of a sentence. Also called a dangling modifier, this grammar problem most often occurs when a sentence starts with a word ending in *-ing*, as in *Trying to meet the filing deadline, my computer crashed*. This sentence is incorrect because it lacks an identification of the subject and implies that the computer was trying to meet the deadline. To remedy a dangling modifier, either identify the actor immediately after the introductory modifier, or reword the modifying phrase so that it identifies the actor, as in *As I was trying to meet the filing deadline, my computer crashed*.

Other dangling participles often result in unintended humor. For example, the following statement was published in *The Westhampton Beach* (N.Y.) *Hampton Chronicle News*: "Boasting a voracious appetite and stocked with both male and female sex organs capable of producing 1,000 offspring per year, officials at the U.S. Department of Agriculture are warning Long Islanders to report any sightings of the oversized escargot immediately."

Incorrect	*Correct*
Entering the darkened room, his eyes slowly adjusted to the dimness.	As he entered the darkened room, his eyes slowly adjusted to the dimness.

g.　Pronouns

(1)　Personal Pronouns

Personal pronouns (I/me, he/him, she/her, we/us, they/them) change forms depending on whether they function as the subject of a sentence or the object of the sentence. When the pronoun functions as or replaces the subject of a sentence, use "I," "he," "she," "we," or "they."

Incorrect	*Correct*
It was me who prepared the document.	It was I who prepared the document.
James and her drafted the appellate brief.	James and she drafted the appellate brief.
Either him or me will do the cite-checking.	Either he or I will do the cite-checking.
Us on the jury voted to convict the defendant.	We on the jury voted to convict the defendant.
It was them who informed the police.	It was they who informed the police.

When the pronoun functions as or replaces the object of a sentence, use "me," "him," "her," "us," or "them."

Incorrect	Correct
You must give John and I clearer instructions.	You must give John and *me* clearer instructions.
We urge you to release Susan and he from their employment contracts.	We urge you to release Susan and *him* from their employment contracts.
She has provided the committee and we with the budget analysis.	She has provided the committee and *us* with the budget analysis.
The prisoner was released into the custody of Janet and they.	The prisoner was released into the custody of Janet and *them*.
Between you and I, the defendant is liable.	Between you and *me*, the defendant is liable.

As an aid to determining which form of pronoun to use, omit or cover up the noun and the word "and" accompanying the pronoun, and this will provide a clue as to which pronoun to use. For example, in the sentence "you must give John and *I/me* clear instructions," omit "John and" so the sentence reads "You must give _____ clear instructions." This reading makes it clear the correct pronoun is "me."

(2) *Reflexive Pronouns*

The reflexive pronouns are the "self" pronouns such as "myself," "yourself," "himself," "herself," "ourselves," "yourselves," and "themselves." Reflexive pronouns usually reflect back on a subject as in "She injured herself." Do not substitute a "self" pronoun for a personal pronoun (I/me, he/him).

Incorrect	Correct
Susan and myself attended the trial.	Susan and I attended the trial.
The accident was witnessed by Mrs. Hendrix and himself.	The accident was witnessed by Mrs. Hendrix and him.

(3) *Relative Pronouns*

The relative pronouns are "who," "whom," "this," "it," "that," "such," and "which." To decide whether to use "who" or "whom," you need to determine if the relative pronoun is the subject of the sentence. If so, use "who." If the relative pronoun is the object of a sentence, clause, or prepositional phrase, use "whom."

Incorrect	*Correct*
The man whom is being arraigned is 22 years old.	The man who is being arraigned is 22 years old.
This is the woman who I mentioned earlier.	This is the woman whom I mentioned earlier.

Practice Tip

Who and Whom (Remember "m" for Who**m***)*

When using *who* or *whom*, rephrase the question or clause and determine whether you would use *he* or *him* in its place. If *he* would be used, use *who*. If *him* would be used, use *whom*. Remember that the "m" in *him* matches up with the "m" in *whom*. This tip works in almost all instances.

    Example: Who is calling?

    Test: Rewrite as *He is calling*. Replace *he* with *who*.

    Example: Whom do you trust?

    Test: Rewrite as *I trust him*. Replace *him* with *whom*.

Use "who" to refer to humans (as in "the paralegal who was hired"). Use "that" or "which" to refer to non-humans, places, or objects (as in "the deposition that was taken" or "the dog that barked").

"That" is used in a restrictive clause (a clause that is essential to the meaning of a sentence) while "which" is used in a non-restrictive clause (a clause that merely adds an idea to a sentence that would be complete without the clause). For example, in the sentence "The corporation that was formed in Delaware has no assets," the word "that" tells us which particular corporation has no assets (namely, the one formed in Delaware, not the one formed in Iowa). On the other hand, review the sentence "The corporation, which was formed in Delaware, has no assets." In this sentence you are given a fact about one corporation. The phrase "which was formed in Delaware," provides additional information about the corporation but is not essential to the meaning of the sentence. Many writers have difficulty determining whether to start a clause with "that" or "which." Remember these hints:

- If you can drop the clause and still retain the meaning of the sentence, use "which." If you can't, use "that."
- A clause beginning with "which" is usually set off by commas.
- A clause beginning with "that" is not set off by commas.
- "That" introduces essential information; "which" seldom does.

Examples

- My car, which was brand new, was damaged in the collision. (You can drop the "which" clause and the sentence still makes sense. Use "which.")
- The car that was damaged in the collision was my car. (Elimination of the "that" clause causes the sentence to lose meaning. Use "that.")

Writers often substitute pronouns for names in a manner that creates ambiguity. For example, in the sentence "The document Ellen drafted for Teresa was given to her for review," it is unclear whether the "her" refers to Ellen or Teresa. Clarifying such an ambiguous statement usually requires rewriting the sentence. Thus, "The document Ellen drafted for Teresa was given to Ellen for her review" makes it clear which individual received the document for review.

Similarly, the sentence "Don likes these cookies more than me" creates confusion. Because the word "cookies" is used as the object of the verb, the sentence means that Don likes the cookies more than he likes me. To reduce confusion, rewrite such sentences. Thus, "Don likes these cookies more than I do" makes it clear Don likes the cookies more than I like them.

Use "it" to refer to collective nouns such as jury, court, committee, or association unless you are referring to the members of the group. Also use "it" or "its" to refer to non-human entities or institutions such as corporations.

Incorrect	Correct
The corporation held their annual meeting in May.	The *corporation* held *its* meeting in May.
The court issued their opinion.	The *court* issued *its* opinion.

(4) Gender-Linked Pronouns

Avoid the use of gender-linked pronouns. For example, the sentence "A nurse should always keep her thermometer handy" is objectionable because it implies that nurses are always female. Similarly, the sentence "A judge must give his instructions to the jury" is objectionable because it presupposes the judge is male.

There are several techniques you can use to avoid offending readers. One technique is to change the singular nouns to plural. This in turn will necessitate a change in the singular pronoun "he" or "she" to a neutral plural pronoun such as "they" or "their." Thus, the first example would read "Nurses should always keep their thermometers handy," and the second example would read "Judges must give their instructions to the jury."

A second technique is to rewrite the sentence to avoid using any pronouns. The first sentence would then read "A nurse should always keep a thermometer handy" and the second sentence could be rewritten as "A judge must always give instructions to the jury."

Another alternative is to use the noun "one." Using this technique, the first example would be rewritten as "One should always keep one's thermometer handy" and the second example would be "One must always give one's instructions to the jury." As you can see, however, the use of "one" often results in a vague sentence that is stuffy in tone.

Another alternative in some situations is to use the pronoun "you." Thus, rather than saying "The applicant must provide his or her address," say, "You must provide your address."

There are some instances in which none of these techniques will work for you. In those cases you could use "he or she" throughout the document. This, however, can result in a clumsy document if used continually. Avoid the use of "he/she." This construction creates an awkward appearance because slashes are seldom used in legal writing. Their use is noticeable and distracting to a reader. The combination "s/he" is even more noticeable and distracting.

If you are drafting a document, you may use "he" throughout and at the end include a statement that the use of a masculine gender is deemed to include the feminine. Avoid alternating between "he" and "she" in a single document, especially in a single paragraph. This attempt to be fair and gender-neutral is misguided and disruptive to the flow of a project.

When addressing a letter to an individual whose gender is unknown, for example, a letter to the Secretary of State of Utah, check the Internet to see if you can determine whether the individual is a man or woman. If you cannot make that determination, address the letter as "Dear Sir or Madam." While "madam" is an archaic form of address, it is correct in such a situation. Similarly, when you are responding to a letter written by an individual whose name is ambiguous, such as Terry L. Smith, consider calling and asking how the letter should be addressed. Rest assured, you will not be the first person confused by such a name. If contacting the person is not possible or practical, you could address the letter "Dear Terry" or "Dear Terry Smith."

In sum, correct gender-linked pronouns to avoid offending readers *if* you can do so without causing an awkward and distracting document. For example, the use of specially crafted words such as "personholes" (rather than "manholes") is jarring to a reader. Thus, it is still acceptable to use "he" or "him," if changing the pronouns or rewriting the sentence would result in clumsy and distracting writing.

Practice Tip

Following the Old Grammar Rules

Because legal writing is more formal than other styles of writing, and because legal readers are notorious perfectionists, err on the side of caution so readers will not be jarred by your usage. Thus, whenever possible, comply with the "old" rules of writing in legal documents:

- **Don't split an infinitive;**
- **Don't start a sentence with a conjunction such as *and* or *but*; and**
- **Don't end a sentence with a preposition.**

2. *Spelling*

Many persons readily acknowledge they are poor spellers by proclaiming, "I've never been a good speller" as if this is some justification for a writing problem that negatively affects a project and the reader's view of its author. If you know that spelling is your weak spot, you need to work harder on this area rather than shrug it off with excuses. Keep several dictionaries handy — one in your office, one at home, and a pocket one in your briefcase. You may want to go to a professional bookstore that stocks legal books or to the bookstore at a law school to purchase a legal dictionary. A legal dictionary will include words used in legal settings such as "rescission" as well as Latin terms and phrases commonly used. Don't be afraid to write in your dictionary. Circle or highlight words you have reviewed. Chances are you will need to look up the word several times before you memorize the correct spelling. Similarly, you may wish to keep an index card handy with your top ten list of commonly misspelled words. Refer to it often. Over time, you will learn the words on the list.

Using a dictionary is not a sign of weakness. It is a signal that you are striving for professionalism in your work product. When you look up a word such as "canceled" in the dictionary, you may notice that you are given the alternate spelling "canceled" and then "cancelled." Usually the entry given first is the preferred spelling and you should use this form of the word. Similarly, use the commonly accepted spelling of a word rather than some foreign or exotic variety. For example, use "organization" and "behavior" rather than "organisation" and "behaviour," which are British spellings of those words.

One of the wonderful features of many word processor systems is their ability to check the spelling of words. Be sure to use your spell-checking feature to help you catch spelling errors but do not rely on it exclusively. In fact, many experts believe spelling checkers encourage complacency. While the spelling checker will let you know if you mis-spelled "restaurant," it cannot check word usage. Thus, if you used the word "principle" rather than "principal" the spelling checker will not in-form you so long as "principle" is spelled correctly.

Be thorough in your review of your finished project and read through the last draft for spelling errors. You should also keep a list of your own common spelling errors handy and refer to it. If you find it difficult to review your own work, ask a co-worker or friend to read through your project for spelling errors.

One of the most distressing results of misspelling is the effect pro-duced in the mind of a reader. If your aim in writing is to inform or persuade your reader and the reader is confronted with spelling errors, any value your product may have may well be overshadowed by the misspellings. Readers of legal documents, such as employers, clients, attorneys, and judges, tend to be highly critical and perfectionistic. When confronted with spelling errors they may react by assuming that if you cannot be trusted to spell properly, you cannot be trusted to have found the correct answer to a legal problem. Thus, spelling errors cast doubt on more than your ability to spell by causing readers to question the correctness of your conclusions. At

best, spelling errors make readers believe you are careless. At worst, they
may question your intelligence.

Following are some words commonly misspelled in legal or business
writing:

Correct	*Correct*	*Correct*
absence	dependent	occurred
acommodate	descendant	offense
acknowledgment	desperately	permissible
admissible	dilemma	perseverance
affidavit	dissatisfied	persistent
allege	environment	possess
bankruptcy	exercise	practically
basically	exonerate	preceding
boundary	feasible	predecessor
breach	foresee	privilege
brief	fulfill	proceed
calendar	goodwill	publicly
cancellation	grateful	rarefied
causal	grievous	receive
cease	harass	recommend
challenge	immediately	relevant
circuit	inasmuch as	renowned
collateral	indict	rescind
column	irrelevant	rescission
commitment	judgment	seize
complaint	(preferred)	separate
concede	labeled	sheriff
condemn	license	sincerely
conscious	lien	succeed
controversy	lightning	supersede
counsellor	marshaled	statutes
deductible	minuscule	transferred
defendant	mortgage	warrant
definite	occasionally	

Following are some tips to becoming a better speller:

- Learn some rules. Many spelling rules are easy to remember and
  have few exceptions, such as "place *i* before *e*, except after *c*, or
  except when it sounds like *ay*, as in neighbor and weigh."
- Use a dictionary. Always consult a dictionary to check spelling and
  mark and highlight troublesome words. Some dictionaries contain
  no definitions; they only list spelled words. These dictionaries are
  useful and portable.
- Don't over rely on a spell checker. Studies show that papers written
  with the help of a spell checker are only marginally better than
  those that are not.

- Use mnemonic devices to help you remember words, such as "the princi*pal* of your school is your *pal*."
- Pronounce your words carefully. It will be difficult to remember the correct spelling of environment if you pronounce it as *enviroment*.
- Write your misspellings several times. If you catch yourself writing "privelege" rather than "privilege," write it ten times to train yourself.
- Proofread carefully. In many instances, a misspelled word will not look "right" to you and you can then correct the error.
- Use the "find and replace" feature of your word processor to correct common errors automatically. For example, if you routinely type *Untied States* rather than *United States*, the find and replace feature will locate each occurrence of this error and replace it with the correct spelling.

3. *Punctuation*

a. Introduction

When you speak, you use pauses and changes in voice inflection as well as gestures to signal meaning to the listener. In writing, these signals are given through the use of punctuation. Punctuation makes writing more understandable to a reader. For example, a period instructs the reader that a complete thought or sentence is concluded. Without periods, all of a writing would be one incomprehensible sentence. Similarly, quotation marks signal to a reader that the exact words of another are being used.

This portion of the chapter will discuss commas, apostrophes, colons, semicolons, quotations, parentheses, and the less frequently used marks in legal writing such as dashes and exclamation points.

There is some variation in punctuation. Given the same paragraph, two writers may punctuate slightly differently from each other. Nevertheless, the basic rules of punctuation have remained relatively unchanged since about the mid-1880s. While the newer, more modern approach to punctuation, referred to as "open" punctuation, uses fewer punctuation marks than the older approach (for example, many modern writers no longer use the serial comma discussed below), legal writing, like business writing, tends to be somewhat formal. Therefore, just as recommended in the section in this chapter on grammar, when in doubt, err on the side of caution and use the more conventional approach to punctuation rather than some unusual approach.

b. Commas

A comma indicates a brief pause and is considered the most troublesome of punctuation marks due to its numerous uses. Use a comma:

    (i)   After the salutation of an informal letter and after the closing of any letter:

Dear Aunt Kay,	Sincerely,
Dear James,	Very truly yours,

(ii) To set off digits in numbers, dates, and addresses:

> There are 4,182 pages in the transcript. (Note, however, that *Bluebook* Rule 6.2(a) states to use a comma only where numbers contain five or more digits and would therefore write this number as "4182.")
>
> The plaintiff filed her complaint on June 9, 2004, the day she was fired from her job.
>
> The defendant resides at 2202 Oak Brook Terrace, Evanston, Illinois 07816.

(iii) To set off an introductory word, phrase, or clause:

> According to the plaintiff's testimony, the car was traveling west on Burgener Street at the time of the accident.
>
> Nevertheless, the defendant failed to comply with the terms of his agreement.
>
> First, the defendant entered Mrs. Smith's dwelling place.
>
> Although she was quite elderly, she made an effective witness.

(iv) To set off interruptive or non-essential words or phrases:

> While looking for her pen, however, she found the missing checkbook.
>
> The defendant, over the strenuous objection of his counsel, insisted on testifying.

(v) To set off appositives (a word or group of words inserted immediately after another word that explains the previous word):

> William Emery, the noted attorney, consulted on the case.

(vi) Before a coordinating conjunction such as "and," "but," "for," "nor," "or," "so," or "yet" introducing an independent clause, namely, one that can function as a complete sentence. You may omit the comma if the clause is short (five words or less). The comma is not needed after the coordinating conjunction if the clause that follows cannot stand on its own.

> The plaintiff intended to amend the complaint, but the statute of limitations had expired.
>
> The defendant's answer had been amended several times, and the judge expressed impatience with the many amendments.
>
> The attorney argued but the jury convicted.
>
> He argued the case and did so clearly.

(vii)   To set off items in a series. Although the final comma in a series is optional in most writing, in legal writing you must place a comma after each item in the list and before the conjunction. For example, examine the sentence, "I leave my property equally to Susan, Bill, Louise, and Tom." Each individual would receive one-fourth of the estate. Note that the omission of the last comma could cause a completely different result, for example, "I leave my property equally to Susan, Bill, Louise and Tom." The omission of the comma after "Louise" arguably indicates the property is to be divided equally into thirds: one-third to Susan, one-third to Bill, and one-third to Louise and Tom together, rather than in equal fourths to each individual. Because the omission of the last comma in a series (the serial comma) can cause ambiguity, always include it. To determine how many commas to use, some writers count the number of items in the list or the series and then use one less comma than the number.

(viii)   Before and after quotations:
"I need the pen," Bob said.
Lee replied, "I agree."

c. Apostrophes

Apostrophes are used to show possession or ownership or to show omission of one or more letters, as in the contraction *don't*. The use of apostrophes to show possession, especially with regard to proper names, is often confusing.

Use an apostrophe:

(i)   to show possession or ownership. Follow three basic rules:

- Add an apostrophe and an *s* ('s) to show possession for all singular nouns, even if the noun ends in s, k, x, or z.

    Correct examples: the girl's coat
    the shareholder's ballot
    Arkansas's election
    Congress's intent
    Charles's book

- When a plural word ends in *s*, add only an apostrophe (') to show possession.

    Correct examples: the four girls' coats
    the six shareholders' ballots
    the two workers' employment
    benefits

14. Back to Basics

- When a word is plural and does not already end in *s*, add an apostrophe and an *s* ('s) to show possession.
  Correct examples: the children's toys
                         the women's cars

- To form the plural of most names or to show possession for most names, follow the rules given above.

  Correct examples: Ed Smith's papers were filed today.
                         The Smiths moved to Chicago.
                         The Smiths' house is large.

- For names that end in *ch, s, sh, x,* or *z*, however, form the plural by adding *es* and then form the plural possessive by adding an apostrophe after the *es* (es'). The singular possessive is formed by following the first rule above (as in *Tim Jones's car is red*.)

  Correct examples: The Joneses moved to New York.
                         The Lynches are wealthy.
                         The Joneses' car is an Accord.

Practice Tip

Marcus' Pen or Marcus's Pen?

Many grammar books permit the use of an apostrophe alone with a singular word ending in *s* when adding another *s* would make the word difficult to pronounce or look odd. Thus, you may see *Mr. Rogers' sweater* or *Marcus' pen*. Nevertheless, the U.S. Government Printing Office *Style Manual*, Strunk and White, and most conventional grammar books suggest the *'s*, as in *Mr. Rogers's sweater* and *Marcus's pen*. This form is always correct.

(ii)   to indicate omission of letters, as in contractions:

         can't (can<u>not</u>)
         hadn't (had n<u>o</u>t)
         it's (it <u>is</u>)
         don't (do n<u>o</u>t)

One of the most common errors students and beginning writers make is misusing "it's." "It's" is a contraction for "it is" (or "it has"). The apostrophe is used to indicate that the letter "i" has been omitted. To form the possessive of it, use "its." Only use "it's" when you mean to say "it is" or "it has," not when you mean to indicate possession.

Example: *It's* a learned court that has the wisdom to reverse *its* decisions.

Practice Tip

Apostrophes and Plurals of Numbers and Letters

There is some disagreement whether an apostrophe should be used to show the plural of a number or letter. The better practice and that of the *Style Manual* is to follow the general rules for forming plurals and to omit the apostrophe unless the result would be confusing.

Correct examples: *There are two Exhibit Bs.*
The audit shows all 9s.
The LSATs are difficult.
Be sure to dot your i's.

---

d. Colons

Use a colon:

(i) after the salutation of a formal letter:

Dear Mr. Smith:
Dear Sir or Madam:

(ii) to introduce a list; use a colon especially after expressions such as "as follows" or "the following":

The defendant asserted the following three defenses: laches, acquiescence, and unclean hands.

(ii) to indicate that something will follow:

We have instituted a new policy: Goods may not be returned without a sales receipt.

(Do not use a colon after a verb or preposition. Thus, it would be incorrect to write, *You will find the answer in: the case or the statute.*)

(iii) to introduce a formal or long quotation:

The court stated in unequivocal terms: "Liability is founded on this act of gross negligence."

(Note that this quotation could also be introduced by a comma.)

Capitalize the first word after a colon if the material following the colon can stand on its own as a sentence. Conversely, do not capitalize the first word after a colon if the material cannot stand on its own as a sentence.

e.   Semicolons

Use a semicolon:

(i)   to connect two independent but related clauses:

That was his final summation; it was strong and forceful.

(Note that these two ideas could also be expressed as complete sentences separated by periods.)

(ii)   to connect two independent clauses joined by a transitional word or conjunction such as *therefore, however, or nevertheless*:

The defendant was not credible; therefore, the jury voted to convict her.
The attorney argued persuasively; however, the judge overruled her.

(iii)   to separate items in a list containing commas:

Standing trial for embezzlement were Connie Rivers of Portland, Oregon; Samuel Salter of Seattle, Washington; and Susan Stone of Butte, Montana.

(iv)   to separate items in a list introduced by a colon:

The elements to be proved in an action for breach of contract are as follows: the existence of a contract; the unjustified breach of the contract by one party; and damage caused by the breach to the non-breaching party.

(Note that these items can also be separated by commas.)

f.   Quotation Marks

Use quotation marks:

(i)   to indicate the exact words of a speaker:

Patrick Henry said, "Give me liberty or give me death."
"The motion," said the judge, "is hereby granted."

(ii)   to explain or draw emphasis to a word:

> The writer misspelled the word "defendant" in the brief.

Use quotation marks only for quotes of 49 words or fewer. For quotes of 50 words or more, block indent the quote and use single spacing. The indentation of these longer quotes itself indicates a quotation.

Always place commas and periods inside quotation marks. Place colons and semicolons outside quotation marks. When a quotation includes another quotation, single quotation marks (') are used:

> "It was the jury foreman," announced Betty, "who said, 'The defendant is guilty.' "

g. Parentheses

Use parentheses:

(i)   to set off interruptions or explanations:

> His primary argument was *res ipsa loquitur* (a Latin phrase meaning "the thing speaks for itself").

(ii)   to direct the reader to other information:

> The plaintiff has failed to allege justifiable reliance in the fraud cause of action (Compl. ¶ 14).

(iii)   to introduce abbreviations:

> The plaintiff, Southwest Avionics Industries ("SAI"), alleged seven causes of action.

If what is included in the parenthetical is a complete sentence, place a period inside the parenthetical. Otherwise, the period is placed outside the ending parenthesis.

h. Dashes

Dashes create drama and draw a reader's attention to a page. In general, however, they are considered too informal for legal writing, and, in most instances, other punctuation marks, such as commas, parentheses, or a colon would be more appropriate. A dash is made by two hyphens. Use a dash to indicate a break or interruption, as in the following sentence: The defendant — not his brother — testified.

i. Exclamation Marks

Exclamation marks are used to emphasize an idea. They are rarely, if ever, used in legal writing other than when they appear as part of a direct quotation.

j. Hyphens

Use a hyphen:

(i)   to divide words between syllables at the end of a line of text. Avoid hyphenating proper names. Use a dictionary if you are unsure where to divide the word. The use of word processors with their automatic ability to space words evenly eliminates much of the need for hyphens in dividing words.

(ii) between the parts of a compound adjective when it modifies the next word:

> would-be informant
> employment-related injury
> high-tech espionage

(iii) after certain prefixes:

> (a) prefixes preceding proper nouns
>
> > anti-American
> > pro-Israeli
>
> (b) prefixes ending with a vowel when the root word begins with a vowel (other than "re," generally)
>
> > anti-intellectual
> > co-op
> > de-emphasize

(iv) to form compounds:

> ten-year lease
> ex-president
> on-the-job training

k. Slashes or Virgules

The diagonal slash or virgule causes ambiguity and should be avoided. It means "or," *not* "and," when used between two words. Thus, the sentence "The judge/jury agreed to acquit" means that the judge agreed to acquit or the jury agreed to acquit, *not* that the judge *and* jury agreed to acquit.

Dictum

- In choosing "a" or "an," consider the sound rather than the spelling of the following word. Use "a" before all consonant sounds. Use "an" before all vowel sounds except long "u" and before silent "h."

a uniform	an heiress
a house	an IPO
a unit	an eight-day vacation

- Commonly used abbreviations:

B.C.	A.D.
a.m.	p.m.
PST	EDT
Ph.D.	J.D.

- Only one word ends in "sede": supersede
  Only three words end in "ceed": exceed, proceed, and succeed
  All other words with the
  "seed" sound end in "cede": precede, concede, intercede

CyberSites

Numerous Web site addresses for guidance on writing and grammar are provided at the end of Chapter 15. The following are excellent sources of information relating to grammar, spelling, and punctuation:

http://www.gpoaccess.gov/ stylemanual	The Government Printing Office *Style Manual* is one of the most widely accepted manuals on English usage.
http://www.fas.harvard. edu/~wricntr/html/ tools.htm	Harvard University's Writing Center provides useful information as well as links to other writing resources (including English as a second language resources).
http://owl.english. purdue.edu	Purdue University's Online Writing Lab offers numerous guides and handouts as well as exercises and answer keys.

Assignment for Chapter 14

GRAMMAR

SELECT THE CORRECT WORD.

1. The deposition transcript was received by Jill and her/she.
2. For who/whom did the witness testify?
3. The SEC has released its/it's/its' findings.
4. Jack and him/he attended the hearing.
5. Someone has left his-her/their briefcase in the courtroom.
6. The company held it's/its annual meeting today.
7. The subpoena must be served on Tom, James, and he/him.
8. The committee, together with the members, have/has issued the report.
9. Each of the exhibits are/is indexed in the closing binder.
10. Only one of the documents for the hearings have/has been summarized.

SPELLING

SELECT THE CORRECT SPELLING.

1.	admissible	admissable
2.	decedant	decedent
3.	dependant	dependent
4.	privilege	privelege
5.	occasion	occassion
6.	organization	organisation
7.	judgement	judgment
8.	inadvertant	inadvertent
9.	interrogatories	interogatories
10.	the foregoing section	the forgoing section

PUNCTUATION

CORRECTLY PUNCTUATE THE FOLLOWING SENTENCES.

1. Both judges chambers were recently redecorated.
2. The motion was heard on January 3, 2005 and resulted in a change of venue.
3. Following are various remedies that may be granted by a court; compensatory damages, punitive damages and equitable relief.
4. Judge Harris opinion was lengthy.
5. The transcript however was not included with the other documents.
6. Alice Bowen the former senator, attended the meeting.
7. The jurys decision was unanimous.

8.   The first witness was late. Which made the judge angry.

9.   There were two omissions in the agreement they were both in paragraph two.

10. He is an extremely diligent paralegal and he is always prepared to help.

State Your Answer

1.   Access the Web site of the U.S. Government Printing Office *Style Manual*.

   a.   Review Rule 3 relating to capitalization and either correct the following or indicate if they are correct.

   - I live near the lake. Its name is lake Deepcreek.
   - I lived in the west. Travel in a westerly direction.
   - I live in San Diego County. The County is large.

   b.   Review Rule 8 relating to punctuation and either correct the following or indicate if they are correct.

   - Your boss's memo is complete.
   - The mens' cars were parked outside.
   - Jefferson Davis' home was in Richmond.
   - The trial began in June, 2004.
   - Send me the April 15, 2005 report.
   - She was a tense, angry witness.

2.   Access http://www.bartleby.com and review *The Elements of Style*.

   a.   Review Section II.1 and use the correct punctuation to make the following expressions possessives: the friend of Charles, the poems of Burns, and the malice of the witch.

   b.   Review Section II.2 and punctuate the following sentence: He opened the letter read it and made a note of its contents.

Strategies for Effective Writing

There are two things wrong with almost all legal writing. One is its style. The other is its content.

Fred Rodell, *Goodbye to Law Reviews*, 23 Va. L. Rev. 38, 38 (1936)

A. Introduction
B. The Plain English Movement
C. Prewriting
D. Precision
E. Clarity
F. Readability
G. Brevity
H. Order
I. Drafting Techniques
J. Electronic Communications

Chapter Overview

Once you have mastered the mechanics of writing you must focus on making your writing effective. This chapter will present techniques to achieve the five hallmarks of effective legal writing: precision, clarity, readability, brevity, and order.

A. Introduction

The cornerstone of the legal profession is communication — communication with a client, adverse party, or judge. In most cases the communication will be in written form. Even in those instances in which you communicate orally, you will often follow up with a written letter or memo to a file.

Because paralegals do not generally appear in court, they often spend even more time than some attorneys in preparing written documents. Thus, effective legal writing is critical to success as a paralegal.

B.   The Plain English Movement

One of the recurring criticisms of legal writing is that it is rendered incomprehensible to the average reader by its use of jargon, redundancies, and archaic words and phrases. The use of words and phrases such as "whereas," "aforesaid," and "notwithstanding anything in the foregoing to the contrary" confuses and angers readers.

The increased activism of consumers frustrated with the impossibility of understanding an insurance policy, mortgage, or agreement for the purchase of an appliance, led to the requirement in many states that certain documents be written in "plain English." The Federal Trade Commission requires that agreements for the sale of a franchise be written in plain English. Similarly, the Securities and Exchange Commission ("SEC") has issued a "Plain English Handbook" to assist attorneys in creating clear disclosure documents for the SEC (available at http://www.sec.gov/pdf/handbook.pdf). The Commonwealth of Pennsylvania forbids the use of Latin or double negatives in consumer contracts.

Similarly, in 1998, President Clinton issued his Presidential Memo on Plain Language, which requires all federal agencies to write clearly to their customers. The Plain Language initiative rests on three principles:

- Writing should be reader-oriented, clearly showing the author is writing to the customers of the agencies, not to other government employees;
- Writing should use natural expressions, using commonly known and used words; and
- Documents should be visually appealing.

A government Web site at http://www.plainlanguage.gov offers writing tips, writing resources, and numerous samples of documents and letters written in plain language. Although the House of Representatives attempted to follow the plain language principles when it released its simplified rules in 1999, unfortunately, the rules were nearly 100 pages long, demonstrating that writing in a plain style is much easier said than done.

The trend toward plain language has also gained acceptance in legal writing. Law students and beginning writers are now encouraged to avoid "legalese" whenever possible and to write in plain English to enhance readability and comprehension of writings.

The plain English movement rightfully shifts the focus away from you as the author to the reader as the recipient. If you have produced what you believe is a beautifully crafted letter and yet the client doesn't understand it, you have failed. A writer is responsible for ambiguity in a document.

Writing in plain English so your reader understands you is not an easy task. Many legal concepts are very complex, and translating them into plain English is difficult. Similarly, some use of "legalese" such as Latin phrases may be unavoidable in certain instances. Falling into the habit of using archaic phrases such as "the instant case at bar" when you really mean "this case" is easy and you must make a conscious effort to avoid confusing jargon. See Figure 15-1.

Figure 15-1
SEC Guidelines for Plain English

Following is a brief summary of the SEC's guidelines for writing in plain English:

- Use short sentences.
- Use definite, concrete, everyday language.
- Use the active voice rather than the passive voice.
- Use tables and lists to present complex information.
- Avoid legal and financial jargon and highly technical business terms.
- Avoid multiple negatives.
- Avoid weak verbs, abstract terms, and superfluous words.
- Enhance readability through attractive design and layout.

C. Prewriting

Many experts agree that the time you invest in a project before you begin writing can be the most valuable time you spend on the project. Two threshold questions are of particular importance in helping you shape your writing so it is effective and understood on the first reading. Always ask yourself "What is the purpose of this writing?" and "Who will be reading this writing?"

1. Purpose

There can be several reasons for writing something. It is possible that your purpose is to relay information such as notifying a client that his deposition has been scheduled for next month. Another purpose may be to obtain information such as asking a client to explain an answer given to an interrogatory question posed by an adverse party. You may be explaining something to a reader, such as in a letter discussing the results of a settlement meeting. Finally, you may be aiming to convince a reader in a trial or appellate brief when your objective is to convince the court to adopt your argument.

If, before you begin any project, you ask yourself, "What is the purpose of this document?" you will set the stage for the tone of the document. After all, there is no point in using persuasive language when your sole mission is to notify a client that a will is ready to be executed. Conversely, you do not want to adopt a neutral and purely informative style if a client's last chance to succeed is your appellate brief. By reminding yourself of the purpose of your writing, you will be able to shape the appropriate tone and style of the project.

2. *Audience*

In addition to considering the purpose of a document, focus on the intended reader. Who will be reading the project — a client, a supervising attorney, adverse counsel, or a judge?

If the writing is prepared for a client, try to obtain a thumbnail sketch of the individual. Some clients may be novices in the legal world and even a term such as "interrogatory," which is commonplace to you, may be puzzling to a newcomer to litigation. Conversely, a client may be a sophisticated real estate broker and a complex discussion of prepayment penalty clauses in mortgage notes may be easily understood. In general, use a straightforward style for laypersons. Clients will not be impressed by your command of Latin phrases but will be frustrated by their use. Clients expect to be informed, not mystified, by legal writing. Immediately following the reaction of frustration is one of anger: anger that they had to pay you once to write the letter and then a second time to have you explain the letter. The goal of your writing is to communicate, not impress.

The highly respected and renowned financier, Warren E. Buffett, explains that when writing Berkshire Hathaway's annual report, he pretends he's talking to his sisters. Though highly intelligent, they are not accounting or financial experts. Mr. Buffett believes that he will be successful if they understand his writing. Similarly, United States Supreme Court Justice Stephen Breyer says that he tries to write his legal opinions so that they are understandable to high school students.

One of the most difficult tasks can be writing for a supervisor. Often the supervisor has not really thought through the way the project should be structured and as a result your approach will not meet the supervisor's expectations. Sometimes the supervisor may have access to certain facts and information you do not have, and your writing may be criticized for being incomplete. You may find that you adopt one writing style for one supervisor and an entirely different style for another. As you get to know the people you work with, you will be able to understand their writing techniques and be better able to meet their expectations. Obtain samples of documents written by your supervisors or colleagues so you can get an idea of their styles and approaches. One of the most frustrating tasks is writing for individuals who are so committed to their style of writing they are never satisfied with anyone else's approach. They will endlessly revise a document, making insignificant small-scale revisions, such as changing all the "glad's" to "happy's." If you find you can never make such an individual satisfied with your work, try a direct approach and ask outright what the individual likes and dislikes in a writing.

If the letter is to adverse counsel, adopt a neutral and objective style. Avoid language that is confrontational or condescending. While letters to other legal professionals may include certain terms of art ("The Lanham Act," "The ADA," *ex parte*) that need no further explanation, avoid a tone that implies you are giving a lesson on the law. Not only are combative or condescending letters generally unproductive, you never know when they may be made part of a record in a court proceeding. You do not want a letter written in anger to come back to haunt you.

Writing for judges presupposes a level of expertise, and you need not give definitions or long-winded explanations for commonly known terms or phrases. Nevertheless, keep in mind that most judges rely heavily on law clerks to read briefs and then give an initial opinion to the judge. Thus, you need to make a strong and forceful argument because the judge may only scan the brief and rely on a law clerk's review. Moreover, judges are usually overwhelmed with heavy case loads and will not appreciate an overly long document that resorts to jargon and legalese. They will be much happier if you make the points you need to make as forcefully, persuasively, and briefly as possible, and then move on. As an inducement to legal writers to adopt more concise writing styles, more and more courts, including all of the courts of appeal and the United States Supreme Court, are establishing page limits for documents submitted. Thus, it is imperative to be concise.

By asking yourself, "Who is my reader?" you will automatically tailor the document so it is understood by the reader. The critical question is not whether *you* love your project but whether the reader will immediately be informed or persuaded, that is, whether your writing achieves its purpose.

D. Precision

The most important characteristic of legal writing is precision. Clients will rely on the information and opinions given to them by legal professionals. Judges, administrators, and others will assume the information provided to them is correct. Therefore, being right is fundamental to effective legal writing. No judge will render a decision in a client's favor by saying, "The legal conclusions you have reached are faulty and incorrect but the brief is so well-written that I will rule in your favor."

Be accurate with regard not only to the "big" issues, such as legal conclusions and arguments, but also as to the "small" elements of a writing, such as names, dates, and dollar amounts. An error in the client's name or address may attract more attention than anything else in the project. Just as spelling errors cast doubt on your ability, so do accuracy errors have a disproportionately negative impact on the reader. The legal profession has become more adversarial in recent years, and even clients (sometimes, especially clients) are quick to point out an error. Similarly, many of your writings are sent to an adverse party who will be more than happy to call attention to a mistake you have made. Thus, because your audience is highly critical, you must be as accurate and precise as possible.

One cause of imprecise writing is an overreliance on forms. Drafting a contract requires more than merely locating another contract in your office and then changing the names and addresses. If this is your approach to drafting, you will no doubt find yourself explaining to a client engaging in accounting services why his or her agreement refers to restaurants and bars. Using forms as a starting point or guide is perfectly acceptable. Just avoid relying exclusively on forms. When you have used a form originally drafted for another client, proofread carefully to ensure the language is appropriate for this new client's needs. Use the "find and replace" feature in word processing programs to ensure the consistent use of terms.

1. Word Choice

The selection of an improper word or the use of vague words causes imprecision in your writing. Similarly, the use of qualifying language or words can cause unintended meanings. For example, no employee would be comforted by reading "Your department is not in any immediate danger of being downsized." The use of the qualifier "immediate" implies that a danger exists; it simply is not immediate. Select the most descriptive and specific word possible. Descriptive words lend strength and vitality to your writing. Moreover, the selection of an incorrect word can be fatal in legal writing. A document that states "The Buyer may deposit the purchase price into the escrow account prior to May 15" means something entirely different from "The Buyer shall deposit the purchase price into the escrow account prior to May 15." The second statement clearly imposes an obligation on the Buyer while the first statement does not.

The use of "will" or "may" for "shall" causes ambiguity and inaccuracy. One writing professor has estimated that more than 1,000 published cases debate the meaning of "shall." Use "may" for optional action, "will" for future action ("I will appear in court on Thursday"), and "shall" or "must" for obligatory action. Many plain English guidelines recommend the use of "must" rather than "shall" on the basis that "shall" is an obsolete word.

Following is a list of words that are commonly misused in legal writing. Just as you use a dictionary to avoid spelling errors, use a dictionary or thesaurus to help you select the precise word you need.

affect/effect

Affect means "to influence" as in "I was greatly affected by the victim's story."

Effect means "to cause or bring about" (as a verb) or "result" (as a noun) as in "He effected a resolution of the case" or "One of the effects of the judgment was impairment of his credit rating."

If you have difficulty remembering the difference between these words, do not use either of them. Use their synonyms (influence, or produce, or result).

among/between

Among is used to refer to *more than two objects or persons*, as in "The agreement was entered into among Smith, Jones, and Andersen."

Between is used to refer to *two objects or persons*, as in "The settlement was negotiated between Peterson and Powell."

and/or

Many experts criticize the use of *and / or*, which can be confusing and ambiguous. Avoid using *and / or*. Use either "and" or "or."

Unclear   You must provide a reference and/or a resume.

Preferred   You must provide a reference, or resume, or both.

apprise/appraise

Apprise means "to notify or inform," as in "I will continue to apprise you of further developments in this case."

Appraise means to "estimate value," as in "He appraised the value of the property at $100,000."

argue/rule

Courts do not argue cases; lawyers do. Do not write *the court argued* . . . . Similarly, courts do not *contend, believe,* or *feel.* Courts *rule, decide, hold, state, conclude,* and so forth.

beside/besides

Beside means "at the side of," as in "Please sit beside me." *Besides* means "in addition to," as in "Besides leaving Angela his property, Grandfather gave her his jewelry."

compose/comprise

Compose means "to make up," as in "The contract is composed of three sections." *Comprise* means "to include or contain or consist of," as in "Tina's collection comprises rare porcelains." Do not use "of" after *comprise*.

disinterested/uninterested

Disinterested means "neutral" and "impartial," as in "Judges must be disinterested in the proceedings they decide."

Uninterested means "not interested or bored," as in "The jurors appeared uninterested in the masses of statistical evidence presented."

ensure/insure

Ensure means "to make definite," as in "We must ensure the tenant pays all rent due." *Insure* means "to protect against loss," as in "We must insure our valuables for at least $10,000."

fact/contention

A *fact* is something that has occurred or can be verified. Writers often characterize something as a fact when it is merely an allegation or contention. Use the word "fact" only when you are describing an event or something proven. For example, it is a fact that a defendant has blue eyes. It is not a fact that the defendant murdered a victim until the jury or court says so.

guilty/liable

The word *guilty* refers to criminal wrongdoing. *Liable* refers to responsibility for a civil wrong. Thus, it is correct to say that "defendant Smith is guilty of robbery while defendant Jones is liable for damages in the amount of $50,000 for breach of contract."

liable/libel

Liable means responsible for some civil wrong, as in "She is liable for all the harm proximately caused by her negligence."

Libel is a form of defamation, as in "The magazine libeled our client by stating he was a crook."

judgment/judgment

In legal writing and in most American writings, spell as *judgment*. In Great Britain, the word is spelled *judgement*.

memoranda/memorandum

Memoranda refers to several documents (plural) while a *memorandum* is a single document.

oral/verbal

Oral means something spoken, as in "The plaintiff's oral testimony at trial confirmed her earlier deposition testimony."

Verbal means a communication in words and could refer to a written or a spoken communication. Thus, the statement *We had a verbal agreement* is confusing because it could refer either to a written or nonwritten agreement. To avoid confusion, use *oral* or *written* and avoid the use of *verbal*.

ordinance/ordnance

An *ordinance* is an act or resolution enacted by a local jurisdiction, as in "Buffalo recently enacted an ordinance prohibiting smoking in public places."

Ordnance is military weaponry, as in "The troops came under heavy ordnance fire."

overrule/reverse

A court *overrules* prior decisions in its jurisdiction. Thus, "The 1954 case *Brown v. Board of Education* overruled the 1896 case *Plessy v. Ferguson*." A court *reverses* the very case before it on appeal as in "The defendant in *Edwards v. Anderson* appealed the decision rendered against him; the court agreed with the defendant's reasoning and reversed the lower court's holding."

prescribe/proscribe

Prescribe means to order, as in "The physician prescribed complete bedrest for the patient."

Proscribe means to prohibit or forbid, as in "Massachusetts laws proscribe littering."

principal/principle

Principal is the supervisor at a school or a dominant item, as in "The principal objective to be gained is the prisoner's freedom." Another meaning of "principal" is a sum of money on which interest is paid, as in "The promissory note required repayment of the principal amount of the debt as well as interest."

Principle is a fundamental rule, as in "The principles of physics are complex."

respectfully/respectively

Respectfully means "with respect" and is a commonly used closing in a document, as in "Respectfully submitted, Andrew Kenney."

Respectively means in a certain order, as in "The attorneys took their respective positions in the courtroom and the trial commenced."

since/because

Avoid using since as a substitute for *because*; otherwise, ambiguity results, as in the sentence *Since the tariffs were lifted, trade has increased*. It is not clear in this sentence whether *since* means *after a period of time* or whether it means *because*. To avoid confusion, use *since* to refer to the passage of time, as in "It has been four weeks since we filed the appeal," and use *because* to show causation, as in "Because the jury was improperly charged, the judgment was reversed."

2. *Vague Words*

To lend forcefulness to your writing, use concrete and descriptive words. Avoid vague words such as "matter," "development," "circumstances," "system," "situation," "problem," and "process," which provide little, if any, information to the reader. Thus, a sentence beginning "Regarding this matter . . ." offers no guidance to the reader as to what "this matter" might be. A much better approach is to write "Regarding your lease . . .".

Similarly, avoid using words such as "above," "whereas," or "herein." For example, if in an agreement you state on page 18, "As described above . . ." the reader does not know where in the previous 17 pages you discussed the issue. Be specific. State, "as described in paragraph 4(b) . . .".

The words "it" and "this" are often used in an indefinite and confusing manner. Consider the following: "The court ruled the defendant should be granted probation. This enables the defendant to participate in a work release program." The word "this" could refer either to the court's ruling or the defendant's probation. When using "it" or "this," you should, if necessary, repeat the word that "it" or "this" refers to. Thus, the prior statement would read, "The court ruled the defendant should be granted probation. Probation will enable the defendant to participate in a work release program."

Similarly, avoid "made-up" words. While you may have heard of, used, and even written "dialogued," "Borked," "liaising," "mentee," or "strategize," these "words" are not generally found in most dictionaries because they are not yet recognized words in English. Our conversation and writing are often influenced by business and technology terms. Thus, a number of terms, such as "cutting edge," "synergy," and "empower" are overused. Do not say "We need to *interface* to resolve the litigation" when you mean "meet." Do not use "impact" as a verb, as in "His actions will *impact* our ability to obtain a loan." Use "influence" or "affect" instead. While English is an evolving language, do not use a word before it has evolved into an entry in a dictionary.

3. *Word Connotation*

Many words have more than one meaning. When you select a word, consider its connotation, or suggested meaning. There is a great difference, for example, in referring to an item as "cheap" rather than "affordable." The word "cheap" connotes shoddy or low quality while "affordable" conveys either a neutral or desirable meaning. Consider the effect of telling someone he or she is "stubborn" rather than "determined," or "blunt" rather than "candid." Certain words carry hostile undertones and will immediately make the reader defensive or angry.

Use care when selecting words to ensure they have the connotations you intend. If correspondence to an adverse party suggests there is a "discrepancy" in damage figures, rather than simply asking for a clarification of the figures, you can be sure of an immediate, and probably angry, response.

E. Clarity

The second feature of effective legal writing is clarity — that is, ensuring that your project is easily understood by the reader. Your writing style should be invisible. It is bad writing that is noticeable. Because legal writings are read not for pleasure but for function, readers expect you to make your point clearly and quickly. The three primary legal writing flaws that obscure clarity are elegant variation, the overuse of negatives, and improper word order.

1. *Elegant Variation*

Elegant variation refers to the practice of substituting one term for another in a document to avoid repetition of a term. Writers are often loath to repeat a term, in the belief that repetition of a term is boring or unsophisticated. Unfortunately, selecting alternate terms creates the impression that something entirely different is intended. Consider the following sentence: Four of the defendant's witnesses were women, while all of the plaintiff's witnesses were ladies. In an attempt not to repeat the word "women," the writer conveys something entirely different about the plaintiff's group of witnesses

Elegant variation is deadly in legal writing. For example, if you are drafting a document that continually refers to an individual as a "landlord" and then suddenly you refer to this individual as the "lessor," the reader may believe that the "landlord" is not the same individual as the "lessor." You should therefore be cautious about varying words and terms you have used. While you may believe that selecting alternative terms shows your extensive vocabulary and lends interest to the document, you unwittingly may be creating the impression that there is a reason that different terms have been selected and that there is a legal distinction to be drawn based upon this variation. Use the "find and replace" feature of your word processing program to ensure terms are used consistently.

2. *Negatives*

The overuse of negatives can be confusing to a reader. While statutes are often set forth in negative fashion by describing what is prohibited, using more than two negative words in a sentence usually forces the reader to stop and think through what you have said. The phrase "not unlikely" should be converted to "likely" or "probable." Anytime the reader is interrupted from reading the project, your message is weakened. As a writer, your task is to ensure that a reader proceeds smoothly through the document without needing to puzzle over phrases. For example, the statement "No individual shall be prohibited from refusing to submit to a breathalyzer examination" is confusing. It requires a reader to consider three negative words: "no," "prohibited," and "refusing."

In drafting projects, keep in mind that there are many more negative words than the obvious ones: "no," "none," or "never." Many words function in a negative fashion, such as "refuse," "preclude," "deny," "except," and the like. While it is impossible to purge your writing of all negative terms, you should carefully scrutinize your writing to ensure that you have not used too many negative words that obscure your meaning.

The other disadvantage of using negative words is that they are not as forceful as affirmative expressions. For example, it is more effective and shorter to say "the plaintiff was late for her deposition" than "the plaintiff failed to timely appear for her deposition." To give strength and vitality to your writing, use affirmative and positive terms.

3. Word Order

The most common sentence structure in the English language is the placement of the subject first, the verb second, and the object third. Thus, the sentence "The defendant attacked the victim" is phrased in this standard order. While the thought can certainly be expressed in another way, such as "The victim was attacked by the defendant," readers typically anticipate that sentences will follow the expected pattern of subject, verb, and object. Although you may not want to structure every single sentence in a project in the same fashion, excessive variation from the expected sentence structure will cause confusion and lack of clarity. Just as you should avoid exotic spellings of words because they draw attention to your writing rather than to your message, avoid exotic sentence structure. For example, an article written in a national newspaper about the 1991 Tailhook Convention began, "The Navy Thursday asked the Pentagon's inspector general to investigate the 1991 Tailhook incident . . . ." This oddly structured sentence catches the reader's attention in a distracting way.

Vary from the anticipated sentence structure of subject, verb, object only when you want to draw attention to a thought. Thus, if you have a point you want to emphasize, vary the way it is structured. Keep this technique in mind if you need to "bury" a weak portion of an argument: Phrase it in the manner commonly anticipated because this will draw the least amount of attention to it.

One of the other benefits of using "normal" sentence structure is that you will automatically phrase your thoughts in the active voice. When you vary from the anticipated order of sentences, the result is often conversion to the passive voice, which creates a weakened point (see Section F.1).

F. Readability

Because the subject matter discussed in most legal writing is complex, and often rather boring, you need to make your product as readable as possible. Clients will be unfamiliar with legal topics. Judges and other legal professionals will be too busy to struggle through a complex and pompous document. Remember that the more complicated a topic is, the more important is the need for readability. To enhance readability:

1. Prefer the Active Voice

The active voice focuses attention on the subject of the sentence that performs or causes certain action. The active voice is consistent with standard sentence structure of subject, verb, and object.

The passive voice focuses attention on the object of action by placing it first and relegating the subject (actor) of the sentence to an inferior position.

Active Voice	*Passive Voice*
The corporation held its meeting.	A meeting was held by the corporation.
The defendant's attorney argued for acquittal.	An argument for acquittal was made by the defendant's attorney.
The doctor testified that the patient consented to the operation.	Testimony was given by the doctor that the patient consented to the operation.

The active voice is stronger and more forceful than the passive voice. Readers do not have to search through the sentence looking for the actor or subject. Another advantage of using the active voice is that it usually results in shorter sentences.

There are situations, however, in which the passive voice may be preferable. For example, assume your law office represents a defendant accused of fraud. Instead of stating "The defendant deposited checks in his bank account," you could write "Checks were deposited in the defendant's bank account." This use of the passive voice shifts the focus away from the defendant. The reader is informed of what occurred but not who did it. Consider using the passive voice in the discussion of weaker parts of your argument to deflect attention from them. Conversely, be sure to structure the strongest parts of your writing in the active voice because it lends strength and vitality to your writing. A classic example of passive voice is seen in the recent statement of a politician accused of wrongdoing who stated, "Mistakes were made" rather than "I made mistakes."

Practice Tip

Avoiding the Passive Voice

In many sentences, the person or the thing doing the action is introduced *by* the word by as in *The policy was announced by the committee*. This is a tip that you have shifted into the passive voice. Most word processors have a feature that will flag the use of passive voice. This feature is a useful guide but can be distracting.

---

2. *Use Lists*

Another way to enhance readability is to use lists when discussing complex matters. Lists not only enable readers to comprehend information quickly, they also create visual impact and interest because they are usually numbered and set apart from the rest of the text. When setting forth items such as the elements of a cause of action or the components of a definition, use a list.

Lists (sometimes called *tabulation* can be structured in several ways, but to increase interest:

- Set the list off from the rest of your narrative by spaces above and below your list;
- Indent your list;
- Identify the items in your list with numbers, letters, or "bullets" (•); and
- Punctuate correctly by putting a semicolon after each item (except the last item) and include "or" or "and" before the last item.

Not all lists need to be indented. If the list is short, you may separate each item from the other by a comma and include the list as part of your narrative text.

The grammatical structure of all of the items in any list must be identical or parallel. Thus, if the first word in a list is a verb, all of the following items must also be verbs. Similarly, if the first word in the first item ends in "ing," all subsequent items must also begin with words ending in "ing."

Incorrect

The elements of a cause of action for breach of contract are as follows:

- an agreement
- a breach of that agreement by one party
- the act of the breaching party must have caused damage.

Correct

The elements of a cause of action for breach of contract are as follows:

- an agreement;
- a breach of that agreement by one party; and
- damage caused by the act of the breaching party.

Lack of parallel structure is often seen in resumes in which job applicants will describe their experience as follows: "Drafted documents. Prepared pleadings. Assisting in trial preparation." The last item should be "assis<u>ted</u>" to retain parallel structure.

Similarly, lack of parallel structure can be seen within a sentence; for example, "It is more important to write the brief than arguing it." Revise as follows: "It is more important to write the brief than argue it."

3. *Avoid Nominalizations*

A nominalization occurs when you take an adjective, verb, or adverb and turn it into a noun. While the nominalization itself is technically correct, overuse of nominalizations drains your writing of forcefulness and makes it read as if written by a bureaucrat.

	Nominalizations
The defendant argued.	The defendant made the argument.
The witness concluded.	The witness drew a conclusion.
The contract was enforced.	Enforcement of the contract was accomplished.
We considered our options.	Consideration was given to our options.
We applied for an extension.	An application for an extension was made.

As you can see, nominalizations not only take strong action words such as verbs and convert them into dull nouns, they also tend to make your writing overlong.

Avoid overusing nominalizations by proofreading carefully. Generally, if you use active voice, you will greatly reduce nominalizations. While not all nominalizations can be avoided, their repeated use will render your writing unimaginative. To avoid nominalizations, watch for words that end in *-ion*, *-ent*, and *-ant*.

4. *Avoid Legal Jargon*

The use of "legalese" frustrates readers and results in stodgy writing. Legalese or jargon includes not only archaic and stuffy words and phrases such as "accord," "aforesaid," "whereas," "opine," and "hereinafter referred to," but words and phrases that are unfamiliar to a reader, such as Latin phrases or legal terms (*res judicata*, laches, collateral estoppel). The Texas State Bar has recognized this problem and has held an annual contest of "legaldegook" for atrocious legal writing. A recent "Wooliness Award" was presented for the following:

> For purposes of paragraph (3), an organization described in paragraph (2) shall be deemed to include an organization described in Section 501(C)(4), (5) or (6) which would be described in Paragraph (2) if it were an organization described in Section 501(c)(3).

Try to avoid using legal jargon. Often archaic or jargon-filled phrases can either be omitted entirely or replaced with more familiar terms. For example, an agreement may begin as follows:

> THIS AGREEMENT is made and entered into this fourth day of May 2005, by and between ABC, Inc. (hereinafter referred to as

"Landlord") and Susan Andrews (hereinafter referred to as "Tenant") regarding the premises and covenants hereinafter set forth.

You may easily change the sentence as follows:

THIS AGREEMENT is entered into May 4, 2005, between ABC, Inc. ("Landlord") and Susan Andrews ("Tenant") regarding the following facts.

The omission or replacement of archaic words and phrases with familiar ones not only enhances readability but also results in a more concise writing.

You may not be able to omit all of the legalese you would like, particularly when drafting wills, deeds, contracts, litigation pleadings, and other legal documents that have more rigid structures. These documents are often drafted in accordance with standard forms and conventions of many years ago. In any case, simply try to eliminate as much of the jargon as possible. For example, the phrases "enclosed please find" or "enclosed herewith is" are often used in letters enclosing other documents. While there is nothing grammatically wrong with these expressions, they are examples of legalese. If something is enclosed, won't the reader find it? Simply use the phrase "enclosed is" followed by a description of the item enclosed.

If you are using legal terms or Latin phrases, be sure to give a brief definition for your reader. A client may be completely bewildered by a letter informing him or her that "the doctrine of laches precludes your claim." Rewrite as follows:

The doctrine of laches, that is, an unreasonable and prejudicial delay in bringing an action, precludes your claim.

While the insertion of a definition or explanatory phrase produces a longer document, the effect of enhanced readability is well worth the extra words.

Even if a document is prepared for another legal professional who will be familiar with the Latin phrase or legal term, add the definition because it often serves as a smooth transition for any reader. Readers experienced with the terms will not be offended by your inclusion of a definition and will readily be able to skip over it. Other less experienced readers, such as a law clerk or a client receiving a copy of the writing, will be greatly assisted by the "translation" you provide.

5. *Keep Subjects and Verbs in Proximity*

Because the two most critical parts of a sentence are the subject and the verb, readers typically look for these first to make sense of a sentence. Legal writing is known for creating huge gaps between the subject of a sentence and the verb. When too many words intervene between the subject and the verb, readers no longer remember what the sentence is about by the time they locate the verb. They are then forced to reread the sentence and hunt for the subject.

While you need not immediately follow every subject in every sentence with a verb, avoid large gaps between these two parts of a sentence. Statutes are especially notorious for separating subjects and verbs by long word strings.

Example

Any *person*, including an organization, institution or other entity, that presents or causes to be presented to an officer, employee or agent of this office, or any department thereof, or any state agency, a claim, as defined in subsection 2(g) of this paragraph, that the person knows or has reason to know was not provided as claimed, *is guilty* of a class 1 misdemeanor.

In this sentence, there is a gap of 55 words between the subject (person) and the verb (is guilty). To eliminate these huge gaps, rewrite the sentence, moving the verb closer to the subject.

Example

Any *person*, including an organization, institution or other entity, *is guilty* of a Class 1 misdemeanor by presenting or causing to be presented to an officer, employee, or agent of this office, or any department thereof, or any state agency, a claim, as defined in Section 2(g) of this paragraph, that the person knows or has reason to know was not provided as claimed.

Alternatively, you can make the words intervening between the subject and verb into their own sentence.

Example

The *partnership*, an entity organized and existing under Missouri law and formed after the passage of the Missouri General Partnership Act, *is composed of* Smith, Jones, and Kimball.

Rewrite as:

The *partnership is composed of* Smith, Jones, and Kimball. It is an entity organized and existing under Missouri law and was formed after the passage of the Missouri General Partnership Act.

6. *Use Forceful Words*

Because legal writing is formal, writers often tend to adopt an emotionless, pallid tone in their writing. While your writing should not read like a romance novel, the use of vivid and forceful words will not only keep your readers interested but will aid in converting them to your view-point.

Emphasis cannot be obtained by merely underlining or italicizing words or phrases or by adding a modifier such as "very" or "hardly." You need to select a word vivid enough to carry the meaning you desire. Use a thesaurus or dictionary to help you select words that are vivid and forceful.

Weak	Forceful
The defendant *stated* he knew where the witness was *located*.	The defendant *boasted* he knew where the witness was *secreted*.
Smith *misrepresented* the condition of the premises.	Smith *lied* about the condition of the premises.
very sad	sorrowful
not allowed	forbidden, prohibited
disagree with	contradict
raining hard	pouring
acknowledge guilt	confess
could not believe	incredulous
withdraw a statement	recant

Conversely, do not take a concrete word, which is strong in and of itself, and dilute it such as converting "improbable" to "somewhat unlikely" or "rapid" to "pretty fast." In fact, some words stand on their own and are not susceptible to degree such as "unique," which means the only one of its kind. Something cannot be "quite unique" or "very unique."

7.   *Repeat Strong Words and Phrases*

While you want to avoid redundancy in legal writing, there are certain situations in which repetition can add emphasis to your writing. The repetition of a key word or phrase creates interest and adds drama to writing.

Example

The defendant misled the plaintiff. He misled her by promising the premises were quiet. He misled her by promising the premises were habitable. He misled her by promising the premises were safe.

Each repetition of the words "misled" and "promise" builds on the previous reference. When you use this technique, be sure to structure the sentence so you end with the strongest element.

Example
> She was a diligent worker. She was a loyal friend. She was a loving mother.

8. *Vary the Length of Sentences*

Short sentences are easier to comprehend than long, complex sentences. Nevertheless, you do not want a project filled with sentences of approximately the same length. Such a writing would be tedious to read.

Just as you may need to vary the pattern of your sentences from the standard sentence order (subject-verb-object) to add interest, vary the length of your sentences to enhance readability. For example, a short sentence such as "She refused" is concise and powerful. Generally, sentences that exceed three lines are too long for most readers.

Nevertheless, you do not want a writing filled only with short sentences. Such a project would have a choppy and abrupt tone and would read like a telegram. For example, note the clipped tone of the following sentences.

> The landlord sent her the rent statement. She refused to pay. He evicted her. She countersued. He asked for a jury. The jury agreed with her version.

The following version has a much smoother and more readable quality:

> The landlord sent her the rent statement. She refused to pay and he evicted her. She countersued. Even though he asked for a jury, the jury agreed with her version.

G.   Brevity

The length of a project does not necessarily translate into quality. Some of the most compelling and well-known writings are the briefest. For example, the Lord's Prayer has only 66 words. The Gettysburg Address has 286 words. Yet just one federal statute relating to hospital and medical expenses paid under Medicare has more than 700 words. One of the most dramatic yet brief statements about a person is that engraved on Machiavelli's tomb: "There are not enough words to say his eulogy."

While almost all writers agree in principle that brevity is an admirable goal in legal writing, brevity is not easily accomplished. One of the reasons brevity is difficult to achieve is that the legal research that is the basis for your project represents time and effort. After going to the library, researching, writing, re-writing, Shepardizing or KeyCiting, revising, proofreading, and editing, writers are loath to abandon the words that evidence their hard work. Like pets and children, we quickly find fault with those belonging to others and defend and love our own. For example, one of the entries in the annual Texas State Bar "legaldegook" contest was a sentence written by a lawyer that began "Accordingly, in the interest of brevity," and continued for more than 60 words.

Another contributing factor to the length of legal documents is that the topics discussed are often complex, requiring thoughtful analysis. Finally, over-review of a writing causes increased length. Each paralegal or attorney who works on a project will feel a need to improve a writing, generally by adding to it, changing "now" to "at the present time" or "if" to "in the event that." Thus, being brief is difficult.

While judges complain about lawyers' inability to write succinct briefs, some writing experts suggest that judges themselves contribute to the mass of legal publication by writing longer opinions with more footnotes. One solution proposed by one writing scholar is that judges impose page limits on themselves similar to those imposed on attorneys.

You must be merciless. Your reader's time is at a premium and you cannot afford to frustrate the reader by redundancy and long-winded phrases. Moreover, if the reader continually encounters a rehash of previous material and never encounters new material, he or she may simply abandon the project and never read some of your later, more persuasive arguments. Finally, more and more courts are imposing page limits and word count limits for submissions. Documents that exceed the stated requirements are rejected. Thus, failure to be brief may be legal malpractice.

To achieve brevity:

1. *Omit Needless Words*

There are numerous phrases in English that we use simply by habit. Many of these can be eliminated or reduced to a more concise word or phrase.

Long-Winded Phrases	*Substitutions*
Due to the fact that	Because
As a result of	Consequently, therefore
In addition to	Additionally
Despite the fact that	Although
At the present time	At present, now, currently
During the time that	While
At such time as	When
With regard to	Regarding, concerning
In the event that	If
As to whether	Whether
In order to	To

Careful writing and revising will help you eliminate extra words. Ask yourself if you absolutely need a phrase and whether there is an effective substitute for it. Many commonly used phrases can be replaced by single words with no loss of meaning. In particular, avoid constructions that include more than one preposition, such as "*in* regard *to*." Use "regarding."

2. *Avoid "Throat-Clearing" Introductions*

"Throat-clearing" refers to introductions that are mere preludes for the main topic that is to follow. Writers often feel compelled to warm up the audience by preparing them for the main idea rather than simply presenting the idea.

Throat-Clearing Phrases	*Substitutions*
In this regard it is important to remember that . . .	Remember
The next issue to be considered is . . .	[none — state the issue]
Attention should also be called to the fact that . . .	[none — state the fact]
It is interesting to note that . . .	Note

Other overused introductory words are "clearly" and "obviously." Writers often add "clearly" before introducing a topic, believing that this word will lend persuasive force. To paraphrase a famous jurist, adding the word "clearly" to a sentence won't make it clear; and if the sentence is clear, you don't need the word "clearly."

The word "obviously" should be avoided for the same reason as "clearly." Moreover, "obviously" carries a hostile meaning. By introducing a sentence or topic with the word "obviously" you signal to readers that you believe they lack the capacity to discern the meaning of the sentence on their own. When you introduce a thought with "obviously" what you really are saying is "even to a moron such as you it should be obvious . . . ."

3. *Avoid Redundancy*

Those in the legal profession are wedded to redundancy. They cannot resist saying "null and void and of no legal effect." Is all this needed? If something is null, isn't it void? If it is void, can it have legal effect?

The reason legal writing is so prone to redundancy lies in the history of our language. English has its roots in Latin and French as well as in the language of the Celts and Anglo-Saxons. Often word pairings were used to ensure that readers would understand phrases no matter what their background or station in life. Thus, the French word "peace" joined with the Latin word "quiet." The French "devise" joined the Latin "bequeath."

These redundant doublings have persisted long after their need. Their use today is often the result of pure habit rather than necessity.

If you find yourself using these "stock" redundancies, stop and ask whether one word is sufficient.

> *Common Redundancies*
> acknowledge and agree
> alter or change or modify
> basic fundamentals
> cease and desist
> close proximity
> consented and agreed
> covenant, warrant, and represent
> current status
> due and owing
> each and every
> force or effect
> free and clear
> full and complete
> give, devise, and bequest
> made and entered into
> null and void and of no legal effect
> past history
> previous experience
> refuse and fail
> release, remise, and discharge
> true and correct
> unless and until
> vitally necessary

4. *Avoid Repetition*

Once you have stated your contention or communicated the information you need to communicate, stop. Many beginning legal writers believe they should make every point three times by

- telling the reader what the writing or project will say;
- saying it; and
- reminding the reader of what was said.

There is no place in legal writing for such needless repetition. If you write to clients, they will be sufficiently interested in your communication to grasp what you are telling them. Supervisors, adverse counsel, and judges are sophisticated enough or busy enough that they do not need an argument repeated three times. When court rules dictate the maximum number of pages in briefs submitted to that court you will not have the luxury of being able to repeat your argument. The only exception to the rule of avoiding repetition is that in a long document, readers often appreciate a separate conclusion, which briefly and concisely summarizes your analysis.

H. Order

1. Outlines

Just as you would never begin a car trip to a far-off destination without a road map, you should never begin a writing without some idea as to how you intend to approach the project. A project that is poorly organized not only fails to inform or persuade the reader, it may so frustrate the reader that it will not be read.

The best system for organizing a writing is to use an outline. Many writers doubt the benefits of outlining and have resisted using an outline since elementary school. While the most complete outline includes full sentences or topics divided into headings and subheadings, an outline need not be so formal. The looseleaf notebook containing the notes you took while researching or the index cards containing notes of your research results are working outlines. By shuffling the index cards or the pages in your notebook, you are outlining, that is, organizing your approach to your writing.

Similarly, your outline can consist of your thoughts on the project scribbled on scratch paper. It is not the format of the outline that is important; rather it is that the mere existence of any type of outline forces you to consider and organize the structure of your writing. The outline should disclose the basic sections of your project and the order in which they will be addressed.

If the notes taken during research are not helpful in preparing an outline, simply jot down on paper all of the words and phrases you can think of that relate to your project. Keep writing and listing the entries; do not worry about organizing these entries. This outlining technique is usually called *brainstorming*. After you have finished listing every topic you can think of, carefully examine the list and then group related items together. After you have settled on these rough groupings, decide the order in which the groups should be discussed.

Another method of outlining is called "clustering." Place a circle or "nucleus" in the middle of a blank page of paper. Place the key word or topic of your project in the nucleus. Now write a related topic or issue nearby. Encircle it and draw a line back to your nucleus. Continue by either branching out from the nucleus or the new circle. Trust your instincts to select new words and topics. The final product should look like a spider web. Write your project with your web nearby.

When your outline or "cluster" is completed, regardless whether it is a working outline, a formal outline, or your list of topics, you should be able to determine immediately whether you have included all of the items that need to be addressed and whether you are devoting too much time and effort to minor points at the expense of major points.

Another popular outlining technique is storytelling. Talk to a friend or colleague about your project. Start at the beginning by saying, "I have been asked to . . . ." As you tell the story of your project, some organizational patterns may emerge. Allow yourself to ramble a bit. Keep a notepad nearby, and write down ideas as you are speaking. Your notes are then a preliminary outline.

Finally, allow some "down time" before you begin writing so that ideas percolate and bubble up to the surface. Nearly all writers have experienced an "aha" moment while showering or driving that gives them a great idea for a project. Keep your notepad handy so you can capture these ideas.

Some writers prefer to devote substantial effort to outlining. The actual writing stage is then that much easier. In many instances the writer is simply expanding upon the ideas already set forth in the outline, adding citations, and polishing.

2. *Internal Organization*

The way you organize the project can affect the reader's perception of the project. There are four tips to follow in organizing your writing so it achieves your desired objectives.

a. Use Headings

In longer writings, use headings and subheadings to alert the reader to the subject being discussed. It is nearly impossible for a reader to comprehend page after page of narrative containing no breaks or divisions. Similarly, it is very frustrating for readers to suddenly find themselves in the midst of a discussion of contracts when the preceding paragraph related to fraud.

Headings serve as signals to readers to alert them to the topics you are discussing and to show a change in topics. If, for example, your brief states there are four prerequisites to the awarding of an injunction, it will be helpful to the reader for you to label your discussion in four separate parts, each relating to the element to be discussed next.

In persuasive documents such as briefs, try to make your headings as convincing as possible. ("Plaintiff has suffered irreparable harm as a result of Defendant's actions.") In non-persuasive documents, your headings may be neutral and may consist of a mere word or phrase ("Irreparable Harm").

b. Use Effective Paragraphs

Just as you use headings to break up a solid mass of narrative, use paragraphs to break up a discussion into units that are easy to read. Readers will expect that each of your paragraphs relates to a distinct idea and will also expect that the first sentence of your paragraph will "set the stage" for what follows. This first sentence is the topic sentence. Use a thesis statement (described in Chapter 17) to provide structure to your analysis.

Avoid paragraphs that are too long. How long is too long? Most readers have difficulty with paragraphs that cover more than one-half of a page. Not only does the mind crave a break from a long discussion, so does the eye. Remember the visual effect of your writing and create a project that is pleasing to the eye. Also avoid short paragraphs. The traditional rule is that a paragraph must have more than one sentence. On occasion, however, you may want to use a one- or two-sentence paragraph in legal writing for emphasis and visual effect.

c. Use Effective Transitions

To move smoothly from one sentence, paragraph, or idea to another, use a transition word or phrase. Without transitions, writing would be choppy and telegram-like. Transitions connect what you have said with what will follow. Avoid using the same transition words. Two of the favorite transition words of beginning writers are "however" and "therefore." If you find yourself continually introducing sentences and paragraphs with the same words, examine your project and try to find other transitions to lend variety and interest to your writing.

Commonly used transition words and phrases are as follows:

To introduce a topic
- in general
- initially
- primarily
- to

To show contrast
- although
- but
- conversely
- however
- in contrast
- nevertheless
- on the contrary
- on the other hand
- yet

To show similarity
- in the same way
- just as
- likewise
- similarly

To show examples
- for example
- for instance
- in fact
- namely
- specifically
- that is
- to illustrate

To show conclusions
- accordingly
- as a result
- because
- consequently
- for this reason
- inasmuch as
- therefore
- thus

To show additions
- additionally
- again
- furthermore
- in addition
- moreover

To summarize
- finally
- in brief
- in conclusion
- in summary
- to conclude
- to summarize

d. Use Position and Voice for Emphasis

In nearly every persuasive writing project, there are stronger points and then points writers wish they did not have to mention. Use the location or placement of information as well as voice to draw your reader's attention to the more compelling parts of your writing and to minimize the impact of "negative" or weak sections of your argument.

The most prominent parts of a writing are its beginning and its ending. Readers tend to start projects with great enthusiasm, lose interest in the middle, and then become attentive again when the end is in sight. Therefore, put your strongest arguments and information at the beginning and ending of your project, your paragraphs, and your sentences.

Bury negative information in the middle of your project, in the middle of your paragraphs, and in the middle of your sentences. These locations will attract the least attention and may even be overlooked. This is another compelling reason for crafting strong topic sentences in each paragraph. These topic sentences, typically placed at the beginning of paragraphs, not only convey the main idea of each paragraph but may be the only parts of a project read by a busy reader. Thus, if the first sentence of each paragraph may be the only portion of your project that is read, put favorable information in these prominent positions.

Negative information that is buried in the middle of a project, the middle of a paragraph, or in the subordinate clause of a sentence will be less likely to be noticed. Be extremely careful when including these unfavorable portions of your writing because a careless spelling error or typo will immediately draw your reader's attention to them.

There are other techniques you can use to "hide" flaws in your argument. Because active voice is much stronger and more forceful than passive voice, use passive voice in discussion of information you believe is negative.

For example, if your client sold a house with known defects to the plaintiff, this fact can be disclosed in the following two ways:

Active Voice	The defendant intentionally sold a house with known defects to the plaintiff.
Passive Voice	The house was sold to the plaintiff.

You can easily see that the plaintiff would prefer the first sentence while the defendant would prefer the second. By using the passive voice you deflect attention away from the actor (the defendant) and onto the object of the action (the sale of the house). Note how the use of the passive voice here eliminates any reference whatsoever to the defendant.

Similarly, the techniques discussed above for making writing vivid, such as selecting descriptive and concrete words and avoiding nominalizations, should not be used in discussions of negative information. Selecting vague words ("situation," "matter") and including nominalizations ("The plaintiff underwent an operation" rather than "The doctor operated on the plaintiff") will de-emphasize negative information.

Finally, use detail in describing facts and issues favorable to you and discuss unfavorable facts and issues in general fashion. For example, consider the following two descriptions of an accident, one from the plaintiff's perspective and one from the defendant's.

Plaintiff's version:

As the plaintiff was safely driving within the legal speed limit, defendant's car careened down the hill and collided with the left front door of the plaintiff's car. The plaintiff was pinned behind the steering wheel for three hours. After being forcibly removed from the totally damaged car by the police and firefighters at the scene, the plaintiff was rushed to the hospital by ambulance, where she was treated for her severe and disabling injuries, including a broken pelvis, a concussion, and internal bleeding.

Defendant's version:

The accident occurred as defendant was travelling westward on Adams Avenue. After the collision, the plaintiff remained in her car until she was transported to the hospital, where she received treatment for her injuries.

Note the detail in the plaintiff's version, which paints a vivid picture for the reader. In contrast, the defendant's version glosses over the event by summarizing it in a general fashion. In fact, the defendant's version doesn't even make clear that the defendant was involved in the collision.

Remember that documents submitted to court are persuasive documents, and their style differs from the objective style used in legal memoranda. As discussed in Chapter 17, in such objective projects the writer must disclose possible weaknesses in the case. Consequently, in these writings, you will not bury negative information but will give it as much emphasis as positive information.

I. Drafting Techniques

1. Getting Started

For most writers, the most difficult task is getting started. The research is completed, the deadline is looming, and yet the writer cannot begin.

The best cure for this common disease is to write something. Write anything. Just get started. If the idea of beginning an argument paralyzes you, don't begin there. Start writing the section of the document you are most comfortable with, even if this is not the correct order. If you are familiar with the facts, begin with a statement of facts. If you know how you want to conclude a letter, memo, or brief, begin with the conclusion. The mere act of writing any section of a document will relieve some of your anxiety about being able to write.

Use the storytelling technique discussed above to help you organize your thoughts and give you ideas on how to begin writing.

Set a goal for yourself. Tell yourself that the statement of facts must be completed by noon. Challenge yourself to complete a task within an hour. These techniques may help you get started.

2. Finishing on Time

You will often be given deadlines for finishing projects. Similarly, documents prepared for courts may need to be filed by a specified date. If you have a deadline date, you may find it helpful to work backward from this date and establish a schedule for yourself. Set a date by which all of the research will be done, another date for completing the first draft, another for cite-checking, and another for revising.

If you are a habitual last-minute worker, always finding yourself operating in crisis mode, it may help to announce a deadline date to someone. Go public. By telling your supervisor, "The first draft will be on your desk by Wednesday morning," you will commit yourself to meet this self-imposed deadline. If there is no deadline for filing the document with the court, ask your supervisor, "When would you like this completed?" Without some deadline date, the project will languish on your desk and continually be relegated to the back burner while you work on other projects.

Once the deadline is established, allow yourself some time for emergencies. The copier may break down, you may get sick, or someone else's project may have a higher priority. If you don't allow room for these last-minute crises, you may fail to meet the deadline.

Set small goals for yourself. Tell yourself, "I will have the statement of facts done by 11:00 A.M. today." These self-imposed deadlines will help you tackle the project bit by bit and meet the real deadline.

If you draw a blank while you are writing, just keep going. Move to another section and return to the difficult section later. Mark blank or troublesome sections with sticky notes if writing in longhand and with "xx's" or some other signal if you are word processing. You can use the "find and replace" feature to locate these troublesome passages later.

Avoid self-censoring. Don't worry at this stage that something will sound awkward or unsophisticated. Similarly, don't obsess about spelling and grammar, and so forth. You can clean up these problems during your revision process.

If you are interrupted while writing, put a sticky note on your notepad or computer screen to remind yourself what you want to write about next. When you return to the project, these notes will help you return to your project efficiently and effortlessly.

3. Methods of Writing

There are three primary methods used for the actual writing process: writing by hand, dictating, and writing on a word processor.

a. Writing by Hand

Some people are most comfortable writing in longhand. While this can be a very effective technique, its primary drawback is that it is extremely time-consuming, especially for a long memo or brief. In fact, some law firms are vehemently opposed to writing in longhand and will insist that a faster method be used. Despite this, projects written in longhand often need less revising than projects dictated or composed on a word processor.

b. Dictating

Dictating is probably the speediest method of drafting. It can take some time, however, to shed self-consciousness when you dictate. Initially, dictating may seem painfully slow. Confidence is rapidly gained, however. Stick with it until you become comfortable.

In the beginning, you may prefer to prepare a mini-outline for your dictating efforts and follow that as you dictate. You may also find that your initial attempts include repetitious sentences and poorly organized paragraphs. With time and practice, however, you will acquire skill at dictating together with a certain mental discipline enabling you rapidly and effectively to organize your thoughts. This skill at verbalizing complex thoughts may translate into ease and confidence in speaking as well. This enhanced competence in oral presentation is one of the hidden benefits of dictating.

If you dictate, you will need to insert punctuation and paragraphing so the transcriber knows how to prepare the document. Similarly, you will need to spell certain words.

The popularity of dictating in law practice has declined in recent years as writers have become more comfortable composing with word processors. Nevertheless, it remains an effective and efficient way to draft for many writers.

c. Using a Word Processor

The most popular method of writing today is composing using a word processor. While this method may be very speedy, and allows much flexibility in changing the placement of sections, individuals tend to spend excessive time revising as they go along. Revising is a task better left until the end of a project. Your project need not be perfect with the first draft. Your initial draft should be focused on including the major issues and arguments needed to be addressed. Try to fight the temptation to engage in micro-editing as you draft on a word processor. Allow your first draft to flow smoothly and then devote effort to revision later.

If you use a word processor, consider the following:

- Save your versions frequently. Use the functions on your computer that allow you to select how frequently the document will be saved.
- To ensure that you don't lose important information, back up your versions on discs, print paper copies of the document frequently in case the disc is corrupted, and e-mail your documents to your personal e-mail account or to a friend for safekeeping.

- Use the features of your word processor to help you. Consider using the "track changes" feature to show changes between drafts. With a single keystroke, you can then accept (or reject) all changes. This technique, called "redlining," is used when legal professionals negotiate the form and content of a document because it allows each to see the changes made by the other.
- Understand that viewing the project one screen at a time allows you to see only a small slice of the document. Thus, headings and other items may become inconsistent. Carefully review a hard copy to check for consistency in the presentation of such items.

J. Electronic Communications

New forms of communication, namely, electronic communications, have arisen in the past several years, changing the way people communicate at the workplace. While many of them are great timesavers, others are traps for the unwary. Consider the following when using any of the newer forms of electronic communcations.

1. Phones and Voice Mail

Although conference calls and voice mail can both reduce the time you spend on communications, there are a couple of guidelines that will assist you:

- When setting up a conference call, treat it as a meeting and be prompt in dialing in to the conference number.
- Make sure that introductions are made for all participants and that all participants can hear each other.
- Always ask for permission before placing someone on a speaker-phone.
- Always disclose that another is listening with you if you are on a speakerphone.
- Do not leave overly long or rambling voice mail messages.
- Clearly and slowly state your name and phone number in voice mail messages. Repeat at the end of your message for those unfamiliar with you so they do not have to replay the message to obtain your name and number.
- Avoid using voice mail to "dodge" callers and to evade bad news.
- Avoid disclosing confidential information over a car phone or cell phone. Messages may be easily intercepted.
- Check your office policy to see if cell phones can be used for business while you are driving. After a large law firm was sued in 2001 for an accident caused by one of its attorneys who was driving while using the cell phone for firm business, many firms now prohibit such use.

2.   *Communication by Facsimile*

Communicating by facsimile is so commonplace that many firms use "real" correspondence only for more critical matters, such as opinions and status reports. Check your firm or office policy as to documents that may be sent by facsimile. Most facsimile cover sheets will include a confidentiality notice indicating that if someone receives the communication in error, he or she should return it to the sender. Such notices are used to maintain attorney-client confidentiality and privilege. Consider sending voluminous materials by mail because even the best facsimile machines produce a copy that is less readable than an original. Always double-check the facsimile number before pressing "send." Once the document is sent, it cannot be recalled.

3.   *E-mail*

E-mail is becoming an increasingly common method of communication, both within the workplace and to clients. E-mail creates an air of informality and the ease with which a message can be composed and sent causes countless errors. We have all heard stories of people who, much to their chagrin, have mistakenly replied to an entire "list" rather than solely to the sender of a message. Many firms and offices have policies as to the types of communications that can be sent via e-mail and will include confidentiality notices at the conclusion of each e-mail message. Follow these guidelines:

- Spell-check all e-mail and proof for accuracy. If necessary, print a hard copy of the message, proof it, correct it, and then send it. It is far better to be overly cautious than to be perceived as sloppy.
- Because e-mail is generally "dashed off" without a great deal of thought, it often results in brusque and abrupt communications. The reader will not be able to see your expression, gauge your body language, or hear any intonation. Thus, attempts at sarcasm and humor may be misperceived. Consider receiving a communication saying, "I resent your message." You may be tempted to respond in a curt or hostile fashion before you realize the writer meant to say, "I re-sent your message."
- Never pass along inappropriate e-mail at your workplace. Politely inform the sender that you do not care to receive such information.
- Do not assume e-mail is confidential. Many employers monitor e-mail communications.
- Be brief and to the point. Many people receive a great number of e-mail messages each day and won't bother to read a long, rambling message.
- Make the subject line specific. Let the recipient know at a glance what the message discusses. Add "no need to respond" to the subject line to save yourself from receiving excess e-mail messages.

- Be a charitable reader. Resist overreacting to an e-mail communication that may seem abrupt. The writer may have been trying to be brief.
- Avoid using e-mail to resolve disputes or for delicate matters in which tone of voice is important.

CyberSites

http://www.sec.gov/ pdf/plaine.pdf	The Web site of the Securities and Exchange Commission offers excellent guidance on writing in "plain English," with numerous samples, explanations, and tips.
http:// www.plainlanguage.gov	This is the Web site of the Plain Language Action & Information Network, a government volunteer group working to improve communications by the federal government. Numerous samples and tips are given for writing user-friendly documents, and various links to other useful resources are provided. The guidance document "Writing User-Friendly Documents" is available.
http://www.archives.gov	The Web site of the National Archives and Records Administration offers materials on drafting legal documents. Enter "Drafting Legal Documents" into the search box.
http://www.ualr.edu/ cmbarger/ RESOURCES.htm	This Web site of a law school professor offers links to references and a varity of resources for legal writers, including tips on grammar, style, and composition.
http://www.ccc.commnet. edu/grammar	This site offers helpful and specific guides to grammar and writing.
http://www.bartleby.com	This site offers direct linking to numerous writing resources, including dictionaries, thesauri, *Bartlett's Familiar Quotations*, and portions of Strunk and White's classic book, *The Elements of Style*.
http://www.quintcareers. com/writing	This site offers a collection of writing essentials.
http:// owl.english.purdue.edu	Purdue University's Online Writing Lab offers handouts on general writing concerns, achieving conciseness, using active voice, developing an outline, overcoming writer's block, parallel structure, and other writing topics.
http://www.dictionary.com	This site includes a thorough dictionary and thesaurus to help with accurate word selection.
http://www1.law.ucla.edu/ volokh/legalese.htm	This site provides a thorough list of archaic and stuffy legal terms and suggested replacements.

Assignment for Chapter 15

PRECISION

SELECT THE CORRECT WORD IN THE FOLLOWING SENTENCES.

1. The effect/affect of the expert's testimony was negligible.
2. The company's principle/principal office is in Atlanta.
3. She agreed to the terms of the parenting agreement during our oral/verbal telephone conversation.
4. The settlement was entered into between/among all four litigants.
5. The jury found him liable for/guilty of malpractice.
6. All attorneys must insure/ensure their clients are prepared for their depositions.
7. The jury was affected/effected by Ms. Lane's testimony.
8. Tina prepared the only memoranda/memorandum this week.
9. Beside/Besides the bailiff, the marshal also performed security checks in the courtroom.
10. "It's the principal/principle of the thing," the client told her attorney.

CLARITY

REPHRASE EACH OF THE FOLLOWING TO PRODUCE A CLEARER SENTENCE.

1. The contract was signed on April 4. The parties' agreement was later amended in May.
2. We are not precluded from claiming that Dr. Smith failed to adhere to a not unreasonable standard of care.
3. We do not deny that scandalous trademarks are unprotectable under the U.S. Trademark Act.
4. The witness arrived early for her deposition. The deponent later tired in the afternoon.
5. We cannot fail to allege that the defendant refused to repair the leased premises.
6. Although the seller paid taxes on the property, the vendor failed to obtain title insurance for the parcel.
7. The defendant's motorcycle collided with the pedestrian. The motor vehicle was then sold for scrap metal.
8. We cannot forget to ensure that Ms. Smith is not unprepared for trial.
9. Mr. Phillips told Mr. Ruiz that he must attend the settlement conference.
10. The bank released the financial statements on Friday. This was a violation of its obligations to maintain the records in confidence.

READABILITY

REWRITE THE FOLLOWING SENTENCES TO MAKE THEM MORE READABLE BY USING THE ACTIVE VOICE.

1. A decision was announced by the Supreme Court that affected all claims brought under the new legislation.
2. The election held by the corporation resulted in approval of the directors nominated by the committee.
3. An agreement to settle the case was approved by the judge.
4. A confidentiality agreement was signed by all of the company's employees.
5. The transcript was prepared by the court reporter after a hearing was held by the judge.

REWRITE THE FOLLOWING SENTENCES TO MAKE THEM MORE READABLE BY USING PARALLEL STRUCTURE.

1. The critical characteristics of effective paralegals are attention to detail, organizational skills, and being flexible.
2. Indexing documents and preparation of letters to clients were two of Mary's job duties.
3. The settlement agreement required the defendant to pay $50,000, sign a confidentiality agreement, and refraining from making any further statements to the media.
4. The clients were instructed to sign the promissory note, depositing the money into the escrow account, and file a copy of the deed of trust with the clerk's office.
5. Careful proofreading and making edits to documents is key to ensuring their accuracy.
6. There are two steps to closing the file: first, returning the original documents to the client; and secondly, preparing the summary of the file contents.

REWRITE THE FOLLOWING SENTENCES TO MAKE THEM MORE READABLE BY ELIMINATING JARGON.

1. Until such time as they execute the agreement, the parties have agreed and consented to cease and desist from any and all activities related to discovery in the instant case at bar.
2. In the event that the document evidences fraud or deceit in its inception or making, the plaintiff shall be required to apprise the defendant antecedent to commencing litigation.
3. The first parcel of land is contiguous and adjacent to the second.
4. At her deposition, the defendant will be required to elucidate her reason for failing and refusing to consummate the purchase transaction relating to the real estate in question.

5. In reference to your lease, we opine that the remainder of the rent that is due and owing must be paid to the landlord.

State Your Answer

1. Review the handout *Writing User-Friendly Documents* at the Plain Language Web site at http://www.plainlanguage.gov. Review page 19. What is a "noun sandwich" and how can it be avoided?
2. Review the SEC's guidance document *Plain English Handbook* at http://www.sec.gov. Review Chapter 6. What are the most common writing problems that the SEC has encountered?
3. Access Purdue University's Online Writing Lab at http://owl.english. purdue.edu. Review the handout entitled "Parallel Structure."
    a. What is the third rule that the Lab recommends to avoid problems with parallel structure?
    b. What proofreading strategies are recommended to avoid problems with parallel structure?
4. Access Professor Eugene Volokh's site at http://www1.law.ucla. edu/~volokh/legalese.htm. What substitutions are recommended for the following terms of legalese: "evince," "negatively affect," and "substantiate"?
5. Access the site http://www.ccc.commnet.edu/grammar and review the information on Writer's Block. What is the worst part of the writing experience for many writers?

Legal Correspondence

I didn't have time to write a short letter, so I've written a long one instead.

Usually attributed to Blaise Pascal

A. Letterwriting
B. Conclusion

Chapter Overview

While television and movies would have you believe that lawyers spend all day arguing interesting and exciting cases in court, the truth is that much of a lawyer's time is spent writing. Lawyers often rely on paralegals to assist in the writing process and often delegate an entire writing task to paralegals.

This chapter will introduce you to one of the most common forms of legal writings: legal correspondence. Letters are written for several purposes, and thus the style and tone you use will vary according to the purpose of the letter.

As you work and have the opportunity to review the writings of others, start collecting samples of the writings you find most effective. Use these samples to build up your arsenal of writing tools.

A. Letterwriting

1. Introduction

Unlike other legal writings, such as contracts, wills, and court briefs, there is no rigid list of elements that must be included in a letter. While letters should, of course, contain the basics (date, salutation, body, and closing), you will be able to exercise great creativity in letterwriting based upon the goal you seek to achieve in your letter. The tone you adopt and the order in which you elect to discuss items are at your discretion. To beginning legal writers this flexibility can be intimidating. Without a rigid format to follow, some writers become paralyzed.

Letters can be extremely effective tools. The first letter you send to a client or adversary often establishes the basis for a relationship. If your letter to adverse counsel is hostile and arrogant, you will be responded to in kind, and this will mark the tone of future correspondence. Thus, you need to do some planning and thinking before you write.

The two most important questions to ask yourself before you begin a letter are "Who will be reading this letter?" and "What will this letter say?" The answer to the first question will set the tone for your letter, and the answer to the second question will tell you what type of letter you should write.

a.   Who Will Be Reading This Letter?

The tone or style of your letter must be appropriate for the reader. If the letter is directed to an individual who is relatively inexperienced with litigation, you will need to explain the information you present in the most clear and complete fashion possible. If the letter is directed to another legal professional, such as a judge, attorney, or other paralegal, you will know that your discussion of some matters need not be as detailed or elementary as for a layperson.

If you find your letters are becoming stuffy and legalistic in style, there are a few techniques you can use to warm up the tone. One is to use personal pronouns, especially "you." Therefore, rather than saying "tenants have a right to withhold rent if the leased premises are not habitable," try saying "as a tenant you have the right to withhold rent because your premises are no longer habitable." Similarly, contractions such as "can't" and "wouldn't" rather than "cannot" and "would not" tend to make a letter slightly less formal and more personal, although contractions are not commonly used in legal or business writing.

The fact that you will adapt your tone in legal letters to suit different readers is no different from what you already do: A letter written home to your family is written in a style entirely different from a letter responding to a job announcement.

b.   What Will This Letter Say?

Before you begin drafting any letter, focus on the central purpose of your letter. Try to distill this to one or two sentences. For example, some purposes may be as follows:

- The client needs to know a deposition has been scheduled for next month.
- The debtor needs to understand that failure to repay the client will result in litigation.
- The adverse counsel needs to be persuaded to dismiss the client from litigation.

- The client needs to be provided advice regarding cutting down trees on a neighbor's property.

These four examples represent the most basic types of legal correspondence: *general correspondence* or *informative*, *demand*, and *opinion* letters. Once you decide what type of letter you need to write, a style will come almost naturally.

Before discussing techniques for writing these varieties of letters, we will examine the format and elements of legal letters in general.

2. *The Elements of Letters*

While there are different types of letters you will write, there are certain "basics" that are common to all legal correspondence. The components of legal correspondence are similar to those used for general business letters.

a. Letterhead

Law firms, government offices and agencies, and corporations all use special stationery, called *letterhead*, that serves to identify the office by name, address, telephone and facsimile numbers, and other relevant information. While usually placed at the top of a page, some businesses and firms place letterhead information in a column running down the left side of the page or at the bottom of the page. Law firms (unless they have a large number of attorneys) usually list the attorneys associated with the firm on the letterhead. Be careful when drafting and setting up a letter that you recognize how much room the letterhead takes up because you need some space between the letterhead and your writing. Use letterhead for all correspondence connected with your employer because it conveys the message to the recipient that the correspondence is "official." Letterhead is used only for the first page of a letter. The remaining pages match the color and quality of the letterhead page but are not imprinted with the letterhead.

b. Date

Every item of correspondence must include a date, written out by month, day, and year (for example, August 12, 2005). The date is usually centered three lines beneath the letterhead, although occasionally it is placed at the left margin. Because dates in legal matters can be critical, be sure the date given is the date the letter is actually mailed, rather than the date of an earlier draft.

c. Special Mailing Notations

If your correspondence will be sent to the recipient by any means other than first class mail, indicate such as follows: "Hand Delivered," or "Registered Mail," or "By Facsimile." This notation should be placed at the left margin two lines below the date and two lines above the address. Similarly, any other special notations such as "Attorney-Client Communication — Privileged and Confidential" should appear before the inside address.

d. Inside Address

The addressee's name and address should appear two lines below the date or any special mailing notations. Always follow the addressee's or organization's preferences for spelling, capitalization, and punctuation. Use titles if appropriate, such as Ellen Cochran, M.D., Stanley L. Williams, Esq., or David P. Kimball, Executive Vice President. If you do not know the marital status of a female addressee, use "Ms." unless you are directed otherwise. The form "Mrs. William Trainor" is acceptable only in social letters. Use "Ms. Madelyn G. Trainor." See Figure 16-1 for sample addresses.

e. Reference or Subject Notation

The reference notation indicates the subject matter of the correspondence. The notation may refer to the title of a case, the topic to be discussed in the letter, or a file or claim number. The reference notation gives the reader an immediate snapshot of what is to be discussed and also helps you later if you need to locate a letter you previously wrote. The reference notation (abbreviated as "Re:") is usually placed two lines below the inside address. As a courtesy to your reader, include his or her file or reference number if you know it, following your own reference notation. If your office uses internal file numbers, indicate those as well, because they often assist in mail-sorting. See Figure 16-2 for sample reference notations.

Figure 16-1
Sample Addresses

Ms. Donna A. Higgins
4529 Grandview Avenue
San Diego, CA 92110

Mr. Allan N. Navarro
President
ABC Distributing Company
1429 Burgener Boulevard
Chicago, IL 96104

Janet F. Sanderson, Esq.
Mills, Arnold and Smith
2900 L Street, NW
Washington, D.C. 20006

Director of Human Resources
Smith Management Company
2800 Arlington Avenue
Irving, TX 75247-3159

Figure 16-2
Sample Reference Notations

Re: *Calvin v. Temple Motors, Inc.*
    Civil Action No. 92-696-VMA

Re: Estate of Boyer
    Our File: 9204\04-646
    Your File: CN-9220

Re: Punitive Damages in Fraud Actions

f. Salutation

The salutation, or greeting, usually appears two lines beneath the reference notation. Unless you are acquainted with the addressee, err on the side of formality and address the letter to Mr. Brown or Ms. Taylor, for example. Once again, unless you have been directed otherwise, address letters to females as "Ms." Letters to an unknown recipient such as the attorney general of a state may be directed to "Dear Sir or Madam:" Follow the salutation with a colon in business letters and with a comma in personal letters. See Figure 16-3 for sample salutations.

Practice Tip

Unknown Addressees

If you do not know the name of the recipient of a letter, for example, the Commissioner of the Internal Revenue Service, consider the following:

- **Use a title, such as *Dear Commissioner*; or**
- **Do some research on the Internet to find out the name of the Commissioner. In other situations, use the salutation *Dear Colleague.***

---

g. Body

The body of the letter begins two lines below the salutation. The body is the critical part of your correspondence because it conveys your message. The first sentence and paragraph should set the stage for the rest of your letter by indicating the purpose of the letter.

Business letters and legal correspondence are usually single-spaced and then double-spaced between paragraphs. The second and following pages will not be on letterhead but will match the color and quality of the first letterhead page and will usually contain information such as the following (a "header") in the upper left-hand corner of each page:

Mr. Elliot Anthony
December 14, 2004
Page Two

Figure 16-3
Sample Salutations

Dear Mr. Smith:
Dear Ms. Anderson:
Dear Sir or Madam:

h. Closing and Signature

Most letters close with statements such as the following:

> Please do not hesitate to call me if you have any questions.
> Thank you in advance for your cooperation and courtesy.
> If you have any questions or comments you may reach me at the
> number given above.

The complimentary closing is usually "Very truly yours," "Sincerely," "Best regards," "Yours truly," or something similar, followed by a comma. "Very truly yours" is generally regarded as more formal and is used less frequently than "Sincerely." If the letter is addressed to a judge, senator, or representative, the complimentary closing is typically "Respectfully." Capitalize the first letter in the complimentary closing and place it two lines below the body of the letter. The closing is usually centered.

Avoid informal or unusual closings such as "Affectionately," or "Successfully yours." Do not merge your complimentary closing with the last line of your letter. These merged closings were fashionable hundreds of years ago but have a stilted and archaic look. An example of a merged closing is as follows:

> Thanking you for your attention, I remain,
>
> Yours very truly,
>
> Suzanne Forrest

For letters that you will sign, be sure to indicate your title underneath your signature so the reader will know your position in the firm. Allow four lines between the complimentary close and your typed name. Some individuals prefer to use blue ink for their signatures, so readers can easily tell the document is an original rather than a copy.

> Very truly yours,   Sincerely,
>
> Matthew K. Lyons   Paula L. Wagner
> Legal Assistant   Senior Paralegal
>
> Best regards,
>
> Elizabeth A. Murphy
> Legal Assistant to Kenneth Trainor

i. Reference Initials, Enclosures, and Copies

Most letters include a few final notations. Generally, the arrangement of final notations is as follows: reference initials (placed two lines below the writer's typed name and title); indications of enclosures (placed one line below the reference initials), and indications of copies (placed one line below any indications of enclosures). All final notations appear at the left margin, but their presentation styles may differ from author to author.

Reference initials indicate who wrote the letter and who typed it or prepared it. If the author is Maria M. Adkins and the secretary who types it is Gregory L. Huntingdon, the reference "MMA/glh" would appear at the left margin, two lines below the signature block. The use of "mmg:glh" is also common.

If you are enclosing something in a letter, indicate this by the word "Enclosure" or the abbreviation "Encl." (or "Enclosures" or "Encls." for more than one enclosure). Some writers list or identify the item enclosed, so the reader will quickly know if the correct item has been included. You may also see the notation "Enclosures (2)" for multiple enclosures. Some authors use the word "attachment" rather than "enclosure" when material is physically attached to the letter rather than merely enclosed.

Copies of the letter you write may be sent to others. For example, the client will routinely be provided with copies of letters you write to adverse counsel because this is a way of keeping the client informed of the progress of a case. To indicate the recipients of copies use "cc:" followed by the names of those who will be receiving copies. While "cc" stands for "carbon copies," which have universally been replaced by photocopies, the signal "cc:" remains in use.

There may be instances in which you do not want the reader of your letter to know who received a copy of it. In such cases, simply sign your letter, mail it, and then mark the copies that will go to the unidentified individual (assume Theresa Stone) that will be placed in the file: "bcc: Theresa Stone." This is a reference to "blind carbon copy." See Figure 16-4 for sample notations for copies and enclosures.

j. Format Considerations

Letters are written on standard 8½″ × 11″ paper and are usually single-spaced and then double-spaced between component parts (for example, between the date and inside address, between the inside address and reference notation, between the reference notation and salutation) and between paragraphs.

Figure 16-4
Sample Notations for Reference Initials,
Enclosures, and Copies

TLB/amk
Encl.
cc: Susan M. Everett
     Thomas L. Cruz
cc w/encl.: Stephen S. Neal

Some letters show no indentations for paragraphs because new paragraphs are clearly indicated by the double-spacing between paragraphs. This style is referred to as "block form" or "left justified." In block form, all elements of the letter, including the date and complimentary closing, begin at the left margin.

Other firms and authors prefer to indent five spaces for new paragraphs even though they are set apart by double-spacing. This style is called "modified block form." Here the date, complimentary closing, writer's identification, and signature are all centered or placed just to the right of center.

When the right-hand margin is even and every line ends at the right at the same space, this is referred to as "right justification" or "full justification." Such letters present a very crisp appearance. One drawback to right justified margins is that the spacing in some words will be cramped while others may be slightly spread out. Reading studies have documented that word-processed right-justified documents are more difficult to read because the added spaces eliminate distinctive word spatial characteristics, which aid comprehension and ease of reading. To a reader, the use of right justification is often distracting. Continuing improvements in word processors are eliminating these spacing problems. Neverthless, some writers prefer a "ragged edge" at the right margin, believing it has less of a "computer" look and more of a "personally typed" look. Many word processing programs now offer letter templates for business letters in which spacing and common closings are already included, allowing you to "fill in the blanks" of the form. Spacing is pre-set as well.

Never allow a page to begin or end with one line by itself or one heading by itself. Referred to as "widows and orphans," these single lines or headings present an unprofessional appearance. Use 12-point or 10-point typeface for readability. Twelve-point type is preferred. Use a common typeface such as Times New Roman or Courier.

3. *Types of Letters*

a. **General Correspondence**

General correspondence or informative letters may include letters requesting information or responding to requests for information, cover letters that accompany some document or other enclosure, confirmation letters that confirm some agreement or arrangement reached with another party, or status or report letters providing a report to a client or insurance company of the progress of a case. Except for status letters, these letters are often brief and may be only one or two paragraphs in length.

These letters should contain the components of all letters (date, inside address, reference notation). They also should conform to the elements of good legal writing set forth in Chapter 15, namely, precision, clarity, readability, brevity, and order. If you misspell the client's name or send the letter to the wrong address, this will attract far more attention than the content of the letter.

If you are unsure whether a letter should be sent to confirm some matter or clarify some detail, err on the side of caution and write the letter. This will keep the file complete and help establish the progress of the case if you aren't there to explain it. Always send a confirming letter to opposing counsel to confirm dates, amounts, or any other matter. If adverse counsel has offered to settle the case for $20,000, immediately confirm this in writing and then notify the supervising attorney, who will likely conduct negotiations or give you instructions regarding such negotiations. If adverse counsel has granted you an extension to answer interrogatories or produce documents, immediately confirm this in writing so no dispute can later arise as to the dates. See Figure 16-5 for several sample general correspondence letters, including confirmation, cover, and status letters.

b. Demand Letters

Demand letters set forth a client's demands. The most common type of demand letter is a collection letter, which outlines the basis for a debt due to a client and sets forth a demand that it be paid. Other demand letters, however, demand that certain action be taken, such as a demand that a landlord repair a leaking roof or a demand that one company cease using a trademark similar to one owned by another company. Your tone should be firm and business-like, not strident or nasty. To eliminate any disputes whether the letter was received, send the letter by some verifiable type of delivery, such as registered mail. The only portion of a demand letter that will differ from a general correspondence letter is the content of the body. Include these elements:

- *Introduction of your firm.* Identify your firm and specify your role. A simple sentence stating "This firm represents James K. Matthews regarding the automobile accident that occurred on January 8, 2004" is sufficient.
- *Recitation of facts.* You must include the facts upon which the client's claim is based. Because your aim is to motivate the reader to pay your client or take some action, phrase the factual statement as persuasively as possible.
- *Demand.* Set forth as clearly as possible your client's demand. If this is a collection letter, specify the exact amount due. If you are demanding that the reader take some specific action, such as repairing a leaking roof, say so. If there are several components to your demand, you may wish to set them forth in a list.
- *Consequence of non-compliance.* Because your aim in a demand letter is to persuade the reader to pay your client or take some action, you should include a statement telling the reader of the consequence of not complying with the demand letter. These consequences may include the institution of litigation, the cessation of work on a project, or some other adverse action. While most readers will be offended by heavy-handed threats, there is nothing wrong in clearly and concisely explaining to a reader what will occur if the client's demands are not met.

Figure 16-5
Sample General Correspondence Letters
A.   Sample Confirmation Letter

LAW OFFICES
OF
MICHELLE L. MONACO
2300 BIRCH DRIVE
PHOENIX, ARIZONA 60234
(609) 788-4000

November 8, 2004

Stephen L. James, Esq.
6200 Tenth Street
Phoenix, AZ 60244

Re: *Brownell v. Kaplan*

Dear Mr. James:

This letter will confirm that you have granted us an extension to respond to the plaintiff's complaint in the above-referenced action until December 6, 2004. As I explained, the additional time is needed due to my client's hospitalization. Thank you for your courtesy and cooperation.

Please feel free to call me if you have any comments or questions.

Sincerely,

Michelle L. Monaco

MLM/pmr
cc: Sharon J. Kaplan

Figure 16-5 *(Continued)*

B.   Sample Cover Letters

SMITH, CHURCH, AND UPSHAW
1414 SOUTH ADAMS STREET
SUITE 1000
BOSTON, MASSACHUSETTS
(214) 649-1200

January 14, 2005

Ms. Ann B. Milstead
2001 Elysian Fields Avenue
New Orleans, LA 70015

Re: *Sanderson v. Milstead*

Dear Ann:

I am enclosing a copy of the transcript of the plaintiffs' deposition in the above-referenced action. Please review this carefully and call me with any comments you may have. As you know, we are particularly interested in the plaintiff's version of the events in the two hours preceding the accident. Any inconsistencies that you may find in the plaintiff's testimony would be extremely helpful. We look forward to hearing from you.

Very truly yours,

William B. Church

WBC/swa
Encl.

Figure 16-5

B. Sample Cover Letters (Continued)

LAW OFFICES OF THOMAS N. MILLER
1600 ELM STREET
SUITE 202
PORTLAND, OREGON 60102
(402) 657-1990

February 6, 2005

Mr. and Mrs. James E. Bailey
2002 Artesia Boulevard
Portland, OR 60435

Re: Execution of Wills

Dear Mr. and Mrs. Bailey:

I enjoyed meeting you last week and discussing the preparation of your wills. I have prepared the first drafts of the wills. They are enclosed for your review. After you have examined the wills, please call me with any changes or corrections you have. I will then revise them according to your instructions and schedule a date for you to come to my office to sign the wills.

Please feel free to call me if you have any questions or comments.

Sincerely,

Thomas N. Miller

TNM:scg
Encls.

Figure 16-5

B. *Sample Cover Letters*   *(Continued)*

LAW OFFICES
OF
TAYLOR AND GILBEY
4305 WILLETT STREET
KANSAS CITY, MISSOURI 45609
(421) 678-1299

September 14, 2004

Cynthia A. Chan, Esq.
5000 Missouri Avenue
Kansas City, MO 45609

Re: *Anders v. Patterson*
Your File: CV 1895

Dear Ms. Chan:

In reviewing my correspondence to you of yesterday, I noticed that I neglected to include a copy of Exhibit A, which should have been enclosed with the letter. I am enclosing Exhibit A with this letter and apologize for any inconvenience this may have caused you.

Please feel free to call me if you have any questions or comments.

Sincerely,

Francis K. Taylor

FKT:wlm
Encl.

Figure 16-5 *(Continued)*

C. Sample Status Letter

FENTON, HOGUE AND HOGUE
1200 B STREET, SUITE 1900
LOS ANGELES, CALIFORNIA 90234
(405) 765-1400

July 16, 2004

Dale L. Curtis, M.D.
3200 Montana Avenue
Los Angeles, CA 90256

Re: Fontana v. Curtis, et al.
     Our File: 94081

Dear Dr. Curtis:

This letter will provide you with a brief status report on the progress of the above-referenced action. As you know, we have provided interrogatories, or written questions, to the plaintiff, which he is required to answer under oath and return to us within thirty (30) days. After we have had an opportunity to review the plaintiff's answers, we will be in a better position to evaluate which documents we should request and which individuals and witnesses should be deposed so we may obtain their testimony regarding the acts of professional negligence alleged against you.

The Superior Court has recently notified us that a settlement conference has been scheduled on the matter for Wednesday, August 12, 2004, at 2:00 p.m. in Room 2404 of the Los Angeles County Courthouse, located at 1212 Wilshire Boulevard in Los Angeles. You are required to attend that conference, at which time the judge assigned to the case will explore the possibilities of settlement. The plaintiff will also attend and will be expected to make a reasonable demand for settlement. If we are unable to settle the case at that time, a trial date will be assigned. We expect that the trial will occur after the first of the year.

As soon as we receive the plaintiff's answers to the interrogatories, we will provide you with a copy for your review and comment. Please contact us if you have any questions.

Very truly yours,

Linda J. Fenton

LJF:sfk

- *Date of compliance*. You must set forth in explicit terms the deadline for compliance. Do not say "You must pay the sum of $10,000 immediately." When is immediately? Two days? Ten days? Three weeks? Set forth an express date so the reader will know exactly when compliance is expected.

Follow these guidelines in drafting demand letters:

(i) *Know the facts.* Be sure you have all of the relevant facts. It is not enough to have most of the facts. If the client has informed you that a debtor has breached a contract, determine if the contract is written or oral. If written, you need to obtain a copy of it and review it. A mistake in reciting the facts will immediately call forth a response by the recipient pointing out your error, and any momentum you may have had, along with your credibility, will be lost. To be sure your recitation of the facts is correct, send a copy of your demand letter in draft to your client asking that your client review the letter and approve it before it is sent to the other party. If it later turns out that the facts recited in the letter are incorrect, you have protected yourself from your supervisor's or client's wrath by having obtained the client's approval.

(ii) *Know the law.* You cannot send a letter demanding money for breach of contract if enforcement of the contract is barred by the statute of limitations or some other law. You must perform some minimum amount of research to ensure that the client's claim is valid and enforceable. Similarly, review the code of ethics for your state. It is unethical to correspond with a person who is represented by counsel. Therefore, once you know an individual has retained counsel, all correspondence must be directed to counsel. Most codes of ethics set forth other rules you should be familiar with, such as that it is unethical to threaten criminal prosecution if a demand is not met.

Many states have consumer protection or debt collection statutes, and demands for payment of debts must comply with the requirements of these statutes. Be sure to research any such requirements in your state because failure to follow the statutory requirements may invalidate the demand.

(iii) *Don't argue the case.* A demand letter should set forth the facts underlying the demand, state the demand, and outline the consequences of non-compliance. You need not, and should not, present all the evidence you would need to prevail at a trial of this matter. The debtor will undoubtedly know some of the facts relating to the claim, and you need not provide copies of every item of correspondence and the names of every witness who supports your client's version of the matter. If the problem cannot be resolved by direct negotiation, your firm will have ample opportunity to argue the case at trial. Don't tip your hand at this juncture. While a few legal authorities may be cited in some instances, routine collection letters rarely include legal analysis.

(iv) *Do what you say.*   If you have told the recipient of the letter legal action will be instituted by December 10 unless the amount of $10,000 is paid to the client, you must be prepared to follow through. Nothing jeopardizes credibility more than empty threats. If December 10 comes and goes and you issue another demand letter setting forth another deadline date, the reader will know you do not mean what you say and will understand there is no reason to comply with the renewed demand.

This issue of doing what you say is often a matter of communicating with the client. If the client has no intention of suing or is aware the reader may have certain counter-claims, the letter can be structured appropriately. For example, rather than stating a deadline date, the letter could leave the issue open and state any of the following:

- We look forward to receiving your prompt response to this demand.
- Please contact us to discuss this matter further.
- Unless we receive a satisfactory response from you by December 10, we will take all appropriate legal action.
- We invite your response to this claim and hope this matter can be resolved amicably.

Note, however, that if you write, "We look forward to a counter proposal from you," you have made a serious concession and have invited the recipient to play "let's make a deal." See Figure 16-6 for a sample demand letter.

c. Opinion Letters

Letters offering legal advice or opinions can only be signed by attorneys. Nevertheless, you may find that you are given the task of researching the law and writing the letter. Thus, while the letter is reviewed, approved, and signed by an attorney, you may be the author. While these opinion letters are usually requested by clients seeking advice on a particular matter, on occasion they may be requested by a third party, such as an accountant who requires a legal opinion as to a client's progress in litigation before the accountant can prepare financial statements.

In addition to the standard components of a letter (date, reference line, and so forth), there are eight key elements to an opinion letter. Opinion letters share many elements in common with legal memoranda, although their analysis of legal authorities is more simplified, and they are written to a client rather than to another legal professional.

Figure 16-6
Sample Demand Letter

DOUGLAS, FRANK, KELLY AND MORGAN
5600 K STREET, SUITE 2500
ALBANY, NEW YORK 12004
(612) 567-8999

August 9, 2005

Mr. Peter M. Todd
Todd Contracting Co.
1255 Stanley Avenue
Albany, NY 12966

Re: *Harry Engineering, Inc.*

Dear Mr. Todd:

This firm represents Harris Engineering Co. ("Harris") regarding its legal affairs. As you know, on January 4, 2005, Tood Contracting Co. ("Todd") entered into a written contract with Harris. This contract required Harris to provide engineering services for Todd for the construction of Nathan Public Park in Albany, and Todd was to pay the sum of $24,550 to Harris for those services. That contract was signed by you on behalf of Tood.

Our client has informed us that it has provided all engineering services required by the contract. Those services were critical to the improvement performed at Nathan Public Park and no objections were made by any individual at Todd regarding these services. Our client has further informed us that while it received one payment from Todd in the amount of $15,550 on March 1, 2005, no further payments have been made to it, despite numerous requests therefor.

This letter is a formal demand that the sum of $9,000 be paid to Harris on or before August 19, 2005. Our client has asked us to inform you that if this sum is not paid as directed, it will institute litigation against Todd for the remaining balance of $9,000 due to it as well as interest and attorneys fees as provided in the written contract which you signed.

Please contact us within the time provided to confirm your compliance with the terms of this letter and to avoid litigation being filed against Todd.

Sincerely,

Anthony P. Kelly

APK:tmb

665

(1) Date

While all letters include dates, the date of an opinion letter is especially important because the opinion will relate to the status of the law on that date. Changes in the law after that date may well affect the correctness of the opinion.

(2) Introductory Language

It may be a good idea to remind the client why he or she is receiving an opinion letter. An opinion letter may take several hours to research and prepare and may well be costly. Reminding a client that he or she specifically requested the opinion may protect you from a client's refusal to pay the bill on the ground that this work was never requested. Consider the following introductions:

- We enjoyed meeting you last week. As you requested, we have researched whether a landlord is liable for injuries sustained by a tenant. . . .
- Per our telephone conversation of March 10, 2005, we have reviewed the issue. . . .
- At your request . . .
- You have asked for our opinion whether . . .
- According to your instructions of July 18, 2005 . . .

This introductory language not only protects you from a client's faulty memory, it also sets forth the scope of the letter by stating the issue that is addressed by the letter.

(3) Review of Facts

An opinion letter should always set forth the facts upon which it is based. Facts are usually given in a narrative (sentence-by-sentence) form rather than in an outline or list form. Including the facts gives the client the opportunity to correct you if any of the facts are wrong. Even a minor factual change such as a change in a date or dollar amount can cause an opinion to be incorrect. Thus, include the facts so the reader understands that the accuracy of the opinion depends upon these facts and that changes in the facts may cause changes in the legal conclusions reached. Consider introducing the facts as follows:

- You have informed us you entered into a written lease on August 18, 2005 . . .
- As we understand them, the facts are as follows: On June 24, 2005, while traveling west on Ash Street . . .

(4) Conclusions

The essence of an opinion letter is the advice given to the client. Clients are particularly eager to get to the "bottom line," and many writers immediately give their opinion or conclusion after a recitation of the facts, and then follow the conclusion with an explanation. This is an effective technique if the opinion you give is one the client wants to hear. If, on the other hand, you will be giving the client bad news, such as informing him or her that a lawsuit cannot be initiated because the statute of limitations has expired, you may want to lead the reader to this unfavorable news gradually. By explaining the law first you will be preparing the reader for the unfavorable outcome, so by the time you actually give the bad news, the reader understands exactly why the outcome is unfavorable. Consider introducing the conclusion as follows:

- Based upon the facts you have provided us and the applicable law in this state, it is our opinion that you may initiate an action for wrongful death against Timothy Allen.
- We have concluded that you may bring an action for wrongful death against Timothy Allen. Our conclusion is based upon the facts set forth above and our analysis of the law in this state.

You may have observed that many opinion letters use "we" and "our" rather than "I" and "my." For example, an opinion is often introduced as follows: "It is our opinion" or "Based on the foregoing, our advice is. . . ." This use of "we/I" is a matter of preference by attorneys. Some attorneys believe it is cowardly to hide behind the royal "we" and insist on using the first person "I/me" as in "It is therefore my opinion. . . ." Other attorneys believe the opinion is actually issued by the firm itself rather than by any one particular attorney and thus the "we/our" form is appropriate. You must learn the preference and policy of your supervisor and firm to determine which form to use. If you are working for a sole practitioner, however, "we/our" is never correct.

(5) *Explanation of Conclusion*

This portion of the letter explains and summarizes the law upon which your conclusions are based. Because most opinion letters are received by laypersons who may not be familiar with the law, avoid detailed discussions of statutes and cases. It is sufficient to summarize the legal authorities in a general fashion.

Should you include citations to cases and statutes? Generally, avoid giving citations unless your reader is sufficiently sophisticated to understand the citations. Similarly, do not merely set out the text of a statute or case; rather, explain what the case or statute means. Refer to the legal authorities as follows:

- Applicable case law provides . . .
- We have researched the pertinent statute that governs this issue. It provides . . .
- The legal authorities in this state are in agreement that . . .

Use headings and subheadings if this portion of the letter is long and you can divide your explanation into easily understood separate sections.

(6)   Recommendation

After you have explained the law that governs the conclusion you have reached, provide a recommendation to the client. Be sure that your recommendation is not unduly optimistic. Never inform a client that he or she will recover a substantial amount of money or that he or she "cannot lose" because you will seldom be able to deliver as promised. Phrase your advice as a probability rather than a certainty. Thus, say "a court would likely hold that" rather than "your claim is undoubtedly valid." Do not include any language that could be viewed by a client as a guarantee of success. Similarly, if you need to give the client bad news, try to soften your approach by saying, "Success is extremely unlikely" or "The chances of a favorable outcome are remote at best," rather than a blunt "Taking your case would be a waste of time and money." Be sure, however, that you clearly deliver the bad news. Don't soften your approach so much that you haven't accurately conveyed your meaning. Readers often perceive what they want to, and there is no room for ambiguity in delivering unfavorable news to a client. If you must give bad news, try to find an alternative avenue for the client, as follows:

> Because the statute of limitations has expired, you will not be able to bring an action against your neighbor for trespass. We would suggest, however, that you attempt to negotiate directly with your neighbor. If this approach is unsuccessful, contact the company that issued your homeowners insurance because it may offer coverage for the damage to your property.

Use wording such as "we regret" or "unfortunately" when delivering bad news.

(7)   Instructions

The last portion of an opinion letter should be a clear direction to the client to contact the office or take some other action. Consider the following:

> Because the statutes governing this matter require that a claim be submitted to the city within 100 days of the wrongful act, please contact us immediately and provide us with your instructions. Failure to file the claim by May 10, 2005, will bar any action against the city.

(8)   Protection Clauses

On occasion, you may not have all of the information you need to provide a complete opinion. For example, the client may have informed you that he is a tenant under a written lease and yet has not provided the lease to your office for your review. In such cases, protect yourself by explaining that you lack certain information, and that the opinion may change depending upon the information you receive. Similarly, if certiorari has been granted for the authorities you rely on, explain this to the reader so if the cases you rely on are reversed or limited, the client will have been forewarned. Finally, think ahead and consider what defenses or arguments the other party may assert. Prepare your client to meet these arguments.

Consider the following examples:

- This opinion is based upon the facts you have provided us. Once we have had an opportunity to review the addendum to the lease entered into between you and your landlord, we will be better able to provide you with our opinion and analysis. Assuming the addendum does not materially alter the original lease, however, it is our opinion . . .
- The landmark case in this area of the law is *Wolfson v. Dana Point, Ltd.*, 929 P.2d 817 (Cal. 2001). That case is presently being reheard by the California Supreme Court. An adverse opinion by the court could affect the conclusions in this letter. We will continue to monitor this case before the court and notify you once the court has issued its decision.
- While your employer may argue his business is not subject to the provisions of the Family Medical Leave Act, we believe such an argument is without merit because . . .

B. Conclusion

Always write your letter with its intended audience in mind and clearly understand your goals in sending the letter. Do you want to inform? Convince? Settle? This will help you achieve the correct style and tone.

After you have finished the letter, re-read it, putting yourself in the recipient's place. This will allow you to focus on whether the letter conveys the information it needs to, whether it will be readily understood by the reader, and whether the tone is appropriate.

Because you have the opportunity to review correspondence from others, keep copies of those that you feel are well written and adopt the techniques you believe make the letters effective. Notice the way others order their paragraphs or conclude their letters. Learn from others.

CyberSites

http://www.business-letter-writing.com	This site provides information on writing formal business letters with checklists and links to numerous other recourses.
http://writing.colostate.edu/references/documents/bletter	Colorado State University provides a guide to writing business letters.

Assignment for Chapter 16

You have been given the following fact pattern by Alison Keane, one of the senior partners in your law firm.

The firm represents Outdoor Artists, Inc., a corporation formed in our state and which is engaged in landscape design in our city, near the state border. The president of the corporation is Edward Davis. For several years the corporation provided services only in our state. During the past year, however, because the city is so close to the state border, the corporation has also been providing services in the adjacent state. Specifically, the corporation opened a bank account in the adjacent state and performed landscaping services for five different customers in the adjacent state. One customer, Leo Mahony, has refused to pay for the services and the client wants to sue Mr. Mahony to recover the money owed. Another customer, Jill Lopez, has sued the client, alleging that the client damaged her drainage system when it performed landscaping services for her.

Ms. Keane is concerned because the client has not qualified to transact business as a foreign corporation in the adjacent state (as required by state statute) and would like you to prepare an opinion letter (for her signature) to the client regarding the possible effects of the client's failure to qualify to transact business. By way of background, the Model Business Corporation Act provides that before a corporation may transact business in a state other than the state of its incorporation, it must qualify to transact business as a foreign corporation, a fairly simple process involving filing a form and asking the foreign state's permission to conduct business in its borders. Our state has adopted the Act in its entirety and the Act is available on the American Bar Association's Web site at http://www. abanet.org. Assume there are no cases interpreting the applicable provisions of the Act.

State Your Answer

1. Access the site http://writing.colostate.edu/references/documents/ bletter/index.cfm.
   a. Review the section relating to formatting letters. How should the complementary close be punctuated?
   b. Review the section called "Effective Letter-Writing Principles." Why do many executives prefer written documents to other forms of communication?
2. Access the site http://www.business-letter-writing.com. Review the checklist for writing business letters. What four tips are given?

Legal Memoranda

[W]riting is the action of thinking, just as drawing is the action of seeing . . . .

Brenda Ueland (1939)

A. Introduction
B. Format of Memoranda
C. A Blueprint for Preparing a Memorandum

Chapter Overview

An office or legal memorandum is a well-known document in legal writing. It calls for you to research an area of law thoroughly and set forth your findings, both positive and negative, in a specific format.

It is only by being completely knowledgeable about the strengths and weaknesses of a case that the law firm can make a fully informed decision whether and how best to

- represent the client
- prepare pleadings and motions
- settle the case
- proceed to trial
- appeal an adverse decision

Thus, office memoranda or "memos" are used to guide those representing the client in every aspect of a case—from the initial decision whether to accept a case to a final appeal. If the law firm knows in advance the weaknesses of a case, it can adopt certain strategies to overcome these weaknesses and prepare the client for a possible negative outcome. If the memo shows the weaknesses are fatal, the memo saves the client time and money that would be expended in a trial and assists in making a decision to settle the case. A well-written memo can form the basis for motions to be made later in the case or even a trial or appellate brief. Thus, skillful

671

research and careful analysis at this early stage of a case will contribute to the successful management of a case throughout its progress in your office.

Paralegals frequently prepare legal memoranda, and your employer will expect you to be familiar with the purpose, style, and format of an office memorandum. Preparing and writing a memorandum is often a challenging and satisfying task because it calls for you to integrate both your research and writing skills and to present them in such a way that a reader has a complete and objective "snapshot" of the case, including both its strengths and weaknesses.

A. Introduction

An office memorandum is a research document designed to provide information about a case or matter. You will be asked to research a question, and your answer will be provided in the form of a written memorandum. It is an internal document, meaning it is prepared for use within a law firm, corporation, or agency. While a copy of the memo may be provided to a client, it is generally protected by the "work product" privilege and thus is not discoverable by an adverse party.

Because the office memo is not usually discoverable and will only be read by those representing the client (and possibly the client as well), its distinguishing feature is its objectivity. It should set forth not only the strong points of a case but the weak points as well.

Focus on the following three guidelines for effective memoranda writing:

1. Be Objective

The most difficult part of writing a memo is remaining neutral and objective. Once we hear the words "our client" we immediately tend to ally ourselves with the client's position and ignore the negative aspects of a case while focusing only on the positive. Thus, phrases such as "I believe" or "I feel" have no place in a memorandum. You should be informing the reader of the findings of the authorities you have located, not interjecting your opinions and judgments.

If you are not objective in pointing out weaknesses and flaws in the client's case, you do the client a disservice. It is much better (and far less costly) to determine early in the representation that the other party has a complete defense to your client's action than to find this out at trial.

Force yourself to play devil's advocate. Approach the project as your adversary might and closely examine the cases that appear unfavorable to your position. Your adversary will certainly do so, and you should be as prepared as possible to overcome weaknesses in your case.

2. *Be Specific*

If you are asked to determine whether a tenant may sublease rented property when the lease fails to address such an issue, focus on this specific question. You need not address the issue as if you were writing a text on the history of landlord-tenant problems from the feudal period to the present. If, during the course of your research, you come across other issues that you believe may be relevant, simply note them and include them in a section at the end of the memo entitled "Additional Research" or "Recommendations."

3. *Be Complete*

The supervisor who assigned you the task wants a finished project, not a sheaf of notes or series of photocopied cases. Anyone can locate cases and photocopy them. Your task is to read and analyze these cases, apply them to the facts of the client's case, and present this as a finished professional research memorandum. Put yourself in your supervisor's place and consider what you would need to know to understand fully the client's case. Assume the supervisor expects a final, polished product that will need no additional work.

B.   Format of Memoranda

Unlike documents filed in court, there is no one rigid format for an internal office memorandum. Some law firms have developed their own formats, and you may wish to ask to review memos previously prepared because these will serve as a guide for you. If you cannot locate a previous memo, use the format suggested below, which is a very common and standard format.

There are usually seven components to an office memorandum, each of which should be set forth as a heading and capitalized and centered or in some other way set off from the narrative portion of the memo. In large part, the elements of a memorandum are similar to those of a case brief, discussed in Chapter 4. See Figure 17-1.

1. *Heading*

The heading identifies the document, the person for whom the memo is prepared, the person who prepared the memo, his or her position, the subject matter of the memo, and the date it is prepared. The subject matter of the memo (found in the "Re:" line) should include a brief statement of the topic of the memo as well as a file name and number. Thus, a topic description such as "Injunctive relief" will help facilitate indexing and later location of the memo. See Figure 17-2.

Figure 17-1
Elements of a Typical Memorandum

MEMORANDUM

To:

From:

Re:

Date:

ISSUES

1.
2.

BRIEF ANSWERS

1.
2.

STATEMENT OF FACTS

ANALYSIS

1.
2.

CONCLUSION

2. *Issue(s) or Question(s) Presented*

This section of the memo sets forth the issues that will be addressed by the memo. In some memos, only one issue will be discussed. Other memos may address several issues or questions. If your memo will discuss more than one issue, number each one. Do not number a single issue. Drafting the issues can be very difficult. In fact, you may not be able to formulate the issues until you are almost finished researching the law to be discussed in the memo.

The issues are normally set forth in a question format. They are usually one sentence, although they may include subparts. Be careful that a one-sentence issue is not so long as to be confusing. The issues should be phrased so that they relate to the particular fact the problem presented. For example, questions such as "What is a sublease?" or "What are a landlord's duties?" or "What is burglary?" are far too broad. Incorporate a few facts from your case. Consider the following:

- Under Massachusetts law, may a tenant sublease rented property when a written lease fails to address this issue?
- Under Illinois law, does a landlord have a duty to disclose to tenants information about crimes that have occurred on the premises?
- In New Jersey, has a burglary occurred when an intruder enters a residence through an unlocked and open door?

Some writers prefer the issues or questions to start with the word "whether," as in "whether a tenant may sublease rented property when a written lease fails to address this topic" or "whether a battery occurred when parties involved in a fistfight consented and agreed to fight." Because questions that begin with the word "whether" result in incomplete sentences, many attorneys disfavor this form. Whichever format you choose, be consistent, and use the same format for all questions.

The questions presented should be phrased in a neutral manner so that an answer is not suggested by the question itself.

Figure 17-2
Sample heading for Memo

MEMORANDUM

To: Michael T. Gregory, Esq.

From: David H. Hendrix, Legal Assistant

Re: *Smith v. Jones*
        Our Ref.: 94061
        Sublease of Rented Property

Date: July 15, 2005

3. *Brief Answer(s)*

This section of the memo sets forth brief answers to the issues you presented together with the reasons therefor. Try to avoid answers that merely repeat the question in a declarative sentence. For example, statements such as "Subleases are common arrangements" or "A landlord has duties to tenants" are hardly helpful to a reader.

Much better answers would be as follows: "A tenant may sublease property rented from another unless there is an unequivocal written lease provision forbidding subleasing" or "Inherent in a landlord's duty to provide habitable premises is a duty to inform tenants of crimes that have occurred at the leased premises." Avoid answers that merely respond "yes," "no," or "maybe." Your answers should incorporate the reason for your conclusions.

Keep your answers brief—no more than one or two sentences. Do not include citations in the brief answers. This section of the memo is only a quick preview of what will be discussed in greater detail later in the body of the memo.

Maintain symmetry in your brief answers. If you have set forth three issues, you must have three answers, each of which corresponds in order and number to the questions previously asked. See Figure 17-3 for sample issues and brief answers.

4. *Statement of Facts*

The statement of facts may precede the issues or follow the brief answers. Either approach is acceptable. Many readers prefer the facts to be given first so they can make sense of the questions the memo will address.

The statement of facts will be based upon what you know about the case, what your supervisor and client have told you, and your review of the file. In brief, you are telling the client's "story." The factual statement

Figure 17-3
Sample Issues and Brief Answers

Issues

1. Under New Jersey law, may a written contract be rescinded due to one party's fraud?
2. Under New Jersey law, can a failure to comply with the terms of a consent agreement entered in court be the basis for contempt?

Brief Answers

1. Yes. A contract may be rescinded if one party procured the contract through fraud and the other party was misled thereby.
2. Yes. Failure to obey any order of a court, even one based upon the consent of the parties, is contempt of court.

must be neutral and objective. Therefore, you will need to include even unfavorable facts. Do not allow your opinions about the case to color your presentation of facts. For example, the statement "He endured four years of employment by Smith" includes an opinion or judgment. State "He was employed by Smith for four years."

Do not include argument in your memo or conclusions that are not supported by the file. If you are unsure whether a statement or event is true, refer to it as an "alleged" statement or event. If there is a dispute as to the facts, include both versions. It is perfectly acceptable to state, "Although the tenant alleges she provided notice to the landlord of the leaky roof, the landlord disputes this."

While only relevant facts should be included, the factual statement should be thorough. Do not omit the facts on the assumption that "surely the attorney who gave me this project knows the facts." It is possible a new paralegal or attorney may be assigned to the case and your memo may be the first source consulted to become familiar with the case. Therefore, the Statement of Facts should be self-contained and not require reference to other sources, such as pleadings or correspondence. To eliminate unnecessary facts, reread your Statement of Facts after you have completed your first draft of the memo. If the Statement of Facts includes facts that are not later mentioned in the Analysis or Discussion section, those facts can probably be omitted.

The best presentation of a factual statement is narrative, that is, sentence after sentence, paragraph after paragraph, written in the third person. Presentations of facts in outline form, for example, in separate bullets or numbered sentences, appear choppy and rigid. Use the past tense to present your facts unless facts are developing as you prepare the memo. Finally, while other approaches are acceptable, the most typical approach is to present a statement of facts in chronological development. In other words, relate the facts in the order in which they occurred.

At this point, you probably realize that a legal memorandum is unlike any document you have yet prepared. The presentation of questions, followed by answers, followed by facts, is indeed unusual. Remember, however, that your final project will include these critical elements within the first page or two, allowing your reader to review only a portion of the memo and yet comprehend a total view of the project. These three elements provide a snapshot of the essence of the client's situation. The critical questions in the case are enumerated, answers to these questions are provided, and an overview of the facts is given. Simply by reading these first three sections, the reader will know the strengths and weaknesses of the client's position.

5. *Applicable Statutes*

Many memos include a section describing or setting forth any applicable statutory provisions that will be discussed in the memo. This section is optional and need not be included. If you include applicable statutes, you may either paraphrase the statutes or quote from them. If the statute is short, set it out in full. If the statute is long, set forth the pertinent parts and consider attaching a copy to the completed memo. Provide citations to any statutes in *Bluebook* or *ALWD* form.

6. *Analysis or Discussion*

The heart of the memorandum is the analysis, or discussion, section. This portion of the memo provides an in-depth analysis of the issues presented. Cases, statutes, and other authorities will be presented and discussed. Citations should appear in the body of the memorandum, not as footnotes. See Chapter 18 for additional information on footnotes. Citations should be prepared according to *Bluebook* or *ALWD* form unless local or other form is used. Keep in mind the critical distinction between primary and secondary sources: Primary sources are mandatory and binding authorities, which must be followed, while secondary authorities are persuasive at best. Thus, rely on secondary authorities only when there are no relevant primary authorities.

There are several things to keep in mind as you write the analysis section of your memo.

Using thesis statements. Many writing experts suggest that authors use a thesis statement when writing projects. A *thesis statement* distills the central ideas and arguments in your project into one or two assertive sentences. It usually appears at the beginning of a project or issue to give focus and direction to the analysis to follow. Sometimes a thesis statement is called an *umbrella statement* because every part of the discussion to follow must fit beneath it. A thesis statement is not the same as a topic sentence. It is far more assertive than a topic sentence, which generally announces the subject matter or theme of a paragraph to follow; a thesis statement, on the other hand, provides a specific conclusion. Consider the following thesis statements:

- To state a cause of action for false advertising, the plaintiff must show that a statement is either literally false or implicitly untrue in that the statement is likely to deceive consumers.
- In order to be enforceable, a noncompetition agreement must be reasonable as to its scope, duration, and geographic area.

You can see that a thesis statement is a strong, conclusory assertion and that it serves to frame the discussion to follow. For example, using the second illustration given above, after providing the thesis statement, the writer would then proceed to discuss the scope, duration, and geographic area of the noncompetition agreement in his or her case. The thesis statement thus provides the applicable rule and a preview of the analysis to follow.

Using the cases.   It is not enough to merely locate authorities and summarize them. Almost anyone can read a case and then restate its holding. You will be expected to do more: to analyze the authorities and discuss how and why they relate to your particular problem. This requires you to interweave and compare the facts of your case with the authorities you rely upon. If the client's particular situation can be distinguished from the situation in the case law, say so. Explain *why* cases apply and why they do not. Be sure to give some of the facts of the cases you rely on so readers can see how and why they apply to your issue. One warning sign that you are merely providing case summaries rather than analysis is that each paragraph in your memo discusses a single case. If you find this happening, restructure the memo to ensure the cases you rely upon are being analyzed and compared with the client's fact situation rather than merely being summarized. Do not mention a case unless you discuss it at least briefly by explaining how and why it applies to the client's issue.

This section of the memo will require all your effort to remain objective. Thoroughly discuss not only the authorities that support the client's position, but also those that do not. If you find weaknesses in a client's case, continue researching to determine if there are ways to surmount them. If new issues are disclosed by your research, discuss them.

If a direct quotation is particularly apt, use it. Be careful, however, to ensure that your analysis consists of more than a series of quotations. It is easy to read cases and then retype what the judge has stated. Use quotations but make sure you explain their relevance to your research problem.

Ensuring readability. Retain symmetry in your memo. If you have identified three issues and provided three brief answers, divide your discussion into three parts, each of which corresponds in number and order to the issues you formulated. Each section should be labeled with a descriptive heading. Brief headings, such as "Elements of Contract," "Fraud," and "Damages," are acceptable and clearly alert the reader as to the topic to be addressed. If desired, you may repeat your issues as headings, although this will add to the length of your brief. Use subheadings if these would be helpful to a reader.

Be sure your discussion is readable. If every paragraph starts with a phrase such as "In *Smith v. Jones* . . . the court held . . . ," your finished project will have a choppy, stodgy style and appearance. The most important part of the memorandum is not a dull recitation of facts and holdings of several cases, it is your analysis of the effect these cases and other authorities will have on the client's particular situation.

Most effective discussions contain the following three elements:

- A discussion of the relevant authorities;
- An analysis and comparison of these authorities to the client's issues and facts;
- A conclusion as to the effect of the authorities as they relate to the client's problem.

In many instances, while writing style and techniques should vary to enhance readability, the analysis can be reduced to the following basic format for each separate issue:

According to . . . [citations], the law is . . . [explain and discuss]. In the present case, . . . [compare with authorities]. Therefore, . . . [conclude] . . . .

Analyzing using the IRAC method.   In discussing and analyzing authorities, many writers follow what is referred to as the "IRAC" method. "IRAC" is an acronym for *I*ssue, *R*ule, *A*nalysis or *A*pplication, and *C*onclusion. Many writers, whether writing memos, letters, or briefs for courts, use the IRAC approach in discussing a legal problem.

First, the *i*ssue being considered is presented. Introduce the question or topic you will be analyzing. In a memo, the issue is originally set forth in the form of a question, such as "Does the Uniform Partnership Act govern a partnership that has no partnership agreement?" In a discussion section, the issue is often set forth in the following form: "The key issue is whether the Uniform Partnership Act governs a partnership that has no written agreement." This serves to frame the discussion that will follow.

Next, provide the *r*ule or legal authority that you rely upon to respond to the issue. The authority can be a case, a statute, or some other primary or secondary authority or authorities. If you rely on a case, give sufficient facts from the case that the reader will understand why and how it governs your case. If your rule is a statute, set forth the applicable provisions. Several authorities may be used. In fact, you should have at least one primary authority for every conclusion you reach. Complex matters will require more authorities, including secondary authorities.

The most critical part of an IRAC discussion is the *a*nalysis or *a*pplication of the rule to your case. Explain why the rule you have set forth does or does not apply to your particular case. Do more than merely summarize a case or statute. Summarizing should have taken place when you set forth the rule. Analyzing requires you to compare and contrast the facts of your case to those in the case you rely upon or to review a statute and show the reader why your client's situation falls within (or without) the activity described by the statute. Apply the reasoning of the case or other legal authorities to your case.

Finally, after a thorough analysis, present the reader with a *c*onclusion based upon your analysis of the rule. If the rule has been set forth clearly and the analysis is complete, the reader will likely be able to draw a conclusion even in advance of your stating it. Nevertheless, presenting a conclusion wraps up your analysis and serves as reinforcement of prior discussion as well as a signal that discussion of a particular topic is complete and that a new topic will likely be presented next, once again using the IRAC method. Readers need closure on one issue before tackling the next. Many beginning researchers are reluctant to draw a conclusion. They simply summarize applicable cases and then move on to the next topic. You will need to synthesize the authorities you discuss by comparing and contrasting them to each other and then applying them to the client's particular case to reach a conclusion. For example, after discussing the authorities relating to sexual harassment in the workplace, you could conclude by saying, "Because the authorities are in agreement that the conduct an employee complains of must be severe to constitute harassment, it is highly unlikely that a court would find a single passing remark such as the one made to our client to be actionable." See Figure 17-4 for an example of an IRAC discussion.

Figure 17-4
Sample IRAC Discussion

Issue	The central issue in this cas is whether a single remark made in a workplace environment (namely, "Hey babe— looking good") constitutes sexual harassment.
Rule	The cases interpreting the Civil Rights Act of 1964 are in agreement that while a single utterance can constitute harassment, the remark must be so severe and outrageous that it creates an intolerable and hostile work environment.
Application	[Discuss cases and give citations.] In the present case, the remark, while offensive and inappropriate, is not "severe" and "outrageous" as those terms are used in the cases governing this isssue.
Conclusion	Thus, the remark is unlikely to rise to the level of actionable sexual harassment.

Following the IRAC approach to discussing problems helps ensure that you conduct a thorough analysis of an issue and is a commonly accepted writing approach both for law students and legal practitioners.

Analyzing using the CRAC method. Some experts suggest a variation of IRAC, often called "CRAC" (for *C*onclusion, *R*ule, *A*pplication, and *C*onclusion). In this analysis, the conclusion is given first, followed by the principal rule of law that supports the conclusion. The rule is applied and illustrated through analysis of cases and other authorities. The rule is then applied to the client's particular case, and the conclusion is restated.

Some writing experts dislike IRAC and CRAC because they believe these methods encourage a rigid and formulaic approach to writing. Others believe that IRAC is more useful for writing objective projects such as legal memoranda (because it requires the writer to state the issue in a neutral manner) and that CRAC (with its assertive conclusion given at the beginning) is more useful in persuasive writings, such as court briefs.

Practice Tip

Using Quotations and Paraphrasing

Many beginning writers wonder when to use direct quotations and when to paraphrase. Consider the following guidelines:

- **Use a direct quotation when what has been said is so articulate and apt that to paraphrase it would dilute its meaning.**
- **Use a direct quotation when the author of the quotation is so well known that a quotation from this person would provide instant credibility.**
- **Avoid overlong quotations.**

(continued)

Practice Tip *(Continued)*

- Use quotations sparingly so that they grab the reader's attention and interest.
- Paraphrase when the original quotation is difficult to understand or would require so much restructuring (for example, with ellipses and brackets) that it would be distracting to the reader.
- Always provide a full citation, with a pinpoint cite, for every quotation and paraphrase in your document.

---

7. *Conclusion*

The conclusion should be brief and should be a highlight of the conclusions you reached earlier in the discussion or analysis section of the memo. In many ways, the conclusion will resemble your brief answers, although it tends to provide more information than the brief answers do. Do not include citations in your conclusion. Simply sum up your analysis. The conclusion should not present any material that has not previously appeared in the body of the memo.

If you cannot draw a conclusion because the authorities are in conflict, say so. It is not your function to predict the client's chances, but rather to report and analyze the authorities.

It is possible that during the course of your research you determine that certain information is needed or that a certain course of action should be followed, such as locating witnesses or propounding interrogatories to the adverse party. You may include these recommendations as part of your conclusion, or you may prefer to create a new section titled "Recommendations." Similarly, if certain issues have not been discussed, identify those excluded issues. In some instances, tables, photographs, or copies of cases or statutes will be attached to the memorandum in a separate appendix. If your memo is unusually long, you may wish to add a table of contents to help the reader. See Appendix A for a sample memorandum.

C. A Blueprint for Preparing a Memorandum

Although legal professionals will invariably adopt individual approaches in preparing a legal memorandum, there are several steps you can follow to ensure you provide a thoughtful, complete, and objective analysis of a client's case. The process usually begins with an assignment from your supervising attorney. The assignment may be written but will usually be given to you orally. Take careful notes, ask when the memo is due, and whether it will be sent to the client. Do not be reluctant to go back to the attorney if you later discover you need additional facts or information. Take the following steps:

1. Consider whether the issue is governed by federal law or state law. Next, consider whether it is a matter more likely to be covered by statutory law or case law.

2. Draft a preliminary issue statement based on the information you have. For example, your initial issue might be written, "Under California law, are non-competition agreements entered into by employees valid?"

3. Develop a research plan. If the matter is likely to be covered by statutory law, review the applicable statutes and then examine the case annotations following the text of the statutes. If the matter is likely to be covered by case law, consider starting with an encyclopedia or reviewing digests to find cases. If you are unfamiliar with the topic of law, initially consult a treatise or encyclopedia to "get your feet wet." Prepare a list of key words or search terms using the indexes to the statutes, encyclopedias, treatises, digests, and other authorities. For example, terms might include "employment," "employer-employee," "noncompetition," and "competition."

4. Conduct research, paying attention to leads to other sources, such as law reviews, A.L.R. annotations, and Restatements. Take careful notes as you read the authorities you locate.

5. Shepardize or KeyCite the primary authorities to ensure they are still valid and to direct you to other authorities on point.

6. Brief the cases you locate if this is helpful to you.

7. Organize your notes, using index cards, notebooks, sheets of paper, or computer files. Use these to construct a working outline.

8. Begin writing. If you have difficulty getting started, begin with the section that is easiest to write. In many instances, this will be the Statement of Facts. Proceed to other sections, always checking to make sure your writing is balanced and objective. Consider using the IRAC method in the discussion section to ensure you are analyzing cases rather than merely summarizing them.

9. Revise the memo. Check for content. Make sure each conclusion you have drawn is supported by legal authority. Review to ensure that the cases you discuss include sufficient facts that the reader will immediately be able to discern why they do or do not apply to the client's situation.

10. Edit the memo to eliminate unnecessary material and clarify ambiguous portions. Proofread to omit spelling and typographical errors. Do a final check of citation form. Present the finished product to the assigning attorney, along with copies of cases and other authorities. Place a copy in the client's file, keep a "chron copy" (a copy placed in a chronological file you maintain showing your work throughout the year), and place a copy in the firm's memo bank, if applicable. See Figure 17-5.

Figure 17-5
Examples of Elements in Legal Memo

	Poor	*Better*
Issue	Does the client have a cause of action?	Under the Civil Rights Act of 1964, does harassment occur when a single remark is made in the workplace — namely, "hey, babe — looking good"?
Brief Answer	No	Because courts consistently require that conduct be severe in order to constitute harassment, the single remark made in this case is highly unlikely to rise to the level of sexual harassment.
Facts	Our client, Grace Parks, was subject to intolerable conduct in the workplace when a co-worker leered at her and teased, "hey, babe — looking good" when Grace entered a conference room full of employees. Grace was thoroughly humiliated by this remark.	Our client, Grace Parks, is an employee of ABC Inc. Two months ago, when Ms. Parks entered a conference room, a male co-worker stated to her, in front of others, "hey, babe — looking good." Ms. Parks would like to know if this remark constitutes sexual harassment.
Discussion	A poor discussion will: • Merely summarize cases • Fail to include facts from cases • Rely upon non-similar cases, such as those involving physical conduct and touching rather than verbal utterances • Lack objectivity and examine only cases in which harassment is found and ignore cases unfavorable to the client • Finish with mere summaries of cases and fail to draw conclusions as to whether harassment is likely to be found	A better discussion will: • Provide text of governing statute • Discuss and analyze cases with similar fact problems, focusing on cases involving verbal remarks rather than those involving physical conduct and touching • Discuss caes holding that a single remark can constitute harassment and compare and contrast these to client's case in order to reach a conclusion • Use the IRAC method to analyze cases
Conclusion	A poor conclusion will: • Be overlong • Include citations • Include topics not previously discussed in the body of the memorandum	A better conclusion will: • Quickly summarize the major points of the memorandum

Tips for Memo-Writing

- Do not use first person pronouns. Avoid statements such as "The next case I found . . ." or "I believe . . . ."
- Use complete *Bluebook* or appropriate citation form so that if the memo becomes the basis for a document submitted to court, you will not have to return to the law library to track down cites.
- Some law firms maintain files or "banks" of previously prepared memos. Before beginning a new project, check the memo bank to see if a memo on your topic has previously been prepared. If no memo bank exists, offer to establish one. Similarly, check with your fellow legal assistants to see if anyone else in your office has prepared a memo on a similar topic.
- Some attorneys prefer that all cases cited in the memo be photocopied and attached to the memo for ready reference. Check to see if the individual assigning the memo prefers this practice.
- Gather all documents and materials before you begin to write.
- After you Shepardize or KeyCite, provide your supervisor with copies of cases that negatively affect any cases cited in the memo so thay can be reviewed.
- Save memos you have prepared and others you come across in your own mini-memo bank. You may be surprised how often you will need to retrieve previously prepared memos to verify certain legal issues or to use as a starting point for a new project.

CyberSites

http://www.law.stetson.edu/ lawrev/rowe.pdf	This site provides an excellent article about legal writing and analysis.
http://www.lawnerds.com/ guide/irac.html	This site provides a thorough discussion of analyzing issues using IRAC.

Legal Memorandum
Assignment for Chapter 17

Two years ago, our client, Tina Wolf, was divorced from her husband of twelve years, Tom, a successful investment banker. As part of the divorce judgment (which incorporated Tina and Tom's voluntarily agreed upon divorce settlement agreement), Tina was awarded monthly spousal support. This spousal support has been sufficient to meet Tina's needs. The couple's two children reside with Tina, and Tom pays monthly child support, which is also adequate to meet the children's needs. Six months ago, Tom won the lottery in our state. Tom will now receive approximately $700,000 per year from the state lottery for the next thirty years. Tina would like to know if she can seek a modification of her spousal support and receive increased spousal support based on Tom's significant change in circumstances.

Please prepare a memorandum for me regarding this issue. The memorandum should be no more than eight pages in length and should be double-spaced. Use *Bluebook* or *ALWD* citation form. Our state has no cases or statutes regarding this issue. Therefore, do not restrict your research to the law of any one jurisdiction.

State Your Answer

1. Access the site http://www.lawnerds.com/guide/irac.html.
   a. What is the key to issue spotting?
   b. Review the section called "Conclusion." What is a common mistake made by many students in conclusions?
2. Access the site http://www.ccc.commnet.edu/grammar. Review the information relating to thesis statements. Give the definition of a thesis statement.
3. Access the site http://www.yourlawprof.com/21f/law34/legalmemonotes. htm. What are the three functions of a legal memorandum?

Legal Briefs

[W]e must insist that parties not clog the system by presenting us with a slubby mass of words rather than a true brief. Hence we have briefing rules.

N/S Corp. v. Liberty Mut. Ins. Co., 127
F.3d 1145, 1146 (9th Cir. 1997)

Chapter Overview

This chapter will introduce you to documents submitted to court. These documents, commonly referred to as "briefs," differ from letters and memoranda in their purpose and audience. While letters and memoranda are intended primarily to inform and explain, briefs are intended to persuade judges. The writing techniques used for briefs are therefore different because each element of a brief must be crafted with its objective in mind: to persuade a court to rule in your client's favor.

A. Introduction

Briefs are formal written legal arguments submitted to a court. Briefs attempt to persuade a court to rule in favor of a party. On occasion, such a brief is referred to as a "Memorandum of Law" or "Memorandum of Points and Authorities." Be careful not to confuse these with the internal office memoranda previously discussed. Similarly, be careful not to confuse the briefs discussed in this chapter with the case briefs or case summaries discussed in Chapter 4.

The fact that the document submitted to a court is referred to as a "brief" does not necessarily mean the document is concise. A common joke is that only a lawyer would call a 50-page document a brief!

Briefs are submitted in pending actions and may relate to a variety of issues, including the following:

- a motion requesting a preliminary injunction
- a motion to dismiss a case
- a motion to change venue
- a motion to exclude evidence
- a motion to compel a party to answer interrogatories
- a motion for a new trial
- an appeal of a judgment

There are several types of briefs. Most are submitted to trial courts to persuade the judge to rule a certain way. After a trial is concluded, the losing party may appeal the judgment and will submit a brief, called an "appellate brief," to the reviewing or appeals court. Finally, briefs may be submitted to administrative agencies or other government units.

If an office memorandum has been prepared in a case, it may be a good starting point for a brief because it will contain an analysis and discussion of the authorities pertinent to the case. While the memo then may serve as a source of cases and other authorities, the manner in which these were discussed in the memo and the manner in which these will be discussed in a brief vary greatly. The style of writing used in a memo is informative because your function as a memo writer is to explain the law. The style of writing used in a brief is persuasive because your function as a brief writer is to persuade the court.

One effective way to learn to write better briefs is to review those of others. A number of Web sites offer free access to briefs, including http://www.legaline.com/freebriefslinks.html, and Westlaw now provides a "Brief Bank," which offers instant access to hundreds of thousands of briefs submitted to appellate courts. Searching is easily accomplished by topic (for example, medical malpractice), enabling researchers to locate briefs on the precise point of law for their own cases.

B. Tips on Writing Briefs

1. Be Persuasive

In some ways, you may find it easier to prepare a brief than a memo. Most writers find it difficult to maintain the neutral and objective tone required in a memo. It is often easier and more natural to advocate the client's position.

Aim at being persuasive throughout every portion of the brief. Even the Table of Contents and headings provide an opportunity for you to persuade the court. Consider the following two headings:

PUNITIVE DAMAGES

DEFENDANT'S FRAUD ENTITLES
PLAINTIFF TO PUNITIVE DAMAGES

While both headings inform the reader that the next topic will deal with punitive damages, the second one is considerably more forceful. Many writers include a "reason" in their point headings throughout their briefs. This is an extremely effective technique for drafting point headings. Consider the following point heading:

THE TRIAL COURT SHOULD AWARD PUNITIVE DAMAGES
BECAUSE DEFENDANT'S CONDUCT WAS INTENTIONAL,
WILLFUL, AND RECKLESS

Each point heading should have all capital letters, be centered, and assigned a Roman numeral placed directly above the point heading. Use parallel structure so if a reader reads only the point headings in a brief, the headings provide a clearly written outline of the argument. Maintain consistency in your headings. Headings are usually one sentence. Maintain this approach and do not switch to only phrases. Do not include citations in your headings.

If your headings appear as elements in a Table of Contents, you have another opportunity to reach the reader. The Table of Contents will be the first part of the brief to be viewed. Use this opening as your first attempt to convince the reader to rule in favor of the client.

To achieve a persuasive tone, remember the techniques discussed in Chapter 15:

- Use active voice;
- Use parallel structure;
- Use strong, forceful, and descriptive words;
- Use sentence structure to achieve strength, placing the strongest part of the sentence in the dominant clause;
- Use placement to achieve attention, placing the strongest parts of your argument in the beginning and ending of the brief;
- Use repetition, but sparingly, for drama and emphasis;
- Use positive statements rather than negative statements.

After you have completed the brief, review it carefully to eliminate words such as "clearly" and "obviously," which are overused, ineffective, and often insulting words inexperienced writers believe will persuade a reader. Similarly, omit vague and equivocal expressions such as "it would seem that" or "apparently," which have no place in a document aimed at persuading a reader.

While accuracy, brevity, and clarity are always required in legal writing, these characteristics are mandated by the United States Supreme Court, which has stated, "The failure of a petitioner to present with accuracy, brevity, and clarity whatever is essential to ready and adequate understanding of the points requiring consideration is sufficient reason for the Court to deny a petition." Sup. Ct. R. 14(4). In May 2000, the *National Law Journal* reported that the Kentucky Supreme Court suspended an attorney for 60 days for submitting a "virtually incomprehensible" brief.

2. *Be Honest*

While you need not present the adversary's argument, you have an ethical duty to be honest and bring to the court's attention anything that would assist the court in reaching a decision. If, in the course of your research, you discover cases that do not support your position, mention these in a straightforward fashion and then show the reader why they do not apply to your situation.

Act on the assumption that your adversary will discover these cases and that if you introduce these problem areas first, you will decrease the effect of the adversary's "smoking gun." Moreover, the integrity shown by an honest and direct discussion of these issues will carry over to the rest of your argument. Assertions you make in other sections of the brief will then be likely to be believed and trusted by the reader.

Discussing these authorities does not mean you need to highlight them and make the adversary's case for him or her. Use placement in the brief to assist you and "bury" the most troublesome parts of your argument in the middle of the discussion. Use passive voice to minimize the impact of these weak spots.

3. *Know the Rules*

Most courts issue rules relating to briefs filed before them. Some of these rules relate to the size, color, and quality of the paper used, while others relate to citation form, length of the document, and the elements required in a brief. Many courts establish maximum page limits and require that briefs exceeding certain page limits include tables of contents and authorities. For example, the First Circuit Court of Appeals now requires a copy of all briefs submitted to be on a 3.5-inch disk as well as in hardcopy form. Similarly, a newly revised federal rule has reduced the page allowance for principal briefs from 50 pages to 30 pages. Fed. R. App. P. 32. Make sure you have obtained a copy of the court rules and have thoroughly read them before you prepare your brief because failure to follow the rules may be fatal. Many courts have posted their rules on the Internet. The rules of the United States Supreme Court can be found at the Court's Web site at http://www.supremecourtus.gov. Each state's judicial Web site is given in Table T.1 of *The Bluebook*. Additionally, your law firm may have a copy of the rules in its law library. If not, contact the court clerk and order a copy of the rules. Always check the date the rules were issued and verify that the rules are still current.

C. Trial Court Briefs

1. *Introduction*

Briefs submitted to trial courts are aimed at persuading the judge to rule in a certain way. These briefs may be accompanied by other documents, such as deposition transcripts, declarations, or exhibits. They may be written in support of a certain position or in response or opposition to an argument. On occasion, they are written in response to a judge's request for legal argument on a certain issue.

In some jurisdictions this brief is referred to as a Memorandum of Law or Memorandum of Points and Authorities. While some jurisdictions have rules relating to the format, citation form, or length of these trial court briefs, these rules tend to be far less formal than the rules for appellate briefs.

As in all legal writing, remember your audience. The judge who will read the brief will be busy and will become frustrated with a lengthy and repetitious document. The other reader, opposing counsel, will have a hostile attitude toward your brief and will scrutinize the brief looking for errors and flaws in everything from citation form to Shepardizing and KeyCiting to the conclusions you draw from your research. While it is a futile effort to believe you can persuade opposing counsel, aim at presenting a brief that at least cannot be attacked by opposing counsel. A sample trial brief is found at Appendix B.

2. *Elements of a Trial Brief*

The elements of a brief submitted to a trial court will vary to some degree from jurisdiction to jurisdiction. The following elements are found in most briefs, but you should be sure to review your local court rules to determine if there is a required format.

a. Caption

Because the brief submitted to the court is a pleading, it must display the "caption" of the case. The caption identifies the pertinent information about the case: the court, the parties, the docket number, and the title of the document, such as "Defendant's Memorandum of Law in Support of Motion to Change Venue." Table BT.1 of *The Bluebook* and *ALWD* Appendix 3 provide instructions for abbreviations and capitalization in court documents.

b. Introductory Statement

The party submitting the brief typically begins with a brief introductory statement such as the following: "Defendant Vincent T. Parker respectfully submits the following Memorandum of Law in support of his Motion to Change Venue."

c. Statement of Facts

To save the judge the bother of reviewing all of the pleadings submitted in a case to determine what the case is about, the brief should include a statement of facts. While these facts must be accurate, you should strive to present these facts in a manner most favorable to the client. Use active voice and descriptive words to emphasize facts supporting your position. Use passive voice and placement of unfavorable facts in less noticeable positions to minimize facts that are troublesome. For example, consider the following two ways of describing a defendant's experience with the law:

- Defendant's version: The record discloses some prior convictions.
- Plaintiff's version: The Defendant has a long history of serious criminal conduct and victimization of innocent parties, including three separate convictions involving violence to women and two additional convictions for assault with a deadly weapon, specifically, a ten-inch jagged-edge hunting knife.

Most facts are presented in chronological order, though you may depart from this order and discuss facts by topic if you wish to emphasize certain facts. Present the facts in the third person and in past tense unless they are still unfolding as you write the brief. Be careful not to jump the gun and argue your case. This section of the brief should be devoted solely to facts, for example, events that have occurred, not legal theories and analysis. Personalize your client by referring to him or her by name (Ms. LaPointe) rather than role (Plaintiff). Although most writers present their statement of facts in a narrative, some courts require numbered paragraphs, each of which includes a reference to supporting materials and documents.

Do not overlook the importance of the statement of facts. Because most judges have a thorough understanding of the law, they may begin forming impressions and drawing conclusions even as they read the facts. Moreover, at this stage of the brief, the reader is still enthusiastic and fresh. Do more than merely recite the facts in a dull fashion. Use the statement of facts to win over your reader.

d. Argument

The argument section of a brief is the heart of the brief. This section contains the analysis of the legal authorities that support the client's position and demonstrates why and how those authorities support the position advocated.

Divide your argument into sections, giving each section a heading and a Roman numeral and centering the heading on the page. The headings should be as persuasive as possible. You may need subheadings. These can consist of short phrases or even single words. Subheadings are usually preceded by capital letters (A, B, and C). Citations should appear in the body of your brief. While footnotes are popular with some writers, they are distracting to most readers.

The use of footnotes in legal documents engenders vigorous debate. Footnotes are commonly seen in law review articles and in legal treatises; however, they are seen far less frequently in published cases. There are two schools of thought on the use of footnotes in legal memos and court briefs. Some experts believe that the placement of a footnote number at the end of a sentence jars curious readers who are then compelled to glance at the bottom of the page, leaving the narrative discussion in the body of the text. These experts believe that if the point of a logical argument is to carry the reader through seamlessly from the first sentence to the last, footnotes detract from this objective. Conversely, if some readers are so disciplined that they ignore the footnote notations and continue reading the narrative text, of what use are the footnotes? Despite these criticisms, footnotes continue to be used. Recently, in fact, some writing experts have advocated more extensive use of footnotes on the basis that citations and extraneous comments clutter arguments and are better placed at the bottom of a page. In fact, some judges in California are experimenting with writing citation-free opinions, placing all citations and extraneous comments in footnotes in an effort to create more readable opinions. Other judges have reached the opposite conclusion, believing that if something is important enough to be discussed, it should be discussed in the body of the text; if a point is not important enough to be in the body of the text, it probably doesn't merit any discussion whatsoever. Check your firm or office policy or practice, but in any event avoid "talking" footnotes (those containing argument or discussion) and footnotes that "wrap" from one page to the next, or even beyond. Some readers will leave the narrative discussion, review the footnote that meanders on for several pages and then simply resume reading where they are, rather than returning to the page on which the footnote began. Endnotes are seen in other disciplines but seldom, if ever, in legal documents.

As you discuss cases and other authorities, emphasize the extent to which favorable cases are similar to the client's case. In the interest of credibility, point out unfavorable authorities and then distinguish them from the client's position by showing why and how they are different and thus inapplicable. Discuss cases in the past tense because references to "this case states" or "the plaintiff argues" will be interpreted as references to your brief itself rather than precedents. Avoid referring to the court by the name of a case. For example, assume you are discussing the case *Horn v. Wagner*, 382 U.S. 116 (1988). In discussing this case, do not say, "The *Horn* Court held . . . ." While this approach is common, it is nonetheless disfavored by some writing experts. The only way a court is referred to is by its title ("the United States Supreme Court") or by the name of its chief or presiding judge or justice ("the Rehnquist Court").

Review your arsenal of writing tips and organize your argument so it flows logically. Consider which techniques make for a strong and persuasive document and give care to techniques that allow you to minimize cases unfavorable to the client's position. Be definite. Avoid expressions such as "it seems" or "it is likely," which immediately convey the message to the reader that the writer is not sure of the position taken.

Avoid any use of the first person. Do not say "we argue" or "it is my contention." Instead use expressions such as "Defendant will show" or "Plaintiff has contended." This keeps the focus on the parties, not on you as the writer.

Be sure you have done more than merely summarize a series of cases. Analyze and apply the cases and other authorities to the client's case so the reader can readily see why these cases mandate the result you advocate. Consider using the CRAC approach (discussed in Chapter 17) to ensure you thoroughly analyze and discuss each issue. It is perfectly acceptable to rely upon cases in which a different result was reached than the one you desire. Simply say, "Although the Court denied injunctive relief in *Gray v. Smith*, 508 U.S. 110, 112 (1995), that denial was directly related to the plaintiff's failure to take prompt action. In the present case, however, ... Thus, the decision reached in *Gray* is not applicable to this case." Use an assertive thesis statement (discussed in Chapter 17) to give focus to your argument.

While the aim of your document is to persuade, you need not denigrate the adversary's position. A logical and well-reasoned argument will command respect. A hostile and sarcastic diatribe will destroy your credibility and render your brief suspect.

Practice Tip

Responding to an Adversary's Brief

When you are responding to briefs filed by adversaries, review the authorities cited in the brief. Dissents in the cases cited by your adversary often provide good ammunition for drafting a reply or response brief.

---

e. Conclusion

The conclusion should be a very brief recap of the highlights of the argument. Because it is a summary, no citations should be included. The last sentence of the conclusion should remind the reader of the relief requested, such as the following: "For the foregoing reasons, Defendant Vincent T. Parker respectfully requests the Court grant his Motion for Change of Venue."

Many writers use this request for relief as their entire conclusion. While this is easy for the writer because it eliminates the difficult task of condensing a complex argument into a readable summary, do not forgo this last opportunity to persuade, especially because a reader often picks up interest at the end of a project and will thus pay special attention to the conclusion. The conclusion should be no more than half a page. Any conclusion longer than this will likely be ignored.

f. Signature and Date

The brief is typically "closed" much like a letter. The favored closing is as follows:

Respectfully submitted,

Dated: _____   _____

Sandra Taylor Jones
Jones and White
Attorneys for Defendant
Vincent T. Parker

Jones and White
162 C Street, Suite 1725
Chicago, Illinois 97205
Bar No. 764110

g. Certificate of Service

For all pleadings filed in court you must verify that all parties have received copies. A Certificate of Service is placed at the conclusion of a pleading and states that a copy of the pleading has been served on all parties. The method of service, such as hand delivery or first class mail, and the date of service must be specified.

h. Exhibits

It is possible you may have attached exhibits to the brief for review by the court. These may consist of correspondence, transcripts of deposition testimony, answers to interrogatories, affidavits, or other documents. Each exhibit should be fully described in the brief itself and then should be appended after the end of the brief and clearly labeled. Do not insert exhibits into the middle of your argument because they will disrupt the flow of your narrative and detract from the persuasive nature of your brief. Use tabs to make it easier for the judge to locate your exhibits. If there are several exhibits, prepare a table of exhibits.

Remember these three techniques for effective brief writing:

(i)   Be scrupulously accurate in your statement of the facts of the case. Include unfavorable facts and resist the temptation to over-emphasize facts in your favor.

(ii)   Focus on your best arguments. If some arguments are "long shots," do not include them. Inclusion of weak or ludicrous arguments causes readers to question the writer's credibility.

(iii) Analyze the cases you rely on rather than merely summarizing them. Describe the cases relied upon, giving sufficient facts so the reader will see how and why these cases are similar (or dissimilar) to your case. Give the holding and reasoning from the cited cases. Then compare and contrast the cases you rely on with the facts of your case. Convince by applying the holding and reasoning from the cited authorities to your case.

See Appendix B for a sample brief for a court.

D. Appellate Briefs

1. Introduction

After a trial court decision or other final ruling, the losing party may appeal the decision. While the trial court judge who rules on a motion supported by a memorandum of law may be familiar with the case and the facts presented in a trial brief and may, in fact, have been assigned to a case from its filing, appellate judges will have no such familiarity with cases before them. You will thus have to be as articulate and persuasive as possible to convince the appellate court to rule in your client's favor. An appellate brief is a formal document filed with a reviewing court. The appellate brief seeks reversal, affirmance, or some modification of a lower court's action. A sample appellate brief is found in Appendix C.

2. Steps in the Appeal Process

After a judgment is entered in a case, the losing party, usually called the appellant but sometimes called the petitioner, initiates an appeal by filing a notice of appeal. This serves to notify the adverse party, called the appellee or occasionally the respondent, that an appeal has been instituted. This notice of appeal must be timely. In federal court, the notice of appeal must be filed within 30 days (60 days if the United States is a party) after the date the judgment is entered. Most state courts have similarly limited time periods for filing the notice of appeal. Failure to timely file the notice of appeal is fatal, and usually no relief can be granted from the untimely filing of the notice. The notice of appeal is usually filed not in the appellate court but with the trial court.

A filing fee is required when the notice of appeal is filed. The appellant then must order the transcript (or selected portions of it) from the court reporter who transcribed the trial proceeding because it is this record of the proceedings upon which the appeal is based. The trial court record also includes all pleadings filed in the case together with all exhibits entered at the trial.

Rules governing appeal briefs are usually more stringent than rules for any other documents submitted to courts. Moreover, these rules are rigidly adhered to, and a brief that is too long or lacks the proper color cover sheet will be rejected. Briefs submitted to appellate courts may be required to be commercially printed rather than merely typewritten or word-processed. Know the rules.

The appellant sets forth his or her grounds for the appeal in a document called the appellant's brief or opening brief. The appellee will then prepare and file his or her response brief. The appellee's brief must usually be filed within a specified time period (often 30 days) after the appellant's brief. Some courts allow the appellant to submit a brief in reply or rebuttal to certain issues raised by the appellee's brief. This is uncommon, however, and in most cases the appellate court will determine the appeal solely on the basis of the appellant's brief, the appellee's brief, and the record from below. No testimony is received.

The clerk of the appellate court will then schedule oral argument. Each side typically has only a half-hour to present the oral argument. The appellate judges usually sit as a panel of three and may ask questions of the parties. Parties should not make the mistake of believing they will save a persuasive issue for oral argument and omit it from the brief. Briefs should contain *all* of the arguments to be presented to the appellate court because a party may be interrupted by questions from the judges and never have the opportunity to present a certain issue during oral argument.

After oral argument, the appellate court will take the case under advisement or submission and will review the briefs and records, reach a decision, and write the appellate opinion. This may take several months. The parties will then be notified of the decision. If the losing party believes the appellate court has overlooked something, he or she may request a rehearing. Requests for rehearings are usually denied.

The losing party may then proceed to the next higher court, if it exists. In most states, there is an intermediate appellate court, and then the highest state court, usually called the supreme court. Adverse decisions of the highest court in a state may be appealed to the United States Supreme Court only if a federal question is at issue. Even then, the United States Supreme Court may deny certiorari and refuse to take the appeal.

In federal cases, after a party loses a trial in the district court, an appeal is taken to the appropriate circuit court of appeals. For most litigants, this is the end of the process because an appeal from the circuit courts of appeal to the United States Supreme Court is dependent upon issuance of the writ of certiorari by the Court. As you will recall from reading Chapter 2, issuance of the writ is discretionary with the Court, and the vast majority of petitions for writs of certiorari are denied. Because appellate work is complicated, some firms specialize solely in appellate practice and prepare appeals for cases tried by other firms.

3. *Standards of Appellate Review*

The appellant is not entitled to a reversal of the trial court decision simply because he or she is unhappy with the outcome. The appellant must show that an error of law occurred at the trial. For purposes of appeal, the appellate court will assume that the facts found at the trial were true (unless these facts are totally unsupported by the record). Thus, if a jury determines a defendant was driving at a speed of 70 miles per hour and this caused an accident injuring a plaintiff, an appellate court cannot substitute its judgment for that of the jury and determine the defendant's rate of speed was 45 miles per hour. It may, however, decide that a prejudicial error of law was committed at the trial and that this affected the jury's verdict. Examples of such errors of law include admission of evidence, such as hearsay, that should have been excluded, errors given in the instructions to the jury, and exclusion of evidence that should have been admitted.

Even if an error of law occurred at the trial, the appellate court will not reverse the lower court decision unless this error was clearly erroneous or prejudicial to the appellant. Many errors can occur in a trial. Harmless errors, however, are not reversible. A prejudicial error is one that likely affected the outcome of the case. Additionally, appellate courts review only those errors that were raised at trial. Otherwise, trial judges would not have the opportunity to correct their own mistakes.

Generally, appellate courts give great weight to the trial court's conduct of a trial because the trial court was in the best position to evaluate the credibility of witnesses and to make "on the spot" determinations. Only if the trial court clearly erred or abused its discretion will its decisions be reversed.

Because of the difficulty in meeting these strict requirements and because of the high costs involved, the vast majority of trial court decisions are not appealed.

4. Amicus Curiae *Briefs*

On occasion, an issue being appealed is of importance not only to the litigants, but also to a wider group of people. The case may involve constitutional issues that will have a substantial impact on a significant number of individuals. In such cases, these individuals, companies, or entities who were not parties to the suit may request that the court allow them to file *amicus curiae* ("friend of the court") briefs. Appellate courts have discretion to accept or reject such requests, though they will permit *amicus curiae* briefs if it is believed such briefs would be of assistance to the court.

5. *Elements of an Appellate Brief*

Many of the elements of an appellate brief are the same as the elements of a memorandum of law or trial brief. In some instances, portions of an earlier memorandum or trial brief may be used for the appellate brief. (See Figure 18-1 for a comparison of the elements of trial court briefs and appellate court briefs.)

Following are the elements typically found in an appellate brief, although, as always, you should carefully review the rules of the appellate court to which you are submitting the brief to determine whether there are required rules as to format or elements for the brief.

a. Cover Sheet

The cover sheet or title page identifies the following information about the case:

- the specific appellate court hearing the appeal
- the names of the appellant and appellee

- the docket number of the appeal
- the lower court that handled the trial or prior appeal
- the title of the document, such as "Appellant's Brief"
- the attorneys representing the party submitting the brief

Some courts require the party instituting the appeal to be identified first in the caption. This often results in a reversal of the plaintiff's and defendant's names. For example, if the original case was *Davids v. Stephenson* and Stephenson appealed the trial court's decision, some courts require that Stephenson's name be listed first. Due to the confusion caused by this rule, most courts retain the original listing of the parties, no matter who appeals.

Many courts require that the cover sheet be a certain color. For example, the United States Supreme Court requires that the appellant's cover color be light blue, the appellee's cover color be light red, and an amicus curiae brief (in support of the petitioner) cover color be light green. This assists the justices reading the briefs because they can identify at a glance whose brief they are reading.

b. Identification of Parties

Unless all of the parties are identified on the cover sheet, a list of all parties to the lower court proceeding usually must be given, including parent companies and wholly owned subsidiaries. This corporate disclosure statement allows justices to review for conflicts and disqualify themselves from cases involving parties they know or with whom they have financial involvement.

Figure 18-1
Elements of Trial Court Briefs and Appellate Court Briefs

Trial Court Briefs	Appellate Court Briefs
Caption	Cover Sheet
Introductory Statement	Identification of Parties
	Table of Contents
	Table of Authorities
	Jurisdictional Statement
	Constitutional and Statutory Provisions
	Questions Presented
Statement of Facts	Statement of the Case
	Summary of the Argument
Argument	Argument
Conclusion	Conclusion
Signature	Signature
Certificate of Service	Certificate of Service
Exhibits	Appendix

c.   Table of Contents

A Table of Contents or Index must be included. While the primary purpose of a Table of Contents is to identify for the reader the location of each element in the brief, a secondary purpose is to serve as an outline of a party's contentions. Many software programs will automatically generate a table of contents.

The Table of Contents should include all of the headings and subheadings contained in the brief. These should be phrased as persuasively as possible. Thus, a heading such as "The best evidence of likelihood of confusion of trademarks is evidence of actual confusion" is considerably stronger than the neutral heading "likelihood of confusion." Headings are usually presented in uppercase letters. Subheadings appear with initial letters capitalized and are usually underlined.

Judges reviewing the Table of Contents will be able to comprehend quickly the scope of your argument. If you organize your brief effectively and phrase your headings persuasively, you are able to make a favorable impression on the judges reviewing the brief even before the argument is begun.

d.   Table of Authorities

An appellate brief must include a list of every primary and secondary authority referred to in the brief together with an indication of the page(s) on which it appears. Complete citations in *Bluebook* form must be given (unless court rules provide otherwise).

Authorities should be grouped together so that all cases are listed together, then all constitutional provisions, followed by statutes, followed by secondary authorities. Within each group, arrangement is alphabetical (or numerical, for statutes).

The Table of Authorities allows readers to identify quickly the location in a brief of a discussion of a certain case or statute. It may be helpful for a reader to compare the appellant's discussion of *Smith v. Jones* with the appellee's discussion of this same case. The Table of Contents and Table of Authorities cannot be prepared until the brief is in final form because it is only then that you will know on which page a certain topic or case is mentioned.

Paralegals often play a major role in preparing the Table of Contents and Table of Authorities. The task requires painstaking care to ensure you have carefully noted each time a case is discussed and the exact location of each authority. Moreover, because this task cannot be completed until the brief is completed with no insertions or deletions to cause changes in pagination, it is often a pressure-filled task done at the eleventh hour.

Many software programs will automatically generate a table of authorities from your document. The program "reads" your document, locates the cites, sorts them, alphabetizes them, and then notes where the cites appear in your writing. They also correct some common citation errors. Because the programs extract citations from your document, case citations will undoubtedly appear in both "stand alone" and "textual sentence" format, meaning that, depending on your usage and placement of citations, the word "Technology" may appear as "Tech." in one case name and as "Technology" in another. Thus, you will need to do some revising to ensure consistency in appearance.

Neither *The Bluebook* nor *ALWD* include any guidance on preparing a table of authorities. Many authors prefer to write out case names in full rather than using abbreviations such as "Sur." or "Hosp." in the Table of Authorities, although citations in a table are clearly in stand-alone format. The preference toward using full case names is based upon the fact that the table will be one of the first pages reviewed by a reader, and the presentation of full case names is polished and complete.

If your word processor does not automatically prepare the Table of Authorities, use index cards to list each case and then shuffle them until they are in alphabetical order. Be sure to note if a case is discussed on more than one page. Carefully review the footnotes because they may also include citations you will need to include in the Table of Authorities. While most word processors will automatically compile a table of contents and a table of authorities, you should always double-check for accuracy. See Appendix D.

e. Jurisdictional Statement

The appellate brief should include a concise statement of the grounds upon which the court's jurisdiction rests, including a reference to the pertinent authority. This jurisdictional statement simply tells the appellate court which statute allows the appeal.

A sample jurisdictional statement would read:

> This Court of Appeals for the Eighth Circuit has jurisdiction to hear this appeal pursuant to 15 U.S.C. § 1071(b) (2000).

f. Constitutional and Statutory Provisions

If the case involves constitutional provisions, statutes, ordinances, or regulations, they must be set forth in full together with their citation in *Bluebook* form. If the provisions involved are especially lengthy, you can set forth their pertinent parts. Alternatively, their citation alone will be sufficient so long as they are set forth verbatim in an appendix to the brief.

g. Questions Presented

Many courts require the parties to set forth the issues presented for review. Some writers prefer true question format while others rely on the "whether" format. These questions are somewhat similar to the questions presented in an office memorandum but should be drafted in such a persuasive manner that the desired answer is obvious. An example would be as follows:

> Whether the trial court erred in excluding evidence showing the Plaintiff provoked the disagreement between the parties.

This question includes sufficient facts so the reader understands the issue you intend to address. It suggests an affirmative answer and is written persuasively from a defendant's point of view. The plaintiff's version of such an issue might read thus:

> Whether the trial court properly excluded hearsay evidence relating to Plaintiff's alleged involvement in the incident in which Defendant battered her.

While questions in an office memorandum are immediately followed by brief answers, there is no answer section in an appellate brief.

h. Statement of the Case

Next to the argument itself, the Statement of the Case is the most important part of the brief. This Statement of the Case or Statement of Facts includes neither argument nor allegations. The only facts to be included are those that have already been proven at trial. Thus, each fact you state must be followed by a reference to the location in the record or clerk's transcript where such fact was established, as follows:

> Defendant Smith was found to be driving at a speed of 70 miles per hour at the time the accident occurred. (R. at 74.)

While you are restricted solely to facts established at trial, you should still strive to present these in a persuasive manner.

In many ways, the statement of the case for an appellate brief will parallel the statement of facts for a brief submitted to a trial court. You must be honest and straightforward. Establish credibility by being accurate and including all facts, even those unfavorable to the client's position. Remember the techniques of passive voice and placement to de-emphasize unfavorable facts.

The facts are best set forth in a narrative rather than outline form because a narrative is more readable. Present your facts in chronological order in the past tense. Use descriptive words, verbs, and adjectives to describe favorable fact scenarios. Use parallel structure and careful repetition for drama and impact.

Because the justices reading the brief will be unfamiliar with the case, introduce the statement of the case by including background information or procedural history of the case. Some courts require this procedural history to be provided in a separate section. An appropriate statement of procedural history is as follows:

> This is an appeal from a final judgment entered October 12, 2000 by the United States District Court for the District of New Jersey. (R. at 79.) A jury found Defendant and Appellant ABC, Inc. ("ABC") to have defrauded its customers in the resale of certain automobiles. (R. at 70.) ABC filed a timely notice of appeal on October 20, 2000. (R. at 80.)

Do not include argument or legal conclusions in your statement of facts. Thus, do not state that the defendant "battered" the plaintiff (unless such a conclusion is supported by the record below). You can, however, recite the facts that the defendant "pushed and shoved" the plaintiff, which will lead the reader to the logical conclusion that a battery occurred.

i. Summary of the Argument

A concise summary of the argument is often included. This is a preview or condensation of the argument to follow. This is the first section of the brief that allows advocacy, and you should take advantage of this opportunity to persuade the reader to rule in favor of the client.

Because justices are so busy, they may only have time to skim quickly the entire argument. This summary of the argument, then, may be the best opportunity to win the reader over. Avoid citations in this summary and keep it brief—no more than one page if possible. A mere recitation of the point headings is not sufficient. Present the summary in a narrative fashion.

j. Argument

Like the argument in a brief submitted to a trial court, the argument in an appellate brief is the heart of the document. This section analyzes the authorities and convinces the reviewing justices to rule in favor of the client.

Divide the brief into separate sections with each section receiving its own point heading. These point headings should correspond to the questions or issues you set forth earlier. Work at making your point headings persuasive and relevant to your case. If possible, discuss topics in the order in which they were presented in the statement of the case. Compare the following point headings drafted for a plaintiff:

A BATTERY IS AN INTENTIONAL AND UNPERMITTED
TOUCHING OF ANOTHER.

DEFENDANT SMITH BATTERED EVELYN WOODALL BY
REPEATEDLY PUSHING HER AND SHOVING HER
TO THE GROUND.

The second point heading is far more likely to grab the reader's attention and persuade the reader that Smith is a horrible fellow. This impression is conveyed as follows:

- By the use of a label, the reader is reminded that Smith is the defendant, that is, "the bad guy";
- The plaintiff is personalized by the use of her name and a reminder of her gender;
- Smith's acts are described in vivid detail.

Written from Smith's perspective, the point heading may read as follows:

BECAUSE PLAINTIFF PROVOKED THE MUTUAL DISAGREEMENT,
DAMAGES FOR BATTERY WERE IMPROPERLY AWARDED.

This point heading focuses on the plaintiff's actions rather than the defendant's and provides the critical fact to the reader that the plaintiff provoked the incident. Moreover, the vivid description of the fight is now minimized to a mere "mutual disagreement." Remember to ensure your point headings have parallel structure so that, read in sequence, they provide an outline of the argument.

Use subheadings within your point headings if needed. While the point headings should consist of one persuasive sentence, subheadings are typically mere phrases consisting of just a word or short phrase such as "provocation" or "punitive damages."

Through analysis and discussion of legal authorities, the body of the argument will demonstrate to the reviewing court the errors of law made by the lower court. Do more than merely summarize cases you have located. Compare and contrast the authorities with your particular fact situation so the reader can readily see why the authorities are controlling. Use the CRAC method and set forth your Conclusion and the Rule that applies; Analyze and Apply this rule; and then reiterate the Conclusion. Always analogize and compare the facts in the cases you cite to the facts before the court. Use a thesis statement (see Chapter 17) to encapsulate the central argument to follow.

Because your argument will be more credible and respected if you discuss unfavorable precedents and because the adversary will undoubtedly raise them, acknowledge these problem areas. Do so, however, only after you have set forth the strongest part of your argument and have, perhaps, already gotten the reader "on your side." Discuss why these precedents are not applicable. Explain that the fact pattern in the unfavorable case is so different from the fact pattern in the case being appealed that it cannot serve as precedent; or you may argue that public policy or public interest favors the result for which you argue. If the unfavorable case is older, you can challenge it as antiquated or outmoded. Of course, expect your adversary to characterize it as the landmark or seminal case on the subject. If there are no legal authorities to support your position, argue that public policy and the interests of society compel a change in the law.

k. Conclusion

The conclusion of an appellate brief often does not summarize the argument section. This summary has already been given before the argument. Instead, the conclusion may merely specify the relief sought, such as requesting that the court affirm or reverse the lower court's decision.

l. Signature

The name of the attorney representing the party is set forth after the conclusion together with an address and telephone number and an identification of the party on whose behalf the brief is submitted.

m. Certificate of Service

All documents filed with a court must also be served on all other parties in the action. This certificate demonstrates to the court that the brief has been provided to all parties and specifies the date and manner of such service, such as hand delivery or first class mail.

n. Appendix

Appellate briefs often include an Appendix. This may consist of portions of the transcript, pleadings and the judgment from the lower court action, or exhibits entered as evidence in the trial. When you refer to these materials in your argument, set forth the relevant portions in the argument and then refer the reader to the Appendix, where the entire document can be found. Do not interrupt the flow of your narrative with pages of testimony, maps, or graphs. Your aim is to present a logical, persuasive argument. Insertions of extraneous materials disrupt the argument and distract the reader. Make it easy for the justice by using exhibit tags, including a table of contents for the appended materials, and highlighting relevant material. See Appendix C for a sample appellate brief.

E. Ten Pointers for Effective Brief Writing

Whether you are submitting a brief to a trial court or to an appellate court, remember the following ten tips:

1. Know the rules of the court to which the brief will be submitted.
2. Do more than summarize cases. By following the IRAC or CRAC methods, show the reader how and why the cases and other authorities apply to the client's situation. Use a strong thesis statement to give direction to the argument to follow.
3. Write from the client's perspective. Omit any references to yourself as the writer, such as "we believe" or "we argue." The brief is not a forum for your personal opinion but a logical and persuasive argument. Use the third person.
4. Avoid a rote or routine method of writing. If each paragraph discusses one case and ends with a citation to that case, the brief will have a rigid appearance and tone. Variety in the method of analysis of the cases will enhance readability.
5. Avoid string-citing unless there is a definite need to do so. Select the best case supporting a contention and use that case.
6. Avoid sarcasm, humor, or irony. While these techniques may provide drama in oral argument, they are often misinterpreted in written documents. Maintain a respectful tone toward the court.
7. Avoid the overuse of quotations. It is often the case that a judge has said something so articulately and eloquently that you prefer to use a direct quote. Used sparingly, quotations give force and

impact to your writing. Overuse of quotations, however, dilutes their strength. Anyone can retype language found in a case. Do more: Analyze why this language applies to the case at hand.

8.   Keep the focus on your argument. If you spend too much time refuting the opponent's position you will shift the focus of the brief from the client's point of view to that of the opponent. Fully argue the client's position before you respond to the opposition.

9.   Do not distort or overstate your position. If any portion of the brief is not supported by valid authority, the entire brief is undermined

10.   Use prominent placement to emphasize the strongest arguments. Bury weaker portions of the argument in the middle of the brief, the middle of paragraphs, and the subordinate clauses of sentences.

Appellate Brief Errata

1. The highest number of *amicus curiae* briefs filed for one United States Supreme Court case is more than 90. Eighty-five percent of all United States Supreme Court cases include at least one amicus brief, often filed by organizations such as the ACLU or AFL-CIO.

2. The United States Supreme Court accepted its first brief in CDROM form in 1997. Such CD-ROMs allow direct access to court transcripts, records, and other documents through hyperlinking, making review easier for many justices. Local Rule 32 for the First Circuit Court of Appeals requires that when a party is represented by counsel, one copy of its brief must be submitted on a CD-ROM disc.

3. The private company that printed most briefs for the United States Supreme Court ended its hot-metal printing process and went digital in mid-2000. Printing a brief using the hot-metal process generally took three weeks, while digital printing enables reproduction of a brief in three days.

4. Supreme Court rules recognize brief writers' tendency to try to squeeze additional wording into a brief by using a small typeface. The rules provide that "increasing the amount of text by using condensed or thinner typefaces, or by reducing the space between letters, is strictly prohibited." Sup. Ct. R. 33(b).

CyberSites

http://www.ualr.edu/ ~cmbarger	Professor C.M. Barger offers numerous resources and excellent information on legal writing and advocacy, including tips and links relating to appellate briefs.
http://www.legaline.com/ freebriefslinks.html	This site provides direct links to numerous free briefs filed with trial and appellate courts.

Court Brief Exercise
for Chapter 18

To: Paralegal
From: Daniel L. Lodge, Partner

Our client, Marisa Bailey, is an 18-year-old high school senior who attends James River High School ("James River"). James River is operated by Rio Grande Unified School District (the "District"), a school district that operates elementary, middle, and secondary schools in the district. In planning its graduation ceremony and program, James River notified parents of the graduating seniors that student-led and student-initiated non-denominational prayers would be offered at the graduation. School officials at James River will review any prayers before they are offered at the ceremony. Attendance at graduation is voluntary.

Ms. Bailey has sued the District on the basis that such prayers violate the First Amendment's prohibition against laws relating to establishment of religion. We intend to move for summary judgment on behalf of Ms. Bailey. Please prepare a brief (or memorandum of law) in support of a motion for summary judgment that will persuade the United States District Court for the Anywhere District that any such prayers offered at the school graduation would violate the First Amendment to the U.S. Constitution.

Court rules impose a ten-page limit on all briefs. In addition, court rules require that the brief be typewritten, double-spaced, and that current *Bluebook* or *ALWD* citation format be followed.

Assignment for Chapter 18

You have been asked to prepare the table of authorities for an appellate brief to be filed in the United States District Court. There are no special rules for citation form. You should use the rules set forth in the current edition of *The Bluebook* or *ALWD*. Do not worry about the page numbers. The following citations will appear in the brief.

> Daly v. O'Brien, 109 F.3d 111, 121 (Eighth Circuit 2000)
> 15 U.S.C. § 1051(a)
> Forrest v. Sullivan Insurance Indemnity Company, 520 U.S. 16, 230 S. Ct. 790, 189 L. Ed. 2d 42 (2001)
> Lehman v. Moore, 909 F.2d 550 (3rd Cir. 1998)
> 15 U.S.C. § 1051(b)
> Nelson v. Lyons, 15 F. Supp. 3d (District Court New Jersey 2001)
> DeLansing v. Kirk, 525 U.S. 909 (2002)
> State v. Reynolds, 789 N.E.2d 199 (N.Y. 1989)
> In re Walsh, 799 N.E. 2d 42, 44 (New York 1991)
> New York Domestic Relations Code Section 445
> 42 U.S.C. Section 2242
> Gregory v. Young, 121 F.3d 889 (8th Circ. 2002)
> New York Commerce Code § 330

State Your Answer

1. Use MegaLaw (http://www.megalaw.com) to access the local rules for the First Circuit Court of Appeals. Review Rule 32. What is the maximum length for a reply brief?
2. Access the site http://www.ualr.edu/~cmbarger. Select "Appellate Resources" and then "Persuasive Strategies for Appellate Brief-Writing." What is the first strategy?
3. Access the site http://www.appellate.net/briefs. Review the *amicus curiae* brief filed in *Anderson v. General Motors Corp.* What is the argument heading for Argument I?
4. Access MegaLaw. What cases can be found for your state?

Postwriting Steps

The best writing is rewriting.

E.B. White

A. **Reviewing and Revising: Stage One**
B. **Reviewing and Revising: Stage Two**
C. **Proofreading**
D. **Proofreading Projects by Others**
E. **Proofreaders' Marks**
F. **Polishing Your Writing**
G. **The Final Review**
H. **Conclusion**

Chapter Overview

Paralegals not only engage in the drafting of documents for themselves, but also they are often asked to review and revise the writing of others or perform proofreading for others. While these tasks are typically accomplished at the end of a writing project, their importance cannot be overlooked. It is at this stage of the writing process that unclear passages should be revised, redundant phrases should be omitted, and spelling and grammatical errors should be corrected. Even a typographical error will impair the professionalism of your project.

This chapter focuses on reviewing and revising your writings, proofreading, and polishing the finished product so its appearance enhances readability.

A. Reviewing and Revising: Stage One

When you have the first draft of your project in hand, the difficult tasks of reviewing and revising begin. Your initial review should be to ensure that the writing accurately conveys all the information needed. At this stage, focus on content. Try to review the project from the perspective of the intended reader and ask if the reader will understand the writing. Consider the following strategies:

- Keep the purpose of the project in mind. If the project is a brief, its purpose is to persuade. If the project is a memorandum, its purpose is to inform. Ask yourself if the writing meets these goals. Consider whether the tone is appropriate for the reader and whether the project is either too formal or too informal.
- Review to ensure the writing flows smoothly and that its organization assists the reader's comprehension. Move paragraphs and sections to other locations if you believe they would be better placed elsewhere.
- Be careful not to engage in micro-revision during the writing process itself. Agonizing over the choice of each word and continually striking out or rephrasing sentences may be a waste of time and energy because you may eventually omit a section you spent considerable time revising during the first effort.
- Do not interpret this advice to mean that no revisions should be done during the writing stage. It is both necessary and helpful to revise throughout the process of writing. Do not, however, write your initial draft expecting that the first typed version will be suitable for submission to court. You may even wish to insert reminders to yourself in the initial draft such as "work on this" or "revise" to remind you that further work needs to be done for a certain section. When writing, if you cannot decide between two ways of expressing an idea, initially include them both. When you read through your completed first draft, you can then decide which version to retain.
- Try to allow at least a few hours (and, if possible, overnight or longer) to pass between the completion of your first draft and your initial review. It is extremely difficult to review effectively a project with which you are too familiar. If you can come to the review "cold," you will be better able to detect flaws and gaps in the writing.
- Focus 100 percent on the review. Ask someone to hold your calls and find a quiet space where you can concentrate on your task. If you attempt to review a project and are interrupted by phone calls and meetings, you will be unable to devote the effort you need to make a critical evaluation of the project and may unintentionally skip over sections.

- You may find it helpful to close the door to your office or the library and read aloud. This will enable you to hear repetition or awkward phrasing or to realize something is missing from the project. Make sure each draft of a project includes a date. Often, several versions of a project will accumulate in a file. Because some drafts will vary only slightly from each other, sorting out the current version can be nearly impossible unless each draft is identified by date, and perhaps even time, for example, "DRAFT 12/16/04 10:30 a.m."
- If you have collaborated on the project with another writer, be especially alert to ensure your headings, numberings, and presentations of lists are consistent.
- If you are aiming to improve your writing skills in general, focus on one or two problem areas (such as overly long sentences or overuse of nominalizations), work on correcting these, and then move on to other weak spots.

B. Reviewing and Revising: Stage Two

The first review and revision of your project should alert you to major problems in content and organization. Use the second review to focus on four specific areas.

1. Sentence Length

Go through your second draft and place a red slash mark at the end of each sentence. Observe if a pattern of overly long sentences emerges. If most sentences are several lines in length, you need to trim your writing. Use sentences of varying length to create interest. Various software programs assist by informing you of average sentence length in a project.

2. Needless Words and Phrases

Read through the project looking for unnecessary words. It is easy to become attached to your product. Writers often have difficulty omitting words and phrases because they are reluctant to omit anything after hours of research and hours of writing. Be merciless. Most writers are far better at adding words than at deleting them. Watch carefully for modifiers such as "clearly," "obviously," or "naturally." These should be omitted for two reasons: They add nothing to a sentence, and they often create a patronizing tone.

3. *Legalese*

Keep alert to the use of jargon and legalese, including the overuse of archaic words and phrases and the overuse of nominalizations such as "discussion" or "exploration" instead of strong words like "discuss" or "explore." You can detect nominalizations by looking for words ending in *-ent*, *-ant*, and *-ion*.

4. *Passive Voice*

The overuse of passive voice will result in a distant and weak project. The active voice, coupled with the selection of forceful words, will lend strength and vigor to your writing. You can detect passive voice by looking at a subject introduced with the word *by* (as in "The report was filed by the company").

C. Proofreading

The third and final review of your writing should focus on technical errors such as grammatical errors, spelling mistakes, and typos. The more familiar you are with a project, the more difficult this task becomes. Your mind will automatically supply the word you intended, and you will not be able to see errors. Do not rely exclusively on the spelling and grammar checker programs of your word processor. A spelling checker will not inform you to use "from" rather than "form" because both words are properly spelled. Do not proofread on a computer screen. Print a copy of the document and work from that. Reading a hard copy is easier on your eyes. Moreover, it is presented in the way it will be to the ultimate reader, allowing you to see it as it will be seen by its audience. Consider photocopying the document in an increased size, for example, to 120 percent of its original size, to allow you to read the document easily and make notes in the margin.

While there are a few techniques you can use to assist you in proofreading, the best tip is to allow as much time as possible, preferably two to three days, to elapse before you begin this final step in writing. This will allow you to come to the project with a fresh approach and will counterbalance the familiarity that hampers a careful scrutiny of your writing. Energy levels are often higher in the morning, so try to schedule your proofreading as the first thing you do in the day.

Do not underestimate the difficulty of proofreading and editing. All major publishers require that writings be edited by professional editors and proofreaders for the very reason that authors are notoriously unlikely to catch their own errors.

Because a normal reading of your project will naturally focus on content and you will read groups of words and phrases rather than isolated words, you need to force yourself to slow down and focus on each word. Try the following techniques:

(i) Place a ruler under each line as you read the document. This will prevent you from jumping ahead to the next sentence or thought and force you to focus on each word.

(ii) Read the project backwards, from the last page to the first page and from right to left. While this technique is excellent for finding typos and spelling errors, it will not help you pick up a missed word or ensure that you have used a word such as "united" rather than "untied."

(iii) Read the document aloud with a partner who has a copy of the document. Each of you will then focus on isolated words, and the listener, in particular, will concentrate on the mechanics of the project rather than the content. Additionally, if your partner stumbles over certain sections, you will know these need to be fixed.

(iv) Read sections of the project out of order. Read Section V first, then the Conclusion, then Section III, then the Statement of Facts, and so on. You will not be able to focus on the flow of ideas, and your concentration will then be aimed at the mechanics of spelling, grammar, and typos.

(v) Devote extra attention to the parts of the project that were prepared last. More errors occur when you and the word processor are tired.

If you find yourself getting tired or losing concentration, stop and take a quick break. Get up and walk around the office. Get some juice or a fresh cup of coffee and then return to the task. Because you are not reading for content, but for mechanics, these interruptions will do no harm.

You can also ask someone else to proof the project for you. Having someone else review the project can be extremely helpful because this newcomer will have no familiarity with the writing. He or she will be able to review the writing with a fresh approach and no preconceived ideas or expectations. If you only want the reader to review for mechanical errors, say so, or you may receive a project with substantial corrections and suggestions. It is an intrusion on someone else's time to review your work; therefore, if you have asked for help, you should give the reviewer the courtesy of considering his or her comments or suggestions without becoming defensive. If you have difficulty accepting comments and criticism from others about your writing, do not ask for help. It is a waste of the other person's time if you are not able to keep an open mind about accepting suggestions.

Be alert to the dangers of overreliance on word processor spell checking programs. While these programs can be of great assistance and even offer suggestions for word choice, they do not recognize contextual misspellings. Thus, if you mistakenly referred to the complaint as "compliant," the spelling program will not alert you because the word "compliant" is correctly spelled. Although spell checking programs help speed up the editing and proofing process, they also encourage complacency. There is no substitute for human proofreading, as witnessed by the fact that a review of some recently published court decisions disclosed 23 cases referring to "Santa Clause" and 817 cases referring to the "trail court."

Similarly, the use of templates and forms prepared for an earlier transaction increases the risk of importing incorrect terms into later documents. Thus, a document prepared for a tenant needs to be scrupulously checked when it is later used for a subtenant. Make sure that defined terms are used consistently. For example, if an agreement uses the term "Franchisor," check to make sure the term is defined in the agreement, that it is always capitalized, and that it is consistently spelled and used. Use the "find and replace" feature in your word processing program to check for consistent presentation and use.

D. Proofreading Projects by Others

If you are asked to review someone else's work, obtain clear instructions so you know if you should review for content or review only for mechanics such as typos, spelling mistakes, and grammatical errors. Reviewing for mechanical errors in someone else's writing is fairly easy. If you are not familiar with the content, the errors will fairly leap off the page at you (just as they will for the ultimate reader, such as the client or the judge).

If you are asked to review for content, be judicious. All writers are sensitive about their product and overcriticizing may result in the writer believing you have a grudge and then discounting everything you suggest.

Recognize that each writer has a unique style. Just because a thought is not expressed in the exact way you would express it does not mean it is inaccurate or vague. Limit your corrections to meaningful items. It is unproductive to change "glad" to "happy" or "concerning" to "regarding." Your credibility as an effective reviewer will be jeopardized if you engage in such meaningless changes.

Comments such as "weak," "poor," or "expand" placed beside a paragraph are nearly useless. Specifically explain to the writer why the section is weak and make a suggestion for improving it. Harsh comments such as "What are you thinking?" or "ridiculous!" will cause the writer to avoid seeking your help and to become a passive writer. Try phrasing suggestions diplomatically, such as "have you considered . . . ?" or "let's discuss some alternatives . . . . " These approaches focus on the two of you as colleagues committed to producing a quality product rather than on the writer's perceived inadequacies.

In some instances, a letter to a client or a memo may bear the notation "dictated but not read," which means that the author dictated the project to someone else but has not reviewed it for errors. Avoid such a notation. The message it conveys to a reader is either "I'm too busy for you" or "don't blame me if there are errors in this document."

E. Proofreaders' Marks

While there is some variety in the marks writers use to show errors, most legal writers employ the standard marks, called proofreaders' marks, used by professional editors. Many attorneys learned these marks while writing articles for law reviews. Their use in law firms and among legal professionals is common.

Most dictionaries will provide descriptions and illustrations of proofreaders' marks. These marks are designed to show clerical staff where and how to make corrections in your project. Be sure all of your working drafts are double-spaced so you will have sufficient room to note corrections. The most commonly used proofreaders' marks are shown in Figure 19-1.

F. Polishing Your Writing

Even if your project is well written, clear, and readable, it should be presented in such a manner that it creates a favorable impression on the reader. One of the reasons many appellate courts insist that a brief submitted must be commercially printed rather than merely typed is that printed briefs are easier to read and present a uniform appearance.

Many factors play a part in making a project readable, including quality of paper, typeface, margins, and headings. If your goal in writing is to communicate, you must avoid producing a document so messy in appearance that it frustrates a reader or one that is simply not read because of its physical appearance.

Visually appealing documents are easier to understand. Replace blocks of text with headings, tables, lists, and more white space. Make sure the layout of your project is uncrowded.

1. Paper

Use the highest-quality paper possible. Some courts require that the paper used for documents submitted be of a certain quality. The United States Supreme Court, for example, requires all 8½ by 11 documents to be produced on unglazed opaque white paper. Sup. Ct. R. 33.2(a).

Select a paper of sufficient weight so that page two of a document doesn't show through to page one. While some law firms use cream or ivory colored paper, most use white. White is the more traditional color and many readers find it easiest to read because black type provides a greater contrast on white paper than on cream colored paper.

Figure 19-1
Commonly Used Proofreaders' Marks

Mark	Explanation	Example
≡	Capital letters	president bush
/	Lowercase letters	the eleventh Juror
∿	Boldface	April 16, 2001
‿	Close up space	in as much
⁋	Begin new paragraph	⁋ The plaintiff
ℰ	Delete	The hearing was was
stet	Let original text stand	Many courts have concluded
∧	Insert item	The plaintiff and his attorney argued
#	Add space	the court.The defendant
∼	Transpose	complaint
⊏	Move left	⊏ any jury
⊐	Move right	⊐ any jury
∧	Insert comma	the Plaintiff John Brownell argued
∨	Insert apostrophe	its a fact that
⊙	Insert period	the court The jury also requested
◯	Spell out	Jan. 10, 2005
or SP		

716

2. *Typeface*

Use ordinary Roman type for most of your writing. Italics (or underscoring) must be used for case names, book titles, law review article titles and other publications, citation signals, and foreign words and phrases. Italics (or underscoring) may be used to emphasize certain words or phrases. Use boldface (letters that are struck two or three times for extra darkness and contrast or through the use of the boldface tab (the "B") on your word processor) only for headings or special purposes, such as emphasizing a deadline date in a letter to a client.

Word processors can easily create italics. Some writers prefer italics to underscoring because it creates an elegant look. Other writers believe underscoring draws more attention to a word or phrase.

As to type of font, many experts prefer a "serif" style, which is one that adds small decorative strokes to the edges of letters. Serif styles are generally viewed as enhancing readability because they draw the eye from one word to the next. Old-fashioned typewriters always used a serif style. Well-known serif styles include Garamond, Times New Roman, and Century Schoolbook. This text is presented in a serif style. "Sans serif" styles (those without extra brushstrokes) such as Arial might be acceptable and dramatic for headings. In any case, do not select a font style that is so different as to be distracting to a reader. Do not use all capital letters, except for short headings, because they are difficult to read.

Practice Tip

Document Design

Consider the following tips to ensure the design of your document enhances its readability:

- **Don't mix typefaces in a document. Variations in typeface make a project look too much like an advertisement. Moreover, readers assume that headings in the same size and font style signal information of the same importance.**
- **Use visuals (graphs, charts, and so forth) sparingly. Keep visuals simple, and make sure they are helpful rather than merely "eye candy."**
- **Typefaces may be monospaced (meaning that every letter takes up the same amount of room) or proportional (meaning that, for example, a capital M takes up more room than a capital I). Most readers find proportionally spaced typefaces (such as this text) easier to read.**

3. *Type Size*

Word processors can provide you with numerous choices for type size. Type size is measured in "points," such as 10-point type or 12-point type, with the larger the number showing larger print. Some courts require documents to be printed in a certain size type. Similarly, some statutes require certain information, such as language disclaiming a warranty, to be of a specified type size. If there are no rules you must follow with regard to type size, select either 10-point or 12-point type, both of which are easily read. Rules of the United States Supreme Court dictate that the text of documents submitted to the Court be typeset in "Roman 11-point or larger type." Sup. Ct. R. 33.1(b). Many readers prefer 12-point type due to its ease of readability.

On occasion a client may insist that certain information be included in a contract, invoice, or other form. In order to fit all of the information or terms in the document, you may need to use a much smaller type size, such as 6-point or 8-point. Alternatively, many photocopy machines will reduce an image. These reductions, however, impair readability.

4. *Length of Document*

If court rules require that a document not exceed a specified page limit, you will need to be able to calculate and estimate the length of a project. The average typewritten or printed page, measuring 8½×11 inches, double-spaced, contains 250 words. If you are handwriting a document, count the words on any one sheet of your handwritten draft. Multiply this by the number of pages in your draft and divide this figure by 250. This will provide a rough estimate of how many typed pages your handwritten draft will produce. Some courts exclude certain sections, such as tables of contents and tables of authorities, from the page limits. Always check your court rules. Word processing programs easily provide statistics on document length and word counts.

If your project exceeds a maximum length requirement, you have several alternatives:

- Revise the project, omitting extraneous material.
- Alter your margins so that more words fit on each page.
- Use a smaller point type size to include more text on each page.

While these last two techniques will allow you to squeeze extra material into the document, some court rules mandate margin size and type size. The rules of the United States Supreme Court flatly state, "Increasing the amount of text by using condensed or thinner typefaces, or by reducing the space between letters, is strictly prohibited." Sup. Ct. R. 33.1(b).

The other disadvantage of squeezing material into a document is that it creates a more cramped appearance, and few, if any, readers will be fooled by artificial techniques adopted to meet length requirements. Pages filled with text from the upper left corner to the lower right corner cause eyestrain and frustration. Using adequate white space will cause headings and quotations to be more easily noticed. While the technique of leaving ample white space on a page, including adequate or generous margins, may seem like an artificial device, reading studies have demonstrated that it results in a more readable project.

Another formatting device that contributes to a pleasing appearance is the use of right justified margins. A right justified margin is one in which all of the words end at the exact same location at the right side on the page. This type of margin creates a clean and crisp-looking document. The only disadvantage is that to ensure the margin is even at the right side, uneven spacing between letters and words may occur. This ragged spacing can reduce ease of reading. Carefully proofread any document with right justified margins to make sure the spacing is acceptable. If it is not, use a ragged right edge.

5. *Headings*

Headings not only provide the reader with an idea as to what will follow, but also create visual drama on a page. Main headings should be in all capital letters, centered, and single-spaced. Each should be given a Roman numeral. Some writers use boldface print to make sure the headings stand out. Subheadings that occur with a main heading should use capital letters only for the first letter in each major word, such as nouns, verbs, adjectives, and adverbs. Do not capitalize the first letter in articles and prepositions, such as "in," "of," or "the," but be sure to capitalize "is," "its," "be," and other short verbs, nouns, and adverbs. Follow *Bluebook* Rule 8 or *ALWD* Rule 3 for instructions on capitalizing words in headings. Label each subheading with a capital letter and underline or use boldface for emphasis. All headings should be separated from the remainder of the narrative by double-spacing above and below. If the heading is a complete sentence, follow it with a period.

The structure and labeling of headings and subheadings should be as follows:

I.
    A.
    B.
        1.
        2.
        3.
            a.
            b.
            c.
    C.

II.
    A.
    B.
    C.
        1.
            a.
            b.
            c.
                (i)
                (ii)
        2.
    D.
III.

Do not use an "I" or an "A" unless a "II" or a "B" follows. On your final proofreading effort, scan through your project examining only the lettering and numbers of the headings to make sure you haven't skipped over or repeated a letter or number.

6. *Quotations and Lists*

Quotations and lists can serve to provide relief from a long narrative. Select quotations with care and be careful not to overquote. Follow *Bluebook* rules and keep quotes of 49 or fewer words in text. Indent quotes of 50 words or more.

Lists also create interest and are an effective tool for presenting information. Overuse of lists, however, can make your project have an outline-look to its appearance. Be consistent in presentation of lists. Don't use bullets in some lists and dashes to introduce others. Review lists to make sure the presentation of the material is in parallel structure.

G.   The Final Review

Just before your writing is sent to the reader, check these four items:

    (i)   *"Widows and orphans."* A "widow" or "orphan," respectively, is a heading or isolated line occurring at the bottom of a page or an isolated line occurring at the top of a page. Omit that awkward placement. It is distracting to the reader and results in an unprofessional-looking project.

    (ii)   *Hyphenated Words.* Do not hyphenate a word between one page and the next. Most software programs automatically correct this error.

    (iii)   *Numbering.* Quickly scan the project to make sure the page numbering is correct. If the document has a table of contents, review it to make sure all references to pages are correct. If footnotes are used, check their accuracy.

(iv) *Exhibits*. Make sure all exhibits or attachments to the project are included and are properly marked.

H. Conclusion

While the foregoing comments relating to paper quality, type size, and white space may seem inconsequential, remember that if your objective is to inform or persuade your reader, any device that keeps the reader's interest is significant. View these techniques as weapons in your arsenal of writing tools. Your goal is to produce a writing that is accurate and readable. Errors and typos impair the accuracy of a writing and an unpresentable project impairs the readability of a writing. If you discover errors, don't be afraid to send the document back for correction. Better that you are viewed as a perfectionist than as someone uninterested in quality.

Strive for excellence. Make every project something you and your fellow legal professionals will be proud to sign.

Common Writing Errors

Watch for the following common errors:

- Repeated words at the end of one line and the beginning of another.
- Errors in figures, dates, monetary amounts, and names.
- Substitutions of letters in small words, such as a change of "now" to "not" or "of" to "or."
- Transpositions of letters such that "complaint" becomes "compliant" and "trial" becomes "trail."
- Misspellings of compound words such as "every one" rather than "everyone" or "can not" for "cannot."

CyberSites

http://www.unc.edu/depts/ wcweb/handouts/ proofread.html	The University of North Carolina provides information on proofreading and editing.
http:// owl.english.purdue.edu	Purdue University's Online Writing Lab provides strategies to improve proofreading and editing.
http://www.prenhall.com/ author_guide/proofing.html	Prentice Hall provides examples of common proofreaders' marks.
http://www.sec.gov/pdf/ handbook.pdf	The SEC offers information on document design in its Plain English Handbook.

Assignment for Chapter 19

CAREFULLY PROOFREAD THE FOLLOWING PASSAGE AND MAKE THE NECESSARY CORRECTIONS.

Our client, Jack Patterson is a convicted sex offendor who was convicted of incest. Patterson pled guilty and was given a ten year sentence to be followed by three years' of supervised probation. As part of his setnece, the court barred Patterson from using a computer or any other device with Internet capabilities, even in the performance of his job. The judge who imposed the sentence stated that the risk of Pattersen reoffending is to great to allow him to have any Internet access. The court noted that Pattersen could use the internet to lure young victims and engage in porngraphy.

There have been a number of cases in this circuit and other circuit tht have discussed this issue. Most of those cases have held that restrictions on computer and internet use are overly braod and are unreasaonble if they are not related to the convicts crime. In the pesent case, Patterson did not use the Internet to engage in the criminal act of incest. Its been held that it makes no more sense to deny an offender Internet access than to bar a wire fraud perpetrator access to their telephone.

Patterson's bakground in information technology and to provide for himself he will need Internet access upon his release from prison. Patterson has asked us to research the following two issues: do they have the right to bar him from using the Internet, may the bar be permanant, and whether the sentence is reasonably related to his crime.

Please prepare a written memoranda for my by Friday morning a.m.

State Your Answer

1. Access the site http://www.ucc.vt.edu/stdysk/proofing.html.
   a. Why does it help to read aloud?
   b. How many times do professional editors proofread a document?
2. Review the Federal Rule of Appellate Procedure 32 for the Ninth Circuit at http://www.ca9.uscourts.gov.
   a. What type styles may be used in documents?
   b. What word counts are imposed for principal briefs?
3. Review the proofreading marks found at http://www.prenhall.com/author_guide/proofing.html.
   a. What does the mark "flush" mean?
   b. What does the mark "Eq #" mean?

Sample Legal Memorandum

<u>**MEMORANDUM**</u>

TO: Adam S. Sawyer, Esq.

FROM: Joanna Roache, Paralegal

RE: Reginald Nelson
         Visual Artists Rights Act

DATE: January 30, 2005

<u>ISSUE</u>

Under the Visual Artists Rights Act, do destruction and removal of sculptures and destruction of posters violate a freelance artist's rights to prevent destruction or modification of his works of visual art?

<u>BRIEF ANSWER</u>

Under the Visual Artists Rights Act, a freelance artist has the right to prevent destruction of his sculptures but not removal of them to another location. Moreover, an artist has no right to be compensated for destruction of posters because these are not works of "visual art" as defined by the Act.

<u>FACTS</u>

Our client, Reginald Nelson ("Nelson"), is a nationally known free-lance artist and sculptor. Nelson works primarily with granite and bronze forms although he has also created lithographs and posters. Four years ago, Nelson signed a written contract with Stonegate Development Company ("Stonegate") by which he agreed to create a variety of sculptures to be placed in a small park owned by Stonegate and located outside of a commercial building Stonegate was developing. Working in his studio, with a few of his long-term assistants, Nelson created six original bronze sculptures for placement in the park, all of which displayed his traditional curving motifs. The park included a variety of other elements not designed by Nelson, such as benches and picnic tables. After the sculptures were unveiled, a number of art critics and artists hailed them as having significant artistic merit. Nelson then created posters of the sculptures, which Stonegate placed in the building lobby. Stonegate fully paid for all of Nelson's work.

Two months ago, Stonegate began to redesign its park. It plans to destroy two of the sculptures and move the remainder to another one of its parks. Stonegate also destroyed the posters in the building lobby and replaced them with those by another artist.

DISCUSSION

The Visual Artists Rights Act and Works Made for Hire. In 1990, Congress passed the Visual Artists Rights Act ("VARA" or the "Act") to allow artists to prevent any intentional destruction, mutilation, distortion, or other modification of their works of visual arts. 17 U.S.C. § 106A (2000). These rights are often referred to as "moral rights" and are intended to allow artists to protect their artistic reputations, even after they have sold their works.

The Act provides three specific rights: the right of attribution, which is the author's right to be known as the author of a work; the right of integrity, which ensures that the work not be distorted, mutilated, or misrepresented in a way that would injure the artist's reputation; and in the case of works of visual art of "recognized stature," the right to prevent destruction.

The Act, however, is quite limited and applies only to works of visual arts such as paintings, drawings, and sculptures that exist in a single copy or in limited editions. *Id.* In the present case, the original sculptures are works of visual art covered by the Act. The Act, however, excludes from its protection works made for hire. *Id.*

A work made for hire is one that is presumed to be authored by an employer because it was created by an employee on company time or authored by a party specially commissioned to create the work when the parties have agreed in writing that the commissioning party will own the copyright and the work falls into one of nine statutorily enumerated categories. 17 U.S.C. § 101 (2000).

In the present case, Nelson was a freelance artist and not Stonegate's employee. If Nelson were an employee, Stonegate would be the presumptive owner of all rights in the works. Nelson was an independent contractor who was specially engaged by Stonegate to create the works in question. Although some cases have examined whether freelancers are, in fact, employees rather than independent contractors, the Supreme Court has held that the term "employee" for purposes of determining authorship of works made for hire should be interpreted according to general common law agency principles. *Cmty. for Creative Non-Violence v. Reid*, 490 U.S. 730, 740 (1989). The Court identified certain factors that characterize an employer-employee relationship: control by the employer over the work, control by the employer over the employee, and the status of the employer. *Id.* at 738-39.

If the employer has a voice in how the work is done, has the work done at the employer's location, and provides equipment and tools to the person to create the work, such tends to show an employer-employee relationship. Similarly, if the employer controls the worker's schedule in creating the work, has the right to have the worker perform other assignments, and has the right to hire the worker's assistants, such shows an employer-employee relationship. Finally, if the employer is in business to produce such works, provides the worker with benefits similar to those received by other workers, and withholds taxes from the worker's compensation, such is supportive of an employer-employee relationship. *Id.*

These factors are not exhaustive, but all or most of these factors characterize a regular, salaried employment relationship. In the present case, Nelson created the work at his studio using his own tools and equipment and using his own long-term assistants. Moreover, Stonegate is in the real estate development business, not the art business, and Nelson was not a regular salaried employee of Stonegate. Accordingly, Nelson should be held to be an independent contractor and thus entitled to moral rights under the Act.

A work not prepared by an employee but rather one prepared by an independent contractor can be deemed a work made for hire and thus owned by the commissioning party (in this case, Stonegate) if the parties agree in writing that it is to be a work made for hire and it is specially commissioned for use as a contribution to a collective work, as part of a motion picture or other audiovisual work, as a translation, as a supplementary work, as a compilation, as an instructional text, as a test, as answer material for a test, or as an atlas. 17 U.S.C. § 101. Both statutory conditions (the specially ordered work must fall into one of the nine enumerated categories *and* the parties must agree in writing that it is a work made for hire) must exist. In this case, the works (sculptures and posters) do not fall into any of the nine specially enumerated categories of work, and thus the works are not ones made for hire. Therefore, Nelson has retained any moral rights in the works because they were not "made for hire."

Destruction of Sculptures. The Act allows an author of a work of visual art to prevent any destruction of a work of "recognized stature." 17 U.S.C. § 106A(3)(B). Thus, determining that the sculptures are of "recognized stature" is necessary in order to protect them from destruction. The phrase "recognized stature" is not defined in the Act, and thus, its interpretation has been left to the courts. In *Carter v. Helmsley-Spear Inc.*, 861 F. Supp. 303, 325 (S.D.N.Y. 1994), *aff'd in part, rev'd in part, vacated in part*, 71 F.3d 77 (2d Cir. 1995), the court formulated the following test: a work of visual art has "stature" if it is meritorious and is recognized by art experts, other members of the artistic community, or by some cross-section of society. In the present case, because of the critical acclaim afforded the works by art critics and others, the sculptures are likely to be found to be of "recognized stature" such that Nelson can prevent their destruction.

Removal of Sculptures. In *Phillips v. Pembroke Real Estate Inc.*, 288 F. Supp. 2d 89, 99-100 (D. Mass. 2003), *aff'd on certification*, No. SJC-09181 (Mass. Dec. 21, 2004), Phillips, the creator of 27 sculptures placed in a park, argued that his work was so site-specific that moving it to another location would be an intentional destruction or modification under VARA. He contended that taking his sculptures to another park would be like painting over the background landscape in the Mona Lisa. The court, however, agreed with the defendant's assertion that moving the sculptures to another location was permissible, just as a museum curator could move the Mona Lisa from one wall in the Louvre to another.

The Act permits the modification of a work of visual art that is the result of conservation or of the public presentation and placement of a work, and specifically states that such is not a destruction. 17 U.S.C. § 106A(c)(2). This "public presentation" exception would permit Stonegate to move Nelson's sculptures from one location to another. As one court noted, the focus of VARA "is not . . . to preserve a work of visual art *where* it is, but rather to preserve the work *as* it is." *Bd. of Managers of Soho Int'l Arts Condo. v. City of New York*, No. 01-CIV-DAB, 29 (S.D.N.Y. June 17, 2003). Accordingly, Nelson has no right to the placement of the sculptures. Stonegate is not obligated to display the works in the park and may remove them to another location because VARA provides no protection for a change in placement or presentation.

Destruction of Posters. The U.S. Copyright Act specifically provides that a work of "visual art" does not include "any poster." 17 U.S.C. § 101. Thus, Stonegate's destruction of the posters in the building lobby was permissible because posters are not works of "visual art" and accordingly are not protected under the Act.

CONCLUSION

Under VARA, Nelson can prevent the planned destruction of the sculptures he created for Stonegate but cannot prevent their removal to another park. Moreover, because posters are not works of "visual art" covered by VARA, Nelson cannot receive damages for their destruction.

Sample Brief
for Court

The following trial court brief was submitted by the United States government in the Microsoft Corporation antitrust case.

IN THE UNITED STATES DISTRICT COURT
FOR THE DISTRICT OF COLUMBIA

UNITED STATES OF AMERICA,
          Plaintiff,
 	
        v.
 	
 MICROSOFT CORPORATION,
          Defendant.
	Civil Action No. 98-1232 (TPJ)

STATE OF NEW YORK *ex rel.*
 Attorney General ELIOT SPITZER, *et al.*,
          Plaintiffs,
 	
        v.
 	
 MICROSOFT CORPORATION,
          Defendant.
	Civil Action No. 98-1233 (TPJ)

PLAINTIFFS' RESPONSE TO MICROSOFT'S OBJECTION TO PARTICIPATION BY PROFESSOR LAWRENCE LESSIG AS AN AMICUS CURIAE

Microsoft has objected to participation by Professor Lawrence Lessig of Harvard Law School as an amicus curiae. Professor Lessig's participation in that role is proper, and Microsoft's objections are ill conceived and unfounded.

I.

Background

By Order dated November 19, 1999, the Court invited Professor Lessig to participate as amicus curiae. The Court also permitted the two plaintiffs and Microsoft each to designate an amicus curiae. In a conference with counsel the day before its Order, the Court explained that it asked Professor Lessig to submit a brief that addresses the legal issue of technological tying. Transcript of Proceedings, November 18, 1999, at 10-11. The Court's Order followed the entry of the Court's detailed findings of fact. There is no suggestion in Microsoft's papers, nor could there be, that the amicus process has anything to do with issues of fact.

II.

Legal Standard

Although there is no federal rule or statute governing participation by amicus curiae at the district court level,[1] *see United States v. Gotti*, 755 F.Supp. 1157, 1158 (E.D.N.Y. 1991), a federal district court has the inherent authority to invite participation by amicus curiae to assist the court in its proceedings. *United States v. Louisiana*, 751 F.Supp. 608, 620 (E.D. La. 1990); *United States v. Michigan*, 116 F.R.D. 655, 660 (W.D. Mich. 1987). The decision to invite or accept participation by an amicus is committed to the sound discretion of the court. *Alexander v. Hall*, 64 F.R.D. 152, 155 (D.S.C. 1974).

The classic role of the amicus curiae is to assist in a case of general public interest, supplement the efforts of counsel, and draw the court's attention to law that may otherwise escape consideration. *Miller-Wohl Co., Inc. v. Commissioner of Labor and Indus.*, 694 F.2d 203, 204 (9th Cir. 1982); see also *New England Patriots Football Club, Inc. v. University of Colorado*, 592 F.2d 1196, 1198 n. 3 (1st Cir. 1979) (historically, the role of an amicus was "to aid the court in resolving doubtful issues of law"). There is no requirement that an amicus be disinterested. *Funbus Systems, Inc. v. California Public Utilities Commission*, 801 F.2d 1120, 1125 (9th Cir. 1986); *Hoptowit v. Ray*, 682 F. 2d 1237, 1260 (9th Cir. 1982), although in this case there is no reason to believe that Professor Lessig is other than disinterested.

---

[1] Federal Rule of Appellate Procedure 29 governs participation by *amici* in the Courts of Appeal.

III.
Argument

A. Microsoft's Arguments

First, Microsoft asserts, without any explanation of its foundation or reasoning, that the Court's Order inviting Professor Lessig's participation is sufficiently broad to constitute a request for proposed conclusions of law. Microsoft also contends that Professor Lessig does not meet requirements to participate as an amicus because he does not have a "particularized 'special interest'" in the legal issues presented in the case, but then goes on to argue, seemingly paradoxically, that he should not participate because he is not impartial. These objections are specious.

B. Legal Argument By Amici Will Not Usurp The Judicial Function

The intended import of Microsoft's puzzling suggestion that the invitation to Professor Lessig to submit an amicus brief "is sufficiently broad as to constitute an invitation to submit proposed conclusions of law from a non-party," Microsoft's Objection at 2, is unclear and, in any event, does not provide any basis for revoking the invitation. First, Microsoft's suggestion ignores the Court's clear statement to counsel that Professor Lessig was being specifically requested to address the issue of technological tying. Transcript of Proceedings, November 18, 1999, at 10-11. Indeed, the Court made clear the straightforward purpose of its invitation of the limited brief of Professor Lessig and those of other amici: "I am asking for amici help." *Id.* at 10.

More importantly, that Professor Lessig and the other potential amici may discuss how they believe that the Sherman Act should be applied to the facts as the Court has found them is neither unusual nor improper, and indeed is the traditional role of an amicus. *See, e.g.,* *Funbus Systems, Inc. v. California Public Utilities Commission*, 801 F.2d 1120, 1125 (9th Cir. 1986) ("perfectly permissible role" for amicus to "take a legal position and present legal arguments in support of it"). Submitting a brief as amici involves *no* delegation of judicial authority or duties, raises none of the same concerns that appointment of a special master would raise, and is unobjectionable.

C.   If The Court Believes That Professor Lessig Would Bring A Helpful Perspective To Legal Issues In The Case, It Is Appropriate For Him Participate As Amicus

"There are no strict prerequisites that must be established prior to qualifying for amicus status; an individual seeking to appear as amicus must merely make a showing that his participation is useful to or otherwise desirable by the court." *United States v. Louisiana*, 751 F.Supp. 606, 620 (E.D. La. 1990). Although some courts have required that the amicus possess some "unique information or perspective," this does not require any particular quantum of expertise beyond the expectation that the amicus will add significantly to, not merely parrot, the contributions from the lawyers from the parties. *See Ryan v. CFTC*, 125 F.3d 1062, 1063 (7th Cir. 1997); *see also United States v. Gotti*, 755 F. Supp. 1157, 1158-59 (E.D.N.Y. 1991) (rejecting proffered amicus brief that merely parroted arguments of defendants).

In this case, Professor Lessig has written at length and taught law school and multidisciplinary courses on the Internet and the law. Contrary to Microsoft's current assertion, *see* Microsoft's Objection at 3, Professor Lessig does possess expertise in antitrust law, having taught antitrust law at Harvard and elsewhere. *See* Microsoft's Memorandum In Support Of Its Motion To Revoke Reference to the Special Master, CV-94-1564, at 7. If the Court believes that he brings a special perspective to the issues raised in this litigation and that his contribution would be useful to the Court, it is appropriate and well within the Court's discretionary authority to invite him to submit his views.

D. Microsoft Has Not Demonstrated That Professor Lessig Is Biased Against It

Microsoft again raises the issue of Professor Lessig's purported bias against it. These allegations are not only wholly meritless; they also are irrelevant as there is no requirement that an amicus be impartial in order to participate.

When Microsoft first raised the issue of Professor Lessig's purported bias in connection with the consent decree enforcement proceeding, this Court found that Microsoft's bases for its allegations of impartiality were "both trivial and altogether non-probative." *United States v. Microsoft*, CV 94-1564, Memorandum and Order, at 2 (January 14, 1998). Having scoured Professor Lessig's record since that time, Microsoft renews its allegations of bias based on two items: (1) that Professor Lessig serves on the advisory board of a non-profit organization devoted to open-source software which is affiliated with, and has received financial support from, Linux vendor Red Hat Software, and (2) that he has expressed the view that the experience of *United States v. AT&T* may be of some interest when thinking about the instant case. Underlying its specific allegations of bias seems to be Microsoft's concern about one theme of Professor Lessig's work, that the open nature of the Internet has engendered tremendous competition and innovation, that this openness is neither accidental nor inevitable, and that society will benefit if this openness continues.

Like Microsoft's previous allegations about Professor Lessig, its current allegations of bias are unfounded. Professor Lessig's affiliation with a non-profit organization devoted to open source software is a non-issue. Microsoft has not shown that this organization has any purpose beyond its stated one, *i.e.*, "to take the principles of open-source software and apply them in a variety of scientific and educational projects 'for the greater good of the general public.'" Exhibit A to Microsoft's Objection, at 1. Indeed, the article Microsoft attached to its motion notes that the group will have a "board of academics and technology experts." *Id*. That the group has connections with Red Hat, a participant in the open-source movement, is also of little moment. Microsoft has not alleged, nor are the plaintiffs aware of, any economic interest of Professor Lessig in the outcome of this litigation. At most, Microsoft has shown that Professor Lessig has views about the public welfare implications of developments in the software industry. None of this indicates that Professor Lessig has any bias against Microsoft that would disqualify him to participate as an amicus.[2]

Microsoft's allegations concerning Professor Lessig's comments about the AT&T break-up are even more puzzling. Read in context, Professor Lessig's comments merely reflect his recognition of the seriousness of the issues presented by this litigation, not any animus toward Microsoft. Exhibit B to Microsoft Opposition, at 3-4.

IV.

Conclusion

For the foregoing reasons, the plaintiffs submit that it is entirely proper and appropriate for the Court to invite Professor Lessig (and others solicited by the parties) to participate as amicus curiae in this important case. Microsoft's motion is nothing more than an attempt to manufacture some appellate point to use to distract attention from defendant's clear and continuing violation of the antitrust laws. Having no plausible basis for appealing any of this Court's findings of fact, and having no plausible

---

[2]In any event, there is no requirement that an amicus be impartial or disinterested. *E.g., Funbus Systems, Inc.*, 801 F.2d at 1125; *Hoptowit*, 682 F.2d at 1260; Krislov, *The Amicus Curiae Brief: from Friendship to Advocacy*, 72 Yale L.J. 694 (1963). Indeed, "by the nature of things an amicus is not normally disinterested." *Strasser v. Doorley*, 432 F.2d 567, 569 (1st Cir. 1970); *see* Tigar, *Federal Appeals: Jurisdiction and Practice*, at 133 (1993) ("An amicus brief is rarely disinterested; usually it supports one party or the other.") For example, to the extent that Microsoft and the plaintiffs invite amici who are themselves or who represent participants in the software industry, these persons will have economic interests that may be affected by this litigation or by Microsoft's conduct far more directly than the non-profit board position that Professor Lessig holds. Thus, even if there were any merit to Microsoft's allegations of some degree of partiality, those allegations would provide no grounds for rescinding the invitation to participate as an amicus.

In an excess of caution and in the interests of full disclosure, the plaintiffs suggest that the Court may wish to consider whether there is any merit in Professor Lessig filing a statement of interest, such as that required by Fed. R. App. P. 29, or disclose in some other format any interest he may have in the litigation, including any relevant information about his role in the Red Hat Center for Open Source.

argument that those findings do not make out a clear violation of the antitrust laws, Microsoft resorts to an attempt to create an appellate question by unfounded attacks on Professor Lessig and this Court's procedures. The Court may wish to consider whether it should accede to Microsoft's tactics simply to avoid adding another issue to this case. However, the law is clear that either decision is well within the Court's discretion.

DATED: December 20, 1999

Respectfully submitted,

_____/s/_____

Christopher S Crook
Chief
Phillip R. Malone
John F. Cove, Jr.
Jeremy Feinstein
Attorneys
David Boies
Special Trial Counsel
U.S. Department of Justice
Antitrust Division
325 7th Street, NW, Rm. 615
Washington, DC 20530
(202) 514-8276

Sample Appellate Brief

The attached appellate brief (a Brief in Opposition to a Petition for a Writ of *Certiorari*) was submitted to the United States Supreme Court.

No. 03-878

In the Supreme Court of the United States

PHIL CRAWFORD, INTERIM FIELD OFFICE DIRECTOR,
PORTLAND, OREGON, UNITED STATES IMMIGRATION
AND CUSTOMS ENFORCEMENT, ET AL.,
PETITIONERS

v.

SERGIO SUAREZ MARTINEZ

On Petition for a Writ of Certiorari
to the United States Court of Appeals
for the Ninth Circuit

BRIEF IN OPPOSITION

Christine Stebbins Dahl
Assistant Federal Defender
101 SW Main Street, Suite 1700
Portland, Oregon 97204
(503) 326-2123
Counsel for Respondent

QUESTION PRESENTED

In *Zadvydas v. Davis*, 533 U.S. 678 (2001), this Court considered the government's authority under 8 U.S.C. § 1231(a)(6) to continue to detain for the purpose of removal those persons whose removal from the United States could not be accomplished in the reasonably foreseeable future. This Court interpreted the statute to limit such detention to a "reasonable time," and applied it to former permanent residents. In this case, the Ninth Circuit Court of Appeals, citing *Lin Guo Xi v. INS*, 298 F.3d 832 (9th Cir. 2002), summarily affirmed the application of *Zadvydas* to Sergio Suarez Martinez, a Mariel Cuban who had been paroled into the United States in 1980 and was ordered removed in 2001. Although it detained Mr. Martinez under section 1231(a)(6) for nearly two years, the government made no effort to remove him, conceded it was unable to do so within the foreseeable future, and ultimately asked the Ninth Circuit to summarily affirm the district court's conditional release order pursuant *Lin Guo Xi*.

Given that section 1231(a)(6) draws no distinction between individuals who are removable on grounds of inadmissibility and those removable on grounds of deportability, this case presents the question whether the Ninth Circuit correctly applied *Lin Guo Xi*, in which it adhered to this Court's statutory construction of section 1231(a)(6) in *Zadvydas*.

TABLE OF CONTENTS

TABLE OF AUTHORITIES

FEDERAL CASES

FEDERAL STATUTES

BRIEF IN OPPOSITION

Petitioners Phil Crawford, Interim Field Office Director, Portland, Oregon, U.S. Immigration and Customs Enforcement, and John Ashcroft, Attorney General of the United States, seek a writ of certiorari to review the judgment of the United States Court of Appeals for the Ninth Circuit. The government has asked this Court to hold its petition pending final resolution of the petition to review *Benitez v. Wallis*, 337 F.3d 1289 (11th Cir. 2003), *cert. granted*, 2004 WL 67860 (U.S. Jan. 16, 2004) (No.03-7434). The respondent, Mr. Martinez, opposes the issuance of a writ in his case. Although the question presented here cannot seriously be distinguished from that in *Benitez*, the Ninth Circuit resolved it correctly and the Eleventh Circuit did not. Because his conditional release is at stake, Mr. Martinez opposes holding this petition pending final disposition of *Benitez*. Instead, Mr. Martinez requests consolidation with *Benitez* for argument should the Court grant the writ.

OPINIONS BELOW

The order of court of appeals is unreported and appears at 1a of the Appendix to the Petition for Writ of Certiorari. The order of the district court is unreported and appears at 2a of the Appendix to the Petition.

JURISDICTION

This Court has jurisdiction to review the judgment by writ of certio-rari under 28 U.S.C. § 1254(1). The government's petition appears to have been timely filed.

STATEMENT

Certain errors in the government's statement require correction. The government has never before suggested that Mr. Martinez attempted to enter the United States illegally. *Petition* at 2 ("Respondent is one of approximately 125,000 Cuban nationals, many of them convicted of crimes in Cuba, who attempted to enter the United States illegally during the 1980 Mariel boatlift."). In fact, he did not. He fled Cuba by boat as part of the "Freedom Flotilla" that enjoyed U.S. government approval.[1] Mr. Martinez arrived in Key West, Florida on June 8, 1980, and was immediately paroled into United States pursuant to 8 U.S.C. § 1182(d)(5). *Gov't Supp. Mtn. to Hold in Abeyance* (CR 12) at 2.

---

[1]Comments by President Carter at a press conference in Miami on May 5, 1980, indicated government approval of the flotilla:

> [L]iterally tens of thousands of others will be received in our country with understanding, as expeditiously as we can, as safely as possible on their journey across the 90 miles of ocean, and processed in accordance with the law . . . . But we'll continue to provide an open heart and open arms to refugees seeking freedom from Communist domination and from economic deprivation, brought about primarily by Fidel Castro and his government.

United States v. Frade, 709 F.2d 1387 (11th Cir. 1983).

The government omits to state that it identified section 1182(d)(5) as an independent source of authority to detain Mr. Martinez for the first time before the Ninth Circuit. *Compare Petition* at 3. In its district court pleadings, the government identified only section 1231(a)(6) as the source of its authority and made no attempt to distinguish *Lin Guo Xi. E.g., Gov't Supp. Mtn. to Hold in Abeyance* (CR 12) at 4; *Appellants' Response to Petitioner-Appellee's Motion for Summary Affirmance and Request for Summary Affirmance* (CA 03-35053) (July 9, 2003) at 2. The government did not suggest section 1182(d)(5) provided independent authority to detain Mr. Martinez until it moved for summary affirmance in the Circuit. *Appellants' Response to Petitioner-Appellee's Motion for Summary Affirmance and Request for Summary Affirmance* (CA 03-35053) (July 9, 2003) at 7.

Finally, while noting annual custody reviews pursuant to parole regulations applicable to Mariel Cubans, 8 C.F.R. § 212.12(g), *Petition* at 8, the government omits to state Mr. Martinez alleged these regulations were constitutionally deficient and yielded an unreliable result because they do not provide detainees a meaningful opportunity to challenge continued detention and are so lacking in important safeguards as to create a significant risk of erroneous deprivation of liberty interests. *See Brief in Support of Petition* (CR 9) at 25. The government never addressed this argument, and the district court's order granting the habeas petition did not disclose whether this argument informed its decision. *Compare Order Granting Petitioner's Motion to Dissolve Stay and for Immediate Release* (CR 24).

REASON FOR DENYING THE PETITION

The petition should be denied because the Ninth Circuit correctly concluded it was bound by this Court's statutory construction of section 1231(a)(6) in *Zadvydas*, and applied the same statute in the same manner. Because Congress chose to treat all of the categories of aliens the same in section 1231(a)(6), this Court has no occasion to rewrite the statute. It has the same meaning for everyone to whom it applies.

Contrary to the Eleventh Circuit's analysis in *Benitez*, the Ninth Circuit began with the statutory construction issue, and having resolved the issue in favor of the petitioner, concluded it had no occasion to address the underlying constitutional issues.

Just a year ago the Supreme Court held that 8 U.S.C. § 1231(a)(6) "limits an alien's post-removal-period detention" to a reasonable time period and "does not permit indefinite detention" by the Immigration and Naturalization Service ("INS"). *Zadvydas v. Davis*, 533 U.S. 678, 689 (2001). We are now presented with the question of whether this statute bears the same meaning for an individual deemed inadmissible to the United States under 8 U.S.C. § 1182. The answer is yes. Our analysis of § 1231(a)(6) begins and ends with *Zadvydas*. Because the Supreme Court construed the statute, we are bound by that framework and thus are not called upon to address the scope of any constitutional claims of an inadmissible alien.

Lin Guo Xi, 298 F.3d at 833-34.

The Ninth Circuit, employing traditional canons of statutory construction, looked first to the language of the statute and concluded that it expressly applies to both inadmissible (formerly referred to as excludable) and removable (formerly referred to as deportable) aliens. *Id.* The plain language of the detention statute provides:

> An alien ordered removed who is [A] *inadmissible under section 1182* of this title, [B] removable for violations of [nonimmigrant status or entry conditions, violations of criminal laws, or threatening national security,] or [C] who has been determined by the Attorney General to be a risk to the community or unlikely to comply with the order of removal, may be detained beyond the removal period and, if released, shall be subject to the terms of supervision in paragraph (3).

8 U.S.C. § 1231(a)(6) (emphasis added).

The Ninth Circuit found that although *Zadvydas* only concerned the second category (removable aliens), this Court's construction addressed the statute as a whole, and thus, the holding of *Zadvydas* was not limited to the second prong:

> Although *Zadvydas* concerned the second prong of the statute — relating to deportable aliens — the Court's ultimate holding addresses the statute as a whole: "we construe the statute to contain an implicit 'reasonable time' limitation, the application of which is subject to federal court review." 533 U.S. at 682. In assessing the applicability of the statute, the Court spoke broadly, noting that it "applies to certain categories of aliens who have been ordered removed, namely *inadmissible* aliens, criminal aliens, aliens who have violated their nonimmigrant status conditions, and aliens removable for certain national security or foreign relations reasons . . . ." *Id.* at 688 (emphasis added). Concluding that the

statute "does not permit indefinite detention," the Court point-
edly used the term "aliens" as opposed to "deportable aliens":

> [W]e read an implicit limitation into the statute before us.
> In our view, the statute, read in light of the Constitution's
> demands, limits an alien's post-removal-period detention
> to a period reasonably necessary to bring about that alien's
> removal from the United States. It does not permit inde-
> finite detention.

Lin Guo Xi, 298 F.3d at 835 (quoting *Zadvydas*, 533 U.S. at 689).

The Ninth Circuit rejected the INS's argument that the statute
should be construed differently depending upon the category into which
the alien fell. The Ninth Circuit found the plain language of the statute
forbids such a "bifurcated construction," and such an approach would be
"untenable." *Lin Guo Xi*, 298 F.3d at 836-37. Because the statute no longer
distinguishes between "excludable" and "deportable" aliens, there is no
sound or principled basis to interpret and to apply it one way for one
category, but a different way for the other. *See Zadvydas*, 533 U.S. at
710 (Kennedy, J., dissenting) ("Section 1231(a)(6) permits continued detention not only of removable aliens but also of inadmissible aliens, for
instance those stopped at the border before entry. Congress provides for
detention of both categories within the same statutory grant of authority").

The INS argued as much in its briefing to this Court:

> [The Supreme] Court has long recognized that, when Congress
> uses the same language even in different parts of the same

> statute, it generally intends the language to have the same
> meaning. That rule is "at its most vigorous when a term is
> repeated within a given sentence." *Brown v. Gardner*, 513
> U.S. 115, 118 (1994). *A fortiori* here, where Congress enacted
> a single grant of authority to the Attorney General over several
> categories of aliens, *Congress must be understood to have*
> *intended the same language to confer the same authority with*
> *respect to each category.*

Brief for the Petitioners at 47, *Ashcroft v. Ma* (No. 00-38) (U.S. June 28, 2001) (emphasis added). Any argument by the government that the statute should now be interpreted differently for inadmissible aliens must be rejected. *See also Zadvydas*, 533 U.S. at 710 (Kennedy, J., dissenting) ("[I]t is not a plausible construction of § 1231(a)(6) to imply a time limit as to one class but not to another. The text does not admit of this possibility."); *id.* at 717 ("[T]hat Mariel Cubans and other illegal, inadmissible aliens will be released . . . would seem a necessary consequence of the majority's construction of the statute.").

The Ninth Circuit properly concluded it was bound by this Court's construction of section 1231(a)(6).

> We thus abide by the Supreme Court's interpretation of
> § 1231(a)(6) and hold that Lin may not be subjected to indefinite
> detention. *See Rivers v. Roadway Express, Inc.*, 511 U.S. 298,
> 312-13 (1994) ("It is [the Supreme Court's] responsibility to say
> what a statute means, and once the Court has spoken, it is the
> duty of other courts to respect that understanding of the govern-
> ing rule of law. A judicial construction of a statute is an author-
> itative statement of what the statute mean[s] . . . ."); *Elmendorf*
> *v. Taylor*, 23 U.S. (10 Wheat) 152, 160 (1825) ("[T]he construc-
> tion given by this Court to the constitution and laws of the
> United States is received by all as the true construction . . . .").

298 F.3d at 836. The Ninth Circuit's having correctly applied in *Lin Guo Xi* this Court's binding precedent and the clear language of section 1231(a)(6), there is no reason for this Court to disturb the order pursuant to which the government released Mr. Martinez on reasonable conditions.

CONCLUSION

The petition for writ of certiorari should be denied. In the alternative, Mr. Martinez requests consolidation for argument with *Benitez*.

Respectfully submitted,

Christine Stebbins Dahl
Assistant Federal Defender
101 S.W. Main Street, Suite 1700
Portland, OR 97204
(503) 326-2123
Counsel for Respondent

January 2004

Sample Table
of Authorities

The following Table of Authorities is from an actual brief filed with the United States Supreme Court and offers guidance on compiling a table that refers to numerous sources.

TABLE OF AUTHORITIES

STATUTES AND REGULATIONS   **Page**

OTHER

Glossary

A.L.R.: *See American Law Reports.*

ALWD citation system: A system introduced in 2000 by the Association of Legal Writing Directors ("ALWD") to provide an easier, more readily understood citation format.

Act: A series of statutes related to one topic.

Adjudication: An administrative proceeding before an administrative law judge.

Administrative agencies: A governmental body that enacts rules and regulations on a specific topic and settles disputes relating thereto, for example, the FCC, FDA, or NLRB.

Administrative law: The law relating to administrative agencies.

Administrative law judge: An individual who presides over an administrative adjudication.

Advance sheets: Temporary softcover books that include cases prior to their publication in hardbound volumes.

Am. Jur. 2d: A general or national encyclopedia published by West covering all United States law.

American Digest System: West's comprehensive set of digests designed to help researchers find cases.

American Law Reports: Sets of books publishing appellate court decisions together with comprehensive essays or annotations relating to the legal issues raised by those cases.

Amicus curiae: Literally, "friend of the court"; a brief submitted to a court by one who is not a party to the action or proceeding.

Annotated: Literally, "with notes"; generally, a reference to one-sentence descriptions of cases that follow statutes in codes such as U.S.C.A. or a state code.

Annotated code: A set of statutes organized by subject matter that contains material accompanying the statutes, chiefly references to cases.

Annotated law reports: *See American Law Reports.*

Annotation: A one-sentence description of a case; an article or monograph about a legal topic published in A.L.R.

Appeal: Review by one court of a lower court's decision.

Appellant: A party who initiates an appeal; sometimes called a petitioner.

Appellate brief: A document presented to a reviewing court to obtain

affirmance, reversal, or some alteration of a lower court's ruling.

Appellee: A party who responds
to an appeal; sometimes called a
respondent.

Attorneys general opinions:
Opinions by executive officials on
various legal topics; opinions by the
U.S. Attorney General or individual
state attorneys general.

Auto-Cite: A computer service provided by *Shepard's* showing the appellate history of a case, used primarily to
confirm that the authority in question
is still good law.

Bicameral: A two-chamber legislature.

Bill: A proposed law.

Bill of Rights: The first ten amendments to the Constitution.

Binding authority: Legal authority that must be followed by a court.

Blawg: An online journal related to
legal topics.

Block form: Style of letter writing
in which all the elements, including
the date and the closing, begin at the
left-hand margin.

Block quotation: A quotation from
another source of 50 words or more,
indented (typically ten spaces) left
and right, that appears without opening and closing quotation marks.

Blog: An online journal or diary.

Blue and White books: Books
published by West for individual
states that include conversion tables
for locating parallel cites.

Bluebook: The best-known and used
guide for citation form; subtitled *A
Uniform System of Citation*, now in
its 18th edition.

Boolean searching: A method of
conducting research online using symbols and characters rather than plain
English.

Brainstorming: A pre-writing
strategy that results in a type of
outline listing all words related to a
project.

Brief: A summary of a case; or a
written argument presented to a court.

Browser: Software that helps access and review information on the
Internet and translates HTML-encoded files into text and images that
one can read and view; Netscape and
Microsoft Explorer are examples of
browsers.

CALR: *See* computer-assisted legal
research.

CCH Congressional Index: Sets of
books used to compile legislative histories.

CD-ROM: Literally, "compact disk,
read-only memory"; a hard disk containing thousands of pages of information.

C.J.S.: West's general or national
encyclopedia covering all United
States law.

CRAC: An acronym for *C*onclusion,
*R*ule, *A*pplication or *A*nalysis, and
*C*onclusion; a method used to analyze
legal authorities and issues in a brief
or other document.

Cable modem: A cable line used
to connect to the Internet, allowing
faster connection than a telephone
line.

Case of first impression: An issue
not yet decided by a jurisdiction.

"Case on point" approach: System
used by a researcher following West
Group's headnotes and Key Numbers
to locate other similar cases by inserting a topic name and Key Number into
the various units of the Decennial
Digest System.

Certificate of Service: A verification that a document or pleading has
been "served on" or presented to a
party.

Certification: The process by
which a court of appeals refers a question to the United States Supreme
Court and asks for instructions and
direction.

Certiorari: Writ of *certiorari*; the
most widely used means to gain review
of a case by the United States Supreme
Court; issuance of the writ (meaning a
decision to review a case) is discretionary with the Court.

Cert pool: The group of U.S. Supreme Court law clerks who takes turns evaluating petitions for *certiorari* and writing memos.

Cert worthy: A case for which *certiorari* has been granted.

Chamber opinion: An opinion written by a United States Supreme Court justice in his or her capacity as the justice assigned to a particular circuit rather than in the capacity of writing for the majority of the Court; also called "in-chambers opinion."

Charter: The governing document for a municipality.

Chat room: A location in cyberspace fostering real-time communications among several people.

CheckCite: A software program providing automatic validation of all cases cited in a document.

Checks and balances: The system whereby each division of the United States government is to exercise its own powers and function separately from the others.

Chief Justice: The presiding justice of the United States Supreme Court.

"Chron" copy: A copy of a legal document placed in a chronological file for law office purposes.

Circuit: A geographical area in which courts are located; the United States is divided into 12 numbered circuits, each with its own court of appeals.

Citators: Sets of books published by Shepard's or Westlaw's KeyCite that direct one to other materials discussing or treating legal authorities.

Cite-checking: The process of verifying that citations in a document are accurate and in compliance with rules for citation form and then verifying that the authorities are still "good law."

CiteFinder: A search engine that uses the databases in the CD-ROM to generate a statistically ranked list of relevant authorities.

CiteRite II: A citation checking software program that checks citations for proper form using *Bluebook* rules or the *California Style Manual*.

Civil law: A body of law depending more on legislative enactments than case law, often seen in non-English-speaking countries.

Code: A compilation of statutes or regulations arranged by subject or topic.

Code of Federal Regulations: The codification of administrative rules and regulations, by subject, into 50 titles.

Codification: The process of organizing laws or regulations by subject matter rather than chronologically.

Committee print: A report or study prepared for a congressional committee.

Committee report: Document reflecting decisions reached by legislative committees considering proposed legislation.

Committee transcript: Report of proceedings before committees considering proposed legislation.

Common law: The body of law that develops and derives through judicial decisions rather than from legislative enactments, usually seen in English-speaking countries.

Complimentary close: The ending of a letter, such as "Sincerely."

Computer-assisted legal research: The process of conducting legal research through computer rather than conventional print sources.

Concurrent jurisdiction: The sharing of jurisdiction over a case by federal or state court so that a litigant can select which forum in which to bring the action.

Concurring opinion: Opinion written by a member of the majority who agrees with the result reached in a case but disagrees with the reasoning of the majority.

Congress: The lawmaking body of the federal government, composed of the Senate and the House of Representatives.

Congressional Information Service: Sets of books used to compile legislative histories.

Congressional Record: A publication that publishes the remarks of the speakers debating a bill prepared for each day Congress is in session as well as other remarks and speeches made on the floor of the House or Senate.

"Congressional": Source provided by Lexis-Nexis on the Internet offering more than 25 years of congressional information, including bills, hearing transcripts, committee reports, and the *Congressional Record.*

Constitution: The document that sets forth the fundamental law for a nation or state.

Constitutional courts: Courts such as the United States Supreme Court that exist under the United States Constitution and whose judges are protected as to tenure and salary reductions.

Convention: A type of treaty, usually relating to a single topic.

Court reports: Sets of books that publish cases.

Courts of Appeal: Intermediate appellate courts; in the federal system, these are sometimes called circuit courts.

Courts of first resort: Trial courts.

"Current Awareness Commentary": A section of the monthly issue of U.S.C.S. *Advance* that includes summaries of pending legislation.

Current Law Index: Separately published index designed to direct researchers to periodicals, such as articles in law reviews.

Cyberspace: The electronic or computer world in which vast amounts of information are available; sometimes used as a synonym for the Internet.

Dead-tree publishing: The publication of materials in conventional print form.

Decision: Technically, the final action taken by a court in a court case; generally, the term "decision" is used synonymously with "opinion," "judgment," or "case."

Demand letter: A letter setting forth a client's demands or requirements.

Depository library: A library designated by the United States government to receive selected government materials and publications.

Descriptive word approach: A method of locating legal materials by inserting words describing a problem or issue into an index that then directs the reader to relevant information.

Dictionary (legal): An alphabetical arrangement of words and phrases providing the meaning or definition of those words and phrases.

Dictum: Technically, "obiter dictum"; a remark in a case said for purposes of illustration or analogy; dictum is persuasive only.

Digests: Books or indexes that arrange one-sentences summaries or "digests" of cases by subject.

Directory: A list of lawyers.

Dissenting opinion: An opinion written by a judge in the minority who disagrees with the results roached by the majority of a court.

District courts: The 94 trial courts in our federal system.

Diversity jurisdiction: A basis upon which federal courts take cases, due to the different or diverse citizenship of the parties in the case.

Docket number: A number assigned to a case by a court to track its progress through the court system.

Domain name: The name that identifies an Internet site, such as "www.ibm.com." Domain names have two parts: the "generic top-level domain," which is the last part of the domain name, such as "com," or "gov," and which usually refers to the type of provider of the information; and the "secondary domain," which is more specific and is to the right of "www," such as "ibm" in the above example.

Download: Transferring files or information from the Internet to your personal computer.

E-mail: Electronic mail or messages sent through the computer rather than in physical form (which is often called "snail mail").

Ellipsis: Three periods separated by spaces and set off by a space before the first and after the last period, used to indicate omission of a word or words.

Embedded citation: A citation appearing in the middle of a sentence, often introduced by a phrase.

Enabling statute: A statute that creates an administrative agency such as the FDA or FCC.

En banc opinion: Literally, "in the bench"; an opinion in which all judges in an appellate court participate.

Encyclopedias: Sets of books that alphabetically arrange topics related to legal issues; treatment of legal issues is somewhat elementary; the best known general sets are C.J.S. and Am. Jur. 2d; some state-specific sets exist.

Engrossed bill: A final version of a bill passed by one legislative chamber.

Enrollment: A process wherein a bill that has been passed by both the House and the Senate is then printed by the Government Printing Office, following which the bill is certified as correct and signed by the Speaker of the House and by the vice president.

Exclusive jurisdiction: The basis upon which a court's ability to hear a case is exclusive to the federal court, such as a bankruptcy case, and which cannot be heard by another court.

Executive agreement: An agreement entered into with a foreign nation by a president acting without Senate approval.

Executive branch: The branch of the United States government that enforces laws.

Executive order: Regulations issued by a president to direct government agencies.

Extract: A *Shepard's* tool that automatically extracts all citations in a legal document and Shepardizes them.

Extranet: An internal company or law firm intranet that provides access to select outsiders on a case-by-case basis.

FAQ: "Frequently asked questions," often included on Web sites and that respond to the most commonly asked questions about the site or about the information provided by the site.

FTP: File Transfer Protocol, a common method of moving files or communicating between two Internet sites.

FULL: A feature of "Shepard's for Research," a software program provided by LEXIS that lists every authority that mentions a case.

Federal Appendix: West's set of books that prints unpublished federal courts of appeal cases.

Federalism: Sharing of powers by the federal and state governments.

Federal question jurisdiction: The power of a federal court to hear a case based upon the fact the case arises under the United States Constitution or a United States law or treaty.

Federal Register: A pamphlet published every weekday relating to administrative law and publishing agency rules and regulations.

Federal Reporter: West's unofficial publication containing cases from the federal courts of appeal.

Federal Supplement: West's unofficial publication containing cases from the federal district courts.

FindLaw: Internet site providing free access to many legal authorities.

Form books: Sets of books including forms for use in the legal profession; may be general or related solely to one area of law.

Freestyle: *See* Natural language.

G-8: A group comprising the major industrial democracies.

GPO Access: Online source offering free direct links through its *Manual* to information about government agencies, their addresses, appointees, staff members, and functions, as well as direct links to the Federal Register, C.F.S., congressional, and executive materials.

GlobalCite: LoisLaw's citation validation service.

HTML: Hypertext Markup Language, a standard language of computer code.

HTTP: Hypertext Transfer Protocol, a common method of moving files or communicating between two Internet sites.

Header: Information found on the second and any following pages of letters in the upper left-hand corner listing the addressee, page, and date.

Headnotes: Short paragraphs prepared by editors, given before a case begins to serve as an index to the points of law discussed in a case.

History references: References provided by Shepard's relating to the subsequent history of a primary authority.

Home page: The first or main page sent when accessing a person's or business's Web site.

Hornbook: A one-volume treatise devoted to one area of the law, such as contracts, torts, or real property.

Hyperlink: A method of instantaneous transport to another destination; hyperlinks are often underscored or appear in different color on the computer screen; by clicking the colored line, you will be immediately transferred to that particular site or page.

IRAC: An acronym for *"I*ssue," *"R*ule," *"Application"* or *"Analysis,"* and *"C*onclusion"; a method used to analyze authorities and legal issues in a memo or brief.

Id.: A signal used in citation form to direct a reader to an immediately preceding citation.

Indefinite pronoun: A pronoun that does not refer to a specific person, such as "anyone."

Index: An alphabetical arrangement of words and terms designed to direct researchers to relevant cases, statutes, or legal information; usually contained in the last volume of a set of books or in separate volumes after the last volume.

Index to Legal Periodicals & Books: Separately published index designed to direct researchers to periodicals such as articles in law reviews.

Infra: A signal used in books or citation form meaning "below" directing a reader to a later (though not immediately following) citation.

Interfiling: An updating technique used in looseleaf binders or sets by replacing individual pages.

International Court of Justice: A court under the responsibility of the United Nations, created to hear and decide disputes between and among nations; also called the World Court.

International law: The law relating to relations among nations.

Internet: A collection of worldwide inter-connected computer networks originally developed for defense purposes and which are linked together to exchange information; the Internet is not owned by any one person or company.

Internet Service Provider (ISP): A company that provides Internet access, such as America Online or Roadrunner, for a monthly fee.

Intranet: A private network inside a company or law firm that provides access only for internal use to those in the company or firm and not to outsiders; for example, a law firm's intranet could be used only by those in the firm and could not be accessed by any member of the general public.

Judge: Individual who sits on a lower court.

Judiciary: The branch of the government that interprets laws.

Jump cite: *See* Pinpoint cite.

Jurisdiction: The power of a court to act.

Jurisdictional statement: A statement in a brief explaining the grounds upon which the court's jurisdiction to hear the case rests.

Jury instructions: Sets of books containing proposed instructions to be used to charge a jury in a civil or criminal case.

Justice: Individual who sits on an appellate court, especially the United States Supreme Court.

KWIC: A computer program offered by LEXIS that provides subsequent appellate history of a case; used primarily to confirm that authority in question is still good law by showing negative history only. Also a method of displaying a band or window of words around a requested search term or phrase.

KeyCite: A citation service offered through Westlaw providing valuable and automatic information relating to the validity of primary authorities cited in a document.

KeyCite Alert: A software clipping service that automatically notifies a researcher of changes in treatment of a case.

Key Number: West's assignment of a number to a particular topic of law, allowing researchers to retrieve numerous cases dealing with the same point of law.

LEXIS: The computerized legal research system offered by Reed Elsevier.

Law: *See* Statute.

Law review: The periodic publication by a law school providing scholarly treatment of a legal topic.

Legalese: The overuse of legal terms and foreign words and phrases in legal writing.

Legal Looseleafs in Print: A publication that identifies which topics are covered by looseleaf publications.

Legal Periodicals & Books: The online version of *Index to Legal Periodicals & Books.*

Legis: A LEXIS database library for legislative information.

Legislative courts: Specialized courts, such as the United States Tax Court, which do not exist under the Constitution and whose judges are appointed for specific terms.

Legislative history: The documents reflecting the intent and

activity of a legislature at the time it enacts a law.

Legislature: The branch of the government that makes law.

Letterhead: Information printed on stationery identifying the correspondent.

"Library References": A feature of U.S.C.S. comparable to that of U.S.C.A. in that it provides cross-references as well as directing the researcher to books, encyclopedias, annotations, and a wide variety of law review articles.

Link: *See* Hyperlink.

Listserv: A system that allows groups of people to e-mail each other and participate in group discussions, usually about a topic of common concern; for example, there may be a listserv comprising law students and when one message is sent by a user, it is automatically sent to all others in the group; sometimes called "newsgroup."

Log in: (n.) the account name used to gain entry to a computer system and which is not secret, as is a password; also called a "user name"; (v.) the method of accessing a computer system.

Loislaw: The computerized legal research system offered by Wolters Kluwer.

Looseleaf (or looseleaf service): A set of materials collected in ringed binders due to the need for frequent updating and related to a specific area of law such as labor law or tax; includes both primary and secondary authorities.

Majority opinion: Any judicial opinion written by a member of the majority after a court reaches a decision.

Maroonbook: A citation manual published by the University of Chicago and used in the Chicago area.

Martindale-Hubbell Law Directory: A comprehensive directory of lawyers in the United States and in foreign countries, which also includes summaries of law for the states and various foreign countries.

MegaLaw: Internet site providing free access to many legal authorities.

Memorandum (legal): A document explaining legal issues involved in a case in a neutral and objective manner.

Memorandum of Law: Document presented to a court to persuade the court to rule in a party's favor; also called Memorandum of Points and Authorities.

Memorandum of Points and Authorities: *See* Memorandum of Law.

Memorandum opinion: An opinion that provides a result but offers little or no reasoning to support that result.

Merged closing: The disfavored combination of a complimentary close with the last sentence of a letter.

Microfiche: Celluloid strips of film used in cataloging or archiving documents.

Microfilm: 16-mm or 35-mm film containing images displayed on screens and often used for efficient storage of voluminous records.

Microform: A type of technology embracing microfilm, microfiche, and ultrafiche, based on photography and that stores material more efficiently than print sources.

Modem: A device that connects to your computer and to a phone line, allowing the computer to communicate with other computers, much the way telephones allow humans to communicate with each other; *see also* Cable modem.

Moot: Resolved; cases that have been resolved or settled in some manner are said to be moot.

NEXIS: An online library affiliated with LEXIS offering the full text of almost 700 general news, business, and financial publications.

National Reporter System: A set of unofficial court reporters published by West and including federal and state cases.

Natural language: A "plain English" computer method of conducting legal research offered by LEXIS; also called "Freestyle"; in contrast to using Boolean connectors.

Netiquette: The code of etiquette or conduct for the Internet.

Network: The connecting of two or more computers so that they can communicate with each other and share resources and information.

Neutral citation: A citation that does not refer to a particular vendor or to a particular type of source; also called *public domain citation*.

Newsgroup: Electronic communications method allowing its participants to view, post, and reply to messages.

Nominalization: The conversion of an adjective, verb, or adverb into a noun, for example, the conversion of the verb "decide" into "render a decision."

Obiter dictum: *See* Dictum.

Official: Publication of cases, statutes, or other legal materials as directed by a statute.

On all fours: *See* On point.

Online: The process of being connected to the Internet through electronic communication.

Online catalog: An electronic database used by libraries in place of a conventional card catalog to catalog materials owned by the library.

Online journal: A journal that is published exclusively online, not in print form.

On point: A case that is factually similar and legally relevant and that controls another case; sometimes called a case "on all fours."

Opinion: A court's explanation of the law in a particular case; also called "case" or "decision."

Opinion letter: A letter setting forth advice to a client.

Ordinance: A local law.

Original jurisdiction: The ability of a court to act as a trial court.

Overrule: The overturning of a case by a higher court considering a different case on appeal.

PDF: Portable Document Format, a format that duplicates on a computer screen what a conventional print source looks like.

Parallel cite: Two or more citations to the same case allowing researchers to read a case in two or more sets of reports.

Parallel structure: The requirement that the grammatical structure of all items in a list be identical or parallel.

Password: The secret code used to gain access to a computer system.

Per curiam: An opinion by the whole court.

Periodical: A publication issued on a periodic, such as monthly or quarterly, basis; for example, the *Computer Law Journal*.

Permanent law: A law that remains in effect until it is expressly repealed.

Personal digital assistant (PDA): A handheld computer device such as the Palm Pilot, which provides wireless access for updating and validating through both *Shepard's* and KeyCite.

Persuasive authority: Legal authorities that the court is not required to follow but might be persuaded to do so; secondary authorities are persuasive.

Pinpoint cite: A reference to the exact page in a source to which a reader is directed; also called a "jump cite" or "spot cite."

Plain English movement: A modern approach to legal writing calling for the use of plain English and an end to stuffy, archaic, and jargon-filled writing.

Plurality opinion: The result reached when separate opinions are written by members of a majority.

Pocket part: A booklet or pamphlet inserted into the back of a hardbound volume to provide more current information than that found in the volume.

Popular name: The practice of calling certain statutes or cases by a popular name.

Popular name approach: A method of locating cases or statutes by looking up their "popular names"; generally the names of the sponsoring legislators, the parties to the case, or a name assigned by the media.

Posting: The entering of information or messages into a network, for example, cases are "posted" to the Web site of the United States Supreme Court and legal professionals "post" messages on a listserv.

Primary authority: Official pronouncements of the law, chiefly cases, constitutions, statutes, administrative regulations, and treaties, all of which are binding authorities.

Private international law: The law relating to which country's law will govern a private contractual transaction or arrangement.

Private law: A law affecting only one person or a small group of persons, giving them some special benefit not afforded to the public at large.

Proclamation: A statement issued by a president having no legal effect.

Proofreading: The process of reviewing a writing to correct errors.

Public domain system: With regard to format- or vendor-neutral citation systems, the citation appears the same whether the reader has accessed the case by conventional print format or by electronic methods, such as CD-ROM, LEXIS, Westlaw, or the Internet.

Public international law: The law relating to the conduct of nations.

Public law: A law affecting the public generally.

Quick Index: An easy-to-use one-volume index published by West that directs the researcher to annotations in A.L.R.3d, A.L.R.4th, and A.L.R.5th. Note that there is also an A.L.R. Federal Quick Index.

Ratio decidendi: The "reason of the decision"; the holding of a case.

Redlining: A method of showing changes to a document.

Reference notation ("Re"): An indication of the subject matter of a document.

Regulation: A pronouncement by an administrative agency; sometimes called a rule.

Regulatory body: An administrative agency.

Report: Set of books publishing cases, generally official sets.

Reporter: Set of books publishing cases, generally unofficial sets.

Resolutions: *See* Ordinance.

Restatements: Publications of the American Law Institute designed to restate in a clear and simple manner legal doctrine in specific areas, such as contracts, torts, or trusts.

Reverse: The overturning of a lower court decision by a higher court considering that same case on appeal.

Root expander: A device provided by LEXIS in computerized legal research, such as an asterisk or an exclamation point, that substitutes for a character or any number of additional letters at the end of a word, respectively.

Rule: *See* Regulation.

Rule of Four: The decision by four of the nine Supreme Court Justices to grant *certiorari* and take a case.

Rules of court: Procedural requirements issued by courts and that must be followed by litigants.

Rules of procedure: Rules governing practice before a court, such as the FRCP, which govern significant matters.

Salutation: The greeting in a letter, such as "Dear Ms. Howard."

Sans serif style: Print style without embellishments of extra lines forming letters, such as the Arial font.

Scope note: A brief paragraph outlining the matters treated in a legal discussion and those to be treated elsewhere.

Search Advisor: A service offered by LEXIS designed for research in a known area of law; ideal source to begin researching an issue because it assists in selecting a topic or jurisdiction by suggesting terms to search.

Search box: A blank box on a computer screen, in which you type or key in the word or terms you are interested in researching.

Search engine: A particular service that helps one locate useful information on the Internet, usually through the use of keywords; common search engines are "Yahoo," "Google," "Lycos," and "AltaVista." A search engine is a Web site that looks for and retrieves other Web sites. Search engines look for words in the millions of Web pages on the Internet and direct you to pages that include the search words or keywords you enter in a search box.

Secondary authorities: Legal authorities that are not primary law and which explain, discuss, and help locate primary authorities; persuasive authority; includes encyclopedias, A.L.R. annotations, law reviews, texts, and treatises.

Selective enforcement: A defense raised whereby a party asserts that he or she has been singled out for prosecution.

Selective publication: The process whereby not all cases are published but rather only those that advance legal theory are published.

Serial Set: Conventional bound pamphlet set of books publishing congressional committee and subcommittee reports.

Series: Newer or more recent editions of cases or other legal materials.

Serif style: A style of print that adds small decorative strokes to the edges of letters, generally viewed as enhancing readability, such as Garamond and Times New Roman fonts.

Server: A computer or software package that provides or serves information to other computers.

Session laws: The chronological arrangement of laws prior to their arrangement in a code.

Shepard's: Sets of books that allow researchers to verify that primary authorities are still "good law."

Shepardize: The process of ensuring that authorities are still "good law."

Short form citation: An abbreviated form of a citation used after a citation has been given in full.

Signal Indicator: A symbol showing on the computer screen that informs the user of the precedential status of a case by indicating through colors or letters the history and treatment of the case.

Slip law: A piece (or pieces) of looseleaf paper containing language of a law; the manner in which laws are first published.

Slip opinion: A court decision available on looseleaf sheets of paper; one not yet available in a published reporter.

Spamming: Sending blanket, unsolicited messages to others, similar to "junk mail."

Spot cite: *See* Pinpoint cite.

Standing: Personal injury or damage sustained by a plaintiff enabling the plaintiff to bring suit.

Stare decisis: The concept whereby courts follow and adhere to previous cases.

Star paging: A technique to convert page numbers in cases published in unofficial sets to page numbers in cases published in official sets.

Statute: An act of a legislature declaring, commanding, or prohibiting something.

String citing: The somewhat disfavored practice of citing more than one authority in support of a proposition.

Supplement: A softcover pamphlet that updates material found in a hardbound volume.

Supra: A signal used in books or citation form meaning "above," directing a reader to a preceding (though not immediately preceding) reference or citation.

"Supreme Court Update": A feature of U.S.C.S. *Advance* that includes summaries of recent United States Supreme Court cases.

Surfing the 'Net: The process of moving or linking from one site to another in the course of reviewing information.

Syllabus: A comprehensive but unofficial summary preceding an opinion of a court, prepared by the court's reporter of decisions or the publisher.

Synopsis: A brief summary of a case prepared by editors to provide a quick overview of the case and given before the case begins.

TAPP: An acronym for "*T*hing, *A*ction, *P*erson, and *P*lace" and referring to a technique used to determine words to insert into an index to locate relevant research materials.

THOMAS: Web site for legislative information provided by the federal government that offers text of proposed and enacted legislation, committee information, calendars for hearings scheduled, and House and Senate Directories.

Table of authorities: List of authorities cited in a brief or document and that must be arranged in a certain order.

Temporary law: A law that has specific language limiting its duration.

Thesaurus: A book providing synonyms and antonyms for words and terms.

Thesis statement: An initial sentence or two at the beginning of a project that encapsulates the central argument to follow; also called *umbrella statement*.

Topic approach: A method of locating legal materials by bypassing the general index and going directly to the appropriate title or topic in a source.

Total Client-Service Library: Collectively, the sets of books published by the former Lawyers Co-op and including U.S.C.S., Am. Jur. 2d, A.L.R., *Proof of Facts, Am. Jur. Trials*, and various form books.

Transitions: Words or phrases that connect preceding language with that which follows.

Treatise: A scholarly book (or set of books) devoted to the treatment of a particular legal topic, such as *Treatise on the Law of Contracts*.

Treatment references: References provided by *Shepard's* relating to the later treatment and discussion of primary authorities by other cases, attorneys general opinions, law review articles, and so forth.

Treaty: An agreement between two or more nations.

URL: Uniform Resource Locator, one's address on the Internet. Most Internet addresses begin with "www" or "http://www." The URL of IBM is "www.ibm.com."

Ultrafiche: An enhanced microfiche holding a great many images.

Unicameral: A one-house legislature.

Uniform law: Model legislation prepared by the National Conference of Commissioners on Uniform State Laws on various legal topics, such as the Uniform Commercial Code, and designed to be adopted by the 50 states.

Uniform Resource Locator: *See* URL.

United States Code: The official publication of all federal laws, arranged by topic.

United States Code Annotated: West's annotated version of the *United States Code*, including all federal statutes arranged by subject.

United States Code Congressional and Administrative News Service: A publication including public laws, legislative history of selected bills, summaries of pending legislation, presidential proclamations and executive orders, various federal regulations, and

court rules.

United States Code Service: Annotated set of federal statutes arranged by subject and published by LEXIS Publishing.

United States Government Manual: A manual or handbook providing information about the United States government, particularly the administrative agencies.

United States Law Week: A weekly publication that prints the text of significant public laws.

United States Reports: The official publication containing cases from the United States Supreme Court.

United States Statutes at Large: The set of books containing all federal laws, arranged in chronological order.

Universal Citation Guide: The citation system promulgated by the American Association of Law Libraries.

Universal symbols: Symbols and characters used in constructing a search on LEXIS or Westlaw; sometimes called root expanders.

Unofficial: Publication of cases or statutes not directed by statute.

Unreported case: A case marked "not for publication" by a court; persuasive authority.

Unwritten law: A reference to the common law tradition of dependence upon cases.

User name: *See* Log in (n.).

V ("Versus Law"): A commercial legal research system offering cases via the Internet for a moderate fee.

WWW: World Wide Web, commonly used to refer to the entire collection of resources that can be accessed in cyberspace, through the Internet.

Web: *See* WWW.

Web page: A particular file or "page" included in a Web site.

Web site: A collection of Web pages; for example, IBM's Web site (www.ibm.com) will consist of numerous Web pages, each of which is devoted to a specific topic. A Web site always begins with a "home page," which is the first screen viewed when the Web site is accessed.

Weekly Compilation of Presidential Documents: Publication including materials relating to the executive branch.

WestCheck: A West software program providing automatic validation of all cases cited in a document.

West Document Retrieval: A fee-based service established by West providing public records and court documents by overnight delivery, e-mail, or fax.

WestFind&Print: A fee-based Internet service established by West allowing one to download cases and other authorities and KeyCite cases.

Westlaw: The computerized legal research system offered by West.

Widows and orphans: A heading or isolated word or line occurring at the bottom or top of a page.

Words and Phrases: A multivolume set of books directing researchers to cases that have construed certain terms.

World Court: The United Nations court, officially named the International Court of Justice, which provides final decisions regarding international disputes.

World Wide Web: *See* WWW.

Written law: A reference to statutes.

Resources

Legal Publishers

Aspen Publishers
111 Eighth Avenue
New York, NY 10011
(212) 771-0600
www.aspenpublishers.com

Bureau of National Affairs (BNA)
1231 25th Street, N.W.
Washington, D.C. 20037
(800) 372-1033
http://www.bna.com

The Bluebook
The Harvard Law Review
   Association
Gannett House
1511 Massachusetts Avenue
Cambridge, MA 02138
http://www.legalbluebook.com

CCH Incorporated
2700 Lake Cook Road
Riverwoods, IL 60015
(800) 525-3335
http://www.cch.com

Congressional Information
   Service, Inc.
See information for LEXIS
   Publishing
http://www.lexisnexis.com/
   academic/3cis/cisMnu.asp

Findlaw
See information for West Group
http://www.findlaw.com

Foundation Press, Inc.
See information for West Group

LEXIS Publishing
9443 Springboro Pike
Miamisburg, OH 45342
(800) 227-9597
http://www.lexisnexis.com
http://lexispublishing.com

Loislaw
105 N. 28th Street
Van Buren, AR 72956
(479) 471-5581
http://www.loislaw.com

Martindale-Hubbell
See information for LEXIS
   Publishing
http://www.martindale.com

Matthew Bender
See information for LEXIS
   Publishing

The Michie Company
See information for LEXIS
   Publishing

Pearson Prenctice Hall
One Lake Street
Upper Saddle River, NJ 07458
http://www.pearsoned.com

Shepard's
See information for LEXIS
   Publishing
http://www.lexisnexis.com/shepards

West Group
610 Opperman Dr.
Eagan, MN 55123
(800) 328-4880
WESTLAW Customer Service:
(800) 937-8529
http://www.west.thomson.com

William S. Hein & Co., Inc.
1285 Main Street
Buffalo, NY 14209
(800) 828-7571
http://www.wshein.com

Government Agencies and Offices

Attorney General of the United
   States
Department of Justice
950 Pennsylvania Avenue, N.W.
Room 4400
Washington, D.C. 20530-0001
(202) 514-2000
http://www.usdoj.com

Department of Commerce
1401 Constitution Avenue, N.W.
Washington, D.C. 20230
(202) 482-2000
http://www.commerce.gov

Commission on Civil Rights
624 Ninth Street, N.W.
Washington, D.C. 20425
(202) 376-7700
http://www.usccr.gov

Equal Employment Opportunity
   Commission
1801 L Street, N.W.
Washington, D.C. 20507
(202) 663-4900
http://www.eeoc.gov

Executive Office of the
   President
1600 Pennsylvania Ave., N.W.
Washington, D.C. 20500
(202) 456-1414
http://www.whitehouse.gov

Federal Judicial Center
One Columbus Circle, N.E.
Washington, D.C. 20002
(202) 502-4000
http://fjc.gov

Federal Register
U.S. National Archives and
   Records Administration
8601 Adelphi Road
College Park, MD 20740
1-86-NARA-NARA
http://www.archives.gov

Government Printing Office
732 North Capitol St., N.W.
Washington, D.C. 20401
(202) 512-0000
http://www.gpo.gov

House of Representatives
Washington, D.C. 20515
(202) 224-3121
http://www.house.gov

Justice Department
950 Pennsylvania Avenue, N.W.
Washington, D.C. 20530-0001
(202) 514-2000
http://www.usdoj.gov

Department of Labor
200 Constitution Avenue, N.W.
Washington, D.C. 20210
1-866-4-USA-DOL
http://www.dol.gov

Library of Congress
101 Independence Avenue, S.E.
Washington, D.C. 20540
(202) 707-5000
http://www.loc.gov

National Archives and
    Records Administration
See information for Federal Register

United States Senate
Washington, D.C. 20510
(202) 224-3121
http://www.senate.gov

U.S. Supreme Court
U.S. Supreme Court Building
One 1st St., N.E.
Washington, D.C. 20543
(202) 479-3000
    Opinion Announcements:
    (202) 479-3360
    Public Information Officer:
    (202) 479-3211
    http://www.supremecourtus.gov

U.S. Courts, Administrative Office
One Columbus Circle, N.E.
Washington, D.C. 20544
(202) 502-2600
http://www.uscourts.gov

Bibliography for Legal Research and Writing

*Aspen Handbook for Legal
    Writers: A Practical Reference*
Deborah E. Bouchoux
Aspen Publishers
(212) 771-0600
http://www.aspenpublishers.com

*Bieber's Dictionary of Legal
    Citations* and
*Bieber's Dictionary of Legal
    Abbreviations*
Mary Miles Prince
William S. Hein & Co., Inc.
1285 Main St.
Buffalo, NY 14209
(800) 828-7571
http://wshein.com

Effective Legal Writing by Gertrude
    Block (4th ed.)
West Group
http://www.west.thomson.com

Grammar Gremlins
Don K. Ferguson
Glenbridge Publishing Ltd.
http://www.glenbridgepublishing.
com

Legal Writing in a Nutshell
    (3d ed. 2003)
Lynn B. Bahrych and Marjorie
    Dick Rombauer
West's Nutshell Series
http://www.west.thomson.com

Plain English for Lawyers
Richard C. Wydick
    (4th ed. 1998)
Carolina Academic Press
700 Kent Street
Durham, NC 27701
(800) 489-7486
http://www.cap-press.com

Index